Forbidden Science 5

Also by Jacques Vallee

Novels in English:

FastWalker, novel (Frog, Ltd.)
Stratagem, novel (Documatica Research)

Science & Technology:

The Network Revolution (And/Or Press, Penguin, Google)
Electronic Meetings, with R. Johansen & K. Vian (Addison-Wesley)
Computer Message Systems (McGraw-Hill)
The Four Elements of Financial Alchemy (Ten Speed Press)
The Heart of the Internet (Hampton Roads Publishing Company, Google)

UFOs and "Paranormal":

Anatomy of a Phenomenon (Regnery, Ace, Ballantine)
Challenge to Science (Regnery, Ace, Ballantine)
Passport to Magonia (Regnery, Contemporary, Daily Grail)
The Invisible College (E. P. Dutton, Anomalist Books)
Messengers of Deception (And/Or Press, Bantam, Daily Grail)
The Edge of Reality, with Dr. J. A. Hynek (Contemporary)
Dimensions (Contemporary, Ballantine, Anomalist Books)
Confrontations (Ballantine, Anomalist Books)
Revelations (Ballantine, Anomalist Books)
A Cosmic Samizdat (Ballantine)
Forbidden Science, Vols. 1 to 4 (Documatica Research, Anomalist Books)
Wonders in the Sky, with Chris Aubeck (Tarcher-Penguin)
Trinity: The Best-Kept Secret with Paola Harris (Amazon)

In French:

Le Sub-Espace, novel (Hachette – Jules Verne Prize)
Le Satellite Sombre, novel (Denoël, Présence du Futur)
Alintel, novel (Le Mercure de France)
La Mémoire de Markov, novel (Le Mercure de France)
Les Enjeux du Millénaire, essay (Hachette Littératures)
Au Coeur d'Internet (Balland, Google)
Stratagème (L'Archipel)
Science Interdite, Vol. 1 (O.P. Editions)
Science Interdite, Vol. 2 (Aldine)
Trinity - Le Secret le mieux gardé, with Paola Harris (Amazon)

Forbidden Science 5
Pacific Heights

The Journals of Jacques Vallee 2000-2009

Anomalist Books
Charlottesville, Virginia

Forbidden Science 5: Pacific Heights
Copyright © 2023 by Documatica Research, LLC.
ISBN: 978-1-949501-24-7

Front cover image: Godruma/iStock
Cover design by Seale Studios

With deep thanks to Patrick Huyghe for his long-standing support and superb editing, and to Flamine de Bonvoisin for her extensive documentation work.

All rights reserved. No part of this book may be reproduced or transmitted in any form or by any means, electronic or mechanical, including photocopying, recording, or by any information storage and retrieval system, without the written permission of the Publisher, except where permitted by law.

The author can be contacted at:
P.O. Box 641650
San Francisco, CA. 94164

The author's website: www.jacquesvallee.com

For information about Anomalist Books, go to AnomalistBooks.com or write to: Anomalist Books, 3445 Seminole Trail #247, Charlottesville, VA 22911

Contents

Introduction..8
Part Seventeen: Athanor Transition............................10

    1. Paris (Mabillon). 6 January 2000
    2. Athanor. 30 April 2000
    3. Hummingbird. 14 August 2000
    4. Hummingbird. 8 January 2001
    5. Athanor. 2 June 2001

Part Eighteen: September Eleven..............................99

    6. Hummingbird. 11 September 2001
    7. San Jose, Costa Rica. 19 April 2002
    8. Athanor. 4 January 2003
    9. San Mateo. 20 March 2003
    10. Detroit. 19 August 2003

Part Nineteen: Pacific Heights..................................219

    11. Sacramento. 10 February 2004
    12. Hong Kong. 9 October 2004
    13. Honolulu, Hawaii. 22 June 2005
    14. Athanor. 28 January 2006
    15. Athanor. 8 July 2006

Part Twenty: Labyrinths..367

    16. Hummingbird. 29 September 2007
    17. Hummingbird. 22 May 2008
    18. Hummingbird. 29 September 2008
    19. Las Vegas. 23 January 2009
    20. Mabillon. 1 October 2009

Reflections..518
Notes and References..523
Index..537

Figures

1. With Dr. Doug Englebart and Elizabeth Feinler at SRI, Dec. 2000
2. Launching the research with witnesses at Haravilliers, 2001
3. Inner sanctum: Janine at Denderah Temple, Egypt. October 2001
4. Collecting water samples at Laguna Cote, Costa Rica, April 2002
5. NIDS Science Board meeting in Las Vegas, May 2002
6. Working with Ron Brinkley at the Athanor Library, 2003
7. Compiling *Wonders* with Chris Aubeck, Porto, October 2003
8. Modern view of the site of the Fatima apparitions, Oct. 2003
9. With Dr. Kelleher and Janine at the NIDS building, April 2004
10. Reviewing Oceania sites with Prof. Swift, Honolulu, July 2005
11. The Bunnies: NeoPhotonics in Shenzhen, China, Oct. 2005
12. *The Lady at the Orient window*, December 2005
13. Janine at Chartres, installing the stained glass, September 2006
14. Birthday party (no.67) at "Cradle of the Sun," September 2006
15. Kennedy Space Center: The Shuttle Endeavor, Dec. 2006
16. At the site of the Soissons encounters, March 2007
17. Hard traces: preserving the imprint from Soissons, 2007
18. The labyrinth outside Grace Cathedral, San Francisco, 2007
19. Boulevard Saint-Michel 1959-2009: Fifty years have passed!
20. Marley Woods: with Ted Phillips and Doug Trumbull, Apr. 2009

Introduction

Les souvenirs que l'on croit fanés	Those memories we thought wilted
sont des êtres vivants	are living entities
avec des yeux de mort	with the eyes of the Dead
vibrant encore	yet vibrant
de passé…	with the past….

Charles Aznavour, *Jezebel*

As I picked up the materials I had saved in the expectation to compile and edit this volume—all those notes and transcripts and bits of correspondence, or notices of events that brought back smiles or tears—I couldn't chase away poet Grace Paley's remark that "there is a long time in me between knowing and telling." She went on to write: "That long time may best be experienced alone." (1)

Before her, Girolame Cardano, the sixteenth century scientist, hermetic philosopher, and medical doctor, used to teach that "the studious man should always have at hand a clock, and a mirror"—a clock to measure the passage of time, and a mirror to observe the changes of his own personality.

At the dawn of the worldwide web, clocks and mirrors became obsolete, mere devices of the past, replaced by streaming videos and online calendars with built-in alerts; yet the technology did nothing to heal solitude in the face of sorrow, or to eliminate the urgent and permanent need for introspection in a rapidly changing world.

In this decade it became fashionable to write "blogs," journals published on the web. I could have shifted to that mode, and indeed I kept such a blog in 2003 and 2004 to make available the "Letters from California" I published in *Le Figaro*.

As Tom Dolby observed: "Blogs… remove the skin and reveal the skeleton and the guts of creative life. Unlike previous eras, in which artists divulged such intimate details in their journals, through letters, or in cafés over a glass of wine, they now do it online, writ large on a cyber screen." (2)

Thus, the context and the very fabric of life changed radically with the rise of new media that were "free"—or appeared as such to naïve users of the Internet, unaware of the actual price they paid by relinquishing privacy and the subtle control of their lives. My own focus remained the mystery of human existence: I wanted to witness and analyze it, even if ultimate understanding escaped me, or *especially* when it did, in the loss of those dearest to me. I could only gain precious bits of wisdom through what I experienced, and what a few trusted friends could teach me.

And what friends they were! The scientists I admired, the writers of Silicon Valley, the entrepreneurs, and the rising teams of bright financiers who built the first "unicorns," those were my teachers. They changed the world and accelerated it, sometimes for the better and often for the worst. Oddly enough, in the inebriation of the rise of Apple, Google, and Genentech, everyone has forgotten that the period of 2000-2010 turned out to be a very bad time indeed, a lost decade in finance following the Dotcom Crash, with a stupendous 54% drop in market value from August 2000 to February 2009.

Research on paranormal realities and witness reports of puzzling phenomena in the sky did not slow down. It remained a major focus of mine, but the work was now riding on new media that removed the observations further away from the human experience they represented. You had to look for it on the SciFi channel and on scattered sites where bits and pieces of testimony were posted, short on evidence but loud in argumentation and vibrant in controversy; cries for "Disclosure" (a term always left undefined) became strident while mutual accusations of trickery drowned out the physical content of actual observations. Fortunately, I was able to preserve a few trusted sources of veridical data, and to control the technologies that could help decipher them (3).

At the end of the decade, we were all ready for something new, in part because our lost innocence needed to be rebuilt from scratch, but also because a young Black President came to power with welcome glimpses of charisma and the promises of renewal. The world paused and waited for magical gifts.

Paris, July 2021.
San Francisco, August 2022

Part Seventeen

ATHANOR TRANSITION

1

Paris (Mabillon). Thursday 6 January 2000.

Rolling clouds threaten rain over Paris but they don't burst, so the deceptive winter sky just hangs over us, every hint of sunshine quickly blotted out by overcast. The world tumbles headlong into the third millennium but some 250,000 homes are still without power throughout France as the storm abates; its ravages remain evident in scarred roofs and severed branches. The level of the Seine is getting lower; workers are ready to re-open the shoreline. They have yet to clean up the slopes and broken trees.

Fighting the gloom, Professor Bokias, our neighbor, surprised us with a *galette des rois* for breakfast. We walked over to a café to sample it with him, leaving our daughter asleep at the apartment. We love this area, its little secrets and picturesque corners. Last night we had dinner at Les Charpentiers near Saint Sulpice with friends from the Genopole, France's leading biotech and biotherapy-dedicated science and business park. The restaurant keeps its traditional flair as a place dedicated to the old craft, adorned with wooden masterworks.

There's a new spirit among French entrepreneurs, heady excitement. I just visited a company (Arisem) that makes a semantic search engine for the Web, in new offices squeezed between second-hand clothing stores and the sex shops of Rue Saint Denis. I left them to their coding and had lunch alone; I needed some private time.

This morning I saw my mother at the rest home for what I am certain was the last time. She was asleep in her armchair by the window, very drawn and thin. She woke up, surprised to find me there. I warmed up her hands in mine. She told me of a recent dream in a halting voice, occasionally catching herself, mixing up words: *Sommeil, Soleil*... In the dream her two closest sisters, Louise and Huguette, who died recently, had walked into her room. They asked, "What will happen to us, when you're no longer there to protect us?"

I left when she fell asleep again, feeling inadequate because I had been unable to say the right things. Yet there were no "right things."

A presence was all that remained, all that mattered. The sun was warm and gay in her room, putting a bright touch on her paintings hanging behind her bed. I must fly to San Francisco this weekend. My brother tells me no one can predict when the end may come.

Hummingbird. Saturday 8 January 2000.

Back at work in California, I've signed the book contract for *The Four Elements of Financial Alchemy* and started plans for our third Euro-America Fund (1). I met with my new business partner, Graham Burnette, a bright attorney and financial executive with whom I had the pleasure to work when he was the CFO at Mercury Interactive (2). Among my messages is a feeler by Mark Rodeghier from the Center for UFO studies in Chicago, who inquires about the files of the competing APRO (Aerial Phenomena Research Organization) group; shouldn't these files be put "at the disposal of serious researchers" at last? Perhaps, but who are the "serious researchers?" (3)

Hummingbird. Thursday 13 January 2000.

The first transfer into the Fund has been cleared; the system is falling into place. The first UFO reports of the year have also arrived; my friend Ren Breck sends me a notice of a sighting in Millstadt, Missouri: last Wednesday, in the company of three other officers, a policeman observed an arrowhead-shaped object at 4 am. They saw a typical dark triangle with three bright lights and many dimmer lights that appeared to simulate a star field. It moved slowly like a blimp; it seemed about two stories high and three times as long.

Yesterday Janine and I enjoyed an early music concert of harpsichord and viola da gamba at the Stanford Church: Telemann and Bach; Couperin's *Pièces de Viole*; then a beautiful sarabande, and especially Marin Marais' *Labyrinthe*, a wonderful piece "for people with peculiar tastes," as the conductor said when presenting it.

Hummingbird. Friday 14 January 2000.

At Stanford University last night, my former mentor Doug Engelbart gave the second lecture in his formal series on "The Unfinished Revolution."(4) It felt like a return to the old days of SRI. Doug had even brought in his old friend Hew Crane to talk about the future of energy.

A mathematician and brilliant operations research pioneer, Crane was full of the kind of clever but useless statistics that give academia its wonderful weirdness. He pointed out that the semiconductor industry was turning out 10 million transistors per person per year, that the world consumed a trillion gallons of oil (which was equivalent to a cubic mile), and that ants numbered 100 million trillions on the Earth. Nobody asked the obvious question: "So what?"

Wired for sound and firmly in control of his many slides, Doug looked as I had always known him, a man with fixed ideas and vast but unfocused vision. This was all the more bizarre because in the magnificent multimedia amphitheater with video, webcast capabilities, and online hookups at every desk, the 45 technically savvy people in the room were all taking notes on paper.

His sparse white hair carefully coiffed, Doug looked the part of the wise old visionary as he recalled his online computer library, the community Journal and its complicated numbering system. While such a dynamic repository was revolutionary at the time (an SRI vice-president had told him "IBM, DEC, and HP don't know anything about that shit," so the research was surely misguided and should be dropped!), such an online record is hardly news in the Stanford of the third millennium, so Doug's point that "something like this is surely needed in the world" drew blank stares from the participants.

Doug still wants to "boost mankind's collective capability for coping with complex, urgent problems," adding that the purposeful pursuit of this goal is itself a complex, urgent problem. In typical Engelbartian fashion he attacks this by coming up with new acronyms, DKR for "Dynamic Knowledge Repository" and CODIAK for something I missed. To this are added ICS for "improvement communities" and ODS for "open document systems." What the world needs, he finally revealed to us, is more NICS (Networked ICS) or even a multi-nation

META-MetaNICS. Jorge Luis Borges would have cried, or laughed, recalling the Library of Babel.

After wallowing in this pursuit of purposeful complexity, I felt drained by Doug's intact vampiritic power. I was happy to drive home in the night, all velvety dampness along the Crystal Springs reservoirs, reality at last.

Spring Hill. Saturday 15 January 2000.

We're finally selling this ranch. My observatory is empty, except for the books of the paranormal section to be packed up tomorrow. We drove to the storage place under the rain to store away a truckload of my field investigation cases. Hunting for cardboard boxes, we drove in the gray rain along the streets and alleys of Ukiah. We circled the liquor stores and auto parts shops.

The reason we must leave is depressingly obvious. In 25 years, the town has sprawled like the fat-bellied unemployed men we see, leaning against the fenders of broken-down Chevy trucks; shop windows are empty, many stores boarded up; crack cocaine has displaced pot and LSD as the drug of choice, driving away the hippie communes. Idle teenagers look for trouble; roaming gangs have confiscated the future.

Away from the main streets, sidewalks are deserted—even on this Saturday night. Some dark monster of boredom and disease hovers above the flat roofs and the sick short trees. The public library is permanently closed. The only original happening we ever saw here, Janine recalls, was a Christmas afternoon when Santa Claus arrived by helicopter in the K-Mart parking lot.

Now I write by the crude light of a naked bulb, ready to spend my last night at the ranch. I feel sad at leaving this land, yet certain that we can take with us the good memories and some unique lessons.

At the next meeting at NIDS, the National Institute for Discovery Science, founded in Las Vegas by Robert Bigelow, they record an interview for the Discovery Channel. "I thought we were going to do some science," I told them (5). Where is the line between research and advocacy? They answered, with some justification, that publicity would increase reporting, and generate cases to investigate.

Spring Hill. Sunday 16 January 2000.

A blue jay sings just outside my window in the tower. I am running out of boxes, having underestimated the size of the library again. I throw away armfuls of the stuff, a collection of the *MUFON Journal*, newsletters and fanzines, the puffery of organizations that claimed to do "research" but never got much farther than their own egos, or simply sank into the cesspool of the Internet.

I called my mother an hour ago. A nurse picked up the phone, simply handed it to her: "It's your son."

She spoke slowly but recognized me. We had a brief, yet normal conversation. She said she was very tired, about to sleep. She asked when we were leaving Paris. She hinted she was getting better, but she was obviously sedated, under pain medication. We said goodbye. So I sit in the last chair in this tower and tears keep flowing because so much is lost.

Hummingbird. Monday 17 January 2000.

The call from my brother Gabriel came in just before midnight, 9 am for him; Maman had not woken up. The nurse found her, still warm, as she came into her room this morning. My brother is weary and sad like me. We spoke for a long time of practical details. Oddly, our father had died almost at the same date, on 18 January, back in 1958. I fly back to Paris this evening. There will be a ceremony on Thursday, then we will drive to Pontoise together.

Mabillon. Tuesday 18 January 2000.

Her neighbors on Rue de la Clef used to call her *La Dame aux Fleurs*, the Lady of the Flowers. Every evening she cared for the plants hung over her balconies, a gift to the street. The colors were splendid; even from far away you could see those reds, those purples catching the setting sun, for everyone to enjoy.

We have lost La Dame aux Fleurs. In her 100th year she left this life in her sleep, in the Paris retirement home where we visited her. On Thursday my brother and I will accompany her to Pontoise for the last time, along this familiar road. We made that trip together in January 1958 when my father died. She survived him for 42 years.

She has succeeded in forcing the door to the new century, with that intensity of presence we knew so well, her passion to live in spite of obstacles. Born in 1900, she grew up in a family of fourteen children; her parents were ruined by the disastrous Paris floods of 1910; she lived through two world wars. Yet she was able to keep intact her enthusiasm for the future. She was a witness to the explosion of science and technology. She was passionate about their potential and the perspectives they opened up. It is no wonder that both her sons embarked on scientific careers.

That science she admired so much fails to account for the major puzzles of life. It would be reassuring to believe that the Lady of the Flowers awaits us in a cluster of perfections, a garden similar to the one where she used to greet us in Pontoise, resplendent with delphiniums and dahlias, smelling of roses and *muguet*! Yet she placed no trust in such visions of the Beyond. It is to terrestrial life that she held fast, with a willpower we admired, surprising even the nurses and doctors who attended her last few months. All that good care would have been in vain without the interior force that brought her back again and again from the edge of darkness. That force even turned against the shadows she invented to give reality to an invisible battle, increasingly difficult, pathetic and intense.

It is to that inflexible will that all those she touched owe the renewed sense of courage that we take into the future for exploration and innovation. Her legacy includes her intense love for children, for innocence, for anything creative and new.

One anecdote illustrates her indignation before any form of abdication. At age 80 she began auditing courses at the Sorbonne, where young students spoke of the future with that fatality characteristic of the generation that came after the war, discouraged by the complexity of the modern world, perhaps because they haven't experienced the horrors of the old one.

Those disabused students, she chastised them with all her might. She was the youngest in spirit in that group. She would get up to remind them they were about to live through extraordinary events, medical miracles, and the voyage to Mars, new adventures and discoveries they barely imagined. A long time before the Apollo project she had no doubt that man would reach the Moon. She came from a family with wide roots throughout Europe. She had travelled to Russia, England and Germany, and faraway California.

She leaves us with a treasure: that practical wisdom accumulated in a century. Her secret? Never allow despair or existential melancholy to take over our spirit. She often suffered, always fought. The mere idea of abdication before pain, adversity, or the meanness of others never touched her. She also leaves us with flowers, her many paintings. We keep them in simple frames.

Mabillon. Friday 21 January 2000.

Adieu. It was disorienting to see you asleep yesterday, your fine hands folded, your dear face so drawn (that curve of your forehead, that white hair) when you should have been up with us, our children, grandchildren, family all gathered to talk softly of the last time we visited you; the group of those you illuminated with life and kindness and many-faceted love; those who stood briefly before you one by one, then turned their faces away to hide their sorrow.

On the way to Pontoise with my brother, his wife and daughter, the bright dawn lifted to sunshine worthy of an early spring. We walked to the town park, talked of our father, the war years. When we saw the old house everything seemed faded and remote. We ate lunch on the Place du Grand Martroy, the square behind the church of Saint Maclou where medieval criminals used to be mercifully tortured.

The cemetery scene was modest, just the four of us and four red carnations thrown over the bier. Down there now, two wooden boxes side by side in darkness. A chill seized us in spite of the sunny sky. Several large trees, uprooted and broken by the recent storms, still lay in heaps. Gabriel drove us back through the slow traffic of Paris.

It does feel good to cry, if only because it underlines the absurdity of your absence, the silence, the dignified end of a long and beautiful life. So why this gag in my throat, why the tears that keep welling out of nowhere, whenever I recognize a street where we had walked together? You do not belong inside this earth where we left you.

Mabillon. Saturday 22 January 2000.

I just walked over to Place Monge, a dark silent void at 2:30 am. I sat on a low wall across the place where Maman lived these last forty years. No conclave of petunias radiates in purple robes from the fourth-floor balconies. The stone building is closed. Looking up, my face is wet with the cold drizzle of Paris and salty with tears. This lump in my throat won't go away, the sorrow a slow silent wail deep inside. Even now when I write about this ultimate pilgrimage (I just had to go back and look at that street once more, walk around the neighborhood) it is just a big emptiness I feel; there's nothing meaningful to do, or say.

Someone came by, so I felt awkward, got up, and walked on. The little bars along Rue Mouffetard harbored late drinkers. City workers in yellow trucks were taking down the garlands of lights hung up for the Year 2000 celebrations. I reached Place de la Contrescarpe. As a silent and confused young math student at the time, I had mourned my father there. Now I see the same streets where my mother did her daily shopping, her routine walks on the way to buy pastries for us and our children. This cannot have any meaning for anyone but me now. Like those of Pontoise, these streets just tear my heart. A few years ago, I could have met her coming around one of these corners. I would have helped carry the groceries up to the apartment.

When I look at her paintings, copies of major artists, they speak to me more than the originals. It is obvious that Edouard Manet painted flowers, but it is for us alone that my mother painted his *pivoines*: they radiate an unconditional love that has no bounds.

Mabillon. Sunday 23 January 2000.

8:30 in the morning. Paris barely stirs. At Spring Hill ranch, Janine, Catherine, and a friend are wrapping up the move, cleaning the empty rooms. In a demonstration of ultimate spite, our dear old, supposedly "New Age" neighbor, the widow Cleveland, member of the Institute of Noetic Sciences (IONS) and local luminary of all things spiritual, has penned a mean letter threatening barriers in the driveway and lawsuits in court: no road easement, no access to the ranch for the next owners! She tries to upset our sale to extort some money.

Back in Las Vegas, the NIDS board must have finished its work. It is the third meeting in a row I have missed, and perhaps I should just call Bob Bigelow and resign. Created with an objective of discreet scientific inquiry, I feel NIDS is too media-conscious. Am I biased because I missed those early sessions?

Hummingbird. Monday 24 January 2000.

Janine called me after her last night at Spring Hill. She was awakened in the middle of the night by a very bright, large, unidentified "thing" that bathed the front of the house in white light as it flew by.

It is ironic to think our long experiment may have worked after all.

The next call came from Nomura in London, an invitation into a potential investment in a biotech company. Other deal proposals are pouring in. Everything has begun to move again.

I spoke to Bob Bigelow this afternoon. He patiently gave me a summary of the Board meeting, stressing his plans for Congressional Hearings where he counts on my contribution. The idea came from Jim West, president of SARA, a high-tech company. He put Bigelow in touch with Congressman Dana Rohrabacher and his district director Kathleen Hollingsworth. They hope for a government program that would be a sequel to Blue Book, but the first Blue Book project was not worth repeating. Military expert John Alexander had the same reaction: "Be careful what you wish for, you might get it!" he told the Board (6). This is a political minefield. Kathleen Hollingsworth stated the goal would be "to make the study of UFOs scientifically acceptable," adding that Congressional attitudes ranged from outright ignorance to mild interest.

Hummingbird. Saturday 5 February 2000.

John Alexander called me in connection with the Congressional Hearings. He plans to organize small panels on science, military aspects, and "implications." He would like me to lead that third panel, so we spoke about who should be invited, reviewing names of some intelligent skeptics. John is thinking of Colonel De Brouwer from

Belgium and Neil Daniels, the pilot of United flight 94 involved in a UFO encounter affecting his autopilot.

John asked Professor Sturrock to take part in the Hearings but Peter reacted: "I wouldn't know what to say." "For Heaven's sake," John countered, "Sturrock just wrote a whole book about it!" (7)

Hummingbird. Sunday 6 February 2000.

When I called him, Peter Sturrock shared his reactions to the contact with NIDS. "It's a most interesting group," he said, "I was impressed with the staffers, and of course the Board is diverse, intelligent and articulate; that's all pretty nice, and with this kind of money behind them they should have a ground plan, but what is it? And the ranch they bought in Utah...Why this particular project?" (8)

I defended the ranch concept, both as a way of engaging the phenomenon and as an exercise in methodology, because I do think that is an intelligent move. We agreed any plan for restarting the Blue Book project was a waste of time. "And that staffer, Colm Kelleher, giving two media interviews a day...Again, what's the goal? Is that sensible if you really want to do science?"*

This morning I returned a call from Dr. Peter Banks in Michigan (9). We spoke of the Environmental Research Institute of Michigan, a government-sponsored think tank he's transformed into a private enterprise, selling it successfully to General Atomic. We touched on web-based intelligence and the knowledge market, what all that technology does to privacy:

"No, it's not George Orwell, with the government as Big Brother," he said. "Everybody is a Big Brother now, everybody has these tools... Anything inside the Earth or on its surface leaves some mark, and we've got the capability to find it."

Today, as Janine and I drove along the ocean, the sunshine made it feel like the first day of spring. The small towns of El Granada, Moss Beach, Montara, and Pacifica sparkled in the surf and the spray.

What are we looking for? Nothing big; a quiet retreat, easy to reach;

---

* In fairness, there was a chicken-and-egg issue; NIDS needed to increase the flow of reports to assemble an adequate sample.

a secure harbor for the research collections and the archives; a little corner for two by the fireplace.

Portland. Friday 11 February 2000.

My sleep, deeply disturbed for the past couple of years, has become even more fragmented. On Wednesday night, barely two hours, then uneasy rest until dawn. Janine says I worry for no reason. The death of my mother and the loss of Spring Hill have created this emptiness. I have become discouraged with paranormal research to the point of indifference to events that just a few years ago would have stimulated or angered me. Am I betraying what was best in myself: my ability to dream, the occasional glimpse into the multiverse that led me to this frontier?

I started on an article for the *Journal of Scientific Exploration* (*JSE*) about the Haravilliers case (10), then I dropped the project, because JSE seems to turn into a dry repository for academics. Here in Portland, I sleep better, however. About the venture business and innovation in technology and life sciences, I am as excited as ever.

Hummingbird. Thursday 17 February 2000.

Yesterday I met again for tea with Peter Sturrock at the Duck Club in Menlo Park. He was relaxed, dressed in a beautiful wool sweater. He was very sharp in his thinking, although when we discussed Ingo's book *Penetration* (about a mysterious contact named Axelrod) I was surprised to find him credulous, even about the Moon being used by Aliens (11). I know three of the men who walked on the Moon, and why would they lie about its structure?

Peter said rightly that one should abandon the notion of ever influencing the government and especially the Air Force. Velasco (12) has sent him a request for a documentary on UFOs, Pocantico, Hynek and everything else. Peter laughed at this. I told him I had turned down similar requests; it's time to return to science. We talked about the Ubatuba magnesium, a Brazilian UFO sample about which he's hoping to publish a letter in *Nature*. There is no question it's made up of terrestrial elements, but the composition is unusual.

Peter said something else that struck me: "This is a really interesting time in any science," he argued, "when you have enough data to show there's something, *but not enough to find an explanation. That's what real research is all about.* Once you have all the data, the conclusions are easy to draw. When you have too little, there's nothing to say." Why not look for correlations between sightings and geophysical parameters? But later I learned that Peter had never joined the NIDS Advisory Board, and the argument was dropped.

Today I signed our second investment for the new Fund.

Hummingbird. Saturday 19 February 2000.

Over lunch with Dick Haines in Palo Alto we discussed Russian cases, his proposal for a system of information about pilot sightings, and a new observation by three witnesses in Oakland.

Thanks to an invitation by the Ravenheart clan, I spent Friday evening at a conference on Alternative Religions. Luisah Teish arrived late, dressed in yellow and gold, sending wavelets of excitement through the crowd as she walked down the aisle. Her presentation, partly improvised, was funny and moving, inspiring and earthy (13).

Later I met Dr. Rasmussen again, out for a walk and stopped in a bar to enjoy the luxurious display of the San Francisco night scene he enjoys. Then I went back to work, finalizing the Fund documents. I anticipate next week's discussions in Paris with my mercurial mentor, Fred Adler, with the usual mix of pleasure and apprehension.

Hummingbird. Sunday 20 February 2000.

As we discussed research, my trusted friend Roger Brenner (14) told me about his work recording videos of New Age lectures hosted in millionaire Henry Dakin's building, around the corner from us, offered at low rent. In the same building is ISSO, Joe Firmage's new space-oriented venture. He funds about 20 different groups or projects. Sound Photosynthesis gets $4,000 a month to film every meeting, including those of Jack Sarfatti and Saul-Paul Sirag.

The science director for ISSO is Creon Levitt, on leave from NASA, who supervises "free energy" space propulsion concepts. Recently, some Russian genius showed up with stories of a device that could mysteriously propel itself without visible means of support, the whole thing being related to the "third derivative of motion," allegedly a sorely neglected corollary of Newtonian physics. Roger was amazed to see the ISSO team taking all this seriously, ready to embark into space propulsion.

Over at NIDS, discussion has been raging about the MEDEA Committee, a group of experts (including my friend Peter Banks) with access to surveillance satellite data. Physicist Eric Davis would like to join on behalf of NIDS, an idea that John Alexander finds unrealistic given the level of secrecy (15). Recalling the structure of Special Access Programs like our remote viewing work at SRI, Hal Puthoff reminded us that Special Access Programs (SAPs) were not really above top secret, they're just compartmentalized in a special way. In that vein, John Alexander spoke mysteriously about a form of secret access called "Blue Border," which he claimed "can get people killed."

Hummingbird. Monday 21 February 2000.

President's Day. I read Dick Haines' latest research proposal, finding many parallels with Peter Sturrock's idea of geomagnetic monitoring. The correlations would be applied to different data (pilot sightings for Dick, historical records for Peter) so there's no conflict, but they would have gained from combining their efforts and ideas.

Aside from such respected friends and NIDS scientists, I shun exchanges with ufologists because their world keeps getting weirder: In October a Tucson jury found a man named Robert Joseph Moody guilty of the 1993 murder of two women. He stated in court that Aliens would raise him from the dead if he was executed.

Another man named Wesley Nunley, 73, has built a $10,000 saucer landing pad on his property near Dallas, thus fulfilling a long-time dream. The pad is in a quarry surrounded by mud much of the year; apparently he doesn't think the Aliens will mind. And a grand jury on Long Island has returned indictments against John J. Ford and two other men who plotted to kill Suffolk County officials thought to be covering up the truth about a UFO crash there in 1995. The District

Attorney commented: "This all convinces me that there is a side to humanity that defies definition."

If people want to go on believing that a very big destroyer was discombobulated into another dimension out of the Philadelphia Navy Yard under the eyes of Carlos Allende (16), or a thousand other tales, I have no business interfering with their beliefs.

Apart from skeptics who reject everything, no one challenges the unscientific notion that abductees should be hypnotized. Those who understand the perils are too intimidated to step forward.

Mabillon. Saturday 26 February 2000.

One of my favorite haunts in Paris, the quaint bookshop La Table d'Emeraude, has closed up, replaced by a brightly-lit, exotic fabric and jewelry shop for tourists. The dark green frame of the window still reads "Esotérisme, Traditions," but the busy shop is full of Japanese girls rummaging through yellow scarves and orange drapes.

Mabillon. Sunday 27 February 2000.

Thrilled by the fresh morning sun rising over the roofs of Paris, putting flames and sparks on the gold of the domes, I shake off the tiredness of the long flight. I must be sharp to cross swords with the terrible Fred Adler at the Ritz this afternoon (17).

I am surprised at my current lack of enthusiasm for paranormal research. Is it cowardice, laziness...or wisdom? Why pursue an ill-focused goal in a domain so often taken over by publicity seekers and dreamers? Even Gilbert Payan is busy with plans for one more documentary (18). He'd do better to investigate his backyard; there are new sightings of UFOs in France, never reported to his office.

Mabillon. Wednesday 1 March 2000.

The first Métro rumbles, somewhere underneath us. Fred Adler has come and gone; our investors are a happy group. Yet everything in the New Economy seems fragile and irrational to me. It is suspended in a gossamer frame of insane stock valuations driven by people who just discovered the Internet but don't understand what it really does.

There are pictures of Spring Hill on these walls. I see them with nostalgia, missing the sublime waterfalls in our secluded canyon.

Mabillon. Thursday 2 March 2000.

I just made a presentation of the new Fund to a young analyst who works for the Sultan of Brunei. Seated in a salon of the Intercontinental Hotel, I presented our track record (which is excellent) and my current deal flow, which is large. But he had one reservation: none of their money can be used for investment in Israel, for political reasons back home.

In the evening, Gabriel Mergui and Jean-Louis Escary wanted me to mediate a legal dispute at Genopole about Genodyssée, which specializes in genomic mutation control.

Mabillon. Friday 3 March 2000.

The case in Haravilliers still bothers me, so I called Gérard Deforge and spoke again to the main witness, Mr. Delangle. They continue to track events, including two new sightings at the same place. Most remarkable is an observation on 20 August 1999 at Le Ruel by a woman engineer. She saw a colored triangle with a yellowish circle underneath, like a small moon. The object hovered over the field where Delangle saw his craft. She tried to use her cellphone and it failed. She did see two tractors in the field, spotlights aimed at the object. Gérard Deforge checked with the landowners: no tractors working that night. Another "impossible" observation.

I catch myself thinking of things to tell my mother, articles I would have saved for her, or some amusing piece of news. Visits to her were a difficult duty at times, a great joy at others; they defined continuity, a fullness of our lives, a world of kindness.

Hummingbird. Sunday 12 March 2000.

We're back in dreamy California. Yesterday, continuing our search for a retreat to replace Spring Hill, we visited a property on a steep bluff overlooking Tomales Bay and fell in love with it.

Janine often recalls the very first impression we had in Belmont, the aesthetic shock when we opened the door onto the wide living room with the light of the limitless Bay and the sky beyond the wide glass doors. This new house (I call it "Athanor," in honor of alchemical pursuits) has the same feeling as Belmont did, with a breathtaking view from Point Reyes in the South all the way to Bodega Bay in the North. The sound of the surf is all around us.

We made an offer today and it was accepted, so we're making plans to re-arrange our books, the research files, and the personal things we saved after selling the ranch, all in storage now, gathering dust. We're tired, Janine working with such energy, and me preparing the new Fund, caught in a whirlwind of Internet follies, slowly recovering from jet lag, and silently mourning my luminous mother.

Hummingbird. Sunday 19 March 2000.

The pace has slowed a bit. Janine has the transactions under control for the Athanor. When we made the inspection with Catherine, the wind howled mournfully along the metal eaves of the roof. The sound caught on the guardrails. The glorious foghorn of Tomales Bay whined and complained in the glow of the Pacific haze.

Last night we saw *The Ninth Gate* again, catching more tantalizing details in this splendid Roman Polanski movie with its flawed ending. The landscapes of Pontoise, the Ile Saint Louis, and Puivert came back hauntingly. Too bad the end is abrupt and a bit silly. It seems clear that Stanley Kubrick plagiarized the same theme in *Eyes Wide Shut*, one of the silliest films I've seen in a long time. Kubrick's plot can be summarized as "Handsome, young millionaire doctor in Manhattan tries to get laid for four days and fails!"

I understand that he attempted to say something profound about the erotic and magical, but he only produced gratuitous gropings. Like Umberto Eco in *Foucault's Pendulum*, he tries to come to grips with the occult and fails, while Polanski has hermeticism in his blood and soul, and the exquisite aesthetics of an Adept.

Polanski has recognized the power and genuineness of his cause, his story, his landscapes, while Kubrick exemplifies the well-trained intellectual who scrutinizes the magical from the outside and just "doesn't get it." This raises the whole question of esotericism, and why it is so difficult to explain its relevance to academics.

In Las Vegas, NIDS is blossoming nicely, thanks to Colm Kelleher and Eric Davis. The latter is a physicist who works on a theoretical development of wormhole theory. He tells me:

"The Fastwalker is a dimensional portal or dynamic wormhole. We can dispense with the particular physics basis for now, whether it's Hal's model or one based on Einstein's general relativity, since I'm working on proving that the two models are the same for wormholes, much as Hal has showed that the models were the same for Schwarzschild-stellar spacetime metrics. My laser experiments address Hal's model directly. Recent cosmological observations showing the universe to be flat also support him."

Eric, who just read my novel, goes on to explain why he thinks UFOs could turn out to be wormholes: "*FastWalker* presents a technology of portal generation and manipulation. In our space, the portal (the UFO or craft) is several tens or hundreds of feet in linear dimension. But when you step into it, you are in a vast landscape possessing eerie qualities.

"This landscape is of a space that is either 3-D and orthogonal to ours, or is a hyper (more than 3-D) space of another separate or nearby universe. In either case, *these spaces are intersecting ours under control*.

"The act of intersection manifests itself into bursts of very bright light, distorted visual effects through the portal. A wormhole has the beautiful topological property to do just this, and this property is simply governed by the invariant Gauss-Bonnet relation between the sectional space curvature of the wormhole surface and the Euler number derived from the wormhole genus.

"Wormholes can connect distant regions within the same space or connect distinct spaces within distinct universes, either orthogonal or hyperdimensional. The visual effects from such connections are just as in your novel."

While discussing the physics, Eric doesn't lose sight of the other aspect of the observations that makes them so tantalizing: "We have yet to explore the facet of human consciousness that potentially extends into hyperdimensional space. Acausal effects empirically known, like synchronicity and quantum entanglement, teleportation and correlations, are indicative of this potential."

Hummingbird. Wednesday 22 March 2000.

On Sunday Eric said that Olga Karatidi's experiments, Hal's SRI research, Ed Mitchell's research, etc. showed that the "mind field was like a universal quantum field but was acausal, a field of Fisher Information. Our minds 'random hash' information patterns throughout the manifold (your words): We gain conscious information a-causally."

On Monday I discussed this at the California Institute for Physics and Astrophysics (CIPA) over lunch with Dr. Bernie Haisch and his wife, Marsha Sims, always friendly and informative. Bernie keeps running into patentable inventions he tries to get financed, so I asked about models of inertia and zero-point energy.

Bernie said he was impressed with Eric, although not to the point of embracing his laser experiments. Eric has spoken openly at CIPA about NIDS and his efforts to track down a woman who'd worked at TRW in Roswell days, and might be able to confirm UFO crash data. But I was amazed to learn that NIDS was not supporting any of Eric's work in physics, demanding that he pursue it on his own time.

About Hal's theory Bernie was positive, adding that the work done so far (including his own) was limited to quantum electrodynamics, while there were more fundamental ways of formulating the problem. We went on to talk about Joe Firmage, who is coming for dinner at our place in two weeks. He'll be alone because he lacks a life partner, Bernie said, "He doesn't have the bandwidth for it." Yet in this field as in many others it is difficult to keep one's balance unless love is part of the equation. What would I do if I didn't have the treasure of Janine's presence?

Joe was looking for scientific papers on breakthrough physics and found Bernie's work. He read it and the next day had his encounter with the being of light. That led to his commitment of $10 million to CIPA.

But Joe's efforts to raise millions for fundamental research subsequently failed, as I had predicted to Kit Green (19).

Squaw Valley. Monday 27 March 2000.

Lake Tahoe in early spring finery offers scenes of unimaginable beauty. This afternoon at Emerald Bay the sun was warming up the snow on every summit around. From the mountain road that circles the lake the view plunges over granite blocks and deep forests to a rocky island. In 1929 a gifted woman built a replica of a ninth-century Norse fortress on that island. She ordered old Scandinavian furnishings to complete it. She was rowed daily to her stronghold in the middle of the bay, where she took her afternoon tea.

Hummingbird. Wednesday 5 April 2000.

Last night Janine and I drove up to Penngrove to spend the evening with the Ravenheart family. We were warmly received by Oberon (the new magical name of Tim Otter Zell) who was relaxed and generous with his wisdom, as usual. Morning Glory was in good spirits, loquacious and clever even as she fought with a recalcitrant Hollandaise sauce for the asparagus and the roasted chicken. Liza, a vivacious brunette, spoke of her efforts to organize "polyamory" communities among Pagan groups. After dinner I described the Haravilliers case, which led to a good discussion about reality.

The stock market has been gyrating wildly. NASDAQ and the Dow Jones index both dropped a vertiginous 500 points yesterday.

Hummingbird. Friday 7 April 2000.

Last night I had a leg cramp, jumped up to squash it and collapsed by the side of the bed. It had happened before, a simple syncope, the only injury a scratch on my cheek, but my brain a horrible void. Janine's hand holding me brought me back, a bridge to life. I won't work today; I've learned my lesson. I catch up on little things, reading John Carter's excellent biography of Jack Parsons (20).

Hummingbird. Saturday 8 April 2000.

Awake in the middle of the night, I got up for a glass of water and walked through the apartment, the lights of San Francisco filtering through the fog. Our place reflects Janine's taste, orderly beauty, only marred (or enhanced?) by my overflow library. It spells soft comfort and peace, suspended above the wondrous City. I felt silly to doubt destiny, to question our future: my professional situation is stable for several years. Janine chides me about my anguish.

"You own all these books that talk of mysticism," she reminds me. "What good are they if they don't help you rise above the human garbage?" She is right, of course. So I steal silently into bed, seeking her breath, the touch of her skin.

Hummingbird. Friday 14 April 2000.

We leave for France in an hour. Yesterday I drove over to Sacramento with Graham Burnette for a presentation to Calsters, 110 billion dollars, 70% of it in stocks. We listened to advice from Réal Desrochers, the French Canadian who heads it up.

Reconnecting with long-neglected friends, I have called George Kuchar (21), Roger Brenner, all good guys on the artistic margins of the chaotic mess into which California is turning.

Joe Firmage came over for dinner. He was sharp, intense, likeable, and obviously sincere. We discussed the Corso puzzle and Ingo Swann's bizarre stories in his book *Penetrations*.

Joe is struck by the absence of any spiritual fiber in Silicon Valley. I told him the Valley will quickly rediscover strong moral values if the NASDAQ drops another thousand points. This morning it's down by 300 and dives, so there's hope for sanity. Yet lots of naïve people will get hurt as the economy wakes up from past excesses with a hangover.

We also discussed the claim that the government may possess Alien hardware. Joe has spoken to a NATO general, one of Hal's "iron posts," who said "I do know there's a crashed saucer because I've touched it."

"What does that actually mean?" I asked him. "What's the 'it'? We still don't have any tangible data, do we?" All we have is another general with a story. Was Hal there when Firmage heard this? Could it be that too many of the people involved have psychotic traits, as some experts say? The story explains nothing.

Mabillon. Tuesday 18 April 2000.

Upon arrival on Friday, dinner with my partners at Cercle Interallié. Yesterday Janine and I roamed pleasantly through the flea markets with Olivier under gray skies and sprinkles. The stock exchange crashed even deeper last week, sounding a warning that the "New Economy" (assuming there ever was such a thing) actually was missing a few screws. A feeling of emptiness and confusion prevails.

My friends' cocktail party on classy Avenue Marceau attracted an over-capacity, ebullient, smart crowd.

Mabillon. Thursday 20 April 2000.

In spite of an overwhelming bureaucracy, entrepreneurship is indeed alive in France. There's no lack of bright scientists, physicians, and engineers willing to take chances and start companies. At the sprawling Génopole campus in Evry yesterday, our scientific advisory board considered five startup projects in an all-day session.

The plans have to do with genomics or biotech, often over my head, but also with applications of information technology to the life sciences, so I feel at ease with this group (22), a tribute to the indulgence they show for my lapses of biological knowledge.

Janine and I spent the evening at the home of Gabriel Mergui in Antony, with his wife and two daughters. He received us in traditional robes and performed a fine Moroccan version of the Jewish rite of Haggadah.

Gabriel told me that Jacques Attali was launching a French venture fund, and would I be a candidate to run it in Paris? I answered I still loved France but my recent experiences with French financiers' sharp teeth and shark-like maneuvers had left a sour taste. We also spoke of the sighting at Haravilliers, where I return tomorrow to study the site with Gérard Deforge.

On the train back from Pontoise. Saturday 22 April 2000.

When Deforge met me this morning at the train station under a steady fine rain, the anticipation was heavy and the air cold. Once again, we drove up to Haravilliers in his green Rover while I turned on the electromagnetic field tester I had brought along: It beeped every time we passed under a power line, but went flat in the countryside. We recorded no disturbance at all, either on the RF scale or the ELF scale, in the vicinity of the sightings. However, we had a surprise when we drove through the village of Grisy-les-Plâtres: The meter reacted violently. So we parked the car and saw an inn across the street: *Auberge du Saint Graal*, said the sign in gothic letters! We laughed and naturally we ate lunch there, finding excellent food.

2

Athanor. Sunday 30 April 2000.

The Athanor stands on the edge of the Pacific, a tall gray structure of wood and glass, modern assemblage of rectangles and slanted surfaces, a cross between a battleship and a futuristic feudal fort. We learn to live at its special rhythm: the sunset is red behind Bodega Bay as a few street lights appear, scattered along the shore. The wind abates and we are left with the sounds of our rambling home, Sirius and Betelgeuse the points of reference above the haze.

At sunrise the light puts a border of bright white lace on the leading edge of every wave, recurring hemlines on the undulating sea lost in fine haze.

Ahead of us is the Point Reyes Natural Refuge, the green snout of a lumbering crocodile. Catherine will enjoy this house. I had a dream about my daughter. Kindly, earnestly, she was telling me of her plans for life. Nothing she said made sense to me, so the dream left me emotionally moved and mentally frustrated.

I'm starting to understand that this contradiction, a hallmark of fatherhood, doesn't fade away when one's children get older.

Las Vegas. Friday 5 May 2000.

Bob Bigelow took our NIDS advisory group on a tour of his ambitious aerospace company tonight. We saw a model of his space station, planned as a large structure between low Earth orbit and the Moon's vicinity. The lab also holds a full-length mockup of one of the 12 units, each designed for a 12-passenger payload. To avoid the nausea that plagues even trained astronauts, the whole structure would spin at one rotation per minute. Never short of ideas, the group immediately offered some design remarks. I asked about noise reduction, an unsolved problem with Mir and other space habitats. Ted Rockwell jumped in with contacts among submarine designers, experts in silent operations; he went on to discuss the placement of the reactors. The physicists from Los Alamos, Martin Piltz and JohnDale Solem, launched into a detailed discussion of the design's energy requirements.

We all warmed up to this exhilarating experience. It takes a visionary entrepreneur like Bob to work so creatively with NASA and the international space consortia. There was much discussion about the ability of private industry to achieve breakthroughs where governments were impotent. Yet private enterprise isn't necessarily immune to poor judgment, as the failed adventure of the Iridium communications system has shown, even with Motorola's billions.

Much of the discussion at dinner had to do with the ongoing disorganization and poor morale at NASA and Los Alamos. Disappointed, experienced managers take early retirement over bad decisions motivated by politics, taking with them the legacy of an entire scientific generation.

Counter-intelligence expert Jim Westwood has reviewed the MJ-12 documents: a sophisticated "authentic fake," he said, whose authors must be within the Intelligence structure. Jim also believes the Roswell crash may have been invented to flush out soviet spies.

Las Vegas. Saturday 6 May 2000.

We had a full series of meetings today at Park House, headquarters for the Bigelow development operations. We started with my presentation of the Haravilliers sightings, received with numerous questions. Then, a discussion of case statistics compiled by the staff. NIDS is mailing thousands of flyers a month to get the attention of police, airports, and pilot organizations while John Alexander pursues contacts with the FAA, and John Schuessler with his own sources.

Jim Whinnery, whose advice I sought about Haravilliers, recommended that the witness undergo a full neurological examination; a putrid smell he once reported could be problematic. But on the bus back to the motel JohnDale told me he didn't worry that the readings I took at the site would pose any problem in terms of health effects for the witnesses, which reassured me.

Over dinner at John and Victoria's house I met Congressman Rohrabacher's assistant Kathleen Hollingsworth, an energetic Irish-born woman. The Hearings are still being discussed, but don't hold your breath, said John: nobody wants a UFO circus in Washington.

Las Vegas. The Luxor. Sunday 7 May 2000.

Hal and I had a further talk about the ongoing Dulce area sightings with Colm Kelleher and Eric Davis. They hear strange reports from the Indian elders, but stories of underground bases sound silly.

NIDS now owns the John Carpenter abduction files, bought for $14,000, but they're still in a pile of envelopes in the storage room and have not been examined. The Institute is breaking down under the weight of the data, as all of us have experienced. So far, there's nothing of significance in the implants NIDS has analyzed. Many abductees are diabetic, and many have had OBEs, but the relevance of these observations is questionable. Colm is saturated with contracts, administration, and recruiting. Travel requests get denied, and Eric himself does his physics research in his spare time (Firmage pays for it). The agenda and the priorities vary from day to day, making long-term planning impractical.

Hal will conduct an experiment in late June at the synchrotron facility of the University of Wisconsin in an attempt to verify his hypothesis about the structure of the hydrogen atom being related to zero-point energy, potentially a breakthrough (23).

Las Vegas. The Luxor. Monday 8 May 2000.

Hal, Eric, and I spent most of the day together, from the Luxor coffee shop to the Stratosphere, and to a Chevy's restaurant with Eric's family. We returned to the Luxor where the three of us went through the Search of the Obelisk ride, giggling like kids. Later, finding a private setting, we discussed two issues that hadn't been brought up before the NIDS science board.

The first topic concerned the revelations of a former TRW employee. An attorney friend of hers has gathered her testimony. She was part of a secret reverse-engineering project called Zodiac. Eric has compiled his own file, but it doesn't lead to the verifiable, hard facts we need.

More interesting is the story of Kit being briefed at "a very high level" about the UFO situation. He was told that there had been three verified cases of Alien landings, respectively in 1947, 1953, and 1984 (which would exclude Holloman, I pointed out). Kit is puzzled about the briefing; he trusts the people who gave it but is only half-convinced the information is true. It might be a test of his credulity and loyalty because it took place after odd conversations with foreigners at an arms control conference.

Now I relax in the neo-Egyptian splendor of this hollow black pyramid that would have astounded Thutmosis. The illuminations of Vegas are visible through the slanted triple windows on the 23rd floor. The Interop computer communications show begins tomorrow. Ubique, one of my portfolio companies, has an exhibit there.

Las Vegas. Tuesday 9 May 2000.

Stepping into the crowded lobby of the familiar Interop center, I know my way around the halls and the booths, although many aspects of the business bore me. It is the people aspect that interests me: So much energy, so much ingenuity among this crowd, changing the world by simply, quietly, rewiring it.

Hal flew back to Austin yesterday afternoon. I drove him to the airport so we could talk about a story concerning a request by the Secretary of Defense to conduct an audit of all black projects. When the budgets were added up, a discrepancy appeared. A high-level officer (a general) who was Assistant Secretary of Defense was tasked to find out where the difference lay. He dug into the discrepancies and narrowed the gap, but there remained a small difference, "only" a few million dollars, yet an annoying fact: the Secretary was afraid of uncovering another Contra affair, or some illegal activity taking place under his nose. So the general finally obtained a briefing on the rogue project.

The secret had to do with low-level maintenance work at a private contractor entrusted with keeping "some material" from prying eyes. The material, he was told, was from a crashed UFO, but it wasn't being subjected to any tests. The general proposed to take the matter to researchers within the veil of secrecy, but his request was denied. There the matter rests. But when someone offered private funding for decent analysis, he was instructed to just go home and forget it.

We agreed the case could serve as a litmus test for all the stories of crashed saucers we keep hearing about. The general had been offered the job of Chairman of the Joint Chiefs and turned it down. He now serves the US "in a difficult diplomatic capacity."*

Athanor. Saturday 13 May 2000.

This is our second weekend here, upgrading the house. Workers come and go. The deer that roam freely through the neighborhood are as familiar as cats and even more graceful. We overlook the wooded canyons where they love to hide. When Janine and I climbed over jumbles of rocks and hiked to a hidden beach through the high grass, we found a sheltered cove strewn with black boulders, its slopes resplendent with red and purple ice plants.

Today we drove to Bodega Bay, with plans for long walks along the mysterious Estero with its wonderful rock formations, oddly

---

* It was later revealed that the story was quite a bit more complex.

contoured, full of natural caves and dolmen-like turrets, but I don't have much time to enjoy all that. In one week, I'll be in France again.

Mabillon. Saturday 20 May 2000.

Sweet sunshine, alternating with cold periods of rain. I met my son and Max near Notre-Dame in this uncertain French spring. We played around the sandboxes while discussing the Internet. Following up on Haravilliers, I spoke to Gérard again about the woman who'd seen a flying triangle. He confirmed the light beams she saw were straight and sharply-defined.

On the phone from California, Janine tells me she drove to Athanor and spent the night there, soothed by the sound of the surf. She loves the place, as I do, and puts renewed energy into it, inspired by the special light and the ocean.

The sale of the Spring Hill ranch, painful as it was, has lifted a huge weight from her shoulders, and mine.

Mabillon. Sunday 21 May 2000.

In some professions I believe, foolishly perhaps, that I could have excelled. If I had stayed in France, I would have been a writer, both of fiction and non-fiction, because writing is what I do most naturally. A written page is my interface between a devouring curiosity for the world and access to the minds of readers, a rich treasure. I love books like Ossendowski's *Sous le Fouet du Simoun*, an account I just discovered, of his travels in Algerian Sahara, the kind of story that has always inspired me.

With equal passion I think I would have made a fair architect or a publisher. Astronomy suited me, but in time I would have been repelled by its academic arrogance and petty budget skirmishes.

I did have an easy career ahead of me 30 years ago, in computer science and futures research. My projects could have been funded for a long time because applications were wide open (They still are). As an Intelligence analyst, I would have known how to integrate large data sets in context; growing up in the chaos and uncertainty of wartime has provided me with some important, life-long insights.

In most other careers I doubt if I could have made more than a decent living; in particular, my father always urged my brother and me to stay away from studying Law.

Of course, I could have been a professor, as Allen Hynek urged me to do, but I would have hated it, once the realities of bureaucracy caught up with me and crushed the dreams and the students.

In the stock market, my brain wouldn't be quick enough to sustain the quantitative stress, and in most other fields I would have failed. As a chemist or a doctor, my poor memory would have defeated me. As a corporate manager, I lack the passion for negotiating and manipulating one must have in order to outsmart competitors.

Oddly enough, my French partners now embrace me as a good investor in technology because my work in venture capital has helped create some significant companies, but I am no financier.

Mabillon. Wednesday 24 May 2000.

Simonne Servais, former spokesperson for De Gaulle and Pompidou, whom I saw on Sunday afternoon, was as energetic as ever when it came to discussing the revamped official French UFO project, now called SEPRA (24), and the political intrigues behind it.

The French public is excited by the sensational new report called *Cometa*, skillfully marketed as "A Report to the President of France about UFOs." That allegation is a scam, she said, but there is indeed a genuine group of officers behind it. They belong to the Institute for Military Studies in France (IHEDN) and their superiors are upset because the study was never meant to be published. The cover used, without my permission and without analysis, the photograph of an unexplained disk I brought back from Costa Rica, so it turned the scientific community against them. As for the real author, Gilbert Payan, the anonymous puppet master, Simonne cannot find anyone who knows him, so she's more intrigued than ever by the situation.

Lunch today at Pavillon Elysées with twenty potential investors in our new Fund, including senior managers from the French Poste and the Caisse des Dépôts. A major investor, one of the few authentic business angels in France, tells me that for fiscal reasons most of his money is frozen in insurance annuities and cannot be used for startup investments. Thus the French State is creating disincentives to the development of new high-tech companies, even as it pretends to spur venture capital: Yet another reason for us to remain in California.

Athanor. Monday 29 May 2000.

Memorial Day. The wind howls in the superstructures of this house and drives waves across the bay. A ray of sunshine: Catherine came over yesterday. Janine suggested a walk up the hill; on the edge of the cliffs our backs are firmly turned to Western civilization and its frothy problems.

Nature offers us this landscape, those graceful hills of the Point Reyes seashore and the wide expanse of the sand moist with salty spray, the horizon blurry with only a thin layer of luminous bluish haze.

Hummingbird. Sunday 4 June 2000.

Christian Pierret is the current minister for Industry under Laurent Fabius in the Jospin government. A jovial man in his early fifties, he spent the afternoon in casual conversations with us on a terrace overlooking the Valley. We stressed the urgent need for reforms to help French startups; I've joined a group that introduces legislation to facilitate such essential tools as stock options for company founders and clear rules for venture funds. Yet the old culture dies hard. The Unions are fiercely against such reforms, with an unlikely ally in corporate tycoons whose comfortable control is threatened by new technology. Innovation remains a dirty word in France.

Hummingbird. Thursday 8 June 2000.

This afternoon I was visiting Ren Breck in Oakland as a priest arrived to give him communion. The old man was a very courteous, crumpled fellow with an odd tie; he looked a bit lost. Ren's brain scans are alarming: the tumor remains viciously active, extending a tentacle towards the brain stem.

His speech remains clear, however, so we reminisced about my old

InfoMedia Company, his role in civic projects and senior housing, and his achievements with causes where his irrepressible goodness won against developers' greed.

Athanor. Saturday 10 June 2000.

This is our last weekend together before Janine goes off for two weeks in Greece and I fly to France for another trip. A strong wind has risen over Tomales Bay. Large birds play at stalling high over the shore and getting blown backwards past our windows. They drop and drift, all feathers extended. They dive and flip, rise again.

Hummingbird. Sunday 18 June 2000.

The view of the City from this high floor offers an orderly sense of structure, the noises reduced to a distant hum. That's probably why Janine likes it so much, she who enjoys proper order and is so sensitive to sound, music, melody, and the human voice.

I didn't go out today, didn't even shave. I worked on the book and a couple of deals. I watched a rerun of *Tales of the City* and caught the news from Finland on the Internet, in Latin ("Nuntii Latini").

I ate a frozen dinner with a glass of wine while looking at the evening sun over San Francisco. I feel tired, angry at my slow brain, wishing Janine were still here. On Wednesday I fly to Europe.

Hummingbird. Tuesday 20 June 2000.

Why so tired? I dined alone again, reading an article by Gregory Benford in a sci-fi magazine. Then Marcello Truzzi called (25). He's writing about remote viewing, he said, expressing puzzlement at the way information about the secret project had leaked out. I had to laugh, pointing out I was the only participant who hadn't written a book or gone on TV about it!

"But if this stuff works, why did they drop it?" he asked. "Could it still be going on somewhere?"

I couldn't help him: I have the same questions. And I couldn't tell him if I had the full answer.

"But why did the government go to the trouble of publishing a report that dismisses it while admitting the statistics cannot be explained?" he went on. "In the 70s, when the Navy asked my advice about the SRI work, I gave a positive recommendation, but I never thought it would go this way."

He must not grasp the bureaucratic mind as fully as he should.

Mabillon. Friday 23 June 2000.

Thalys, the silver-and-burgundy high-speed train to Brussels, took me to Belgium today with Graham Burnette and our French partners. The city was gray and drizzly, torn up by street works, disfigured by a dreary landscape of derelict façades and obscenely wealthy mansions. We told our story to three smart executives in the multimedia room of an ancient private bank dripping with cash.

Belgium has no serious tax on wealth or capital gains, so it is the logical refuge of French fortunes, only an hour from Paris on the high-speed train.

Mabillon. Saturday 24 June 2000.

Finally, I arranged for lunch at Totem with Simonne Servais and Gilbert Payan. They crossed swords immediately, sparred and tested each other, to my amusement. I introduced the major challenge of the UFO phenomenon: it is so varied and diverse that one can always find enough data among the sightings, if selected appropriately, to "prove" any theory, including its non-existence. For that reason, it's very dangerous to work selectively with reports from the military, or pilots, I said, without taking the context into account.

When I nettled him about the *Cometa* report, the ripped-off picture of my Costa Rica object on its cover, the publication by the same tabloid guilty of the Roswell "alien autopsy" story, and the studious avoidance of all reference to private researchers, Simonne intently studied Payan's face for signs of reaction. *Interestingly, there was none.* He replied in a flat tone that my work hadn't been considered because I had linked UFOs and parapsychology: "When you went to see that general in Washington, at the embassy, you gave him your book *Confrontations*, which talks about the Yeti..."

"*Confrontations* isn't about the Yeti!" I interjected, shocked by such a preposterous lie. "It proposes a classification of anomalies that encompasses all the observed facts..."

He dismissed this with a shrug: "The CNES has 2,000 reports from gendarmes: not one of them mentions paranormal incidents."

"If I had just seen a UFO and called the gendarmes, why would I mention such details?" I countered. I gave him several examples of cases whose blatantly paranormal aspects never appeared in the literature: the Colonel Coyne episode, Father Gill, their private confessions to me. And the Chapin case in California (26).

Afterwards Simonne asked me, in her most serious tone, "*Who does this man work for?* He's extremely well trained, a man of action and discretion, able to control a discussion without betraying his plan. You're right, he's indeed the puppet master behind a lot more than *Cometa*. Something must have happened for these generals to allow him to use their names, while he remained hidden..."

About the TV documentary project, Payan said it was a joke. I mentioned Velasco was at the end of his rope, begging me to participate. "We'll do something for Velasco," Payan dropped for his only answer, suggesting the future of SEPRA wasn't in doubt.

Yet many of the things Payan says are naïve. He believes everything people write about implants, and he's ready to reconsider Adamski "because of what he said about the propulsion system," which is childish.

When it came to abductions—another topic *Cometa* has avoided—Payan said if they decided to approach such a case they would bring in a military psychiatrist.

"Good luck," I thought. So I went on connecting the dots: the very poor American translation of the *Cometa* report was paid for by Laurance Rockefeller and the Fund for UFO Research (27). Then Ira Einhorn, of all people, showed up to market it in the States!

Mabillon. Sunday 25 June 2000.

After midnight. I watched France beat Spain in the Euro 2000 soccer tournament, fell asleep heavily, woke up an hour later. I must drag myself through the days, meetings and phone calls and the drudgery of business maneuvers. I miss Janine; without her my life doesn't make much sense. Will I find the right words to tell her how much I love her, fresh from island adventures and salty swims?

I called up Gérard Deforge about Haravilliers. The French military have visited the area: for what purpose? Then ufological zealots have dragged the witness to a hypnotist, with predictable bad results.

Over the phone, Simonne reiterated Payan was more powerful than he let on.

"But why is the French army so afraid of parapsychology? These generals, are they really such blushing virgins?" I asked.

"They're not blushing virgins, but skilled politicians," she replied seriously. "Don't laugh, Jacques. *These people have an agenda.*"

Lyon. Monday 26 June 2000.

A beautiful day in Lyon, the Saône River resplendent and sparkling. More investors join the project to fund us.

Lunch at Villa Florentine with the group. But I am so tired...

Mabillon. Wednesday 28 June 2000.

Paris remains hot and sticky, under the first assault of summer. One of my meetings was cancelled so I came home to do the laundry, went to the bank, and ran errands among Parisians and tourists in light dress. Janine called from Greece, lifting my spirits. She was waiting for a boat to Naxos, her last island stop with Helen.

An article in *Libération* (22 June) shows a heavy-set and ageing Ira. He speaks of his "continuing campaign against violence in America," posing as an Internet pioneer and target of a witch-hunt. Ira as victim of persecution, poster child for human freedom? The article is designed to portray him as a victim of America's barbarism, rather than the manipulating monster he's become. Laughable...

Pierre Lagrange (away on a visit to a sick friend, Nicolas Maillard) doesn't believe there's any substance behind *Cometa*. Simonne disagrees. Pierre says Payan must simply have written everything and persuaded the other officers to lend their names. But the president of

Cometa is Algrin, an attorney who belongs to a far-right group. The bad translation was published without permission by Stanton Friedman is further embarrassment for the authors. In the face of this garbage, the National Centre for Space Studies (CNES) will be under pressure to quietly move Velasco aside.

Yesterday our Genopole science board met, on the historic occasion of the decoding of the human genome. But only 85% of the job is complete. I joked with Pierre Tambourin that biologists were falling into the same bad habits as computer experts, releasing incomplete products and expecting their users to finish the job.

I have negotiated a commitment for our new investment operations. Graham and I have made enough progress to launch the third Euro-America Fund before the end of July.

Air France flight. Saturday 1 July 2000.

Over the Northern Territories with Janine who came back to Paris last night, tanned from her trip to Greece, enthusiastic about her travels. She threw her arms around me and told stories of sunny, faraway islands that brought back memories of Homer and Herodotus. Another page begins, a peaceful one: a page for music, strolls on the beach, concerts at Old First Church, simple pleasures.

Hummingbird. Thursday 6 July 2000.

Thank heavens for these Journal notes and a fast search engine! I've discovered something today by scanning my notes: My meeting with General Pouliquen in Washington was on December 1994, at a time when General Letty was already at work with *Comité 89*. But Alain Boudier had told me, "Payan wanted CNES to contact the Americans to get access to the hardware recovered at Roswell... Pouliquen was to approach the Pentagon on the UFO issue."

So things go back to that time, six years ago. Then came Greer and his briefings. Among this mix of valid data and made-up tales were high-level reports by Willard Miller, a genuine officer with an authentic record. Was it Miller's visibility that triggered the decision by *Cometa* to go public? Or our Pocantico meetings?

At our lunch with Payan last week, Simonne had remarked, "It looks like something happened..." a shot in the dark to which Payan replied with a tone of finality, "Yes, something did happen."

Eric Davis and Ed Mitchell now tell me that Miller initiated briefings on UFOs with the Intelligence office of the Joint Staff in September 1993, with Congress in April 1997, and with the Director of the Defense Intelligence Agency (DIA) in September 1998. John Petersen of the Arlington Institute, who supports Greer and is familiar with the military, was unimpressed with these briefings. He wrote: "Miller was down at CINCLANT and he arranged for Greer to talk to the Joint Staff J2, an admiral who listened politely until it got weird and then shut down the conversation. When I heard about it, there'd been no follow-up on the part of the military. At the time it was my impression that Miller only knew what Greer told him."

Eric Davis notes that in 1994 Miller retired from active duty as the Current Operations head (J3) of US Atlantic Command, Norfolk, Virginia, where he worked operations, intelligence, and special contingency issues. Now Ed Mitchell provides more details: "I participated in the meeting in the Pentagon with the JC intelligence chief. It was quite factual, discussing credibility of sightings, the possible existence of a covert government organization, and reviewed testimony of a few military eyewitnesses. The particular vice-admiral and staff seemed naïve and uninformed. The admiral promised to look into the issue of a covert, high-level organization. A few weeks later, Miller received a cryptic call from the admiral's office saying only: 'You are correct.'"

Ed Mitchell adds: "Miller is conservative in his approach to the issue—listens a lot more than he talks. His main concern is that the lack of candor from government and the secrecy and covert maneuvering will eventually precipitate a national security disaster when someone mistakes a genuine sighting for an attack."

"Unless Congress or the President really gets busy, the coverup and stonewalling will continue indefinitely. Wherever the control exists, it's not going to be easily revealed at the Pentagon."

Did the French pick up on these rumors, and did they take them at face value? Was that the trigger for *Cometa*?

Hummingbird. Tuesday 11 July 2000.

Today Dr. Peter Banks and I went to the California Institute for Physics and Astrophysics where Bernie Haisch told us that Joe Firmage planned to buy Scientific Applied Research Associates (SARA) and merge it with ISSO. SARA is a $5 million/year operation.

The folks at SETI have reacted violently (in the *Washington Post*) against Firmage's alliance with Carl Sagan's widow to create *Voyager*, the new media enterprise for which he's said to have raised $21 million.

Hummingbird. Friday 14 July 2000.

Peter Sturrock called me last night in search of advice about NIDS. "I've missed two meetings in a row," he said, "and of course the first time I went there I was impressed with the Board. But I've been wondering. I read their emails; it all seems so... puerile."

Perhaps, but he's not aware of all the work investigating dozens of "black triangle" reports and other unexplained events.

The main reason I stayed on, I told Peter, had to do with the Utah ranch. Buying and instrumenting such a property in a "hot" area is exactly what I would've done if I had such resources, and indeed what I began at Spring Hill.

NIDS may slip to become little more than another UFO group, with the usual features: a website, an 800-number for the public, and vague expectations of Congressional Hearings.

Peter was unmoved: "Well Jacques, as you know I believe I can best spend my time doing science. I'm interested in publishing serious papers. I've been neglecting astrophysics. I think I ought to concentrate on that."

Athanor. Saturday 15 July 2000.

Point Reyes is in the fog. As I write I see a steep bluff where a doe and her fawn are grazing, then the trees that frame the beach, and the milky Pacific beyond. The wind brings hints of mysteries and the song of birds. Soon we will retrieve our bookcases and all the research files. The same week, Graham and I will open our new office in Santa Clara, down the road from Intel.

Dominique Weinstein (28) kindly sends me a French tabloid with an item about Willard Miller, distorted news about Stephen Greer and Congress, and well-written accounts of Velasco's visit to Chile.

Athanor. Saturday 22 July 2000.

We loaded the truck with our little treasures and spent the afternoon at a homeowners' meeting in quaint Tomales where an amusing controversy has arisen: a small sect, devotees of Saint Anthony, have purchased 400 acres of prime land they plan to develop, high above our coastal ridge. Local residents have taken up the flag of resistance against these Gnostics: why do they come here, instead of retiring to caves in the desert like their holy founder?

Back home we sorted through boxes of clothes, curtain rods and Victorian lamps, electronics and kitchen utensils, a hundred little things. Some are indeed cherished, like my mother's painting of a doe in Belmont, and family photographs that remind us of Normandy. Other objects simply followed us for no reason.

Hummingbird. Sunday 23 July 2000.

Commander Willard Miller called me tonight. He made it clear he hadn't been very public and remained careful among ufologists: we agreed that 95% of the new data in circulation was disinformation or made-up stories designed to impress the media.

"I've been working mostly with military officers and have given a couple of briefings at the Pentagon, as you're aware," he said. "There's an overwhelming body of evidence, much testimony from people connected with programs, in and out of government."

Hummingbird. Thursday 27 July 2000.

Over breakfast on Tuesday with Peter Sturrock at the Duck Club, he gave me a draft of his newest article about the isotope ratios in the

Ubatuba sample, consistent with a terrestrial origin (29). He showed me his letter to Bigelow, resigning from our NIDS science board.

Prime Minister Lionel Jospin has finally signed the extradition papers for Ira Einhorn, who will appeal, so he may not be returned to Philadelphia yet, assuming he doesn't simply disappear one more time. Jospin was clever enough to sign last Friday, just before the end of the Tour de France, so the media paid no attention.

Athanor. Monday 31 July 2000.

We woke up as the sun put a golden touch over the redwood beams. The fog bank was still hanging over the beach and the trees below, leaving us suspended between two worlds of various light. I spent much of Sunday recompiling the blue files. As the evening crept in I unpacked the parapsychology volumes and rediscovered some treasures, while Janine exhumed our old stereo and joyfully played vinyl records we had long neglected.

The weather has alternated between soft sunshine and cool breeze. Sometimes it swallows everything; other times it recedes or simply pulls a magic act of evaporation in minutes, only hanging a pretty row of cotton balls over the ridge. Then we can see the people on the beach, surfers and fishermen. All night the roar of the surf has engulfed us. We savor the opportunity to be here; thinking of our parents, their own lives and hopes; remembering my mother, who would have enjoyed this house at the edge of a continent.

Athanor. Tuesday 1 August 2000.

The books have been moved to the new shelves: from the grave reflections of Ruppelt, Keyhoe, and Hynek to the fantasies of Adamski and the dark obsessions of Hopkins and Jacobs, they represent a spectrum of human inquiry in the face of the unknown, with more than a pinch of idiocy and the occasional scam.

When I was lecturing on the subject in the seventies and eighties, I spent much time on events like the Dr. X. observation and the Williamette Pass photograph (30).

If I made a presentation today I couldn't use either of them. Dr. X.

may have experienced something but he lied about some key elements. As for the Williamette photo, it was a hoax. What, exactly, can we prove? NIDS' experience in Utah will be an important part of the answer.

Athanor. Saturday 5 August 2000.

We went back to the City for a day to catch up on current business. Electronic mail has slowed down except for a flurry of messages from maverick physicist Jack Sarfatti, writing about his space drive theories. The new book I have in mind would describe the betrayal of the Internet, whose early history has been forgotten or distorted. Those who write about it were not there, and those who were there either cannot write or have become too rich to care. I can write about it credibly because I was there from the beginning and have not been caught up in the games.

Athanor. Tuesday 8 August 2000.

Simonne Servais tells me she's met again with Payan. He claims to be "an ordinary consultant with the Ministry of Research." She isn't fooled by that. He clearly has access to the foreign Intelligence apparatus. Simonne also said there was a front-page article in *Le Figaro* about Gordon Cooper's book, where he speaks of his sightings as a pilot and mentions that his film of a UFO landing at Edwards was confiscated by unknown authorities.

We had lunch in Bodega Bay today, at The Tides restaurant filmed by Alfred Hitchcock. We watched the famous seagulls, the ducks and sea lions, as they played in the silvery light of the harbor and fed in a cool, gray weather where even time seemed blurry.

From rainy Normandy, Gérard Deforge gave me some news of our case at Haravilliers. The caretaker has been interviewed again. He swore *he'd clearly seen an airliner that morning*, flying very low in the early dawn. And a military team (not from CNES) has come over to take "radiation measurements." As I did before them... but who went there?

The mail had brought a bank statement of my mother's modest life insurance policies, to be split between my brother and me. Getting money from her feels wrong. I must think of using it for something good, something she would approve, but not for myself.

Athanor. Wednesday 9 August 2000.

We just took an exploration trip I had long hoped for, to a part of the country ignored by tourists and guides: the heart of Northern California is undocumented mountain land, with few dirt roads and fewer visitors. It extends over an extraordinary expanse, a million acres from Clear Lake to the foot of Mount Shasta. The road that crosses it is little more than a dusty trail, closed during the winter, when the Forest Service can't clear the snow. The region is called Yolla Bolly, a jumble of volcanic hills.

Reaching Covelo itself is not easy. A mountain road rises from Willits over precipitous gorges, all the way to a saddle from which one discovers Round Valley, a marvel among the steep hills that shelter it so well that pioneers of California gave it "generously" to the displaced Indians, foolishly assuming it would contain them. At the eastern end two roads take off into the abrupt hills. One, to the North, moves on towards Zenia, while the other plunges due East, climbing up for miles until my truck, now in 4-wheel drive, seems to hover above the deserted gorges visible through the white dust. The wilderness road goes down, up again, to Black Butte at 7,448 feet. We stopped for a picnic in the forest and continued along the ridge, with a view to precipices above the bad lands of Willows and the central valley. The descent is bleak, the few hamlets ill-kept.

Athanor. Friday 11 August 2000.

Tomales Bay is bordered on the West side (the ocean side) by a long ridge blessedly bare of any development, part of the Point Reyes National Seashore. It holds no human settlement beyond Inverness. Sandy beaches along the small bays are sheltered from the wind. Janine and I paddled out from Marshall in a kayak, landing on one of these secluded coves for a picnic and a hike along the ridge. Abandoned wooden buildings stood in the underbrush, left by an artist colony that tried unsuccessfully to flee civilization.

I thought of Alan Watts writing about the Way of Zen, "the freedom of clouds and mountain streams wandering nowhere," and the aimless life, a concept unfortunately foreign to me.

3

Hummingbird. Monday 14 August 2000.

Graham and I have moved into our new office in Santa Clara, in a beautiful three-story building with oak paneling, heavy wooden doors and an enormous glass atrium, originally designed to serve as headquarters for Intel. Once again I enjoy the unique feeling of a startup, the first day of operation of a new company with an empty suite of offices. Graham wired the communications panel while I unloaded boxes of files, setup the fax machine, and then sat on the floor next to the first working telephone.

"Let's call an entrepreneur! What's the number?" I asked. Graham answered, "In this area, you can just dial at random, you're sure to find an entrepreneur."

So I called the founder of a medical company who had contacted me for financing and we arranged to meet on Thursday.

We don't have any desks or chairs yet, but we've already seen four companies in anticipation of launching the Fund: the prospect of ongoing business is unmistakable.

Bill Moore and Jack Sarfatti try to drag me into acrimonious disputes, innuendoes about Hynek's supposed dark side, and the Paul Bennewitz case (31). Janine asks why these childish debates bother me. With that sharp intellect of hers, she sadly watches the mystery of ufology disintegrate into such futile altercations.

Hummingbird. Friday 18 August 2000.

I managed to track down Dr. Niemtzow, now practicing acupuncture at the naval base in San Diego. He was happy to reminisce about our trip to France. He'd lost touch with ufology, but he did get involved in one episode at Edwards Air Force Base, early last year. Richard heard that a commercial airliner had encountered a large unidentified disk and that a jet from Edwards had been sent up to investigate. Since he knew the general, he went into his office and said, "I understand one of our jets went up after a UFO?"

"If it happened, I'm not aware of it," the man said. "You ought to ask Colonel such-and-such, who's director of operations."

The colonel was adamant: this was not a true story. Yet Richard knew the people at Edwards: "Richard, they did launch an aircraft," they told him. But the trail stopped there: The control tower invoked "Need to Know."

Hummingbird. Monday 28 August 2000.

Janine's brother Alain has come over from his Charleston restaurant for a few days of vacation, so we are eating like kings and enjoying fun memories. At work, we meet new entrepreneurs every day. This afternoon, a board meeting at CyberIQ (32). My energy has returned, and so has better sleep.

I am reading Gorres' *Mystique* for the second time, with renewed admiration. I wouldn't exchange our era for his, but there is much to be said for a time when men could take the time to study the dusty archives of miraculous deeds and compile books like his.

Beaver Creek, Colorado. Sunday 3 September 2000.

The Renaissance Conference is reaching the end after three days of distinguished panel discussions on everything from Internet and religion to environmental concerns, family issues, and investments. I took an active role on three of the panels, although little will come of such rambling talks.

Yesterday, with Steve and Linda Millard, we took the lift to the top of the mountain and walked down the trail, telling stories and making the sort of enthusiastic plans Californians plot as soon as they are away from their computers.

Ex-astronaut Wally Schirra, true American hero, brushed aside the UFO subject when Steve brought up the revelations in fellow-pilot Gordon Cooper's new book, which he called preposterous.

Beaver Creek. Monday 4 September 2000.

Labor Day. We got up at 6 am for a ride in a hot air balloon. In the transparent atmosphere and gentle breezes of the Rockies, we floated up, meeting the sunrise at 9,000 feet, and then gliding down the valley to the astonishment of a few prairie dogs. Being away has helped me make new plans for *The Heart of the Internet*.

Las Vegas. Saturday 9 September 2000.

The science board of NIDS began its meeting with an update by Bob: he's expanding the facility in Vegas after a failed attempt to locate operations in Montana. The major uncertainty is NASA, he said, and its monopoly in the commercialization of space. The discussion left me with deepening admiration for Bob's vision.

Next, Colm led a discussion about relations with the Chilean investigative project, the CEEFAA, housed under the Chilean Air Force and led by General Mario Avila Lobos, a UFO witness.

Today we tackled the ranch events again, reviewing a variety of cases, including mutilations. I pointed out that NIDS had a difficult choice: playing the role of a UFO group (Our "MUFON on steroids" scenario) or becoming a specialized institute supporting the work of others (the "Blue Book with an attitude" scenario). John Schuessler spoke of sensor technologies. Hal commented on the magnetic anomaly Poher and I reported in our 1975 paper for the American Institute of Aeronautics and Astronautics (AIAA) (33).

Colm and Eric are chasing two interesting cases, one in Montana where a terrified couple saw objects land around their cabin in the woods near Noxon, and one in Poughkeepsie, New York, where a truck driver swears he saw an object plow into a hillside. We may never find the secret of Alien visitations, but all this makes for fascinating conversation in Mr. Bigelow's magnificent office.

Hummingbird. Sunday 24 September 2000.

The best birthday present of all: my son arrived yesterday with three-year old Maxim. We've been talking, playing, arguing about everything. There's another quarrel on the web, recalling my skepticism about the Rockefeller-Mack initiative. A writer named Gary Bekkum insists: "Dr. Vallee is, of course, one of Them."

He thinks I belong to a corps of Wonderkids who received cosmic knowledge "beyond their education and years." I can only wish... but I did spend a quiet day with Max, Olivier, and Janine.

Hummingbird. Sunday 1 October 2000.

Dominique Weinstein came over for dinner tonight, along with Dick and Carole Haines, and extraordinary compiler Larry Hatch. Olivier and Max were there as well, so it was a fun evening of UFO jokes: I gave Weinstein a fake Area 51 badge and a map of the "Alien Base."

New York City. Wednesday 4 October 2000.

Two days in Manhattan, the usual combination of suspense, exhaustion, and a long meeting with Fred Adler. On the plane I met a group of distraught computer types who thought I was Senator Kerry (it seems we have the same abundant white hair). They were even happier to hear I was a venture capitalist, hoping I would invest in their scheme. Internet companies are falling out of favor with most investors, once giddily enthusiastic for any "dot-com" plan.

Hummingbird. Monday 9 October 2000.

Over lunch at the Duck Club with Peter Sturrock, he was candid in his assessment of his own book (*The UFO Enigma*), which has passed unnoticed in the scientific media: not a single review, not even an invitation from some university to speak on the subject! We spoke of Velasco's documentary project with Payan, absurdly entitled *The American Secret*, where both Peter and I declined an opportunity to appear. The idea that such a documentary could force official support is as bizarre as the title itself.

Hummingbird. Thursday 12 October 2000.

Flying back from Portland after two Board meetings, I find a message announcing the death of Pierre Guérin on Saturday, October 7, of complications of his cancer treatment. His book *UFOs: The Mechanism of Disinformation* has just been published. Sadly, it is a venomous attack on anyone Guérin regarded as an offender against the Extraterrestrial Cause, especially sociologist Lagrange. Although we're distraught at the news, the fact is that no substantive discussion had been possible with him for years, even on subjects like the Big Bang. He'd become bitter against the entire world.

My friend Ren Breck is dying, too. We have long discussions over the phone, often at bizarre hours because he's lost all sense of time. He's also lost most of his vision and hearing, so he dictates his autobiography to a tape recorder in long ramblings tirades about his victories and hopes, and Cold War politics. Yesterday he felt "vibrations" and a powerful release of energy, due to the drugs that prevent his brain from swelling. The experience he described was reminiscent of VALIS, which long fascinated Philip Dick's readers.

Back in the Middle East, America faces the forces of religious fanaticism. Battles are raging, stones against rubber bullets changing to real bullets against missiles, rifles against helicopters, and a suicide mission against a US destroyer. If that kind of stupidity is the end result of spiritual faith, what does that say for mankind's so-called finer aspirations?

Athanor. Saturday 14 October 2000.

This site speaks to us in many ways. Janine says it is the only place where she's immediately happy, in harmony with a landscape she could contemplate for hours. In the morning, I preciously guard her sleep while savoring the muffled roar of the waves.

I read Thurston's *The Physical Phenomena of Mysticism*, recommended long ago by Aimé Michel, and David Hatcher Childress' *Lost Cities of Ancient Lemuria and the Pacific*, which makes me want to learn about the antiquity of Hawaii.

Athanor. Sunday 15 October 2000.

Friday night at the Ravenhearts, good antidote to gloomy news. A rare full moon on Friday the 13th, which only occurs every 17 years, was a fine excuse for the party. Morning Glory wore butterfly wings; there were fairies and elves, spiders and a unicorn. Oberon wore a leather mask and a metal-studded belt. The crowd arrived with music and a frolicking mood, wearing little more than their imagination.

We lingered to admire Oberon's latest work, and then we drove over to the coast, where Roger Brenner joined us: he was our first guest at the Athanor, and the first fellow-researcher to see the full library. He'd brought us a videotape from Firmage's research organization, heavy on physical theories, light on critical analysis. On Saturday we had a picnic at the beach where the high waves sprayed us. The cold wind eventually drove us home.

Athanor. Saturday 21 October 2000.

We went back to Bodega Bay today and walked all around the Point on the way to the vertiginous cliffs. After yesterday's rains the weather has been very clear, the waves whipped up by a strong North wind. We're celebrating our 40th wedding anniversary. On the phone, Olivier told us he couldn't even comprehend such a number.

Forty years, and so much pleasure at our quiet conversations, or working together to organize this new home: we attack simple tasks, cleaning up the garage, landscaping the hillside before the first serious rains. Heaven, like the Devil, is in the details.

In the downstairs library that threatens to turn into a museum of the paranormal, I've corrected the galleys of *Four Elements* and pursued the manuscript of *The Heart of the Internet*. Many old letters end up in the trash, old controversies too: not enough time.

It isn't the size of this library that's important but its selective value, the result of distillation. It spells out the existence of another level of consciousness within man, and of another level of reality in the external universe. It also hints at one or more secret government projects that neither Kit nor Bob nor Hal have found. But where?

Athanor. Sunday 29 October 2000.

Winter comes early. I write in the library, looking over the beach, drafting a review of a new book on abductions (34) for *JSE*. I had doubts that I could deal with an issue so distasteful to me, but writing proves therapeutic. The authors involved—Hopkins, Jacobs and even John Mack—have the intensity and narrow-mindedness of zealots.

On Wednesday night I went to see George Kuchar, one of the dear friends I'd neglected during the horrible period of my professional transition. He gave me a copy of his Rockefeller digital epic, a two-hour video entitled *Secrets of the Shadow World* that features John Keel at Mount Shasta and Whitley Strieber in San Antonio. There is an ominous parallel between Whitley's childhood experiences and those of "Roger Brenner." Both were fascinated by teachers or acquaintances that exposed them to esoteric skills; both have trouble remembering what took place in those murky encounters.

Janine and I have achieved this certainty, a place of simple beauty at the edge of the world: nothing in front of us but the wooded shore, the cliffs and the sand, wild flowers among the rocky outcrops, and this magnificent bay. Yesterday a falcon perched on the railing near us and surveyed it all with the palpable intensity of his round eyes.

Hummingbird. Wednesday 8 November 2000.

Like all of America we've watched the election results, Bush against Gore, with mounting amazement. Oberon and Liza had come over for dinner. The four of us followed the news, state by state, with deepening concern. At midnight Luc Evrard, of Europe No.1, called me from Paris to elicit comments about Bush's victory, quickly reversed when Florida was thrown into question again.

In San Francisco the air tastes so good, the landscape is so beautiful. After all this time...why does it still feel like inebriation, the first heartbeats of love, pure freedom, the beginning of life? And in the evening, your head on my shoulder.

Hummingbird. Sunday 12 November 2000.

Ramping up for a trip to Europe in a couple of days, the old enthusiasm comes back into my veins. Letters finally get written, including a difficult one to Guérin's wife, reminiscing about Pierre, mentor and friend. I also owe a reply to Roger Corréard, whose amusing chronicles of phenomena in the Durance valley sound so much like ufological *Lettres de Mon Moulin*...

Mabillon. Friday 17 November 2000.

Graham and I took the train to London today for a presentation to the Altius group. We walked near Buckingham Palace in the cold and finally sat for a leisurely lunch at a nearby hotel in plush luxury. I was happy to get back to old Paris after another trip on sleepy Eurostar. The experience with the long tunnel was an anticlimax, the technology so perfect that one hardly notices the heroic plunge under a sea that has divided nations and promoted warfare for centuries. It felt like a brief trip through smooth darkness, only enough time to read a page of *Le Canard Enchaîné* and enjoy one cup of coffee.

Mabillon. Saturday 18 November 2000.

All I've done since my arrival on Wednesday evening: some disorderly sleep in stretches of a few agitated hours, then coffee with our erudite neighbor Christian Bokias at La Palette, his favorite *café littéraire*. Olivier Todd, a disciple of Sartre, sat at the next table.

I had a brief meeting with my brother at Le Rostand for an update on our mother's papers. He was tense, hurried. The weather had turned cold, with snowflakes in the air. Yet I enjoyed those errands that reconnected me with France: the post office, the train tickets.

Mabillon. Sunday 19 November 2000.

My young friend Eric Raulet has invited me to a seminar on the paranormal. Given the near-fanatical cult of "rationalism" among Paris intellectuals, it went surprisingly well. Marie-Thérèse de Brosses was in the audience, as well as researcher Marceau Sicaud from Pontoise. Gérard Deforge brought me news of Haravilliers; the most recent sighting was of cylindrical, collimated beams, moon-colored, unexplained. Other old-timers of French ufology and parapsychology were in attendance, like Françoise Fouéré, Professor Chauvin and his wife, Father Brune, Bertrand Méheust, young sociologists, journalists, science buffs, arguing testily about statistical tests, chi square formulas, all the paraphernalia of many obscure experiments.

A panel on transcommunication (alleged electronic messages from the dead) almost ended in a hilarious brawl, with Professor Lignon haughtily challenging all the claims. I asked why the experimenters did not run their voice recordings through frequency analysis, which would establish whether they matched human voice patterns, or were synthetically-generated. Nobody picked up on this. One could also use dictation or speech-understanding software now in common use. That, too, was ignored, as if the parties didn't really want to know what was in their data. Their controversy is a reward in itself!

Bertrand Méheust is a serious fellow, completing his dissertation on "animal magnetism," the spark for much of 19th-century parapsychology. He's come across some 200 unpublished pages from Aimé Michel (35). I introduced him to Sicaud, who's in touch with Aimé's son. Madame Fouéré assured me René Hardy's death was a suicide: he suffered from kidney failure, had been operated on, knew he was dying. This explanation doesn't fully satisfy me (36).

Mabillon. Monday 20 November 2000.

My colleagues and I were in Lille today for a presentation on high-tech investing: Someone called it "masterful," a word rarely used in financial circles. We spoke in a cavernous 18th century mansion belonging to wealthy industrialists. I discover the region's hidden private wealth, much of it safely hoarded across the nearby border in

Belgium where taxes are favorable.

Only a few hours of sleep, interrupted by phone calls to our struggling companies. Cold weather, gray with occasional sunshine.

Mabillon. Wednesday 22 November 2000.

Paris seems slow to wake up today. In the blackness, the first Métro brings a distant rumble. Last night Gabriel Mergui drove us back from the Génopole science meeting in heavy rain and the chaos of the boulevards. He'd been too busy to replace his windshield wipers, so we stumbled through a crazy world of light streaks and blurred showers of gutter drops. I enjoyed the intellectual stimulation of the six biotechnology deals their founders presented before our panel.

Lyon. Thursday 23 November 2000.

I had a free afternoon in Paris after interviewing Thierry Labbé, ex-president of Cisco France, for a venture position with us. So I walked over to a bookstore to buy Pierre Guérin's book, a last rite in his memory. I found it in the esoteric section, a thick volume with black cover. Pierre would have felt insulted to see his work among ghosts, poltergeist, astrology, crystal healing, and treatises on tarot.

In the train back from Geneva. Friday 24 November 2000.

We made two presentations of the Fund today, along with our diligent and faithful colleague Jean-François Puech. I am amused by the cozy atmosphere of Swiss finance, with its high-tech touches behind thick mahogany doors and elegant design, white pebble corridors, walls of sliding water. The TGV takes four long hours to return to Paris, half of the trip over old tracks, not yet upgraded.

Mabillon. Saturday 25 November 2000.

Researcher Christine Hardy, last seen at Raulet's seminar, met me at Relais Odéon this morning, on her way to a four-month meditation stay in India. Christine works on a theory of "semantic fields," groping for a framework that would account for coincidences. She's an energetic woman with a demeanor of modest reserve that must blend well in India or Iran, where she once studied with a Sufi master. Her work matches my own attempts to describe the universe in terms of information structures.

An hour later I was back at the same café for lunch with Dominique Weinstein. We discussed a little-known French military report (37) issued in 1995, the text that triggered the dubious *Cometa* document. Payan still enjoys playing with ufologists, his puppets.

Mabillon. Sunday 26 November 2000.

Yesterday evening I saw my brother again. This time he seemed relaxed and even happy. We had a warm discussion about the politics of medicine, mad cow disease, and trends in biological research. Driving rain again, wind whipping out the few last leaves.

Hummingbird. Monday 27 November 2000.

I read Pierre Guérin's book on the Air France flight, with mixed reactions. He takes Roswell at face value, which is silly, but he shows a sophisticated approach to mutilations and abductions. He even considers the possibility that witnesses may have been fed false images by the phenomenon itself. Pierre is fair in quoting my reluctance to accept first-level extraterrestrial theories. Yet he falls into the trap of taking ufological rumors for Gospel truth: he regards NIDS as another tool of the "American services," but he trusts the fake Gulf Breeze pictures (38). I was moved by Guérin's book, in spite of these shortcomings. It's a simple, straightforward text. It comes across very differently from his rambling letters, full of bilious epithets boiling in a cauldron of dogmatic prose.

Athanor. Saturday 2 December 2000.

A brief interlude today, a walk to the beach for lunch at the edge of the spray before another trip to Japan next week. The tide was very high, cutting off our access to our favorite picnic place on the rocks.

Tonight, back in the City, we attended a recital by Pepe Romero followed by dinner with Roger who told us that Joe Firmage was tired of funding New Age projects. No wonder: in keeping with the general debacle in Internet deals, the stock of USWeb has dropped from about $60 to less than $2 in six months.

Tokyo. Wednesday 6 December 2000.

Tsuyoki Isobe, an intense Japanese gentleman in his forties who works at Narita airport, met me at the gate with a warm handshake and helped me with the transportation formalities. He is translating *FastWalker* into Japanese for a science-fiction publisher, Tokyo Sogensha, with release planned in August.

My room looks over Tokyo Bay, reached last night after a long bus ride through congested traffic. A series of financial meetings have been setup for Graham and me over the next three days.

Aside from the long journey, trips to Japan now feel easy. I have no apprehension to return to this deeply-cultured city of exquisite politeness, a bit too ordered.

With every trip I try to understand new layers of this island universe. For that reason, too, I look forward to visiting Japan as a writer rather than as an American investor.

Tokyo. Thursday 7 December 2000.

Unsettled time. The US presidential election remains undecided one month after the vote: Is it Bush or Al Gore? Stock markets tumble again after a two-day irrational surge; technology companies vacillate in the wake of bad earnings by Apple and other PC firms. In Tokyo, in the meantime, cranes are at work, skyscrapers go up.

We visited two firms yesterday, starting with our old friends at Nippon Investment & Finance, and we will see three more today, guided by a long-time French expat from Caisse des Dépots.

Over dinner with Tsukoyi Isobe I learned that *FastWalker* would appear in a collection that includes Edgar Rice Burroughs of *Pellucidar* fame. "Gouki" had a large bag full of my books with pieces of paper sticking out of many pages. He grilled me for two hours about the Pentacle Memorandum, thoughts on Roswell, obscure points of

UFO history, and even my family's ancestry, recording me on tape while we ate prawns and raw fish at Attore.

Athanor. Sunday 10 December 2000.

Long walks on the beach with Janine and her visiting sister, Annick. The sky clears up after a rainstorm. The atmosphere is limpid; the sea splashes splendidly over the dark rocks. What makes me happiest is that Janine loves this place, as if she'd found her ideal home, where time no longer matters, where we can be completely at peace.

Hummingbird. Tuesday 19 December 2000.

Over lunch with Dick Haines, I gave him the beautiful French aeronautical charts from Weinstein. Dick begins an international project he calls the National Aviation Reporting Center on Anomalous Phenomena (NARCAP) (39) to assemble pilot reports of UFOs worldwide. He went to see Bigelow for support and spent five hours with him in Vegas, but they disagreed over control. The alternative option of funding by Firmage is fading away. Dick plans to retire next spring and move to Whidbey Island, his late father's home.

Athanor. Saturday 23 December 2000.

Annick and Olivier have joined us for the holidays, leaving Max in Japan with his mother; we forget the cares of the business world.
Yesterday I attended an interesting reunion in Menlo Park, at the SRI International Center, which brought back many memories. Doug Engelbart wore the national medal of technology recently handed to him by President Clinton. Elizabeth "Jake" Feinler (the woman who invented "dot-com"), Harvey Lehtman, Charles Irby unchanged, calm and friendly, and Dave Crocker of ARPA fame were there along with Bob Johansen in a bright red sweater. SRI old-timers shook my hand and spoke of our days in research with the warm sparkle of unforgotten friendship, shared adventures of the mind. Doug, who has a new team of volunteer disciples, was all smiles.

Athanor. Monday 25 December 2000.

Catherine is here for Christmas with the happy news she's been accepted for an MBA program. We feel ready for a New Year, if not a new millennium. Everything changes fast: George W. Bush in Washington, the web everywhere, and the economy in hard landing.
   Reviewing my study of abductions, I am reminded of a remark by Freud: "One should never make the mistake of applying the norm of reality to repressed creations of the mind. By such a process one runs the risk of underestimating the importance of phantasies of imagination in the formation of the symptoms, or the risk of attributing a different source to a neurotic feeling of guilt..."

Athanor. Sunday 31 December 2000.

Richard Niemtzow, who'd travelled to Toulouse with Jacqueline, his first trip to France in ten years, called today. Over dinner with Velasco, he was amused to see he now sported a goatee and cultivated a vague resemblance to Hynek. His budget has been slashed. "Jean-Jacques sees doors closing before him," says Richard. "He wonders whether all this hard work was worth the effort."
   The last few days here have been so happy that we delayed our return to the City. It seems fitting to watch the end of the old century simply facing the great living void of the Pacific beyond Bodega Bay, the turmoil of the world simmering far behind us. The night sky, all purple sunsets and carmine streaks, has turned deep blue, then black, carrying the crescent moon and Venus in the Southwest, Jupiter and Saturn spanning the ecliptic. Away from the crowd, we huddle happily in the folds of their splendor.

4

Hummingbird. Monday 8 January 2001.

Rain feels different here, arriving in Northern California after three weeks of pure springlike poetry. People smile at the sheer pleasure of breathing; the mood is still relaxed in spite of new concerns for the massive layoffs in high tech, overblown digital dreams.

With my new office near Intel, the commute is much too long, but it gives me the luxury of a spectacular drive along the Crystal Springs reservoirs, a plunge into the woods freshly scented by rain on both sides of the ridge on Skyline, then the Pacific Ocean at Daly City and the scenic route to the park. From the lakes, one drives up Portola Boulevard (one of Janine's favorite areas) to the top of the hill, then a plunge along the curves of Market Street to the gay rainbow flag at the Castro intersection and the final trip home to Pacific Heights.

My son left yesterday for Washington and Paris; Alain flies back to Charleston tomorrow. Only Annick remains for another week, nervous at the prospect of the wet grayness of Normandy. Work is almost finished at Athanor, including the wooden staircase I built to the garage loft, new computers, and a high-speed link to the web.

Hummingbird. Wednesday 10 January 2001.

Artist Carlo Bartalini, our friend and neighbor in this building, has just died at 76. We love the graceful sculpture of Pan Janine bought from him. Carlo liked to be surrounded with works of stupendous texture and color, worthy of his operatic talent and booming voice (40). He's created many art objects, gifted as he was with the eye and the hand. The result, in his home, was a visitor's total immersion in a bewildering jungle of imitation swords and cheap tapestries, some ravishing antiques, Italian chairs, a Nefertiti or two, clashing curtains over red wallpaper worthy of a bordello, with the occasional Mesopotamian monster peering from a gaping closet.

We were privileged to sample his wild cuisine and to preserve some of his art. Tomorrow his ashes will be dispersed from a boat beyond Alcatraz; then another genuine San Francisco character will be gone. We will miss Carlo's good humor and buoyant humanity. Perhaps he has now joined his goat-foot god and looks down on us in the same gay pose, a flute in one hand and grapes in the other.

Las Vegas. Friday 12 January 2001.

The weather remains clear in Nevada while another California storm moves on, dumping deep snow as far as Arizona. I arrived early for the NIDS meeting. Eric Davis greeted me at the airport. Recent events: A week ago part of the NIDS operation was cut, letting Dr. George Onet go. Eric and Colm were asked to produce a report (it ran to 17 pages) about the Institute's work.

We reviewed recent cases, notably an apparent near-landing at the Utah ranch on 27 December. There have been multiple mutilation investigations since 1998, in Montana, California, and Arkansas. But the investigation of the Noxon, Montana, case won't proceed further.

Kit has related to Eric and Colm that on one of his missions to Asia, he had a bodyguard who was a tactical helicopter pilot. The man assured him that his unit had flown 1,000 hours in machines disguised to look like UFOs. He gave no details, but made clear the purpose of the flights was to make certain the guards responded appropriately. That may not explain all the cases (especially when launching sequences were tampered with) but we should take it into account.

Ron Pandolfi is an enigma, his office at CIA reportedly filled with fake UFO pictures and Alien jokes.

Hummingbird. Sunday 14 January 2001.

The NIDS group spent Friday evening at Bigelow Aerospace, inspecting the new model of a space habitat module (1/6 scale). Based in part on the group's advice at our last session, the design no longer focuses on a "space hotel" but on a well-designed commercial platform, representing over 80% of the ISS volume.

There are persistent allegations that Pandolfi's office has interfered with Bill McGarrity's clearance and with Martin Piltz' reputation, smearing him at Los Alamos as a UFO believer.

On Saturday we had presentations by the staff about the Minot Air Force Base case of October 1968 where the crew of a B-52 encountered a UFO both visually and on radar, followed by a study of the Montana cases: flying objects, helicopters, and mutilations all over the Northern Tier. Finally, the group reviewed a sighting at the ranch by our neighbors the Garcias a couple of weeks ago. A maneuvering light was caught on videotape by one of our two functioning cameras, however it may have been attached to a low-flying plane, not a UFO.

In the afternoon we discussed theory. John Petersen presented a vast matrix of belief systems that seemed to embrace all New Age ideas, down to the most tenuous. We also discussed my Hilltop Curve (41), sighting strangeness, and John Alexander, who has returned from Peru with fascinating stories of Ayahuasca drug parties, giant snakes, and the Face of God.

Throughout these discussions Bob Bigelow had the savviest comments of us all. He stressed the new reality of dense communications, "things we don't have a science for," and the imminence of reality-changing events. Approving my review of Gregory Chaitin's books on the frontiers of mathematics (42), John Dale spoke of the limits of science: One of Hilbert's celebrated problems is concerned with Aleph Zero, the number of all integers.

"We know that 2 raised to the power Aleph Zero is an integer greater than Aleph Zero, but is there an integer in between?" A mathematician from Berkeley has now proven that *we cannot know the answer to this question*. Perhaps the UFO phenomenon is a problem of the same "unknowable" type?

Hummingbird. Monday 15 January 2001.

We find ourselves alone again after driving Annick to the airport this afternoon. We savor the renewed simplicity of our life.

Eric and Colm are following up on my suggestion to install a radar system at the Utah ranch, but they keep finding obstacles. I recommended an Internet link like the system I have just installed here, which requires no phone line.

The Institute is doing good work in Las Vegas. Obtaining the complete files of Sheriff Wolverton in Great Falls, Montana, was a good step. The lesson is clear, however: Even with all his police resources and investigative skills, Wolverton couldn't catch the perpetrators. NIDS has found a veterinary needle *underneath* a mutilated bull during the Montana wave. Is it a plant, or the tool of a crime? No one seems to know. Many animals were actually exsanguinated.

All this makes me wonder about people who had the opportunity to get the facts right back in the 70s. They blew it by hiring an FBI bureaucrat like Rommel to write a whitewash. Was that deliberate?

Portland. Thursday 18 January 2001.

I made an overnight trip to Beaverton in order to get an update from two investments we made last year. I love the flight to Oregon along the Cascades chain, watching the gorgeous peaks in the snow.

Poor Ren Breck passed away two nights ago. So gifted as an investigative journalist and crusader for the old, the downtrodden, unafraid of powerful people, yet such a hopeless and impractical idealist in other ways... His attempt to restart my InfoMedia business was a failure. His old father seized power and accelerated the demise of the company. Yet Ren's notion of combining recorded news and live information with our conferencing system was brilliant, ten years ahead of the networking industry, yet he could never focus, or manage what little money came in. I ended up paying large network access bills for him. He did single-handedly re-establish links to faraway Armenia after a massive earthquake. In that case at least, our money went to save many lives.

Now a cab has brought me to a non-descript suburban hotel in the dark drizzle of Oregon. An Intel campus grows here, with a joint institute between them and IBM to develop the Linux language. Startups that flee Silicon Valley relocate nearby.

There's an energy crisis in California, blackmail from the Utilities. In the last two days I have attended two Board meetings in the dark after sudden power blackouts, a new experience for a region that thinks of itself as the world capital of Tech.

Hummingbird. Monday 29 January 2001.

Lockheed researcher Dr. Bernie Haisch and his wife wanted some advice, so we had lunch in Palo Alto today. There was sweet sunshine all over, fresh wind from the Pacific and pink flowers all over the trees. Bernie had invited Creon Levitt, the manager of Firmage's ISSO. They are about to run out of cash because Joe finds himself severely overextended. Things are bad: He's selling his boat and cannot keep his commitments to various space startups, even OneCosmos and Voyager, his joint ventures with Sagan's widow.

Many investors face similar problems. The Dow Jones index has lingered between 10,000 and 11,000 for months while the NASDAQ tumbled, barely above 2,500 now, and Joe's left holding the bag. Firmage had assumed that he could simply seed a number of projects for venture capitalists and investment bankers to pick up and launch into the big time, as he once did with USWeb. The Internet debacle has brought back hard reality.

I took the opportunity of the visit to the California Institute for Physics and Astrophysics (CIPA) to review a curious point of statistics with Bernie. Three years ago, a researcher named Spottiswood reported in *JSE* that parapsychology experiments seemed to have best results when performed about 13.5 hours of local sidereal time, when a particular slice of the sky passed overhead. Could this imply a relationship between psychic functioning and a cosmic source? A considerable number of objects (stars, clusters, galaxies, radio sources, etc.) are found in that band running along the 13.5-hour meridian of right ascension, including Spica (Alpha Virginis, at 13h 24m) and Lalande 25372.

In Bernie's library, I looked up the motion of the Sun, and the direction of the galactic center, which could have been remarkable references for psychic functioning, but the result was negative: there was no correlation at all. Curiously, these two directions are very similar. The galactic center lies at 18h of right ascension and about minus 29 degrees of declination, within one degree of the direction towards which the solar system is moving at 20 kilometers per second. Since then, I've checked statistics about UFO data: They don't provide any correlation with any fixed point in the sky.

Hummingbird. Thursday 1 February 2001.

This morning I drove across the bay to pick up the first copies of *The Four Elements of Financial Alchemy* from Ten Speed Press in Berkeley, ran some errands in anticipation of our next flight to Paris, and sat in a booth at the Village Café with the mail I'd just picked up, when a middle-aged fellow came over, coffee cup in hand. He said he recognized me from my books and sat across the table from me. He claimed to be an airline pilot and friend of Fred Beckman. Actually, he hadn't seen him in a while, he added, but they once "got drunk for three whole days together."

He insisted that Fred always spoke highly of me. "In a sober state as well?" I had to ask, laughing.

Over the next hour or so he gave me a summary of his supposed experiences: fellow pilots who saw strange craft, colleagues he'd taken to see John Mack, a Nevada colonel he introduced to Bigelow, and a very disturbed FBI agent who got drunk with him and confessed he'd been put in charge of surveillance for a site where "100 bodies had been found, dropped from the sky, naked."

Nothing is verifiable in these stories. What kind of science can you do with them? More to the point, did he know where he could find me, to feed me these tales? Private detectives have been hired to report on researchers like me, and Pandolfi's office at CIA, among others, keeps spreading these bizarre rumors. What's the point?

Mabillon. Sunday 4 February 2001.

Paris is in a gray winter mood, warming up a bit under dismal rain. Being here with Janine turns the dreary weather into a chance for intimacy, huddling in cozy cafés or visiting apartments for sale in search of a larger place.

The result isn't encouraging. "Modern" French architects design impersonal structures; their owners paint them over with glossy plastic shine; windows open onto other walls, sad perspectives of communal gray; not our style.

Mabillon. Sunday 11 February 2001.

The irresistible smile of Paris returns, even under the dreary sky of February. Alas, an hour later a bitter wind catches me by surprise and chills me. Last week was spent on work, dragging charts and records from meeting to meeting. Now Graham has flown home; Janine has gone off to Normandy with Olivier.

We continue to look for apartments: a cute one-bedroom with a view of the Seine, all twisted orange walls and overpriced ambitions; a modern place near Paris Observatory, more affordable but too remote from our areas of predilection; a cavernous place in the 15th arrondissement, all shiny paint again, no view.

I cornered our neighbor, kindly Professor Bokias. Over coffee at Relais Odéon, we discussed the problems of classical education. Writer Claude Sarraute came into the brasserie as we tackled the *Iliad* and my spotty recollections of Homer.

Claude Sarraute, currently married to Jean-François Revel, is a leading Paris hostess and literary figure. Bokias told me spicy gossip about her. Such casual encounters with cultural icons make the area unique, the atmosphere enchanting, and the price of a garret accordingly lofty.

Mabillon. Monday 12 February 2001.

From the Seine to Maubert and Saint Michel I walk on, wondering where all the erudite bookstores have gone. They were chased away by pizzerias and trendy clothes shops. Taking a stroll through the area used to be like sailing around the Cape Horns of imagination. Little is left: A few New Age shops, their tables loaded with crystals and boxes of fake herbal remedies, have permanently replaced the wonderful metaphysical bookshelves of the Table d'Emeraude.

I still enjoy the guiltless taste of coffee with no deadline before me, no imminent appointments, and I treasure the feeling of idle contemplation, travelling along the streets of the Latin Quarter, heavy with memories like those overloaded barges that drift down the Seine, occasionally washed over by icy waves of nostalgia.

Mabillon. Tuesday 13 February 2001.

The wind before Saint Sulpice feels like early spring today. I paid a visit to Thérèse de Saint-Phalle at Plon, giving her a copy of *Four Elements*. She praised my steady friendship. French publishing, now under the control of big industry or hedge funds, relies on trendy books about vacuous TV personalities, authored by ghostwriters.

Thérèse complained that the sense of place and pride of nation was lost in France. She invited me to summer in Chablis, in sweet Burgundy, to experience genuine French traditions, but my roots are in the Oise valley of Van Gogh and Cézanne, of which nothing is left.

Hummingbird. Friday 16 February 2001.

Gordon Creighton just called from England. In his buoyant voice, he went on to talk about the Ummo hoax and then asked if I knew Joe Firmage. Gordon is worried about Firmage's declining fortunes because *Flying Saucer Review (FSR)* received $25,000 from him, "and that's the only reason we're still able to publish, because the Internet is killing us. People think they get so much more information from the net… they don't understand it's all garbage, unsorted trivia."

Gordon asked me how old I was now (61 years). He said he was 30 years older and still going strong. When I hung up, his cheerful voice and presence had lifted everything around me.

Colleagues at the Society for Scientific Exploration (SSE) urge me to "go public" again. Art Bell wants me on *Coast-to-Coast*, his late-night show. "Your voice should be heard above all this confusion," they say. Yet nothing could satisfy an audience raised on a diet of Roswell crash stories, MJ-12 paranoia, anal probes, and alien autopsies.

Janine tells me I should turn the page, abandon the research if it can't be done right: *The basic tools are not there to tackle the problem,* she says, *there's no rational framework*. "So let's build one," I say. When I speak to her of the clear reality of the phenomenon, she replies that science will just have to pick it up eventually from another angle, when it matures.

"One more reason to screen and preserve the best data," I argue. But she points out the field has been compromised beyond saving by crackpots and frauds, and the absence of serious investigation.

Hummingbird. Sunday 18 February 2001.

We had an all-day UFO meeting at the CIPA yesterday, chaired by Dick Haines. Dominique Weinstein had made a special trip.

To Dick's credit, he's assembled a remarkable group of pilots and aerospace experts. There were media people in the room with their own agenda: A TV reporter arrived with writer Leslie Kean, working on a BBC documentary. Frank scientific debate doesn't mix well with activist claims, and pilots are notoriously afraid of publicity.

The morning went downhill. People wanted to discuss "chemtrails," some secret chemical spread throughout the atmosphere as part of a black project; perhaps, but they had no data, not even a spectrum. Later someone accused the electronic facility of HAARP (High-frequency Active Auroral Research Program) in Alaska of causing harm in terms so absurd he would have been thrown out of an undergraduate seminar.

In the afternoon, in welcome contrast, Weinstein gave a good overview of his statistics on 1,052 visual cases, 206 radar-visual cases, and 61 electromagnetic events in his pilot database. This was broken down into 606 military reports, 444 from airlines, and 193 from private pilots. The electromagnetic effects were seen on both gyros and compasses. In 20 cases a UFO had been seen, round or spherical in shape, from 20 to 200 feet away from the aircraft. In several cases the compass actually pointed to the object. Military aircraft seem immune to such effects, perhaps because they are shielded from EM pulses. Most of the remaining time was spent discussing "organization." When it came to funding, I was happy to hear Dick say wisely that we shouldn't go chasing after billionaires' dreams.

Hummingbird. Monday 19 February 2001.

We had a fine evening at Dick's house, where Dominique, Janine, and I were the guests. I gave Weinstein a clever cartoon by Jean-Pierre Petit: a map of French ufology showing the Gendarmes taking down witness reports and passing them on to SEPRA, pointedly drawn up as a comical little "mailbox" for shadowy figures like Payan.

Dominique laughed and said the real problem was lack of research, even within the weapon laboratories. Yet Payan still plays absurd games: he asked a French ufologist, Gildas Bourdais, to beg Weinstein for a copy of the French Army report on UFOs (the real one, not *Cometa*) as if he didn't have his own copy. Dominique saw through the silly plot: "So typical of Payan," he said, "to ask a civilian to request a military report from me!"

Hummingbird. Thursday 22 February 2001.

Peter Banks and I met at CIPA today with Bernie Haisch, Joe Firmage, and Creon Levitt to look over a proposal for a new type of tunable laser. This is one development that Peter may be interested in funding through his own venture fund, tied to the X-Rite Corporation, so we felt that something concrete might come of the meeting with money flowing to CIPA. The project is probably not appropriate for our own Fund, because any real product from this invention is three to five years away, even as a prototype.

There is resentment about Firmage's financial debacle among people who left their jobs to follow Joe's vision, only to be told a few months later that money had dried out. That Institute spent too much money investigating perpetual motion and antigravity.

Athanor. Friday 23 February 2001.

Today we were fed up with work, tax returns and business plans, so I cancelled a couple of meetings and drove up north with Janine in bright sunshine, eager to put all that behind us.

We had a picnic on the beach at high tide, just us and a hundred sandpipers, always so funny as they jump in and out of the surf with their agile legwork. We watched the grayness return in big horizontal bundles, turning the sea to light pewter with bands of white. I have come to understand why people can live for and with the sea, aboard ships or on desolate shores, with no need for anything else. But I have to hold you very close to me in order to enjoy any of it.

Athanor. Saturday 24 February 2001.

One bright exception to the dismal landscape of UFO research is the work currently going on at NIDS with Colm Kelleher and Eric Davis. Yet the data they uncover may lead us into even more somber conclusions about the phenomena. On February 7 and 8, respectively, Colm recorded interviews with two police officers in Cache County, Utah. Both related a series of mutilation incidents in their area, attended by black helicopters.

Back in 1977 Deputy Sheriff Jerry Simmons, acting under orders from Sheriff Darius Carter, tracked three helicopters involved in a mutilation incident and ran them down at the Logan-Cache Airport. Deputy Simmons tried to block the plane, then...

"A man got out of one of the helicopters. He had a shiny suitcase in his hand. Ran to the fixed wing aircraft. They slid the door open. He boosted the suitcase through the door. Door slams, and this pilot went to full-power, taking off the wrong way towards the patrol car heading down the middle of the runway."

The patrol car driver took evasive action at the last moment, realizing the pilot was prepared to either take off or die in the crash.

As for Deputy Simmons, he was left facing the helicopter:

"The guy who'd gotten out of the Huey was about 6'2", remarkably good-looking, light hair, blue eyes. I asked to see some identification. He said, 'I have none.' I looked at the helicopters: they were dark, either dark green or black. No identifying markings at all. He didn't even have a helmet. There weren't any dog tags. The moment I touched that man, the two other helicopters lifted off the ground and one spread left, one spread right and hovered... I'm a Vietnam vet, I interpreted this as a gun pass. If I attempted to physically arrest that man, they'd kill me right there, with the same mental attitude as the pilot that ran the patrol car off the runway."

Simmons did some fast thinking:

"I told him about the mutilations in Rich County, how he'd been spotted there, how we had riders out in all three counties with high-powered rifles, and that sooner or later we would get a shot at his helicopter and 'we intend to bring you down, Sir, if this type of mutilation doesn't stop.'

"And he looked at me and smiled a little bit. And then he said, 'May I go?' And I had nothing to hold him on and, like I say, you know, I wasn't holding the high card in that deal. So I said, 'Yeah.' He got back to the helicopter and they flew off."

In a separate interview, Sheriff Carter states that "right on the bottom of the door in the helicopter you could see 'Property of US Army,' that little insignia that they have on all their equipment."

Adding to my puzzlement is Kit's reaction to this report: "It still sounds to me like a black US Government (USG) operation. It doesn't sound like it is for good reasons, but that isn't my right to decide. If I believe it is a legitimate USG operation, I am committed to not foil the plan, because of my security oath. We can't second-guess the values of the persons who are more in the need-to-know than are we... I've been involved in dozens of black operations... from the inside they were as pure as the driven snow, and my buddies from the outside said they stank. Since I ain't a bad guy, I always chalked up the bad press as being due to partial information. I bet this is one of them..."

Hummingbird. Saturday 3 March 2001.

The personal retreat of Joe Firmage in the Santa Cruz Mountains is a fine A-frame house hidden in the woods at the edge of a canyon near the summit, not far from the abandoned headquarters of an old California sect in Holy City. Under Bernie Haisch's initiative Joe had invited nine participants to a meeting of his "inner circle," including Bernie, Marsha, and me.

The other five were Hal Puthoff, Eric Davis, Michael Lindemann, with Larry Lemke and Al Holt from NASA.

This was a remarkable group, heavy with experience of classified projects, space operations, and the rumors of 30 years of ufology. But it was also a credulous bunch, motivated by expectation of an imminent breakthrough, government disclosures of an Alien presence in the States, if not the world. We had a light lunch Joe had prepared, some rice with meat, salad, and fruits (but no coffee, in Mormon tradition, which I found unfortunate).

I raised the usual objections: the best physical theories including those of Paul Hill (43) only describe 10% of the craft's physics but fail to explain most UFO behavior; previous rumors of imminent disclosure have proven false or fraudulent; there may be more to the phenomenon than an extraterrestrial intervention; and the idea of a secret project in control of Alien hardware and biological specimens does not match the observed effects on society, or even the pace of our technology. Furthermore, as the mutilation incidents and Colm's recent report show, the government may be all over the landscape with black programs fooling the public, ignoring any outrage.

The group listened politely but they remained unconvinced. Larry Lemke emphasized that we needed two Copernican revolutions, not just one, in order to understand the phenomenon. As a result, ignoring my arguments, the discussion went on under Firmage's guidance as if the extraterrestrial theory was taken for granted.

Joe showed twenty slides to emphasize his point, including the potential impacts of the "imminent disclosure" on society. In desperation, I pointed out again that the same questions he was asking about the history of mankind, its ability to survive in space, and the origin of life in the universe were not new *and were not even ufological. They are asked every day in genetics and in astronomy.*

In the end we didn't learn much. Hal did talk about his contact with a four-star general who once located a unique research project preserving UFO hardware, but it was never clear what the evidence consisted of (44). Four other sources were listed: a technology executive, a field researcher, an intelligence operative, and Larry Lemke's own father who had an "R" clearance at Laurence Livermore Lab; he was once asked to machine some metal samples allegedly recovered from a saucer crash. Eric Davis retold the story of Zodiac, which involves real people like Jerry Rosenberg, currently at IDA, and Dale Graff, who was part of the remote viewing experiments at Wright-Patterson. Eric has been told there are ten Velobind volumes at Wright-Pat with Roswell data concerning two crashed "Manta ray" shaped craft, recovered bodies, foil-type material, and a special study by TRW.

In the absence of evidence, I'm cautious. These rumors are only supported by other rumors traced to "intelligence sources," so in the end we know nothing. We continue to accumulate interesting stories told in fancy homes in beautiful California forests under the quiet rain. But there's no science there, not even the beginnings of investigation, which would demand actual facts, real materials.

San Diego. Shelter Island. Wednesday 7 March 2001.

The plane banks out of the clouds over Mission Bay, the setting sun turns the ocean red, the shore radiant with orange beams. The magnificent ships of the Pacific Fleet are outlined like dark castles towering above the surf. Tomorrow I meet Peter Banks and the team of Photon Control Corporation at the Point Loma submarine base.

Russell Targ has invited me to speak before a psychic research group in San Jose: "Your public needs you," he said cheerfully.

I chuckled and declined: "Ufologists," if there is such a thing, too often want to hear about Area 51 and dead Aliens, not science.

Smugglers' Point. Thursday 8 March 2001.

Trust the military to secure the best real estate on Earth for its exclusive use: the Point Loma submarine base extends to the edge of the peninsula that outlines San Diego harbor. Only the darker outline of Catalina Island breaks the line. Huge Navy tankers and dark gray maintenance ships, as big as city blocks, sail in and out, just outside our meeting room, hiding the sun as they pass. There's a sense of vibrant imminence here, a novelty, an expectation of global resonance, evidence of a dangerous reality the public ignores.

Athanor. Saturday 10 March 2001.

The breaking waves have the colors and translucent beauty of jade and emerald, all the way to the Point Reyes peninsula, which has turned bright green in recent weeks of rain.

We're waiting for Diane, our guest this weekend, while marveling about the upheaval on Wall Street this week. It began with Intel announcing job cuts and an expected 25% reduction in sales; the next day *Yahoo!* collapsed, and then Cisco acknowledged it couldn't meet the expectations of analysts. The most respected, widely-held stocks deflate like punctured balloons, including Oracle.

We're somewhat sheltered from most of that, as we stick to my theory of the *Four Elements of Financial Alchemy*, which serves us well as a framework in the midst of chaos (45). But all this makes it much harder to raise our next Fund: "This is the only business where people stop buying when prices are low," wryly observes my partner Graham. There was a similar debacle in 1984 and '85, when new computer architectures failed to deliver the promised fortunes. Stocks plummeted, ordinary folks were separated from their savings, and venture funds melted in the folly of money managers. Another big collapse took place, of course, in the fall of 1987.

Hummingbird. Tuesday 3 April 2001.

Janine and I attended the inauguration of the Institute of Noetic Sciences (IONS) on Sunday afternoon. It has moved to a beautiful country site in Northern Marin County. It comprises a cluster of redwood buildings, a library, conference center, and fine offices among stately oak trees.

Cheerful Marilyn Schlitz was there, with physicist Fred Wolf, among a relaxed, elegant group of about 200. A lady psychotherapist took me aside to tell me of her concerns about ufology, with all the talk about Alien abductions and hypnosis. "It all begins to sound like cultist beliefs," she said rightly, "delusions reminiscent of the silly satanic scare, twenty years ago."

Paris. Sunday 8 April 2001.

Sitting at Le Train Bleu restaurant inside Gare de Lyon, that relic of 19th-century and Belle Epoque luxury. I don't usually have lunch in such grand style, but trains are on strike, there's only sporadic traffic to Lyon, and I have three hours to kill. The Unions are afraid to lose their stranglehold on transportation because the service may soon be partitioned, privatized, and forced to compete under European rules. So they have picked the Easter holiday to stop traffic, and to hell with folks like us and even their own working-class comrades hoping to get away for a few days of rest with their kids.

Mabillon. Tuesday 10 April 2001.

Paris is rainy, occasionally quite cold, but the atmosphere is vibrant, pretending there's no recession. On the contrary, financial magazines now hawk the "opportunities" of the crumbling *Bourse!*

Dr. Philippe Pouletty, who now lives in a splendid old apartment near Place Maubert, is one bright example of the new generation. He sold his spread in Woodside and is busy starting a French fund, Truffle Ventures, specializing in industrial spinoffs.

My son, who brought little Max to lunch with me on Saturday, has the same profound thirst I feel for the density of Europe, the beauty of this culture. Could I live here again? The country remains a backwater with brilliant eddies of erudition, sadly twisted views of a glorious history, and an elite that blames all problems on others.

There is no doorway to the stars here, no dreamer like Robert Bigelow building space habitats, no venturers inventing paths to intelligence beyond rigid standards of rationalism, no pagan covens raising unicorns in the golden fields of Gaia.

Mabillon. Friday 13 April 2001.

Middle of the night, no sleep. I did have an interesting day with Eric Rauley and Marc Menant, as we recorded a 90-minute radio show for Europe no.1. The field has become so inept that it doesn't make sense to advocate UFO research except in narrow, specialized cases. Dominique Weinstein and his statistical documentation on pilot sightings is a good example of what can be done. He works hard with Dick Haines, just retired from NASA.

Paris had periods of sunshine but the cold and drizzle came back. In a few hours I will be in Normandy, where Annick has just undergone an operation. She is out of danger; fortunately, no cancer was found.

Bayeux. Saturday 14 April 2001.

When we met for dinner (at Arbuci) on Thursday night, Dominique Weinstein brought me a package of documents about the B-52 case of

December 1968. He also told me of his recent lunch with Payan, General Letty, and Gildas Bourdais, where Payan described me as a nice fellow, unfortunately under the control of *"Les Américains."*

Defamation, slander, calumny, innuendo, and "faint praise" sadly remain favorite sports here, poisoning any relationship with French elites; Payan must be a very bad judge of character. On the other hand, it wouldn't surprise me if some US agents were trying to discredit my data because I do step on a few toes. French ufologists close to *Cometa* brag that they can break into email exchanges: official hackers have easy access to the web servers, but nothing I do is sensitive.

Bayeux. Sunday 15 April 2001.

Easter, quiet and sad. Annick is still in the hospital, so Janine and I have taken over her sister's house. We are keeping adorable Max, always in motion.

In Paris the weather was still clammy, drizzly, with a mean cold wind. Here in Normandy, it simply rains and rains. I'm tired, with a flu-like weakness and an earache.

Antony, near Paris. Wednesday 18 April 2001.

There's a meeting of the Genopole science board today, so I took an early train to this town where Gabriel Mergui will pick me up in front of this café. This time of day, 7 am, most of my fellow-travelers are workers from various parts of Africa, the *Strange Strangers* of poet Jacques Prévert. The languages of choice are Arabic and Swahili. The weather remains gray, moist, and cold as Death itself. Tomorrow I'll climb aboard a Boeing 747 bound for California, but I will make the trip alone again and I won't see Janine for several weeks, except in the castles of the mind. My heart is heavy, apprehensive.

When I tell Simonne Servais of the smears propagated about me by Payan, she answers that I just don't understand the suspicious mind of the military: "They only talk to their own sources, so it's easy for them to get the wrong idea about an independent researcher like you, with access to the kind of data you gave Yves Rocard back in the sixties, even knowing that no security was breached (46). Mind you, I had my own clash with Rocard when he tried to convince me the Valensole craft was only an American helicopter!"

Athanor. Sunday 22 April 2001.

Filtered sun over the marshes of Hamilton Field and the hills of Petaluma, the car stereo playing the *Vespers* of Rachmaninoff. I came up here alone, pleasantly detached, my ears still muffled from some virus picked up in France. I rediscover an old truth; this is indeed where I belong: in this freedom, under this open sky, in a world without compartments and preconceived notions of status.

Hummingbird. Tuesday 24 April 2001.

Last night a group of Francophiles from Stanford, about 20 people, gathered at Il Fornaio in Palo Alto for dinner with Dominique Strauss-Kahn. I was seated next to him so I asked, "If you were in Bercy today, would you be concerned about the American recession hitting France later this year?"

A true politician, he laughed, "Are you asking me if I would be concerned as Finance Minister, or if the fact of being at Bercy would give me some negative information I don't have today?"

"As Finance Minister," I replied.

"Well, I think France is pretty well insulated from the US."

That is the general wisdom but will this be true if the American crisis (with the Dow Jones around 10,000, and NASDAQ down to 2,000 and below, from a high of 5,000 a few months ago) impacts sick Japan and the rest of Asia, and then moves on, into Europe?

Strauss-Kahn clearly enjoys his vacation from power, as a lecturer around the world and occasional visiting professor at Stanford. When I asked him about the recent layoffs in French industry, which have triggered reactions from the Unions and the Jospin government, he was clear. "It's absurd to punish a company like Danone," he said, "they handled the layoffs perfectly, trying their best to relocate their workers." In this he showed his independence from the socialist party line, and a healthy sense of economic directions. If businesses can never lay off workers, they must simply stop hiring, or die, and the entire economy will suffer. Unfortunately, France enters a dangerous period with an over-burdened bureaucratic system worthy of the old Soviet Union.

Las Vegas. Saturday 5 May 2001.

Hal Puthoff, as the new chairman of the science board, has brought healthy vision and focus to the NIDS meeting. He began last night by urging us to think of "deliverables" rather than simple hypotheses (I have done that all along) and to pursue analysis to its ultimate degree of precision. He has studied an alleged Roswell sample supplied by Whitley Streiber and Roger Leir that turned out to be ordinary silica, 99% pure, a reject by Silicon Valley standards.

Before the group arrived I spent several hours with Colm and Eric reviewing the old AFFA case (47).

I had brought them a historical treasure: Hynek's handwritten copy of Colonel Friend's account.

Colm and Eric told me that Bob Bigelow was back in cost-cutting mood, moving the Institute to one of his office buildings. I can't blame him: activity is low, not much has happened at the ranch, and there is no breakthrough in view. The field is simply abuzz with silly rumors and the promotional notices of Dr. Greer's press conference in Washington about an unlikely "Disclosure." The exercise will set the research backward again, predicts Ted Rockwell.

Today Hal went around the table to get updates from all members. I spoke about a case in Yuba River in Little Washington, and passed on my file to Colm. In the afternoon we heard from Jim Westwood, the intelligence consultant who has done extensive work for Hal. In a scholarly but cynical way, he spoke about the history of the field and the disinformation associated with it. He left this idealistic group of scientists with an impression of dread mixed with disgust.

Westwood surfaces from the Cold War like a rusty submarine emerging from past eras. He first called our attention to various links with biological warfare, and again dismissed MJ-12 and Roswell as counter-intelligence exercises designed to flush out foreign spies. He'd kindly brought a copy of my *Samizdat* for me to sign, saying he especially liked this book "as a Sovietologist." He'd underlined the passage where Azhazha told me that Soviet experts had long considered UFO rumors as CIA tricks..."and they were largely right," Westwood said, "much of the phenomenon in Russia was phony, part of our own disinformation."

Hummingbird. Sunday 6 May 2001.

Donald Rumsfeld is a guest on *Meet the Press* this morning, speaking about recent friction with China. He brings back memories of treacherous maneuvers that derailed our own work and what Westwood calls the "hypocrisy and ambiguity" that characterize paranormal research in Washington (48). I wonder what we'll find in Asia when we travel there tomorrow on another business trip.

Tokyo. Wednesday 9 May 2001.

The Imperial Hotel: a massive block with hundreds of rooms in this huge tower designed by Frank Lloyd Wright. From the 24th floor, I see a jumble of roofs and streets, a wooded strip near the palace.

I feel invigorated here, energetic even after a 10-hour flight and four long meetings with investment companies: NIF, Asahi, Jafco, and Techno-Venture. Why I should be so at home in Japan is a mystery: I don't speak or read the language, can't find my way around town, and an economic crisis hangs over everyone's mind. But people are friendly, polite, accessible, with a keen sense of humor underneath cool obsequiousness. The Japanese subtle sense of style shows up in everything they touch.

Tokyo. Thursday 10 May 2001.

Over breakfast I just watched a summary of Greer's "Disclosure" briefing on CNN. They selected two impressive pieces of testimony from military witnesses, interspersed with bad videos of alleged disks over Mexico and Beijing, obvious fakes. Greer argued that we shared space with other beings and therefore should not deploy space weapons, in contrast to Rumsfeld who has just proposed "to protect our satellites and deploy an American shield."

The fact that CNN refrained from ridiculing Greer is interesting but the 5-minute news report did conclude with the observation that any action was unlikely until ufologists had more concrete evidence than blurry pictures. The atmosphere changes: a cover story in *Popular Mechanics* this month ("When UFOs Land") quoted Pocantico and my own work, but no UFOs are showing up at the Utah ranch.

Tokyo. Friday 11 May 2001.

The Shinkansen rumbles by, under dark skies. Four more meetings to go with financial companies in their giant buildings. The Japanese economy is at a standstill, or sliding back under enormous debts no one wants to acknowledge. Unofficial figures speak of 12 trillion yen, but the French experts here arrive at 150 trillion yen or so, three times the cost of the Savings and Loan debacle in the United States a decade ago. Who is supposed to pay for all that?

Last night I had dinner with Isobe-san who brought four of my books, a transcript of our previous talk, and questions about Pentacle, Aimé Michel, the Pontoise case...and the novels of René Barjavel!

Tomorrow we fly to Brunei through Singapore. Everywhere we go, executives ask us what we think of the US economy's chances of recovery, and what about Japan's finances? A topic we evade gracefully, insisting with a deep bow that we aren't economists.

Janine is back in San Francisco. "The weather is warm," she says, "which is nice, except for all the sloppy folks, lounging around in shorts and ugly clothes, such a shocking contrast to Europe, bums urinating along Market Street; and George W. Bush always pompous on TV... I'll just stay inside until you get back."

Brunei. Sunday 13 May 2001.

Six hours of shaky flight brought us to Singapore. We waited three hours for the Royal Brunei plane. Before takeoff the crew ran a proper video prayer to Allah to protect us, our families, and our journey. We respectfully joined in praising Mohammed. The navigation system's map had an arrow pointing to Mecca as the plane made its takeoff turns. We landed at midnight in stifling heat and high humidity.

Within walking distance are the royal museum, the ministry of finance, and a few blocks of restaurants, barber shops, and cheap souvenir sellers. The population of Bandar Seri Begawan, capital of Brunei, is a mix of dark-skinned Malays, Chinese, and other races from all over Asia. Most people are short, wiry; they walk around in slacks and T-shirts, standing on the high sidewalks designed to rise above the rainwaters. Women walk in groups, wearing blue jeans and sandals. There's a Pizza Hut at the corner, and a Kentucky Fried Chicken offset from the road by deep trenches covered in ironwork grills: the torrential rains again. This is the equator. Satellite dishes are horizontal. The jungle starts at the town's edge.

Tourist brochures invite a visit to the local mosques, warn against alcohol, and suggest coming over to the Istana palace during the Muslim Hari Raya holiday when "the sultan and his two wives greet thousands of visitors with a handshake and some money for the children."

One must not point at things with the index finger, or shake the hand of a person from the opposite sex, although the smart young women of the ministry of finance, fresh from Harvard, amused to confuse us, do it all the time when we meet them.

5

Athanor. Saturday 2 June 2001.

I fly back to San Francisco on Tuesday night, and arrived several hours before I left, one more disconcerting fact about Asia.

A little fun to dispel the tiredness of our travels: we organized another medieval feast today, our second celebration of Saint Agobard. Our dear friend Oberon Ravenheart (previously known as Otter Zell) came over with Morning Glory and Liza in magnificent magical robes. Writers Gary Shockley and Lori also joined us. Janine wore her medieval dress, and I sported a black Viking jerkin with silver stars and a dagger, worthy of our first Feast at Spring Hill.

This was a chance to stop and take measure, to speak of science fiction and unicorns and witchery and pleasure and superstition and the good Saint Agobard, *Praised be His Name!* And to taste the great repast Janine had prepared, with mutton and flounder in cream, and brioche, and watercress salad with two kinds of cheeses, and two kinds of dessert: a true rite of medieval gluttony.

Now I rummage through old notes and find that poem, Cassilda's Song from *The King in Yellow*, a gift from Anton:

> Songs that the Hyades shall sing,
> Where flap the tatters of the King,
> Must die unheard in
>   Dim Carcosa.

The lines seem oddly appropriate to this research, with all its unspeakable and unknowable data. I resonate with the last stanza:

> Song of my soul, my voice is dead,
> Die thou, unsung, as tears unshed
> Shall dry and die in
>   Lost Carcosa.

It's a song from a play never written, in a book that doesn't exist, yet it sums up the dreadful tiredness that finally emerges from our years of investigation into false secrets and real mysteries.

Yes, we did make some discoveries, but they cannot (should not) be expressed until the right framework exists.

How profound of Anton LaVey, in spite of his enormous faults, when he warned me that *no secret could be revealed to anyone who didn't already know it!*

"Those who uncover certain things are damned by their own audacity," I said. He laughed and replied that Truth had never made anyone free, and anyone who thought otherwise was a damn fool.

La Jolla. Thursday 7 June 2001.

Janine and I are invited to the annual meeting of the Society for Scientific Exploration in San Diego. So we flew down this afternoon, rented an enormous car and arrived at the Radisson in time for the buffet. We're glad we made the trip: The first people we saw were Dick Haines and Dominique Weinstein along with Hal, John and Victoria Alexander, and the well-meaning SSE crowd. Victoria spoke about Peru, still adamant that the drug ayahuasca led to God.

Dr. Federico Faggin (49) was among the crowd, as well as a fellow from China who introduced himself as the founder of the first UFO study group there. He now works for Toshiba in Silicon Valley.

La Jolla. Saturday 9 June 2001.

Bob Wood opened the conference this morning. He's a kind man, very knowledgeable about the history of the subject, yet credulous, in my opinion, when it comes to the Majestic 12 "revelations." Hal gave an excellent talk about relativity, after which Janine and I had lunch with the Alexanders. We listened to their discussion of Amazonian drugs, which left us skeptical. Perhaps I would be more open to the idea of a drug-induced contact with divinity if we hadn't heard the same thing in the days of LSD, and seen all the disappointing results.

In the afternoon I presented the case at Haravilliers as a recent example of the real phenomenon, against the confused background of all the theories (Fig. 2). Dick Haines spoke convincingly about pilot sightings, but when a woman asked him why spacecraft from another world would come all the way here to hit somebody's airplane, that excellent question caught him by surprise.

After lunch the group took a cruise around the bay, passing Point Loma with its boomers ready to dive and the parade of mighty ships of the Pacific fleet arrayed all around the harbor. The sun was shining on that technology of war. The world remains a dangerous place, and yesterday's mysteries have not gone away.

Janine and I had a friendly dinner with John Petersen. He took us to La Valencia in downtown La Jolla, a magical site high above the surf. He told us about the 4-star general who reported visiting a UFO reverse-engineering project conducted by about 150 people in four States, working for a contractor with no line item in any budget.

This must be the same story Hal told me (50).

Hummingbird. Sunday 10 June 2001.

Dominique Weinstein has compiled a remarkable new report on pilot sightings. Back in France, Velasco receives some credit for it, since the CNES logo is on the documents, while Dick Haines is posting them on his US website. Dominique had to replace me as the central character in the French documentary about "The American Secret" where I was supposed to appear, since I'd declined. His face is never shown, but his name will soon be known among the specialists, for better or worse.

We flew back this afternoon and one of the first people to call me was Jim Westwood. Talking to him is to enter a universe of shadows and deception. His information on the "undercurrent" goes back to World War II, when Stalin asked the chief designer of his rockets, engineer Korolev, what flying saucers were. Korolev answered there was a real phenomenon but it wasn't a great threat. Stalin is reported to have told him he'd received the same answer from other sources. Westwood pointed out that the Germans never built a real flying disk, but "the Nazi did destroy and burn a lot of stuff and machinery; so we don't know everything."

Jim assures me that in the course of his research he'd spoken to a 90-year-old gentleman who was involved in government UFO research in the fifties, when there was active classified interest. "We never understood the phenomenon," he told him. "I was against using it to manipulate the silly UFO believers, but the boys on the dark side of the house went ahead anyway."

Westwood said there was still an ongoing collection effort, a low-level project. He tracked down another man, now 84 years old, who worked on the Robertson Panel: "Puthoff really wants to find the hardware. Well, I've been in this business for 48 years, and I know for a fact there isn't any." This squarely contradicts Petersen's statements about his own source, that 4-star general.

"When did the disinformation start?" I asked. "Surely in the forties and fifties it would have been hard to fly a fake flying saucer..."

I am still thinking of what I saw over Pontoise in 1955, a perfect lens with a transparent dome, hovering in the clear afternoon sky.

"Not before the early 70s," answered Westwood. "Or perhaps the late 60s, because I knew a pilot who flew over Cleveland then, carrying special light patterns that simulated a UFO. But the technology wasn't good enough to be effective before the 1970s."

This actually matches what Kit had stated at our meeting.

Westwood may be correct when he doesn't relate mutilations to UFOs but to biological warfare. He went into a long dissertation on the feasibility of infecting farms exploited by the Soviet Army, which is vertically integrated like everything in Russia, producing their own meat, milk, and vegetables.

"You've been there," he told me. "You know their roads are impossible, so everything moves by train: the missile sites are served by trains. Well, we can identify every railroad car in Europe. It wouldn't be very hard to put a canister full of nasty bugs on a railroad car and track it to the vicinity of one of these farms. You can open it at the right moment with a radio signal from a satellite."

The thought chilled me: infecting an enemy's livestock and plant life to paralyze its missile silos is horrible. "You contaminate the tissue with parasites. The operators are going to eat the cabbage from those fields and drink that milk," said Westwood flatly. "The entire site will be disabled when they get sick. You can run the whole operation from a desk in Sunnyvale."

Yes, it's horrible, said Westwood when I reacted in disgust. "But we will do anything, repeat *anything*, not to fight a nuclear war. Or a bugs-and-gas war. That's what fascinated me about your book, *Samizdat*, when you described the sightings in Voronezh. You obviously didn't know it, but Voronezh is a major nuclear site, the most important one outside Moscow. It's like the underground command post we've got in Pennsylvania."

"And those rumors about Roswell?" I asked.

"For over 20 years we had a thing going, it was called Operation Shocker. It was run through a double agent, an Army officer they thought they'd turned, but he worked for us, feeding them data to convince them we had capabilities we didn't have, and that the things we did have didn't work. The UFO business was woven into that."

I decided to push deeper: "What about Bentwaters?" I asked.

"It may have been an American experiment, as you've argued in *Revelations*, but I doubt it. The timing would be right, however. You have to understand, my only theme is chronology. I keep things on little cardboard cards, organized by dates. When you reach a point of data density, you suspect there's more than coincidence."*

Mabillon. Saturday 23 June 2001.

After a few days by myself, wandering through castles of the mind, Janine joined me yesterday in sunny Paris. I've seen startup medical companies at Genopole, then dinner with Gabriel Mergui and Dr. Claude Weisbuch, and a visit to Nautilus Biotech.

The weather is so delightful that we walked all over this morning, first to Max's school on Île Saint-Louis, then across the Marais and along the Seine. We have so many friends here... We had coffee with Professor Bokias, then Simonne Servais called, Elizabeth Antébi contacted us, and there was Weinstein and Eric Rauley too.

Professor Michel Serres, with whom I had lunch on Friday at the Balzar, next to the Sorbonne, says that Americans have no ego in the classical sense, they speak of their own existence as if they had no interior life, no *profondeur*—a hard word to translate into English. Of course, he's exaggerating, but that may explain why we have so few true, long-term friends in America. I did enjoy meeting him: he was bright, optimistic, and spoke with a singing Southern French accent reminiscent of Aimé Michel's.

Now the Internet brings sad news. Larissa Vilenskaya has died, killed by a train on the way to work, clearly a suicide. A few months ago, someone told me that she was depressed. Since SRI days I had always enjoyed her conversation, her Russian sensitivity. For a while, like me, she had frequented the Rosicrucians.

---

* Dr. Kelleher later made the stunning discovery that the Bentwaters incidents happened synchronistically with the notorious Cash-Landrum case when two women and a boy suffered grave radiation injuries.

Bordeaux. Friday 29 June 2001.

Hotel Sainte Catherine stands on a quiet street of this old city, a narrow cobblestone street closed to automobile traffic. Last night I spoke before some twenty selected clients of the Meeschaert financial group in a very discreet old home, the Labottière House, all sober courtyard and exquisite 18th century architecture, so discreet our local cab driver had never heard of it. Our investors look beyond economic concern; the country plunges into the demagoguery of 35-hour work weeks, populist measures, and confiscatory taxes, disincentives to enterprise, even as the economy slows down.

Yesterday we went to see Alain Mérieux, head of the prestigious pharmaceutical company in Marcy-l'Etoile, outside Lyon. He, too, was bitter about France, congratulated me on making California my home, and gave a pessimistic, even savagely negative assessment of the future of France. He slipped into French as he vented his anger, apologizing to Graham that he couldn't say these things in English, berating his own country in front of an American.

Mabillon. Saturday 30 June 2001.

We visited Simonne Servais this afternoon. We found her physically weak but as intellectually sparkling as ever. She scoffed at my statement that I had "turned the page" on ufology. So I told her two major events led me away from public involvement: First, the observation that so many educated, smart people were now ready to believe in every stupid rumor about the origin of modern electronics in the Roswell debris. Yet the inventions of the transistor, the IC, the micro-computer, fiberoptics, are all within human memory. I know several of the people involved, like Federico Faggin.

The second big disappointment was the attitude, from SEPRA to Payan to *Cometa*: nothing has been learned. Even the military responds to irrational beliefs that have nothing to do with research. Yet Simonne defended Payan's position: "There might be Aliens among us on the Earth…" This made me sad, because she was trying to trick me, and she ought to know better.

Forbidden Science 5 93

Fig. 1. With Dr. Douglas Engelbart and Elizabeth "Jake" Feinler at SRI at a reception honoring Doug's contributions, Dec. 2000.

Fig. 2. Launching the research with witnesses at Haravilliers, 2001.

Mabillon. Sunday 1 July 2001.

In Pontoise, the simple color of *coquelicots* along the hedges carried me back to my childhood. The suburban train stops in Saint-Denis, Enghien, St-Ouen l'Aumône, quaint names from the depth of time. Finally, we saw the cliffs of Pontoise with their ramparts. There's a Pissarro Museum where the castle stood and where my parents rented the house that was blown up during World War II.

The church of Saint Maclou has been upgraded to a "cathedral" but the doors are locked. A sense of slovenliness hangs over the town, enhanced by garish advertisements. Once in the park, all is quiet again.

We saw my parents' old house on Rue Saint Jean with its terrace. A young boy dressed in white was playing there. At the bottom of Rue de l'Eperon we found the *Sente des Poulies*, such a pretty name I'd forgotten. The path wanders along the slope between hedges, unkept bushes and fences lined with those humble *coquelicots*.

Further away, near Osny, we took the path to the old water mills so loved by the Impressionists: the *Moulin du Pas d'Ane*, now modernized, and the *Moulin de la Couleuvre* once painted by Cézanne. A park has been developed along the creek, leading to the picturesque Rue des Etannets. We stopped there, the weather balanced between summer sunshine and fresh breeze.

Janine finds such feelings too strong, bringing back forgotten moods and dead people, vertiginous views into time depths upon which we stand so unsteadily. To me, on the contrary, this excursion to Pontoise was soul-nourishing, reassuring: alive with all the turmoil of the waters rushing over the dams of the medieval mills; a happy time, because you were with me.

Athanor. Saturday 7 July 2001.

Janine has flown back to California with Max who brightens everything with boundless curiosity. We took him to the beach today. It had been so long since I'd built a sand castle! I cherish those times, grateful that our little family has stayed so warm.

I did call Jim Westwood again. He pursues his theory that UFO cases and cattle mutilations around military bases are designed to send a message to the Soviets about biological warfare. This is strategic stuff, he claims. In 1972 the Soviets signed the biological warfare convention, and immediately proceeded to violate it. A defector from the Russian delegation at the UN in 1975 gave the CIA the first good information about their program. Jim claims this was followed by confirmation in 1989.

I pointed out the absurdity of it all. Biological tests could be done on the basis of a little blood, or a single hair, with no killing. The psychological warfare argument is not credible either; these events are seldom reported, they only come to the attention of specialists.

Athanor. Saturday 14 July 2001.

Various documents come to light about the Rockefeller Initiative under Clinton in 1993 and 1994, when Laurance approached Jack Gibbons with the suggestion of a new study of UFOs.

As I already knew, Gibbons tried in vain to get any information out of the CIA. They sent him a bland paper prepared by Bruce Maccabee at the instigation of Dr. Pandolfi, rehashing old stuff. The only outcome was an uneasy, misplaced effort to re-open the Roswell case.

When an auditor from the General Accounting Office followed up by contacting the Pentagon for Roswell data, he was instructed by a military spokesman to "go shit in your hat."

The documents report on Steven Greer's approaches to CIA director James Woolsey, introduced by John Petersen. Woolsey and his wife had seen a daylight UFO in New Hampshire in the sixties. Woolsey had very limited access to Clinton, however. When a crazy man crashed a plane on the White House lawn, the joke was that it was a desperate Woolsey, trying to get a meeting with the President!

Yesterday came a report of classic histrionics by Ira Einhorn. Faced with extradition, Einhorn convened a television crew and cut his throat in front of the cameras. He was rushed to a hospital in Angoulême, where his life is not in danger, and he appealed to a European court to stop his return to the States.

The media have finally seen through this. Holly's sister said she had never expected Ira to return quietly, but, as she put it, "I must admit I hadn't thought of that one!"

Portland, Oregon. Wednesday 18 July 2001.

In Portland for a board meeting, I found myself staring at Ira on television. He was being interviewed from France by CBS News after his attempt to slash his throat. His power to fascinate the media is intact; he captured a full ten minutes of the morning news, accusing Jospin of trading him for American political favors!

Hummingbird. Sunday 22 July 2001.

Stephen Greer, Daniel Sheehan, and Carol Rosin of the Disclosure Project are in San Francisco for a big presentation. I didn't go but I joined a smaller meeting afterward at Henry Dakin's center.

It's hard not to like Dr. Greer. He comes across as totally committed and sincere. He's a good storyteller: NDE as a teenager, did transcendental meditation, taught at Maharishi University, spent three years in Israel where he met his wife (a Bahai follower like himself), and became an emergency room physician.

Greer stated that the "UFO Presence" was transformational, that it utilized extraterrestrial interdimensional physics, with direct implications for consciousness. But he loses credibility when he states that advanced propulsion systems using antigravity are already used by the US, and that NASA's Apollo was a cover.

Edgar Mitchell, whom I consulted, told me: "I agree with your assessment, plus one additional item, which those of us who have worked with Greer discovered the hard way: he listens to no one, has become very full of himself as *The Guru* in these matters, and overruns his own data."

Hummingbird. Friday 27 July 2001.

We met George Schultz yesterday at a small reception for François Bayrou, the leader of the UDF centrist party in France, here on a fact-finding tour. Secretary Schultz was with his wife Charlotte Maillard, a well-known San Francisco hostess. He told the amusing story of a dinner at the French embassy for the Bicentennial, where the unevenly-sized tables were set in an incomprehensible pattern, until it was revealed they followed the arrangement of the French ships at the battle of Yorktown against England, indeed a nice touch.

The same evening, Bayrou and his entourage kept Schultz waiting for more than an hour while a few French *notables* arrived at Tom Horn's apartment, with its magnificent view of downtown and the bay. My friends François Laugier and Ken Alwyn were there, and Elisabeth Paté-Cornell, dean of an engineering department at Stanford. Schultz and Bayrou shared memories of Giscard d'Estaing, whom they both admire.

When Schultz left we went to dinner at Le Bistrot with Bayrou, former minister of transportation Madame Idrac, and Jean-Pierre Alix from the Cité des Sciences.

Athanor. Monday 13 August 2001.

A brief vacation: on Saturday Olivier flew back to Paris with Max. Life returned to the routine, no longer punctured by our grandson's giggles and pirouettes. I had rarely seen Janine as happy and alive as during these four weeks. We joked, walked on the beach, hunted crabs and insects, played mad soccer games. I slept soundly with beautiful dreams and the intimacy of magical beings.

My son seemed reluctantly happy here, given his negative views on Silicon Valley and the ills of America. I could tell him volumes about rotten business and the hypocrisy of power plays in Paris, I said. Then the fog was lifting over the Point Reyes peninsula. The grayness is gone. Hundreds of starfish cling to the half-submerged rocks at low tide. They range in color from deep purple to orange amidst the clams, sea anemones, and *varech*. Small crabs scurry around, back away as we chase them, and peer at us from crevices.

Athanor. Friday 17 August 2001.

It's the light that makes this region so special. Yesterday we hiked some ten miles along the ridge through the Point Reyes wilderness. We walked through pockets of diaphanous fog, with occasional sunny windows over the rocky Pacific shore on one side, the beaches and the bay on the other. The landscape opened up on sudden views of meadows, small lakes with herons, herds of elk. Today the waves tossed my kayak around, on blue Tomales Bay.

On the way to Japan. Saturday 1 September 2001.

Michael Briggs of Kansas University Press suggests I should write a UFO book for him. He's a kind, tall man in a dark suit, with silver hair and an impeccably trimmed beard. He asked about the days when Janine and I became interested in the phenomenon. What did she think at the time?

"There was good data to be assembled," she said, "and meaningful statistics to be done: much unexplored territory. Above all, there were honest minds and true friendships: Aimé Michel, Pierre Guérin, Dr. Hynek… now gone…"

Tokyo. Imperial Hotel. Wednesday 5 September 2001.

Another series of visits to Japanese financial institutions is over, an excursion from skyscraper to concrete tower, with plastic meeting rooms only softened by the ever-present, silent assistant in her sharp uniform who brings delicious tea, bows deeply, and turns invisible. We've made little progress in fund raising: the Japanese economy is in chaos. President Koizumi doesn't know whether to jump into the unknown of structural changes or cling to the edge of the abyss, hoping that America will recover and pull up his economy. This seems unlikely as one major firm after another is warning of deeper cuts.

In Tokyo I was struck by the fragmentation of the products and the high prices. If Japan doesn't have a leadership position in consumer electronics anymore, no wonder the country is in trouble.

Now I long to get home. When we drive to the north coast there is a special point where the cares of the ordinary world are forgotten as the road meets the fog through universes of coolness and privileged visions. Our third venture capital Fund is in place for ten years of stable professional operation. We're determined to find a new pace: more focused, with time for long walks and deeper research, drawing lessons from the rich landscapes of the past.

Part Eighteen

SEPTEMBER ELEVEN

6

Hummingbird. Tuesday 11 September 2001.

It had to be an accident, just a horrible accident. When we turned on the TV set this morning, the first thing we saw was a burning tower in New York, a numbing sight, one of those catastrophes you dread in that city of all extremes. Janine had to leave for a meeting. A beautiful late summer day was rising over our City. In New York, too, the sky was blue and radiant. Why such an incongruous sight?

We usually turn on the financial channel over breakfast, but the stock quotes had stopped: no more fancy histograms, no economic commentaries. Instead, journalists were piecing together stories about a plane hitting one of the World Trade Center towers. Suspicions grew. Perhaps this was no accident?

A short time later the second tower was hit, shattering all sense of reality: "Roll this tape back!" yelled a journalist, losing the professional tone that had made the first crash look manageable. "Didn't a piece of that building just fall down?"

Now it looked like a bad movie. People ran in the streets ahead of a huge swirl of chaos, as in some gory Hollywood drama.

In the next minutes, the tragedy unfolded, ugly and irreversible. The twin towers collapsed in a surrealistic plunge, all-engulfing smoke and dust, millions of tons of debris, and all those bodies. By the time the Pentagon was also hit there was talk of war, comparisons with Pearl Harbor, ugly foreboding.

I drove to work, passing the airport just as the police was closing its access routes. The last plane authorized to land, an airliner from Thailand, was escorted to the ground by two Air Force jets.

Hummingbird. Wednesday 12 September 2001.

A stomach-churning sense of horror spreads now, darkening every thought, acutely real. All those people unable to escape from the destruction, and the haunting views of the airliner aiming at the top floors of the tower and penetrating it, embedding itself into it like a bumblebee entering a flower. Then the red-orange explosion, smoke billowing black. People terrified, jumping off windows. I will never look at an airplane in the same way.

Stunned, my French business partners have cancelled their trip to California. We were going to visit our portfolio companies next week but many of our executives are stranded in Hong Kong, Spain, or the East Coast. Peter Banks and his wife had to drive back all the way from Pennsylvania to Michigan where they still have a house. Phone calls to New York don't get through. I wonder if our friend Douglas Crosby is safe. The Pentagon burns on and on.

Athanor. Saturday 15 September 2001.

Douglas called to say he was all right, and so was his brother, but they've lost their best friend in the collapse of the towers. His latest movie set, on a crumbling pier (an ugly place tragically called "Freshkill") in Jersey, has been taken over by the security services. They use it to sort out body parts from the debris they haul by the truckload out of lower Manhattan.

I called Ingo, still in shock, having watched it all from his roof. He was pleased that I'd thought of his safety. Many people are reconnecting in the emergency. Here the fog is rising over the Point Reyes peninsula and Tomales Bay. I can already see a few people on the beach. We're waiting for Teish, to introduce her to Oberon. The house is full of good food Janine has prepared.

I've brought my notes over in order to work on the Internet book (1). We frequently turn on the news to see what Europe is saying and to watch America preparing for a new kind of war. Haunting images of the collapsing towers stay with us, day and night. Janine wonders if we should cancel our plans to visit Egypt next month.

Athanor. Sunday 16 September 2001.

Teish came over looking slim, a fact she attributes to the endemic lack of food in Nigeria, where she has extensively travelled. She was as sharp as ever. Oberon and Morning Glory soon joined us, one of those opportunities for wide-ranging discussion, a chance to combine the closeness of people we admire with the scope of this landscape. All of it was made possible by Janine's work, and the wine, and the tasty pie, and coffee on the deck as I translated an old article about the "Géon" (forgotten ancestor to the "Gaia" concept) for Oberon (2).

Teish brilliantly explained the aspects of Erzulie in cultures and contexts, as a warning against superficial contemporary imageries about African traditions. It was a superb afternoon, the fog receding over the ocean, leaving an underlining of silver light. But we could not forget the ongoing horror in New York, so conversation kept drifting back to the predictable horrors of war.

Hummingbird. Monday 17 September 2001.

I spoke to Fred Adler today, and to the French, about restructuring our plans for investment. Three former associates of the Fulbright, Jaworski legal firm in New York have died in the collapse of the towers. In this new, chaotic world, my own responsibility goes first to refinancing the fledgling companies we support, from San Diego to Portland and Silicon Valley. I called all our CEOs: How can we help them survive in the next few years?

Hummingbird. Sunday 23 September 2001.

Sleeping badly, still obsessed with the television coverage of the attack and its aftermath. Speaking to friends in New York (Joe Blades at Random House, Douglas Crosby) brings me closer to the ugly reality of devastation. Now come the preparations for the inescapable "war against terrorism," the great rumbling of ships and bombers, sabers rattling in the minds of Washington.

Yesterday evening, in honor of my 62nd birthday, Janine and I went to see Lily Tomlin in *The Search for Signs of Intelligent Life in the Universe*. The audience was warmly appreciative of Tomlin's talent and wry humor. Her most articulate and sympathetic character is a bag lady contactee with invisible alien friends: "Trudy" has bittersweet insight into the human predicament; she is crazy, so the contradictions of our everyday lives are an open book to her.

We walked home along twelve blocks of the Tenderloin, slick music clubs and dreary saloons, paper-strewn sidewalks and luxury hotels, shiny limos in waiting. Panhandlers were everywhere among plump painted prostitutes in ill-fitting neon outfits, huge motorcycles parked outside gay bars. An entire block of Polk, in front of the burned-out Leland hotel, consists of boarded-up shops covered with graffiti and tags, an appropriate symbol for this era. But the bag ladies asleep in that alley have nothing to say about the Universe.

Athanor. Sunday 30 September 2001.

As we make plans for a trip to Europe and Egypt, the manuscript of *Heart of the Internet* is off to publishers. Last weekend I stayed in San Francisco to rush through a new rewrite. In the current turmoil that is the most useful thing I can do, raising one voice to preserve the spirit of the network revolution through crises to come. I see myself having another ten years or so of professional activity, with a chance to influence some high-technology directions.

Hummingbird. Monday 1 October 2001.

Our new office is ready, painted and carpeted, with stately oak bookcases and a nice view of San Mateo: water and trees, fog rolling over the western hills, and the San Francisco skyline on the horizon. Airliners streak through on approach to the dual runways.

A correspondent writes to me that Don Antonio Ribera died on September 24 and that I am therefore "the only surviving pioneer" in Europe. This isn't exactly true: Gordon Creighton is still alive. But the remark does throw a new light on an old debate: Where is this research going? I don't expect any breakthrough from the various projects that are tracking abductees or compiling pilot surveys. Even the Utah ranch experiment and NIDS' mutilation study have no conclusion.

Perhaps it is in Antiquity that new hints could be found, if we peered back into the darkness with new tools. We should look into the wide spectrum of human spiritual history, as Aimé Michel and Alexander Kazantsev had surmised. Janine agrees with eager expectation: In a couple of weeks, we will be in Egypt, where I plan to pick up the faint thread of an idea from Maurice Chatelain: Did the mystery obey the same laws in the ancient world?

Hummingbird. Thursday 4 October 2001.

The economy keeps bumping through uncertain waters, the Dow at 9,000 and NASDAQ at 1,600. Unemployment rises, both here and in Europe. Several of our old Euro-America companies are breathing their last in spite of hard-won alliances with industrial partners. Big companies, with their enormous cost structure, sink into this mess even faster than our fragile startups. The airlines are devastated; San Francisco lacks tourists while technology firms lay off workers. Even Intel is affected: In a rare show of humility, it opens up its foundries to smaller companies in need of manufacturing capacity, said John Markoff (of *The New York Times*) when I had lunch with him.

Mabillon. Sunday 7 October 2001.

Sleep doesn't come. Paris is in a cautious mood; antiterrorist measures are visible everywhere: Trash cans welded shut, soldiers on watch. As a taxi drives me to a meeting, rain puts another layer of poetic distance between me and the city.
 Gérard Deforge tells me our witness of Haravilliers now feels alienated and depressed, but that might be a consequence of irresponsible hypnotic sessions imposed on him by silly ufologists, rather than the UFO experience itself.
 Gérard recalls an interesting UFO incident while he was a school principal. Ten of his pupils had witnessed it. Recently he met the mother of one of the little girls at a local bank: "Marie-Paule is 33 now, she's fine, she has several kids. We often talk about you; and about the flying saucer... she always swears to me it was the truth."
 Marie-Paule had seen a saucer with a dome on top, near a construction site in Eragny. She drew it in black and white: "It didn't have any colors," she had told Deforge. It stood on three legs.
 Today Janine and I went to the Luxembourg gardens under the rain with Olivier and Maxime. There's a conference on investment in

Paris. It attracts few visitors. It is incongruous in this financial debacle, when big and small investors have seen their savings evaporate. So the private bankers have hired beautiful hostesses in Dior outfits and bright scarves; they hand out leaflets advising visitors to buy warrants (not shares, but warrants, those elusive pieces of paper) with their last savings. It sounds like a bad joke.

America begins bombing Afghanistan. We have to bomb somebody, don't we? Hit in the dark, at someone.

Mabillon. Friday 12 October 2001.

Yves Messarovitch is back at *Le Figaro*, where I met him this afternoon. We spoke of restarting my column (3). Then we had a very friendly dinner at the home of Dominique Weinstein, with his wife, Mady, and their son.

Tomorrow we fly to Egypt as our study begins in earnest on the trail of the "Ancient Gods." We'll start with a guided tour of Luxor. The Paris-based organizers and the Louvre proposed rescheduling it in view of current events, but enough courageous people committed to keep the original schedule, as we did.

Luxor, Egypt. Saturday 13 October 2001.

We had clouds most of the way from Paris, only lifting for a dramatic view of chaotic mountains in Sicily. We landed at night, minutes after our first clear glimpse of Egypt. Now we rest in the quiet darkness of the New Winter Palace, empty of tourists scared by the threat of war.

The cruise ships that normally would sail down the Nile are all crowded together by the shore and the airport is gloomy. CNN shows bombs falling on Kabul, riots in Pakistan.

Luxor, Egypt. Sunday 14 October 2001.

No sign of imminent tension here, even as we wandered into the darkness of the side streets and the bustle of the souks, but we will be under army protection tomorrow when we drive out of town.

The experience of Karnak is overwhelming. Yes, we've seen the books and movies, and documentaries about the temples, but one must stand among the statues and the obelisks and walk along the sacred lake to comprehend the grandeur of this site.

As a religion, it is clear that the cult of Ammon set the standard for the various beliefs that flowed out of the Nile valley, the Jewish and Christian faiths (including the impregnation of Mary as a form of theogamy), and the Moslem faith, which we hear proclaimed tonight out of three different mosques. One of them is oddly suspended high above the courtyard. It was built at the level of the sand that drowned most of the sanctuary over centuries of neglect and was removed grain by grain by archaeologists. With its plaster minaret, its loudspeaker and garland of colored lightbulbs, it seems as incongruous as the ads for Chinese food, or the McDonald logo blinking in the souks.

Going back in time is the only wise exit. The majesty of the temple reminds me of the ancient principles I once studied and pondered, and discussed so often with Serge Hutin and Allen Hynek. American mystic Spencer Lewis had aptly captured the quiet intelligence of this era. This feels like a circle closed, not with any grandiose design of destiny but with a certain ideal of my younger days when I met Janine and began reading about alchemy. She is still with me today in the Naos of Luxor.

Luxor, Egypt. Monday 15 October 2001.

We left early this morning and were driven under armed escort for two hours, finally reaching the temple of Osiris at Abydos. On the way back we made a stop at the well-preserved temple of Hathor in Danderah. Both sites lie on the western bank of the Nile, dedicated to death and resurrection.

The constructions are astounding in inspiration, in the beauty of their execution, and in the mystical sense they impose on the land. These are not fragmented parts of an exciting story, as in Greece, remarks Janine. They feel sacred *for all time*, still complete in every sense. In Abydos we could take no pictures, with a few exceptions thanks to the well-remunerated kindness of the guards, but we did spend time at the tomb of Osiris and admired the story of his resurrection at the hands of Isis, told in exquisite relief.

The same tale is told again in greater detail at Danderah, built under the Ptolemaic period at the end of Egyptian history, summarizing three chronologies of the Pharaohs. There's a laboratory, an Inner Sanctum where the walls keep recipes for perfume and incense, secret ingredients of magic and who knows what else? That temple has crossed the centuries almost intact, except for the defacing of the Gods by Coptic fanatics who used the temple as a hiding place. They were scared, justly so, by the intense magic from these walls, draped with a mystical beauty they could never approximate.

On the way to Abydos, we passed Nag Hammadi, where Gnostic manuscripts were found. Our guides had nothing to say about it.

The Egyptian government is understandably scared of potential disorders. Not only are we preceded by an army truck with machine guns, but we keep passing checkpoints clearly concerned with more than the safety of a few tourists. One of these crossings is equipped with armored vehicles, as was the heavily-guarded site of Abydos. Every village we pass features local police in *djellabahs*, carrying rifles. Yet the Egyptians are not surly or antagonistic. People smile broadly and spontaneously. They are warm, intelligent, and ready for a joke. Children keep waving at us.

The apparent complexity of Egyptian religion resolves itself, once it is understood there is actually only one god, Ammon, too far away to be seen, heard, or grasped. He's only perceived through his effects such as sunshine, love, fecundity, motherhood.

The manifestations of this primary God are the gods and goddesses of Egypt in their many combinations. Death is not termination but rebirth, as in the resurrection of Osiris that served as a template for later religions, the great myth getting watered down in time and eventually degraded into the Easter story.

Oddly, the Gospel obeys the full scenario of the Egyptian myth: the knock on the door, the revelation: "Indeed it is true; the God has come back to life..."

Returning to Luxor, we went through the mummification museum, putting the practices of the sanctuaries into perspective. But the place to which I would love to return some day is Denderah with its secret laboratory and wondrous chapels. We spent too little time there

Fig. 3. Inner Sanctum: Janine at Denderah Temple, Egypt, October 2001.

Fig. 4. Collecting water samples at Laguna Cote, Costa Rica, April 2002.

because our Egyptian guide was scared of the many bats that hung over the portals. He let us wander into the subterranean treasure of Hathor and climb the staircase to the top of the temple and the place where the first day of the year used to be celebrated. On the ceilings of Denderah complete zodiacs are painted, and the temple roof makes a splendid observatory.

Luxor, Egypt. Tuesday 16 October 2001.

The political context escalated today with the rumor that President Mubarak would come to Luxor tomorrow or Thursday, to inaugurate the restored temple of Hatchepsout at Deir el Bahari.

We were able to see the third terrace today. We began the tour of the Theban necropolis with the temple of Sothi the First and ended it with the obligatory tourist stops at the papyrus museum and the sound and light show in Karnak. We were amused when arguments flared between our French guide, some of the more erudite members of our group, and the director of West Bank monuments who took us into the sanctuary of Queen Hatchepsut, the only female Pharaoh, a fascinating figure.

The curator ranted against western museums for "stealing Egyptian treasures." Our polite group refrained from pointing out that Egypt had neglected these priceless artifacts for centuries, selling precious artwork to anyone for dollars, francs, or shillings until western archaeologists recognized their historical value and started collecting (and thereby saving) them for restoration and public view.

Luxor, Egypt. Wednesday 17 October 2001.

We had lunch at a Theban hotel, its terrace looking down on the Nile. Everywhere we see people fixing roads and repainting the black and white sidewalks, in advance of the presidential visit.

Individual tombs are most interesting: they provide insight into the private lives of noblemen, government ministers, and craftsmen, as opposed to the impressive religious motifs of the major temples or the monuments of the Pharaohs. We visited seven of these tombs today, including that of Ramose who was Akhenaton's vizir, or prime minister, after serving his father, Amenothis III.

Sophie Labbé-Toutée, our guide from the Louvre who leads us through this maze, says that Akhenaton remains one of the controversial topics in Egyptology today.

I asked her about DNA analysis; one of the tombs we saw today kept a desiccated fetus in a glass display. The child was not identified, and some of the filiation of the Pharaohs is in question. In the case of Akhenaton, however, his mummy is unavailable, and so is that of his wife, Nefertiti.

Luxor. Thursday 18 October 2001.

Mubarak remained in Cairo, but his wife replaces him on a mission to revive tourism, so the main streets are draped with fine carpets and vividly-colored tapestries, fabrics with slogans, portraits and flowers, guarded by police in black and soldiers in white.

We crossed the Nile again to see the "twin colossus of Memnon" (in fact, gigantic statues of a Pharaoh) and the Valley of the Kings, including the tomb of Tut-Ankh-Amun. Vendors of trinkets, postcards, and statuettes, some of them nicely made, outnumber tourists. We only saw three buses in the huge parking lot, and when we got to the highest tomb our little group was completely alone.

The reason is simple: Trouble is brewing everywhere. Afghanistan has been thrown into chaos. The Taliban appear to be weakening in Kabul but the assassination of an Israeli cabinet minister yesterday has re-ignited the Middle East. The world is sick, feverish.

The Luxor Museum is small, airy, well-displayed. Madame Mubarak just passed through, opened a hospital and a new library, which is nice.

Tonight, our hotel organized the obligatory Oriental dinner; belly dancers and dervishes but very few stars were in the sky, hidden by the dampness of the air over the river.

Luxor, Egypt. Friday 19 October 2001.

The last day of our trip. We came here as humble history students on a philosophy-inspired quest, in search of a pattern, a geography of ideas that could heal our confusion about the forces beyond ordinary reality. We came here to reflect on the stately figure of Thoth. Stylus in hand, he stands quiet, absorbed in the task of watching and recording. He summarizes the peace, tranquility, and balance that characterizes Egyptian civilization for us, and inspires research.

Perhaps Egypt borrows these qualities from the ever-majestic Nile. This equanimity is best observed in the earliest dynasties, with scenes of stable power and domestic abundance. The tombs exhibit a profound preoccupation with personal integrity and social justice. There was a clear division among classes, evident in the enormous labor required to build these monuments, yet it led to recognition for the craftsmen who were allowed to build their own decorated tombs, their path to the night land beyond.

In these early sites one looks in vain for pictures of bloody battles like the ones our "evolved" civilization will leave behind. Contrary to primitives in America and elsewhere, the Egyptians never used blood sacrifices. They knew offerings to the Gods meant gifts of the same kind in return: *as below, so above*. Therefore, the offerings consist of baskets of food, rings of gold, and representations of life in all its glories. At funerals: more food, protection from demons of the night, and celebrations of life with scenes evocative of graceful dances, young women in transparent veils, blessings from the sky.

At the last tomb we visited, the guard said he didn't like the place: There was a Jinn, a giant, he said, hovering over the Valley of the Kings. Egyptians are not Arabs but a mix of Semitic and African people, with spiritual and mystical concerns from both influences.

Later the same day.

We went back to Karnak this morning to visit several side buildings. The Egyptian builders kept re-using stones from older temples to erect new walls and monuments. Archaeologists, as they examine each block, often discover that it comes from older constructions. Thus with the adorably-proportioned white chapel of Senostris-I and the red-colored chapel of Hatshepsut.

Between these reconstructed monuments and the main temple of Karnak, an open-air museum has been arrayed on concrete platforms, with thousands of blocks still unclassified, fragments of statues, partially-reconstructed scenes. In a faraway corner stands the temple of Ptah, with a fine statue of Sekhmet in the darkness.

Free for the afternoon, we sailed up the Nile in a felucca to an island of banana trees and ended up on the terrace of the Winter Palace for tea at sunset. The sounds here are those of the call to prayer (especially today, Friday) when it seems all the mosques in Upper Egypt keep responding to each other, hundreds of birds sing in chaotic clusters along the banks, and the hooves of the horses resonate, drawing absurdly-decorated *calèches*. This is a land of intense smells, too, of spices and odorant leaves, of teas and carcaret, the juice of the hibiscus. On Banana Island, the smells give the place a rich sense of antiquity. The tools we see along the path, designed to plant and harvest, are the same ones represented on the walls of the Pharaoh's Temple of a Million Years.

Mabillon. Saturday 20 October 2001.

Finally, at home, a familiar, reassuring sound: the rain on the rooftops and courtyards of Paris; the smell of moisture on the trees, walls, cobblestones; nostalgia rising from the streets.

American elite troops are on the ground in Afghanistan, fighting the Taliban—our former allies—around their strongholds. In happier days of anti-Russian resistance, the Pentagon furnished them with the rocket launchers they now use against our guys.

In email exchanges at NIDS, we talk of anthrax vaccines, neglecting our usual themes of paranormal events in Utah, or wormhole travel.

Eurostar to London. Sunday 21 October 2001.

Lumbering through the English countryside on the way to a technology investment conference, the Eurostar is humiliated to a crawl by the tortuous English rails. Here the train meets the ordinary gray, closed sky that seems to prolong the undersea tunnel.

We had dinner with Olivier last night, at Vagenende. He seemed strong and relaxed amidst the financial turmoil of the last few months. He keeps passing new exams in finance, quite brilliantly.

The inspiration of Egypt lingers while the wind and rain make a carpet of fat leaves around Saint-Germain-des-Prés.

London. Tuesday 23 October 2001.

The Cal-IT meetings bring fifty West Coast companies to the City for introductions to European partners. Any element of pleasure to be derived from these conferences has been blown away by recent events: every hotel a fortress, every airport a garrison, every meeting room a high-security area. I attend few such events, and only for the opportunity to renew some friendships, track new markets, and take the temperature of an investment world turning to uncertainty and gloom. The loudspeakers insist on playing big band tunes from the 50s that only contribute to the heaviness of the affair.

Olivier, whose office is only a few blocks away, will join me for lunch today. Then Janine and I fly back to America before the weekend.

Hummingbird. Saturday 27 October 2001.

I found my new office again, with renewed pleasure. Our wide windows look over a graceful landscape of hills, lakes, tall trees, and the sloughs of San Mateo that extend all the way to the Bay.

Abrupt changes at NIDS in Las Vegas. Gabe Valdez is gone and Mindy, the assistant, has not been replaced by Bob Bigelow, who no longer supports independent research. I have not been privy to the analysis of metal samples from New Mexico or rumored studies of "implants." There was an object found in Utah, and some biological studies, but none of that was openly discussed. This is an unfortunate consequence of the team's isolation, in my view, because it compartmentalizes everything, owns everything, and thus risks missing everything.

Our next meeting will be a watershed: Bob wants to merge our science board with Bigelow Aerospace.

Colm just published a clever paper on human endogenous retroviruses and non-coding DNA (4). I introduce him to executives at Handylab, one of our best portfolio companies.

Of all the events NIDS has studied over the years, mutilations have been the most puzzling. We currently have samples from three of the eight cases reported by Sheriff Wolverton's group in Montana. In one of them Colm found Oxindole, a powerful sedative related to a narcotic derivative.

Oxindole and Indole, manufactured in Europe, disrupt the neurological system and muscle-nerve connections and can cause death. The report says: "Our 1999 Utah case found ultra-high levels of KCl (10 times what was needed to kill an adult bovine) and a blue gel within the muscle-blood vessel tissues that remains unidentified even though we ID'ed the atomic elements forming the compound. It's a large macro-molecular compound that GCMS was unable to discern."

A Florida forensic lab also found high doses of European drugs in a mutilated adult cow: amphetamine, barbiturates, B-12, and an antibiotic that is not approved by the FDA. What does it all mean?

Hummingbird. Thursday 1 November 2001.

From my home study, San Francisco looks like a fine painting seen through translucent paper, some parts blurry or barely outlined, the tip of towers lost in suggestive haze. The air, fragrant with hints of Pacific spray, brings my throat and lungs back to life after the roughness of Paris.

Dual late-model computers on my desk allow me to do most of my work here when I don't drive down to the Valley.

Halloween was subdued this year, in spite of a "Blue Moon" in the sky playing with layers of low clouds worthy of Spielberg. We had dinner with friends at the University Club.

When we came out on California Street where cable cars were rumbling by, we only saw one king and one flapper. We walked home along a stretch of Polk Street that looked empty and sad.

Las Vegas. Friday 2 November 2001.

Sam's Towne Casino, where I stay, sits on the Boulder Strip, far from city center. The black cab driver jokes he has heavily "invested" in the place over the years. His business is way down; tourists are staying home. "The country is on its knees, but we just need to get back up on our feet, and nip this whole thing in the bud."

Easier said than done. If Osama Bin Laden could see the security precautions at the airport, he would die laughing. I had to go through the machine three times. My last attempt was made shoeless, my belt and wallet in a plastic box. "Was my suitcase ever outside my control?" the clerk demanded to know. Yes, for 10 minutes, while the rent-a-cops with the X-ray machine were fooling with it.

Two of my friends have had items stolen from their bags by the airport inspectors: Douglas a pair of brand-new shoes, Paul Saffo his class ring.

The America we loved is gone. A nation under law is being turned into a sad approximation of a police state—not by the Taliban, who were invented and armed by Washington, but by our own elected leaders. Bush has just decreed that presidential papers must remain inaccessible to contemporary historians.

Las Vegas. Saturday 3 November 2001.

The NIDS meeting marked a turning point, as Colm had anticipated. Bob opened with a status report, noting that the Utah ranch has been quiet. In reaction, Board meetings will now be semi-annual. Hal Puthoff will continue as chairman, but our activities will merge with those of Bigelow Aerospace; that campus now holds 23 people working in two shifts on Bob's expandable space modules.

"When you go into space, do you bump into things that relate to the UFO observations? Are there new materials you would discover in the process?" asks Bigelow. "Can we start from the UFO topic and go backwards, find the right combination of elements for space propulsion? Can we craft an experiment on the ISS or the Shuttle that would indicate a 'signature,' something that can be made in microgravity but cannot be made on Earth?" What about the titanium aluminide that Battelle was playing with in the days of the Pentacle Memorandum? And what about the classified project called *Pyewackit* in the Fifties and Sixties, when the Navy and Air Force tested a flying disk at Mach 10? A *Pyewackit*, it turns out, is an old name for "a witch's familiar."

Colm followed with a statistical presentation. They have now recorded 150 cases across the US, of large triangular objects that can either jump across the sky or move leisurely at 30 mph. One even took off from Wright-Patterson. They tend to be seen around air lanes between major bases.

Doesn't that argue for a military craft, as in the Belgium UFO wave of 1989-1990?

Later the same day.

At a break, JohnDale Solem thanked me for the review of Chaitin's work I just published in *JSE* (5). A mathematician colleague of his at Los Alamos added that there are true theorems for which the proof would require an amount of information greater than the bit content of the universe.

People at Los Alamos speculate about how to build a super-laser with a beam 100 miles in diameter. If placed somewhere inside the orbit of Jupiter, this device could be used to power a spacecraft close to the speed of light, far into interstellar space.

Bob Bigelow took us on a visit to his aerospace campus, an impressive 50-acre facility where he opened two streets, one called Skywalker Way, the other Warp Drive. In September he went to two shifts to build Voyager XM300, a 300 cubic meter expandable module for a crew of eight, 45 feet long and 22 feet in diameter when deployed. "Going to space is not a technical issue any more," says Bigelow in one of his smart one-liners. "What we need is more 'IBM,' intelligent business management!"

Las Vegas. Sunday 4 November 2001.

Today Colm Kelleher soberly summarized the NIDS data on 67 cases of mutilations, including 13 reports from police since June 2001. The most interesting is case number 607, a 6-year-old red Angus with missing jaw, left eye, tongue, sex organs, and rectum. A green substance was found under the jaw bone; it fluoresced under UV light. The cow had been healthy a day earlier. They requested that the head be mailed to Las Vegas for analysis, again finding Oxindole in the eye fluid and in the green tissue.

"This is not the kind of thing a normal toxicology scan would have discovered," the analysts pointed out. "We did a molecule-by-molecule study, and then we did a control with a cow's head we left out in the same conditions, for the same length of time."

All this continues to point to human activity. We remember the Cache Logan confrontation in Utah in the mid-70s, when strangers in uniform were involved, and where three helicopters confronted a single sheriff's deputy trying to arrest the perpetrators.

NIDS has two instances of law enforcement officers following such helicopters to a military base, one recorded by Kit, the other by Dr. George Onet. As for the alien hypothesis, still proposed by Linda Howe and Dr. Altschuler, "it vaporizes under scrutiny," was the conclusion. Yet some of us are unconvinced: The cardinal case in Saskatchewan that NIDS investigated had multiple mutilation elements along with strange beings; a dozen animals were lost.

But was it paranormal? And if so, was it "Alien"?

The NIDS UFO catalogue now holds 864 cases including 158 large triangular objects, 71 cases with electromagnetic effects, 52 with physiological effects, 235 close encounters. There are multiple eyewitnesses in 435 cases. In one case an object flew over a bed of petunias that changed from purple color to striped white and purple, then to lime green. The Board agreed that this might be caused by UV or IR activation, affecting a set of gene transcription factors. One case, in Carteret (New Jersey) in July 2001, had 120 witnesses, of which 21 were interviewed by NIDS.

Hummingbird. Tuesday 6 November 2001.

Self-proclaimed "prophet of the Patriot movement," ufologist Bill Cooper has died, as he once predicted to me, in a gun battle with a sheriff's deputy in Eager, Apache County (Arizona), after wounding another cop who was trying to arrest him.

William Milton Cooper was 58. In his radio broadcasts, he regularly railed against the federal government and talked of doomsday omens. One of his faithful listeners was Timothy McVeigh, the Oklahoma

City bomber. Their genuinely American streak of violence continues to spread.

Athanor. Saturday 10 November 2001.

Who should call me two days ago but Robert K. Weiss, who now produces a television show with Dan Ackroyd out of New York. The series is called *Out There* and consists of programs on the paranormal for the Sci-Fi Channel. Bob wanted to reconnect after a failed Internet venture: at the height of the dot-com bubble he ran a company called *Blastoff* that proposed to land cameras on the Moon as a space event, to be webcast around the globe. They only raised 16 million dollars out of the 40 they needed to complete the first event. They had to fold the company when the market collapsed.

Bob Weiss and Dan Ackroyd now interview ufologists who talk seriously about Pentagon saucers and Reptilian invaders. I laughed. "How likely do you rate the Reptilian hypothesis," I asked, "on a *scale* of 1 to 10?"

Bob said he'd steal the pun and regretted my decision not to be on the show. But compared to Reptilians, robots busy inside the Earth, Budd Hopkins' naked flying abductees, and David Jacobs' saucer sex, anything I would say would sound boring.

Athanor. Saturday 17 November 2001.

After every trip we rediscover our hidden fortress high above the shore. Yesterday we had a picnic on the hill. Deer grazed along the cliffs and the wind rolled gray cloudbanks towards the fields of Sonoma. A cloudburst caught us on the way.

The rain hasn't stopped since, furthering our blissful isolation. Janine is so happy here...

I put final touches to *Heart of the Internet*, inserting notes from a pleasant lunch with Paul Baran and Steve Millard on Tuesday that helped me understand the true origin of packet networks. Tomorrow I leave for Montréal (a conference on innovation) and on to Paris. Travelling is a burden, terrorism adding delays for searches.

Montréal. Monday 19 November 2001. Hotel Wyndham

The Canadian economy is in a visible recession. This old Meridien is sadly deserted, except for a few dozen attendees to this conference. The city is very bland, the grass dead, the sidewalks sadly strewn with dirty papers. Our investors from the Québec Workers Fund (FTQ) tell me winter is late in coming. All the talk about innovation revolves around ponderous government action and meager budgets.

Back in Afghanistan, music is heard once again in the streets of Kabul as the Taliban take a beating. A quiet woman journalist going back to her TV job after five years of interdiction in the name of some crazed cleric's personal interpretation of the Coran spoke softly, without bitterness, of working secretly at home as a hairdresser, afraid to leave her house. She was more poignant than all the fighting that is redrawing the maps of a continent.

Mabillon. Friday 23 November 2001.

The very notion of international normalcy has vanished, a page turned. Here in France people are unsure about the war. They express relief because their country is not engaged in Afghanistan but feel spite at not being privy to serious decisions. They have a need for order, the receding mirage of socialism or the faded beauties of tradition, while Paris rolls along towards Christmas as if the horrible mess of the planet could somehow be managed. The mistrust of outsiders looms larger as many folks grasp again at the soggy straws of racism.

Mabillon. Sunday 25 November 2001.

There is a saturnine side to my soul that delights in contemplation, walking alone in the darkened streets or standing against a pillar in a cathedral, marveling at incongruous details. I could easily be misled by dreams of ancient castles, the bizarre conversation of freaks and outsiders, the flame of a simple candle, the compilation of marginalia, the chance discovery of an old book, or the arcane knowledge of obsolete artisans and faded courtesans.

At the same time, I treasure life in the gardens of high tech: lunch with Paul Baran, board meetings in San Diego or Portland, inside knowledge of future wireless standards, glimpses of exquisite new materials (erbium-doped silicates, how beautiful!), quiet talks with physicists taming entangled particles in the shadow of Stanford.

From Paris, I call Janine every day. She delights in working with our daughter, fixing houses, visiting clients, dealing with the changing landscape of urban California, not for business alone but an inspired impact on the lives of others she helps gain ownership of their first home. I treasure her wisdom with a pinch of envy, her inspiration so unlike that somber, anxious drive in my heart.

Hummingbird. Sunday 16 December 2001.

Our friends, Dr. Kevin Starr and his wife Sheila, had a party tonight for some sixty people. We spent an hour there, talking to their guests: a mix of academics, judges, a Monsignor or two. This is the season for parties: Americans seek out their friends, relatives, and the novelty of strangers. Everyone is eager for companionship after the recent horrors.

Over the phone, Douglas Crosby tells me workers have just reached the major structural piece at the World Trade Center. They were shocked to uncover "a staircase filled with mummies."

At the Band of Angels party with Fred Hoar and Hans Severiens, we saw Steve Millard and Linda, Amory Lovins, Federico Faggin, people who changed the world. We make preparations for Max's visit tomorrow with his parents: I rebuilt a large closet into an alcove for him, all dark blue with a starry sky and phosphorescent galaxies.

Hummingbird. Monday 17 December 2001.

Colm Kelleher tells me that Howard Cross from Battelle had reported a UFO he witnessed at 6 pm on October 2, 1951, some fourteen months before he penned his secret Memorandum (6). The case is in Blue Book, but I had missed it. He was the contact for Edward Ruppelt. Cross can be tracked all the way back to Vannevar Bush's war research, when he was involved in titanium metallurgy.

Hummingbird. Thursday 20 December 2001.

The executive board of Dick Haines' NARCAP met again today in our new conference room in San Mateo. Larry Lemke of ISSO, Ted Roe, and a NASA engineer joined us.

Much of the discussion had to do with the group's attempts to gain legitimacy for studies of pilot sightings. The difficulty comes from the fact that many airlines forbid their pilots from discussing such incidents.

Six trips to France this year, two to Japan and Brunei, assorted excursions to London and Egypt. In the US, I flew to Vegas 3 times, San Diego 4 times, and Portland 7 times. No wonder I feel a bit tired.

Athanor. Tuesday 25 December 2001.

Christmas Day was mild here, with changing patterns of filtered sun, haze, and drizzle. I spent the afternoon playing on the beach with four-year old Maxime, throwing a ball against the wind. I have converted the NIDS database of reports and Dominique Weinstein's excellent catalog of pilot sightings, as well as the Hatch catalogue into a state-of-the-art "data warehouse." Eventually I will start adding my own lists of unpublished cases.

For Christmas, Janine gave me Brenda Denzler's book *The Lure of the Edge* (7) where I found my own work quoted in the right perspective for once. Yet it's still obvious that this clever author can only present the possible existence of the UFO phenomenon in extraterrestrial terms.

How long will it take for people to come round to the idea that other hypotheses exist, and they open the way to a more profound truth and to more powerful methods to analyze it?

Those contemporary researchers open-minded enough to revisit ancient traditions stumble across the minefield of demonology: They are tempted to explain a stereotype (the modern Grey abductor) with a caricature (the ancient evil monster from Hell). In so doing they obliterate the data. They ignore the dangers and opportunities of interaction with unknown creatures of the mind and the soul.

Athanor. Friday 28 December 2001.

Dr. Richard Niemtzow, whom I called this afternoon in San Diego where he's still stationed (after 20 years in the Air Force), encourages me to go on with my own quiet research: "You have the pleasure of seeing what's going on with the phenomenon, even if others don't recognize it. You have the opportunity to take the next step. You're at the center of the circle; others are just walking around it. What does it matter if you can't get them to come inside and see what you've discovered?"

He says he's reached the same point with acupuncture and alternative medicine: "I've had the experience of being on stage at medical meetings where professionals brought patients they hadn't helped, and after a few minutes I was able to stop their pain. Yet that doesn't convince my skeptical colleagues..."

"They say the patient was healed... for the wrong reasons?" I joked.

"Exactly," replied Richard, "but that doesn't bother me. As I get older I now understand that what's important is to keep doing what you think is right, and not worry about what other people say or do."

Hummingbird. Monday 31 December 2001.

This afternoon Teish invited me to a celebration at her church in honor of Legba. Several attendees became possessed by the Orishas and prophesized. "The coming year will be difficult," channeled Oshun in Spanish through the throaty cries of a young man who danced wildly among the couples dressed all in white, assembled to pray in the rented dining room of a restaurant at Broadway and 23rd street, downtown Oakland, site of mysterious deeds.

Athanor. Saturday 5 January 2002.

It rains and rains, flooding in the North Bay. We can hardly see the shore from here; one can only guess at the Tomales peninsula outlined at the horizon. The sea is white with foam.

Perusing the web, I have found yet another remarkable artist in downtown Oakland, a lapsed astrophysicist named Cliff Stoll who makes and sells clever Klein bottles and lovely "zero-volume" mugs he calls *Kleinsteins* (8).

Sitting by the fireplace, I go on reading Des Mousseaux who quotes Cornelius Agrippa (9), *De Occulta Philosophia*, Ludgd. 1531 p.354: "At Nadhegryn Promontory in Norway, demons allow themselves to be seen publicly (*in aero corpore, in preasentia cernintur ab omnibus*) and similar Wonders take place in Scotland and several other regions. As for myself I refrain from testifying about what I have seen with my eyes and touched with my hands. The astonishment caused by these marvellous facts would make the skeptics call me a liar."

It is vital to place today's paranormal events in the context of such older records. Whatever the phenomenon is, whether linked to undiscovered processes of human perception or to the intervention of another form of consciousness, it has always been with us. It is part of the human sphere of existence. The anonymous author of *Art Magic* insists: "Planetary Spirits respond to invocations from the sincere Spiritualist, and often hold watch and ward over the favored ones of Earth to whom, through prepared conditions, they communicate the great truths of the Universe, unattainable to mortals without their aid."*

Hummingbird. Thursday 10 January 2002.

Our friend Dr. Harary now lives in Portland. He left L.A. with Darlene in fear of attacks after September 11. He went to Vancouver, was horrified by the high crime rate, and settled in Oregon.

Tonight, I had a happy reunion and dinner in La Jolla with Richard Niemtzow and his two sons. Richard is now a full colonel and a military expert on alternative medicine, recognized for his acupuncture therapy. We spoke of the early days of GEPAN (a unit of the French Space Agency CNES whose brief is to investigate UFOs), when he was friends with Poher and Payan, and Kit asked him if the French "were close to finding an ET presence?"

"If you hear something, tell me right away," Kit once said, "I have

---

* The authors of *Art Magic* were William Britten and Emma Hardinge Britten. Emma died in 1899. See also *Ghost Lands*.

a direct link to someone on the President's National Security Council." He wanted to know the French UFO research budget, and how many people were involved. Richard's superior, the Surgeon General, told him with a thin smile that he kept getting mysterious calls urging that Niemtzow be allowed to travel to Paris. Shortly afterwards Richard was invited to lunch at the home of Gilbert Payan, whom he only knew as "a high-level French scientist close to the government." The 7-hour conversation was all about UFOs.

"Do you know why you're here?" Payan finally asked as they strolled in the garden. "We know very well that you report to the US government on what we do. But why don't you come and work for us in France? We'd help your wife find a job at the University, and you'd be with GEPAN..." Richard answered he was an American officer, and would feel he was betraying his country if he accepted.

Back home, Richard recalled a contact through Dr. Richard Neal, of a retired MD rumored to have performed an autopsy of an Alien. He tracked the man down, went to his house. But when he broached the subject, the man suddenly panicked: "His face literally decomposed before my eyes," Richard told me. "He stammered that he couldn't talk about any of that, he'd lose his pension."

When Richard tried to contact him again, the old doctor had died. A similarly strange situation arose when Richard tracked down another MD through Len Stringfield. He was alleged to have photographs of humanoids. Discussing this with Kit, he was told not to pursue it: "Physician to physician, Richard, I'm telling you to drop it. Stringfield will lose his job if he keeps this up."

Richard was never able to confront the doctor, and Stringfield did lose his job.

The most tantalizing story Richard tells concerns the UFO project at McDonnell in the 1970s. He repeated what he'd told me in July 1989: Along with John Schuessler, he met in Houston with the head of R&D for McDonnell. A reservation made at a local hotel got changed at the last moment.

The man smiled: "They keep doing this, perhaps to protect me. Let's not talk in here."

So they spoke in the parking lot. Niemtzow was offered a position with the UFO project. *"What you've been imagining, Richard, wasn't your imagination. There's nothing wrong with your imagination! But if you join us, you'll never practice medicine again."*

Richard said he wanted to remain a doctor, but he's always wondered about that day. Kit was the official monitor, although he only said he was associated with it "out of personal interest."

New York. Sunday 20 January 2002.

The Plaza brings back memories, the rooms small and plush under high ceilings, with the only addition of annoying electronics, incongruous in this luxury: a flat-screen display, a modem, a fax machine. I crawled under the green marble-topped desk, found the switch and disconnected the whole noisy mess.

I haven't been in New York since the drama of September 11. The city has recovered its composure; life seems almost normal although all conversations begin with reminiscences of that horrible day.

There was a thin layer of snow on the ground at Kennedy, but the streets are dry and clean. Tomorrow I meet with Philip Chapman at the Adler office, and dinner is arranged with Bob Weiss and Douglas Crosby at Smith & Wolenski's steakhouse. Janine is in Guadalajara with a dozen people from her office, at the wedding of a colleague from Prudential. Catherine is in Graz, Austria, where her MBA team will present a report on industrial clusters to government officials.

Mabillon. Thursday 24 January 2002.

The mood in Paris is of cautious pessimism, smothered in the grayness of the sky, and a mild winter that could turn mean any minute. As I switch to the euro currency I have just spent my last 50 Franc note at Café Danton. The new bills depict architectural motifs, indifferent bridges and vacuous windows. They are uninspiring, like dusty blueprints faded in dryness. European bureaucracy is growing, costly and inaccessible. Yet the success of the historic transition to euros is a genuine display of administrative acumen. It gives hope that a large enough economic market will be created to erase old rancors and transcend inefficiencies. In the meantime, passage to the euro has resulted in a generalized upward rounding of all retail prices, roughly a 5-to-10% hike on all consumer goods; the government refuses to acknowledge it.

Our neighbor Professor Bokias is tired of Paris, where his main distraction comes at Collège de France lectures attended by erudite retirees like him. Yet he recently left the august institution in disgust, in the middle of a dissertation on "Iconophiles and Iconoclasts."

Mabillon. Sunday 27 January 2002.

This is Janine's birthday; I am sad to spend it so far away. She writes that it rains in San Francisco; she is staying home with a cold. A storm blew over Paris last night, with much noisy wind and shaking, leaving the air cleaner for once. I had dinner with Dominique Weinstein, François Louange, and Joëlle, a smart vivacious redhead. Marriages of many years' standing are breaking up all around us.

At *Le Chien qui Fume* across from CNES headquarters, we spent hours catching up on events since the historic Pocantico meetings and comparing our scenarios for a possible revival of GEPAN.

Louange has been assigned to conduct an official audit of SEPRA, sending him to interview 35 big wheels in French science, administration, and the media. Results were surprising. Even Pellat, who once killed Poher's project, gave an open-minded view. Experts on the high atmosphere said that a new study might lead to fresh insights, "although unlikely to reveal extraterrestrials."

Hubert Curien, another hardened rationalist, offered to send an observer from the Academy of Sciences if a new steering committee was created. Louange reports a strong consensus that real science could be done, as Pocantico had concluded, and that it was time to restart GEPAN. This would mean having Jean-Jacques Velasco report directly to Paris, with expanded staff and a new budget.

Cometa may have played a murky role in all this. The military group has fallen apart, but Payan has recaptured power. There is talk of his long acquaintance with Soviet researchers, so I watch all this with some cynicism. The troubling memory of Belgian triangles and the evidence that UFO claims have often been used to shield American tests of stealth technology over Europe suggest that all is not pure science and innocent research in the new efforts; these people are neither naïve nor stupid. We left the restaurant in the wet breeze, and Dominique drove me home.

Mabillon. Monday 28 January 2002.

Full moon setting on Boulevard Saint Germain, a splendid sight: wet sidewalks under the first flames of the rising sun.

The science city at La Villette, northeast of Paris, where I speak on a panel on "entrepreneurship," the latest socialist fad. It is a vast complex of plastic architecture and meaningless metal "art." The only nice touch comes from water-filled pools lapping to the edge of the concrete. Environment minister Yves Cochet was on my panel, so I asked him if we might greet him in San Francisco soon; he answered he hadn't been in California for over 15 years—not a good record for an ecologist.

Sunday was spent at Olivier's apartment, full of the laughter of kids, and conversation with his friends. He baked a quiche as he spoke of being caught in the economic storm, his employer's firm disbanded, investment banking in disarray.

Things are not going well for venture capitalists, either. Not only are most portfolios under water by a third of their value, but they've hired too many managers, assistants, and secretaries, and made too many hasty investments. The auxiliary funds, a ploy of the French government to fuel company creation, are raised by banks from middle-class folks eager to set euros aside from the taxman, a poor excuse for an investment strategy. The bankers don't know how to manage these funds, turned over to private firms keeping a healthy percentage of the loot. The money must be invested in two years, so it goes into any deal that comes along, with disastrous consequences.

Hummingbird. Sunday 3 February 2002.

I flew back to the States in time to hear our friend Krista Bennion at the Palace of the Legion of Honor, playing on Jasha Heifetz' donated violin that is kept at the museum: Bach's "Partita 1 for Solo Violin," then Mozart's "Divertimento," and Schubert's "Concerto in C Major."

Janine and I especially enjoyed Schubert, but Krista was upset when she discovered that the treasured violin, poorly maintained, had a broken bridge, and her E string snapped in the middle of Mozart, yet she went on and gave a fine performance.

Athanor. Friday 8 February 2002.

Yesterday: Shoenberg and Mahler (Michael Tilson Thomas conducting the Symphony). I was struck by the beauty of Shoenberg's music. I had never found an affinity for his serial and dodecaphonic experiments, but his "Five Pieces for Orchestra" were splendid, especially "Premonitions" and the intricately emotional "Things Past." Mahler, however, is still a challenge for me: his "Songs of the Earth" (based on 8th century Chinese poetry about the virtues of drunkenness and the despair of living, which reminded me of Fred Beckman) are often gripping, at times merely a puzzle to my untrained ears. Janine, whose musical sense is far ahead of mine, loved the performance.

Athanor. Saturday 16 February 2002.

A long weekend, welcome rest, the office closed for President's Day. The North Coast expects some rain so we just watch our old slides of the sixties and seventies, touching images of our children growing up, our parents, and Janine so ravishing. The early sunshine over the bay is hidden by clouds; the blue sea turns to pewter, the blue sky to silver, the green peninsula to a darker tone, almost black. There is no sound, except the surf and the wind in the pine trees that form a screen below us, between the hillside and the rocky coast. We are alone. I love you more than I can say.

Hummingbird. Sunday 24 February 2002.

The Herbst Theater at the War Memorial building in San Francisco was the site of the formal creation of the United Nations in 1945. One of our secret pleasures is to walk down the ten blocks of shops and movie houses to hear concerts there, then to walk back, stopping at some restaurant on Van Ness or Polk. Last night we heard Krista

Bennion again playing Bach, then a profound piece for synthesizer and strings by Terry Riley called "Remember this O Mind," inspired by the gospel of Sri Ramakrishna: "Vain is your wandering in this world..."

It is our great luxury to be able to walk over to such events on the spur of the moment, or just to browse among used bookstores and antique shops when we spend the weekend in the City.

Telephone conversation with Sturrock tonight, about databases. I argued I found no historical peak in UFO reports at a certain local sidereal time, contrary to his calculations, because of redundancies in the files, but he didn't believe me.

Peter continues to do research at Stanford on the internal structure of the Sun. Measurements of neutrinos emitted by the Sun show differential rotation patterns in the interior structure, possibly related to the elusive dark matter that astrophysicists have been trying to fathom. Peter looks at the periodicity in the emissions. One current theory is that weakly interacting massive particles could have collected within the Sun since it formed 5 billion years ago.

Hummingbird. Friday 1 March 2002.

All night, a late winter storm has shaken the glass in the frames of our windows, pulling us again and again out of sleep.

General Exon has recently told Eric Davis that he knew a pilot named Henderson (not "Pappy" Henderson) who'd flown back from Roswell with one of the planes that carried alien samples in unmarked boxes. He managed to hide some of the material in his toolbox. It consisted, as often reported, of two types of things: 1. light material with the consistency of balsa wood, fibrous in nature but metallic in color, that couldn't be broken, didn't crack or dent. The samples were about three by one inch in size, but there were reportedly much larger samples among the recovered debris; 2. foil with burn marks, stiff, purplish and shiny. It could be crumpled by hand when force was applied, but it would spring back to its original shape. Some of the samples, reportedly, were over one foot square although the pilot only had a 3x5 inch piece of it.

General Exon also stated he'd seen photos of the debris including beams several feet long, with inscriptions. He confirmed to Eric that the Ramey press conference with Jesse Marcel was a cover-up, part of a Rawin target. The journalists were kept at the office door to make sure they wouldn't touch the material, switched for the real Roswell debris. This embarrassed poor Jesse Marcel, but Ramey followed orders "to kill the flying saucer story once and for all."

General Exon said he knew nothing about any Alien bodies. Asked about Corso's book, he called it ego-inflated, but the description of the way any recovered material would be handled in a compartmentalized process was absolutely correct.

Eric also told me about a recent conversation with Jim Westwood, who claimed to have located two genuine reports about UFO crashes with hardware recovery, and bodies.

Pursuing my own designs, I plan our discrete April expedition to the area of the Arenal volcano in Costa Rica, where the famous photograph of an emerging disk was taken, a lasting enigma.

Athanor. Saturday 2 March 2002.

Kit tells our group that he was briefed three times on the "Alien" subject and came to the—admittedly unscientific—conclusion that the Roswell autopsy was genuine.* He was first briefed officially at the Pentagon, about 1981, while at CIA. He was told about collected data from a network of sensors camouflaged as environmental monitoring stations. I had suggested this idea to Professor Rocard in the mid-sixties... and it was later implemented by the French, according to Niemtzow, who was told about it when Payan tried to recruit him.

The second briefing was an unofficial invitation to the Pentagon, about 1987-88 when Kit was no longer at CIA. A "person in uniform" asked his opinion about photographs and autopsy reports.
The cadaver was consistent with the later "Santilli film."

The third briefing was an official session at CIA about 1991-92. He

---

* In an Internet message on 7 May 2021, Kit retracted this opinion, saying he had realized the briefings were "meant for disinformation. The perpetrators ... are attempting to disenfranchise me, starting with my very public retraction of the Alien Autopsy report—which report was a hoax played on me—from inside the USG ..."

was asked, once again, to examine some autopsy reports whose nature was ambiguous.

Kit thought they were the same reports he'd already seen. No action was taken, and he "was left hanging."

He now thinks that Alien forensic tissue samples, if they exist, might well be secured at the Walter-Reed Armed Forces Institute of Pathology Medical Museum, a classified facility that he's only visited twice in his career, under escort by the Chief Medical Examiner of the Army, Dr. Charles Stahl. He stated that the two individuals seen on the Santilli film follow a procedure consistent with Army medical practice of the 1940s, yet it seems incredibly sloppy to me, if only given the risks of contamination if the beings had been real Aliens.

Athanor. Sunday 3 March 2002.

One is almost ashamed of confessing to bliss. So many people in the world live in pain or anxiety that any private happiness almost becomes a dirty secret. But our feeling of the last two days is something I would like to keep forever: this timelessness of the sky and the sea, our long walks along the wet sand to the Landing, the flocks of sandpipers filling the air, our intimate conversations about subjects big and small, and finally the overwhelming need to just give in to the heavy, sensuous, fragrant flow of time itself.

Catherine called us at midnight, joyously saying she'd passed her last tests and obtained the international MBA for which she's worked so hard from California to Austria and from France to Belgium. This morning the air is crisp and cold, the landscape so clear we see every crack of the shoreline at Tomales Point.

Both nights, we slept with the windows open, the sound of the surf filtering through. I have plenty to read, original news and thoughts from faithful readers.

My friend and faithful correspondent Chris Aubeck circulates an article called "The Creature in the Comet: 19th Century UFO Crashes" that reinforced my contention that UFO contact is the world's oldest story, not just a recent episode of extraterrestrial exploration.

San Diego. Thursday 7 March 2002.

Richard Niemtzow tells Eric he once met René Hardy, who told him of an incident in which a French military rocket was followed by a UFO that flew around it. There was an investigation, "now lost."

A diary is precious as memory; I find it an indispensable reference when Kit writes about his briefings, and about what happened in the 1970s with Niemtzow, or in the 1980s with the tracking down of alleged autopsy reports. But it's even more important as my personal calibration. Thus, I watch other participants in this game either stuck in frozen recollection of things they witnessed or swept anew by partial views. References to my ideas and mistaken theories, or simply the changes in my assessment over the years, are essential in charting my own course, avoiding useless replay of old records.

While it would be wonderful to join in the chorus of voices that now support real Aliens, real autopsies, real doctors..., I find all that a bit too reminiscent of the days when Ira Einhorn, Puharich, and Bearden were calling for global embrace of an undefined (but of course quite lovely) Alien agenda for Earth.

As I read *The Bureau and the Mole* (10) it encourages me to challenge the ability of "The Intelligence Community" to analyze this phenomenon without distorting it, or simply playing games with it and fooling us. To that point, Dominique writes that the effort to restart GEPAN has run into a brick wall within CNES. He's trying to setup a lunch for me with General Letty during my next stay in Paris.

Athanor. Friday 8 March 2002.

The end of a busy week: Monday in Portland, Wednesday and Thursday in San Diego, and today in Santa Rosa, visiting all our outlying portfolio companies in one week, learning about some extraordinary mathematical and technical breakthroughs. Now I must review the remarkable exchanges we've had with Kit over the last two weeks.

On March 5th he wrote: "I never interviewed the surgeons who did the prosection (can't say "autopsy" if not done by a credited pathologist) but I read their purported notes. They looked fine. In fact, the arcanalia of the way a doctor describes dissection are weird enough, I have never believed the notes were hoaxes.... In this business, high-quality science isn't the first thought of the persons trying to find consultants. Bronk had credentials but wasn't qualified. Stahl was qualified and had credentials but was not on the inside. Hynek was credentialed but had no medical qualifications. The 'surgeons' were cleared but had neither credentials nor qualifications."

Later the same day, he added:

"I do now recall that I spoke with one Air Force physician... Donald Flickinger MD, Brigadier General....about the Alien autopsy material. He was a consultant to me on soviet spacecraft, Apollo-Soyuz and later brought me on as his consultant on the Glomar Explorer project, where he was the medical director, and asked me to take on the job as Forensic Analyst of the remains.

"For about ten years he was the Executive Secretary of the VIP health program in my division of the CIA managed by Myles Maxfield, MD, PhD. Myles was ever-so-much my academic superior, but I was the Administrative Director of the program.

"Don told me he had seen the autopsy material, too... many years earlier, when he was the first Air Force MD to make the rank of General Officer, post the manned spaceflight effort, the medical portion of which he headed. He told me it was all real.

"He told me that in 1994, after I had known him well for 16 years. But he was never able to get me cleared for that program, as he was for the Jennifer program." (11)

This is very important—the first credible hint that there is indeed a secret program with access to biological material. And it is, understandably, recognized by Hal and Eric as the closest thing to a proof of the reality of the Roswell crash, Aliens and all. Colm Kelleher, however, remains on the sideline.

I keep telling the group that I still suffer from what I call the Pocantico Syndrome: "I'm glad I came, I love all the stories, but you haven't given me any material I can carry back to my lab."

Hummingbird. Friday 15 March 2002.

Plans for today: move forward on the Internet book. Splendid weather. Tonight, I speak to a group of French entrepreneurs sponsored by France Telecom; that giant monopoly trying to play venture capitalist is an amusing situation.

In my spare time, I work on sighting catalogs, assembling bits of case histories, completing classification codes, filling the fields about time and space coordinates. Now Eric Davis tells me that a Dr. Robert Parvin Williams (1891-1967) is alleged to have been one of the surgeons participating in the supposed Alien dissection. He was a Lt. Colonel in 1947. Hal has heard other names: Dr. Robert Crowley? Colonel John Grime? The latter retired in 1970, lived in Austin until 1985, moved to Albuquerque, and died in 1995, age 91.

Hummingbird. Monday 25 March 2002.

Russell Targ now works as an independent lecturer on spiritual subjects. He publishes with Hampton Roads Publishing Company under his own imprint. Over lunch in Palo Alto today he handed me the galleys of my foreword for Richard Nolan's first book on *UFOs and the National Security State*. They may publish *The Heart of the Internet*.

As we walked back to the parking lot, he pointed to a large moving van stationed in front of the California Institute for Physics and Astrophysics, Bernie Haisch's research group financed—until last year—by Joe Firmage.

"That's the last day for them," he said. "Joe has pulled the plug, nobody's been paid since the First of the year." Bernie, walking out for lunch, stopped to chat with us.

Hummingbird. Thursday 28 March 2002.

Word has come from Vegas that NIDS has sent away Eric Davis with two weeks' notice and reduced Colm's role to halftime; he'll spend the other half on aerospace business. Hal swears that work continues; a reduced staff will monitor new cases. Bob took him to his aerospace campus: "Guards in camo, new tunnels, new fences with high security...He's putting $500 million into this, yet pharmaceutical companies are not rushing to sign manufacturing contracts for microgravity. He must be planning other applications."

Eric called me, seeking a new job so I put him in touch with Dr. Peter Banks who said Los Alamos was recruiting physicists.

I also had a good conversation with Colm who is speaking with HandyLab, one of our best portfolio companies.

The Athanor. Saturday 30 March 2002.

Rohnert Park, between Petaluma and Santa Rosa, is a sophisticated town close to Sonoma State University and home to many artists, old hippies, software companies, and creative people who like to live away from the big city. Last night, at the fine Performing Arts Center, we attended a play called *The Descent of Inanna*. The rich interpretation of the Sumerian myth of Goddess initiation used beautiful masks and intriguing puppets.

The myth is illustrated by ancient rituals throughout the Mediterranean. The clearest example is the story of Ceres and her daughter Proserpina. While foolishly gathering flowers, the fair Proserpina is ravished by Pluto who drags her into his cavern. In despair, Ceres wanders over the Earth in search of her, *travelling in a car drawn by dragons*. She carries two lighted torches and is begirt with a serpent. At last, she comes to Eleusis and retrieves her daughter from the darkness of the infernal regions. In the end, Proserpina is restored to her divine intellectual nature.

The myth has to do with the peregrinations of the soul, represented by young, innocent Proserpina. Her mother Ceres is the brain's higher intellect. The girl's carefree but thoughtless gathering of flowers shows the soul becoming ensnared in the delusive attractions of sensible form. Captured by Pluto, the soul sinks into material darkness. The lamentations of Ceres represent the misery of intelligence faced with the weakness of the soul.

After the show we repaired to the home of the Ravenheart family for coffee, dessert, and champagne honoring the artists, creators of *The Independent Eye*. Morning Glory was there, displaying her model of Hecate, three years in the making, while Oberon presented us with his splendid statuette of Odin. I took the opportunity to ask Morning Glory about Samothrace, which fascinates me. As usual, she was a source of erudition: the island had indeed been a center of worship of "the Gods before the Gods." It was supposed to be inhabited by a race of dwarves endowed with magical abilities, like the elves of Ireland and the Menehune of Hawaii—or the short Aliens of flying saucer lore. The initiates used electro-magnetism.

Art Magic has more to say about the island: "The Samothracian mysteries date back to the earliest periods of Grecian history, and attempts have been made to show that in these veiled rites the use of the loadstone, the secret powers of electricity, and the twin fires of magnetism were brought into play."

Now the fog is rolling in, creating its own magical eddies of light and grayness around the rocks of a canyon we've discovered a couple of miles away. Fern and moss drape the rounded stones rising from the grass like surfacing whales.

We jumped over the creek at the foot of the cliffs and found a craggy castle with a cave perched over a quiet clearing, as beautiful as a fairy glen.

The Athanor. Saturday 6 April 2002.

Again, the Middle East stands at the edge of the abyss. Israeli tanks roll into Ramallah, knocking down homes and crushing ambulances; soldiers summarily execute Palestinian guards, hatred flares up from suicide bombings.

Despair has erupted like long-repressed lava. The statements made by all sides—Arafat, Sharon, Bush, the Pope, the UN—sound like pointless wordplay, a carpet of lies.

Each side is shamelessly holding "negotiations" in obvious bad faith. It looks like a mock-up of a Greek tragedy directed by toddlers, an ugly game played with the tears of grieving women and the flesh of children torn apart by the bombs that ambulances carry around.

If we must find a single factor in all this, it is the falsity of creed, the abusive power of religion, fanaticism in the name of spirituality. If the believers in Christ and Muhammed were judged on what they do rather than what they pretend to believe, the assessment would be easy. Three religions derived from the single dictate that "you shall not kill" have butchered the world for centuries. *Who's kidding?*

A simple study of the evolution of man on the Earth shows fantastic acceleration, headed for disaster as a species. Whether the end comes from a conflagration triggered by fanaticism, or by the straightforward replacement of human beings by artificial life combined with genetically-modified organisms, this particular animal has run its course on the planet.

Hummingbird. Tuesday 16 April 2002.

In a 19th century book about spiritism, apparitions, and magic, I find two references to a Dr. Passavant who wrote about "spectral light." Mr. des Mousseaux, too, teaches that the spiritual body has a similar nature to the fluid or *ether* that permeates the universe.

Visits from our Limited partners from Europe and Canada have exhausted me. I am not very good at these events. We had 25 people coming from Europe and Québec with their wives, ten companies to visit in two days, one dinner (at the Fort Mason Firehouse) with the French community, and a larger one at the Ritz-Carlton for our company CEOs and venture capitalists who co-invested with us.

One of our entrepreneurs, a young Indian professor of electronics remarked, "I grew up learning about Dr. Federico Faggin, the legendary inventor of the integrated circuit, and all of a sudden, he was right there, at my table!"

Also at the dinner was Chris Ledwith, the husband of my assistant. He grew up with our children in Belmont, so the event held pleasant moments for Janine and me.

We heard Rostropovitch last night, playing Dvorjak. It inspired me to make new plans: we leave for Costa Rica in two days, and shortly after our return, I'll go to Vegas for the very last meeting at NIDS.

Messages keep flowing: a new confidential abduction case from Brazil, fascinating medieval items from Chris Aubeck.

But what stays with us from recent months is the extraordinary inspiration of Egypt, its spiritual lesson still vibrant across millennia.

7

San Jose, Costa Rica. Friday 19 April 2002. Hotel Irazù.

I stayed here seventeen years ago. The same friends, Carlos and Ricardo Vilchez, greeted us this afternoon. They remain faithful to their research and to democracy, a major theme in this beautiful little country where people care deeply about freedom and peace. Costa Rica abolished the death penalty in 1871 and the military after WW2. They care about art: Ricardo presented us with two fine books of local photographs and poetry.

The weather is pleasantly tepid, with a cool breeze blowing from the cloud-shrouded mountains. The hotel, after an 8-hour flight and a stop in San Salvador, was just what we needed, a simple place resounding with joyous Spanish phrases, and a bed into which we dived for long, carefree slumber.

Carlos and Ricardo told us there were few UFO cases of recent interest here, and no news from the Arenal area. They went there with Dick Haines three years ago but found no answers to the mysterious events. Ricardo did tell us he'd done several hundred regressions following abduction claims and was left amazed at the hidden abilities of the mind but had no firm answer. He's keenly interested in the sociological evolution of the problem.

I told him that, back in the US, wholesale conversion to extreme beliefs about extraterrestrials and abductions was only leading to increased fanaticism. As a result, many scientists and witnesses who might have had something to say were no longer interested.

He responded: *"El tributo para la comprehension es la incomprehension de la mayoria."* (The price one pays for understanding is to be misunderstood by most people.)

San Jose, Costa Rica. Saturday 20 April 2002.

We left early to drive up to the top of the Irazù volcano, dormant yet menacing, its three craters black with powdery rock and ashes, a mean-looking yellow-green pool of sulfurous liquid stagnant at the bottom like a half-filled cup of absinthe.

We went through Cartago, the first capital of Costa Rica, and into Pariso Valley where the artificial lake, near Orosi, was very low. We had lunch among coffee plantations and flowering bushes. We saw a small granite sphere in the front yard, about 2 feet in diameter. Nobody seems to know where these spheres come from, or who made them. They've become a popular decorative motif.

The Lankaster gardens are a fine botanical park that holds a collection of orchids donated by an Englishman in the 1950s.

On the way back we stopped at the cathedral of the Virgen de los Angeles. I had visited it with Salvador Freixedo and John Keel. A statuette of a miraculous black Virgin is kept there. Back at the hotel, I reviewed the file on the Lago de Cote photograph and the analysis by Perrin de Brichambaut. It contradicts Dick Haines' conclusions.

San Jose, Costa Rica. Sunday 21 April 2002.

Not much to do today, except wait for the results of the French elections in front of the satellite TV. I have just read John Saul's book *Mort d'un Général* (12) about the assassination of Général Ailleret, so my thoughts about French politics have taken a depressing turn, even as we rest here, sleep and dream.

We were stunned when the live TV news revealed the faces of the two top contenders for the presidency like two cards flipped up on a gaming table: *Chirac... and Le Pen!* Soon afterwards there were demonstrations in the streets of Paris, Jospin declared in a huff that he was giving up politics, and pundits from DSK to Martine Aubry were fishing for words, seeking excuses: they put the blame squarely on the French people, as if the French people had not just spoken massively against the *élite* that has been manipulating them for so long, from both the socialist left and the impotent right.

During dinner in the mountains overlooking San Jose, Ricardo told us there were few mutilation cases in Costa Rica, but he knew of a sheep found dead with two holes in the throat. It was exsanguinated and very light, as if the insides had been removed.

We spoke about the fate of common friends. Freixedo is in Spain now, still active in research. He keeps cautioning the Vilchez against starting an organization: "You can do better work by yourselves." Wise advice. Castillo is back in Venezuela. Carlos told us he'd seen a recent video from England showing two lights quickly making a crop circle, "moving like the beam of a scanner." This confirms the French theory about military experiments, but why do they go on so long, past the point where they are perfected?

Arenal Lodge. Monday 22 April 2002.

Headline in *La Nacion*: "Terremoto Politico en Francia."

Today a 3-hour bus trip took us to San Ramon along the Pan-American Highway, then north on winding roads through fields, small towns, and sections of rain forest; after that it's a wide plain all the way to the foot of the Arenal. We reached it from the green, wooded side, a giant cone of quiet majesty. But as the road winds its way to expose the northwest face, it becomes dark and forbidding.

The lodge is several miles away from the main road, up in the deep forest. From our room and balcony, we face the black lava flows, alive with bursts of vapor and *fumerolles* rising from crevices. From time to time this giant neighbor of ours rumbles and belches.

There are flowers along the road, hibiscus and impatiens on all sides. Birds abound, red and black, yellow and blue, and even one comic character that seems to be wearing a cycling helmet with a black point. It rained as we took the shuttle bus to La Fortuna with hotel employees who were going home. They joked and laughed in Spanish all the way down the hill, speaking too fast for my ear.

Arenal Lodge. Tuesday 23 April 2002.

The principle of deep meditation is easy to grasp here: the many sounds of the forest blend into friendly chaos, broken only by an angry bird, or a playful fish frolicking in the pond. It has rained all night and humidity stays high, the pages of my Journal thick and moist as I write. The volcano, less than 5 miles away, has vanished into a thick curtain of whiteness. We have nothing to do but stop the brain, swim in easy lakes of slumber and hope for the return of the rainbow we saw yesterday, framing the mountain in glory.

Concerned about future research, I wonder how I can preserve and extend my documentation and support our trips in search of the roots of the phenomenon. Wherever I go, I am greeted by fellow-seekers like the Vilchez twins, who tell me they have been influenced by my work and stimulated by some of my ideas. Along with pleasure, such praise brings a feeling of shame because these excellent people expect a lot more of me.

The Lodge has an Internet connection, which brought me news from Russell Targ: Hampton Roads wants to publish my Internet history book if I elaborate on the dream behind the technology and its spiritual implications, something I am happy to do.

Arenal Lodge. Wednesday 24 April 2002.

Today Janine and I finally made our long-expected trip to Lago de Cote, where the aerial photograph of the famous disk was made. It isn't an easy excursion. The 7am shuttle left us in La Fortuna, where we caught the local bus that goes to Pueblo Arenal and on to Tilaran, at the very end of the large lake. The road is twisted and mean; in places it is little more than a dirt path wedged between hills covered with ferns and the blade-like leaves of banana trees. Further along, it widens to offer large vistas of the lake and the mountains beyond.

We reached Pueblo Arenal in two hours, passing with inches to spare on bare bridges whose parapets, low metal fences, had fallen into precipitous creeks. Drivers are very careful in this country, however, so there was no sense of danger. We stopped at random intervals to pick up schoolchildren, hikers loaded with tents and supplies, and local folks on their way to work. In Arenal we stopped at a place that sold cheap paintings, maps, and supplies and doubled as a German bakery.

There are many German retirees in the area, building houses on quiet lots with views of the lake. Given what goes on in Europe these days,

I cannot blame them for choosing birdwatching, fishing, and explorations of the canopy, over hard winters and complicated politics back home. All you need to become a permanent resident here is proof of a regular pension or salary.

We got a driver to take us to Laguna de Cote, close to Pueblo Arenal. I asked him to leave us at a *Finca*, a large horse farm with stables extending to the very shoreline. We walked down the last half mile to dilapidated structures that looked like the outbuildings of a small inn. There were old toilets and a concrete platform with corrugated roof, an open area where sandwiches and drinks may have been served in earlier days. The water of the lake was surprisingly high, flooding the first lines of vegetation, making a swamp around us. Wavelets washed up on the concrete platform. Laguna de Cote is heart-shaped and quite attractive, an ancient volcanic crater alive with the wind and the rain, circled by reeds, small trees, and marshes. I took a water sample from the end of a wooden pier, and we watched a storm blow over the lake.

We tried to imagine a large disk some 40 meters in diameter flying out of the water (in 1971), and 15 years later three cylinders that rose over the surface and sank again, as recalled by a young farmer who filled out a report to the Vilchez brothers. On the way back we stopped at the farmhouse to ask if people there had ever noticed anything unusual. A man recalled fishing with his son, two years ago, when he saw a figure fly down at 5am and sink into the lake.

Arenal Lodge. Thursday 25 April 2002.

At nightfall, birds compete with crickets and toads all around the lodge. Every hour or so the mountain emits a groan, a loud belch, or a series of heavy asthmatic heaves. Rocks then detach themselves from the lava field on the north side, ejecting puffs of white smoke. In my scope, I can see their red-hot surfaces as they tumble down. On the less active western face drift bluish vapors, mostly carbon dioxide according to local guides. No smell of sulfur here, but $CO2$ is just as deadly. In fact, it often comes out in huge bubbles from volcanic lakes: Could this be the explanation for the object seen in the photograph?

Earlier eruptions of Arenal have been devastating, but people at the Tabacon hot springs, a resort directly below the north slope, black and white with ashes that show up red in the night, don't seem worried. "It's a bit like living aboard the Titanic," a waitress joked.

We walked for two hours in the rain forest, stopping to watch wild turkeys, monkeys, and various birds all the way to the lava flow on the relatively safe southwest side. Along the path were huge ant-hills covering dozens of square feet, and a termite colony as tall as me.

Janine is skeptical about what we can learn from Lago de Cote. "Why establish a connection between the photograph of the disk, the observation of dark cylinders coming to the surface, and now the farmer's story of a figure descending into the lake?" she asks, "Why should there be a connection?

Janine observes that she's never seen me so detached and quiet. I do sleep easily and deeply for a change. After years of professional turmoil, I need this sabbatical. Arenal was an ideal setting. Janine has read three books in one week, also a refreshing novelty.

Arenal Lodge. Friday 26 April 2002.

Sitting on the balcony with a view of the valley, we watch the full moon in and out of dark clouds hiding the mountain. The frogs are back in concert and the silly wild pigs howl monstrously. The trees are full of quick lights: one of them came close to our windows last night, beautiful phosphorescent green…a big firefly. There are powerful smells, too: decaying leaves, the distinct odor of wild pigs, and yesterday the stink of a rotting carcass in the underbrush.

For a couple of hours, we walked in the rain forest again today, admiring the butterflies. They look brown when closed, but inside is a luminous blue. Lunch in La Fortuna: The volcano was visible to the top, with its sudden bursts of rolling rocks and low grumbles.

There's no phone here, no television, and we're out of reading material, so I picked up Houellebecq's *Plateforme* again. The first run through the book irritated me, with its facile saturation of sex scenes and the underlying message that we mustn't expect happiness: post-existentialism without the philosophical construct, the sophisticated imbecility into which French intellectuals easily fall.

Reading it again, however, I now find the text richer and more interesting. Houellebecq displays the cruel humor and contempt for his characters that suits the France that the elections have just revealed, the land of Le Pen, of hypocritical young tycoons on power trips like the Vivendi managers I've known, while everyday folks sink in fear, indifference, or decay. Anti-Americanism serves as a cheap replacement for original invention or intelligent critique. It is born of rancor and impotence: the same impotence Houellebecq visits on his characters who work too hard or dream too little to have ideas or erections past the age of forty...

Thus, one of Houellebecq's most interesting characters, Robert, is a retired mathematician of 53, disenchanted with research and teaching. He spends his time in the bars and brothels of third world countries and likes to quote Chamford's stupid observation: "Happiness is a delicate thing, difficult to find within ourselves, impossible to find in others." *Plateforme* is a cruel book about the fallacy of happiness, the pointlessness of its pursuit. Unfortunately, it is also a fair rendering of the pathetic state into which France is sliding.

Arenal Lodge. Saturday 27 April 2002.

We complete our short survey with a spectacular river trip at the Nicaraguan border, up the Cano Negro. We've learned to recognize caimans from dead logs, turtles from simple rocks, cute Jesus-Christ lizards (they walk on water! holding air bubbles on their feet) from green leaves.

Distinguishing sloths from monkeys in treetops takes more training, and howlers from white-faced monkeys; the former are sedentary, the latter nomadic.

When it comes to birds, the nomenclature grows enormous, with all different kinds of aigrettes, ibises and kingfishers, and others of various sizes and colors.

I am happy here with Janine, suspended above time in the home of the god of fire. Chamford's observation is truly absurd: I've always been able to find happiness, both within myself and quite often in others. I am happy when I work. Time has done nothing to blur my love for Janine, my desire of her, and that special awareness of our ability to find balance.

Hummingbird. Monday 29 April 2002.

A brief interlude at home, long enough to repack my suitcase for Las Vegas. It's good to be back in San Francisco where I belong, my mind and body agree. My soul, too: this air, this sky, this lightness of the crystalline mist, and the City seen from our high tower.

Las Vegas. Friday 3 May 2002. Texas Station.

Welcome to Vegas: two men were gunned down next to this hotel, outside my window, in some sort of gang argument. I was at Bigelow's Park House with the group: a good alibi.

The dinnertime discussion began with Bob's assessment of the project. NIDS started seven years ago, he reminded us, with a mandate to study UFOs and consciousness, and survival research. It evolved into the single topic of ufology. Now Bob wants to "resize to the opportunities we have." For the past two years, he said, interesting cases of hard evidence have been lacking. While Colm made contact with many labs for potential analyses, the Institute became frustrated trying to chase stories. In the meantime, the space activity is ramping up and relationships with NASA improve.

Bob made the point that the microgravity environment "defines unique properties that the UFOs must be using, in terms of temperature, stresses, resilience for their materials." He's convinced that going into space is the first step to really understand them.

Colm made a long presentation, his last briefing to the board. He said a rash of new mutilation cases started in June 2001. NIDS collected 30 reports, including two from Utah. He estimates that only one case in ten ever gets reported, the same proportion we see for UFOs. The latest incident involves a Charolais cow, mutilated on April 6th. The tail was cut off and there was a hole in the abdomen. None of it could be a predator attack. Even the trachea was gone, while the bladder and the uterus were left. The investigators could hardly extract one milliliter of blood from the carcass.

Generally speaking, we now have several documented cases where unusual substances were found, including oxindole, but there's no consistent pattern of toxic substances. NIDS was not able to find out who had procured the oxindole: the data was kept private by the labs.

I'd predicted that, as we withdrew attention from the subject, new events would start happening at the ranch, where the cameras were turned off last year. Indeed, a few days ago the people living on the property, Jean and Richard Dietz, recorded some odd events. For a minute and a half, in clear weather, Jean saw a strange circle above the trees, like a wobbling, gray piece of rope.

Colm also described a curious case of alleged contact with entities in Santa Rosa, California. A retired fire investigator claims to be experiencing multiple abductions and entities. His two teenage children "saw something," but his wife is skeptical. A "claw" 16 mm long with some hair attached was found. It failed to show any DNA match to a known species.

Finally, Colm gave a summary of NIDS research, with the help of Kit and Kristin, into the origin of titanium aluminide and the Battelle research into its properties. Howard Cross, the man whose secret significance I revealed in connection with my unearthing of the Pentacle Memorandum in 1967 (13), was involved in the earliest research into the material, which he appears to have brought to the US from Farnborough in England about 1946. There is no indication that knowledge of it came from a UFO crash, however, and no smoking gun has been uncovered at Battelle.

Las Vegas. Saturday 4 May 2002.

Most of today was spent visiting the new aerospace campus and discussing ways in which board members could remain involved. NASA is interested in the Bigelow modules as a stowage unit, but Bob has greater plans with his condominium model. Surprisingly, no large corporation seems to build habitable modules beyond the current space station, lacking usable research space.

Bob's great talent is to envision a reduction in the cost of habitable space by a factor of 50, which he is clearly on the way to demonstrating.

The progress made at the campus facility at 1899 Brook in North Vegas (near the intersection of Cheyenne and Clayton) is striking. It now employs 45 people, including 11 in security behind a sturdy double fence. Everywhere we went, there were guards in fatigues (with the alien-looking logo on their sleeves), standing at attention. In the main facility much of the floor was hidden by black curtains.

Once we returned to Park House, the discussion took a practical turn. Board members could still act as intermediaries to run projects, but there would be no meetings. A big page had simply been closed.

As we were about to disband, I made a plea to analyze our shortcomings. For seven years we had an unprecedented, open-ended chance to try new research directions; the Utah ranch experiment was brilliant, pursued by a competent staff; the mutilation studies, first led by Onet and later by Kelleher, were thorough. Yet most of us hold the same beliefs today that we held then.

One of the physicists answered that ufology resembled acupuncture in the sense that you could prove there was "something" but you couldn't find any physical structure for it. The "meridians" of acupuncture don't match any biological system you can dissect, yet they exist in function.

Then John Alexander wisely reminded us that even after all the funding we gave John Mack, his group could never come up with any solid multiple-witness abduction case.

Later the same day.

The advisory board has just had its last supper (at Texas Station), followed by nostalgic goodbyes and unlikely invitations to stay in touch. I'll miss the great conversations, the intense collective work on a big enigma. I sat between Ted Rockwell and John Schuessler, the latter free from the Mutual UFO Network (MUFON) and reminiscing about his work with astronauts. Ted recalled Admiral Rickover calling him from Rome where he was on an official visit: "I'm having a great time, Rockwell; I'd have made a damn good Pope!"

In later years, as he saw the admiral on his deathbed, he heard him say, "How are we supposed to know what God wanted us to do? I might have been a cellist." Rickover loved music as a child, but his father was too poor to buy him the instrument.

The world would certainly have been a different place.

Hummingbird. Monday 6 May 2002.

I just flew back from Vegas after spending a day with Colm, Eric, and Hal at the new NIDS offices on South Polaris. It is a beautiful neighborhood during the day, a nest of hookers and dealers at night.

Our consensus is that whatever was actually known in official UFO research has been privatized. There certainly isn't any sign that it is held anywhere inside the government.

"Lockheed?" I asked one of my colleagues over breakfast before meeting Eric and Colm. "No," the colleague replied, "I rather suspect the Carlisle Group, revealed after September 11 as the private conglomerate that has absorbed several black project contractors. It has the Bin Laden family as one of its investors. Carlisle is run by Franck Carlucci, a former secretary of defense."

In a cost-cutting measure, NIDS moved from Tropicana to its current location a few months ago. The building is striking, with a UFO-like tower with big white bulging windows all around. It used to serve as the design center for the builders of the Budget Suites, now in full operation. The upstairs offices are splendid. There's a magnificent library room, with few UFO books but a great collection of volumes on parapsychology and consciousness; three offices with modern computers, first-rate furniture; and all the equipment one could wish for. It is deserted now that Eric is gone and Colm reduced to half-time.

We sat in the library with Hal and tried to summarize what we knew, what we thought others knew, and what we knew others didn't know. John Alexander is in contact with a man named Frank Meade, at Edwards Air Force Base, who sponsored research by Robert Forward on matter/antimatter interactions and tried to replicate the work of T. Townsend Brown: "There's nothing to it," said Hal, "at least up to 15,000 volts."

The group noted that Kit's recent emails (supporting the Alien autopsy) had a special subtext. He'd tried to verify his data with two former directors of the CIA and was told by Colby to "go back and check your sources," an indication that he was being misled.

Hal said that Dr. Pandolfi, who has inherited Kit's responsibilities at the Agency, recently came to San Francisco to see Jack Sarfatti, who told everybody afterwards that the government was "validating his work." Jack gleefully joins the colorful characters on the UFO scene, like Dan Smith of "eschatology" fame.

We learned that one plan for the aerospace company might have involved an alliance with Energia, the Russian space corporation, to fly to Mars in eight years. But Colm hadn't briefed the board on this idea, regarded as too ambitious. I said that if anybody was going to build condos on the Red Planet, it would be a developer from Vegas!

In the middle of all that, a call from Janine: Chirac has been reelected with 82% of the French vote, against 18% to Le Pen. The scary thing is that LePen has actually increased his percentage.

Athanor. Saturday 11 May 2002.

After the Vegas meetings, I spoke to John Alexander who wanted to discuss ideas for a new security company. He also told me he'd tracked down stories about the famous Hangar 18 at Wright-Patterson Air Force Base. He had concluded it was a sophisticated training facility for Air Force intelligence officers.

"They were taken there at night," he told me. "They were told to take all the notes they could, then they were shown a flying saucer. And at the end they were asked: What do you think this was? What are the implications? What could you do with it?" This led to all the fancy UFO stories we've heard, John said, adding he'd spoken to the man who had confiscated the film shot at Holloman.

"What happened is that an A-12 prototype, the plane designed to replace the U-2, had a flame-out and was forced to land. They closed down the base and confiscated everything. The next day, the Air Force itself started the rumor that a UFO had landed there."

The book *Mort d'un Général* makes a very strong case that Ailleret was assassinated. Who was minister of defense in March 1968? Which Gaullist politician committed suicide about 9 May 1972?

Hummingbird. Wednesday 15 May 2002.

Lunch at the Fish Market with Sturrock, who came to see my offices in San Mateo. He told me how relieved he was that the impact from

Fig. 5. NIDS science board meeting in Las Vegas, May 2002: Martin Piltz, with John Alexander, Hal Puthoff, Albert Harrison, and others.

Fig. 6. Working with Ron Brinkley at the Athanor library, 2003.

his UFO book had died down. Peter is as disgusted as I am at the state of the field. I told him about our trip to Costa Rica, showed him the photos.

François Louange assured me he had carefully scanned for waves on the lake (in all three frames I'd given him) without finding any. If the object had been an emerging disk or a CO_2 bubble (as Peter Banks suggests), there would have to be waves of some sort, so I'm not making much progress in solving this mystery.

François added that nothing moved within CNES.

Hummingbird. Wednesday 22 May 2002.

In the evening sky, tiny Mercury leads a procession of planets: Saturn, Mars, Venus and Jupiter, and higher still the Moon, as if to invite us to follow them into some glorious sunset.

Over lunch with Dick Haines, I briefed him about our Costa Rica trip and showed him the photographs from Lago de Cote. When he visited the site, he interviewed a young witness who had seen something emerge from the lake; a huge foam formed concentric waves, and then died out. This could be evidence of a CO_2 bubble, but when I look again at "our" photograph of the disk, I cannot see how it would fit this hypothesis.

Hummingbird. Wednesday 29 May 2002.

The world: unstable, bizarre, torn by irrational tragedies. India and Pakistan shooting again across their Kashmir borders, extremists driving to war; any incident may place populations at risk. Conspiracy theories are taken seriously in much of the world, like the absurd rumor that "4,000 Jews were warned not to go to the office on September 11 in New York..."

My own failed experience, trying to bring sanity and analysis to aerial phenomena, has taught me how pervasive paranoia could be. Arthur Koestler argues in one of his books (*Janus*) that humanity is basically insane. It is time to read those words again.

This weekend, the announcement came that Mars did hold water in the form of ice locked in the soil, and lots of it, enough to form an ocean 500 meters deep.

Isn't it the kind of news that, in a rational world, should move men to forget their quarrels and look to the sky?

Athanor. Saturday 1 June 2002.

Catherine was with us today, a bright ray of sunshine and laughter. She brought a bushwhacker, and we tried to bring control to the tall grass around the house. My Internet book is making progress. I am rediscovering Russell in all this. His daughter Elizabeth is in the hospital with a brain tumor. I can imagine what he suffers.

Athanor. Sunday 2 June 2002.

We walked for 11 miles on the wild Tomales Point peninsula with Roger Brenner today, talking about physics all the way. In spite of my lazy approach to exercise, I'm not in bad shape. I have started to sleep well again (cutting travel has helped), and I am hardly aware of asthma any more. Wild flowers are everywhere, the elk are grazing on the hills, and the Point itself is magnificent in a dangerous, savage way. Far below, in the crushing waves, seagulls and pelicans fight over banks of fish. Roger told me that Joe Firmage, Daniel Sheehan, and John Mack were about to get together at Henry Dakin's lab.

Athanor. Saturday 8 June 2002.

We celebrated Saint Agobard today. Gary and Lori came over in bright Chinese vestments while others wore 9th-century garb. Diane arrived late, fighting migraines, accompanied by a UC Berkeley librarian. It was a fun group, knowledgeable about space and anthropology, eager to do honor to Janine's astounding repast. They had never eaten *pets de nonne* (literally, "nun's farts") which ended the meal on a suitably ecclesiastical note; white wine was Chateau Saint Jean and the red was a Chateau des Jacques, followed by Chateauneuf du Pape.

I have started to read Colin Bennett's delightful book on Adamski (*Looking for Orthon*) that adds another layer of bright warmth and indulgent social commentary to the mysteries of alleged contact.

Janine and I stay home today, curious to watch the news. Television is surreal these days: the droning flow of meaningless drivel about sports and entertainment, punctuated by imminence of total war in India and unending bloodshed in Palestine, glimpses of President Bush at work on yet another plan "to save the freedom of America" by slashing individual rights, and the multi-faceted evils of Western good intentions. A scary world now, increasingly meaningless: virtual vacuity, untouched by vision, a condensate of horrors.

San Diego. Wednesday 12 June 2002.

The Sheraton Marina, close to the airport. I flew down from Oregon yesterday for meetings with Peter Banks and Jim Lemke, and the Board of Chaos Telecom. It's a cool, hazy morning on the Pacific shore. California, like the whole country, holds its breath in the midst of terror threats at home and the rumble of war abroad. Countries are moving armies and fleets like pieces on a board.

The word in Silicon Valley is that the attack on Iraq will be delayed until the Pentagon can obtain enough bandwidth to run the Predators. Planners had counted on communications satellites that have not been launched, given the current downturn in the telecom business. These satellites, known as "bent pipes" in the military communications field, serve to transmit real-time images to ground-based pilots of robot drones. They can barely cope with Afghanistan and would be swamped by an Iraqi war.

Athanor. Sunday 16 June 2002.

"Pomp and Circumstance" was played under the warm morning sun in Hayward, and among thousands of people we watched Catherine's MBA graduating ceremony at the California State University commencement yesterday. It was a joyful, moving, and proud occasion, one of the finest days in my life because Janine was with me and everything went right. We had a late lunch at Jack London's Square and clinked our glasses in honor of new beginnings.

Mabillon. Saturday 22 June 2002.

When I landed on Wednesday, I heard with the usual pleasure from my five girlfriends: Thérèse, Caroline, Henriette, Louise, and Marie (14). The Latin Quarter was in a busy mood. I expedited routine visits to the bank and post office and reconnected with all the castles of my mind. The next morning, I attended a conference on nanotechnology in the luxurious salons of the French Senate.

After the obligatory messages of congratulations from absentee dignitaries, several panels of academics and lab directors from large companies spoke of their pressing need for money. Lunchtime came, we all got up, and the first person who approached me was Alain Boudier. His business card now reads "ProteActive Europe." Obviously well-informed, he told me of current sightings in Polynesia (actually, in the Marquises) and of a remarkable Air Force observation of giant triangles on November 5, 1990, over France.

Reading *Michaelmas* again, a deeply intricate novel by Algis Budrys (1977) about an investigative journalist whose portable computer, *Domino*, helps him run the world. In it, I find this remark: "Ah, if men had the self-denial of Suleiman the Wise, to flask the clamorous Djinns that men unseal..."

I went to *Le Figaro*, had lunch with Alain Dupas; then Janine arrived. We went to Maxime's school like doting grandparents.

Mabillon. Sunday 23 June 2002.

Janine and I happily find the way to our old haunts. We were sitting at a café terrace near the Sorbonne yesterday when we saw my brother and his wife walking up Rue Champollion, on their way to a movie, at a relaxed pace. They joined us for a light lunch.

Today, a tepid breeze ruffles the leaves along the Seine. We had lunch with Boëdec, to whom I returned his precious Pontoise files.

Mabillon. Thursday 27 June 2002.

"The danger to the world economy is in the balance of payments deficit of the United States," says Yves Messarovitch over breakfast in the shadow of the church of Saint Germain des Prés. "If you're right that technology won't recover until 2004 or 2005, there's a real problem. High-tech advances have been masking our huge deficit. Now the markets could plunge even deeper."

Janine and I had another dinner with Weinstein, Louange, and Joëlle at *Chien qui Fume*. François gave me a CD with the digitized photos of the object at Lago de Cote. I described our visit there. Velasco is "kept in the cellar" by the CNES bureaucracy in the aftermath of Jospin's political debacle. There are no new cases, and Louange's excellent audit finds no echo at CNES.

Mabillon. Saturday 29 June 2002.

Janine and I had lunch at Brasserie Lipp with Alain Boudier yesterday. He'd brought his friend, Commandant Jean Kisling, a most interesting pilot whose story started with the US Air Force in World War II and went on to a long career at Air France. He told us that early in 1945, while stationed at Selfridge, objects were often reported flying over the air base. They were assumed to be "Japanese balloons," but nobody knew what they actually were. One day he was ordered to chase a formation of five of these "balloons" in his P-47; they were observed by about a thousand people on the ground. He flew towards them as high as he could without reaching them. He was ordered to "empty his machine guns," and as he did so the "balloons" flipped into disk shapes and flew away at high speed. When he landed, he was told that nothing had happened, and that he should forget the incident.

One day in the early Fifties, as an Air France commandant flying the New York to Paris route, Kisling found his Constellation parked in a corner of Idlewild airport under heavy guard. He was told he only had five passengers on the flight. An envelope with instructions had been left in the cockpit to be opened once he was in the air. It ordered him to fly straight to Orly. During the long flight, he went and sat with one of the passengers, an older man with a long beard who told him the group was composed of scientists on the way to various eastern countries, including the USSR, to discuss UFOs.

They were from a secret Pentagon office, he said, which had recovered "out of this world" material from a crash near the Mexican border, close to El Paso, but he refused to provide details.

Born in 1922, Kisling is no ordinary pilot but a man of remarkable intellect and courage, still active in his retirement years. He was delighted to have lunch at Lipp, a place he frequented in his father's days. Boudier also confirmed to me the observation of the giant triangles of November 5, 1990, by the French Air Force. There were twenty Mirages in the formation, and the pilots were able to fly above the triangles.

This, naturally, vaporizes the notion that the case was a satellite reentry. As for the *Cometa* report, it has had no follow-up.

Later, at *Le Figaro*, I was warmly received by Laurent Guez and Yves Messarovitch: Would I resume my Silicon Valley chronicles?

Hummingbird. Wednesday 3 July 2002.

Today the Board of Vivendi ousted Jean-Marie Messier, who had tried by every means to hold on to power. How this brilliant businessman took over a successful, affluent, politically powerful utility company and turned it into a media conglomerate loaded with huge debts is a remarkable study in greed and egotism. Messier gave up a formidable, reliable water and garbage business, tempted by Hollywood cocktail parties and breakfast with actresses in Manhattan penthouses.

I remember my meetings with him in the fancy boardroom of Vivendi, when he supervised our venture investments. The company was a playground for sharks and bullies of every type under the veneer of high finance (15).

Hummingbird. Saturday 6 July 2002.

Technology stocks are at their lowest point in five years. No recovery is in sight for telecoms; even the largest companies like Nortel or Cisco are in trouble. Yet I am surrounded with devices that have indeed changed my life: the cellphone, a set of diskettes holding my work, and a wonderful notebook computer from Fujitsu, the size and weight of a hardcover book, sitting on my bedside table. It picks up the radio signal from my home office radio net and shows me messages from Janine in Paris, Olivier in London, and friends everywhere. It holds the manuscript of *Heart of the Internet* and some 20,000 UFO reports, selected and parsed by an AI screen I've programmed. Technology once reserved for hi-tech labs is deployed everywhere. It poses new problems, hence the economic plateau.

My life is stable here with our budget renewed for two years in negotiations with our partners last week. But time has no special flavor in Janine's absence. It is the density of life, the meaning of a presence that I miss, the simple sound of her steps in the apartment, the brush of her hair, the sound of her voice.

Athanor. Saturday 13 July 2002.

We drove over to Tomales for a town meeting this afternoon. We heard our neighbors discuss street bumps and safety lights, water rights and easements to a religious order with plans for a monastery. But the friendly arguments did nothing to pull me out of my worries. I find the world dull, in a scary frontier overlooking an abyss.

Some of the social crevices are financial; they have already swallowed up many retirement funds and the livelihood of numerous people. Europe is affected, too, with the failures at Vivendi and France Telecom echoing those of Enron and Worldcom in the US. The venture business is frozen shut in the storm.

San Diego. Tuesday 16 July 2002.

The Holiday Inn on the Bay. I am weary of travelling: in Portland yesterday, several hours with Mobilian (16) and a difficult discussion to try to save a company that finds itself out of cash in the dreary economy. The stock market, rocked by scandals and cynical about Bush's administration, is a falling piano nobody dares to catch.

Yesterday I negotiated the contract for *Heart of the Internet* with Hampton Roads, a small publisher long on quality and short on cash. Money is not the point: this book is a simple historical reference.

At the Athanor on Sunday I worked on the aerial phenomena database for several hours, filling in some of the missing data in Larry Hatch's astonishing catalogue. There's still a thrill here for me, surrounded as I am with every reliable source. The books help me probe into faraway lands and long-forgotten reports: I do believe these witnesses! Then the dark areas expand again like an inkblot.

Athanor. Sunday 28 July 2002.

We stayed in bed yesterday morning, savoring the solitude, the gray sky in the morning, the hazy sunshine; then lunch on the patio, the soft wind around the house. Eve Lungren's strange work, *The Love Bite*, gives me credit for early work on Alien abductions. This led us to discuss the nature of the phenomena from our experience of 40 years and our new vantage point, removed from the turmoil of the field as we are now. Janine's advice is close to that of Kit: it is more important to find out what goes on in the brain of witnesses than in the world outside, she feels.

Forty years and not much evidence, not even one credible photograph attested by multiple witnesses. What does that say about the physical nature of the phenomenon? Seven years of intense monitoring by scientists at NIDS and no good observation of a craft, no sign of a credible light effect with physical correlations such as traces on the ground, or even a drop in temperature, properly recorded. Yet we have the case near Soissons, and the mold to prove it. So I testify for the physical side, but my arguments are weak and fuzzy. The phenomenon is absurd and chaotic, but so is much of science, until an organizing principle is found. The problem here is that we haven't succeeded in isolating UFOs from a range of other effects. When it comes to abductions, I could start an uproar if I published my files on victims who reported human involvement in their experiences, starting with Kathie Davis' unpublished revelations, a fundamental witness refuting Hopkins' arguments.

Eve Lungren, a psychotherapist in Marin County, believes the Aliens have an evil plan to manipulate the erotic emotions of those they touch. She lists cases when families were disrupted and hearts broken as a result of events the witnesses perceived as abductions. Her analysis starts from a Christian fundamentalist perspective, Jesus helping her... All that is spiritually respectable and scientifically suspect: studying one bias from the basis of another.

Gabriel Veraldi, from Geneva, sends me translations from Sturrock's book about our Pocantico meeting. As I review them, I am again struck by that brilliant panel, helpless before our data.

Athanor. Tuesday 13 August 2002.

The computers stayed behind today. We caught the Russian River at Forestville and paddled for 10 miles in the warm sun. This being a weekday there were less than a dozen canoes on the river, which made for good comradeship. The landscape along the river is glorious: redwoods and towering oaks, faraway hills resplendent in gold, and the wind playing with the sun to put ripples of silver everywhere. We stopped for a picnic in the shade to watch ducks at play, and grey herons who barely acknowledged our presence.

Athanor. Friday 16 August 2002.

This landscape is so splendid, even in its stubborn grayness, that it makes everything else petty and forgettable. And I am so happy here with you! Whether we travel to Château St. Jean along the rich Valley of the Moon, shop for Mexican chairs and geraniums in Petaluma, lie in the dark to listen to old French songs by Yves Montand, or drive out through the fog of the estuary for a simple dinner at Valley Ford, your presence is all I need, and these simple things of everyday life.

Athanor. Sunday 1 September 2002.

Lunch with Peter Sturrock on Wednesday at the Duck Club. He'd brought me a copy of the CNES database on behalf of Velasco. So today I installed another printer and a zip file reader, only to realize the disk from SEPRA had been written by a Macintosh and was incompatible with my system, another quirk of technology. Peter told me he'd seen Poher, who's moved back to Toulouse where he owns a fine house.

   NARCAP meeting yesterday afternoon at Dick Haines' house. There were ten of us, including Ted Roe, Larry Lemke who now designs airplanes for the Martian atmosphere at NASA-Ames, as well as Jim McCampbell, in better shape. Others were technical types from

Silicon Valley, and an 82-year-old retired United Airlines captain. It was a pleasant afternoon in Dick's backyard. He recounted the reports he'd received, NARCAP's international plans, talks of a book, and various studies of recent accidents, especially TWA 800 and Egyptair, where there's much obfuscation from the US government. Radar tracks do show unidentified objects in the area at the time of both crashes—possibly military missiles, Dick said.

In a conversation with Brian and Tina in Arizona (they've recently moved, but are still in Sedona), I went over their recollection of what took place at Norton AFB back in March 1985. They never saw a film of a landing, aliens or anything of the sort. They did see a "giant Rolodex" filled with military UFO reports, hanging from a machine like a conveyor belt. Many reports were from the Navy. Some had photographs of UFOs coming out of the sea, and a catalog of photos.

Later Tina, Brian, and Allen were taken into a very small vault where they were told, under Generals Miller and Scott's authority, that the Coast Guard had lots of information, that specific contacts would be provided to them, and that an appointment would be made for Allen to see something "in a hangar at Edwards Air Force Base."

This must be the point where Allen called me for advice, and I told him to check with Colonel Robert Friend because I was suspicious that we might be led down to a hoax. Allen spent two hours with Friend and got back to Brian and Tina with the evidence that Miller and Scott didn't even have the authority to get him into Edwards...

Today I am catching up on computer work with the Corpus database. Janine and I walked a few miles through the fields beyond the last houses in the village and down the cliffs to the wild shores of the Estero. We rested on the deserted beach of white sand, watching pelicans playing in a large pond. We have much to celebrate with the approach of autumn. Thanks are due to the gods of the universe, whoever they are. I am in love with the bitter-sweet awareness that in later years I'll remember this as the most shining phase of my life.

Athanor. Saturday 14 September 2002.

A lot of work with our new Fund, bravely supporting our startups through the storm: no less than seven financings or refinancings, from

Portland to San Diego, before month's end. It seems essential to put some distance between us and the world's festering mess. Ridding the world of Saddam Hussein may seem logical, but George Bush's methods are a caricature of everything the world regards as the decay of America, with internal politics reminiscent of a Police State. His opponents of the Democratic Party seem unconcerned.

Discussion with Janine about magic: Why all the esoteric books? Why this extensive library? My answer is another question: How is it possible to be interested in anything else?

We don't know where we come from, where we go, who we are, or even whether the universe, so full of what physicists call "information," has any meaning. The search for patterns, rhythms, and symbolic relationships must precede any true understanding.

Mabillon. Sunday 22 September 2002.

The sun is out, with the special light of autumn on the Latin Quarter. At *Le Figaro,* Laurent Guez is happy with my new chronicles. Dinner tonight at Les Charpentiers with Eric Raulet and his friend Lina. *Forbidden Science* has become their favorite book, so we spoke of our common research interests.

The French Bourse has gone through eight consecutive losing sessions, a descent into hell for those who had been seduced to invest in the pillars of national industry: Alcatel, Vivendi, France Telecom, the traditional portfolio of the average French family.

Mabillon. Monday 23 September 2002.

Lunch with Boudier, whom I met again at Brasserie Lipp. He was as mysterious as ever. He now suspects Payan himself to be an American agent, an amusing twist indeed! Payan once attended a meeting at his house. After an hour or so he went to the bathroom where Boudier's son, from an adjoining room, clearly heard him changing the cassette of a tape recorder...

Boudier is interested in the continuing reports of strange lights near Col de Vence, which other researchers call hogwash. He showed me half-a-dozen recent Gendarmerie reports, evidence that the phenomenon is still active and that Boudier himself remains well-connected. He also showed me an analysis of a piece of alloy allegedly coming from a recent contact: Aliens are supposed to have handed the sample to "a friend of his," another dangling tale.

Later the same day.

In the afternoon we met again with Raulet at a psychology center on Rue Bargue. Under the auspices of a popular young novelist and *Prix Goncourt* winner Didier van Cauweleart, a group of Mexican mediums was holding a series of séances paid for by his publisher.

Dressed all in white, the 23 people in the room (13 men and 10 women) were treated to a two-hour session in darkness, during which a medium, Samuel, produced apparitions, noises, and various musical interludes. The fraud was so blatant that we left as soon as we could, skipping the dinner to which we'd been invited, only shaking the hand of Bertrand Méheust on the way out.

Young Eric Rauley was puzzled by "what we saw." I told him I was not puzzled at all: In the dark we didn't see anything but an interesting display of human credulity. Yet two of the people who travelled with the Mexicans, a French couple whose young daughter had died in Mexico, were in tears after the séance. I did not want to offend them with a public outburst, so I just left quietly.

Mabillon. Tuesday 24 September 2002.

The weather has become quite cold, all of a sudden. I have a sore throat and feel tired. I turn 63 today. I visited an Internet infrastructure company in Gennevilliers (Streamcore) and came back to the Latin Quarter in time to meet my brother and his wife at Café Mondrian. They were warm and relaxed.

Professor Bokias has just returned from Greece. As we were sipping coffee with him, a man strolled by and saw me. It was the co-founder of our old AI Company, Neuron Data. Now an affluent name-dropper, he boasts of advising Messier and the Bronfmans, keeps a boat somewhere in the Cyclades, and generally runs the planet.

Mabillon. Thursday 26 September 2002.

There are strikes at the Métro, so it took me an hour to meet Mergui at Antony. We drove on to the Génopole science board meeting in Evry, always an opportunity to catch up with medical research. Two more venture meetings are planned for me this afternoon, and a phone conversation with Internet guru Vint Cerf.

Siparex offices. Friday 27 September 2002.

A fascinating report in the media: The new management at Vivendi is so short of cash that it reneges on commitments and refuses to answer capital calls for Viventures. The fund I left three years ago amidst such trauma and anxiety has found its demise. "You look like a genius now," people tell me. "You saw this coming."

Lunch with Weinstein at Le Suffren. He speaks about his life, his work alongside the FBI and CIA, then he asks: "And you, have you had contact with *these people*?" Indeed, I've been in contact with intelligence folks through my SRI work, yet discussions of UFOs left me unconvinced about any serious hidden project at their level. The SRI results, by now, are well known everywhere, and no longer secret. Yet it is true, when I review what I know, that I found no genuine UFO research. Neither did Hal, or Jim Westwood, or Kit Green, more cynical than ever. If there is a secret group, as I believe, it is at a different level, and everyone knows that by now.

Kit did mention a group that includes Chris Mellon, involved with advanced aeronautics and "infotainment." He had to resign when legal complexities were found. He gave no details.

Mabillon. Sunday 29 September 2002.

There was an amusing coincidence today. Olivier called us, saying he'd be late for lunch, so we stayed home. We heard a knock on the door. A neighbor came in with two women and a man, introducing them as the owners of the apartment below us, and would we consider buying their place, left vacant by their elderly mother?

Suddenly our problem of the last few years seemed easier to solve.

The two flats, if combined, could make a nice townhouse. Later we did meet our children at Saint Michel and walked to the Vert Galant, Max riding fast ahead of us on his bike with much peril to Parisians.

In the evening we had tea at Deux Magots with consciousness researcher Christine Hardy. We laughed at the silly Mexican séances, still going on, the rage of Paris.

New York. Monday 30 September 2002.

The Plaza. I travelled with my colleague Alain Caffi of Ventech, a group I'd thought of approaching. He too was coming to the conference on Private Equity, a gathering of international funds.

The economic news is bad all over, to the point where Germany has decided to close down their technology market, the *Neuer Markt*. ("They'll have to find it, before they can close it!" jokes Olivier.) Billions of dollars have gone up in smoke and stocks keep plunging. Silicon Valley is in denial. Major companies cut their R&D budgets while rumors of war in Iraq get more precise. The First Cavalry is training in Texas; thousands of tanks and trucks are ready to go rumble across the Euphrates.

I called Janine from the plane. She'd made progress on the apartment project, selecting a *notaire*. When I bought *Le Figaro* at the airport, I saw my third "Letter from California."

Montréal. Wednesday 2 October 2002.

Hotel Wyndham. At the Private Equity conference, Marc Cellier confirmed to me that Viventures was finished: the last unit will sell the portfolio, if they can. A devastating TV documentary has just reported on Messier's misguided investments, with shots of the Vivendi board room I visited several times when the team bragged it would revolutionize French innovation. It's not that easy.

Athanor. Saturday 5 October 2002.

We discovered another series of trails this afternoon and explored a canyon that led us to a splendid view of the meandering Estero. There are pumpkins on porches and orange lanterns under the eaves of roofs. The sun is reflected in the ocean waves; it shines too bright in our faces as we read and softly talk. So we draw the drapes and discuss the future in the pink-golden light of the afternoon.

Hummingbird. Monday 14 October 2002.

Columbus Day. At Ira Einhorn's trial, the defense's arguments are supposed to begin tomorrow. So far, Ira has been uncharacteristically subdued. His court-appointed lawyers don't seem to encourage any rambling about mind control and extraterrestrial spoon-bending. Perhaps they hope to sway the jury into indecision by arguing there was no blood in the apartment and little evidence that Holly was actually killed there.

This is no repeat of the O.J. Simpson affair. The prosecution has built a strong case of Ira's frequent violence, his attempts to remove the famous trunk from his apartment, and even a chilling episode when he went searching for books on mummification. Whether or not he dabbles in the murky world of mind control and covert operations with psychotronic technology seems irrelevant.

My own recollection of Ira does not suggest unique knowledge. He did know about Bob Beck's research, of intense interest to the CIA at the time, but many others knew of it as well. Whatever he pursued in Yugoslavia with alleged Tesla technology was never clear.

Athanor. Saturday 19 October 2002.

Our 42nd wedding anniversary. The day is gray, a good time to cuddle in the warm house, making new plans for Mabillon. Back in Philly, Ira has been heard and sentenced. The jury only took two hours to send him back to jail for the rest of his life.

The world is sick of Ira Einhorn. Witnesses paint him (wrongly) as a foul-smelling freeloader who beat up women and did nothing more than xerox papers to mail them around to what he called his "network." He was asking for this when he fled the country.

Why is he so adored by the media, if he's so bad? *Le Monde* sent a special correspondent to follow the trial, *Libération* painted him as an anti-American hero, victim of capitalism (!). The courtroom was full of reporters. As for those "poor innocent women" he supposedly treated sadistically, I remember them in the mid-70s chasing this supposedly "repulsive" character, fighting among themselves to rub his naked back, and feed him grapes. I was jealous!

Squaw Creek. Tuesday 22 October 2002.

Blue skies over Squaw Valley; it's too early for snow. Two hundred business people are here for yet another investment conference, but the dismal state of the world is the main topic. Janine and I sneaked away to Reno for an exploration of the local economy.

The town boasts one street with casinos, a tiny business district, and a wasteland of parking lots and decrepit pawn shops. But there's a modern campus just north of the freeway, and the residential sections are green, full of trees in autumn colors. Far more hospitable than Vegas, it offers hills and lakes, a feeling of openness; a future?

Hummingbird. Thursday 24 October 2002.

The various events orchestrated by the Podesta-Mattoon agency on behalf of the Sci-Fi Channel (and Spielberg's upcoming series on abductions) are taking a bizarre turn in Washington. First, John Podesta, a high official from the Clinton administration, requested at the Washington Press Club that the government end its policy of secrecy, a move that a skeptical journalist immediately called "the return of the UFO cult."

The Podesta PR firm released a website, a claim under FOIA, and an article against the "UFO coverup" by Leslie Kean. All fair and good, but it gives much play to *Cometa* and a crash in Kecksburg, Pennsylvania, with little data. Games are being played here, beyond the obvious hype for the show.

Hummingbird. Wednesday 30 October 2002

Tom Tulien came over for dinner yesterday. He's a tall bearded fellow, intelligent and intense, a member of the Sign Historical Group, which gathers researchers like Barry Greenwood and Brad Sparks to compile oral histories. Tom enquired about our contacts with Brian and Tina in Arizona and the whereabouts of the APRO files. Tom knows Dominique Weinstein; he's interviewed Robert Friend, William Tompkins, and the B-52 crew from Minot.

Washington. Thursday 7 November 2002.

The Doubletree Hotel on New Hampshire Avenue, near George Washington University. The weather is windy but mild for November. Walking through a bookstore before dinner last night, I picked up a new paperback novel based on the forthcoming *Taken* series. The marketing machine behind the Sci-Fi channel is working well, setting up interviews and documentaries, activating a website and filing pointless lawsuits against "the government coverup."

There's a new mood in Washington following the elections. The Republican Party now has a majority in Congress, paving the way for a probable war against Iraq in the spring.

Taking advantage of this trip, I reconnect with the hard core of computer science: Bob Kahn and Connie McLindon at the Center for National Research Initiatives, and Neil Brownstein at NSF who supported my social network research for the Institute for the Future. This afternoon I'll visit Invicta, a security company in Herndon.

Washington. Friday 8 November 2002.

The conversation I had with Bob Kahn this morning was illuminating. He's the quietest of the "four fathers" of the Internet, while Larry Roberts parades at government parties with Hollywood starlets in risky dresses; Vint Cerf is often consulted on TV, and Len Kleinrock appears so frustrated at not getting recognition that he hired a float at the latest Rose Bowl Parade as "Father of the Internet"!

Kahn, in contrast, is a quiet reflective man, well grounded in his research. He explained to me how the politics of networking had almost prevented the development of the Internet, and how he had to force BBN (Bolt Beranek and Newman) to open up their architecture in 1972, at the time when ARPA designed the first satellite links with important nodes in England.

Next, I went to Herndon for a meeting with Victor Sheymov, former major in the KGB who defected to the US in 1980 and joined NSA. Together with his wife Olga, he eventually formed Invicta, an American computer security company. In a futuristic building next to the Dulles Hilton, a site right out of James Bond, he explained to me why there was no such thing as a firewall.

He showed me so many things about cryptography that I finally understood why I was confused about the field, and why anyone who wasn't confused was a very great fool (17).

In later searches, I discovered that he'd played a role in extraordinary Soviet efforts to spy on the US Embassy in Moscow and had helped expose a high-level FBI official who was paid by Russia to leak critical secret documents. I had no idea this man would be my teacher in computer security, but I won't forget meeting him (18).

United flight home. Later the same day.

The panel organized by Podesta-Mattoon met at prestigious George Washington University, moderated by distinguished journalist Ray Swarez. In turn, Dick Henry (Johns Hopkins, NASA), Michio Kaku (SUNY), Bernie Haisch (Lockheed), myself, Ted Roe, John Callahan (ex-FAA), and Peter Sturrock spoke on UFOs and the prospects for life in the Universe.

The media didn't rush to cover our event. Someone was there from the *Washington Post,* but C-SPAN never came: the panel itself is not "newsworthy," we have no smoking gun, and Washington is still in the midst of post-electoral frenzy.

The panel took a sober, low-key approach to the subject. Rockefeller attorney Henry Diamond was there, as well as cinematographer Paul Davids; Bruce Maccabee was in the audience but he hadn't been invited to join the discussion.

We had lunch with people from Sci-Fi, our host Ed Rothschild, and journalist Leslie Kean. I am flying back on the same plane as Peter Sturrock, who has slowed down a bit, but his mind is as clear and practical as ever.

Mabillon. Saturday 30 November 2002.

Awake at 3am: The cafés I see from my window are still full of carefree groups, cabs come and go; the whole city is vibrant. Yet intellectual life seems to be closing in. Books are predictable, the range of ideas narrows to a few standard thoughts. I paid a visit to Madame Lapautre to bring her the newest version of *Heart of the Internet*. She made the same observation as Lagrange: publishers cut down the size of books, refuse to include an index, and don't pay translators. Odile Jacob turned down my book with a strange excuse: They couldn't think of a well-known French dignitary to write a foreword! Everything is tied to the media, and the public is deemed unable to recognize important ideas.

In the meantime, the economy stinks behind a façade of reassuring statistics. Working folks are worried by pending layoffs in companies large and small.

Mabillon. Sunday 1 December 2002.

Pierre Lagrange tells me that the head of CNES, Alain Bensoussan (whom I used to know as head of INRIA, the French computer science program), is waiting for the first opportunity to kill SEPRA.

Bensoussan asks a reasonable question: can the effort to collect sightings from the public be linked to real research projects? No answer is forthcoming from Velasco or from Payan, the puppet master in the shadows.

Mabillon. Wednesday 4 December 2002.

On Monday the team of *Figaro Entrepris*es invited me to their editorial committee again. The French didn't believe war is coming.

The deep night of Paris is fit for restful sleep: yet I woke up at 3am and I have been tossing ever since, feeling stupid and lonely. Fortunately, I bought a book by Philip Dick in Lyon yesterday, *Flow My Tears, the Policeman Said*, in an excellent translation prefaced by Gérard Klein. It talks intelligently about love in all its forms. "Theory transforms the reality it describes..." So does love. I'll be all right, even if I can't sleep: tomorrow Janine joins me here.

I work on the Internet book: last details, the fight to find a French publisher. Then more work on a dozen portfolio companies with shaky plans.

The world is askew, poised on the edge of conflict.

The winter air of Paris doesn't agree with me. This cold and damp weather exhausts me with asthma and stuffiness. This wouldn't be a healthy place for us when we get older, and I hate Parisian summers even more!

The redeeming beauty is in the festive decorations in the shops, the lights along the boulevards.

Hummingbird. Sunday 15 December 2002.

The first storm of the season is blowing through as I return to California for urgent meetings, wrapping up the financial year. On the way to Dick Haines' party yesterday afternoon, I found the road closed in Palo Alto. A fallen tree had taken down a pole, the street lights, and electric wires.

The members of NARCAP and their friends arrived in good cheer. A few didn't make it, stranded across the bridges.

We were a motley group of ufology survivors: Bernie Haisch and his talented wife; Larry Lemke with notes about his father's career in intelligence; a few pilots with stories to tell; and a man named Patrick Bailey who's joined the Masons in hopes of discovering deep secrets and ended up in a high degree, Commander of the Knights Templar of Northern California, "yet still unable to turn lead into gold, or make himself invisible," he joked.

All were good people and good company, but I have become too analytical, or perhaps too cynical, to believe any breakthrough will come from their efforts to get media support, or to put pressure on the government to release the deep cosmic secrets it doesn't have.

Mabillon. Wednesday 25 December 2002.

Back in Paris, for a quiet Christmas on Ile Saint Louis. We walked back and forth with gifts, food, and cameras under the pewter-colored sky. The weather has been mild, with occasional cameo appearances by the sun. We took Maxime to see the toys in store windows. Tomorrow we sign the papers to acquire the downstairs apartment, a timely conclusion to another comedy of a deal.

Cast of characters: a crooked building manager, a spinster of a notary with a mean attitude, two nosy neighbors trying to kill the deal to get the place for themselves, and Professor Bokias, disappointed that we're not buying his studio after all.

The seller is a kind lady on her deathbed; any delay with her signature could mean complications in the settlement of her estate... But the two flats we plan to join through a new staircase are recorded under different legal *régimes*, all the elements for a fine Vaudeville in the best Parisian tradition.

Christmas celebrations are subdued. The world watches the Middle East with apprehension; another Gulf War is about to erupt.

Mabillon. Friday 27 December 2002.

The Raëlian cult has achieved prominence with the unlikely claim of the first cloned baby in history. Vorilhon's disciple, chemist Brigitte Boisselier, talks about instructions she gets from the Elohim and visions of immortality, trying to steal Christmas.

Amusingly, this has triggered a deluge of "ethical" Christian pronouncements that sound even more phony and hypocritical than the claims of the sect. None of the pundits seem to understand the obvious fact that cloning isn't immortality, since an individual's personality and memories cannot be transmitted to the clone; a clone of Hitler might be a mild-mannered violinist, a clone of Einstein could be a petty crook.

Once again, I had lunch with Dominique Weinstein, as smart, self-effacing and agreeable as always. He said the French had just arrested over 200 Islamists, including a group that planned to blow up Strasbourg cathedral, and another preparing to fly a small airplane filled with explosives into another building.

In this time of Christmas, as we walk by Notre-Dame on the way back from Olivier's apartment, I marvel again at religion: humans are incapable of following the inspiration of Jesus as a man of peace and genius who stated the principles of humanity in such a clear, concise set of lessons. So they follow Christ, not because they are inspired by his beautiful, genuine pleas for love and morality, but because they believe he walked on water, multiplied the fish, revived the dead, turned wine into his own blood, resuscitated after he was buried, and flew up to heaven, none of which backed by any fact. Hollywood wins again.

This realization is maddening because it means that even the most clever and well-intentioned, the most spiritually-developed men and women can be fooled—indeed, delight in fooling themselves—by reference to vulgar magic and clever promotion.

Who knows what horrible tricks those hypothetical Elohim may visit upon the Earth, now that humanity has slipped its few remaining intellectual moorings?

8

Athanor. Saturday 4 January 2003.

December rains have filled up the Estero. The bar along the deserted beach has been breached by the current. We walked to a hilltop in the fine drizzle of early afternoon to watch the renewed flow of the river. Eager for a quiet time together, we have avoided our friends, except for Hans, that incorrigible wanderer, on his way to Argentina.

Athanor. Saturday 18 January 2003.

Today the fog lifted mid-morning. We found the beach strewn with pebbles of every color; the sea carries stones and marble fragments carved out of the mountains by furious rivers. Part of the cliff has collapsed, upsetting the landscape. The flat sand where we played with Max such a short time ago has been overlaid by a chaos of boulders, with varech and kelp left over from the storms.

I spend a lazy time here, walking on the beach, watching the scary news and the demonstrations against an Iraq invasion. People miss the larger threat: their own liberties being strangled, the war for privacy lost in the thunder of hovercraft leaving San Diego harbor.

Athanor. Saturday 1 February 2003.

Reality seems to acquire bizarre qualities: heaviness, unpredictability, like an old bus out of control, its driver drunk or dead, tires squeaking, windows buckling. We are only days away from war in the Middle East. America and its allies may be in control of the attack, but the sequels will be messy because terrorism is a fact of history, fueled not by political passion but by the much more explosive fuel of religious fanaticism. How strange that mankind has taken the best of its ideals, that spirituality that is supposed to make us different from the beast, and turned it into such a poison.

We came to the Athanor last night, slept with the sound of the waves and woke up in a hazy atmosphere that filtered the morning sun on the ocean. Janine spoke softly of the beautiful sky, but I only see the greater beauty in her eyes.

I finished editing *Heart of the Internet*, and as I turned on the European channel I heard the news in French: The Shuttle Columbia had disintegrated over Texas. It carried a crew of seven, flying back from the space station.

The ugliness of reality has gone up a notch. I walked up alone to the wind-swept hills above the Estero. There are small pools from the latest rains, bright green grass, and purple flowers already in bloom. We mourn seven brave people, and face our own defeats.

Hummingbird. Wednesday 12 February 2003.

Mstislav Rostropovich conducted the San Francisco Symphony this evening: *Slava!* by Bernstein, Tchaikovsky's Fifth Symphony (so pompous!), and Benjamin Britten's *Symphony for Cello and Orchestra*, with exuberant solo cellist Steven Isserlis. I knew nothing about Britten and heard the piece with surprise and pleasure, although Isserlis was disturbing in his wild hair and showy manners.

The Institute for the Future has contacted me. They are looking for a director for its technology projects, so I recommended Peter Banks for the position. Over lunch with Bob Johansen, I heard of the tribulations of the previous year, when they almost went under. I saw Paul Saffo there, back from Davos.

Everyone sends us messages clamoring for peace and applauding the French who threaten a veto at the UN, but the arguments sound hollow. It is George Bush's "Ugly American" posture, his contempt for the international community and his appeals to fundamentalists that make people uncomfortable. The architect of this policy is Donald Rumsfeld, the man who once told Hynek he had no "need to know" about UFO records. John David Ashcroft, the Attorney General, and Dick Cheney, the vice-president, seem happy to re-interpret the Constitution in guise of saving democracy.

Marcello Truzzi died a few days ago. I got the news from Loren Coleman. Truzzi had colon cancer but he hoped for a few more years: He sent a message requesting advice on what to do with his extensive library. I hope he found a good home for it.

Athanor. Sunday 16 February 2003.

Always the tension, the rumble of war. The 101st Airborne, the "Screaming Eagles," have embarked for the Middle East. Massive peace demonstrations everywhere, from New York to Rome and Paris. We remain far from all that, watching the storm sweep over Tomales Point, the grayness engulfing us, this house, the world.

The work on four new UFO computer catalogues is making progress. Ed Rothschild called yesterday to recruit me for potential briefings. His contacts are Tom Davis and Mr. Mattoon, chair of the Government Reform Committee of the House.

We agreed to talk when I get back from France. It all sounds very weak.

Mabillon. Saturday 22 February 2003.

Marvelous Paris! At 1 am, a hungry traveler can have a big cup of hot chocolate and buttered *tartines* of fresh bread at *Le Danton*, where a group of Scots in formal kilt and black tie celebrate a rugby victory. A block away, yuppies wait at the door of a disco. Groups form everywhere; people greet each other and laugh, lovers kiss. In one week I will be gone, so there's no time to enjoy my friends. I feel guilty to neglect people who would gladly rekindle the flame of hope. I feel guilty for sneaking into town like a robber. In friendship as in love, one always ends up feeling guilty: not hearing, not guessing, loving too much, too little, or mistaking for love what's actually nostalgia, longing for what we used to know, or used to be.

The idea lingers of spending half the year here when age catches up with us, and I get utterly fed up with business games. What would Janine want?

Writer Jean-Jacques Walter calls me out of the blue. He's concluded that Aliens manifested through false religions—as in my own *Messengers of Deception*, he says.

He's decided the intelligence is demonic. Walter, a charismatic Christian, is the prey of discarnate voices. Yet he may have a point.

Mabillon. Monday 24 February 2003.

Three in the morning. I can't sleep, even after taking a pill. Troubling thoughts: the poor state of venture capital, this stupid war. This weekend I read *Israël Attaque* by Yves Cuau, the story of the Six Day War of 1967 that returned Jerusalem to Israel. It puts the Middle East in a perverse perspective of age-old hatred, ready again for bloodshed.

Mabillon. Tuesday 25 February 2003.

Long conversation with Gabriel Mergui on the way to the Génopole meeting in Evry. We were stuck in a huge traffic jam that froze the entire region south of Paris as the A6 expressway was blocked by a well-armed gang's attack of an armored truck a few kilometers ahead.

It was a fight worthy of old Chicago, two stolen big rigs thrown across all lanes of traffic while the armored car was under fire with heavy machine guns and explosives. Amazingly, the armor resisted and the gang had to flee, leaving vehicles in flames all over the freeway.

Clearly outgunned, a few cops coming the other way had to hide in the bushes until the end.

Dinner tonight with Dominique Weinstein, François Louange, and Joëlle at L'Arbuci. The fate of Jean-Jacques is still uncertain. His office in Toulouse is at one end of a building, his secretary at the other end, and the French UFO files in another building altogether...

Hummingbird. Sunday 2 March 2003.

The news is full of anguish even as San Francisco, like Paris, enjoys an early spring. The skyline of the financial center looks fine, two dozen towers rising against the blue sky, and the Bay sporting white sails. But the heaviness of war hangs over everything.

Athanor. Saturday 8 March 2003.

Rest, and a long walk through the dunes with Janine. Working on my quiet research and on the Internet book, it is hard to imagine that we are so close to war. In Washington, the administration works in secrecy and recognizes no rights to question its motives or methods. It just exudes contempt.

Ordinary citizens are simply expected to fly an American flag from the window of their pick-up truck, and shut up.

San Mateo, my office. Thursday 13 March 2003.

The lassitude that is felt here, in this valley of creativity that is not given to idle moods, now verges on despair. There's the looming horror of a badly mismanaged adventure in Iraq, with the eradication of terrorism a convenient excuse to put the screws on civil liberties. There's also is a deepening slump in the economy. Today again, estate agents brought us brochures offering prime office space at record low prices; every day we hear of new bankruptcies.

Soon American tanks will cross the Euphrates and the dice will be cast. Yet, Silicon Valley keeps finding new inspiration, like the sensor technology I saw yesterday a team in Berkeley builds networks out of disposable nodes no bigger than sugar cubes.

Hummingbird. Friday 14 March 2003.

Demonstrations closed down the Financial District today. Meeting Bill Fuller at the Asia Foundation, I parked my Cherokee a few blocks away and walked through the ranks of placard-carriers. "Down with Bush!" and "No War for Oil" were the main slogans in the crowd of hopeful young faces and stern seniors. Washington's reply is that terrorism has made endless war unavoidable.

Hummingbird. Sunday 16 March 2003.

Three helicopters and the sheriff's plane circle over Mission Street, watching another demonstration. Miscalculations abound: Bush wavers between forcing a UN vote and withdrawing his ill-timed proposals. His hawkish supporters would be happy to do away with the UN altogether. As for Rumsfeld, whose historic hour seems to have come, he keeps issuing misleading statements with great assurance. There will be 90 countries in his coalition, he swore a week ago, but the UK has cold feet. The world holds its breath.

9

San Mateo, my office. Thursday 20 March 2003.

Vernal Equinox: The Sun at coordinates (0,0) and the first bombs fall on Baghdad. Validation for astrologers? Not really, but evidence that the world has exploded again, with angry protests everywhere. Downtown traffic is permanent blocked. It took me two hours to reach Market Street.

    A sense of foreboding hangs over the City. The third Millennium wasn't supposed to begin like this.

Hummingbird. Friday 21 March 2003.

The news jumps at you from every outlet: the car radio, the Internet. Every meeting starts with an excited burst of information: "They think they got Saddam," or "Turkey just opened up its airspace." The stock market initially reacted as if the war was already over, but the underlying mood remains one of anxiety, suspended life. The real battles have not begun; "getting Saddam" may be the easy part.

Claude Poher sends me a theoretical manuscript about *Universons*, particles he's hypothesized to explain gravity and UFOs, still viewed as extraterrestrial vehicles. With precautions of confidentiality, he's also sent it to Sturrock.

I made two attempts to read the book and failed to grasp it. The first section talks about interstellar travel and the probability of life elsewhere; nothing new there. But the second section plunges into particle theory; it pictures Universons as reverse gravitons (an unproven particle) remotely related to the zero-point energy of the vacuum.

The weaker third section tries to link that theory to UFOs that accelerate rapidly, go away in the "blink of an eye," or change color as they move.

Hummingbird. Saturday 22 March 2003.

Peter Sturrock is as puzzled as I am by Poher's book, the result of twenty years of work. "I told him that I looked forward to studying it," Peter said, "but I've set it aside. It's full of circular arguments. The same applies to Puthoff's work. For instance, Hal points to the significance of the ratio e/m, energy over mass. But he fails to see that he's also redefining mass in the process. I've sent Bernie Haisch six questions like this and he never responded."

This made me feel better because I hadn't understood the argument either.

Bernie Haisch himself was sitting next to me this afternoon at Dick Haines' house for another NARCAP meeting. Dominique Weinstein was there from France and Dr. Joao Cardozo from Portugal, who spoke about pilot cases and physiological effects of microwaves, but

Cardozo never defined his "microwaves" in terms of frequency, intensity, or duration of exposure, nor did he seem aware of the enormous literature on the subject.

In all this, as in Poher's book, researchers pick and choose whatever facts seem to support their theory among a vast body of reports. This is poor methodology. I reminded Cardozo that Maurice Masse, with whom I once spent two days in Valensole, assured me that he had remained "paralyzed" in his field for 20 minutes *after* the famous object and its occupants had departed. Can the "paralysis" continue when the field is no longer applied? Perhaps. But current theories don't account for that. Similarly, "blink of an eye" disappearances may be explained by fast acceleration on the part of physical saucers. But what about "blink of an eye" disappearance of hard objects inside a bedroom? Or shrinking in place? Or into a vaporous state? Or into the rocky side of a mountain?

Jim McCampbell, as usual, was urbane. He spoke of physiological effects with some command of the engineering parameters. He took me aside to show me his manuscript on geophysics—another product of 20 years of personal research beyond the fringes of science. He has looked at the hypothesis that asteroid and comet impacts shaped the early Earth (a commonly accepted idea nowadays) but also triggered the events that brought oil and minerals to the surface. The insight is interesting, but I can't tell how significant the hypothesis will turn out to be. Then Dick Haines gave me a manuscript from mathematician Bozhich in Moscow, who challenges the status quo.

Others around the table included Larry Lemke, Ted Roe and his son, Patrick and Nancy Bailey, and Leslie Kean. Sturrock was realistic: "I won't go to any Congressional briefings if they're still trying to pry things out of the Air Force," he told me yesterday. "That will never get anywhere. There are plenty of civilian cases: that's what scientists should study." I agree completely.

At a meeting of the American Association for the Advancement of Science ("AAAS") in Denver last month, Bush's scientific adviser Geoffrey Sommer said the public should not be told of an impending asteroid impact if nothing could be done to stop it. "Ignorance for the populace is bliss," apparently. Does this also apply to UFOs?

Hummingbird. Sunday 23 March 2003.

It's impossible to take one's eyes away from the television news where the war is now shown in real time. There's manipulation by both sides, of course, but it's hard to argue with the basic facts of bunker-blasting bombs as they annihilate Saddam's ostentatious palaces, filling the sky of Baghdad with shreds of marble and steel.

Hummingbird. Monday 24 March 2003.

Louange is still working valiantly to get SEPRA reorganized. Letters have gone out to various ministries requesting cooperation in an advisory committee, notably to the Ministry of the Interior, suggesting that Weinstein be assigned to the group. I briefed Dominique on the Kelleher hypothesis about a possible link between cattle mutilations and BSE epidemics, or rather the possibility that Mad Cow disease masquerades as Alzheimer's. This takes us away from the idea that mutilations are strictly linked with UFO phenomena.

Dominique is on his way to Washington to work with U.S. teams that track the financial dealings of illegal organizations. He tells us that the anti-American campaign within the French administration has taken such proportions in Paris that he's often the only remaining contact at this level.

Athanor. Saturday 29 March 2003.

Combat appears to have halted for a while in Iraq, as armored divisions on both sides dig into position and resupply. Every discourse begins with an invocation either to God or Allah. Bush makes sure he gets introduced by a chaplain when he speaks to the troops. Didn't his God instruct, "Thou Shalt not Kill?"

Alas, God (or Allah) has neglected to take human stupidity into account. No bunker is strong enough to shield us from fanaticism.

Hummingbird. Saturday 5 April 2003.

This afternoon I drove Janine to the airport on her way to Paris, and I came back to pack my suitcase for my own trip to New York tomorrow morning. The battle for Baghdad is raging anew, with mounting death toll on both sides.

Colm Kelleher has sent me a confidential report entitled "The Origin of transmissible spongiform encephalopathy in North America, and Animal Mutilations." It follows an earlier draft presenting evidence of a correlation between animal mutilations and the emergence of a TSE epidemic in North America.

Colm has also spoken with Dr. Toshiyuki Tanaka of the Hiroshima Peace Institute, an acknowledged expert on Japanese war crimes. He learned that in the 1930s and 40s, following the invasion of China, Japanese forces (Unit 731) did conduct epidemiology experiments throughout Southeast Asia under the cover of "water purification" projects. This sophisticated, massive biological warfare program involved injecting sheep serum into prisoners in New Guinea and New Britain. Some of the sheep may have had scrapie, a well-known TSE, leading to the condition known as *kuru*, a specific TSE in humans that overlaps with CJD (Creutzfeldt-Jakob Disease).

In 1942, the US began its own research on biological weapons. Lt. Col. Murray Sanders at Camp Detrick, Maryland, was among the first to interrogate members of Unit 731 when Japan surrendered. In 1957, Dr. Joseph Smadel sent Dr. Carleton Gajdusek to investigate kuru in New Guinea. "Gajdusek started sending multiple kuru brains from the wilds of New Guinea to NIH," reports Colm.

In the 1960s an intensive program of transmission tests began at NIH, encompassing many labs and many types of animals injected with kuru brains, compared with scrapie-infected sheep, to verify similarities between scrapie and kuru brain pathology lesions.

In 1967, researchers at Colorado State University noticed that some of their captive deer began to exhibit strange symptoms. Colm has spoken to the senior authors of the first paper on chronic wasting disease in cervids: "The fact that experimentally infected scrapie sheep were at the same facility from which CWD first emerged is not generally known," he writes. A subclinical BSE infection, possibly a form of mad cow disease, began in the 1960s. "The current epidemic of Alzheimer's disease in the US may be a result of this high level of experimentation on kuru and scrapie," Colm speculates (22).

New York City. Monday 7 April 2003.

"Too busy," Jean-Marie Messier canceled our breakfast meeting at the Four Seasons restaurant. I had hoped to find out what he thought of the demise of his venture fund. Vivendi has reportedly sold it to Global Asset Capital and Hamilton Lane for a pitiful $9 million, against the better judgment of management.

New York City. Kennedy airport. Tuesday 8 April 2003.

My appointments are over: Merrill Lynch, to talk about future funds, then my friends at Adler's office. "You should be pleased, you're still *in the Game*," they observed when I sat in their office near the Plaza and described our portfolio. Many venture funds have been disbanded or returned most of their money after drastically reducing their teams, as Vivendi was just forced to do.

There's snow on the ground at Kennedy. My cab driver, an Egyptian, observes that I must be "very proud to be French." Wall Street financial managers hope "the war will be a short one." Yesterday the Dow Jones shot up 250 points in the first hour, then retreated as people realized that the economy was in bad shape, war or no war.

Monday was an extraordinary day. It began with the siege of Baghdad, the invasion of Saddam's palaces, the discovery of caches of "chemical agents" that turned out to be common materials, and a devastating hit against a bunker where the Iraqi leadership was said to be planning an escape from the besieged city.

Mabillon. Saturday 12 April 2003.

Baghdad is firmly in American hands now. The story that began in "shock and awe" ends in rubble and pillage, a situation worthy of Philip K. Dick in a world where palaces are torture chambers, hospitals are garrisons, and flowers are bombs.

Unforgivable: the failure of the American military to prevent the looting of Iraqi antiquities and the devastation of Baghdad's museums.

Mabillon. Wednesday 16 April 2003.

Janine and I walked past the Opera to Drouot to watch what was left of the sale of André Breton's collections, notably his primitive art statuettes from Oceania and Canada, plus some Arizona Kachina dolls. Then our neighbor Professor Bokias allowed us to visit his own studio, 30 square meters piled up with books, all manners of debris, a stepladder... We had a busy day shopping for toys, then a session with our *notaire* in his ancient office. In France, you always miss one more piece of paper to complete your indispensable *dossier*.

Saintes, in Charente. Friday 18 April 2003.

We left Paris by train, our work done. Denis Bourgeois at Balland signed my contract for *Heart of the Internet,* and we finally obtained the official paper that reclassifies our apartment for a bank loan. Olivier and Max are with us, so we had a fun trip through Tours and Angoulême: flowers are everywhere, bands of deep yellow "colza" fields spread to infinity on both sides of the track.

Annick introduces us to the shores of the Charente River where she has many friends. It is a land of rich food, good wine, and deep red-brown Cognac drunk in wide-mouthed glasses. There are evening walks through the Abbaye aux Dames, and quiet dinners on the patio.

Then we drove to La Rochelle, passing Rochefort, and went on to the Ile de Ré, a long and boring tongue of an island enhanced by old fortifications. At the tip stands the interesting lighthouse of Les Baleines (the whales) with a pleasant view of the ocean.

The land is flat here, only enhanced by the sunny weather that endows it with wildflowers and palms, wonderful "glycines."

Athanor. Saturday 26 April 2003.

We rushed here last night to recover our mental and spiritual balance after the long flight home. We took a drive down the splendid shore of Tomales Bay, stopping at every little cove, and discovered a secluded area at Millerton Beach for a picnic and a stroll.

Athanor. Saturday 3 May 2003.

Prompted by ongoing correspondence with Eric and Colm, I have been re-reading Ray Stanford's book on Socorro (with the odd title *Socorro Saucer in a Pentagon Pantry*). The copy I have belonged to Allen Hynek and includes his precious annotations. Ray had picked up a rock at Socorro that bore traces of metal abrasions from the landing gear of the landed UFO, which turned out to be significant.

In August 1964, a scientist at NASA-Goddard examined the samples under a microscope and told Stanford that the analysis revealed that the slivers consisted of zinc and iron in an unusual ratio. Yet by the time Ray Stanford was able to contact Goddard again, he was told the sample was determined to be silica! This was later confirmed in a letter on NASA stationery, sent to Richard Hall at the National Investigations Committee on Aerial Phenomena (NICAP). The coverup at work, once again, using the old channels.

In our "inner circle" further information has come to light: 1. Ray's wife works at Goddard in the PR office. In the hallway she heard a returning retiree be introduced to someone else with great pride as *"the guy who stole the Socorro sample."* 2. Kit pointed out that "the samples showed up at CIA sometime in 1982. They were analyzed at LANL where we had a metallurgical services contract." The results: "not any aluminum-titanium alloy we ever saw from this earth (?)"

When Kit found himself the executive director of materials research at GM in 1992, he had the samples re-examined: "The main constituents were definitely titanium and aluminum."

On Thursday evening, Janine and I had Morvan Salez as a dinner guest, fresh from a visit to the Institute of Noetic Sciences, where he was impressed by Dean Radin's experiments in precognition. Morvan has read *Forbidden Science*. He wryly comments that he identifies with what we went through because French science remains so sterile; parapsychology is treated even worse today than it was 40 years ago.

I once thought that the scientific generation of the 1968 era would upset things in France once they came to power, but if anything, the old structures have fortified themselves. Morvan, who works on the Herschel instruments at the Institut d'Astrophysique in Paris (where Guérin used to be), is seriously tempted by California.

Athanor. Saturday 10 May 2003.

The dirt road that leads to the Estero is overgrown with wild flowers, the fields on either side fat with moisture; ferns and wild irises cover the coastal cliffs. Janine even discovered tiny yellow flowers known in Normandy as *Sabots de la Vierge*. The path narrows as it rolls over the last hill above the beach. The rains have made a canyon down the middle of it. We jumped from rock to rock down to a slippery trail.

The deserted beach was a paradise under the mild wind of May. Granite boulders that the latest slide had sent crashing down to the shoreline made a comfortable room for us with a floor of sand. No sign of human beings in any direction, as far as we could see.

Reston. Thursday 22 May 2003. Town Center Hyatt.

I'm watching TV until the time of my breakfast with Brian Pinkerton. Later we will go over to CNRI to meet with Bob Kahn and Connie McLindon's staff to discuss new computer projects.

There are brave new plans to brief Congress about UFOs in hopes of starting new research. Tonight, our little group will have dinner with Ed Rothschild, and tomorrow we meet with Congressman Tom Davis. I'll fly back to California with Peter Sturrock.

The weather is as humid as a wet towel, as morose as the diplomatic mood. The US has just "disinvited" France from joining Air Force exercises. Six French journalists on their way to a show on advanced graphics have been expelled from Los Angeles.

Canada has just reported the first BSE ("mad cow") case in North America. Colm Kelleher was in San Francisco on Monday for a meeting with Michael Farmer and the founders of Prosetta. He now considers a link between cattle mutilations and the spread of BSE. There is some speculation that CJD, the human form of Mad Cow disease, may masquerade as Alzheimer's.

On the flight back to San Francisco. Friday 23 May 2003.

Ed Rothschild picked us up at the Arlington Hyatt. The VP for project development of the Sci-Fi channel, Larry Landsman, was with him.

Peter Sturrock, Dick Haines, and I headed for Capitol Hill, where we met Dan Mattoon and Congressman Tom Davis of Fairfax.

Davis (R-Virginia) is chairman of the House Committee on Government Reform. A young, dynamic man with a reputation for a keen interest in science, he called two of his aides (including Peter Sirh), listened to our presentations, and said he'd support the Hearings, and perhaps a small budget for studies. The name of Dana Rohrabacher, chairman of the Subcommittee on Space and Aeronautics, was mentioned. (I pointed out he'd been briefed by NIDS.)

Davis, obviously tired after a late-night debate and vote on President Bush's tax reform act, interjected some humor: "I get letters from a woman who complains the DoE is dumping radioactive moon dust into her well. So I write to the DoE to tell them to stop dumping radioactive moon dust. What else can I do?"

Pleased with our morning work, we headed to the cafeteria in the basement of the Rayburn office building, where Ed Mitchell joined us, as well as a woman named Rhiannon Burrus, assistant for Representative Solomon P. Ortiz of the 27th district of Texas, who had arranged for us to brief another Congressman, Nick Lampson of Houston.

It turned out Rhiannon was a friend of Leslie Kean, helping Sci-Fi with contacts for Ed Rothschild. Rhiannon is an intense believer in Alien presence, saucer crashes, reverse engineering, the grand coverup of new energy systems, and an imminent cure for cancer.

Ed Mitchell told the Congressman he was certain there was a secret project reporting to Pete Aldridge, Under Secretary of Defense for acquisition, technology, and logistics. Rhiannon added that fiberoptics and most high-tech came from crash retrievals.

I could tell Lampson was unimpressed, so I hinted: "You can see why there's a stigma attached to this subject among academics...if we want their attention, we'll have to start from facts."

When we got out of the meeting, Rothschild told me, "It's a good thing Dr. Mitchell wasn't in the morning meeting. It could have been much worse. At least, we didn't hear anyone mention that UFOs cure cancer!"

Athanor. Saturday 31 May 2003.

We spent the day canoeing down the Russian River, lively and sunny, with just the right breeze in the afternoon. We only met a few ducks, who ignored us, and one large turtle sunning itself on a log.

Pete Aldridge has responsibility as Under Secretary of Defense for Acquisition, Technology, and Logistics since May 2001, along with "all matters related to DoD acquisition, research and development, logistics, advanced technology, international programs, environmental security, nuclear, chemical and biological programs, and the industrial base." (Wow...)

Formerly Secretary of the Air Force from June 1986 to 1988, Aldridge later joined McDonnell Douglas electronic systems as Company President (1988-1992). The groups reporting to him include DARPA and the Defense Special Weapons Agency.

The first copy of *FastWalker* in Japanese arrived yesterday, dutifully sent along by my excellent friend Gouki.

Hummingbird. Wednesday 4 June 2003.

We saw *Mysterious Skin* tonight. The play has to do with a young man who is sexually assaulted by his high school coach under distressing conditions, and copes with it later in life in an altered mental state where he feels in contact with Aliens.

Hummingbird. Sunday 8 June 2003.

We just drove down the Sierra from Reno with songs in our heads ("*Now it's guitars, Cadillacs, hillbilly music...*") and pains in my shoulder from a couple of days of hard work helping courageous Catherine with some carpentry. She invited us to a concert by Dwight Yokon.

San Jose. Tuesday 10 June 2003.

I use an empty office to gather my thoughts before a Board meeting at the Neophotonics facility on Zanker Road, previously owned by Lightwave, a company we recently acquired. I feel happy, living in the soft light of Janine's radiance. It is hard to recognize happiness, until it is too late. My parents used to speak this way of the twenties, the early thirties, a creative and vibrant period I never knew.

I have felt happy for the last several years, and I wonder if my holiday from ufology is a factor. I find it hard to become involved again. People keep calling with suggestions for films and documentaries, and I keep answering that I cannot see myself contributing to the current confusion of the field.

Hummingbird. Wednesday 11 June 2003.

Bernie Haisch and Marsha, who now work with Joe Firmage at ManyOne Systems, have their office just two blocks away from me. Ever since Fred Beckman sank into his personal alienation, I've missed our regular gossip about the paranormal and other odd subjects, but Bernie is much better informed than Fred ever was.

The discussion returned to the possible existence of a large secret project. Bernie has heard the same information I have, namely that Pete Aldridge had responsibility for it, but he now thinks there are four projects, not just one, dispersed among contractor facilities. They have hardware from Roswell. One of his sources is NASA engineer Larry Lemke, whose father was assigned to work on advanced hardware that seemed to have come from beyond Earth.

We spoke about reincarnation and remote viewing. Marsha, who believes she recalls her prior lives, sees me both in the past and the future, on the bridge of a spaceship, brightly attired, but I suspect that scene is a reflection of her artistic career as a mezzo-soprano. She has a leading role in *La Belle Hélène* at a local theater.

Athanor. Saturday 14 June 2003.

Twenty copies of *Heart of the Internet* just arrived, along with copies of the Japanese edition of *FastWalker* (they printed 12,000). It's ironic that these two books, so different, arrive in the same month.

I've been reading Jacques Bergier's *Je ne suis pas une Légende* (19), an extraordinary book; it's not easy to be a genius in the France of the 1940s! This sent me back to my computer for some research, and I dug up two versions of *The Strange Case of Vintrix Polbarton,* a novel in English by Ian Marshall. So why does the French version, published on 21 October 1931 as *Le Docteur Frégalle*, bear a fictitious author's name as "Oswald Dallas" in a very bizarre coincidence? (20)

Mabillon. Sunday 21 June 2003.

Solstice: The weather is hot with no sign of rain, fanning the flames of torrid music on every street. At four in the morning, crowds still try to dance a few exhausted steps to the rhythm of lingering drums; a few just sit on the sidewalk, dazed, waiting for sunrise and the green commandos of municipal cleaners who will dispose of smelly hills of beer cans, Alps of plastic bottles, Everests of greasy paper.

All access to central Paris was closed tight: the Palais de Justice is host to dozens of Mujahideen arrested last week in Auvers. My friend Dominique, as part of a raid by 300 agents, interrogated them in Pontoise. The next day three sympathizers set themselves on fire in Paris, so the guards around the Palais are visibly nervous.

Mabillon. Friday 27 June 2003.

Lunch with Thérèse de Saint-Phalle at Monteverdi on Rue Guisarde. Mr. Robert Laffont, retired but still active in literature, sat at a nearby table, so I went over and shook his hand.

Now that there's (some) money in ufology, people want to turn me into a celebrity. Larry Landsman of the Sci-Fi Channel asks me to take part in a Larry King panel. This reminds me of the charade at Norton AFB (21). In those days Sandler and Emenegger were looking for visible scientists who could give credibility… to what? Leslie Kean and Larry are convinced I could re-establish the phenomenon in the public's mind. I politely declined, suggesting a quiet lunch instead.

New York. Tuesday 1 July 2003.

The Plaza now has computer connections in every room, enabling me to stay updated on the venture portfolio. My first thoughts of the day were for Janine, her new projects. Yet I expect no surge of visionary adventure from Silicon Valley.

Those few friends who had an indomitable passion for humanity like Ren Breck have passed on to a better world. Even the Pagans have become rather dull.

Between a meeting with Professor Montagnier and Ed Greger at ThyoPro (22) and an economist's briefing at Merrill Lynch, I walked all over New York today under the glorious sun. It was one of those afternoons when you realize how many beautiful women there are, with perfect skin and flowing hair.

Montagnier works with Dr. Harry Demopoulos in the ThyoPro startup. We had a strange discussion; Demopoulos was so unfocused that I had trouble grasping what his company was trying to do.

United flight to San Francisco. Wednesday 2 July 2003.

Last weekend, the Sci-Fi channel brought together the ufologists, including Colm Kelleher from NIDS and the three major groups. I had excused myself. Bernie wasn't able to travel, and the ufologists didn't want to see Firmage. They discussed "What to do?" over two days, stressing the need to "coordinate data gathering and setup investigations," a fine objective. MUFON will send their field people, NIDS will do analyses.

This reminds me of the failed *National Enquirer* panel of 20 years ago, which found no signal among the mass of reports from the public.

Larry Landsman, from Sci-Fi, coordinates digs at Roswell, investigates abductions and ground traces, and plans Congressional Hearings. But the Sci-Fi Channel itself lies in the ruins of the Vivendi Empire, soon to be sold off as part of the Messier debacle.

Athanor. Saturday 5 July 2003.

Larry Landsman called to say that, at the Washington meeting, there had been much discussion of my role in the field. I had "lots of credibility among these people," he said, and why didn't I pick up Hynek's mantle as a leader of ufology? I told him my credibility in ufology probably comes from the fact that I don't want any mantle.

Athanor. Saturday 12 July 2003.

Janine has returned from Paris. She walked out of customs tired but smiling, with suitcases filled with items from Mabillon and bottles of special wine for our next feast of Saint Agobard. The Paris apartment is empty now, awaiting a few months of remodeling.

Over lunch with Russell Targ at Joanie's in Palo Alto, we discussed books and parapsychology. Remote viewing is still a subject of fascination, but Dean Radin's research into precognition is attracting the most interest. He claims that subjects in an experiment have a significant emotional reaction (detectable with sensitive instruments) about three seconds *before* being exposed to a shocking image. Scenes from the future are being perceived with equal success as scenes from the present. All of that suggests again to me that the major flaw in contemporary science is our incomplete concept of time.

On the way here, on an impulse, we stopped to visit a sculptor's garden filled with colorful figures of considerable mythological variety. We met the artist, Chaz Clover, who showed us his ebullient work in progress. It made me think of a poem I've recently read, "Life is a trader with much to sell," by Robert Kingery Buell (23). It gave me a sense of tenderness and expectation: *Yet the trader will pass you by / unless you come with a questioning mind...*

I never lost my questioning mind, that's the important thing.

Hummingbird. Thursday 17 July 2003.

Jim McCampbell showed up at my office on Tuesday, bringing the manuscript of his book on geology. He was very kind, showing a level of respect I don't deserve. He said he'd lost trace of Fred Beckman, who's been sick, hospitalized, and according to rumor, transferred to a nursing home.

Now a message from Loren Coleman brings sad news of Gordon Creighton's death yesterday morning.

He was 95, a remarkable man to whom I owe much. He translated *Challenge to Science* with flair and enthusiasm and was always a friend of good counsel.

Athanor. Sunday 27 July 2003.

We celebrated the fourth Feast of Saint Agobard yesterday: a medieval meal of vegetable julienne with ham, cod with *salsifis*, venison sausages with cabbage, and a rabbit in prunes and raisins, along with Blue Nun and red wine "from the Saint Agobard reserve."
It was a fun afternoon with many stories and, of course, political diatribes among people dressed in medieval regalia. All of them are published writers, artists, or scientists (Marilyn is still on the astronaut roster), and dear friends. I'm working hard on the French version of *Heart of the Internet*, hoping to convey how the network arose, and what dangers it carries.

Hummingbird. Thursday 31 July 2003.

Lunch with Arthur Hastings, who now teaches at the Institute of Transpersonal Psychology. The Institute develops a subfield of psychology that traces its roots to Maslow and Tony Sutich (24).
Colm Kelleher is in San Francisco for a few days, exploring positions in biotech. HandyLab is interested in talking with him, but Michael Farmer pushes him to join Prosetta, his new company.
Events at the Utah ranch are continuing, and Bob Bigelow's brilliant aerospace projects are moving forward, aimed at a full-size launch in 2007, preceded by the orbiting of a prototype.
Colm reminded me of an incident told in Jim Schnabel's book *Remote Viewers*. Using tips from Bob Monroe's books, Kit once tried to get out of his body in 1982 or 83. He succeeded in separating himself from his prone form "like a crab molting from its old shell."
"He walked across the room," Schnabel writes, "but now there were other beings in the room. There were monsters. Some kind of goblin hobbled up, put its nose right in his face, stared at him." Kit had difficulty getting back inside his body, and swore off.

Athanor. Saturday 2 August 2003.

The four elements converge here: the earth of the rugged North coast, the silvery waters of the Pacific, the air in multiple forms, a bride's veil of fog in the morning, lifting at noon to the burning sun.

Colm rightly questions the phenomena we've studied together. I don't have a better answer than anyone else, but I can state the obvious: 1. *Time is not what we think*; our physics is profoundly wrong about its nature, and 2. *The brain is a screen*; its main function is not to perceive as much as possible of the world, but to filter away what the animal doesn't need for basic survival.

10

Detroit. Tuesday 19 August 2003.

The Renaissance Marriott is all curved concrete and tunnels leading to downtown skyscrapers. The world looked deceptively fine and peaceful as seen from the air, but I reached the hotel in the middle of horrible news: the bombing of the UN mission in Baghdad and yet another bus explosion in Jerusalem, broken bodies everywhere.

I have two professional visits to make, to Handylab and a new energy company, but I'm eager to spend time with Kit, whom I haven't seen in well over a year. This visit opens up a new phase in my research. Now that NIDS operations have stopped, I need to reconnect with those few investigators who are still active.

I also arrive just as Detroit recovers from last week's massive power failure that plunged half of North America into darkness. The western world is precariously suspended between ugly fear and abject hatred, ready to lash out at invisible enemies in the darkness.

Ann Druffel has just sent me her book about James McDonald, *Firestorm* (25). It's quite an achievement, capturing as it does both the personality of her main subject and the complexities of the scientific arguments about ufology. She has done a fair job of reflecting my impressions of Jim as a bright but humorless bull in a China shop, which tempers her adulation of him. The reader will plainly see why Jim and Allen could never have worked together.

Detroit. Wednesday 20 August 2003.

I spent most of the day with Kit and his medical colleagues (we spoke of magnetic resonance imaging and a potential business venture) and just came back from dinner with him and Kristin. The afternoon was spent at the Wayne State University School of Medicine, where Kit has a nice office two floors underground. He jokes that he likes to keep it dark and cozy, making his colleagues uncomfortable. Pictures of Kristin and fine Chinese paintings surround him there, as he works on projects ranging from a GM program on driver distraction to patient reviews and his work on functional brain imaging, straddling MRI research and the psychiatric treatment center.

Using two magnets (1.2 Tesla and 4 Tesla), Kit runs subjects in various states of sensory deprivation through virtual reality scenes. In one study he's recruited people who felt they had communication experiences with Aliens. He presents them with slides of faces in which an Alien face is inserted. When I asked him where that image came from, he said "from the Aliens at Los Alamos."

I had brought my laptop, so I showed him the four catalogs in various states of analysis, notably my universal Law of Times.

Our discussions during the evening and dinner ranged over many topics: UMMO, which may have been a Nazi cutout with its origin in Latin America (26), Colm's study of mutilations and paramilitary units, and finally old topics like the McDonnell-CIA study in the seventies. Kit professed not to know anything about its potential records, referring me instead to John Schuessler.

Interestingly, this old McDonnell study is mentioned in the latest issue of *Inforespace*, the bulletin of SOBEPS (Belgian Society for the Study of Space Phenomena) (27). Investigator Franck Boitte recalls an observation made by a witness in Assas, near Montpellier, on 18 April 1955. Perry Petrakis has also researched the case. About 20 years after the event, five or six investigators, without prior warning, visited the witness, Mr. D., in Montpellier.

"Of various nationalities, most of them physicians, they reported to the defense department of their own countries. There was a Moroccan who was a consultant to this commission; he introduced himself as King Hassan II's personal physician." Mr. D. reported this to J.P.

Troadec in 1988, adding he'd met Richard Niemtzow, but had missed a visit by John Schuessler. This "commission" was clearly monitored by Kit, who refuses to talk about it—even now.

When I asked him what "Aliens at Los Alamos" were all about, he explained that he'd been given data, through Hal, that pointed to a series of analyses "but not from 1947, it was more like 1950, 1951" with photos of live Aliens, autopsy reports and histology slides. He had no way of knowing whether or not the data was genuine. The cells looked like they "could have come from fish."

Kit studied thousands of slides of fish cells for his graduate work; the whole thing could have been a test or a hoax. Kristin, interestingly, thinks we might be fed material that is "ten years or so ahead of the time, from classified research, just as we had 6cm resolution from satellites as early as 1973, but we never knew it."

Detroit airport. Thursday 21 August 2003.

My morning was spent in Ann Arbor learning about modern Stirling engines, and the afternoon at a Handylab board meeting. The weather is muggy. Black limousines glide to and fro among the big trucks that deliver industrial parts to car factories in the area.

At the airport, all the TV screens show the latest devastation in the Middle East, suicide bombs and retaliatory missile strikes, men proudly brandishing Kalashnikovs, a planet on the brink again.

Athanor. Saturday 23 August 2003.

Reviewing my visit with Kit, I find many questions left hanging, as well as lingering contradictions about supposedly "secret" projects. If there is only one black UFO operation, as Hal and John Petersen assure me, and if it has to do with hardware, then why is so much biological data floating around, purportedly about live Aliens at Los Alamos?

Kit told me he'd discussed the existence of the data in meetings with Director Colby ("You deserve to know," he said, but he didn't confirm the data) and senior physicians. But could those particular UFOs be WMDs, "weapons of mass deception"?

Athanor. Saturday 6 September 2003.

Larry Landsman tells me that nothing is happening in Washington regarding future Hearings. The Sci-Fi channel plans two new films, one in October about the alleged Kecksburg, Pennsylvania, "crash" of 9 Dec. 1965, the other in December about Rendlesham Forest. Larry must have sensed my doubts because he mumbled something about lack of actual evidence.

Colm Kelleher has received a formal offer from Michael Farmer to come work in San Francisco once Prosetta is funded. Handylab in Michigan may offer another choice for him, but he'd be very valuable to either firm.

Hummingbird. Wednesday 10 September 2003.

According to Bernie Haisch, Hal has tried the "front door" approach by writing to Pete Aldridge, sending along his physics papers. He also copied Under Secretary Jacques Gansler. He got no answers. Bernie had confirmation from another source there was a project "that was cut off into four parts." This source was not shown any object or craft, but he saw the list of people with access, which contained 200 names. As for "The General," he was retired and working for an oil company when he met with Hal and Joe at the suggestion of John Petersen.

Hummingbird. Sunday 14 September 2003.

A disturbing follow-on conversation at the Duck Club with Petersen, upset that Joe Firmage spoke loosely about his meeting with the general, which happened, he said, seven years ago, about 1996. The purpose of the meeting was to "try to get some money" and was confidential. I had to point out that Joe, Bernie, Hal, and Ed Mitchell, plus the Greer people were all talking about it freely, even mentioning there were "one or more secret UFO projects" under Aldridge. Petersen retorted this made no sense: the general in question doesn't even talk to him anymore.

The initial meeting had to do with several black projects, but *he never said that he'd seen any hardware and certainly not a craft.*

Petersen said he there was "zero chance" of my getting any information because it was so highly classified. But then, why Firmage? Was someone leading him on with fancy stories?

Hal Puthoff confirms that he was at the meeting but that *nothing specific was said about seeing hardware*, confirming what Petersen told me. The meeting did have to do with money. Joe had plans to raise lots of it, and there was talk of hiring this officer to run the project. What Ed Mitchell refers to is altogether different (the "four projects"), and I'm told it comes from a new, "impeccable" source.

Hal has been part of a John Petersen semi-official scenario exercise that included role-playing (the press, the government, the military, etc.) in various situations of potential ET contact.

Hummingbird. Thursday 18 September 2003.

Over dinner with Joe Firmage at Chantilly, the following came to light: A second top-level meeting took place in London two years later, in the early summer of 1998. The officer in question, a 4-star general, was Jack Sheehan, then in a senior role at NATO. (Wasn't he already retired then?) Sheehan is now a vice-president with Bechtel, dealing with oil exploration. There was a subsequent meeting, about a year later, where Sheehan volunteered more information to Hal and John.

At the first (1996) meeting, Joe and Hal had started the discussion by showing the MJ-12 documents to Sheehan. He vaguely said he "had seen something like that," then told the story of his boss instructing him to take a flight to a certain facility (presumably a Lockheed site) where he saw and touched a "craft." He also said he would honor his secrecy oath and not reveal more, but he did acknowledge he found a $9 billion discrepancy in some budgets which led him to uncover the project. He seemed disturbed at the absence of oversight: private industry is completely in charge, he reportedly said. Which raises the question, "Could the project(s) in question be using DIA money without oversight or even knowledge," which wouldn't be very kosher in purely accounting terms, if not on legal grounds?

Joe's extrapolations are surprising. He believes an Alien contact with the US took place on a ship in 1915. He also thinks the Roswell craft may be a "gift" rather than a disabled vehicle...Here I tend to concur. We also agree metallurgy development is a key, given my discovery of the "Pentacle Memorandum" and the Battelle Institute work, before and after 1947.

Hummingbird. Friday 19 September 2003.

This is an interlude, reading *Le Canard Enchaîné*, one of my few luxuries. Janine is in Nevada to help Catherine with a property.
 The Internet reveals General John J. Sheehan as Supreme Allied Commander, Atlantic from October 1994 to September 1997. A graduate of Boston College and Georgetown University with degrees in English and government, he saw combat with the Marine Corps in Vietnam and Iraq, served as director of operations for the Joint Chiefs, and joined Bechtel in 1998 to manage overseas petrochemical operations.
 Sheehan's official photos project an intense figure who transpierces you with icy eyes behind his glasses. A close adviser to Donald Rumsfeld, Sheehan has commanded military operations from Haiti to Bangladesh and from Serbia to Kuwait.
 If this man has actually stated that he touched an Alien craft, then a new chapter needs to be written and, as Joe rightly says, so does the history of the 20th century. But I must remind myself that I haven't had the opportunity to ask direct questions of first-hand sources, and I have not touched any craft, so I have no basis for judgment.
 Now the rising sun fills this apartment with gold dust made of light. The calm order of the place, this home that Janine has made for us, feels like a star suspended in the murmurs of the awakening city.

Montréal. Monday 22 September 2003.

Today Graham Burnette and I had three meetings with investor groups, in brand new buildings and fine autumn weather.
 These huge pension funds are confused about their strategy, so they hire "gatekeepers," as if expensive consultants could tell them where the next wave of innovation is going to come from.

New York. Tuesday 23 September 2003. Waldorf Astoria.

This hotel is the center of the world today. The UN General Assembly is in session, so heads of State are staying in Manhattan, with George W. Bush in this very building. Hence the street closures, the canine units in the elevators, patrol cars and black limos all over the place, and the secret service people running around.

We're attending the annual Private Equity conference, which also attracts hundreds of financial executives to this city. Consensus: the corporate funds are gone, and the angels out of cash. Many funds are turning to LBOs (28). The venture industry is in disarray.

United flight. Wednesday 24 September 2003.

On the way back to SF. This is my 64th birthday. I look in some puzzlement at my recent notes of the trip. I wrote: "Will faux humans confuse smart dust? The world changes fast, with blurry terminology moving at Internet speed.

Hummingbird. Monday 29 September 2003.

I am reading a "background" document dating from the late Clinton administration: "The near $5 billion in black programs in the USAF research and development budget are in the acquisition category. They are overseen within the DoD by Maj Gen Marshal H. Ward, director of special programs in the office of Dr Jacques Gansler, undersecretary of defense for acquisition, technology and logistics."

General Ward heads up the SAP coordination office* and, along with his counterparts in the policy and C4ISR offices, is part of an SAP Oversight Committee (SAPOC), chaired by the Deputy Secretary of Defense, John Hamre, with Dr. Gansler as vice-chair.

"The SAPOC is responsible for approving new SAPs and changing their status; receiving reports; and, among other things, making sure that they don't overlap with each other. This was a major criticism in

---

* Only three government organizations can have SAPs. But the topics are so secret that the funding may overlap without anyone's knowledge or auditing power, an obvious waste of money.

the 1995 report: 'If an acquisition SAP is unacknowledged,' the commissioners remarked, 'others working in the same technology area may be unaware that another agency is developing a program. The government may pay several times over for the same technology or application developed under different special programs.'"

So those are the Guardians of the Treasure. But do they really understand what it consists of?

Austin. Thursday 2 October 2003.

Hal picked me up at the airport; on the way he told me frankly that he thought Joe and Bernie should never have spoken to me about the general. Actually, Joe shouldn't even have spoken to Bernie, but Hal thinks I should have been part of those meetings from the beginning.

He also made it quite clear he wouldn't tell me everything because he had to protect his own sources, or at least one critical "deep throat," and this would also protect me in case I was ever polygraphed about the whole business; if I have no source to reveal, my position will be a lot cleaner. I did agree to that, of course; good ground rules. A lot of that stuff, I don't need or want to know about.

The thread begins in the late 80s when Hal was part of a supposedly top-secret UFO study group for Army Intelligence started by John Alexander. This is the ill-fated, ill-conceived group I'd heard about, the early childish papers I saw through Col. Ron Blackburn of Lockheed, and nicknamed "the Secret Onion." Ridiculous or not, they went high into Abramson's space command.

"We didn't learn anything new by reviewing the evidence, including Fastwalkers," Hal told me. "But we all became convinced the UFO phenomenon was real and we went out to brief highly-placed military and government people. That didn't lead to the research we hoped for. Instead, the whole project was killed. At the time I thought this happened for fear of ridicule and political power games. I was wrong: *It was killed because there was already another project, deeply black, and somebody didn't want it exposed. Or duplicated."*

One of the people at those so-called "advanced physics" meetings, which took place between May and August 1985 at the offices of BDM (now part of Raytheon) along the Washington beltway, was somehow related to two intermediate sources: Commander Miller, who now lives in Florida, with whom I have briefly corresponded, and Oke Shannon, a naval officer who went to work at Los Alamos in April 1997. These connections were not made completely clear because of the need to protect those "iron post" super-sources.

At the Pentagon briefing organized by Greer, Commander Miller, who is a firm believer in UFOs, managed to meet with Admiral Tom R. Wilson, who was deputy director of DIA and J2, in charge of all military intelligence for the Joint Chiefs of Staff.

Wilson was unimpressed by Greer, and he was upset at the meeting with Miller, who "sounded flakey," but he was reportedly influenced by Shannon and agreed to look into the existence of a possible secret project involving UFO hardware. William Perry, Secretary of Defense at the time, authorized his review of black project budgets, and Wilson did find a multi-billion-dollar discrepancy that he tracked down, as General Jack Sheehan had done a few years before.

All this simply confirms what many of us already knew.

At the time, activist-journalist Leslie Kean published an article in the *Boston Globe* that mentioned Wilson's name, and he was ridiculed by colleagues as a result.

This is where the real story begins. The details are written down in a transcript of an interview that Wilson gave to "an Air Force officer who was hoping to join DIA." The man in question was Eric Davis. They met in April 1997 in the parking lot of EG&G in Las Vegas at Grier and Paradise (29). The transcript is stupefying. Here is Wilson explaining that he searched through the records of special access programs under the authority of the SAPOC (oversight committee).

He found not one but *three* programs related to UFOs. None of the three would talk to him, but they referred him to a fourth group, and he insisted on talking to that project. The meeting took place with the head of the group, plus an assistant and an attorney. It became clear that all they wanted out of the meeting was to know how Wilson had learned of their existence! They also made it clear that, J2 or not J2, *he wouldn't be given access*. Admiral Wilson reportedly got very, very mad at that point and insisted on knowing "why they were spending his (DIA's) money." The answer was that the project was not under his jurisdiction because it was not a weapons program; nor was it an intelligence program or a special ops program.

"So what is it?" Wilson reportedly insisted.

The project leader groaned and didn't answer but his attorney said he had to, so he said: "We're a reverse engineering program." At that point Wilson thought he got it: "Russian? New Chinese device?"

No, they said, *they had an Alien craft*. They had been studying it for many years, and they were getting nowhere. They gave him no details. They said they had "almost been outed once," evidently referring to General Sheehan's inquiry, so they were nervous.

The security budget for the program was six or seven times the research budget. Wilson was shown the bigot list. It included between 400 to 800 people, depending on the years and budget, but no President, no member of Congress, no intelligence agent, only scientists, managers, and engineers. Hal remarked that to be invited one had to have something to contribute: "What are our chances?" We don't even know who the major contractor is."

"What about biological material?" I asked.

"There were no biologists on the list," was the answer. We agreed there must be another project dealing with biology, but *where is the coordination*, I asked?

Tom Wilson went back to SAPOC and raised hell. He was "livid at the lack of oversight," he told his interviewer (Eric Davis) but he was told that if he didn't drop it, he'd lose two stars and would never be director of DIA. Wilson did drop it, but he remained mad. He was director of DIA from 1999 to 2002.

At this point he's taking over as president of ATK missiles in Edina, Minnesota. He is being polygraphed and may be concerned to be accused of unknowingly leaking privileged information.

Austin. Friday 3 October 2003.

Today I saw a cold fusion experiment in progress at the Institute for Advanced Studies, and also the last remaining Nazi Shauberger saucer, which EarthTech hasn't been able to fly. I showed them my four databases, my ongoing analyses, and the trends resulting from it.

Then I read again the Wilson interview and reviewed the physics meetings of 1985 that led to a briefing of the Army Science Board on 18 November 1987. Blackburn was there, as was Kit (as Chair). The meeting with Greer, Ed Mitchell, and Miller took place on 4 April 1997. They briefed Admiral Crawford and General Patrick Hughes, then director of DIA. Wilson was in contact with the NNSA (National Nuclear Security Agency) and the AFIO (Association of Former Intelligence Officers) who helped him dig into the black programs.

My friends believe the hardware reverse engineering project in question is not a simple special access program but belongs to "a special subset of the unacknowledged/carve-out/waived programs." In other words, there is no way to know the codeword and the budgets hidden inside other SAP budgets stacked like Russian dolls.

The interview of Wilson mentions other names, like Paul Kaminski, Brigadier General Kostelnick, director of SAPOC, at OUSDAT in 1994-97, and Judith Daly, assistant deputy, OUSDAT. Bill Perry was involved, as was Jacques Gansler again, who told Wilson that "UFOs were real, and abductions were not."

Confused, I went over some of the chronology again. Evidently the program was inside the government at some point. Under Nixon it got transferred to a private contractor in order to secure it. As in the remote viewing program at SRI, the parts that the managers wanted kept secret were handled as "proprietary," not subject to FOIA. Classified papers are subject to review and reclassification, while proprietary data can be kept secret forever.

Later the same day.

Where does all this leave Bob Lazar's story? It smells of official disinformation, my friends say, like the doctored MJ-12 documents, serving the purpose of confusing the casual researchers and wasting their time. I think Jim Westwood is wrong with his idea of linking ufology with biological warfare; *it must be even bigger than that.*

I sketched out a list of who might know the truth, and who probably doesn't. Ed Mitchell has no details. Based on what Bernie Haisch learned at Lockheed, Kit must know a lot, as do Joe Firmage and John Petersen. Bigelow and his foreign friend are smart outsiders, and John Schuessler's access is probable but dated, given his participation in the McDonnell study of the late seventies. Colonel Blackburn, too, is an enigma. He once told to me that he'd seen a piece of UFO metal that looked like a wing section. Those who worked on the project were doing so under extreme hardship conditions *because of the time distortion induced by the craft.* But didn't he also try to convince me that the US had a base on Mars?

We spoke of MJ-12 and Menzel.* There's an article by him entitled "Superstars and the Black Hole Myth" (11 June 1975) that predates Hal's work on zero-point energy. Menzel cites one Hüseyin Yilnaz, of the Perception Technology Corporation (30). Hal and I discussed Corso. And what about our unique data: Should we go to our graves with it (my first choice), or pass it on securely? And if so, to whom?

Athanor. Saturday 4 October 2003.

Some things are not changing: this ocean, this blessedly infinite landscape. Relaxing with Janine today, I try to gather my thoughts. Together with Annick, her husband, and Alain, we walked along Millerton beach, the wind clearing up my brain after this intense trip, admiring the iridescent colors of beached medusas, and the flight of the cormorants going against the wind and the tide.

Hummingbird. Monday 6 October 2003.

Over lunch, Paul Saffo asked me what I thought of the stories about government cover-up. "I've heard the same rumors you have," I only replied, evading his question. Paul knows John Petersen and regards him as a clever man with a peculiar set of beliefs. Like Janine, Paul believes the government cannot keep a secret very long, but Hal has now convinced me otherwise: *They don't have to keep any secret.*

All they need to do is confuse everybody about what it means, by planting crazy people and fake stories, manipulating the credulous, destroying good people's careers, and derailing research.

---

* Professor Donald Menzel's work was done under Air Force Cambridge Research Laboratories contract F19628-75-C-0016.

Incline Village, Nevada. Thursday 9 October 2003.

Fancy hotels have never impressed me, but this Hyatt resort, next to Lake Tahoe, is a splendid place. It manages to enhance the magnificent lake, all emerald and night blue, rather than desecrate it as most luxury developments do. The wind makes the waves resound against the shore; it carries its music deep into the forest. I am here for the Golden State investment conference, as one of a dozen panelists on software and communications.

Gayle Crowell, former CEO of RightPoint (one of our companies, acquired by Epiphany), gave a vibrant talk on the economic recovery. I hope she's right.

Reno. Silver Legacy. Friday 10 October 2003.

We drove down from the Sierra paradise with Annick and Michel. Over lunch at Denny's with Catherine, during a swing through streets with old apartment buildings and a drive alongside the campus, the challenges of this fast-growing area were obvious.

I am attracted to Reno in spite of the blatant roughness of its Western posturing. The North side of the city is all ravines and dry boulders, but the southern part is enlivened by trees and grass. In between, one finds a mosaic of unfinished blocks, streets that end in mere dust, and empty lots that reek of decay. Then a whistle blows, a train passes majestically in the canyon between the casinos.

I'm amused by Reno because it is so greedy and even more void of substance than its wicked cowboy image would suggest.

Soon it will be time to pack our suitcases again for Europe, and a conference in Portugal for a distinguished panel on consciousness, science and religion. It's an opportunity to see Professor Meessen again and Chris Aubeck with whom I have been exchanging data, files, and insights about ancient sightings.

Paris. Saturday 18 October 2003. Hotel Clément, near Mabillon.

We're selling Mobilian, Inc. to Intel, so I stopped over at an Internet café to catch up with the deal and with friends. Paris is a true delight, sunny and brisk, in love with life. People stroll and smile as they wander among medieval marvels, gliding in velvety shadows, ignoring a political system that destroys what's left of ancient loyalties: to workers, to citizens as human beings, in the name of modern micro-management. France has 35-hour weeks, but its youth is badly educated, the old sacrificed. 13,000 died of heat exhaustion over the summer while ministers splashed in their swimming pools.

Janine lands this afternoon. I'm eager to show her the progress at Mabillon, where the old walls have been torn down and the new floor plan is taking shape. A metal ladder joins the two floors; the air smells of plaster; thick cables hang from the ceiling: It's wonderful.

Porto. Tuesday 21 October 2003.

Hotel Fenix, in the area of Bom Suceso. It's a modern part of the city, the business area, medical buildings, a few parks. Janine, who notices so many details I miss, pointed to an older section barely visible beyond modern shops, where we found the real people.

I hope to meet Joaquim Fernandez, one of the organizers, a fervent student of Fatima. I've written a book preface for him. Chris Aubeck, who teaches English in Madrid, promised to come over as well. He has compiled an extraordinary collection of ancient UFO cases, a "Return to Magonia" in which he successfully enlisted the assistance of librarians, historians, and collectors around the world.

Porto. Wednesday 22 October 2003.

There's an Internet café next door, in the basement of a modern shopping center, all neon and chrome: thirty consoles occupied by teen-agers with headphones, playing shoot-em-up games. (Fig. 7)

This morning we took a long walk through the city in balmy weather, until darker clouds built up over the Atlantic. By then we had traveled over the medieval streets to the Crystal Palace for a magnificent view over the Douro from the high cliffs and down to the river itself for a lunch of grilled salmon.

Porto has few commercial centers, so modernity has not yet killed small shops crowded together in the old town; narrow tunnels are filled with tools and simple machines where craftsmen repair furniture and appliances. An old woman walked up towards us, a large, flat basket over her head, with a dozen fresh fish. She cried out to alert customers as she hobbled into an alley. There is good taste everywhere, especially in the care and disposition of the fine parks. Past opulence is obvious, the façades covered with blue ceramic tiles and boasting ornate wrought-iron balconies.

Porto. Thursday 23 October 2003.

Nobel Prize winner Christian de Duve opened the proceedings with a fine lecture on "Listening to Life." He said life was no longer left to natural evolution; it will change based on what we do with our new knowledge, "a watershed of unfathomable historical importance."

He was followed by a panel on society and values, fundamentalism and survival.

The first speaker, Muzzafar Iqbal, was a colorful, tall Arab in traditional clothes, head of an Islamic science institute in Alberta, Canada. He spoke of civilization's fragmentation, of deepening imbalance among countries.

The clearest message he delivered had to do with what he called the failure of scientific progress, too often equated with material progress: If the predictions of the progressives were true, we would all be living in a golden age by now. *What went wrong?*

He was followed by Hebraic scholars and the discussion expanded with citations of Freeman Dyson ("The universe must have known we were coming!") and Stephen Gould's amazement that humans exist at all. Buddhists like Mathieu Ricard added their comments.

Porto. Friday 24 October 2003.

The second day of this conference on "Consciousness, Science and Religion" started with a panel on biology and medicine, referencing Qigong, remote viewing, and healing, so we heard plenty of New Age talk about chakras. Professor August Meessen was there to give a straightforward physics lecture interpreting the Fatima "Miracle of the Sun" in terms of the physiology of the eye. He was followed by Brian

Lancaster (mysticism and neuroscience).

Chris Aubeck arrived from Madrid today. We liked him immediately. He's a warm and lucid researcher, tall, dressed in black, filled with historical insights and stories from innumerable archives he has been compiling. With him and Meessen we had a marvelous time arguing about various theories.

Porto. Saturday 25 October 2003.

Today we heard talks by Chris Corbally, a Jesuit who directs the Vatican observatory in Tucson ("Will organized religion survive an encounter with extraterrestrials?" he asked) and Steven Dick of the Naval Observatory, who spoke of post-biological evolution.

This city has kept its provincial atmosphere, its conventional families with well-behaved children. People don't seem to be in very good health, however, and many buildings show the kind of disrepair American real estate agents call "deferred maintenance."

Lisbon. Monday 27 October 2003.

We left Porto in a rented Ford and two hours later we arrived in Fatima. The roads are lined with woods: many pine trees and other greenery, in spite of the advancing season. The colors of vineyards, red, purple, and yellow, were the main signs of autumn, amidst the ever-changing pattern of showers and sunshine. At Fatima the Church has made no effort to preserve the pastoral setting of the Virgin's apparitions in 1917. Only one large oak remains at the spot where the little shepherds used to wait for the "Lady."

We heard the midday Mass at the basilica, then watched a small crowd assemble at the nearby chapel built on the site where the Virgin is said to have manifested, every month on the 13th day from May to October. This is where people come to pray (5 million each year) and ask for celestial favors, going around the sanctuary on their knees.

The landscape has been flattened, cemented, asphalted, and equipped with loudspeakers. The general effect is that of a Stalin-era communist monument combined with a sacred shrine.

The visit made me wonder about the "Miracle of the Dancing Sun"

Fig. 7. Compiling *Wonders* with Chris Aubeck, Porto, October 2003.

Fig. 8. Modern view of the site of the Fatima apparitions, October 2003.

and the sudden parting of clouds that the crowd watched in awe.

During our short stay, two hours or so, we were treated to a constant alternance of dark skies, sudden cloudbursts, followed by patches of blue, and radiant, blinding sunshine, causing all sorts of after-images. If this is typical of Fatima weather in October, Meessen may have a point about physiologically-triggered visions.

We drove into Lisbon in the rain, following the road around the industrial section: warehouses, refineries, factories, and maintenance yards, until we reached the Tagus River, the magnificent Tower of Belem, and the narrow streets of Bairro Alto.

We got lost again, but the experience was fun. Dodging buses, trams, taxis, and pedestrians, we found a hotel and quickly went out again for coffee and pastries at Nicola, a walk to the river, and a climb to the magnificent battlements of St. Georges' castle. Again, the spectacular sky was boiling with dark and light gray, splashes of red and purple sunset with spots of blue that brought out every detail of the city below us, its orange roofs and the silver Tagus River. Ships bound for the ocean steamed by.

A poet has said that Porto was a "vertical" city while Lisbon was horizontal, a courtesan awaiting her sailors. But from the towers of the fort equipped with heavy guns, this city seems more eager for the gold of Eldorado than for any lazy embrace.

Paris. Thursday 30 October 2003.

Thérèse de Saint-Phalle, in typical fashion, launches into a story as soon as I call her: "We're just back from Rome. I've seen the Pope!" At publisher Balland, I met the editorial team and made final arrangements for the design and printing of *Au Coeur d'Internet*. Now I'm waiting for my son on Place Saint Michel.

Weinstein recently visited Velasco at SEPRA in Toulouse. Instead of following up on serious cases, like the pilot reports Dominique is getting from Air France, Jean-Jacques is writing a book for a publisher who will sensationalize it: The same fellow made a bundle from the absurd claim that the September 11 attacks were an American dirty plot. As for Poher's recent book, with its difficult theory of universons, it is not likely to revive the subject either.

At Mabillon, the workers are busy. We move frantically from the architect to the bank, the selection of tiles for the new kitchen, all of it a welcome break from the high-tech world. We sleep in a tiny *mansarde*, a fun return to our starving student days.

Hummingbird. Thursday 6 November 2003.

Exceptional solar activity the past few days: A flare of gigantic proportions was detected two days ago, affecting satellites.

Researcher Brad Sparks thinks the most important date in American UFO research was 28 July 1952, when Blue Book was turned into a PR operation while the "real project" approved by General Stamford decreed that only instrumental cases would be seriously considered, and the flow of public reports was ignored.

They also decided to start a psychological operation to prevent panic. Brad is intrigued by the coincidence of dates between Roswell (4 July 1947) and the secret decision to begin stockpiling atomic bombs in the US. That decision, made just three days before, marked the beginning of the big arms race. LaPaz, too, suspected there was a link between the green fireballs and secret military activity in the Southwest, but he was never told about the stockpiling project going on at four locations—including the little town of Hopkinsville in Kentucky (31).

Athanor. Saturday 8 November 2003.

Winter has come to the Athanor with great blows of wind and sheets of rain. It turned the ocean into slabs of pewter and the sky a rich boiling mass of gray with white fringes. Janine is tired, slowly recuperating from the trip and a virus that has made her cough for the last three weeks. The storm is an excuse to spend the day by the fire, watching television news and an occasional soccer game, typing my notes, cleaning up our papers.

The Institute for the Future has asked me to join their Board of Trustees, to help solve a crisis of management and finance that threatens their survival. I will help if I can, for old time's sake.

Hummingbird. Thursday 13 November 2003.

Brad Sparks sends me a summary of his research:
"Dr. Howard Cross, your *Pentacle*, witnessed a Daylight Disc officially listed as a Blue Book *Unknown*, among Ruppelt's 63 best cases he kept on top of his desk, none of which were given to the CIA or the Robertson Panel. This sighting was withheld, along with all the best Unknowns."

He adds: "Hynek may have known of Cross' sighting because he represented Battelle to Blue Book and the CIA Robertson Panel (32). But maybe that was kept from Hynek, too.

"Years of complaints that the AF was not properly analyzing these reports fell on deaf ears because of a willful, secret policy decision to ignore them: UFO intelligence had focused on instrument data instead of 'worthless' civilian sightings. So you're quite right that it looks like an underground branch had a visible counterpart, but it did not *go* underground, *it was always underground*.

"It had been run by Gen. Samford's deputy, Gen. Garland, since Dec. 1951. Gen. Garland started a highly classified 'black' project on March 26, 1952, to track UFOs with sensors."

Brad believes the Air Force told the CIA it emphasized instrumentation, but it said nothing about a black project, or about a radical change to high-tech intelligence methodology, and nothing about the most sensitive collection systems being developed. CIA had no authority, then or now, to insist on AF disclosure.

"Harry Woo, the Navy analyst of the Tremonton film told me in 1975 how upset he was that Panel members were 'picking' on him, and how appreciative he was that Hynek came to his vocal defense."

Athanor. Friday 28 November 2003.

The calm before another stormy trip to Paris. Venture investments are not doing well, in Silicon Valley or in Europe. The Thanksgiving holiday gives us an opportunity to rebuild frayed nerves and recapture the long view.

Yesterday Janine and I walked some four miles along the beach to the fishing harbor, full of boats and trailers. Today is uniformly gray and cold, but we will go out again along the higher trails. At home Janine is sorting out boxes of old letters from our kids, full of wit, life, and love.

The tenderness of slowly passing time is obvious here. Another emotion rises from the gray Pacific, telling us that nothing really matters except the ability we have to love even when it hurts, even when it complicates our lives and makes us so vulnerable.

Paris. Friday 5 December 2003.

Hotel des Deux Continents, on Rue Jacob. I arrived in France in time to celebrate my son's birthday, spending the evening in the warm atmosphere he creates, with Max's laughter in the background. I saw Dominique Weinstein at Le Suffren. General Letty has introduced him to Colonel René Giraud, one of the witnesses of a remarkable encounter with a luminous object on 7 March 1977 from the cockpit of his Mirage IV, a nuclear bomber.

Research into UFOs is not dead in France, but it goes on in the unhealthy atmosphere that has condemned it to marginality, like the group organized by Morvan Salez that meets at a research center in Gif-sur-Yvette for presentations by Pierre Lagrange and Jean-Pierre Rospars. They plan for email confidentiality: is there such a thing?

Paris. Sunday 7 December 2003.

The city is gray, cold, and dry; also morose: the country finds it hard to claw its way back from the economic ravine, a big drop in business for the tourist industry. Several investment funds are in trouble; my partners react as French professionals always do, by hardening their complicated bureaucracy.

Our own results in the US are disappointing as well. At *Le Figaro* my friends are cutting down the pages they print. The *Entreprises* section is financed by recruiting ads, which have fallen precipitously.

Lunch with Gérard Deforge. He tells me of a paranormal research group around Marceau Sicaud and a woman psychic in Paris. General Letty and Rear Admiral Gilles Pinon attend the meetings but, as Sicaud says, "they don't know anything more than we do!"

Paris. Friday 12 December 2003.

Dinner last night with Janine at Dominique Weinstein's new house, a gentle old structure on three floors where Dominique has reorganized his files. Dr. Georges Leftheriotis was there from Angers, as well as François Louange and Joëlle. Louange believes SEPRA will continue in some form within CNES if only because, as he says, "It's difficult to setup something like this in our bureaucracy, but it's even more difficult to stop it!"

We discussed medical cases and the premature publication by Velasco of confidential cases with sensational headlines. "A UFO above a nuclear plant!" claims a recent issue of the *VSD* tabloid. That object may have been a balloon. Why push for such publicity?

Athanor. Sunday 14 December 2003.

We woke up this morning to the news of Saddam Hussein's capture. It closes an era of confusion and self-doubt for America, while Europe is still unable to agree on its Constitution.

Hummingbird. Thursday 1 January 2004.

A storm moved over during the night; it howls around the building, shaking rain-soaked windows. This is a day for rest and reflection after the warm holidays, the joy of having our family around the white tree.

The rain kept me inside much of the time, reading, writing dragon stories for Maxime, and watching films. Yet I dutifully drove to my office between the holidays.

New buildings keep going up in Silicon Valley, financed during the bubble. They stand empty, towering over desolate Sunnyvale or the sprawl of San Jose. Along El Camino, from Belmont to San Carlos, every other storefront is boarded up. The jobs destroyed during the crisis are not coming back; the challenge is to create new ones. The companies that survive have either reduced their staff to part-time specialists, or shifted activity to places like India.

Yesterday I spoke to Colm, who'd met Kit at a recent conference.

"Kit surprised me," he said. "He seems to believe in the core story now, although there's no evidence for it."

"He was impressed by a briefing he got, about actual bodies," I said.

"Two briefings, actually," Colm corrected me, "including autopsy reports, and schematics of saucers."

"I've got a few books here with autopsy reports and schematics of saucers," I countered. "Why the briefings, if he was never inducted into the real project? Doesn't that sound like disinformation?"

"I think he's aware of that. He speculates his critical attitude may have disqualified him from the real project."

The phenomenon remains at a low point. The Sci-Fi Channel group that gathers reports has found nothing worthy of a follow-up.

"I keep coming back to the Noxon, Montana, case," said Colm, obviously puzzled. "Two sincere witnesses described pandemonium, 'spaceships' landing in the forest, and Alien entities around their house. They called a neighbor, *who saw nothing* but "lost" a two-hour period that night. We went there several times and couldn't find anything physical: no disturbed vegetation, no traces! That was a turning point for Bob. That's when he decided to move on and concentrate on aerospace, just building space modules."

"I don't blame him," I said. "I've had that feeling many times."

"I don't blame him either, although I'd rather go back to biotech work," Colm said. "The UFO field is dead. It will take another generation to pick up the problem again. They'll have to re-invent the wheel, and they'll start wrongly, from the ETH. By then there won't be any reliable archives, and no trace of what we've done."

Athanor. Saturday 3 January 2004.

Colm's statements remind me that the disposition of my own archives is a perplexing problem. We toy with the idea of selling this place and moving the files into a proper office, perhaps even setting up a research Trust to preserve them. Yet every time we come here the view is so stunning, and the house so inviting, that those ideas evaporate.

My next project is a new venture Fund. The economy recovers slowly after two years of carnage. The Dow has just reached 10,000, the NASDAQ index 2,000. There are new worries, though, with the threat of terrorism that grounded six Air France flights over the holidays, and the first cases of mad cow disease in the US.

Bob Bigelow finds it hard to hire someone to continue the UFO work. People insinuate he's antagonized the aerospace community through his personal style, yet I admire what he's accomplished. In a field dominated by politics and big company competition, he has introduced bold, novel ideas I believe in.

Athanor. Saturday 17 January 2004.

Popular Mechanics carries a cover story by Ian Wilson implying that several countries, including the US, already have a plan "in case E.T. arrives." It would include the FBI taking control, and any Aliens quarantined in biowarfare isolation, while the Department of Energy nuclear teams investigated their saucer...one more bizarre scenario.

Over 100 planets have now been discovered outside our solar system, and the definitions of life have been expanded with studies of extremophiles. Ironically, at the same time, the growing database of UFO events keeps diverging from the extraterrestrial theory.

Later the same day.

Back on July 24, 1952, a man who was fishing at night in the Serchio River near Vico, Italy, saw a disk hovering nearby. A protruding hose plunged into the water. A man in a diving helmet looked at the witness through a window. The man received an "electric shock" as a ray of light hit him. His strength failed, and it was with difficulty that he looked up to watch the object leave.

Six days later, the witness was again fishing at the same spot when a tall, thin man who spoke Italian with a foreign accent approached him and asked if he had seen "airplanes or flying saucers" from that spot. The witness said no. The man offered him a long, gold-tipped cigarette. The witness began smoking it and thought he was about to die as his head reeled. The stranger took the cigarette away and threw it into the river, leaving the witness weak and helpless (33).

I put this in parallel with the Dr. X case, or that of Kathy Davies.

Now Ron Brinkley, who used to live and work in Alaska, sends me a perceptive analysis of Ingo Swan's book *Penetration*: "Ingo's description of his trip with Axelrod to 'the Far North' doesn't match the reality of the Far North at all. The episode with Axelrod was a theatrical production to inculcate a belief system in Ingo."

Hollywood. Saturday 24 January 2004. Hotel Roosevelt.

This hotel has been modernized, but it retains the feeling of informal convenience we enjoyed years ago, with its wonderful painted ceiling. We've spent three hours at the Getty Center.

We're always amused at the glitzy shops of Hollywood, Elvis impersonators, folks hawking maps of star homes, and the new symbols of Goth: glistening motorcycle helmets, belt buckles with skulls, and an insignia of "Area 666," a Short Gray with horns…

San Diego. Monday 26 January 2004.

The second "Spirit" robot has just landed on Mars. It receives instructions from Pasadena, not far from here, while a European probe has now transmitted evidence of water ice at the pole of the planet.

That would have pleased Gérard de Vaucouleurs, who predicted it a long time ago. We had lunch with actor Jamie Cromwell at Urth Café in Beverly Hills, and today we drove down from L.A. after lunch with Pamela de Maigret at the Renaissance. We spoke about Brazil: a return expedition? Reluctantly, I now find myself in sympathy with Aimé Michel's views at the end of his life, when he gave up research. Janine disagrees. Like Colm, she says, we're simply too early to understand.

Hummingbird. Tuesday 27 January 2004.

Today is Janine's birthday. Our friends will give a surprise harpsicord concert for her in Palo Alto.

We are happy, and aware of our happiness, to the point where Janine often wonders why we have this enchanted life we may not entirely deserve. Worries over jobs, finances, or children do arise, but they never mar the wonderment of every instant together.

Part Nineteen

PACIFIC HEIGHTS

11

Mabillon. Monday 16 February 2004.

Paris seems empty this week, many families away on ski vacations. The crowds that commonly assail department stores have moved away, so it was easy to shop for furniture and drapes for our new French home. On Thursday, they delivered the all-important bookcases; windows open to an amusing view of Saint Sulpice and the blue Norman bedroom overlooks Rue de Buci.

The place is not large, but it has a cozy library, red walls, and double glass doors.

This afternoon I walked over to Balland's office and signed press copies of *Au Coeur d'Internet*. I'm restarting my research, in new directions. It's fun to be a Frenchman again, to buy the morning paper and find the political news and Chirac's pomposity in full display as a generation of colorless leaders passes from the scene.

This is a new beginning, in other ways. I enjoy writing a weekly column for *Le Figaro Entreprises* (400,000 copies every Monday), while the media reconnect me with former friends.

Mabillon. Tuesday 17 February 2004.

Cousins from Normandy came over this morning to help assemble a traditional oak provincial wardrobe and a sculpted cabinet. Annick has given us a very old *confiturier* from Bayeux. There is something wonderful about a country that finds it necessary to have a special piece of furniture to store strawberry preserves…

The electrician who reconnected our phone line was Portuguese. He cheerfully unscrewed plates and twisted wires all over the place. The painters were from North Africa, the cabinetmakers were Italian. Others were from Poland or Turkey. All have done a superb job.

Mabillon. Friday 20 February 2004.

The cold North wind is back; sidewalks were wet with sprinkles when I walked over to *Le Rostand* to see two emissaries from a semi-mysterious group, the "European UFO Survey." I met Marina L. Lecomte there, a tall blonde with a soft hat. She was with a man named Philippe-Alexandre Gaugain, a computer consultant and author of an interesting paper on Dirac-Maxwell equations and their implications for multiple universes.

They didn't dispel the bizarre secrecy about their group, assuming, of course, that there is a real organization, so I couldn't see how to be of help. We ended up rehashing generalities and stories of unsolved encounters.

Mabillon. Sunday 22 February 2004.

Nine o'clock in the morning. We could play softball on boulevard Saint Germain without seeing a single car. Parisians get up late on Sunday, except for proper old ladies going to Mass.

I saw my brother yesterday. He marveled at Max and his Japanese robots spilling over the table. Gabriel is entering his 80th year, which must mean I'm almost 65. He worries about his wife, in therapy after spine surgery, but he has kept his sense of humor and his kindness—as long as the conversation stays away from politics.

Mabillon. Thursday 26 February 2004.

The smell of coffee has replaced the odors of fresh paint, carpet glue, and tile grout around the apartment. The old dining table from Pontoise with the sculpted lions that fascinated me as a toddler has found a new home here, along with my father's red armchair. Family photographs, old furniture: a sense of a circle closing, but not the end by any means.

Sitting in the Norman bedroom with a good book, one can survey the animated streets below and the Buci market. Every instant has meaning and surprise—every precious moment with you.

Over lunch at *Le Suffren* today, Dominique Weinstein was eager to talk, fully engaged in a catalog of pilot sightings that he keeps enriching through his contacts with sources in aeronautics.

One interesting observation has come out of that research: The behavior of the objects seen by civilian pilots is different from that in military cases. In the former, the UFO simply crosses the path of the plane; in the latter, closer attention is often displayed by the lights, including maneuvers, pursuits, and occasional dogfights.

Mabillon. Friday 27 February 2004.

Over another private lunch with General Letty (at La Chaloupe), I had a chance to get acquainted with this remarkable man and to better understand the process that led to the *Cometa* report. The shadowy group assembled by Payan is going nowhere, and its *Cometa* report hasn't led to any new action (1). Letty confirmed to me there was no connection between the report and IHEDN, other than past membership by some of the officers. He hand-carried a copy over to the Elysée Palace but has no indication it was seen by Chirac or anyone close to him. Velasco took a copy to Jospin. All that activity in and around CNES has done nothing to help SEPRA, where Velasco is as frustrated as ever; he now reports vaguely to a director he's never been able to meet.

I confirmed to the general that the report had created a stir in the US. It is one thing for civilian ufologists to speculate about possible Alien hardware recovered by the Pentagon, and quite another for high-level officers to state a similar claim in a *faux*-official report. Americans have naturally assumed France must have secret evidence for such a bold statement. No, Letty told me, it was "just a hypothesis," part of an appeal for sharing data. Then I learned that the *Cometa* members were all politically far to the right, starting with Aigrain, their attorney and spokesman. This puzzles me.

Athanor. Saturday 6 March 2004.

Back home by the Pacific shore, we drove to a secluded beach where acacias in bloom spread yellow blossoms. We had our quiet picnic there and walked around a peninsula where two ospreys fed their young in a huge nest atop a utility pole. Local park authorities have wisely given the birds a wide sanctuary.

James Westwood has a hypothesis about cattle mutilations being related to attempts to calibrate strategic factors of the Cold War. Westwood has covered the same investigative ground as Hal Puthoff and Eric Davis, even identifying their four secret "iron posts:" sources they believe to be unimpeachable, well-connected in the Intelligence establishment. They confirm the existence of a hidden project for reverse-engineering of Alien hardware.

As Westwood writes, they are: "two senior flag officers, one defense industry/high OSD official, and one civilian high official of the Reagan and Clinton administrations, all pretty much telling the same story, three of them helping manage the Defense budget." The two officers I already know to be Wilson and Sheehan.

Westwood writes (2): "Unfortunately, NIDS would not keep me on as consultant in 2001 after a written report that there is no 'ET' flying saucer hardware extant to be studied..." He's certain that, in the early 1950s, Dr. Vannevar Bush supported a strategy that cynically used the public's expectation of UFOs as a psychological warfare tool.

Reno. Friday 12 March 2004. The Silver Legacy.

On a business visit to Nevada, we heard that Kenny Rogers had a show tonight, so we bought three tickets as soon as we were settled. Undoubtedly he will be singing "The Gambler," one of the greatest songs of all time. There's still snow on Sierra peaks but the weather is mild. A sense of the future in motion can be felt here.

Chris Aubeck's latest messages speak of the carnage in Spain after the latest Al Qaeda attack, and the anger of the crowds against their government for lying about the reality of terror.

Hummingbird. Sunday 14 March 2004.

We came back yesterday morning, a three-and-a-half-hour drive through some of the greatest scenery anywhere: Donner Lake in a crown of pure snow, the forest along the slopes to Auburn, and San Francisco Bay opening up to the sound of Santana. More music last night: Krista Bennion and her New Century Chamber orchestra played Mendelssohn, William Walton, and Bartok.

Hummingbird. Friday 19 March 2004.

A reporter for *O Globo* has come over with a cameraman and news about the Lead Mask mystery (3). Their TV channel in Brazil has re-opened the case as part of a "true crime" series. They used our interview to give an international flavor to the case. For me, it's an opportunity to renew contacts in Brazil and to stimulate independent witnesses. What I said may advance the case, but it's still a mystery.

On Wednesday night, I drove to Monterey for dinner at Roy's with John A., a military strategist friend of Paul Saffo. I arrived early, having driven over the coastal range in the splendid light of Spanish Bay before the sunset. Pebble Beach had the inspiring perfection of a sacred site. John came over, walking awkwardly, "still recovering from his latest trip" but he did not elaborate about his military assignments. We spent three hours talking about remote viewing (he wanted to know the inside story), abductions, and my quiet work with John Mack, and finally my evaluation of Colonel Corso.

John has worked on computer security, cyberespionage, and the RV data. I told him my remote viewing scans suggested that Bin Laden's nerve center wasn't in the desert but at a place with communications facilities, "hidden in plain sight, in a city," still too vague.*

Having attended Russian-US meetings on remote viewing, he said the Russians confirmed the subject was taken seriously at high levels. But he's become skeptical of abduction stories, given the high proportion of cases attributable to sexual abuse in childhood, including those covered up by the Church.

I told him at length about the case related by Lindner in *The Jet-Propelled Couch*. I also took the opportunity to relate what I thought about the phenomenon itself: physically real but extending so far in history and material complexity that the ET connection was at best an

---

* Bin Laden's home was a modern complex in Abbottabad, hidden in plain sight; he had full communications facilities. In my scan I had only seen an urban site: no secret grotto, no mountain retreat with special couriers on camels...

incomplete hypothesis, one among many. John pressed me: What about the undercurrent of disinformation and manipulation? Is there a third level?

Yesterday we had radio producer Moira Gunn and her assistant Nancy for dinner to discuss her *TechNation* show and their plans for a "Summit on global challenges." Something very odd—one of my "intersigns"—happened during our discussion about mythology.

Nancy was speaking of various orders of angels, pointing out that Cherubims were not cute little babies with wings but formidable entities of light and energy. She added that Adam's first wife was not Eve but Lilith, but she couldn't recall who Litlith's consort was after Adam. "It was Samaël," I pointed out.

We were finishing dinner when the phone rang. I didn't pick it up, but once our guests had departed I found a message from the operator. Someone named Steve had put the most urgent pressure on her to pass on his phone number, so I called back and a man's voice told me breathlessly that he needed help. He was seeing Aliens on Twin Peaks and he'd just spoken… to *an apparition of Samaël* that left him terrified! He'd called to ask me to join him at the top of the hill to verify his experience…

More prosaically, one of our companies, Nanogram Devices (4) has just been acquired by Wilson-Greatbatch for a nice amount. This relieves a bit of the pressure on me because we'll be able to return money to our investors and move forward more steadily.

Athanor. Saturday 20 March 2004.

At the end of the week, I'm scheduled to fly to Las Vegas for the Bigelow reunion. One of our trusted sources wrote to me: "I gave them permission to tell you what I've discovered regarding the MJ-12 documents, the identities of Mr. X and Falcon, the issue surrounding the Holloman Air Base UFO landing film, as well as new info on the 'material' that Corso handled when he worked for General Trudeau. They will brief you on everything. I lost one of my key sources when he passed away last Fall. I have another source, but he is hard to move, due to his stature in life."

In preparation for our Scientific Advisory Board (SAB) meeting, I also read the summary of an Advanced Propulsion project for the U.S. Air Force.

Las Vegas, Friday 26 March 2004.

The Fiesta Rancho Casino Hotel on Rancho Drive. Hal and I had taken early flights in order to meet at the airport before others arrived. Without preamble, he told me Eric's story. Eric was the person who interviewed Wilson in the EG&G parking lot. He'd contacted the admiral about his project to restart a chapter of AFIO (Association of Former Intelligence Officers) in Las Vegas, and the topic drifted to ufology.

Eric is now in touch with the vice-chairman of the association, who is none other than former president George Bush, Sr. They've spoken twice on the phone. The first phone call was initiated by Bush who gave Eric some advice about AFIO and his future career. Eric told him about his interest in the Corso revelations: "Could it be that Corso was mistaken in dealing with the material he was handling? Could that have been Nazi hardware?" Eric asked.

"Impossible," replied Bush. "The two topics were clearly separated. By that time (1947) all German secrets had been processed and filed away; they were not used as cover for anything else."

Bush remembered General Trudeau. He showed interest in pursuing the discussion, asking Eric for his recent physics papers. He knew of the remote viewing project, but didn't recall Hal's name.

The second conversation was more interesting because it got into the Holloman film, which remains a fixation for Hal, Eric, and me. The former President was aware of it. Was it a training film, a special ops exercise? No, he replied, "it was 'the real thing.'" There was a secret project, and the security was "obscene."

Eric developed other sources, notably a former DIA senior officer who confirmed that DIA had a UFO collection project at one time. He promised to provide more information but died before they could meet again. His secretary found an envelope inside his desk, sealed and addressed to Eric. It contained the man's notes about the project, and the real source of the fake MJ-12 papers, with which the field of ufology remains fascinated.

The story I was told is this: In 1961, the UFO project inside the government was taken over by DIA. By the early 1980s Rear Admiral E.A. Burkhalter, Jr., who was chief of staff and acting assistant vice director in the Directorate for Collection Management, and his deputy Col. Roy K. Jonkers, USAF, were in charge of the project. They are shown in these positions on an org chart dated March 1981. The same document shows Dr. Jack Vorona as assistant vice-director for scientific and technical intelligence.

Burkhalter, calling himself "Mister X," and a man named Polko, introduced as "Falcon," decided to spread disinformation about UFOs. Apparently Dale Graff, who monitored Hal's project on behalf of DIA, wasn't in the know. The remake of the Sandler-Emenegger documentary in which I participated was the convenient platform, with the Norton episode, but when Pentagon P.R. man Colonel Coleman told us to "go out on a limb" to draw out sensational revelations, I fortunately convinced Hynek we shouldn't take the bait.

After I had derailed this first attempt to turn us into "useful idiots," Rear Admiral Burkhaklter and Polko contacted Bill Moore and Linda Howe, and reportedly spread their "revelations" through a frequently-used disinformation channel.

By then the MJ-12 documents had been re-purposed as "genuine" false documents, based on data that came from the old Eagleton's disinformation files at CIA, and ufologists the world over swallowed the bait. So everything now ties together. I still fail to see the ultimate point of such shenanigans, however.

Later the same day.

The SAB has assembled. Twenty members had dinner with Bob Bigelow tonight at the Fiesta, packed with retirees trying their luck at blackjack and one-arm bandits. Bob leaned towards me and asked what I thought would happen if the Chinese went to Mars and established a real estate empire there, neatly dividing the planet by township and range, and selling parcels: Wouldn't a new world economy be created? It would, I replied, but they're years away from such a capability.

Bob disagreed: "Microgravity will change history," he said. Yet he knows astronauts lose 2% of their bone mass per month in orbit, so we're not ready for that trip. Not to mention the DNA damage, I said. Or the unknown psychological effects so far from Earth.

Las Vegas. Saturday 27 March 2004.

We've spent a memorable day at the Bigelow Aerospace campus that now occupies some 80 acres near the North Las Vegas Airport. Only Ed Mitchell missed the meeting. Dean Judd, whom I had only met once at the beginning of the SAB, was with us again.

The day began with badging and an excursion to the explosion testing cages where Bigelow's staff (60 people now, including 20 in security) do the destructive experiments on the space modules. We were given a tour of the first hangar-like structure where the offices are, and where various models from quarter-scale to third and full-scale hang from two 15-ton cranes (nicknamed Tom and Jerry...)

In the afternoon we gathered in another building (the lobby large enough for three 18-wheelers delivering supplies) behind a double door the size of a basketball court. The desert wind was shaking it, making a loud sound that reverberated throughout the structure.

We spoke in turn about what we had been doing for the last two years. It was an interesting retrospective. JohnDale is retired but keeps an office at Los Alamos. Jim Whinnery heads up the air research program at the FAA and sits on the Air Force Reserves board. John Schuessler lectures about space exploration and still helps MUFON. He reported that UFO incidents had picked up in the US.

Warren teaches pharmaco-genetics and consults in forensic psychology. Al Harrison works on a new book about SETI. John Petersen's Arlington Institute has the defense department of Singapore as its main client. Colm Kelleher heads up Bigelow's Space Sciences Inc., reviewing experiments with NASA and microgravity tests with Bristol-Myers Squibb and Amgen.

John Alexander continues his work on non-lethal weapons but his most interesting stories are about Afghanistan, where he just spent three months as a mentor for the defense minister. Marty Piltz, also retired from Los Alamos, spoke of lasers, nanomachines, and new materials. Jessica pursues her teaching and lectures in statistics and psychical research. Dean Judd, also retired from Los Alamos, consults on missile defense, asteroids, space surveillance, and hypervelocity. He spoke of North America and Western Europe as "singularities" in today's world: on other continents, the allegiance is to a tribe, not to a national leader or an organized State, he said.

Next, Ted Rockwell launched into a long, interesting speech on nuclear misconceptions, and Kit followed with a presentation on the promise of functional MRI and magnetic resonance spectroscopy. After serving as CTO for GM in China and later for Asia-Pacific, he now runs the various medical projects I recently saw in Detroit. Hal spoke of his "clearinghouse for maverick inventors" and of cold fusion. His "zero point" research is slowly getting accepted.

When Bob Bigelow asked us if our beliefs had changed regarding UFO reality, abductions, and the potential for a secret project within the government, the room was quite divided. Dean Judd, John Alexander, and Jim Whinnery were negative on the question of "physical presence and influence of ET on Earth today," while John Petersen was a believer. Kit said abductions were a mental, not a physical process, and implants nothing more than normal, localized accumulation of fatty tissue. He left us puzzled, because there are many contradictions in the hard data.

Bigelow has scheduled his first module launch in November 2005, out of Vandenberg, on a rocket owned by Space Exploration, Inc. The package will be a one-third scale model of the human module.

Las Vegas. Sunday 28 March 2004.

This morning Hal, Eric, Kit, Kristin, and I had a long private breakfast in the hotel restaurant. Kit wasted no time in telling Eric that he shouldn't spread hypothetical stories: "Don't even try to ask about CIA, that's not where it's at, and that would be a disaster."

Eric said "the Admiral" was willing to meet with him again, but not until he'd gotten his own clearance at his new company, which takes over the manufacturing of critical space hardware. Later I heard that Dr. Pandolfi, for unknown reasons, had tried to get Hal, Kit, and even Marty stripped of their essential clearances.

Later the same day.

My own speculation is that some powerful group is trying to change reality, as in Borges' extraordinary story, "Tlön, Uqbar, Orbis Tertius." In fact, when I hear Professor Sturrock seriously considering that microelectronics could have come out of the Roswell crash, I have to realize that like so many people, he no longer relies primarily on critical analysis to build his models. They've already forgotten.

I told the group about details of my March 1985 Norton visit, when APRO leaders Tina and Brian were shown hundreds of military UFO files (5), suspended from a laundromat-type belt machine. So where are these files now? Hal and Kit replied that a few years ago there was a meeting about the disposition of those same archives, and Bob was there, possibly invited through Nevada Senator O'Donnell, whose father used to oversee the Nevada Test Site.

Kit recalled two occasions when he was told he could see the Holloman film... both of them mysteriously withdrawn the next day.

"I contacted five former DCIs about this issue," he said. Helms gave me an appointment: 'Be in front of the National Academy of Sciences at 10 am.' I went there and he never showed up. I contacted Bill Colby, about 6 months before he died. He asked me to come to his house in Georgetown: 'I'll make some coffee and we can talk.' Colby is humorless, hard to read. He once mentioned a classified project I was working on, in an open Congressional meeting, and killed it without warning me. I told him the whole story, the Holloman film, everything. He spent two hours with me, and sent me away with a single recommendation, *to go find out...*"

How likely is it that such a project would have 800 cleared names on its list? Surprisingly, that's possible. Kit said that "Project Jennifer, the Glomar Explorer, had over 5,000 names. That doesn't mean these folks knew what was going on; the levels were severely controlled. I was never cleared for it while at the Agency. General Don Flickinger kept telling me he was working on getting me cleared, but he never did.

"Once I was at GM, and got the clearance, a lot of people with whom I had been working before, some of them for twelve years, tapped me on the shoulder with congratulations: 'Glad to have you on board!' but

I had never suspected they were part of it. The funding was interesting: Jennifer was a CIA project but it was funded laterally out of the National Reconnaissance Office (NRO) budget, and even the Director of Central Intelligence was not cleared for it, although he knew there was 'a project.' This may be similar. *Typically, the integrating contractor is not the operating contractor."*

So where is the real UFO project, and how is it run? We speculate the four logical contractors would be Lockheed-Martin, the Aerospace Corporation, Raytheon (which now owns Hughes), and Northrop-Grumman, which owns the old TRW. Are they working, like my fictitious Alintel, on a genuine Alien craft, under the "obscene security" mentioned by a former President of the United States?

Athanor. Saturday 10 April 2004.

A blanket of fog weighs on us, hiding the trees and the shore. I enjoy this quiet time among the books, rearranging my records, and preparing the transfer of my parapsychology archives.

I am upset about a completely fictious "controversy" involving statements I'm supposed to have made about some investigations in Montana. So I called Grant Stapleton in England: evidently Marina Lecomte and Gauguin are repeating what I confided to them about the bizarre Montana case, and misquoted it. It is curious to see that Puthoff is also under attack, his theories about ZPE and the Casimir Force ridiculed by Sarfatti who goes so far as accusing Hal of stealing his "intellectual property." The disinformation seems orchestrated from some inside office (possibly by rogue elements around Dr. Pandolfi's office, from what I hear).

In any case the purpose is just to muddy the waters, get people upset, stimulate controversies, compromise goodwill, and generally disrupt any budding research within the community.

Athanor. Saturday 17 April 2004.

Every Thursday evening, I take a class in stained glass from Dan Gamaldi at Cradle of the Sun, a break from my venture work. I'm far from producing great beauty, but the cuts on my fingers are healing nicely and the thrill of the technique and the material is wonderful. My first piece: a simple representation of an alchemical athanor.

Athanor. Saturday 24 April 2004.

In the year 830, Caliph al-Mamun, son of the illustrious Harun-al-Rashid of *Arabian Nights*, was passing through Harran, south of Edessa (in a region that now lies at the border of Syria and Turkey) at the head of his army, on the way to fighting the Byzantines.

Observing some men in unfamiliar costume, he asked them if they belonged to one of the peoples protected by Islamic law.

Since they confessed they were neither Christians, Jews, nor Zoroastrians, he told them they must be infidels, so he would kill them all when he returned unless they adhered to one of the religions protected by the Koran.

The men were Pagans with no intention of changing their ways, so they read the tradition and discovered that it also protected the "Sabians," except that everybody had forgotten what the Sabians were all about. So they took over the name.

Tobias Churton writes: "The law required a divinely recognized prophet, together with a book to support the new nomenclature. In this regard, the learned Pagans of Harran settled on the *Hermetica* as their scripture, with Hermes as their prophet.

This timely ruse brought Hermetic gnosis to the very heart of eastern and western intellectual, practical and spiritual experience: a momentous decision whose ramifications reverberate to this day."

Indeed, it does. From 830 onwards the Arabs learned Greek science and philosophy from the Sabians of Harran, and in 856 al-Mutawakkil re-established the Baghdad library and a translation school, from which the early sciences like alchemy and astrology would flow, eventually filtering into the West centuries later and forming the foundation of all our sciences today.

It also established the basis of Western esoteric philosophy, which would flower in Rosicrucianism. I find all that in *The Golden Builders* (6), a historical fact illuminating some events all of us should have learned about in school.

Las Vegas. Thursday 29 April 2004.

Monte Lago Village, near Green Valley resort, on Lake Las Vegas. A developer has created an artificial lake here with a fake Italian town on its shore and a carillon that rings every hour. Céline Dion's helicopter flies over, taking her to the Mandalay Bay casino.

On the way here we stopped over at NIDS headquarters. I wanted Janine to see the new building and to meet with Colm and Bruce Cornet, whom I hadn't seen in years. We shared a Chinese lunch and Bruce showed us a study tracking unknown objects in Pine Ridge.

This evening a small group of venture capitalists and entrepreneurs assembled for the first conference on high-tech innovation held in Las Vegas. Lieutenant Governor Lorraine Hunt extolled the virtues of Nevada for our benefit, supposedly as a haven for startup companies running away from California's big taxes and crowding. Not a smart idea: Las Vegas is crowded, polluted, and crime is high.

Hummingbird. Saturday 1 May 2004.

Robert Bigelow very kindly invited Janine and me to his home at the Las Vegas country club today. We met in his beautiful study, a separate building with an office and library with tall shelves and inspirational sculptures by a Montana artist.

Over the next two hours Bob spoke to us freely of his interests, of incidents on the ranch (the case of the four bulls and the case of the severed cable remain especially puzzling) and of Nevada real estate trends. It was a memorable conversation with a man we admire.

Bob speaks like someone who recognizes no limit, except for the barriers of our own bureaucracies, which he detests. "My grandfather was born in a covered wagon, yet he lived to see Man landing on the moon," he observed. In 18 months, a rocket will lift up from Vandenberg (7) with the first Bigelow module deployable in space.

Mabillon. Saturday 15 May 2004.

Paris is already warm; the heat brings a close, unpleasant stillness. In the new apartment, there are toys for my grandson, books for his father, and framed family photographs. Even our old tapestry of a lady gathering roses has returned to France after its long journey.

There's a storm brewing among ufologists about electronic evidence of a string of unidentified objects by Mexican military pilots. Unfortunately, the objects were not seen visually. They were only detected in infrared by a drug-chasing plane. (8)

Friends in England have reconstructed how my brief meeting with the two emissaries of a ufology group in Paris inspired Sarfatti's spurious claim of a "war with ET" on the Utah ranch. Marina Lecomte turns out to be a childhood friend of Grant Stapleton, who introduced her to Sarfatti with stories of a sect inspired by the mythical Priory of Sion. I'd be wiser to leave my curiosity about such groups unsatisfied.

Mabillon. Sunday 16 May 2004.

The sound that rises from the boulevard is a mix of crowd voices, the roar of tires on pavement, noisy motorcycles, and people arguing loudly or calling out to friends. The bells of Saint Sulpice majestically spread their magic above it all, imposing order.

Confused by jet lag, I can't resist the urge to sleep in the afternoon, a muddled sleep fed with the anxiety of business meetings, Janine's absence, and a disorientation that is not unpleasant but simply awkward. I am, as the English would say, "out of sorts."

In the slow evening, the noise becomes more subdued. I watch the Louvre and the Institut de France turning pink as the last flames of the sun throw long shadows over these temples of culture. The first notes of a saxophone rise over the bustle of Rue de Buci; another night begins in Paris.

Hummingbird. Monday 24 May 2004.

An amusing message from Tokyo tells me that *FastWalker* is nominated for the Japanese 2004 science-fiction award. That is nice news indeed; very few novels are ever translated from French to English, and almost none into Japanese. It is ironic that *Alintel*, now recast as *FastWalker*, should find its greatest audience in Tokyo.

Athanor. Friday 28 May 2004.

Colleagues tell me that Velasco's media statements have backfired: "His book is used by Alain Bensoussan and the direction of CNES as an excuse to get rid of SEPRA. The agency is the butt of persistent requests for access to the UFO archives and attacks from both 'ufoologists' and skeptics, now united to destroy the research."

Kit talks about alleged implants: "All the ones I have reviewed (the scans and the removed objects) are collagen protein ceramic insect hairs and none are metallic... either magnetic or paramagnetic. Often, the 'implants' are not really there, or are blips in the scans. I have seen or done a dozen MRIs to date." I believe him.

Over lunch on Thursday (at our favorite place, the Fish Market in San Mateo), Bernie Haisch reminded me that Admiral Wilson had been briefed about the existence of recovered craft, although, unlike General Sheehan, *he hadn't seen anything.*

Janine drove home last night after two days helping Catherine. Her radiance amazes everyone; life with her, a magical journey.

Athanor. Sunday 29 May 2004.

Our friend Bogdan came over today with Tia Elena and his Romanian family. We spent the evening by the fire arguing about religious history, Gibbon's *Decline and Fall of the Roman Empire*, and the split between the Western and the Eastern church, defined by that missing "iota" in a Greek text of the Apostle's Creed.

They taught me that it all goes back to Arius (256-336), a Berber who was a pupil of Lucian of Antioch. He taught in Alexandria that Jesus Christ and God the Father were of a different essence (*"homoi-ousios"*) rather than of one, single essence (*"homo-ousios"*). This implied that Jesus was a created being, which denied the doctrine of Trinity since there must have been a time when Jesus didn't exist. This made man's deification impossible, a huge problem!

The controversy became significant enough that Emperor Constantine called the First Council of Nicaea, Turkey, in 325. It condemned Arius' doctrine. The great schism between the Eastern Church and the Western "Catholic" Church took place in 1054 when

Rome claimed papal supremacy and added the *filioque* clause into the *Credo*, claiming that the Holy Spirit proceeds from the Father "*and also* the Son." This became part of the official Catholic creed in Lyons in 1274, but the Orthodox Church has never accepted it.

Hummingbird. Monday 31 May 2004. Memorial Day.

Last night our young Iranian friend, harpsichordist Mahan Esfahani, finished his Stanford concert with a *Sad Pavane for these terrible times of war*. The revelation of the use of torture by Americans in Iraq, supported by horrible photographs, shows how sordid the Bush administration has become. The US has lost the moral high ground it was supposed to hold in the Middle East.

Interestingly, the news reports have briefly mentioned that the torture and intimidation project was an SAP, a *Special Access Program*, setup by Donald Rumsfeld. Even though this item quickly vanished from the media, and no journalist had the guts to follow-up, it served as another interesting glimpse into the black world.

I have spent the morning sorting out old correspondence and photographs. Much beauty has passed, and much sadness, and attempts noble or foolish to touch the edges of human vision.

At the Athanor too, I streamline the files and the books. Some of the items I dredge up deserve special attention, like the case of old Mr. Dale I once met in Oklahoma City. He told me about a sighting in 1938 on his grandparents' farm near Joplin, Missouri. As the object landed, flames came out of the bottom while sparks flew around. They observed this for four minutes, noticing a door, but no windows or occupants. The object rose straight up, veered east, and vanished over the horizon with a roar heard by neighbors. A freshly slaughtered hog was found near the landing site and a large burned ring in the grass. In later life the witness served as ground crew in the Air Force for 17 years, then became a security guard.

Such stories spray cold water on current theories about cattle mutilations, including those of Colm Kelleher and Jim Westwood. Among the letters I throw out, some readers urge me to continue my research even as they confess they have become too scared or too disgusted to pursue their own work on such topics.

Hummingbird. Thursday 10 June 2004.

After a staff meeting at the Institute for the Future, Peter Banks took me aside today and said he received a curious visit from a CIA staffer who wanted to talk about China. Just as he was about to leave, he mentioned me. "You have an interesting man on your Board of Trustees," he said, seemingly as an after-thought.

Peter assured him I was well respected in the field, but he now wonders what that was all about.

Now the news brings word of the death of Ray Charles. Janine and I will always remember the enthusiasm that filled the room when we heard him in Austin a few months after we arrived in Texas in 1962.

Paris. Wednesday 16 June 2004.

Restaurant Le Suffren. I am early, waiting for Dominique Weinstein. Paris is moist and too warm, fortunately tempered by a breeze today. I have four more meetings this afternoon, including a briefing for one of our main investors, in a strange atmosphere for business.

France is caught between ambitious center-right politicians like Sarkozy who try to accelerate reforms, and the entrenched forces of the large unions, spurred to action by alienated workers.

There was another street demonstration yesterday, underlined by multiple power failures. The public is not rallying behind the demands of the fat-cat electricians, who have cozy pensions and secure jobs—hardly poster children for a hypothetical, long-suffering French proletariat.

A man named François Parmentier has published a book on UFO disinformation, clearly inspired by Payan. He lives in Nancy and seems obsessed by "Intelligence," yet his text is well documented. He even quotes John Arquilla appropriately ("The next war will not be won by those with the best weapons but by those with the best story"), but his biases lead to absurd conclusions.

Payan was at one time close to "eastern powers" and did extensive work on advanced lasers with soviet scientists. But for whom does he work now? And why is he hiding it?

Anti-American sentiment has never been so strong in France,

including in police circles. As for the members of *Cometa*, they do lean to the political extreme: Algrain, their spokesman, was a local candidate for Le Pen's Front National in recent elections.

Paris. Thursday 17 June 2004.

Restaurant Le Madrigal. Yesterday, Électricité de France (EDF) workers cutoff electrical power for 15 minutes throughout the business section of Paris, just to make a point. I was in the middle of a meeting with an executive at a large insurance company. We continued our discussion in his office, still stately but darkened, made silent as all the equipment switched off.

Over dinner with four executives of EDF who invited me to join the board of Easenergy, their innovation subsidiary in California, I learned that striking workers had turned off power to their headquarters and rang the alarms, prompting evacuation and throwing their bosses into the street—the supreme insult for Utility executives.

In their own call centers, the striking workers have found a clever way to freeze operations: they remove the balls of the computer mice, a process they humorously call "deratization," throwing client records into chaos.

With or without electrical power, Paris is wonderful, the late spring putting a touch of excitement on every casual encounter.

Mabillon. Sunday 20 June 2004.

Apart from a sudden cold front and a cloudburst yesterday morning, when we attended Max's school party, Paris has remained sunny and the air clean. The surprising fact is the energy of the crowd: vital, happy, and bent on spending. So all is well after all.

Over lunch with Dr. Pouletty, who has new offices at Truffle Ventures, I spoke of my future Fund.

He warned me that everything was political in France, especially money, and there's no progress on the funding of venture capital by major insurance companies that represent the only large source of long-term financing for innovation.

Mabillon. Monday 21 June 2004.

My Manhattan partners, Fred Adler and Philip Chapman, are already in Paris, at Hotel George V. Our meetings will determine our strategy for the next year, so I am staying focused on investment priorities.

My brother came over for lunch with Jeannine yesterday. We had a relaxed, warm afternoon together, talking about family history, reflecting on our parents' exceptional courage when they returned from Normandy in the midst of war, having lost everything they owned under the bombs, including a few treasures: the piano from my father's younger sister Valérie, who had died in '36, and a country clock made from the wood of a cherry tree that grew in their grandfather's garden, in Mesnil-Rogues…

Mabillon. Thursday 24 June 2004.

My meeting today at *Caisse des Dépots*, heart of French finance, on a high floor of the Montparnasse building that towers above Paris, as CDC dominates the French economy, provided an ironic window into the bureaucratic mind. The building itself is an arrogant disgrace and an insult to the former artistic, vibrant cultural center that was Montparnasse in the early part of the 20th century—razed to make room for this monstrosity of asbestos and concrete.

I told Monsieur Dupont that I had two choices for my next Fund: either a pure American project, investing primarily in Silicon Valley, or a true transcontinental fund with a French team and an American team working on the same deals to support technology startups. He looked at me skeptically and, instead of discussing the merits of the idea, simply asked how old I was. I answered that the question would be illegal in the US and that I was 10 years younger than Warren Buffett, the wise man of Omaha, who is fine.

Then I politely took my leave and walked over to the Métro.

Mabillon. Saturday 26 June 2004.

The weather is perfect now, balmy with a touch of pleasant breeze. All along the Seine people are lounging, lovers kissing, kids playing.

So why is it that I long to be back in California, where my heart and my lungs always seem to expand to their full dimensions, and my mind to its potential? I mistrust the system here. It is as if there was a barrier I could not breach, a level of hidden decisions I could never grasp, manifesting the deeply corrupt *nomenklatura* that rules the country under the glamor of its old culture.

Another important factor is the extinguishing of the spiritual flame. Any expansion of the mind is censored, attacked, interdicted. My young friend Eric Rauley, who organizes a conference on science, was told there must be no reference to parapsychology (although the French co-invented it). Yet it would take little for the spirit to blossom because great talent is there, and so is the money. The obstacles have to do with cultural points of view that are inflexible.

Later the same day.

Gérard Deforge comes over with news from Haravilliers: Our main witness, Mr. Delangle, has become convinced he's an abductee, heavily influenced in this direction by a cohort of ufologists who plan to hypnotize him again, much against my advice.

Franck Marie, whom I hadn't seen in many years, had lunch with me at *Le Départ* with more details about the observations of November 5, 1990. This man has done extraordinary work, cataloging and classifying thousands of cases by himself. Then our waiter, hovering around us during the discussion, volunteered he'd seen a shiny, flying metal disk as a kid, near Oléron Island. Unreported.

Hummingbird. Sunday 18 July 2004.

We just hosted a conclave of scholars worried by mysteries and teased out of their rational work by horrible tales of abduction, rape, and the end of civilization. David Jacobs, who came to our home this evening with his son Alex, regaled us with story after story of hypnotically-regressed victims testifying to an invasion of flying saucer Insectoids and the Short Grays under their command. The Grays are impregnating women against their will, he claims, to create a race of hybrid babies that will gradually replace humans on Earth. This started in the late 1800s, as he computes it.

Peter Sturrock was here with local members of our defunct Science Explorers Club: graceful Marsha Adams, Federico Faggin and his wife Elvia, real estate tycoon Dick Adams and his wife, and Dr. Richard Blasband, an orgone therapist. There were few questions because David spoke incessantly, as if driven by the theory.

This made for a colorful *soirée* as the guests enjoyed the coffee, the various teas, and the food. Janine supplied exquisite Chinese pastries, an almond tort and an Italian chocolate cake, then she leaned back in amused contemplation of Jacobs' spectacle. *If the Earth is about to be taken over by horrible hybrid creatures, we might as well enjoy our last few days on the planet*, we thought as the fog rolled up to our windows, sealing the apartment from the world, with shadows creeping up the spines of the old books lining the walls.

We felt like challenging Jacobs' theories, but we were the hosts and preferred to maintain a harmonious atmosphere. Everybody else seemed too stunned, or too intimidated, to raise any question, so images of Insectoid invasions kept pouring out until David decided it was time to leave.

Athanor. Saturday 7 August 2004.

We woke up engulfed in fog again, but it lifted just before noon, when we walked onto the beach with a picnic lunch and scrambled at low tide over piles of rocks. Janine is full of energy, both mentally and physically. She ran up the cliff ahead of me.

I have been watching two recent exchanges of electronic mail that made me think about an old theory of Fred Beckman's. He believed that the Black World of intelligence was run by a cadre of very smart men who knew about UFOs and studied them in secret. I have always discounted this idea as far-fetched; any such system of closed knowledge would soon dry up, as was the case with soviet science.

The first document came from one Andrew D. Basiago of Vancouver, who calls himself a "solo legal practitioner": "During the years 1967 to 1972, I was a child psychic and early time-space explorer in a set of classified, defense-related research and development activities undertaken by the United States government under a project named Pegasus. The involved agencies included ARPA, the US Navy, and NASA. The Ralph M. Parsons Company was one of the involved defense contractors. In said capacity, I participated in several advanced technical activities that remain secret and that are believed by the general public to exist only in the realm of science-fiction. Supposedly, the 140 schoolchildren involved were selected because ARPA wanted to test responses to quantum technologies it was developing; the children were used as participant-observers in remote viewing activities; innate psychic and cognitive abilities were cultivated and enhanced, and they were trained for future time-space exploration programs."

I did ask Hal Puthoff and Kit Green about the claimed project. Hal answered it made no sense to him: "Seems like a fellow who wants to develop a book/TV series and needs to try out the ideas on someone like you. I have no evidence that ARPA ever got that advanced on quantum concepts, since they still fund much more mundane things they wouldn't need if they already had that in place."

Kit, however, gave a different response: "There was an actual project. It failed. This guy is seriously exaggerating. One of the reasons the project was killed is because it actually yielded no results at all, other than in the delusional minds of many subjects."

This brings us to Jack Sarfatti and the 1953 phone call. ("I am a conscious computer on board a spacecraft from…We have identified you as one of 400 young bright receptive minds we wish to … You must give us your decision now. If you say yes, you will begin to link up with the others in 20 years.")

Sarfatti did write, on July 31: "I was recruited as a kid in Walter Breen's group as part of a covert operation by Eugene McDermott, a co-founder of Texas Instruments using William Sheldon at Columbia University psychology department and an intelligence bigwig from WWII. We kids were tested for psychic powers by Breen and were told that the saucers were real and that we would figure out how they worked later on. Men in black from 'New Mexico' showed up to monitor Walter Breen's progress with us kids. Puharich was in the background back then, as were L. Ron Hubbard, Ayn Rand and even Isaac Asimov whom I met, with Breen, when I was 14."

He goes on to claim that Hal Puthoff's Austin lab is only a front, and that the real lab is underground "as described in Jacques Vallee's *FastWalker*."

Four days later a man named Terry Arbegust sent Sarfatti a reference to interviews of John J. Ford and Walter Breen that mentioned "Superkids" in the period 1955-56. (If nothing else, I thought, this would tie in with Roger Brenner's experiences.)

Terry Arbegust writes: "Around the early 1950s I was part of an after-school group of gifted kids (including Johnny Glogower who worked with me, and Lenny Susskind at Cornell later on) conducted by the late Walter Breen. Breen was a graduate student at Columbia and well-known numismatist associated with psychologist William Sheldon. Breen had a connection with the nuclear weapons laboratory, Sandia Corporation, because we were visited by two men from Sandia who lectured us on 'patriotism' and 'anti-communism' when they took us to dinner in New York's Germantown.

"Breen was closely connected with people in Ayn Rand's circle. I was recruited into Breen's group by another kid in my Junior High School named Robert Bashlow. Breen arranged a full scholarship for me to go to Cornell at age 17 by writing an extensive psychological profile...he predicted I would make revolutionary discoveries.

"My professors at Cornell like Hans Bethe, Robert Wilson, Phil Morrison, all were major figures in the Manhattan Project at Los Alamos near Sandia. Breen recently died in prison, convicted of child molestation. I was definitely never molested by Breen or any of the other adults that I met in his apartment and I never heard any suggestions of that by the other kids. Indeed, Breen had two children with the well-known science-fiction fantasy writer, Marion Zimmer Bradley who wrote *The Mists of Avalon*. Breen told me he did much of the scholarly research for that book. I would run into him about every 10 years, or so, up until about 1990..."

Athanor. Saturday 14 August 2004.

Patricio Abusleme, a young Chilean journalist who researches UFO cases, has come over for dinner with his brother. He has been investigating the famous case of Corporal Valdes, an Army officer who was confronted with luminous objects that landed close to his unit's position on 25 April 1977. The event involved the fact that Valdes returned from his investigation of the lights with five days' worth of beard, and his digital watch showed five days' elapsed time, when he had only been away for a few hours.

Morgane is back in California, so she came up to the Athanor with us. We went to lunch in Bodega Bay. We showed her the cliffs and our foggy shoreline, the rocks and the caves, worthy of hypothetical Lemurians. We spoke of books and of the Angels of the invisible planes where she says she travels in her spiritual work.

Most of my focus now is on the launch of our next Fund, in close connection with a group of industrialists and financiers from Silicon Valley. We met with Calsters on Thursday and will go to Montréal on Monday and Tuesday, to visit major investment groups. I am returning alone through Washington to spend some quiet time with my good friend Bob Chartrand, the only person currently in a government position whom I can trust, to assess what I've learned of the supposed deep project.

Back in France, Velasco is now re-attached to the director's office with an empty "mission" that deprives him of any ability to do research work, as a delayed result of the backfiring *Cometa* fiasco.

Washington, D.C. Thursday 19 August 2004.

Chevy Chase Holiday Inn. After a long day of meetings in Montréal I landed at National Airport (now Ronald Reagan Washington National Airport), passing the dark shape of the Pentagon. An "orange alert" is in effect in Washington. Bob Chartrand came to pick me up in his fine vintage white Cadillac and drove me to the Kenwood club, where he and his wife go for lunch. Our conversation started with pleasant recollections of the Al Gore Hearings on emergency management. I have followed the conclusions of the 9-11 Commission, I told him, and it reminded me of the recommendations we made in our own report 20 years ago (9), which of course were never followed by the Administration.

Bob is skeptical that much change will take place this time either, because the restructuring of the intelligence community means establishing yet another bureaucracy, with the creation of a Department of Homeland Security.

Erecting one more layer of complexity is a poor way to solve the problem of having too many heavy layers of complexity, but in Washington this kind of reasoning is meaningless.

Over tea in the deserted lunchroom (I was beginning to understand why this is the ideal place for a confidential discussion, more secure than any SCIF), I gave Bob the brief memo I had prepared about my findings and those of Hal and Eric. He was silent for a long time and then commented, very systematically, on the political history of the phenomenon, point by point, with an amazing recollection of all the names and details. He laughed as he recalled the Mendel Rivers Hearings to which Hynek had contributed, and for which Bob had prepared briefing papers on behalf of the Congressional Research Service. Everyone thought it was going to be a breakthrough, given all the luminaries ready to testify.

Mendel Rivers had opened the Hearings by saying, "I don't know about UFOs but my wife believes in them, and by God, we're gonna get to the bottom of this!" to the amazement (or amusement) of the Joint Chiefs, who were sitting in the front row.

Bob laughed, and I reluctantly joined him in his amusement, recalling all the effort that had gone into preparing Hynek's testimony, and all the wasted time.

Coming back to my memo, he focused on the name of John Hamre, former Assistant Secretary of Defense and head of SAPOC. Bob works for Hamre at CSIS, the Center for Strategic and International Studies. Another potential contact is Porter Goss, currently designated but not yet confirmed by Congress, as the next director of Central Intelligence. They are well acquainted through various task forces on emergency management. Goss has asked Chartrand to serve as an informal "conduit" to him on information that might not reach him through ordinary official channels, so this is in fact the ideal way to get my memo to the top of the establishment.

Naturally the only significant breakthrough would come from the realization that, after so many years of pointless studies, perhaps it's time to try a different approach.

Over the next hour Bob and I spoke about Donald Keyhoe, whose book *Flying with Lindbergh* he's long admired, and of Art Lundahl, about whom he told me more anecdotes. He also mentioned a little-known piece of history he had preserved: the recovery of US bombers sent over Okinawa during World War II, intercepted by Russian fighters and forced to land at Vladivostok.

Brentwood Heights. Saturday 28 August 2004.

My friend Pamela has a fine old house on Bundy Lane in this exclusive western suburb of Los Angeles, a few blocks away from the notorious mansion where O.J. Simpson was arrested after the murder of his wife, and a few short miles from the Getty Museum. We arrived after a pleasant lunch at Mirabelle in Hollywood. I was eager to ask about her contacts in Brazil; she had a close friend (João) with access to their Air Force, who promised to look for the missing reports on the Amazonian sightings.

"First, he was told very officially that there were no such reports," said Pamela. "So he insisted and gave them the published details from your book. Well, perhaps there had been one incident. And what about the reports? Well, perhaps there had been documents but they weren't available: *Nobody knew where they were*."

She went on to tell me the real inside story, and how the clumsy American attempts to get the information had pitifully backfired.

Tracy and Robin's wedding reception took place at Mel Tormé's old house on Hidden Canyon Drive, down from the gorgeous vistas of Mulholland. On every trip to Hollywood, I recall the mystical and disturbing atmosphere of my intense first visits there. The spiritual sense gets eroded quickly, however. After a couple of days, I just want to leave, so we returned to the quiet beauty of Brentwood Heights, where Pamela told us of the recent Mexican sightings. She happened to change planes in Cancun shortly after the news hit the media, so she innocently walked over to the parked military aircraft to take some pictures. As expected, a man in uniform stopped her, so she engaged him in conversation (in her fluent Spanish) and found out he was the co-pilot of the leading plane during the night in question. The crew did see three of the lights; they were anything but bubbles of hot air over some drilling platform, as the fake official explanation went. *So there were visual sightings after all.*

What makes the journey so special is the luxury of Janine's presence. To some extent the exploration has succeeded, the research led to a few certainties, yet my ambition is more focused now. I am less of a rebel, even if I still hate the bloody mess of politics and the hypocrisy of much of the posturing that passes for science.

Janine has taught me how to look at all this through the quiet stability of conscience and the simple perspective of love. Such is the sense I bring back from every trip with her, whether it is a walk down the block to see a movie or an expedition to the Amazon to talk to the Brazilian Air Force.

Yet I still want to know what it is they saw, flying around Colares back in 1977, and why the real reports have been kept under lock and key for so long.

Athanor. Saturday 4 September 2004.

Labor Day weekend. A thick band of fog has now swept in from the north, blurring the shore, filtering the sun. The light has turned to a golden tint, while the atmosphere has become still and stifling. The world is breathless, suffocating, waiting for something.

The news is filled with the raging aftermath of a terrorist attack in Southern Russia where Chechen extremists have taken over a school. Children and teachers have now died by the hundreds, as Russian troops stormed the place.

The planet is witness to an escalation of horrors so simple and brutal that there is nothing to say about it.

We walked up to the monastery lands and over to the Estero under the honey-colored light. One could look at the sun directly through the high cloud that takes the color of pewter at the edge of the horizon, yet seems so thin overhead that blue sky pierces through it. It is a miraculous light, a glow worthy of Fatima, the stuff of apparitions. Then back home, the television news, the horror of the slaughter of hostages in Russia.

The death toll keeps escalating, over 300 now.

Athanor. Saturday 11 September 2004.

At the Technation Summit yesterday, an invitation-only event held at the Lone Mountain College of USF under Moira Gunn's efficient direction, I had a chance to meet several people I had wanted to contact for a long time. Larry Lessig and Dan Gillmore were there and Robert Kennedy Jr. gave the keynote speech.

It was a sparkling September day, with splendid views of San Francisco, as we ate lunch with the clerics and discussed the future under the trees of this Jesuit University, well detached from the sinful world below.

It amused me to recall that Anton LaVey once started a rumor that the Atlanteans had consecrated the Lone Mountain to Jupiter.

New York. Monday 20 September 2004. Times Square Westin.

Fred Adler received us this morning at his splendid apartment where we had his full attention and plenty of good advice for our future fund. This is UN Week: Many heads of state are in NY with dozens of security people, blocking the East side. The fine weather in this city fails to move me. If New York was a meal, it would be a three-egg omelet with bacon and melted cheddar, followed by a pint of vanilla ice cream, washed down by beer.

I've had friends here over the years but nothing remains of the emotions that were attached to them, or our meetings. This giant city just moves on. *Who the hell cares?*

Hummingbird. Wednesday 22 September 2004.

It is San Francisco I love, breathing that "succulent wind" Jolie Holland sings about so well; or taking in the sights of Noe Valley, where I still go every Thursday night to learn the techniques of stained glass at Cradle of the Sun; or simply strolling down the street to a movie with Janine. The other day (we were on our way to see *Intimate Strangers*), we walked behind a young man who pulled a strange wooden box, the size of a human body, awkwardly balanced upright on two small wheels. A horrible odor exuded from it. A decomposing cadaver? It couldn't be, could it, rolling down the sidewalk in the middle of the city? The fellow who was heaving it paused at every block, looking anxiously over his shoulder at the street. Whatever vehicle was supposed to arrive was lost somewhere, the scene more bizarre than anything in a horror movie.

Bob Chartrand has called me back. He wasn't able to connect with John Hamre: the Center is fully involved in developing a strategy for Iraq, he said. But he had three questions. (1) Was it my intention to personally meet Hamre? I answered I would drop everything and fly there if that was possible. (2) Should he give him my memo? The thought had actually kept me awake. Although it mentions no names of sources (other than the obvious ones of Sheehan and Wilson, and Ed Mitchell who has spoken publicly on the issue), people could be traced and ostracized. I trust Bob, however. In telling him this story I am only doing my duty: if my friends are right, the project in question is a misuse of national assets and possibly illegal, dangerously so. Perhaps Bob could let Hamre read the memo but not keep it, so it wouldn't be entered into an official record. (3) Would I recommend that he contact someone within the project now? I hadn't thought of that, but Hamre might not have the clearances for access any more.

Hummingbird. Friday 24 September 2004.

Jim Westwood, in Virginia, has come up with new data, looking up archives and inspecting government documents. He's close to Fred Durant (of the old Robertson panel) and his contemporaries. He's uncovered a third official trail into the secret UFO project through Charles Bowsher, Comptroller General of the United States under President Reagan from 1981 to 1996. He may be one of the four "iron posts" beyond Sheehan and Wilson. Bowsher found a crashed UFO program during a massive audit of classified projects: "Less than a handful of officials knew about it."

In the period 1984-85, Bowsher uncovered a bizarre special access program coverup which surely violated every classification, executive order, regulation, and Congressional rule.

They contemplated turning it over to Justice for prosecution, but "a powerful person in DoD quenched it." The program, according to the

Fig. 9. With Dr. Kelleher and Janine at the new NIDS building, Apr. 2004.

Fig. 10. Mapping Oceania UFO sites with Professor David Swift, Honolulu, July 2005.

reviewers, had to do with *an exotic, non-Earthly vehicle.*

I am 65 today and generally in good shape. I've cut by half the only medicine I use. I still get out of breath easily, and my legs get more tired than they used to, but that is due more to my laziness and lack of exercise than to age. As for Eric Davis, he now has a job in Austin with Hal, working on three projects: plasma propulsion, zero-point energy, and advanced communications.

Mojave Spaceport. Tuesday 28 September 2004.

The Xcor Corporation, a neighbor of Burt Rutan's Scaled Composites, has invited me to their big barbecue at Hangar 61. Tomorrow, SpaceShipOne will take off with pilot Mike Melville and the equivalent weight of two more passengers. It will have to repeat the exploit within two weeks (on October 4, anniversary of Sputnik), reaching 100 km altitude, to win the $10 million X-Prize. I cannot help but reflect that yesterday would have been my mother's birthday. How she would have loved to see this!

Just now, a terrible message from Hal says that John Mack has died, crushed by a car in England...a big shame, a setback to research. He just heard it from Joe Firmage, and we're all in shock.

Mojave. Wednesday 29 September 2004.

Melville bravely took the spaceship up beyond 100 kilometers, but not without anguish when the craft started spinning wildly before the top of its climb. Then we witnessed true American spirit, intact and undiluted, as he ignored instructions to land, risking his life.

What the news reports cannot convey are the emotion and the swelling feeling of camaraderie, the magnificent rise of innovation, and daring exploration that infused the entire crowd.

At Xcor, I met Rich Pournelle and their president, Jeff Greason. Sally Rayl, whom I had last seen in 1996, was at the barbecue, held on the runway among parked F-4 jets. In the breakfast line at dawn, I saw Bob Bigelow and an enthusiastic Pamela, who wouldn't miss such an event. They were with their friends from Vulcan Ventures.

Athanor. Saturday 2 October 2004.

More news of John Mack's death at age 75 in a deserted London neighborhood, at 11 pm after a conference on T. H. Lawrence. He was run over by a truck driven by a drunken man now held for manslaughter. Sarfatti and his group are already busy inventing dark conspiracies around the accident. Here, more prosaically, we put things in order in anticipation of our trip to China next week.

12

Hong Kong. Saturday 9 October 2004.

We landed at the new airport, far from the city. The bus follows long bridges and tunnels, evidence of formidable changes since my first visit. The view is split between cliffs of thin vertical buildings on every island and the jumble of lighted ships in the harbor, cranes and containers everywhere.

On the day before our flight, I had breakfast with Bob Theleen of Chinavest at Silks, in the financial district. He gave me the perfect introduction to the trip, a lecture on the history of China as seen from the West, and guidelines to use when speaking with entrepreneurs:

"In the 15th century, China was the largest power on Earth, over 25% of global GDP, but it never had a *Renaissance*! In Western history, the trial of Galileo marked the decisive moment when factual observation of nature became divorced from blind belief, but China didn't have a similar epiphany until the 1970s, under Deng Zhao Ping. Even Maoism was in many ways a simple continuation of imperial structures, a veneer of communism over the Chinese mindset.

"Mao had never set foot outside China, but Deng had worked in France and he never forgot his days at Renault, his experience in a major industrial power. When he was asked how a particular decision could be reconciled with Marxism, he famously answered, 'I don't care if a cat is black or white, as long as it catches mice!' That policy marked the turning point, the intellectual birth of the new China."

Bob urged me to pay attention to the universities; they will be the cradle of modern Asia. "Shanghai is the business center, the New York of China, but the future will be spelled out in Beijing."

We began our stay in Hong Kong with lunch at the top of Victoria Peak and a tour of the New Territories, north of Kowloon, from the Bamboo Forest Monastery to the Shenzhen River. The next day, our business meetings began across the galleries and various skyscrapers, in the elegant offices of law firms for a panel of investors that included the ever-present Carlyle Group, and then an interminable lunch of Chinese delicacies. In the afternoon, a boat took us through the harbor and beyond Aberdeen in the haze and the smog of a hundred factories, in the wake of countless container ships. The sun set, deep red in a sky veined with heavy fumes.

Shanghai. Wednesday 13 October 2004.

On the "Bund," the large boulevard that borders the Huangpu Jiang River (10), the stone buildings of old China stand as stately reminders of the European presence with their columns and balconies. Across the river surges a science-fiction landscape, Manhattan meets Las Vegas in weird towers and massive skyscrapers. Our hotel, the Shangri-La, is recessed from the river by ostentatious gardens, while the surrounding area remains a construction zone. Taxis race against cement trucks, buses, and weird contraptions pulled by bicycles.

Chinavest has offices on the Bund. Very efficiently, they had called me in Hong Kong to arrange a meeting, and directions were waiting at the hotel. Their entire Shanghai team met with us to speak of our respective projects, our early-stage investments, and on their side, the massive changes in Asian cultures.

Janine and I returned to the Bund for dinner. Both sides of the river were illuminated in neon, giant ads flashing. Chinese masses are discovering the magic of modern brands and the joys of fast living. All is not rosy in this explosive Asian miracle. In a prominent local family who'd bought several Ferraris, husband and wife promptly killed themselves in style on the busy road. Hong Kong records several suicides a week by failed real estate speculators.

Beijing. Thursday 14 October 2004.

I had been warned about this, but the contrast is stunning after Shanghai, with the heavy influence of the State most obvious here. This is a city of bureaucrats, designed by bureaucrats, with huge square buildings on both sides of straight avenues that go on forever to the edge of the smog. Everything is oversized and overbuilt, with sparse reminders of the old China in a few dark alleys, and the odd red pagoda still standing among bulldozed suburbs. Pollution is overwhelming, traffic a nightmare.

In spite of this, the enthusiasm of the young crowd is infectious. Dozens of fragile software companies are being created. We're approached at every turn by entrepreneurs thrusting forward their business card: "Pleased to meet you, my name is Bill." Forget the inscrutable East and the ritual innuendoes of Japanese financiers: the Chinese frankness is refreshingly blunt. They are well aware that corruption among their elders and local officials will restrict their growth. They tell us frankly how they view us as both competitors and colleagues—language Californians love to hear.

Entire sections of the city have been razed to make room for technology parks with ecological design and futuristic lakeside vistas reminiscent of Silicon Valley, while the bars of Beijing are filled with fashion models and the new stars of Asian media, signs of excess after decades of restraint. We came back to the Hyatt tired and fairly stunned, carrying a stack of business cards and glossy brochures. It was too late to visit the Forbidden City, but a stroll across Tiananmen Square gave us a taste of the scale and ambition of the country, a brief initiation to a lasting lesson.

Hummingbird. Sunday 17 October 2004.

A fruitful trip has ended. Everything was in place when we got back to our love nest in the clouds. The City is cool, ready for rain. In London, John Mack's body has been cremated. Silly rumors of his assassination have been replaced by equally silly stories that he now communicates psychically from beyond the grave. We learn of the death of Betty Hill. Sadness has deepened.

Another page turns: Colm Kelleher has accepted a job with Prosetta (through an initial contact at HandyLab). He'll leave NIDS in November. The website has already been shut down, with a terse message blaming the low level of UFO activity: no field investigation for the last two and a half years...

I am hard at work with Chris Aubeck in Madrid, compiling *Wonders in the Sky*, having always thought that the best time for research was the quiet period, when no one was looking.

Hummingbird. Friday 22 October 2004.

Colm tells me that Bob Bigelow pulled the plug on the NIDS website within an hour of his resignation. All investigation reports, all the papers, all the data we collectively published vanished from the web.

The rain has come over the Bay in wide blades of wetness that washed away any trace of dust and fog ahead of the elections. The media echoes with statements, exaggerations and accusations exchanged between George W. Bush and John Kerry. The candidates and their parties promise grandiose reforms and glorious deeds they are plainly incapable of delivering. I will vote for Kerry because there's a greater chance of shoring up public liberties under his administration, but he's done or said nothing to indicate that he could assemble a credible team, or solve real problems.

The only source of clarity in America today is the team around Bush with their simplistic statements about a "polarized world." The word "polarization" itself is a trap: it only involves two players. Can global politics be reduced to that? How silly! But Kerry, in response, only makes vague statements of tepid integrity under layers of wishful thinking.

Athanor. Saturday 6 November 2004.

The country has elected Bush to a second term, so California woke up in a deep funk on Wednesday. As Janine kept reminding me, John

Kerry never had a program, not even the beginnings of a plan. This wouldn't be too scary, because economics find their own level and even the Iraq war will be a passing episode, unless deep divisions over religious issues drive the country further into fanaticism.

Eric Davis' report to the Air Force on advanced transportation concepts, which include traversable wormhole theories inspired from Hal Puthoff and our joint paper given in Porto, has only triggered strident criticism among academic physicists.

Now the fog closes off our view of the ocean. At our office, life revolves around a constant parade of bright teams with new ideas in engineering, medicine, or energy systems. Soon I'll be in Paris again for a whole month in Europe, but this is a time of happiness for me in California, with Janine at my side, her soft presence and sharp mind, and the fine balance we have engineered between work and play, travel and leisure, the City and the mystical peace of this Athanor, overlooking the blessed "Coast of Dreams" our neighbor Dr. Kevin Starr has just described in his new book about California (11).

Hummingbird. Tuesday 9 November 2004.

Often, I wake up about 5am and fall again into an exhausting false sleep. The world intrudes as soon as we turn on the TV. First, the French news with their falsely sophisticated analyses, then the American networks with their simplistic vision of events abroad. Arafat is dying in Paris, praised fanatically by the Palestinian people. When will they pick a hero who isn't a bloodthirsty killer? There's a civil war in the Ivory Coast, punctuated by the haggard look of displaced families. The crushing of Fallujah goes on in Iraq, another demonstration of American military prowess with a very thin coat of rationality, ready to be punctured by the next car bomb, the next kidnapping, the next global strike by terrorists.

It could come in the guise of a new virus. At a breakfast meeting this morning in Palo Alto, I heard the CEO of Anacor discuss biowar and the need for novel vaccine technologies. The panel included a physician from Chiron and a woman partner with In-Q-Tel, the VC fund of the CIA.

Perhaps because I was so tired, I got impatient and stood up to offer pointed comments. "Are you guys kidding? A vaccine against what?" I asked. "The basic data is hidden away. The Soviets have many variants of their smallpox weapon; and by the way, why wasn't the perpetrator of the anthrax attack in Washington ever identified, since he must've been an American scientist, *one of us*? The healthcare system is so mismanaged that we don't have enough respirators in California to face the next 'ordinary' flu epidemic!"

At once, I regretted this outburst, but to my surprise the rest of the discussion focused on my arguments. Some only shook their heads, while others came up to give me a business card. One of the participants was Larry Brilliant, a co-inventor of the Well, who remembered Notepad.

Athanor. Saturday 20 November 2004.

After years of promises, the government has released the so-called "Star Gate Archive," a massive collection of 12,000 documents, or 90,000 pages devoted to remote viewing. According to Joe McMoneagle, "it's been thoroughly picked through and there is nothing of material value. It's mostly routing and reference slips...."

Joe adds: "Most of the reports have been separated from what they were targeted towards. Everything is shuffled hopelessly and all the dates and reference numbers have been removed. So it's all useless data. They've had nine years to cull through and trash the materials. Some of the better stuff was shredded back in the late 80s and early 90s. Expect none of the materials pertinent to the CIA, NSA, NSC, SS, or White House. This is only DoD materials."

In the last few weeks three influential ufologists have died: Betty Hill of lung cancer; John Mack run over by a truck in London; and Gordon Cooper of an undisclosed illness. With the abrupt closure of NIDS, the departure of Colm Kelleher, and the loss of interest among the major media, what is left is a loose association of researchers and a few journalists who compile documentaries for the cable channels, like Nick Cook. They argue about pet theories and rediscover this or that old episode, suddenly popular again, because few people have the perspective of the early years, or even know where the golden data is resting in the archives.

Today, Catherine is with us, ready to celebrate Thanksgiving in advance of our trip to Paris next week, so we listen to old songs and talk about projects for next year. The world in which George W. Bush has just been reelected is strange and unstable.

Bob Johansen, with whom I had lunch yesterday, plans a new project on the future of religion. He's starting from an odd place, doing work with the War College, which now calls itself VUCA University for "Volatility, Uncertainty, Complexity and Ambiguity."

American generals don't really believe the US is fighting a war on terror, Bob said. Instead, they tell the Bush administration that advanced countries should be engaged in a long-term combat against poverty and alienation. Taking over Iraq is one thing, but fighting the conditions that lead to despair should be the hard, real goal.

Mabillon. Sunday 28 November 2004.

Our Paris apartment has the true feel of a home now, sweet and functional. Three suitcases sit in the hallway, filled with books (including the old trashy *Fleuve Noir* science fiction collection, for nostalgia's sake) and fabrics, old photographs, presents for Olivier.

Not only are the dime novels safely lined up on the shelf, but family portraits find their place on the walls, lit by a round window that overlooks Saint Germain des Prés. Janine will join me here in a week, bringing more little treasures from our past.

Sophia-Antipolis. Thursday 2 December 2004.

It rains all over the Midi. Our hotel is a cold place, a product of French rationality, all metal and weird angles. The conference is another venture capital "Summit" with friendly faces and cheerful reunions. I gave a keynote speech before a lively audience, and this evening we had dinner with the group in Juan-les-Pins at a luxurious casino dripping with tinsel, overlooking a darkened beach.

Over the web, a computer conference on parapsychology to which Russell Targ has invited me goes on with some interesting insights, notably a long message by Joe McMoneagle that he calls "a short essay on the differences between remote viewing for science and support for applications, specifically in the security or intelligence area." It makes it clear the social environment of paranormal research hasn't improved much, even after the SRI work.

"In order for [security firms] to consider using psychics or remote viewers," said Joe, "They need to be convinced that it works. This takes an enormous amount of time and effort. Usually, it takes a lucky break or a chance meeting with someone within the organization who sees something happen, or experiences something. But the subject is still taboo for politicians, afraid of exposure."

Mabillon. Saturday 4 December 2004.

We've just watched a documentary about psychiatrist-philosopher Derrida, which left me confused and cold. People (like Walter de Brouwer yesterday in Nice) occasionally quote me as having applied his "deconstruction" concepts to the paranormal. I do try to use rigorous thinking in statements about UFOs or ghosts, but it seems the filming of Derrida missed the point of his teaching.

I have resigned from the Society for Scientific Exploration, with regrets. I'd sent them the proof that UFO events didn't happen at a particular local sidereal time as they claimed. (That supposed "discovery" came from a catalogue which contained massively duplicated cases for one particular slot of time, on 5 November 1990.) Not only did the Society withhold an answer for six months, but they sent me a single-line reviewer's advice...about redrawing one figure. John Alexander, checking the facts, told me there had been four reviews, none of which was sent or shown to me.

I can't stand this practice, so I've uploaded my article to the Internet where it has already recorded 7,000 hits. Yet academic "experts" will continue believing there's a special arc of the sky that is sending us those infamous gray Aliens.

Lyon. Friday 10 December 2004.

My French partners hold regular dinners where notable personalities are invited, generally industrialists or political leaders. Last night the guest was Monseigneur Barbarin, Cardinal Archbishop of Lyon.

About 60 members assembled in the fancy surroundings of hotel Sofitel, including the rector of the Catholic university.

Monseigneur arrived in a simple black cassock with a priest's collar and silver cross. He spoke on the topic of "Entrepreneurship and performance." His speech was clever but filled with generalities, so I didn't feel touched by any special grace or insight. His values emphasize the spreading of joy and the recognition of human dignity, but they use a narrow definition of joy and gloss over the many indignities of business life. The result may be to give good conscience to tycoons of industry as they navigate the spiritual shoals of finance, but a fair solution to the inequities of society remains out of reach here, after all the talk about ethics.

I was left with some amusement at having met a successor of Saint Agobard, having enjoyed a very good dinner in Lyon with my colleagues, and little else.

Mabillon. Sunday 12 December 2004.

After two weeks I have finally caught the French rhythm. This morning, Janine and I went shopping amidst the colors, the smells, and noises of the market on Rue de Buci. Local communists handed out leaflets among itinerant chair repairers lining up furniture on the sidewalks. Gérard and Lisou Deforge came over for lunch, our first meeting on paranormal topics at Mabillon. I learned they had witnessed a strange phenomenon themselves, an aerial ballet of lights in Eragny, back in October 1988, that left them baffled.

Mabillon. Saturday 18 December 2004.

A message from my friend Douglas Crosby tells me he handed over *Heart of the Internet* to Steven Spielberg on the set of *War of the Worlds*: "He expressed his fondness and respect for you."

The wind has come, astride a rainstorm that blew dead leaves all over the streets, even inside our local bank. The storm also brought us Catherine, fresh from California, eager to see Paris again. Annick, on a short excursion to Saintes with Alain, tells me she's found the tomb of Saint Agobard in the roman crypt of the ancient church of Saint

Eutrope de Saintes.

Philippe Pouletty and Gabriel Mergui came over for dinner on Tuesday, with their wives. Philippe is pushing for the creation of a dedicated French research agency. The system is flawed, he says, with money sloshing around for the wrong reasons, burdensome taxes, and a huge bias on the country's economy that discourages innovation.

Mabillon. Wednesday 22 December 2004.

Winter gave us a dusting of snow, fast melted, on the roofs and gutters of Paris. Dominique Weinstein and François Louange (just back from South Africa) came over for dinner last night. Janine, unfortunately, had a cold that made her feel miserable.

The main news from CNES is that an oversight committee is finally being formed to steer whatever project will succeed the defunct SEPRA. In true French bureaucratic form, it was eliminated *retroactively* as of January 2003! Velasco will be reassigned. In Toulouse, the poor archives were moved again. Dominique hopes to save some of the essential data.

The only real research work on UFOs at CNES is what Weinstein does at home in his spare time, as he compiles his pilot sighting catalogue. He will soon move to Brussels where the first Europe-wide security agency is being created. Whether through my French partners or other investors, my assessment of national economic innovation is flat. There's a distressing drop in recruiting for positions in business and management, says Laurent Guez, new editor in chief at *Figaro Entreprises*.

Mabillon. Saturday 25 December 2004.

Over lunch at Brasserie Lipp with Thérèse de Saint Phalle, I brought up the late François de Grossouvre, whose interest in my work still puzzles me. She remembers him well. "I met with him on March 15, the year of his death," she recalled. "He told me he had a 200-page manuscript to show me, that many people wouldn't like. We made an appointment for April 15. He was dead before I saw him again."

She believes he was killed the way Alexandre de Marenches once explained to her: He was found holding a 2-pound gun somebody must've put it in his hand, as the force of recoil should have separated the gun from the dead man. Did the manuscript expose the financial manipulations around Mitterrand, with the commission kickbacks for military procurement and other contracts? As for his son, he wouldn't know anything about his father's interests. Grossouvre had a mistress and neglected his six children, who reportedly hated her—and him.

Our apartment at Mabillon has been filled all week with light, laughter, happy kids. Annick's son came over with three of his children, an emotional reunion. Happiness consists of making others happy, doesn't it? Tonight, we all went to Olivier's apartment, listened to the music of Santana, and watched the full moon rise over the Île Saint Louis. Tomorrow, I fly back.

Hummingbird. Monday 27 December 2004.

California is engulfed in the first serious rains of winter. The urban landscape is a painting of grayness, car headlights glimpsed through raindrops, flashing like so many tiny flames amidst the great wash of the sky. I relish the sweetness that is San Francisco, where I can hope and create. I look forward, eagerly, to the New Year. France is a wonderful place, nothing more. On good days it purrs like a happy cat and glistens like a polished piece of art, all pricey crystal and brass. But it doesn't suggest expectation and the smell of freedom.

If I were a painter, I would try and catch the extraordinary lightness of a Pacific morning, the last of the rain, or the stillness born of the fog caressed by sunlight. I find it nowhere else. Turning away from museums, Janine reminds me that the deepest feeling is found in watching nature's work, her infinite wisdom and grace. The best an artist can do is to acknowledge the failure to approximate it.

Hummingbird. Tuesday 28 December 2004.

Amazing views of the Indonesian earthquake and the fantastic tsunami it has triggered keep rolling off the news reports from Jakarta, with mounting casualty figures.

As if the misery of poverty and disease was not enough, walls of water have also devastated coastline communities as far away as Africa.

Hummingbird. Thursday 30 December 2004.

More images of rushing water, black with filth and dense with debris, fill the news and our heavy dreams. A disaster of "biblical" proportions continues to unfold as rescuers manage to reach some of the isolated areas. Entire towns have been washed away, islands have vanished, and the infrastructure of several nations is caving in. Even the military has been disabled in some zones where men and matériel were submerged by the massive tide. Seen from California, the scale of the disaster is hard to contemplate. Even the number of the dead, four days after the quake, is only a weak approximation.

Dr. Richard Niemtzow called me this afternoon. He now lives in Washington, still with the Air Force. He's been asked to open an acupuncture clinic for them, so he works between Andrews AFB, the Pentagon, and other places. Most personnel to whom Richard talks don't even know that Project Blue Book ever existed. He mentioned Allen Hynek to another officer who told him, "Look Doc, I'm not that old!" A sobering thought as our generation of researchers passes into history—or oblivion. But what about the golden data?

Athanor. Saturday 15 January 2005.

Janine and I had a fine dinner last night at the home of Dr. Patrick Bailey and his wife, Nancy, in the exclusive Emerald Hills section of Redwood City. Their house is a fine new structure they have patiently turned into a museum of New Age pictures, sculptures, and art objects from east and west, a striking assemblage of embroidered cushions, wall-size television sets, floor-to-ceiling loudspeakers, shimmering butterflies made of fiberoptics, and framed portraits of Kuthumi, Jesus, Saint Germain, and other Ascended Masters, in a large living room with a gorgeous view of Emerald Lake.

Our hosts live easily amidst these displays of spiritual contradictions. Nancy is an expert in Chinese herb medicine and spiritual healing, while Patrick is president of the International Association for

New Science, concerned with cold fusion and alternative energy. He's also involved in several organizations that have their seat at Mount Shasta, including the I AM movement: He listens to their channeling but doesn't lose his rational sense, as when he sees Joe Firmage as driven by ambition and Dr. Greer as lacking objectivity.

A past Master of the Masonic Lodge in Los Altos, Patrick has much respect for traditional rituals, but he downplays his own mystical achievements, joking that on the way to the high degrees he developed the ability to organize annual picnics, but no great magical powers. With many of its members in their sixties or seventies, American Masonry is concerned with deserted buildings, their former glory largely dissipated.

Patrick has acquired a stunning perspective on ideologies from every cult in California, so we discussed everything from Billy Meier's Pleiadians to the denizens of the Moon and the teachings of Ramtha. This left us too confused to reach new creative conclusions, but we agreed to meet again and explore the mysteries in greater depth.

Friends confirm that Patrick is a respected scientist (12) as a manager since 1986, with a specialty in electrical systems and nuclear-powered spacecraft.

Hummingbird. Friday 21 January 2005.

Tonight, at Patrick Bailey's kind invitation, I attended the Installation of Officers of Commandery no.1 of the Knight Templars of California. The ceremony, preceded by a simple dinner, took place at a "secret" Masonic location in the Mission district. I had been given the confidential instructions to the place, but they were wrong, like most secrets, so I wandered through a large Taqueria where I stumbled upon Patrick and his wife, as lost as we were. He finally remembered the right address, and we climbed some stairs to the large nondescript structure that housed the Lodge.

About 200 people had congregated there, including a chapter of the Royal Arch Masons, who were also installing their officers, so I watched that fine ritual as well and met many well-meaning, smart people. About half the members were Chinese Americans.

The proceedings were quite impressive. Everyone was in full

regalia, with colored jackets indicating their rank, special ties, and traditional decorations and insignias. Puzzled, I came away with the conclusion that the array of impressive symbols embodied the process on the material plane, as opposed to any genuinely profound secret on the higher ones.

I was told that Masons never recruited actively, yet it was hinted that my application would be welcome. I have always respected Masonry, in France as in America, as a group driven to rectitude, assistance to their fellow men, and social achievement. I also admire their historical role, but I would lack motivation to participate because I don't think they hold the knowledge I seek now, any better than alternative traditions. Besides, Janine would probably object if she saw me wearing a hat with ostrich feathers.

Another issue for me is the heavy, narrowly defined link to Christianity. Accepting and affirming spirituality is a fine idea, but looking for a universal key to consciousness through a single religious path makes no sense to me. If I wanted pictures of Christ and sermons from the Gospels, I wouldn't go to a Lodge but to Grace Cathedral, which has fine stained glass and a beautiful labyrinth. Then, I was told Masons travelling the world were always welcome in foreign Lodges, except for members of the French Grand Orient who don't demand allegiance to God, and are generally shunned by other initiates in spite of their remarkable history and generous record. So, what's the point?

Athanor. Saturday 29 January 2005.

On the occasion of Janine's birthday, Catherine joined us to see *The Gamester* at the American Conservatory Theater, and later had dinner at the nearby Clift Hotel. After the rains of the past week, California has already adorned herself in the emerald dress of spring. All is quiet, the surf and the wind in the trees the only sound as I work.

Athanor. Saturday 12 February 2005.

A curious time has come, the winter of our sadness. Our daughter-in-law now refuses to speak to us altogether; she leaves us without news of our grandson.

Who said Christmas was a time to bring families together? We don't even know what the problem is, so we spend sleepless nights trying to guess. Did we say something wrong? Did we fail to do something that was expected of us?

We try in vain to move beyond this heart-gnawing, brain-freezing worry. It leaves nothing but torture in its wake.

Later the next day.

In spare moments, I continue to update, verify, and refine my database on ancient cases, merging together the historical sources that line the walls of this house with whatever comes through the web from Chris Aubeck's astonishing research with his Magonia group. We now list over 400 cases before 1800. Chris demonstrates that abductions and Roswell-like crashes are nothing new, and that Charles Fort was only scratching the surface when he researched things from the sky.

In the last few weeks, the Brazilian air force has released a version of the Project Prato 1977 report, the first-level document we reviewed in the office of Colonel Hollanda Lima. Bill Calvert tells me that the most interesting documents (the two higher-level secret reports) will now get buried deeper, since US intelligence discredits the doctors who inspected the injuries and the hospitals that verified the wounds caused by the objects over the Amazon.

Brazilians, even more than Europeans, resent being ridiculed by experts from "Norte America," so they withhold their data with smart excuses. Agobar himself now seems terrified of the subject, perhaps as a result of Colonel Hollanda's recent death.

Rain has fallen all week over California. In the silence and the peace and the majesty of this place, I realize how happy we have been the last few years. But such happiness is only measured at the gauge of the trust of those we love, and now that trust is crumbling.

Athanor. Sunday 27 February 2005.

Janine has driven off to a piano recital in Cupertino, while I came here alone to complete the archiving of my research correspondence. It's still raining hard; I feel inexplicably sad as I look out over the bay, the distant rocks of Tomales Point battered by waves and the deserted beach drenched with foam. I've written to Fred Adler in honor of his 80th birthday. Doug Engelbart, too, has just turned 80, like my brother Gabriel, who tells me he doesn't go out into the world any more.

Yesterday I took Janine on a pleasant boat ride on Stow Lake, in Golden Gate Park. I rowed out to a place where a tree made a shelter. We ate our sandwiches there as ducks and seagulls circled our boat, begging for crumbs.

Sacramento. Monday 28 February 2005.

Steve Sawyer, a voice from past decades, contacted me with the claim he had new information on UFO history. We met for lunch at the Sheraton, where I attend a two-day conference on new ventures. Steve is a tall, lean fellow with dark hair and glasses. His father, as an Air force pilot, once saw a mile-long object that was also observed by fellow officers and the crew of a B-52, off the coast of Virginia. They were debriefed as soon as they landed, interrogated in separate rooms, and told they'd seen... a weather balloon. Nothing changes.

Athanor. Saturday 5 March 2005.

Dr. Green and a colleague of his, a professor from Brazil, try to validate medical data about Brazilian witnesses. As they attempted to setup meetings with local doctors, he reported that "most are not really physicians, but were said to be in the news reports. The ones who are physicians say the reports are bogus; they refuse to see us."

Well, what did they expect? The social distance between local folks and academics in many Latin countries is such that any report of strange events in the provinces gets brushed off.

The same has been true in the US, with Sagan and Menzel speaking *ex cathedra* about theoretical projections, never bothering to travel to any muddy farm to understand what the rancher had experienced.

Kit goes on: "I was going to resource the trip from a grant on neurodegenerative disease in a program of diagnostic radiology I manage. The trip was cancelled by me last night... no one to see."

He adds an update on his abduction research: "I have a colleague receiving MRI and CAT-scan data from abductees. Last month there were three. When he asks if I can evaluate the scans as a specialized physician, free and confidentially, most are not forthcoming. To date the score is: 8 scans, 2 interesting and 6 clearly not interesting."

Mabillon. Friday 11 March 2005.

Janine and I landed yesterday, in time to attend an amusing meeting of homeowners of our building, a microcosm.

I was promptly elected as president for the meeting, fortunately a meaningless formality. The roof is in need of repairs and a dozen issues have to do with new regulations of the City of Paris.

Our neighbors are a quiet, friendly group, including retired professors. Yet local political reality reasserts itself amidst strikes and mounting malaise.

It took most of the day to make reservations to London. Then Janine spoke to our son's wife about a visit, hoping to see our grandson.

"Out of the question!" wrote his mother in a blunt email response, *"for a couple of years, as least!"*

It hit us like a knife through the heart: the injustice, the absurdity of sudden spite, yet so stunningly painful.

Janine went off to shop for furniture near Alesia, still in a daze, so stunned and hurt that she stumbled in the path of a car whose driver hit the brakes in panic, missing her by a miracle. She only realized where she was when she heard screams, the screeching of tires, and felt the bumper against her body.

Mabillon. Saturday 12 March 2005.

To change our mood, we went out to see a movie about the life of Mitterrand, *Le Promeneur du Champ de Mars*. The old President's remark, recommending indifference in the face of emotional adversity, was stunning. Mitterrand joked he would be "the last French monarch." After him, he thought French presidents would be subject to supranational European authorities.

Yet the nostalgia of an older France lingers unavoidably, as a great reactionary force. If a terror attack similar to the train station bombs in Madrid targeted Paris, would any government be able to prevent a massive shift to the racist, isolationist extreme right, away from France's European destiny as a modern country?

Mabillon. Sunday 13 March 2005.

I am reading (off the Internet) a troubling account of the death of expert remote viewer Pat Price, written by Terry Milner and publicly posted by Gary Bekkum.

Milner cites "Frank," a former Marine who served in Vietnam, who knew of the SRI experiments and was aware of Price's whereabouts in the two days prior to his death:

"Price had flown from West Virginia to Washington, D.C. where he'd met with people from the Office of Naval Intelligence and NSA who were involved in his work at SRI…. He did say he was bringing documents with him, and that should anything happen to him while he was in Las Vegas, Frank was to secure the material and forward it to Dr. Puthoff before the local police took possession of it.

"On 13 July 1975 Price flew from Washington to Salt Lake City where he met his son before flying on to Vegas. As he registered at the Stardust a man bumped into him, an apparent accident. He had dinner with Frank and his wife, and then complained that he 'felt lousy.' He was in pain all night with stomach cramps and had trouble breathing. At 6:30 am, Frank went over to his room, finding Price sitting upright in bed, his face flushed but otherwise normal, until his body went into an arc 'so that only the back of his head and his heels were actually touching the bed.' He went into a convulsion and then reverse-arced again. Frank heard what he described as a 'death rattle' breath sound. Repeated CPR by Frank and paramedics brought Price to life again, but each time, the body went into an arc, and he stopped breathing again."

Frank called Hal, who could only confirm the instructions. The funeral took place in L.A., attended by Dr. Puthoff and Price's Office of Naval Intelligence (ONI) case officer. Frank intended to drive up to Portland with his wife, so Hal asked them to stop by in Palo Alto. When they called him in the morning, however, he said he'd be "right over," but he only arrived two and a half hours later. According to

Milner, once at Hal's house, Frank and his wife were told that Price's work didn't have anything to do with Intelligence. A call to someone introduced as "Price's doctor in L.A." then told Frank that Price had a history of heart problems and that he'd suffered a "myocardial infarction."

After this episode, Frank and his wife noticed bizarre events at their home in Portland. Their phone acted strangely; once they heard someone talk about "the tape running out," another time they were followed by a white van, and documents related to a project involving Frank with Pat Price were stolen from their car.

At that point, Frank decided it was safer to withdraw from the field.

Mabillon. Monday 14 March 2005.

Dinner last night at Le Suffren with Dominique Weinstein, who now spends the week in Brussels as a member of the European security group. We spoke of the fate of SEPRA and my proposed meeting at CNES, where I'm invited by Arnaud Benedetti, director of public affairs. They contemplate a new project, not exactly a scientific project but a French Blue Book, to respond to citizens' questions with honesty, but it will hardly be a serious tool for investigation.

London. Wednesday 16 March 2005.

Hotel Britannia Hampstead. This is an old English pile of stones on Primrose Road that someone has attempted to modernize, but the creaking lift with its solid wooden doors rubbed and scratched by generations of visitors shows no willingness to move into the 21st century. Even if it did, the faded carpets and antiquated furniture would foil the attempt. I woke up at the sound of soldiers passing on horseback, had a decent breakfast, and called Janine in Paris. She was vibrant and clear, although she harbors much private sadness, as I do.

Mabillon. Saturday 19 March 2005.

Our friend Tia Elena arrived from Stanford on Thursday; Annick joined us. Their warm presence has lifted Janine's spirits.

This afternoon, walking along the Seine and looking at books, I found Robert Lomas' history of the ancient (and Royal) "Invisible College" and a wonderful analysis of stained-glass iconography by a modern master, René Champs, entitled *Miroir et Lumière*. Then I stepped inside Notre Dame to study again the three fine roses of stained glass, the southern one in flamboyant sunshine at the time.

The Christian Cross has often made me uncomfortable because of its lurid, tragic, even masochistic undertone and the unbalanced way in which it divides space. As opposed to Tibetan mandalas, representations of yin and yang, or Indian medicine wheels, the Cross awkwardly quarters the universe, dividing spirits instead of gathering them. It is, quite blatantly, a symbol of torture, all uneven arms and off-center sections, as analysts have often noted.

Thérèse de Saint-Phalle and Jean-Daniel Belfond, the publisher of *Presses du Châtelet*, came over for dinner last night. We spoke of my new novel called *Stratagème*.

Hummingbird. Tuesday 22 March 2005.

The plane landed in a San Francisco rainstorm. The distress in my heart is made deeper by distance from my son. I have many things to say to him, and I dream about Maxim. Thus, the absurdities of life seem increasingly obvious as I grow older.

Jim Westwood, on Hal's payroll, has now determined that the Robertson Panel report was drafted by Frederick C. Durant III, cited as a consultant with Arthur D. Little. In fact, according to Westwood, Durant was "a full-time, paid secret agent-employee of the CIA, under cover." The CIA and the Air Force (and AFOSI) had also penetrated NICAP, notably through Colonel Joseph Bryant, chief of CIA's psychological warfare staff during 1947-1953.

Hummingbird. Saturday 26 March 2005.

Another rainstorm is coming, ready to engulf the City. From my study I see the light change over Russian Hill with colors that might announce the end of the world: crimson and black, ominous and heavy, like an inescapable catastrophe.

During an interview with recruiters who want me to join a new international Fund, I heard them refer to my "ideal profile": a science background (the other partners come from sales and marketing), strong software credentials, respect in the venture community, and valuable ties to France, plus "gravitas." But does that carry any real weight today? I hadn't heard that Latin word in a long time.

Reno. Saturday 16 April 2005. The Silver Legacy.

The air is crisp here, the pace of life simpler. More importantly for me, as I go about business, I rediscover a sense of freedom, an open invitation to think and live that is unique to the American West. Back in Palo Alto, the Institute for the Future, briefly lifted from the dangers that almost left it bankrupt, goes through troubled times again. Peter Banks has not emerged as a long-term leader, and various cabals agitate the staff.

Reno. Sunday 17 April 2005.

Dinner at the Nugget with our local friend Bob Handy, who looks like an old uncle. A former driver for Budweiser beer, he's full of stories about the past of this "little city in the desert" that has no major industry and very thin culture. Yet Reno attracts big crowds to hear Willie Nelson, Kenny Rogers, and other icons of popular music, creating an atmosphere of bright lights and cheerful folks that only lasts until the bleak reality of dawn.

The Art Bell show is big here. Hawking miracle cures and strange mysteries, it follows in the tradition of Old West charlatanism and frontier radio. Major Ed Dames is heard predicting nuclear explosions. Remote viewing, once so carefully calibrated at SRI that it deserved a special place in science, is becoming stale and suspect.

Athanor. Saturday 23 April 2005.

The rains linger over the silver bay; everything is green, fat and blooming. I had lunch yesterday with Colm Kelleher, newly installed in San Francisco where he now works at Prosetta. We met at the

Garden Court. He autographed his book *Brain Trust*, and we reminisced about NIDS and the mutilations research project. As we reviewed the book, he recalled that Richard ("Rick") Doty had been a CIA agent all along, and that an abduction study conducted by Hal using small recording instruments had been done in connection with John Schuessler's second in command at MUFON, a former NSA employee. I had never known the full story about that project whose results, according to Colm, were unfortunately inconclusive.

Last night, Janine and I went to the Institute for Transpersonal Psychology, where I was to talk about my current research. It was an opportunity for a sober, integrated presentation, which wasn't advertised beyond the membership. Steve Millard was there, as well as Arthur Hastings, Bernie Haisch and Marsha, Russell Targ, Ron Blackburn, and people who had guided my work from the early days of the Parapsychology Research Group, 30 years ago. Walter Bowart, the author of *Operation Mind Control,* was there as well as a young man dressed all in black who confided to us he belonged to the Temple of the Vampire, the latest "occult" flavor.

Hummingbird. Tuesday 26 April 2005.

This is the season for French politicians to come and visit our remote Provinces. This morning six senators (including Jean-Léonce Dupont, former mayor of Bayeux) came over as a delegation visiting Easenergy, the EDF subsidiary where I serve as an outside Board member. This evening Ambassador Levitte was back at the Consulate, along with another delegation that included former Budget Minister Alain Lambert. When I spoke to Levitte about California's interest in rapidly-developing China, he took pains to minimize its relevance. Japan, he said, had once grown even faster. Yes, I thought, but one must look beyond the numbers, at the irreversible cultural changes those refined politicians fail to notice.

Hummingbird. Wednesday 27 April 2005.

Roger came over tonight, bringing books (*Eight Keys to Eden,* and a treatise by Dunne) and his sharp memory of investigations, people, and events. I opened for his benefit our files on Betty and Barney Hill, our visit with them in New Hampshire in 1967. The whole episode deserves to be reviewed: the beeping sounds that bracket their experience, the details like that skin scraping—a standard anthropological technique...

Athanor. Saturday 21 May 2005.

Today is my daughter's birthday. She puts light and warmth in our lives at a time when we have reason to feel sad and lost, and lonely.
On a trip to Detroit earlier this week (for the board meeting of HandyLab), I was unable to see Kit, who was ill with a very high, most unusual fever that raised much concern.
In the larger world of physics, research has lost its compass. Academic attitudes are more hypocritical, unimaginative and cowardly than ever. I read in *New Scientist* (13): "The Theory of Everything is proving elusive. But perhaps the mainstream approaches are heading the wrong way, and what we need are some radical ideas..." All right then, this must be the right time to look at the range of phenomena that don't fit in the narrow catalogue of today's science, like UFO sightings, survival of death, telepathy? No, of course not: The writer goes on to discuss another version of the old theories.
In a few days I will be in France again, with the usual stress of financial meetings. I plan to refresh myself in body, spirit, and soul with a trip to the stained-glass wonders of Chartres.

Chartres. Saturday 28 May 2005.

The train from Montparnasse only takes an hour to get here, although it halts enroute in Versailles, Rambouillet, Maintenon, those names of the France of yesteryear. Chartres is something else, rising out of the plain like a single flame in the gray, monotonous morning.
In contrast with its glorious exterior, the cathedral is cavernous and dark, in need of repairs and a thorough cleaning. The walls have accumulated dust and grime for centuries, except for the Western side with its statue of Melchizedech, where the golden stone has been scrubbed. Inside, the feeling is cool and gloomy, even ominous.

Stained glass is the only relief, but what stained glass! So fine and precise, especially in the high *verrières* that spread their glory eight stories above the stone floor where I walk.

The local museum also speaks of later works, of the innovations of Tiffany and of modern stained glass with abstract designs, even fused materials, dressed up and painted; but those do not appeal to my spirit. It is the combination of naivety and mastery in this art that I cherish, even the cartoon-like character of the ancient scenes: In the folds of a formal robe falling off the shoulders of some grand personage, one finds cute lions, stylized cubs grinning at us. What seems like naivety is actually freshness and authenticity.

The river Eure flows quietly to the North of the cathedral, past the remains of ramparts and rotten platforms of old *lavoirs*. You almost expect to see women in long dresses bringing their baskets to the river and washing the laundry while arguing about the price of eggs.

Mabillon. Sunday 29 May 2005.

The French people have spoken, and the word is NO! A clear majority, 55%, reject the proposed European Constitution drafted by Giscard d'Estaing. Something like this had to happen. This Europe built by politicians serving big industry (it started with steel and coal) became a fairly successful financial federation when the Euro was introduced, yet the citizens of Europe have only been allowed to become involved as remote participants in multi-tier elections, mere spectators. Today was the reckoning. France is one of the founders of the Union, but her people are afraid, unsure of themselves and the future, tired of being lied to by politicians.

I called Janine when the news came, then I went for a walk in the Latin Quarter, where everything was quiet under a cold, steady rain.

Mabillon. Tuesday 31 May 2005.

This afternoon I met again with Arnaud Benedetti to discuss the future of GEPAN at the CNES headquarters building in Les Halles. An efficient secretary led me to a basement room equipped with a video hookup, a teleconference with Toulouse, so I was "tele-introduced" to two regional managers: David Assemas, in charge of future plans and planetary protection, and his assistant Fernand Albi, in charge of space debris and unexplained aerial phenomena, "PAN" in French. Velasco has been replaced by a man named Jacques Pathenet. CNES has not forgiven Jean-Jacques for his book with Payan. (14)

After the video presentations and a summary of my involvement and current interests, Arnaud explained that CNES intended to restart collection activities as well as external communication. Professor Sillard will preside over the steering committee, where public bodies will be represented: civil aviation (DGAC), Army, Air Force, Weather Bureau, CNRS, Gendarmerie, and Police, among others.

Once we were alone again, Arnaud took me to his fine office with a view over the park where the huge market of the former Halles once spread out in a jumble of wrought-iron pavilions and tortuous passages. He explained the CNES' problem in terms of the "passions" of both sides. While eminent French scientists like Brock and Charpak are incensed at the idea of any public body studying UFOs, the believers are equally sanguine, convinced that CNES runs a conspiracy to deny the Alien presence. Both sides want access to the public archives, which CNES does plan to make available, minus the names of witnesses. Benedetti asked if I would be available to brief the new committee.

Mabillon. Friday 3 June 2005.

California novelist Rob Swigart met me for lunch and a long conversation at *Les Editeurs*. He's on his way to Turkey to survey a prehistoric settlement; he has a contract for a book set in Paleolithic time. The conversation turned to the disintegration of Europe and our concerns about the Institute for the Future, where Peter Banks has just been replaced as president.

Mabillon. Monday 6 June 2005.

On Saturday, Gérard Deforge drove into Paris to have lunch with me at Le Départ. As a former Union leader among educators, he's kept a sharp view of French society and its many contradictions and injustices. The socialist party is blowing up, he said, torn between Hollande and Fabius, and the political landscape is being reshaped, like the plan of a city to be redrawn after an earthquake.

Dominique Weinstein stopped by today on his way to Brussels, so we reviewed my meetings at CNES. Evidently, Velasco's publisher has a habit of filing for bankruptcy to avoid paying his bills, a regrettable *penchant* among French publishers. Jean-Jacques lost control of the book, got embroiled in lawsuits.

The economic turmoil in France extends to the media. Even well-heeled *Le Figaro* is under stress, so I no longer write my column, having published the last weekly "Letter from California" a month ago, after 87 consecutive pieces.

Today my neighbor, Professor Bokias, resplendent in a green jacket, invited me to dinner at a *crèperie* on Rue des Canettes. He spoke of the decay of Greece, where covetous orthodox priests now grab everything of value, and of the unease of Europe, with that mounting rage among the young.

I was only able to speak briefly to my son. He was on his way to Luxembourg and couldn't see me.

Mabillon. Wednesday 8 June 2005.

Spring-like weather returns. Over breakfast with Yves Messarovitch, I hear him say: "There's no quality left in journalism here. It's impossible to conduct real investigations, or in-depth analyses. Costs are being cut everywhere; salaries are frozen. The business isn't interesting anymore." As for the government, it has nothing to offer, Yves added. He's even critical of his former economics professor, socialist leader Strauss-Kahn, whom he blames for encouraging the fuzzy thinking on the Left.

At noon I walked over to *Editions de l'Archipel*, near the Châtelet, where I saw Jean-Daniel Belfond. The two of us had a fine literary lunch with Thérèse de Saint-Phalle at *Le Chien qui Fume*, famous restaurant across the square from CNES headquarters. I had brought them the first complete draft of *Stratagème*, which I've been writing furiously since arriving in Paris, taking advantage of my strange waking hours and jet-lagged reveries. I walked all the way back, through the little streets where the art galleries had their doors open to the sunshine.

I dream of returning to California, to the north coast where the sky is pure and the sea hums and roars. The grass of Tomales Point will already have turned brown by the time I get back.

We make preparations for our first, too long delayed introduction to the Pacific, an opportunity to better understand its vanished cultures, and perhaps to heal the pain in Janine's heart.

13

Honolulu, island of Oahu, Hawaii. Wednesday 22 June 2005.

We flew in early this afternoon. Once settled in our portside cabin aboard the *Norwegian Wind* (1,700 passengers, 700 crew), we went ashore again to meet with Professor David Swift at the Aloha Tower. A young woman named Donna, an art student who takes his sociology course, joined us there. She'll move to San Francisco as soon as she can, she says, happy to leave the island.

David is the kindest man I know, and he looks increasingly like a wise old bird. We had coffee and pastries at Zippy's, a popular family restaurant downtown. David recalls visiting us at our home in Belmont ("the house with the huge map of California on your wall"), but he feels isolated in Hawaii where the culture is "stagnant and dull." He tells stories of failed efforts to find intellectual stimulation, or interesting colleagues.

He remains well connected, however, to Dick Haines, Bernie Haisch, and Bill Gough, founder of the Mind-Brain research group. But nothing is happening on the islands, in terms of serious psychical research.

Hilo, island of Hawaii. Thursday 23 June 2005.

Shortly after breakfast we saw the Big Island under a sky of rolling gray clouds. We left the ship as soon as it docked in Hilo and spent the day studying calderas, craters, and vents of this volcanic land.

This town of some 50,000 people has an agricultural base (papayas, Macademia nuts, and gorgeous flowers) and sad memories of two devastating tsunamis. The only other significant place on the island is the town of Kona, which we save for the return trip. A warm rain came as we got back to the ship after our excursion over the black landscape and the waterfalls. We slept quietly, in deep oblivion.

At sea. Friday 24 June 2005.

As night fell, the captain took us alongside the southern coast of the Big Island to watch the bright red lava oozing out of the darkened cliffs. Now the ship sails smoothly, straight south towards Fanning Island, at the center of the Pacific.

At sea. Saturday 25 June 2005.

I've begun reading *What the Dormouse Said*, John Markoff's essay on the role of the counterculture in the birth of the personal computer. It covers the same period as my *Network Revolution*, with greater detail about the protagonists, but John has trouble making it all come to life. There's too much detail and not enough of the real-world stuff of passion and conflict that gave that era its texture and color. Perhaps it has become an impossible task to recapture what was a discontinuity in spirit as much as it was a fracture in culture and a dramatic breakthrough in technology.

We still enjoy perfect weather, already some 3,000 miles away from the nearest land. Out of the satellite footprint, we have lost all news of the outside world. I am also losing sense of time, not an unpleasant sensation. Silicon Valley would only be a distant memory if I wasn't reading Markoff's book, with its gallery of pioneers I knew well: Charlie Rosen and Bill Harman, and of course Doug Englebart, larger than life in the early days of personal computing.

Now the captain comes on the public address system, telling us our position in his comforting Norwegian accent, together with such important technical details as the temperature of the water in the Jacuzzi on deck twelve.

Fanning island. Sunday 26 June 2005.

Lost in the middle of the Pacific, we found this unique spot enchanting. Inhabited by about 2,000 people who emigrated from the Gilbert Islands, this little ring of volcanic rock was once used by the British as a cable relay. It is now part of the Republic of Kiribati, with the Australian dollar as its currency. The lagoon is unspoiled, a perfect blue, circled by palm, the ideal spot for sea kayaking or just floating on foam rafts. Still no news from the civilized world, so I work on *Stratagème*, putting meat on the bones of my story.

Nawiliwili, Kauai. Wednesday 29 June 2005.

Back to the Hawaiian archipelago, it felt good to leave the ship and go kayaking down the Hule'ia River, into a tame jungle with vines and flowers, wild roosters and tales of the Menehune: They are white dwarfs, said to have occupied the island until the Polynesians arrived in 800 AD. Like the Fairies in Europe, the Menehunes are said to have vanished suddenly, perhaps into one of the hidden valleys along the Na Pali Coast. There are examples of sophisticated, yet unexplained fitted stone on Kauai found nowhere else in the islands. We paddled past a supposed Menehune fishpond, but the mysterious dwarfs did not display any of their magic to advance our research.

Lahaina, Mauai. Thursday 30 June 2005

A royal seat since the 16th century, the city of Lahaina became the residence of King Kamehameha in 1802. In the 19th century, this quaint port was the whaling capital of the world: "To the raffish sailors who favored it for its superb anchorage, grog shops, and uninhibited women, Lahaina was heaven itself. To the stiff-collared missionaries who arrived in 1823, however, the town was a hellhole, a place of sin and abomination. When the Congregationalists prevented naked women from swimming out to meet the whalers, their belligerent brethren anchored in the harbor, cannonballed Mission homes and rioted along the waterfront," according to the brochure I'm reading.

Nothing quite as dramatic happened during our visit, unfortunately, but we can see Molokai, a gray shadow, the only major island we will not visit on this trip.

Kona, Hawaii. Friday 1 July 2005.

We are anchored off the Big Island again, on the southern coast this time, under a warm sun that becomes more bearable as one drives up into the hills, topped by a cloud forest. We were able to call Catherine, deeply saddened by the illness of her childhood friend.

This side of Hawaii is superb, with fruits and flowers growing wild everywhere, from coffee and papaya to bananas and pineapples. We visited the obligatory coffee plantation overlooking the bay where Captain Cook met his death at the hand of Polynesian warriors.

The white "painted church" of Saint Benedict built by a Belgian priest is distinguished by the biblical scenes he depicted on its humble wooden walls, for lack of a better way to communicate with his illiterate parishioners. More appropriate in the Pacific setting is the ancient sanctuary, with its fine examples of massive Polynesian walls made of volcanic stone.

Once again, here as in Luxor, we are curious to detect the sources of inspiration that have defined human civilization. We are no experts in archaeology, but we need to see the sites, the people, and the tangible remains of their greatness as testimony to their spiritual teachings, hoping to take these lessons with us.

Now the ship is steaming towards Oahu. Before flying home tomorrow, we will visit David Swift again at the University of Hawaii to help him spur research ahead.

Hummingbird. Friday 8 July 2005.

Islamic terrorists have struck London: three bombs in the subway (including at Russell square, an area I know well) and one on a bus.

School children everywhere are taught about religious wars as an aberration of the past, an ugly period in history when Mankind had not yet been "enlightened by progress" and rationality. Yet here we are, watching bloody scenes perpetrated in the name of faith, a poor excuse for hatred and carnage.

Athanor. Saturday 9 July 2005.

After spending a week reorganizing my office in anticipation of several business trips, we drove up to our North Coast library where I was at peace to study some interesting correspondence from John E. in Tacoma, James Westwood in Virginia, and researchers Jean-Marc Gillot and Jacques Maniez in France.

Today we went to the Russian River and rowed 10 miles under a pleasingly warm sun and clear skies.

The water was full of tourists who swam and splashed, turned, overturned, and made complete fools of themselves, as we did.

Ann Arbor, Michigan. Monday 11 July 2005.

On the way to Montréal to brief our investors, my partner and I stopped here to attend a board meeting of HandyLab. I was hoping to see Kit and Kristin on this trip, but they are away for a couple of weeks as he recovers from an illness that turned out to be a case of poisoning.

From what he told me on the phone he suspects it was deliberate, and related "to things we've discussed before."

Montréal, Québec. Tuesday 12 July 2005.

Politics and pollution, ozone burning my lungs. Canadian investment funds are caught in permanent intrigue with government ministers trying to control the flow of money, and local interests clamoring for more technology jobs.

The TV brings news of an early breakthrough in the investigation of the London explosions, with a sobering surprise: The first suicide bombers in a Western country turn out to be ordinary, soccer-playing young men who lived quiet lives in England.

Hummingbird. Thursday 14 July 2005.

Catherine's friend Edgar died today. She spent hours at his bedside, every day and night. We all feel devastated.

Redondo Beach. Monday 18 July 2005.

Yesterday Janine and I drove south to the Portofino resort where the board of Easenergy meets with top-level managers from Electricité de France and energy experts from major California companies.

This morning I met with Bob Bookman, one of Spielberg's agents, at the Creative Artists Agency (CAA) offices across the street from the Beverly Hilton. He was amused when I gave him a copy of Marcia Seligson's 1977 article in *New West* describing my first conversation with Spielberg (15). Belfond, who likes *Stratagème*, recommends adding another 50 pages: I plan to complete the book in August. Putting what I really think between the lines of a novel is the best way for me to advance research into the phenomena that interest me, rather than waste time arguing in academic circles.

Redondo Beach. Tuesday 19 July 2005.

In 100-degree heat, my EDF investment colleagues, freshly arrived from Paris, decided to visit the monstrous CalSteel factory in San Bernardino. We drove back along ugly freeways and increasingly intense smog, barely able to see the mountains to the north.

The company presents an example of "negative electricity" generation I hadn't seen in action before. It is under contract to stop using current (compensated in dollars) and turn off the huge furnaces when the region is close to a blackout, especially during heat waves. This saves the local Utility from buying expensive current from other networks, or building new nuclear plants at enormous cost.

Athanor. Saturday 30 July 2005.

It is Janine's turn to be sick, coughing and tossing much of the night, shaken by the alienation of our daughter-in-law and a new awareness of our own physical fragility. We are not of a mind to collapse under such insults, however. We'll restructure our existence once again, ready to sell this house, streamlining daily life.

Two recent books intrigue me. Greg Bishop's *Project Beta* claims to expose the role of disinformation agents like Doty and Moore, guided by handlers in the intelligence community, who unfortunately include some of my friends, acting from the shadows. Nick Redfern's *Body Snatchers in the Desert* claims to pin the blame for the Roswell saga on men who wanted to bury the files on unethical medical experiments done by the US military in the 1940s, testing the resistance of humans to radiation, space capsule environments, and the phenomena of the high atmosphere. The role of "three-letter agencies" and their managers in the myth-making that followed is murky at best.

Hummingbird. Sunday 31 July 2005.

I've asked Hal what he thought of the Bishop and Redfern books.

"*Project Beta* is interesting," he said. "Especially the part where one of his sources, 'the Colonel' describes the chaos that marked the whole Bennewitz affair. That rings true!"

Hal is similarly impressed by Redfern's detective work. Stanton Friedman has issued a rebuttal to it, but it ignores the medical experiments at and around Roswell.

So where does that leave the "core story" of alien hardware? "It could mean that the hardware is not from Roswell at all," said Hal, who sticks to his belief that the secret UFO project is deeply buried. I forgot to ask him if he knew who was sponsoring Doty's actions.

Hummingbird. Thursday 11 August 2005.

This afternoon Bob Johansen invited me to the Institute for the Future where he was briefing Doug Engelbart on our futures research. Doug came in quietly, wearing an old Institute for the Future blue shirt, and smiled when he saw me. He spoke softly of his models for solving society's problems, then complained of being misquoted, most recently by John Markoff.

Doug, at 80, is conscious of his poor short-term memory. He thinks of selling his house in Atherton (his wife, Ballard, died eight years ago) and moving into a retirement community. He told us about his childhood, discovering an old Model T Ford in somebody's barn and refurbishing it with help from local mechanics who took pity on the half-orphan (his father had died when he was four or five). He is rightly proud of his "country boy" background.

As a young engineer, Doug worked on control systems for wind tunnels at Ames Research Center, where he got the idea for models of problem solving for the great issues that face society. I told him the main products from his work were the colleagues that he had influenced, myself gladly included. That seemed to please him.

It pains me when people react to his name by saying, "Oh yeah, the mouse man!" Doug has achieved so much more…

Athanor. Saturday 27 August 2005.

In need of a retreat, I got here last night in the cold fog, woke up even colder. For a week I have been alone, building our next Fund project. Janine is in Normandy, reunited at last with Maxim. I put a favorite record on the stereo (*Missa et ecce terrae motus* by Antoine Brumel) and began catching up with accumulating documents.

Over the Internet, I've been following a parapsychology discussion list, a closed group of some 40 leading experimenters that include Stephan Schwartz, Ed May, Russel Targ, Dick Bierman, and others all over the world. Trailing the Parapsychology Association meeting in Petaluma last month, much of the discussion concerns the attitudes of the academic community towards psychic phenomena, more negative than ever.

Schwartz summarizes the state of the field by writing (26 August): "SRI and Mobius both began during the early 70s; so did Chuck's psycho-physical lab, and Mind-Science in Austin. Also, of course, PEAR began (16). To my way of thinking the real crunch came in the early 90s. SRI/SAIC closed, Mobius closed, Mind-Science was gone, ASPR ditto. Today there is PEAR, UVA, the Rhine (to a limited extent) and IONS, and individual researchers under the umbrella of what might be called virtual labs. I'd guess that the collective US budget for psychical research is less than 1.5 million."

On Wednesday I had dinner with Roger Brenner in San Francisco. We walked over to the fancy Culinary Academy where we cut a funny figure among the elegant diners, me in a casual sweater and disheveled Roger in his cycling clothes, both carrying armloads of books and magazines we were going to discuss.

A day or so later he had a strange episode on the subway, when four strangers suddenly engaged him in conversation...about UFOs.

Hummingbird. Wednesday 31 August 2005.

Peter Sturrock called me tonight after a long silence, possibly caused by my rebuttal to his statistical study. He has redone the analysis of UFO frequency, failing to replicate his published correlations with sidereal time in the French data, as I had pointed out.

Hurricane Katrina now hits New Orleans with devastating fury, reminding me of many discussions about models of emergency management and civil engineering with Bob Chartrand and the Al Gore hearings in Washington. There's been no progress, except for government buying lots of useless computers. Nobody seems to focus on the key question: Will the levees hold, or break under the pressure of all that water draining towards the city?

On the way to Paris. Friday 2 September 2005.

Federal and local authorities are losing control in New Orleans. Neglected for a very long time, the levees have been washed out by the storm. Dirty water from the lake and the swamp floods the city; the poorest sections, of course, are the most exposed.

Mabillon. Sunday 4 September 2005.

Paris was very hot today as a group of researchers gathered for lunch and a good afternoon discussion at our apartment. Dominique Weinstein came with Dr. George Leftheriotis and François Louange. George gave me his copy of a dissertation by one of his students. Then I mentioned Greg Bishop's and Nick Redfern's books, urging them to read both of them.

A dedicated French ufologist, Jacques Maniez, sends me four photographs of a ball of light taken in Provence. My friends had never seen them, or even heard of the case.

This illustrates the poor state of affairs in this research, even with an official government team in Toulouse. Louange said that the new structure, chaired by Yves Silliard, has taken a long time to get to work.

London. Victoria Park Plaza. Friday 9 September 2005.

London waits for rain, the turmoil of recent bombings a sober memory. Our last presentation of the week is scheduled today at HarbourVest as we lay the groundwork to raise our new Fund.

My old friend, publisher Gérard Klein, invites me to the regular Monday literary lunch of French science-fiction writers, conveniently held at *Les Trois Canettes*, a few steps away from Mabillon.

Mabillon. Saturday 10 September 2005.

Janine wouldn't mind coming back to France permanently, to a life spent between Paris and some quiet country home in Normandy. I cannot fault her impression that America is sinking into simplistic religious notions at home and disastrous pretensions of badly-timed domination abroad, while poor Americans are left to die in the flooded areas of New Orleans.

The image of corpses floating in polluted waters among the alligators of Lake Pontchartrain will remain as a symbol of what happens when little minds try to run a country like the United States with policies based on obstinacy and greed rather than intelligence. Will France fare much better, defined as it is now by the expanding egotism of its supposed elite?

Chirac is hospitalized, allegedly with a "minor stroke." Not one but two alligators are hoping to feed on that particular corpse: Sarkozy, all sharp teeth and ruthless ambition, and Villepin, a vaporous diplomat who has found an easy constituency by fanning the flames of anti-Americanism: both men products of modern-style demagoguery.

Mabillon. Monday 12 September 2005.

Janine's voice on the phone, from the West coast, so profound and clear. She is my horizon, my guiding light, the standard of my mind. I can survive alone, as I do here, but it's a dull sort of life. Fortunately, I will be home in a few days.

Now a victory: Thérèse de Saint Phalle has convinced Belfond to send me a contract I can sign for *Stratagème*.

Athanor. Saturday 17 September 2005.

Thick fog is rolling past my windows. A record is playing, again Antoine Brumel's wonderful mass. Catching up on accumulated news, the computer brings me the announcement by Bob Jahn and Brenda Dunne, of the closing of their parapsychology lab at Princeton:

"For more than a quarter century, the Princeton Engineering Anomalies Research (PEAR) laboratory has engaged in a broad range of experiments on consciousness-related physical anomalies and has proposed a corresponding selection of theoretical models that have combined to illuminate the fundamental nature of the provocative phenomena that emerge."

While it is sad to see psychical research stalled around the world, it is the stunning lack of results, contrary to the convoluted claim above, which made it unavoidable. Parapsychology is stuck in old models; it repeats the same experiments with the same marginal results. Even the impressive SRI/SAIC results which came as a systematic extension of the French research by Warcollier before World War II, were the victims of Washington bureaucracy and failed to explore the higher levels Ingo and I had suggested to them.

The official reports, at CIA and other agencies involved, falsely claim that such insights had never been contemplated before.

Hummingbird. Saturday 24 September 2005.

We were hiking along the trail to Tomales Point, with sublime vistas of the Pacific crashing at the foot of vertiginous cliffs, when Janine surprised me with a bouquet of wild flowers and gave me a kiss. Today is my birthday, no. 66. We walked along the 10 miles through the brush and the sand in the blessed, misty light unique to the North coast. This is my favorite place in the world. The fog, so dense all summer-long, stayed far offshore all day. The elks in rutting season challenged one another with their curious whistle.

Roger came along for the long hiking trip, full of good stories about the world of the paranormal, outer space, and beyond.

Hummingbird. Friday 7 October 2005.

Email from Kit, today, about noon: "I leave in an hour. The contacts of the well-known Brazilian UFO hunters have failed. They are flakes, nut cases, and mostly selling books and magazines. It has been hard not to laugh. Why are they all overweight and in tennis shoes, and want me to be sure to have their photos? They don't seem to have day jobs, either."

Of course, if we start with so much prejudice against the local culture, we will easily conclude that the sightings were just rumors among the peasants. In the same way, the investigation of cattle mutilations became intractable in the 1970s. Kit and his colleagues do advocate going after the truth, but as John le Carré writes in *Absolute Friends*: "In his profession, he should know that the truth, as he finds it, is always a lie."

Hong Kong Marriott. Sunday 9 October 2005.

Fourteen hours over the sunny ocean, cramped in coach, to attend the first joint US-China Board meeting of NeoPhotonics, one of our portfolio companies. It will take place at Photon Technology in Shenzhen, a local company we're absorbing in a complicated series of stock-and-cash transactions. I arrived at the Marriott on Pacific Place, my briefcase heavy with documents, my trusted Fujitsu laptop and a battered copy of Le Carré's novel. Every TV channel shows the devastation in Pakistan, where a massive earthquake has just collapsed buildings, erasing entire villages over an extensive area.

The lesson from recent disasters, from 9-11 to the Tsunami, to the floods in New Orleans to this earthquake, is clear: Populations can place no trust in governments, bent on empowering themselves, or on charity organizations driven by inadequate, idealistic visions as they fiercely compete with other faiths to exploit the blood and the dust. Then, the pitiful sight of mothers in tears, and fathers digging into rubble with their bare hands to find children, or their bodies, under the concrete of poorly designed, sloppily-constructed schools.

Hong Kong Marriott. Monday 10 October 2005.

Two meetings with financial executives today, both friends of ChinaVest. At Wells Fargo, an experienced man told me that raising money in China was even harder than Europe or the US: "Money is in the hands of rich families and company founders who've become wealthy. They have no patience, no clear process for investing."

He stressed the Chinese attraction to brands and designer names: Carlisle, Cisco, Newbridge... which fascinate them with their billions. Governments are in the business, too, notably Singapore, Korea, the Chinese provinces and the Kuomingtang ("KMT"), but it's hard to decipher the actual source of the money, and corruption is rampant.

Edgar Cheng, former chairman of the Hong Kong stock exchange, dashed my hopes to find a placement agent in China. He characterized Shanghai as the center of business, Beijing as the center of expertise, while Hong Kong is the vibrant financial center for the continent, "a city where many knowledgeable people can write a $3 million personal check." As for Singapore, it is barely relevant, he believes, while Japan has missed the boat, and Taiwan is becoming secondary; its major industries are moving their manufacturing centers to the mainland. I gave him an overview of our technical strategy.

"You should bring your ideas to Hong Kong," he said, because it is the center for investing into the mainland, especially in this post-Enron period when legal obstacles have become overwhelming in the States. "The Chinese Bank of Construction is raising $6 billion in Hong Kong, not in New York," he pointed out.

He pushed aside the reports I had brought as part of my presentation. *"We must let our minds flow,"* he added warmly, "rather than work from documents. I admire that you are still so active at your age. My own background is in traditional medicine and yoga; I follow my own interests. You'll need someone else to help you reach the second-generation layer, in the Pearl River Delta."

Edgar Cheng wanted to hear my ideas about Asian flu, not only the medical consequences, which he knows, but the financial and societal ones. Can the crisis be solved by foresight, as the potentially disastrous Y2K computer bug was averted? What form of investment will survive, he asked, and what form of government, if 20% of the world's population gets incapacitated some day?

Shenzhen. Wuzhou Guest House. Wednesday 12 October 2005.

Two of my co-investors in Neophotonics joined me today, and after much confusion our driver took us to the Shenzhen industrial zone through security gates with armed border guards who scrutinized every passport. He spoke no English, but gave his name as "Henry."

First impression: a nasty mix of gray collectivism and frenzied shopping, East Berlin meets Vegas under a sky heavy with brown pollution. The hotel is staffed by armies of identical little girls in blue uniforms, busy at phones and computers. Luxury, in this hotel for distinguished foreign guests with money, is naturally perfect. But why is it impossible to plug in my own computer and get on the Internet? And why do I already feel the walls closing in?

Shenzhen. Thursday 13 October 2005.

After the board meeting of Neophotonics, we were invited to visit the Huawei factory, main global competitor to Cisco. They occupy a huge campus with a curious main building that resembles the Louvre and a White House-like rotunda stuck in front. Oddly enough, in this landscape it all seemed to make sense.

Our group went through one of the multiple factories on silent electric carts. It took us 20 minutes to drive from one end of the three assembly floors to the other. Hundreds of uniform-clad workers were inspecting circuit boards, stuffed components, and tested products.

Shenzhen is a heavily-polluted city the size of Paris with 11 million people, walls of skyscrapers, cranes as far as the eye can see, a huge golf course with 108 holes "for distinguished guests" of the elite, and newly-made Chinese millionaires. While we were impressed, last year, by Shanghai and Beijing, and while Hong Kong can actually be stimulating, inspiring, and even fun, this city simply leaves me cold and scared. In the evening we are treated to fancy dinners: four different soups, including "Monk jump over the wall" soup and monkey-head mushrooms, fish lips and concoctions of various animal parts, said to be "good for the men." We had a very refreshing yogurt-like drink, and also "Chinese water," an alcoholic drink that tastes like motor oil and burns belly and brain alike.

Instead of hors-d'oeuvres, we had four tiny delicacies: something sweet, something sour, something bitter, and something spicy, the four components indispensable "to those who have lived a full life."

Athanor. Saturday 15 October 2005.

Two 14-hour flights in six days with long tours of the Photon factory where 1,500 technicians, engineers, and administrators work very hard. In the evening, most go to bed at the company's dorm, a cinder-block building with four or six beds per room, no privacy, no place to wash or dry clothes. They lead a life of intense competition in a war-like atmosphere.

Chinese industrial facilities resemble warships under full steam. As I prepare to leave for home, I am still under their dark spell.

Reno. The Peppermill. Wednesday 19 October 2005.

An interesting investment conference takes place in this hotel. Eager entrepreneurs, enthusiastically demonstrating their latest products, meet with financial types and "angels."

The big funds are not here, so the egos are muted, the conversations friendly. Reno is especially lovely in the fall, but the contrast with China is brutal. The air is clean here, the lakes sparkle in the mild breeze from the mountains. The trees are changing to rich new colors, including a fauve-orange tint that borders on pink.

Janine is with me, dashing downtown for her own business. I have a few hours in the room to work on the *Stratagème* translation. This is our 45th wedding anniversary, and time passes too fast.

Hummingbird. Saturday 22 October 2005.

We drove up to Healdsburg today for a happy reunion of the team of women who worked at InfoMedia as account managers and executive assistants. They've stayed in touch for the last 25 years, through marriages and divorces, relocations, many children, and multiple jobs. They call themselves the "Infomaniacs." Ruthie and her husband, who organized this event, run a successful beverage operation and own a fine house close to the historic square, so we had a hearty dinner with the group. Ruthie proposed a toast to me as "the man who had the vision," but I had to check her: "I'm cured now, Ruthie, I don't have any more visions…"

Hummingbird. Wednesday 26 October 2005.

Kit has returned from Brazil, blasé as ever. "Did the trip change any of your conclusions?" I had asked. His email to me this afternoon is worth quoting.

"I never had any conclusions except that the medical data and sources were poor," he replied. "I actually found them to be non-existent… and the hospitals were worse. The most important briefings I had were with seven members of the heavily-armed and very bright members of the Brazilian Floresta Military Police who cover three states of high sightings. They emphatically denied anything had occurred…under their watch…and that while everyone knew of the cases 'made famous in our tabloids,' they were all the result of what they called 'those thinkings of the peasants.'"

Yes, I said, we heard the same thing in Brazil, and the assessment is accurate. This was to be expected, was it not, given the social distance between the authorities and the lower classes? We ran into this bias everywhere during our own trips. It is the same distance one would find between New York sophisticates and Alabama share-croppers. Kit lacked a reliable guide to the complexity of Brazilian culture, but that's not all there is.

"Nothing is true of what has been said," Kit went on. "Several contacts have asked us: 'Don't you find it odd that thousands of people are reported to have had these events, but in the heart of the locations, you can't find a single one who has an education?'"

Again, I had to wonder: "Why not go directly to these 'uneducated' peasants, to find out what it was they saw, as we did with Bill Calvert and Agobar? As for the Air force intelligence team under Colonel Hollanda Lima, calling them 'uneducated' is an unnecessary insult."

The area explored wasn't even near the places where we had documented over fifty close encounters, many with physiological sequelae. So what game is being played? By which side? Both sides?

Hummingbird. Thursday 27 October 2005.

Lunch with Russell Targ (at Joanie's). We have the same publisher, so we spoke about *Heart of the Internet* and a reversion of rights to me that will enable me to release the whole text, without charge, on Google. He told me that Ed May's experiments confirmed what Dean Radin had found about precognition signals: a subject's heartbeat shows a three-second anticipation of sudden scary events.

Athanor. Saturday 5 November 2005.

France is in the grips of riots in the poorer suburbs; hundreds of cars are burning. The government's control of the situation is slipping. This had to happen. The country has swept the sub-population of immigrants and unemployed under the rug of its complacency.

Here at home, my first stained glass window is in place. It is a *lancette* of four panels showing the Queen of Heaven emerging from a parallel universe; Earth and Water signs are above her as she holds an alchemical retort. The bottom panel shows a furnace, the athanor with three vials. The top panel completes the ogival design with a rose that will repeat in the four other *lancettes* I plan, whispering: *sub rosa*.

Hal and I have discussed Kit's Brazilian comments. He is puzzled, as I am, by the denials and negative statements. He thinks the local military may not have put him in touch with the actual places or the doctors who did the investigations, so all we have is an indirect approach, once again.

Hal saw Bob Bigelow about seven months ago at a NASA planning meeting to map out various future projects with the staff. The main idea is a very conventional return to the Moon rather than (1) exotic propulsion research, or (2) a novel plan to blast supplies to an orbital station using electromagnetic thrust. Bob's plan to test his modules has been delayed because the Falcon rocket from Space-X is not yet fully tested, so he now considers a back-up plan with the Russians.

Air Canada flight to Montréal. Monday 6 November 2005.

Many American friends, dazzled by the beauty of central Paris, fail to see reality. Our neighbor, historian Dr. Kevin Starr, returned enchanted from his French vacation. He visited museums and lingered in Monet's garden, blind to the trouble brewing from Nanterre to Evry, where biotech workers get assaulted by gangs in the parking lot of the Center for Sequencing. Cab drivers won't take you to those suburbs after dark, while firemen only venture to "the Projects" under police escort. That is the situation I've witnessed for years, yet no measures are taken to improve the lot of the young, the displaced, the idled workers.

Tonight, Janine and I watched a French television debate about the riots. It featured a minister charged with patching the "social fracture." He had 30 billion euros to modernize the suburbs *"but it takes time to bring the cranes,"* he said.

"How long would it take for Bob Bigelow to assemble those cranes and solve that problem?" I wondered. So we just turned off the set and went back to our Sunday routine, but feelings of loneliness hit us. Once again, we have no news of our grandson. The separation is hard on me and especially cruel to Janine. I often wake up in the middle of the night in an empty bed. I get up and find her sobbing alone, desperate in the dark kitchen, defeated, head resting on her crossed arms. I am at a loss to change her mood because I feel no better than she does. There's nothing to do in the face of such meanness.

Hummingbird. Wednesday 9 November 2005.

Eric Davis has asked Kit about his fMRI (functional magnetic resonance imaging) experiments: "Do you see a particular signature in the brain of abductees that's indicative of sleep paralysis? Or do you see the classic signs of paraphrenia? If not either of those, is there a unique signature corresponding to an abduction event at the time of the scan, which can be identified as a 'daimonic' event?"

Kit answered tersely: "No difference from normal subjects."

Hummingbird. Friday 18 November 2005.

Another lunch with Bernie Haisch and Marsha. A new company launched by Joe Firmage is getting traction, offering a valuable information source on the web with participation by the Sierra Club and *National Geographic*.

To my surprise, Bernie wanted to talk about Meier, the Swiss hoaxer who keeps producing fake saucer pictures. I had the feeling I often get among zealots, that nothing I can say will inform the conversation, so I talked about something else.

In the evening, Janine and I attended a concert where Krista Bennion was leading her orchestra in several baroque pieces, notably the admirable *Bells of Sainte Geneviève* by Marin Marais.

Hummingbird. Thursday 24 November 2005 (Thanksgiving).

We spend a quiet day alone, just the two of us, a bit sad, reviewing notes, sorting papers in anticipation of the end of the year. Keith Harary has surfaced with an article in *Psychology Today* (December) entitled *Mind Games*.

The cover introduces it as "The Confessions of a Star Psychic," a title he surely detests because it detracts from the real thing, a capability present (but often submerged) in all of us.

Athanor. Saturday 26 November 2005.

Chris Aubeck writes that Bob Pratt just died of a heart attack. Bob had sent me a nice message, just one week ago, that the daughter of General Uchoa planned to attend my lecture in Virginia Beach.

Then Bob Bigelow sent me five pages of reports from the Utah ranch, where one employee has witnessed poltergeist phenomena: things flying off, strange smells, whitish presences—still no craft

Virginia Beach. Ramada Hotel. Friday 2 December 2005.

Gregory Little, a co-organizer of the conference, picked us up at the airport. He reminded me that Northrop had flown a magnesium "battering ram" dual jet engine aircraft in 1945, called the XP-79B. It killed test pilot Harry Crosby when it crashed. He believes this is an indication that could help explain the Ubatuba UFO crash, although the Northrop magnesium wasn't quite as pure as the samples I have.

Janine and I have made new friends at the Edgar Cayce Foundation, including Cynthia Luce, a friend of Bob Pratt who has lived in Brazil for 30 years and chased UFOs with him. Stanton Friedman is here, stressing his work on MJ-12 and Donald Menzel's autobiography.

We visited the ARE (Association for Research and Enlightenment) and its excellent library, meeting the managers of the well-organized foundation, then spent yesterday evening with Stephan Schwartz, whom I had met in the early days of the SRI work on remote viewing. At his fine house on the shore, we discussed the Navy's role in the early history of American parapsychology (Rickover, Deep Quest and the Nautilus) and the likelihood that Roswell was indeed an illegal medical experiment gone horribly wrong, which will be denied forever.

Virginia Beach. Sunday 4 December 2005.

We fly back to California this afternoon, but I will jump into another plane tomorrow morning to rush to Texas, where Hal and Eric tell me they have news about "the project" and request my assessment.

I spent over an hour this morning with Denise Uchoa Slater, the granddaughter of General Uchoa. She's in her early 40s, married to an American, raises two small daughters and teaches languages to Navy Seals. As a teenager, she interpreted for Allen Hynek and was his guide in Brasilia in the 1970s. Her father is three-star General Paulo Roberto Uchoa, head of drug enforcement for the Interamerican organization, currently based in Washington.

A pleasant and intelligent woman, she told me her grandfather had been trained in mechanical engineering and studied at West Point in 1954. He retired in 1967 and moved to Rio. His remarkable experiences with UFO cases on a farm outside Brasilia are a close parallel to events at Bob Bigelow's Utah ranch.

Austin, Texas. Monday 5 December 2005.

Hal and Eric picked me up at the airport and we went directly to the Fonda San Miguel. With them was McGarity, a friend of John Alexander, former manager of operations at the Nevada test site after working at EG&G Special Projects, and later at Los Alamos. Now retired in Miranda, he serves as a Baptist minister and teaches school.

Hal showed me a patent for a ramjet disk, a picture of a disk on the ground codenamed "Senior Soda," and of the same disk aloft, all from a confidential film. The contractor believes UFOs derive from such pre-existing hardware, which led Hal and Eric to seek my help.

We reviewed the factors involved, but the data is poor. The source has no background in physics and his information is typical of a beginner dredging up old engineering ideas. Hal is well aware of Admiral Radford's involvement in project "Winter Haven" and T. T. Brown's flying disks. We spoke of the episode with the other general's visit to the famous black project, where he touched a disk.

Reluctantly, Hal granted that it proved nothing.

Later the same day.

The conversation with McGarity was valuable. He told me he'd seen a UFO on 23 October 1987, along with Gabe Valdez and "a French physicist and his wife" on the Archuleta mesa. (If the date is correct, this couldn't have been Velasco, in Toulouse at the time. So, who was it?) They saw a large triangle that came over rapidly, hovered above them, turned, and zipped off before they thought of using all the cameras they had brought. There were markings under the craft, possibly a drone, which was silent and bore bright white lights.

While working at the test site (Summer 1980), Bill volunteered when a manager in a business suit came to his team, asking for two people to stand watch on Black Mountain. He went there with night vision equipment and spent three days scanning the sky and the valley. During the day it was simply boring desert, but "everything came alive at night." Large trucks and balls of light as big as the vehicles seemed to come out of the side of the mountains. The spheres of light flew off, came and went. It seemed the trucks were "bringing something to the lights, which were as bright as the truck headlights, but even more intense in night vision binoculars."

Hal and I speculated they might be directed energy or ionization regions of the type Roger Rémy once described to me, but Hal has attended briefings where the head of that project reported only tentative, preliminary success. It's hard to believe the technology would have been so well developed as early as 1980.

McGarity could go anywhere on the site except for Papoose (an NSA site) but never found out what the lights were, or why he had been sent out to watch them. He laughed when I mentioned Bob Lazar, to whom he'd been introduced by Don Ware. When he probed his actual experience, Lazar failed to show any real knowledge of the situation at Area 51 and S-4. Later, Bill tracked down his role at Los Alamos as a simple technician with no clearance.

McGarity also told me that the strange radiating object in the Cash-Landrum case had been tracked as coming from the Gulf of Mexico.

San Mateo. Euro-America offices. Tuesday 6 December 2005.

The weather has turned cold. It froze overnight in Austin. Eric Davis kindly drove me back to the airport for the flight to SFO. I told him I thought he and Hal were grasping at straws, like all of us, seeking validation in an artificial vacuum.

Hal was recently part of a panel assembled in Washington under semi-official auspices to discuss the potential impact of publicly revealing the reality of UFOs. Attendees were broken up into 64 societal sectors and eight subcommittees. Initially open to disclosure, all members ended up recommending secrecy because violent reactions to disclosure would be uncontrollable: religious zealots would go on a rampage, clamoring for witch hunts. Hal doesn't know who organized the workshop, or why. As for Kit, he now believes the "Alien Autopsy" to be genuine, a rare operation on a human sub-species specimen: not an Alien, "but not a Progeria patient either." (?)

Upon landing I called Hal again to thank him and to ask about the workshops. They involved John Petersen, but "they went much higher." The participants were told that the US, Russia, and China all had custody of Alien hardware.

For now, I hold to my working hypothesis that the psychological warfare boys are playing games, as they've done consistently since at least 1952. Of course, both assertions could be true at the same time.

Mabillon. Sunday 11 December 2005.

Real investigations in France are conducted by men like Jean-Claude Venturini, Gérard Deforge, and Rear Admiral Gilles Pinon, who spent the afternoon here. The contrast with "official" ufology is striking. The private studies address close encounters and abductions; they treat social and physical implications as significant, along with live debates about our old case of Haravilliers. Pinon and Venturini even attended a recent international conference in Châlons, where several remarkable cases were discussed, the witnesses comparing notes in person. None of that feeds into the cut-and-dry CNES files.

Mabillon. Tuesday 13 December 2005.

Janine was able to get the last two tickets for tonight's performance of *Boris Godounov,* so we heard Valery Gergiev's magnificent rendition of Mussorgsky's genial work. Music and singing were sublime in spite of the ugly backdrop and props (banks of neon lights? Spiders?!). Why am I so moved by that opera, when I know so little about music?

Paris is sunny but cold. A brisk walk from one meeting to another freezes the ears and warms the heart, a much-needed distraction from lingering sorrow, kept in the dark again about our grandson.

Mabillon. Friday 16 December 2005.

In the rush to Christmas, Parisians seem to have forgotten the events of a few weeks ago, the suburbs in flames. I spent the evening in long and unproductive negotiations with my French partners about our budget for next year. Many books are published about the decline of France, but no one tries to tackle the real problem, an obsolete cultural outlook, badly in need of overhaul, and a cast-iron bourgeoisie soldered into a network of privileges.

Today is formal, with our annual meeting with our investors at the Cercle Interalliés, then I'll be free. Annick is coming over from Saintes. I look forward to dinner at Les Charpentiers with the two sisters, and more conversation, meetings with researchers.

Mabillon. Saturday 17 December 2005.

We had wanted to do this for a long time: gathering some of our Parisian friends for a long afternoon of tea, hot chocolate, coffee, and pastries, and lively debates. Rob Swigart was there, as well as François Imhoff and Martine, and another painter, Jean-François Deluol who brought his wife Christine, and of course Annick.

Deluol sat down in the old red armchair and warmly recalled his many conversations with my mother. We joked about *les goûters de la rue du Four*. It was our first opportunity to dwell on literature and the gossip of Paris. Tomorrow my brother and his wife, whom we haven't seen in almost a year, will come over for coffee.

We fly back to San Francisco next Thursday.

Hummingbird. Friday 23 December 2005.

A quick trip to the office to sort out recent mail and put the files in order. One of our Funds, Euro-America-II, comes to an end next week after 12 years of work, notable personal victories (among those, the IPO of Com21, some accomplishments in medicine, and the acquisition of Class Data Systems by Cisco), and a rough time during the Internet bubble crisis. Nobody lost money; our investors made a profit, in contrast with most funds of that period that saw the collapse of Vivendi, Worldcom, Enron, Lucent, Alcatel... We can hold our heads high.

San Francisco is tightly wrapped in fog. I nurse the cold I caught in Paris, unable to find a thread for a novel I would like to start.

George Soulès, writing as "Raymond Abellio," has published a novel called *Les Yeux d'Ezékiel sont ouverts* that keeps me interested, a mixture of visionary esoteric knowledge and messy geopolitical ramblings. His insights about the human condition in the days of Marxist ideology and anarchist passion explode throughout the text like the guns of saboteurs. Yet, in today's atmosphere of nuclear terror, suicide bombers, worldwide datamining and biowar, even Abellio's bravado sounds puerile.

Hummingbird. Saturday 24 December 2005.

My head is clearer today. I am coughing less, yet I still go through phases of exhaustion. Our daughter is off to L.A., so we spend Christmas alone.

What I dreaded as a depressing end to the year has become sheer pleasure, having Janine with me, a selfish joy. I love her mystically, even as she lightly dismisses my emphatic declarations.

Athanor. Saturday 14 January 2006.

The house was battered by a rainstorm all night. I slept evenly, the night punctuated by the sound of waves and squalls. I had a dream of playing with my children as I remember them: Catherine so bubbly, Olivier tender and curious, inquisitive, trustful...how I miss my son!

I feel sorry for those who do not have the luxury—or the courage—to keep a diary, or at least orderly notes. The events of the last few months would already be just a blur if I didn't have such a record.

Mabillon. Sunday 22 January 2006.

My third day back in Paris, where the weather is mild, sunny again; time passes, even and lazy, with sleepy afternoons and mornings that drag on, and vague musings of a new book. I have found an inspiring little volume by Bernard Thirian, talking about the art of stained glass as initiation, quest for ultimate truths. It helps me learn the French terms for the craft of the *maîtres-verriers*.

Three more days in Paris for the launching of *Stratagème*. I have spoken on the phone to Gérard Deforge, and to Chris Aubeck in Madrid, to discuss our progress on *Wonders*. I already miss Janine's presence, the routine of our days.

Mabillon. Tuesday 24 January 2006.

The party for the launching of *Stratagème* was held last night in the fine vaulted medieval cellars of the former Hotel de Villeroi. It was an opportunity to gather many of my friends: Gabriel Mergui from Génopole; Elisabeth Antébi; Gérard Deforge and Jean-Claude Venturini; Simonne Servais and Thérèse de Saint-Phalle; François Imhoff and Jean-François Deluol; Dominique Weinstein and François Louange with members from Institut Métapsychique including Mario Varvoglis and Stephan Schwarz, Stéphane Alix (author of a documentary about John Mack), and magician Majax…

Some ufologists are upset with the novel. Let them, I thought, another page has turned.

Now I put my papers in order, starting new projects. I should be inspired by this fine building with its wonderful pedigree. Erected in 1926 by the architect Etienne Lorrain, it long served as a hotel for intellectuals and literary figures. Tolstoi, Pasternak, Waldo Frank, and Brecht came here for long evenings of passionate debate about culture, according to a memoir by Léon Paul Fargue (*Le Piéton de Paris*).

Perhaps the timeless echo of their discussions will filter to my small library on the sixth floor, and educate me.

Paris is cold. France braces for a winter storm that will bring snow and ice. My work here is done.

14

Athanor. Saturday 28 January 2006.

The rain is silvery like the sea, soft and steady as your body against mine. We watch the waves and linger in bed after breakfast. I must be in fair physical shape because I've recovered from the trip, short jet-lagged nights, long flights, and the cold of Paris. Here I catch up with my partners, news of the ever-expanding web, and the latest *New Scientist* talking about Newton's manuscripts (surprise, surprise, he was serious about alchemy), the enigma of dark energy that supposedly makes up two thirds of the universe, and a new book I should get about the laws of information: *Decoding the Universe* by Charles Seife.

I have new supplies for my stained-glass panels; I brush them clean in the quiet seaside air. I hope to complete the third one soon. It will show Saint Agobard blessing a man who has emerged from a vessel flying in the clouds. The celestial ship sends down beams of pure iridescent heavenly light. In the lower panel, a little devil (inspired by the cute demons at Chartres) holds up reflectors that scatter the light, breaking it up into dirty colors to fool our ordinary minds...

Hummingbird. Sunday 12 February 2006.

This is a time to enjoy our friends, like Paul Gomory and Béatrice, seen on Friday night at the War Memorial Theater for a concert by Philharmonia (Tartini, wonderful on ancient instruments). We had dinner with them at La Jardinière. And yesterday we drove over to Menlo Park for dinner with Rob Swigart, Jim Fadiman, Harvey Lehtman (a colleague from SRI days), and their friends, discussing novels, new drugs and old computers, Doug Engelbart, the Tech Museum, the Wayback machine, the special artefacts and secrets of the Valley...

The phone rang this morning as I worked on *Wonders*. A man named John "E" was calling from Tacoma, bluntly offering big money for research. He rambled on about large projects, his links to millionaires, and ambitious ideas for extraterrestrial studies. I was on guard at once because he reminded me of Allen Hynek's would-be patrons who used to call him out of the blue with such offers, but never followed up with concrete steps.

Mr. E's vision includes a "Defensers Fund, non-profit, with money from a 50-billion-dollar Stonewood Fund with a for-profit subsidiary to study UFOs, paranormal phenomena, crisis management..."

Here it gets a bit complicated because he mixes in emergency preparedness, Bob Wood's own plans, and what he calls my "wonderful" research, but he was oddly evasive as soon as I suggested that we meet in person.

Hummingbird. Thursday 16 February 2006.

Ingo Swann called. He praised my recent interview for the magazine of the Edgar Cayce group, where I acknowledged my participation in remote viewing and my training by him at SRI. So he wants me to give a talk at the forthcoming conference on remote viewing in Las Vegas. Ingo said he was 72 now and had suffered a bad fall.

Athanor. Saturday 18 February 2006.

Our plans for a new venture Fund are at a standstill. My Canadian investment contacts are caught in an intractable political mess of their own making and bureaucratic disputes among the financial giants of Québec. For the second time in my life, I will have been tempted, and then discouraged, to go live there.

If they had funded our team, Janine and I would have found a place in Montréal and I would have opened a Canadian office to support local hi-tech startups, but that idea now seems foolish.

Yesterday I had wonderful visits at the Presidio, which is turning into a focus of high technology. Rob Swigart and Harvey took me to meet Brewster Kahle and his staff at the Internet Archive. Afterwards we strolled over to see David Sibbet at *The Grove*. These two visits flashed before me the wide opportunities of the Bay area, its unlimited talent and imaginative projects with worldwide impact. Why would I even think about moving away?

Athanor. Saturday 25 February 2006.

Winter has returned to Northern California with a hailstorm on the shores of Bodega Bay. I work hard on *Wonders*, enjoying exchanges every day with Chris Aubeck in Spain. The book is taking shape nicely, after some compromises on both sides.

We had dinner in Petaluma with Peter Banks and Mary to plan a proposal to NASA regarding their future venture fund, Red Planet Capital, a new opportunity to work together on aerospace projects and to do good work for the space program, sadly bogged down in bureaucracy.

The phone rings again and Mr. E reiterates that he's contacted Robert Switch of the US Patent office "and another friend of his, Tom Ward of Brookhaven's DoE weapons program. The UFO study would be funded by a for-profit subsidiary of the Defensers Fund, itself part of a $50 billion trust, setup with oil wells as guarantee."

It all sounds as positive progress, but whose pockets does the money actually come from? He lost me when he spoke of a vague "indenture trust relying on bonds floated in Europe, with discount measure financing under the Roe program." Why all the foreign complexity?

Again, I suggested a face-to-face talk, but Mr. E pleaded he was an old man, unable to meet. What games are being played here? The financial setup makes little sense, and I won't touch any money my partners and I can't document fully.

Hummingbird. Sunday 5 March 2006.

More about the enigmatic Mr. E, who called me to say he was in touch with Roy Mann, "*an associate of Reagan and Casey who has seen the crashed ones.*" He went on about one Ed White, who "wants to talk to you," implying he had something to do with a huge Trust for humanitarian projects handled by the Federal Reserve. White, of Columbia, Mississippi, is an 80-year-old Mormon, "friend of Tom Delay and Trent Lott..." Mr. E went on to name a bewildering series of other people who might be assembled to help his hypothetical project. My searches on the web about them raised concerns about political connotations but didn't reveal any serious grounding in advanced technology.

I have not worked in venture capital for 15 years to be fooled by a friendly name-dropping voice who casually talks on the phone about billions, so I requested to be kept outside of any public fund-raising promotion.

Athanor. Saturday 11 March 2006.

More strange goings-on. Recent postings on the web initiated by Starstream Research comment on the role of Ron Pandolfi, "Project StarGate," and others. Reports are floating around, asserting that Dr.

Pandolfi is involved in the development of a new type of radar using a passive system designed to detect unwanted intrusions of stealthy craft: "The TIGER DIA committee at the National Academy of Sciences received a briefing from Ron in November 2005, with a demonstration of the system: The Chinese have used it to counteract Stealth…the software is key, it is classified."

As stated, it makes no sense, so much of the data must be classified.

I am told that Pandolfi, reputedly chief phenomenologist at the CIA, met Bigelow at the Los Alamos National Laboratory (LANL) and at John Alexander's house in the formative stages of NIDS. Starstream wrote: "In 1993, the DIA StarGate project initiated a pilot study into the feasibility of using telepathy for command, control and communication." That confused me even more.

When I asked Kit's advice, he was less sanguine: "My lab in Detroit and a think tank in Arlington (Petersen) and a private medical foundation are also working on the program… but no results yet. No, it doesn't require telepathy. Think RF, and modulated B-fields."

Athanor. Saturday 18 March 2006.

Robert Bigelow called me on Tuesday to say he had no objection to a translation of the NIDS mutilation report that a correspondent of mine wants to publish in France. Unexplained phenomena continue at the Ranch along with voices, shadows, and luminous objects. I told him about my current investigations of the San Jose area sightings, where very similar things were reported in 1974-75.

We went on to discuss the proposed NASA venture capital project, of which he was unaware, and his own plans for two launches this year and two more next year. He said NASA was becoming "little more than a job employment program for risk-averse bureaucrats."

On Thursday, I drove to the Valley again to visit a woman who'd written to me about unexplained flashes of light, small luminous objects hovering around her husband's car, and rumors in the area about "ghosts and saucers."

She once saw a red and green disk in her room after suddenly waking up, and another time a black, seven-foot creature with red eyes receded into the wall when she reacted in anger at the intrusion. Significantly, she's not alone with that type of experience, but most observations by people in the neighborhood remain unpublished.

Mabillon. Thursday 30 March 2006.

There are only four customers with me at Café Danton, gloomily staring out at the rain-swept boulevard. It shows no trace of recent demonstrations, yet the general atmosphere is oddly reminiscent of impending riots: the same heaviness in the air, discontent in the minds. A repressive government parades its obsolescence.

Following a Black Tuesday of strikes and demonstrations, which I spent among my colleagues at Genopole in Evry, people seem mentally stumped and economically lost, worried about their future. Students risk losing a year of study as they rise to defend basic rights.

Peter Banks called on Wednesday with the good news that we were among just a handful of teams screened by NASA for a presentation in Washington on April 19th before the Red Planet Capital selection team. It rains in Paris, and even more in San Francisco, says Janine, eager to join me here soon.

Mabillon. Friday 31 March 2006.

Huge trucks of the riot police rush down the boulevard, sirens blazing, large metal screens bolted to their front bumpers. They are followed by a convoy of buses, blinking blue lights as far as I can see. Prime Minister Villepin, at his lowest point, implements a new labor contract full of traps for young people eager for their first job; unhappy, they can be fired at any time and replaced by cheaper fresh meat, with no positive economic exit. Roaming bands of students confront the police; 57 universities are closed; colleges are occupied; railroad stations disturbed. Tonight, all of Paris is upset. Overturned cars in flames light up the evening news.

Janine arrives tomorrow, flying through Chicago, in time to share the turmoil with me, and a strike on Tuesday. Things are looking up in the US, fortunately: Peter Banks, Graham Burnette, and I just had a phone conference to plan our presentation to NASA.

Mabillon. Sunday 2 April 2006.

Following the advice given long ago by my friends from Chartres, we took the subway to Saint-Denis to visit the basilica, the crypt with what remains of the royal legacy, and the wonderful sculpted tombs. After lunch on the little square we looked at the stained glass in more detail. Some of the panels date from the time of Suger (the consecration of the church was in 1144), the earliest examples of the art in Europe.

It is that early stained glass I love over everything else, sharing Abbé Suger's view that through light, "mournful spirit rises towards truth through the material and, at the sight of that light, is reborn out of its interior submersion."

Medieval windows only used three fundamental colors, namely blue, red, and yellow, and two composed colors, green and purple. Yet they conveyed a sense of transcendence that has rarely been equaled.

Mabillon. Tuesday 4 April 2006.

France is on strike again but some major services are still running. We overlook the boulevard, always animated, vibrant with shouts, protests, drunken songs, or jazz music spontaneously erupting at all hours. I fly back to San Francisco on Friday, but Janine will stay behind, patiently trying to mend family ties. Over lunch with Thérèse at Brasserie Lipp, I heard good advice about publishers and politics.

Tonight, I had the surreal experience (at the invitation of my colleagues, who stayed safely home in Lyon) of joining a dinner given at the Salons France-Amérique in honor of American pension funds visiting Paris. The theme was "investing in France," but the Americans in attendance were obviously bewildered at the political scene that greeted them.

Timing could not possibly have been worse, as about 100 guests assembled under the dripping gold and white sculptures of the elaborate dining rooms. Looking at the list, I quickly added up the sums involved. There were billions of dollars in the room; the California pension funds alone hold hundreds of millions.

Unfazed by the gloom of the strike and the screaming patrol cars in the street, the US Ambassador made an encouraging speech. Pieces by Gershwin and Debussy (*L'île Joyeuse*) were played, songs by Ravel and Reynaldo Hahn were beautifully sung, while our jet-lagged guests wondered what all that fuss was about, tired eyelids dropping.

The drinks were served late and there was no way to save the food (*tartare d'avocat et tourteau, médaillon de lotte, risotto crémeux à l'huile de truffe blanche*) that had gotten cold, or burned.

Mabillon. Thursday 6 April 2006.

Rachmaninoff's *Vespers* sung at Saint-Germain-des-Prés by two extraordinary choirs have sent chills down my spine. Sacred music, to me, is the ultimate art form, combined here with sculptures of light and color. Other artistic disciplines compete in beauty or greatness, but only those two are capable of forcing the spirit to rise to that point where that unique truth is grasped, the evidence for the other levels.

Hummingbird. Sunday 16 April 2006.

Back in San Francisco, a dull Sunday morning without you. It rains throughout the Bay Area, and Easter snow falls on the mountains. Yesterday, you were about to leave Normandy with Maxim.

Catherine and Becky came over to the City yesterday and cheered me up. We had a brunch of chicken crêpes on Polk Street. In the afternoon, Graham and I finalized the NASA slides for our presentation in Washington. By coincidence, on Tuesday Janine and I will fly in opposite direction and land at Dulles airport within minutes of each other. She will be on the way home, while Graham, Peter Banks, and I will be headed to NASA.

Washington, D.C. Tuesday 18 April 2006.

Janine was surprised to find me waiting for her when she came out of Customs to transfer to the San Francisco flight. She'd finally had a chance to discuss the family situation in Paris, but she was met with a flood of needlessly cruel words.

Spring over Georgetown, cherry blossoms, and a major meeting tomorrow as we compete for the opportunity to run the $75 million Red Planet Fund. I'm eager to be done with this phase of it.

Hummingbird. Wednesday 19 April 2006

We cannot predict what NASA will do, but our presentation in Washington yesterday was the best one we've ever made. Graham and Peter were both in splendid shape, and the two-hour interrogation session by the senior evaluation team passed quickly.

At stake is nothing less than dominance in space for the US, even if the technologies we bring are still in infancy; they will need to be deployed within ten years, while Russia and China catch up, or try.

Athanor. Saturday 22 April 2006.

At the invitation of Béatrice and Paul Gomory, Janine and I attended yesterday's concert of the Philharmonia Baroque Orchestra for the North American première of Christian Cannabich's *Mozarts Gedaechtnis Feyer*. The orchestra distinguishes itself by playing on historically accurate instruments. The resulting sound is quite unlike what our ears have learned over hours of recordings, radio, or other concerts.

San Francisco's art community is thriving again. It feels good to be in a city where culture is an important part of life. Symphony Hall was packed, so were the Opera house, the Ballet.

Mabillon. Sunday 7 May 2006.

In France again, I just read the 200 pages of correspondence between Aimé Michel and Bertrand Méheust recently recovered, feeling as if I was sitting with them again in some country inn, arguing about the soul, the universe, and Man's ability to comprehend the world (17).

Under a light gray sky, I walked over to the Sainte Chapelle to bathe in its otherworldly light and to decipher its message, now that I am better able to read the glasswork and see the skill of the craftsmen.

A short storm has just burst over Paris, changing the mood. In the warmth of this apartment, it would be insane to complain. On the south side, I have the quiet courtyard and the view of Saint Sulpice. To the north, Montmartre shimmers far away like a fresh cream pie in a pastry shop. Now some good news: I'll be able to see Maxim this week.

Yet this is Paris without you, so many things noticed, that I point out to you in silence, in imaginary dialogue. I miss you, our quiet way of planning each day, every hour together, so that it never matters if it rains, or the sun shines, or if a sudden noise in the street awakens us in the middle of the night.

Mabillon. Tuesday 9 May 2006.

Rain drips from rooftops, from the gargoyles of Notre-Dame. I walked over to Max's school and gave him the dragon stories I've written and illustrated for him. He'd prepared my next assignment, a list of seven future chapters he wants me to write and draw, so we sat in a bistro and made plans. He is a calm boy now, well organized and smart.

Mabillon. Wednesday 10 May 2006.

The area around Les Halles was still deserted when I drank my second cup of coffee in a bistro across from CNES headquarters and walked in to meet Jacques Patenet, who's replaced Velasco. We set up the projector and waited for members of the steering committee to arrive at 9am: urban, smiling Yves Sillard; David Assemat from CNES; Arnaud Benedetti; Jérome Béquignon, Bruno Rivière, Pierre-Henri Digeon, and Dominique Crosasso from Intérieur; Pascal Bernaud and Patrick Michel from Recherche and CNRS; Jacques Goas from Météo-France; Emmanuel Jacquemin from Aviation Civile; an officer or two from Armée de l'Air; and Jacques Zlotnicki from the *Université de Clermont*.

Two papers were distributed: my 1975 AIAA presentation with Claude Poher, and the more recent "Six-layer" model with Eric Davis. There were few questions, mainly clarification inquiries from Yves Sillard, an impressive man I immediately appreciated.

After my presentation, Dominique and I had lunch at *Chien qui Fume*. We savored a glass of White Sauvignon to celebrate the occasion, without exaggerated expectations of a breakthrough. I recalled my visit in similar circumstances with Hynek and Niemtzow on 24 June 1985, when we saved GEPAN from being disbanded. None of the members of that old group was present today, so there's very little institutional memory left in the French project. In fact, Patenet took me aside, suggesting we stay in touch "since you seem to have better files than we do on many French cases." Fortunately, François Louange is still around, as a valued consultant.

Mabillon. Friday 12 May 2006.

Spring has draped the boulevard in greenery, scented the air, and cleared the sky. Parisians drown in such sweetness, a smile on their lips again. They walk lazily around, taking pictures of each other with no care in the world, ignoring the Clearstream scandal (18), and all the vile quarrels. It is a sad, slimy time for Chirac's mediocre government that should simply slip into oblivion.

Mabillon. Saturday 13 May 2006.

Over a drink at Deux Magots, Messarovitch said many French politicians had been tainted by the scandals of Thomson-CSF's Taiwan frigates and the hidden "retro-commissions" that came with them through banks like Clearstream: a billion dollars, spread over the entire, corrupt French political spectrum. Mitterrand himself, who retired in 1995 after his second term, had grabbed a big slice of it. Is that what de Grossouvre wrote about, and why they gunned him down in his own office?*

I spent another delightful hour and a half with my grandson on Ile Saint-Louis, reviewing his homework at the corner café, an activity that involves ice cream and heady arguments about flying dragons. The weather, so fine yesterday, has already turned hot and sticky. Spring feelings never last here because any extended sunshine smothers the city in its own fumes.

"Why do you have to go back to California?" asks Max.

How can I explain that my real life is over there, with you?

---

* Sarkozy replaced Chirac in 2007, defeating Ségolène Royal.

My office in San Mateo. Tuesday 16 May 2006.

There's a message on my phone from Lisa Lockyer at NASA Headquarters: "*I am pleased to inform you that the eval team has finished our evaluation and we thought your response was the best one we received for Red Planet Capital. And so I wanted to let you know, and start talking about a Space Act Agreement and see how we can make all this work...*"

Athanor. Sunday 28 May 2006.

Whether from fatigue, stress, or our new responsibilities at NASA, my health has been shaky the last few days, starting with random muscle pains, blurred vision in one eye, and finally, that Friday evening, an episode of amnesia.

I was driving to the North coast, but, halfway across the Golden Gate, told Janine I couldn't go on.

The next thing I remember is returning to the apartment with her at the wheel. She assured me I'd driven quite properly to a parking area and never lost consciousness during the episode. I spoke and behaved normally, but my face was tired and ashen. Once at home, I unloaded a few things, undressed, and went to bed, but I couldn't remember what had happened, or why I hadn't gone to work that day, or even the fact that we'd had visitors from France the previous evening, Yves Messarovitch and my partners from Lyon.

I couldn't even recall that we were starting the new venture fund for NASA.

Hummingbird. Tuesday 30 May 2006.

After breakfast yesterday I had another episode. I had to ask Janine what day it was. Then the pains came back.

After 24 hours of tests at St. Francis, I seem in fair overall shape, so I will go back to work tomorrow while doctors pursue other hypotheses: small seizures? It felt good to leave the hospital, knowing I'd wake up next to you...Memories of the NASA work came back.

Hummingbird. Friday 9 June 2006.

Another alert, the third one. After a restful weekend and a normal workweek only marred by tension headaches, I fainted on my keyboard last night while working on a book.

When I came to, Janine was cradling my head with her arm while calling emergency, but the new tests were normal as before: excellent blood pressure, equal in both arms, no evidence of stroke or seizure, so they released me again, quite puzzled.

Hummingbird. Sunday 11 June 2006.

More scary time last night, near fainting and some confusion, but my heart and brain remain physically fine, arteries intact. Today I feel shaken but alert, seriously planning the organizational phase of our new fund with Graham and Peter. Janine works with her clients while I relax by watching the World Cup (Portugal-Angola).

Now the pain in my neck comes back whenever the effect of Tylenol fades away, and confusion sets in periodically; it infuriates and terrifies me.

Hummingbird. Tuesday 13 June 2006.

These attacks seem to happen early at night, just as I enter sleep. Last night was terrifying—confusion again. Yet Janine tells me I spoke rationally and was able to recall, with some effort, what I had done during the day.

The worst thing is not to know what's happening. Will I be able to go on working at the high level the venture business demands? Why is this hitting me just as I have a new plan, the best partners?

The blurred vision hasn't returned and the pains are getting milder. Janine is wonderful, keeping our ship afloat through the storm, but I feel ashamed to let down those I love.

Hummingbird. Wednesday 14 June 2006.

How I long to feel well again! To enjoy thinking new thoughts, learning new things…I certainly do not feel diminished by the dark episodes of the last two weeks. Catherine took time out of a busy day to come sit by my bed and talk to me; her visit, a great blessing. The neurologist runs a sharp toothy device over my legs, reads my file, and tells me I'm fine, I haven't suffered any sort of ischemia, and I should "resume my normal activities." Easy to say: I woke up with sharp headaches again. I have a board meeting this morning, which I can do by phone, and an EEG this afternoon followed by blood tests, but I still experience occasional confusion.

Hummingbird. Sunday 18 June 2006.

Every day we make progress with NASA and both teams of lawyers working on Red Planet Capital. Two days have now passed without any headache or medication. I made arrangements to spend a couple of weeks in France in late August. Through Yves Messarovitch and his friend Philippe Favre, an invitation came to work for a week in the *atelier* of Didier Alliou, the stained-glass master based in Le Mans, in charge of the restoration of the ancient panels at Chartres and Sainte Chapelle—my favorite places in the world!

Athanor. Saturday 24 June 2006.

I've worked normally all week. The neurologist tells me everything is fine with my EEGs, so my hopes return.

He's finally diagnosed TGA, *Transient Global Amnesia*, a serious but not incapacitating condition from which most patients recover fully. "It might happen again, and you'd probably recover again," he says a little too cheerfully. I still have the occasional cramps, however, and I need more sleep than I did before this crisis.

Yesterday, somewhat reassured, I finally reached my son in Paris. I told him we wanted to make peace in any form they wanted. He answered calmly but missed the fact that my call was a cry for help.

15

Athanor. Saturday 8 July 2006.

Day by day, I regain confidence amidst the blizzard of legal documents that will set up the complex structure for Red Planet Capital. It's not easy to have the US Government as a venture partner. We hold daily conference calls with NASA headquarters, their adviser from JP. Morgan, and two teams of lawyers in Detroit and Boston. I develop the website, I draft deal memos about technologies already brought to us by startup companies: smart manufacturing, innovative displays, and new types of rocket propulsion.

There are two new books on my bedside table about scientific discoveries on Mars, as I catch up with recent work. Much time has passed since I plotted the first computer-based map of the planet Mars under Gérard de Vaucouleurs, back in Texas!

There was sharp anxiety this week about the launch of Discovery, one of only two surviving Shuttles. After weather delays, followed by the realization that an external fuel tank suffered a gap in its foam insulation, NASA finally made the difficult decision to launch the spacecraft with its crew of seven. It took off on Independence Day and made its way to the Space Station, where it is docked today.

There's been no news from the mysterious Mr. E. and his money, so I may never know what that assemblage of elderly tycoons, curious experts, weapons dealers, Republican politicians, and assorted executives had in mind.

Las Vegas. Friday 21 July 2006.

The Flamingo has been taken over by a few hundred space enthusiasts, members of the Space Frontier Foundation. The organizers have invited me as one of the judges on a panel for the business plan competition. Five finalists presented their ideas about rocket engines and airship relays for communications. Some of the members recognized my name, including Jim Oberg, one of the intelligent skeptics in ufology, and Robin Snelson, a journalist and writer who told me that a boyfriend of hers who worked in Hollywood on a new TV show back in the 1980s once borrowed, but never returned, her copy of *Messengers of Deception*.

"The show turned out to be the X-Files!" she said. "Did you ever get a check?"

I could only laugh with her; we both know how Hollywood works.

There were sessions on lunar base infrastructure, Cisco's plans for interplanetary communications, and grand visions for space tourism, which leave me skeptical; nobody is funding that. The audience was the usual blend of young men with orange hair, serious engineers in formal suits and ties (the temperature was 108), and journalists with wires in their ears and recorders hanging from shoulders.

Bob Bigelow was the star of the show. His first spacecraft, Genesis I, launched atop a converted SS-18 soviet-era rocket on July 12, has now deployed in orbit and is circling the earth. Cameras on board show test objects inside in weightless motion. I had a private lunch with him at McCormick & Schmick, to brief him on Red Planet Capital, a surprise to him.

Naturally we spoke about UFOs, the Utah ranch, and his own investigations. He once tracked down a nurse who had been on the scene, in the sixties, after a crash near Sainte Marie outside Albuquerque. The Highway Patrol had secured the scene and called the hospital, telling her to bring stretchers to take away "injured children." She got there before the local doctor and saw that the "children" were not normal humans.

A colonel arrived with troops, pushed everyone aside including the cops, barked some orders, and took away all the hospital's equipment, including the stretchers, the sheets, the sponges, and anything that had touched the bodies.

Bob mentioned a book written by Clinton's assistant attorney General Webster Hubbell, who was sent to jail for a year or so and wrote up his experiences (19). He mentions one of his major regrets: not completing a presidential order to find out the truth about UFOs.

Bob had shown the passage to Senator Harry Reid and encouraged him to ask Clinton about it. The former president confirmed he'd tasked Hubbell with two special projects: find out who killed Kennedy and "Are there UFOs?"

"Clinton had never been briefed. George Bush must know, because his father knew, given his position."

"What is Mike Griffin's attitude on the subject?" I asked Bob.

"Reserved," he said. "He's very self-conscious about it."

Bob, on the contrary, speaks openly of his interest. He told journalists at the conference that it was his curiosity about UFOs, triggered by unexplained sightings in his own family, that pushed him to build up his wealth and dedicate it to space exploration. "I could have retired at 35," he told me with a smile as we finished our meal in a quiet corner of the restaurant, "but I just kept working so I could finance *all this stuff*."

Athanor. Saturday 22 July 2006.

A heat wave is spreading over California, with temperatures well above 100 in Santa Rosa. To escape from that oven, crowds have discovered our secret cove using Google and weather maps, creating traffic jams along the coastal road. In Europe the hot weather causes casualties, as it did in 2003.

Peter Banks points out that scientists project average temperature increases of one degree, which doesn't sound big, but that figure doesn't take into account the fact that much of the Earth is ocean, so the true increase in land temperature will actually be much higher.

Peter also tells me that the Bush administration has just yanked observation of the Earth out of NASA's mission, effectively blinding the US when it comes to monitoring global warming from satellites, in step with Washington's idiotic denial of the impact of its flawed energy policies.

Now the Middle East is in crisis again. Israel has entered Gaza to crush the Hamas extremists (who, absurdly, deny the very existence of those who crush them). Now it bombs Lebanon to put an end to rocket attacks from Hezbollah.

Hummingbird. Sunday 30 July 2006.

An evening reception at the new de Young Museum gave us a chance to admire the magnificent building with its twisted copper tower high above the trees and the hills, as proud as the superstructure of an aircraft carrier. The event included collections of American art and a Chicano exhibit vibrant with humor, bright colors, and intense social commentary.

We now have a date (next Monday) for a decisive meeting in Washington with NASA Administrator Mike Griffin. Much work has gone into the legal structure and recruiting trustees for the non-profit corporation that will control the money. I've prepared files on our first series of ten attractive investments and met in Sausalito with Gilman Louie to discuss his own experience as the founder of In-Q-Tel, the fund setup years ago by the CIA.

Athanor. Saturday 5 August 2006.

Last night Peter Banks and Mary met us for dinner in Petaluma. We reminisced about earlier days of science, the first Russian images of the hidden side of the Moon, what has been learned and what remains to be discovered. The North coast is clear and bright this morning, the sky immensely blue.

I feel pages turning, past concerns fading away. My mind returns to my early fascination for space and the planets—the passion that brought Janine and me to Texas, many years ago.

Washington. Monday 7 August 2006.

Yesterday my two partners and I went to the harbor for dinner (at Sequoia) and walked home the two miles along Virginia Avenue, past the Washington monument and along the Mall, the Smithsonian, and the Air and Space museum. It was a good evening. It helped us get into the spirit of tomorrow's big meetings.

The Space Act Agreement between NASA and Red Planet Capital was signed this afternoon by Assistant Administrator Rex Geveden and by Ms. Ruann Ernst as one of our Trustees.

The meeting with Mike Griffin, a bright engineer with no time for idle talk or humor, was tense at times. He spoke of his success at In-Q-Tel, the CIA venture fund he ran as president under Gilman Louie. While that project seems to have helped the agency acquire valuable technologies, it is regarded in Silicon Valley as an unwelcome intrusion of spooky government into the venture business.

Earlier in the day, we'd spent time with the scientists of the NASA Interface Center. In the evening Scott Pace invited us to the Cosmos Club for dinner, reviewing the Fund and joking about the name. I pointed out that Mars was not quite red, rather butterscotch in color, but the name "Butterscotch Ventures" wouldn't sound quite as good as "Red Planet Capital."

The club, situated in a glorious old mansion with painted ceilings and golden moldings, has the same stale atmosphere as San Francisco's University Club, populated by slow-moving dignitaries who play dominoes or attend the occasional wine tasting.

Athanor. Saturday 12 August 2006.

Celebrated some delayed birthdays and the inception of Red Planet, Janine and I had dinner last night at Sutro's, the restaurant at the Cliff House, with Catherine and Rebecca. The sunset beyond Seal Rock is a powerful sight, and the pelicans flying over the ruins of the Sutro Baths never cease to celebrate it. The fog stayed offshore, the view along the beach was perfect. Now I must spend time in my library, digging up references to complete *Wonders in the Sky*. Chris Aubeck, back in Madrid, has found updates to our manuscript, now close to our target of 500 cases recorded before the year 1880.

In Erwin Chargaff's book of scientific reminiscences, *Heraclitean Fire,* (20) the celebrated biochemist recalls being invited to Moscow for a conference. Before leaving he was visited by several strange people from American Intelligence, notably a strange woman he called Mrs. Grizzly, "looking very much like an underpaid mother with several difficult children." He adds: "At this occasion, no money was offered; everything was strictly scientific, although the poor woman was clearly out of her depth as a spymaster. Mrs. Grizzly asked for my help with difficult questions which she had trouble spelling correctly. It was not clear why she had come. She was pleasantly confused, exuded warmth, wished me a pleasant trip, and added, unfortunately, 'See you again.'"

This was the summer of 1957, and the spooks' request for Chargaff to "keep his eyes open" had the opposite effect: Not eager to become some sort of spy, he avoided all contact with his soviet colleagues, spending much time in museums, learning nothing. When he came back, there was Mrs. Grizzly, waiting for him: "Her people wanted to know whether the Russians had succeeded in creating a homunculus, and tiny men with whom to populate their spaceships."

Manoir du Chêne. Friday 25 August 2006.

In the Norman countryside, a mile or so outside the village of Nonant, we have joined Annick's son in his large country house. Maxim came with us on the train from Paris. We visited the new house that Annick—fed up with the heavy climate and inhospitable atmosphere of Charente—has just bought in Douvres la Délivrande. Nine-year old Maxime has matured into a keen observer of nature, expert on cartoons, explorer of country lanes. Tomorrow, Janine and I take the road back to Paris, leaving him with his cousins and six cats.

Saint Rémy du Val. Sunday 27 August 2006.

Our friends Philippe and Kathryn Favre, introduced to us by Yves Messarovitch, are restoring this old abbey with its large chapel and the lodge of the Abbot of Moullins, a fine little castle. They invited us to dinner in 15th century splendor.

Philippe gave us a tour of the buildings, highlighting the improvements of the last 20 years, and those of the next 20 years, an enormous project conducted with a deep sense of historical and artistic precision. One of his artist friends, Didier Alliou, joined us for dinner in the grand library room with its beamed ceiling. We spoke of history, of UFOs, and the Internet. Favre is semi-retired after a career in banking that took him to Saudi Arabia, Sweden, and England in top positions for IndoSuez. He follows the markets for his private clients from this country home and serves as manager of a group of Stanford alumni. His energy seems inexhaustible.

The conversation moved on to space projects, parapsychology, and survival. Philippe confided to us that he'd died at age two and a half, was revived, remained in a coma for six months, and woke up recalling details of the operating room, which he'd seen from above.

Le Mans. Monday 28 August 2006.

We slept well behind the thick walls of Moullins Abbey. After a rich breakfast, Philippe drove us to Le Mans, where Alliou and his team were expecting our visit at their workshop of Vitrail France. The stained-glass panels from the axial bay at Chartres (the main window of the Annunciation, high above the main altar) were laid out on broad light tables, a true splendor expecting cleaning and restoration. We looked at them with reverence and wonder.

Over the next hour, Didier and his wife, Béatrice, detailed for us their work of exquisitely precise preservation of these treasures: the removal of old lead from fractured pieces to be patched, the new protective measures for every panel. Didier set me to work with his team that same afternoon.

I had planned a window inspired by the Melchizedek of Chartres, as the fourth *lancette* for the San Francisco study, but this requires techniques of *grisaille*, or painting on glass, as done in the 13th century, so they taught me the materials and the use of their tools.

The weather cleared up in the afternoon as we toured the old town, where Didier took us to the cathedral where he had done much work. He gave us a detailed lecture on the evolution of stained glass from the 12th to the 20th century, all of it accessible in that single magnificent building. I looked at them with stunned reverence.

Le Mans. Tuesday 29 August 2006.

Janine has taken the car to return to Normandy and Maxim, while I walked over to the studio in the light rain to work on the pieces I cut yesterday. The technique has not changed since medieval times: I was patiently initiated into *demie-teinte,* painting with a paste of crushed bone and glass powder. I was shown how to mix it into *mousseline*

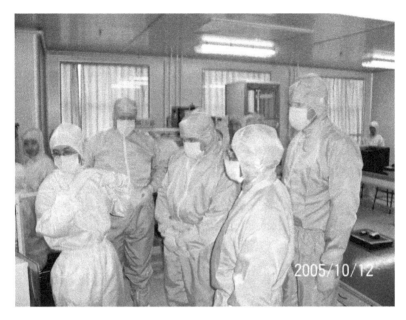

Fig. 11. The Bunnies: Board members of NeoPhotonics inspecting the clean room. Shenzhen, China, October 2005.

Fig. 12. The "Lady at the Orient window" in my study.

and apply it with fat brushes amusingly called *trainards*. Soon the big oven (at 680 degrees C) was at work, fixing the stern attitude of "my" Melchizedek and the motion of his fine hands.

I am happy here, enjoying the privilege of work among leaded panels eight centuries old, a guest of a team of craftsmen whose quiet, anonymous life and vision I admire. Once they saw I knew enough about glass not to get confused about the various tools, and did not cut myself with the sharp edges, they adopted me as a trusted colleague, or at least as a promising apprentice.

The aesthetic shock I feel whenever I look at Chartres has two powerful causes: sheer admiration and empathy for the achievement of the craftsmen who dedicated their lives to such marvels in the primitive conditions of a rugged era and, more importantly, the realization that the glass, interposed between man and the unknown, or rather the unknowable splendor of the sky, acts as a translator, a compiler of infinities, a mediator, a vector for the soul.

Le Mans. Wednesday 30 August 2006.

Didier and I drove over to Chartres and we climbed up to the top of the scaffolding to inspect the job site. He patiently showed me how the ironwork held the panels, the *barlotières*, the *feuillards*, and the *clavettes* invisible to the tourist—and most of the clergy!

From the top of the eight-story catwalks tied to the eastern side of the cathedral, the eye sweeps across the plains of the Beauce region beyond the town. Up there it's another world, a forest of stone, copper drains, and lofty *arc-boutants*.

Didier strolls confidently on the stone ledges that line the tall windows. Seen from the back, the stained-glass panels show their age and the battering of centuries of storms, insects, bacteria, furious attacks by Protestants, and bad modern repairs with cement and rusting metal braces.

We detached one of the plywood panels that obstructed the wide bay. The cathedral, seen from that point high above the main altar, was revealed as a forbidding cavern with only the dim glow of a cluster of candles and the filtered light from the great western rose.

Le Mans. Thursday 31 August 2006.

Today, Didier took me over to visit his friend Jousse, the ironwork master who has travelled with him to job sites all over the world. We had lunch with two young computer entrepreneurs who wanted to talk about technology. Then, over dinner in the Old Town with Béatrice, Didier presented me with some rare samples of ancient glass. I enjoy these few days by myself, the walk over to the workshop in the morning and the calm of the narrow streets.

Mabillon. Saturday 2 September 2006.

Yesterday, Didier had a party for his neighbors and regional dignitaries to show them the final panels he'll be re-installing at Chartres on Monday. Janine joined me from Paris for the evening, bringing Maxim.
 This was the only opportunity any of us will have in our lifetime to touch these panels again, so I wanted my grandson to be there. I took him on a tour of the workshops, with the vast reserves of glass sheets of all colors, then we listened as Jousse spoke about the intricate mountings and locking systems.
 Max is still with us today, sleeping in the blue "Normandy" room where he can play and paint to his heart's content. He comes and sits on our bed in the morning to tell us his night's dreams.

Chartres. Monday 4 September 2006.

We came back to be with Didier and his team who needed help to reassemble the glass panels and to mount them onto the cathedral. Rain clouds came and went; the wind stopped the work for a while, but the sun eventually won over the storm.
 For several hours, Janine and I carried the panels up the tall metal ladders to the workers above, then Didier handed me the heavy mallet and offered me the honor to re-attach the four bottom panels. They represent the bakers who donated the money for the monumental stained-glass window that towers 20 feet above us.

Chissay Castle. Friday 8 September 2006.

The Stanford Executive group assembled by Philippe Favre meets here for two days. I gave two lectures in the luxurious accommodations of this restored castle on the banks of the Cher River, in barter for the opportunity to work with Didier's stained-glass team.

Philippe recalled for us his meeting with Osama Bin Laden during his stay in Saudi Arabia. "I used to fly to Geneva regularly to meet with members of his family," he said. "The Saudi royal régime is surrounded by a court of a few selected families, but the Bin Ladens are the closest ones to the king. They supervise state-owned buildings, so they have special access."

He explained that Osama's hatred of America was secondary to his desire to overthrow the Saudi régime itself: "It all goes back to the day in 1979 when Islamist extremists took over Mecca, the most sacred site in the Muslim world."

The king sent his guards, but they were summarily mowed down by machine guns as they approached across the plaza.

"The Saudis then asked the French to send their elite troops, the GIGN. The French demanded the plans of the building, held by the Bin Laden family as a State secret. Osama was furious when his family released the plans."

"So, did the French take over the building?" I asked.

"That's never been officially acknowledged," said Philippe. "But that episode is the root of Osama's hatred of the West, of his family and of the Saudi royalty. The main reason he attacks Americans is to force them out of Saudi Arabia, so he can take over the kingdom, and eventually rule over Islam."

Hummingbird. Thursday 14 September 2006.

The new Pope, Benedict XVI, has just made inflammatory remarks about Islam and Mohammed, thus playing into the hands of extremists who believe in an imminent clash of civilizations. Ironically, I have just resumed my work on the stained-glass panels of Melchizedek, the ancient priest-king from whom all three Western religions flow. The Pope could have used such a figure to highlight the common spiritual origin of the various faiths and their search for peace. On the contrary, the world seems eager to seize every opportunity to aggravate misunderstanding.

Athanor. Saturday 16 September 2006.

The North coast is quiet, bathed in warm sunshine, the sea slow and peaceful. I came here with a glass panel to complete and my notes from the French trip. I also dug into the blue files for references to ancient cases to be included in the final draft of *Wonders*. It's a fine day for a picnic and a walk along the beach, a tour of the hillside, a chance to put some distance between us and the world before plunging back in. This is the last weekend before the formal announcement of Red Planet Capital in Washington. Our website goes live on Monday, Peter flies to San Diego for an aerospace industry conference, Graham to the East Coast for a venture panel, and I'll to speak on a panel with Lisa Lockyer of NASA at the meeting of the American Institute of Aeronautics and Astronautics.

Hummingbird. Friday 22 September 2006.

A big day, a turning point: Catherine is buying her first house; Janine is closing a long-standing deal; and Red Planet Capital was announced this morning before hundreds of space experts assembled at the AIAA conference. Bob Bigelow was there, as was Pete Worden, the director of Ames Research Center. Entrepreneurs continue to send us their smartest business plans.

I have gone around the Sun 67 times, a tiny creature carried by a small planet in the unthinkable infinity of space. Mankind is on the verge of exploring the neighborhood, but the obstacles are immense. Bob Bigelow stunned the audience on Thursday when he announced his plan to launch a full-scale space station ahead of schedule to stimulate a race to orbit. We shared the table with General Pete Worden and half a dozen executives from Lockheed and Boeing.

Yesterday I went boating at Stow Lake in the fog of autumn, relishing the smells and the freshness from the trees in the beautiful park. The stresses of the past weeks and months are receding at last.

Hummingbird. Monday 25 September 2006.

David Swift sailed into my office today, looking frail but his mind sharp as ever. He'd come from Hawaii to speak at the AIAA conference. David asked my opinion on psychical research. "Why does the reality of the effects have to rest on such razor-thin statistics, when the claims are so large?" I asked.

I have recovered from the episodes of last June, as my neurologist had predicted. I hadn't suffered a stroke but a "transient metabolic event" (as opposed to a "transient ischemic event"). The warning is there, however, beyond the medical terms. It colors the plans I make, my priorities. It puts ideology in perspective. It makes me less willing to fight quarrels that now seem irrelevant, whether they deal with UFOs, parapsychology, or venture capital. Most importantly, I have learned that things and people tend to find their own level. What we must treasure along the way are those rare magical moments when human contact reveals its beauty, its true powers.

Hummingbird. Wednesday 27 September 2006.

Kit, looking very trim in a black shirt and dark jacket, met me for breakfast at Fisherman's Wharf. He was in town for an Air Force science meeting. He told me he was now convinced that "the totality of the UFO conundrum was contained in a single delusional model."

"Why do you take the time to study it," I asked, "if the players are so delusional?"

"Because so many of them are in top positions in government and industry, that's why! I don't spend any time any more with folks like Dan Smith and Falcon, marginal players. The people I'm talking about include a vice-president of BAE systems."

He was surprised to learn about Red Planet Capital. He reacted quickly to the news, providing advice for the medical and psychiatric area. When I pointed out I was finally able to contribute directly to the study of the solar system, the very topic I had come to research when I came to Texas in 1962, he looked at me with his good smile: "You're like me, Jacques. You're a slow learner! I'm finally doing the research I wanted when I was in my twenties, looking inside the brain."

The same day I had lunch with Bernie Haisch and Marsha, still active with Digital Universe, the latest Internet creation of Joe Firmage: "Joe said I should tell you, if you invest $500,000, he'll tell you everything he knows."

"I don't believe Joe knows anything," I laughed as we ordered lunch. "I hoped to renew friendship, but he only talks about money."

"Well," said Bernie, flustered, "Joe has spoken to the General."

"I don't believe the General knows anything, either," I answered.

Marsha, a talented lady, said again she was seeing me in her visions, in a maroon uniform, piloting a spaceship of the future propelled by the zero-point energy of the vacuum...

Houston, NASA Clear Lake. Sunday 15 October 2006.

The vast landscape of the Gulf Coast under the tepid rain glistens from one expressway to the next, washing over the sprawling urban galaxy that calls itself Houston. The hotel looks out to the Galveston shore. A few sailboats are forlorn at anchor, all quiet. Tomorrow morning we'll be at the Johnson Space Center, Mission Control, and the Space Station mockup to meet the top manager and understand their technical expectations. Then I fly to Austin to spend Tuesday morning at Hal's new offices and labs. Last week it was Ames on Thursday and JPL on Friday, both marked by excellent introductions by Scott Pace and lively discussions of the Fund, its purpose and methods. I learn much about current and future problems of space exploration, but even more about the politics inside NASA and its relationship with the far larger military establishment: At Ames, the Air Force had taken over the wind tunnels.

On my visit to Pasadena, I had dinner with Mark Benton and his wife, Karen Fry. Both are engineers at Boeing who've seen UFOs and wanted to discuss the subject. They had even brought an old copy of *Confrontations*.

Janine tells me the skies are gray over San Francisco, and she feels the place empty without me. Our love has reached a plateau of quiet intensity, with a touch of urgency, because we're increasingly aware of the cruel passage of time.

Austin, Texas. Tuesday 17 October 2006.

A major storm rolled over Houston yesterday, flooding the bayous, turning major intersections into lakes and halting traffic. Four people died in submerged cars. Driving to the airport with Lisa Lockyer, we lost two hours waiting for the roads to drain and we drove through a foot of water before reaching Hobby, where all the planes were late.

Hal's new office is a convenient square, two-story brick building in an area of light industrial development. The newly paved parking lot was empty when I arrived, so I sat on a step reading Ken Follett's *Pillars of the Earth* until I saw Hal's black VW Jetta drive up. He took me through the new lab with its calorimeter used to test claims of cold fusion. A few sporadic instances of heat generation, he said, but none of the big theories hold up. Next, he has setup his experiment to test the nature of dark matter—the unexplained source of a force that seems to spin the outside stars of galaxies in a way inconsistent with the inverse square law. Upstairs are offices for Hal, Eric, and Hal's son Brendan, now his part-time manager. The library holds Hal's physics notes and his UFO books.

When Eric arrived, I briefed them about Red Planet Capital, our structure and goals, and they brought me up-to-date on their own work, collaborating with an industrialist from North Carolina. This man and his family have a keen interest in automobile engineering and space. They work with John Petersen to setup a futuristic study of planetary exploration.

The "weird desk" of the CIA came into the conversation because Dr. Pandolfi had become highly placed under Negroponte in Homeland Security. He openly discusses ufology over the Internet with various provocateurs and even got involved in an altercation with Richard Doty. Pandolfi reportedly accused him of being a foreign agent and is supposed to have gotten him suspended without pay.

When Kit went to his former boss and mentor, Julian Knoll, with stories of UFOs, Knoll (now retired and working at IDA) recommended that he deal only with top people: 4-star generals, not 2-star, and chairmen, not presidents of companies.

"What should I tell them?" asked Kit.

"Ask them why they care!" was the answer.

Over lunch, we spoke of nano-bacteria (on Mars and in Martian meteorites) and of the "Day After" futures study panel where Hal had participated: it had been setup by a senior advisor. As we enjoyed the fine Texas autumn day and excellent Mexican food, Eric mentioned that Bush senior recalled being briefed by Trudeau at the time of the 1968 Mendel Rivers Congressional Hearings. On the golf course, Colonel Trudeau told Bush (then a congressman from the 7th district of Texas) that one of his men, Colonel Corso, had been asked to testify before Congress and was about to reveal he'd received Alien hardware from a UFO crash and distributed it to industrial labs. As a result of this golf course conversation, the Corso testimony was quashed.

Athanor. Saturday 21 October 2006.

We have our Saturday ritual. I bring another stained-glass panel to be cleaned while watching a football game (today Lille-Lorient, a boring affair) on the TV5 French channel; I work on it in the morning air on the patio, and then we go down to the beach for our picnic and a leisurely walk to shake off the tiredness of the week.

On Thursday evening Alain Dupas and Philippe Richard (of Onera), on the way to the special "New Mexico space race" came over for dinner. I introduced them to my partners. They are stunned at the news of Red Planet Capital and hope to bring the idea back to Paris.

The Trudeau-Bush senior conversation mentioned by Eric Davis would have related to the Hearings before the Committee on Science and Astronautics of the House of Representatives held July 29, 1968. It was presided by J. Edward Roush, and George Miller was the chairman of the full committee where Allen Hynek was introduced by none other than Donald Rumsfeld. Miller had given a short address in the form of a warning, stressing that the committee wasn't set up to criticize the Air force in any way.

Washington. Tuesday 7 November 2006.

Last week the French financial daily, *Les Echos*, published an article about Red Planet Capital that rippled through the political sphere in Paris, causing much surprise. I went on visits to the Goddard

Fig. 13. Janine at Chartres Cathedral, working on the scaffolding setup by the stained-glass restauration team, September 2006.

Fig.14. Birthday party (no.67) at the "Cradle of the Sun" glass workshop. San Francisco Noe Valley, September 2006.

Spaceflight Center, then on to NASA headquarters where we'll meet with Doug Comstock, head of the innovative partnership programs. The news of the resignation of Donald Rumsfeld has just broken; Robert Gates will replace him. On Sunday, I fly to Paris for the annual meeting of our investors and a presentation at Genopole about microgravity.

Mabillon. Tuesday 14 November 2006.

The cab's radio is playing Johnny Cash. The weather is surprisingly mild. I met nine-year-old Max after school. We sat in a café to go over his homework, study the map of France, and learn geometry. I gave him some toy astronauts, a present from NASA.

A few months from the presidential elections, the French government is eager to extinguish the flames that threaten big city suburbs. A recent attack against a bus in Marseille has left passengers terrified and a young woman with critical burns.

The French economy was flat last quarter. The middle class stagnates or regresses. Paris, however, remains full of surprises. I am completing a few projects here, including the transfer of the French and American versions of *Heart of the Internet* to Google.

Mabillon. Sunday 19 November 2006.

In a nostalgic moment, I called my brother Gabriel to suggest lunch or a drink. He spoke kindly to me but didn't feel like meeting. We spoke of our late uncle Maurice. He said his grave was in the plot of our grandfather's family in Nogent-sur-Marne, adding he had renewed the tenure there for his wife and himself someday.

Rainy Sunday. Dominique Weinstein, whom I met this afternoon at the Suffren, told me that François Louange and his former company were caught in the reorganization turmoil of the European Aeronautic Defence and Space Company (EADS). François is not far from retirement and has given up hope of influencing the research. He may offer his photographic interpretation services to Sillard, whose proposed book is taking shape, with the best chapter (about pilot sightings) authored by Dominique.

Mabillon. Wednesday 22 November 2006.

People I meet in academic or journalistic circles are stunned at the news of the creation of Red Planet Capital because such a development could never happen in France. During an interview at Cité des Sciences for the Senate's TV channel, shot against a simulated Martian landscape, I wasn't asked about creative technologies but only about the "brain drain." It remains an obsession here, as if science wasn't a global pursuit. They see me with suspicion and envy. Even though I'm bringing much of my work to France, they still accuse me as a traitor for having left. Yet everything I have achieved would have been impossible in France.

Cape Canaveral. Wednesday 13 December 2006.

Mild rain. Of the space facilities we have visited so far, Kennedy is the most intense, with a sense of urgency I hadn't felt at Ames and Goddard, or even in Houston. As for JPL in Pasadena, it carefully preserves its campus atmosphere and wisely keeps the NASA bureaucracy at arm's length. At the Cape, we went through all the major buildings, including the facility where Endeavor is being prepared for launch in a couple of months. (Fig.15)

The Shuttle Discovery is in orbit, docked to the ISS. We watched it on all the screens as the crew tried with difficulty to fold the solar panels of the space station.

Washington-Dulles. Friday 15 December 2006.

The Marriott suites, a welcome pause before I catch a KLM flight to Amsterdam and Paris. This morning I am scheduled to meet a man from DIA who wants to show me a new holographic display technology. At Kennedy, our presentation was part of a formal briefing by Scott Pace. I met him again at Orlando airport, so I had a chance to ask him how I could join the Mars planning group.

"You're part of the family now," he said warmly. "Go talk to the folks at Ames." He added, "We can dream all we want about going to Mars, but keep in mind we don't have any money to do anything!"

Mabillon. Sunday 17 December 2006.

Back in Paris, I found Janine's brother Alain diminished by a recent fall and a new treatment. Maxim is here too, making plans with me for a new episode in our jointly authored book of dragon adventures. The city is cold, with occasional rain, but the joy of the holidays is real, mixed with the rumblings and tensions of imminent political change. The presidential campaign injects welcome thrill into the drab social reality of France.

My immediate concern is technical; the sheer incompetence of the phone services makes broadband connections a complex administrative challenge. I also need to supervise our first investment (in Alter-G, a medical equipment company) before I can relax.

Mabillon. Monday 18 December 2006.

Le Cabinet Noir by Frédéric Laurent, my current reading, fills important gaps in my understanding of De Grossouvre and the Mitterrand years. Then, I'm busy with telephone meetings with my US partners and Dr. Jeffery Hoffmann, a professor at MIT who flew into space five times.

Thérèse de Saint-Phalle tells me that *Le Seuil* has turned down my book on the future of French culture. "We don't need any lessons from Americans," they said. This reaction was predictable, even if I took pains to explain that I wrote as a Frenchman who has seen the world, not as an American looking at France.

The fragile fabric of the social and economic culture here shows signs of wear. It is pulled in various directions by forces of irrational violence; people are unhappy, suspicious, unsure of themselves. The country looks for vision (Sarkozy? Ségolène Royal?) and finds none.

Mabillon. Wednesday 20 December 2006.

Our esteemed friend and good neighbor Professor Bokias came over for coffee last night. He sat down in my father's red armchair and told us how happy he was in retirement, free from the drudgery of slaving in the decaying establishment of French education. His dream, ever-postponed, is to sell his studio and live the rest of his days in the wonderful light of Athens, close to the sea praised by Homer. He would miss Paris, of course, auditing lectures at Collège de France.

Dominique Weinstein, on the phone from Brussels, told me his doubts about Sillard's forthcoming book. It quotes *Cometa* extensively and leaves little doubt UFOs can only be extraterrestrial. Like me, Dominique is astounded at the conversion phenomenon that spreads even among sophisticated scientists. He even regrets contributing his own chapter.

Max has come back to spend the night at Mabillon, bringing his friend Nicolas, so the apartment is filled with laughter.

Douvres-la-Délivrande. Saturday 23 December 2006.

A weak red sun barely pierces the fog of Normandy, while the countryside only brings the muffled sounds of a few cars. Alain is here, still fighting an illness that slows him down. For Janine and me, it is a time of quiet retreat. Friends and relatives come over, the Christmas tree is ready, presents are wrapped; the house is filled with good wine and good food.

I also spoke to Chris Aubeck, urging him to complete our chronology. One of his correspondents has uncovered a possible explanation for the famous 1927 Roerich sighting in Mongolia. It turns out that Dr. Leon Davidson, back in 1976, found out that an expedition was in the Himalayas at that time. That Sino-Swedish group was led by Sven-Hedin, on its way to Sinkiang through Inner Mongolia. On behalf of Lufthansa, it prospected a route and landing fields to enable a commercial line from China to Berlin (21). The group released some 350 pilot balloons along the way, to a height of about 70,000 feet. Was that the bright round object Roerich so famously observed with his Sherpa?

The lesson is that we must re-examine everything we had long taken for granted.

The main contribution I can make is to help younger researchers get published, inspiring new methods and a cautious approach to documentation and analysis.

Douvres-la-Délivrande. Monday 25 December 2006.

We haven't seen the sun in three days. Even at Ouistreham yesterday, when Janine and I had lunch at *La Broche d'Argent*, the breeze from the Atlantic could not dissipate the grayness of everything. Today, Michel took us on a long drive through Franceville and Deauville to Honfleur and its mythical, picturesque harbor. Signs of arrogant recent wealth are everywhere, in an opulent décor stinking of bad taste. I remember these sandy shores in the mid-fifties, when my parents took me there for a few weeks in summer. The German concrete fortifications of the Atlantic Wall were still standing. The superstructures of sunken American ships were visible at low tide and there were huge ammunition dumps in the dunes. Nobody had taken the time or trouble to fence them in.

My father showed me the rockets, the bullets, the bombs piled up all around us, as high as a man. He emptied the powder from a couple of clips and took them home as a paperweight.

Austin, Texas. Friday 5 January 2007.

On the way to visit Zebra Imaging, a startup company that makes a holographic printer for 3D navigation, I had dinner again with Hal at San Miguel. We spoke of the changes in Washington as Democrats take over Congress and try to reverse the Bush era. On other topics, I was puzzled by Hal's interests. He and Eric are pursuing a peculiar Lockheed technology for a jet hovercraft tested in the 1960s: So what if it looks like a flying disk? And what about Eric Julien, alias "channel" Jean Ederman, arguing about time dimensionality? He reportedly left his wife, Eve Marchal, and secretly flew to Réunion Island to bolster his claim of joining ET friends aboard a flying saucer. In 2002, Julien began publishing theories of three-dimensional time that reflected the former work of Russian physicists, notably Kozyrev, Albert Veinick, and Vadim Chernobrov...When the French police started looking for him, he sent his wife an email to stop the search. The message was traced to the island where, as he said, "he was hoping nobody would ever find him."

In his "UFO pilot" persona, Julien asked the people of Earth to hold a telepathic referendum to call down the ETs. The news was picked up by John Petersen, who seems to take it seriously.

Austin is delightful, crisp and relaxed, but the receptionist at Zebra told me the city had become too big, losing the charm and easy-going ways of the friendly town we once knew.

Hummingbird. Sunday 7 January 2007.

Timothy Good's latest book names the people who were part of John Alexander's "Onion" group in the 1980s. It included both Kit and Pandolfi, several generals, high-level military and intelligence people, all cleared at the Top-Secret level. (22) They discussed sightings and parapsychology, reviewed the Tehran case, and classified testimony on Fastwalkers, but nobody mentioned any captured hardware. In the end, the group got nothing done. This doesn't discourage Hal, who still thinks there is such data somewhere, but probably not from Roswell. I agree with him when he argues the information may be so secret it wouldn't be brought up, even in that setting. He cited several cases when top-level people in Washington were kept in the dark about the SRI remote viewing study. There may be a similar situation here.

I made the trip to Texas in spite of a cold and paid for it with a flare-up of asthma that has kept me home all weekend. I did send Chris Aubeck two annotated sections of our book on *Wonders*.

As I now review my Texas visit with Janine, though, I have to concede we have nothing new; the likelihood of the government releasing genuine information on UFOs is thin. If we ever get to the truth, it will be through some sensational new case or, more likely, very patient, independent analysis of the worldwide data.

Reno. Thursday 11 January 2007.

The AIAA holds a conference in this town. Peter Banks is on a panel about the new role of the Space station as a national laboratory, so I've accompanied him to speak with the NASA managers and with Jeff Bingham, the senior staffer for the Senate space subcommittee.

The day started badly with a series of phone calls informing us that, among others, the funds for Red Planet Capital had been cut from the President's budget for this year. Not only NASA but all Federal agencies are to stop investing in startup Funds.

The news reminded me of the warnings by senior venture capitalists in the Valley, telling me it was futile to work with the government. Later inquiries revealed that the decision came from political ideologues in OMB (Office of Management and Budget) and OSTP (Office of Science and Technology Policy), yet Red Planet Capital was the tool NASA counted on to enlist the help of the entrepreneurial community, which today doesn't give a damn about space.

Since the Shuttle will stop flying in 2010, and other programs cannot supply a vehicle until five years later, NASA has to rely on commercial companies to take astronauts and supplies (15 tons a year) to the station.* Bureaucrats keep 'forgetting that venture capital is the "pilot light" of American industry.

Athanor. Saturday 13 January 2007.

We're all disgusted and hurt at the government's decision. So much work and hope wasted! In five months, we found 45 companies having novel technology products of interest to NASA, and we made a first investment, half a million dollars in the new physical training and therapy machines of Alter-G.

The blow came from Dick Cheney's office. The individuals behind the OMB's request to terminate private equity investments by all government agencies are Richard Russell, assistant director of OSTP in the executive office of the President, and David Addington who has replaced the disgraced Scooter Libby in vice-president Cheney's office. Addington is a government lawyer, who articulated the idea that some forms of torture, in Guantanamo and elsewhere, were justified, even in the light of the US Constitution. He is accused of war crimes in Europe and theoretically could be tried in Germany, but such accusations are mostly a matter of international posturing.

---

* Actually, there was no follow-on human flight from US soil for another 13 years, until Space X started flying US astronauts again in 2020.

Mabillon. Wednesday 17 January 2007.

I landed in Paris in time to learn that Maurice Papon, the notorious Nazi collaborator responsible for the deportation of so many Jews in World War II, had finally died after thumbing his nose at French justice for the last 60 years. Cynically protected and even promoted by De Gaulle, he was the man in charge of the police when the Charonne massacre took place. He will be buried with his medal of the Légion d'Honneur... Nothing changes in France, least of all official hypocrisy...

Mabillon. Saturday 20 January 2007.

As soon as I arrived, I returned a call from a senior television executive who knew of a remarkable French landing case that has been kept quiet since 1977. He will bring me the documents when we have dinner next week.

The street cleaners had already washed the sidewalks when I went out for breakfast. The rising sun had put an orange fringe on dark branches of the trees lining the boulevard. I arranged for lunch at Lipp with Alain Dupas of Polytechnique, Philippe Richard of Onera, and Paul Eckert of Boeing. We discussed the idea of a new global Fund to replace Red Planet Capital, the forthcoming conference in Strasbourg on lunar exploration where I'm invited to speak, and French politics remarked on the steady rise of Bayrou in the polls.

Strasbourg. Sunday 21 January 2007.

I landed here in heavy fog, Janine's absence making the trip long and dreary. When I called her to lament the absurd decision by the Bush administration, and my unhappiness, she said in her calm and quiet voice, "Perhaps it's time to move on, and do something else."

I wish I had her steady confidence, but I still hope to fight and build on what we've already done.

Later I called Peter Banks to discuss the terms of our eventual legal settlement with the agency.

Strasbourg. Monday 22 January 2007.

Several delegates walked with us through the darkened old city to the church of Saint Thomas to hear a Bach and Mozart concert: *Allegro* from Bach's Concerto in A minor and *Allegro* from the Sonata in B minor for flute and organ, then Mozart's *Tu Virginum Corona* for soprano, flute, and organ, followed by his Adagio KV 356 in C major for organ, and ending with Debussy's Syrinx for flute solo and three more pieces by Mozart. He once played in that church, praised the great organ, and possibly was influenced by the statue of Maréchal de Saxe atop his tomb, oddly placed where the main altar should be. It is said to have inspired the statue of the Commander in Don Giovanni.

The ancient houses were illuminated, reflected in the dark river. Afterwards, Philippe, Alain, and I had an Alsatian dinner I would have enjoyed if I didn't suffer from a cold that triggers asthma again.

I am learning a great deal about future settlements on the Moon, the challenges of human support away from the planet, and the plans of various countries to explore near-Earth space. The Chinese are here as well as the Japanese, the Russians, and a strong NASA group. Characteristically, while everyone bragged about the size of their rockets, neither biology nor nanotechnology were mentioned during the proceedings. Yet those will be the key technologies in ten years; they were my main targets for Red Planet Capital.

Tomorrow, Alain Dupas and I will present our idea in Strasbourg for a global Fund with a European component.

Mabillon. Tuesday 23 January 2007.

I got back to Paris in time for dinner with my new research colleague. We met at Le Suffren. What this urbane, exquisitely polite gentleman told me in perfect French was a stunning observation by two very reliable witnesses in August 1977, of a series of phenomena that escalated over three weeks and were clearly seen by a team of Gendarmes they alerted. They took pictures and tested for radioactivity (negatively). After he had contacted authorities, he'd rushed to the site and was authorized to take plaster molds of the imprints, which he still has.

I now have the verbal testimony of the main witness, age 64. He stated to me that the property belongs to his parents. It overlooks two valleys and has excellent visibility. On the first night, his wife was at the window. The time was about 10:30 pm. When he asked her why she was staying there so long, she just said, "I'm watching a shooting star."

Two minutes later he was watching the phenomenon with her, obviously not a shooting star. Both saw it as a bright light approaching, and they made three observations: (1) They were petrified and could not take their eyes from it; (2) There was total, utter silence, no air vibration, no animal noises, no wind; and (3) They became terrified as the unknown object went into a field beyond the gate and "seemed to watch them" as it changed color and eventually took off.

When the witnesses went to the site, they found the vegetation crushed into the soil, forming three imprints, each 80 cm to 1 meter in diameter. The gendarmes visited the site, oddly accompanied by…the Army!

"An officer came to interrogate us. He pulled out a 6-page questionnaire from his briefcase," stated the main witness. *"The questions corresponded precisely to what we had experienced and included items such as 'Have you heard any sound? Was there a change in the level of ambient noise? Did you feel any pricklings?' It was obvious the officers had a clear idea of the physical and physiological correlations to UFO sightings."*

The Army stayed on site for several days, taking extensive measurements. So why is it that no one at CNES seems to know about the case? Was it not researched by GEPAN?

Athanor. Friday 2 March 2007.

Paris was beautiful and quiet when I left with new plans and fresh hopes. Today, after a couple of hours spent working on a stained-glass panel of Sainte Hildegard that gives me some difficulty, I joined Janine on a hike to the boat landing and back along the beach. Few people were out, even at the fishing pier. The air was so limpid we could see every house in Bodega, across the wide bay. Birds played in large noisy groups along the water, and a seal swam leisurely near the shore. Everything was pristine and steady. It felt like the universe had just been created, and everything was right.

Athanor. Saturday 17 March 2007.

A layer of fog hugs the North coast again today, so we had our picnic in the truck, high up on top of the cliffs, watching the filtered light play with the waves and the spray. Next weekend we will be in Paris again for the Genopole science meeting, so I've planned a trip to the "shooting star" landing site with my research contact.

The manuscript of *Wonders* is taking shape; we should have a first draft by May 1st. This work has been a joy, covering a subject I had visited when I wrote *Passport to Magonia* but with far better documentation, thanks to a group of Internet-based scholars led by Chris, and a more critical attitude, better guided, sensitive to the setting of the various eras.

Discussing scientific discoveries with Peter Banks the other day, he pointed out that the celebrated Van Allen radiation belts had actually been discovered by one of James Van Allen's graduate students, Carl McIlwain at the University of California, San Diego. As is often the case in science, the sensors attached to rockets had been set to work in *the range that scientists expected to find*, never paying attention to the fact that the readings were saturated at certain altitudes. It took McIlwain to realize that they failed because the radiation was much higher than scientific belief had predicted...I think the same pitfall exists with UFOs. Scientists assume that, if there were UFOs, they would behave in certain ways; not finding the right parameters, they dismiss the phenomenon.

Similarly, believers have their own set of parameters, so they select and twist witness testimony and censor other researchers when they present alternative facts or theories, losing most of the valuable data. No wonder the two communities have nothing to discuss!

The same applies to *Wonders*. Since ufologists "know" that Aliens only became interested in our planet after the first nuclear explosions (hence Kenneth Arnold's sighting and the Roswell crash in the summer of 1947), there's very little attention to the literature of former centuries and miss the fact that the same phenomenon manifested throughout history. Chris and I are now able to list 500 documented cases prior to 1880.

Hummingbird. Tuesday 20 March 2007.

Lunch with Peter Sturrock at the Duck Club today. I had not seen him since the death of his wife, Marilyn, months ago. I found him gentler, nicer. In retirement, he has lost the British restraint that made him seem a bit aloof, even when one knew it was only a cultural code. He asked me how much I knew about "orbs." He has taken digital photographs that show "psychic" globular lights. We disagreed about what they could be.

Paul Baran came by as we were arguing, so I introduced them to each other. Peter didn't know Baran had originated the Arpanet. So much for scientific communications in our "modern" era!

Mabillon. Friday 30 March 2007.

Breakfast at Deux Magots with Thérèse de Saint-Phalle. No progress on my proposed book. We reflected that, while Americans may disregard social graces and appearances, they are rarely as mean-spirited and jealous as the French. It is a characteristic found at all levels of society here, well hidden under the sheen of superficial politeness. Hatred of anyone who succeeds, or gives the appearance of lifting his existence above the dreary rubble of working life, surges easily through the cracks in the veneer.

Later the same day.

Didier Alliou took me to the top of the scaffolding above the altar at the Sainte Chapelle this afternoon, and I remain under the spell of that special place. He taught me about the extraordinary windows on either side, including the Ezekiel panels, a hundred feet or so above the floor. Didier showed me how they were mounted from the inside, and how sophisticated the entire ironwork structure was. Most astonishing, all the windows were done in only ten years.

One of Didier's secret pleasures is to stand in a corner and watch the expression on visitors' faces when they emerge from the staircase into the chapel, and discover they have entered a mystical jewel box of immense proportions.

Mabillon. Saturday 31 March 2007.

Janine and I took the train today to meet my investigator friend. Annick joined us for the excursion and a very good lunch at the brasserie across the station, and then we all drove off to meet the town's mayor, who introduced us to a deputy and to local people who remembered the events quite vividly.

We went over to the site in two cars, over a dirt trail in the muddy fields. There, after I recounted some of our research, the farmer who owned the field stepped forward and recalled that, when he was a teenager, his parents wrote to him somewhat anguished over seeing a "flying saucer" in Provence. This was in 1954 or 55. They were driving along when they clearly saw an object landed by the side of the road and two short silhouettes that walked near it.

Such spontaneous testimony, never told before and only triggered by that spur-of-the-moment recollection, is the most reliable class of data, untouched by the media. Back in town for the evening train, I spoke on the phone to the retired gendarme who had conducted the main investigation. He told me that the grass was burned all over the places where the object had touched down. He also said that the official statement he typed would have been destroyed after ten years if Gendarmerie regulations were followed. He thought the Army would have buried the case. Does CNES have a copy?

Mabillon. Sunday 1 April 2007.

Over our regular Sunday afternoon meeting at Le Suffren, Dominique Weinstein gave me an early version of Professor Sillard's book and reiterated his concern. Single-minded, the text leads the public towards the expectation of space visitors, he said, ignoring other possibilities. As for Patenet, his role as spokesperson takes much of his time, now that he is on television, as Velasco before him.

Fig. 15. Kennedy Space Center: The Shuttle Endeavor, Dec. 2006.
(With Graham Burnette and our NASA guide)

Fig. 16. At the site of the Soissons encounters, March 2007.

Sleep is still difficult, in part because I haven't shaken off the jet lag, but also because somebody plays the hunting horn under our windows. He does play quite well for once, but how wise is it to go hunting on Boulevard Saint Germain at 3 am?

Mabillon. Tuesday 3 April 2007.

Our science committee of Genopole assembled today at their new location in Evry. It is good to see a real science center, intelligently planned, being built up in France. Yesterday I met with Francois Auque, the president of Astrium, one of the biggest aerospace companies in Europe. In the evening Janine and I took the train to Antony to celebrate Seder (the Jewish Passover) with the Merguis and their nine-year-old daughter, Pasha.

Mabillon. Thursday 5 April 2007.

A final flurry of meetings: auditors at Grant Thornton, astronaut Jean-Jacques Favier at CNES (he once secretly took 17 Picodon cheeses aboard the ISS as a joke), meeting with former Industry minister Christian Pierret, then lunch today at *Le Bistrot d'André* and a visit to Jacques Zyss at SNPE (Société Nationale des Poudres et Explosifs), which manufactures powders and explosives for the French nuclear missiles and for Ariane. We gathered his advice about a possible new Fund for space startups. Then, packing my suitcase for the trip home tomorrow.

I look forward to a couple of quiet days of recovery at Hummingbird, a quick trip up North to retrieve the rare books, and an Easter dinner at my daughter's house.

Manhattan. Tuesday 17 April 2007.

Paul Eckert, from Boeing, has asked me to chair the first panel at this invitation-only Space Investment Summit, held on Wall Street. I spoke after an address by Buzz Aldrin and introduced prepared papers by five speakers who described the prospects for space as a business as well as their legal issues. I was amused when one of the panelists, John Vornle, pulled two of my UFO books out of his briefcase, and asked me to autograph them for his daughter's birthday.

Athanor. Saturday 21 April 2007.

Janine and I went to the Consulate this morning to vote in the French elections (François Bayrou for me, because I am equally disgusted with Sarkozy's manipulations and distrustful of Ségolène Royal's economics) and walked home under a gray sky. Then we drove away from the City for a picnic atop the cliffs.

The road north of San Francisco goes through Petaluma, where we usually turn towards the coast and the Athanor. A few miles beyond that town, you find yourself in a region of wide pastures at the foot of Santa Rosa Mountain where open fields alternate with orchards and wide cow pastures.

Hidden among trees and flowers, the new home of Oberon and Morning Glory is full of books and magical artefacts. The famed Goddess Collection and several altars to pagan deities give the house the flair of a medieval wizard's retreat, an impression reinforced by Oberon's own appearance: older and wiser, with a stringy white beard and kind, intelligent eyes in a face as chiseled as mine. I promised to write a foreword for his next book (23).

Oberon is a good man and a good friend, looking sadly at old age and the illness of his long-time companion, Morning Glory, who has a debilitating cancer. That did not stop that courageous woman from cooking a feast for the group.

Then Artemisia played the *vielle à roue* while the sun was setting on the arbor with its purple and white wisteria, a crowd of fairies hidden in the foliage.

Hummingbird. Tuesday 1 May 2007.

Among the items I brought back from Paris after my mother's death was a bundle of letters from her brother Charles Passavant, who lived in the Bronx. The folder holds a series of long essays on the lives and memories they shared, the history of their parents, their journeys and joys.

In his declining years, alone in New York, he found his great pleasure in the classics, writers and philosophers from Balzac to Schopenhauer whom he quotes in elegant, carefully crafted phrases. He was amazed, he said, at my mother's energy and steady enthusiasm for the future and for art.

I had lunch today at Stanford with Peter Banks and Elizabeth Paté-Cornell, a tall, distinguished woman who chairs the department of engineering economics. She's on President Bush's intelligence board (having had to renounce her French citizenship in the process).

Hummingbird. Wednesday 8 May 2007.

A page has been turned in Paris. France enters a new era as Nicolas Sarkozy prepares to take over as President next week after beating the divided and confused Socialist Party, where the new generation of leaders is undermined by obsolete survivors from Jospin days.

Bayrou got almost 1,000 votes among the French living in the Bay Area, and 7 million overall in the elections, but not enough to qualify for the second round. So I stayed home on Saturday, unable to support Sarkozy and even less the Socialists because their victory would mean economic chaos and years of further confusion for a nation already in decline. Sarkozy's program is filled with needed reforms. They can improve the situation if they are fairly applied, but I'm leery of the sharks that swim in his wake; my memory of the Vivendi disasters in venture capital is still too warm and painful. Indeed, the first thing the new president-elect did yesterday was to jump into a private jet loaned by Bolloré, media tycoon and corporate raider, to be whisked aboard a super-yacht in the Mediterranean. The move reveals who will really pull the strings.

Hummingbird. Monday 14 May 2007.

I allow myself a one-week holiday. I just finished re-reading Simenon's *Liberty Bar* in which Commissaire Maigret investigates a sleazy murder on the Côte d'Azur. With nostalgic amusement, I recall the pleasure I once had reading books by writers like him and even, many levels down, the improbably trashy sci-fi novels of Jimmy Guieu. I used to buy them second-hand, for a few francs, on the Boulevard des Italiens across from the big Rex Cinema. I was broke, but I collected these like first editions. I still have most of them and vaguely envy such popular authors who can enjoy the secret pleasure to sit on the train next to some suburban commuter consuming their pulp to escape the stress and worries of the day.

Janine is off to Reno to inspect a property. Chris Aubeck has returned our text with all his notes. On the phone with Madrid yesterday, we reminisced about *Passport to Magonia*, which some friends of mine urge me to reprint (the old ones sell for $160 on eBay). It will have taken 40 years to reach the next step, this well-documented reference catalogue of ancient cases.

Athanor. Sunday 27 May 2007.

A meeting of the NARCAP group (the first in five years) was held yesterday at my new office in Palo Alto. Since we served as hosts, Janine and I had made arrangements for plenty of food, a telephone conference bridge, and our large interactive board for presentations. Dick Haines was there, as well as two active NASA managers, Brian Smith and Larry Lemke. Ruben Uriarte, the Northern California MUFON director, had been invited, as well as Bernie Haisch and a retired pilot and instructor with an early career in the Air Force, Robert Stahl. There were nine of us. We discussed NASA's interest in the Fermi Paradox (24), then spent most of the afternoon on the analysis of last November's O'Hare sighting, NARCAP's 18th case, where a gray disk had been seen, hovering over an airport terminal.

Larry Lemke had done a calculation of the energy required for the object to vaporize a "cookie-cutter" hole in the clouds when it seemed to take off vertically. He found 100 MW, almost twice the energy of a Boeing 747 at full cruising speed.

During the discussion, I learned that Brian had had a sighting at Langley during a lunar eclipse: He was looking at the Moon, equipped with stabilizing binoculars, when he saw two objects in a break in clouds. One was on a straight trajectory, the other in a zig-zag, sawtooth pattern alongside it. They were white, half a dime at arm's length in size. The observation lasted about 20 seconds.

Bernie is pursuing an experiment in extraction of zero-point energy sponsored by DARPA at the University of Colorado. The results have been negative so far. As for Dick Haines, he still lives on beautiful Whidbey Island with Carol and her elderly parents. He complains of having no one to talk to about current scientific, social, or political issues, yet his meeting was well prepared, friendly, and constructive, a rare event in the study of this elusive phenomenon.

Mabillon. Monday 4 June 2007.

The week begins softly after a weekend of flamboyant light, tourists in T-shirts, the cafés overflowing, but now the skies turn gray again.

Sarkozy, in power for hardly a month, charges ahead with reforms while his opponents scramble to save precious seats in Parliament in the face of his "blue wave."

The Left has contributed nothing to a renewed debate, while the Greens are in disarray. The extreme right, under Le Pen, has disintegrated. No great loss there.

Mabillon. Tuesday 5 June 2007.

Having learned that SOBEPS, one of very few sane, well organized UFO groups in Europe, was about to give up research, I called its president, Michel Clérebaut in Brussels to express my regrets at seeing this excellent institution, along with *Inforespace*, its fine magazine, disappear in the confusion of the field.

Clérebaut had a lot on his mind, so he spoke non-stop for half an hour. "We only have about 200 subscribers left," he said, "and 40 of them get the magazine free. There are few good cases, only about two a year and we don't want to publish junk. Our members have a low motivation to invest their time in investigations, and they don't see any progress." Since he owns the headquarters building, some papers will be preserved, especially the 20,000 pages of reports on the 1989 Belgian wave.

Professor Meessen has saved copies of everything, but he's getting old, as we all do.

Mabillon. Saturday 9 June 2007.

A week filled with company presentations with Peter and our new French partners (EADS in internal turmoil, then our Siparex colleagues, and attorney Daniel Schmidt). A sudden storm blew over Paris last night. It woke me up with the pleasant sound of rain and wind on the shutters. I speak with Janine daily, sometimes twice a day, nine hours out of sync, yet so close. Today I must finish the illustrated Dragon book for my grandson.

Mabillon. Sunday 10 June 2007.

I keep rediscovering Paris, a city that keeps changing its castles of the mind and its palaces of dreams. In a popular area of art exhibits and smart shops, Jean-François Boëdec, with whom I had not spoken in a long time, introduced me to an elegant tea and coffee shop near the Beaubourg museum. He'd agreed to meet me to discuss a remarkable case of close encounter in Landévennec in Brittany with physical effects on vegetation.

    We discussed the CNES study group. The question lingers: Is it only a depository for public reports, while more serious work goes on elsewhere? Who keeps records on the real cases?

Mabillon. Monday 11 June 2007.

Rob Swigart came over for lunch with me at *Bon Saint Pourçain*. We walked around the fair on place Saint Sulpice, admiring overpriced baubles, ugly paintings of dogs, and some very nice old books. Later in the afternoon I had coffee with Professor Bokias, who still thinks about selling his apartment, which he only uses to store his hundreds of books. It has a balcony on the seventh floor and a splendid view of the entire north side of Paris.

Mabillon. Tuesday 12 June 2007.

In quiet moments I read the *Mémoires of Madame de la Tour du Pin* (25) with fascination for her adventures. Here is a refined, intelligent woman caught in the smoke and blood of the French Revolution. I admire her spiritual strength, and that beautiful writing style.

Last night Alain Dupas and his wife, Dominique, invited me to Club Eratosthène at Hotel Meurice, where we listened to a lecture on world economic trends by Thierry de Scitivaux, a financial pundit who challenged many common beliefs about the US deficit and the impact of India and China on world commerce. He predicts that many French "leveraged" investment deals are about to collapse.

Mabillon. Wednesday 13 June 2007.

Last night I spent a delightful hour with my grandson after picking him up at school. I gave him the book of *Dragons* with its final chapter, certainly the work I had the most fun in writing. Seated at a café down the street before a cup of steaming chocolate, he insisted on reading the whole thing aloud from the beginning.

NASA has given us the final verdict from the Office of Management and Budget (OMB). Terminate Red Planet Capital, they said, rejecting our proposal to put to work the money they have already disbursed and return the proceeds to the government. Now we have to consider legal options. Our trustees, Gilman Louie and Ruann Ernst (26), are thoroughly disgusted but any direct appeal by us or even by NASA would be fruitless.

Walking through Beaubourg on the way home, I found four small original paintings by Jérôme Garrido (27) that will put a touch of adventure on our library walls.

Mabillon. Saturday 16 June 2007.

Unstable weather brings sudden downpours now, with a cool breeze in the evening. I enjoy the change. Last night the air was finally clean and fresh. Astrium, the big aerospace company, has unveiled its concept of a space plane for wealthy tourists, actually a suborbital rocket plane the size of a business jet. The presentation took place at a funky old market in the Marais, the Carreau du Temple.

Thinking of the data in our venture files, I asked the chief engineer, "If there was one technology or tool you wish you had to make your job easier, what would it be?" he thought for a minute, then he said, "Nothing—we know everything we need to know."

I admire his brave French confidence, and wish him well with a suborbital prototype that, three years after the successful achievements of Spaceship One in Mojave, has yet to make its maiden flight.*

Mabillon. Wednesday 20 June 2007.

The warm weather has returned, lung-stinging pollution in its wake. I don't think I would be comfortable spending more than a few weeks at a time here. On the way to the air show at Le Bourget, once the mythical site of Lindberg's landing, I only saw a decrepit suburb where dusty roads are jammed. Nothing is done to fix the cracked sidewalks or the heavily graffitied cement walls.

Add to this the closure of expressway ramps reserved for VIPs, company CEOs, Arab sheiks and their motorcycle escorts, and you have a perfect picture of a French society where the rich have all privileges while ordinary folks line up for hours under sunny, humid weather to catch the bus that will crawl back to Paris.

We did meet with OHB, a German firm whose CFO expressed interest in our plans. I saw Alain Boudier briefly, at the chalet of Aérospatiale where an exclusive reception was held while jets roared overhead in demonstration flights.

Mabillon. Saturday 23 June 2007.

There is a special moment of quietness, the evening before I leave France, when the suitcase is packed, the clothes are back from the cleaners and in their place in the closets, the computer is turned off, and the TV set unplugged. I spoke briefly to Thérèse de Saint-Phalle who gave me the tired litany of the poor publishers: Too many books get returned; people don't read any more because of the Internet…As if the web wasn't creating a literary explosion before our eyes, from

---

* That particular Airbus prototype designed by engineers who "knew everything" never left the hangar.

Amazon to the new Lulu software.

But Thérèse does not believe in the blogosphere.

Air France flight 084. Sunday 24 June 2007.

Sign of the times: today is the 60th anniversary of Kenneth Arnold's sighting of "flying saucers" over Mount Rainier.

General Simon ("Pete") Worden, director of NASA-Ames, has encouraged his staff to hold a weekend seminar on the Fermi Paradox: Since life must exist throughout the universe, how come "they" (the Aliens) are not here yet? Larry Lemke, Peter Sturrock, Bernie Haisch, and I volunteered to join the SETI researchers to present the view that the hard UFO data may be an indication of non-human entities in our environment.

This created an uproarious scandal among the straight-laced rationalists, so Sturrock and I decided to stay home. We were told we could attend if we wished but would not be allowed to present papers, or offer any remarks.

Athanor. Saturday 21 July 2007.

The manuscript of *Wonders* is taking shape, but my first attempts to find a good publisher for it have gone nowhere. I took a day off to see Peter Beren at Palace Press, which produced such amazing books as *Dressing a Galaxy*, a special edition volume inspired by the Star Wars saga. I found Peter in the company's kitchen, correcting page proofs. He was pessimistic.

"The American public has lost much interest in UFOs, discredited by the fake documentaries on TV showing the same stupid Alien autopsies, the MJ-12 hoax, the Roswell circus, the abduction absurdities," he said.

I replied those were old theories, while Chris and I were bringing new wood to the fire.

Peter just laughed: "Look, Americans get 500 channels on their home cable system. Whenever they want a new theory, all they have to do is push a few buttons!"

Hummingbird. Saturday 28 July 2007.

Incapacitating headaches hit me again yesterday, as bad as last year. I stayed in bed most of the day.

Dominique Weinstein has come to the same conclusion I did in *Messengers*: Someone is in the background to promote a particular version of a new extraterrestrial ideology, while hiding the real files.

Along similar lines, Colin Bennett circulates a paper ("The Meme Wars: We have an Agenda") which he says I inspired, where he develops the idea of Borges in "Tlön, Uqbar, Orbis Tertius," about the merging of the physical world with a virtual construction promoted by a hidden group.

A man named Mark W. Allin is involved, but who is he? We haven't found any citation.

Hummingbird. Thursday 2 August 2007.

Graham and I had lunch in Burlingame with Steve Millard and two co-founders of a new group called Pathfinder, Phil Ghoia and General Norman Scott, previously at NRO.

We are not really colleagues, since our hope is to build commercial space enterprises away from the vagaries of government funding, of which we've just had a burning example. But the conversation came to UFOs and Phil Ghoia again related his own frustration at the fact that nobody in the military or the science community followed up on sightings, even when an Army division was involved, as happened in Vietnam:

"We were on a ridge, shelling Viet Cong positions on the opposite ridge of a deep valley," he said. "This was at night, and they were firing at us in return. All of a sudden a light appeared on the floor of the valley, where there was nothing but a few primitive hamlets. The light expanded to fill the valley. All shelling stopped, and I heard someone on the radio ask, 'What the hell is that?'

The light simply lifted off the valley floor, rose in the sky and flew off. There was a period of stunned silence; then the battle started again."

Athanor. Saturday 4 August 2007.

There must be ways to access information about real UFO hardware, beyond the small fragments we have. Hal thinks he knows where "the right people" hide; but they're in the same position as Leonardo da Vinci handling a garage door opener.

When I mentioned a statement by Kit who said the government itself was not involved (some years ago he made the opposite comment, in connection with Doty's role, that he was satisfied the government had proper authority and oversight), Hal clarified the situation: "The government provides a funding path and a security umbrella." If so, I suspect the control of technical items has been passed on to the private sector—so much so that the contractors are probably able to trump government requests, the classic "our way or the highway" scenario, with the government rolling over. That would be consistent with what I've found when I analyzed the structure.

Hummingbird. Saturday 11 August 2007.

Along with Oberon, Morning Glory, Artemisia, Diana Hall, Becky and Catherine, Janine and I celebrated the traditional Rites of Gluttony for the Feast of Saint Agobard.

Once again, we had invited Reverend Robert Kirk, the author of *The Secret Commonwealth*. We had a plate for him but he failed to come, possibly because the fairies abducted him in 1641.

Hummingbird. Wednesday 15 August 2007.

In the real world, stocks have dropped over 1,000 points in one month, with the Dow Jones average now below 13,000 points, the result of the "sub-prime" crisis and the follies of hedge funds that sought to speculate on it.

I note that Thierry de Scitivaux, whom we heard at Hotel Meurice, predicted this two months ago. But our thoughts are on our trip to Paris, with hopes to see Maxim on his 10th birthday, and attend some exceptional concerts in Germany.

Mabillon. Tuesday 21 August 2007.

Over the weekend the boulevards were empty, traffic blissfully fluid, and the night was silent, but today the French have started to return from rain-soaked holidays, so Paris finds its usual rhythm. Sarkozy has rushed back to the Elysée Palace to accelerate his reforms, with the added challenge of a suddenly degraded economic outlook and financial rumblings. It isn't only the absurd excess of subprime loans in America that triggered this crisis, but the speculation built on top of it by careless banks seduced by mythical hedge funds.

Janine arrived in Paris yesterday while I sorted through the news: Claude Poher claims that he has successfully demonstrated the power of *universons* in his laboratory. His writing blends brilliant insights (good arguments that his devices overcome inertia and tame quantum gravity) with tirades against those who fail to support the progress of science in France. Claude has remained isolated too long: When is the last time the French Establishment supported visionary research that might undercut old financial interests?

Mabillon. Wednesday 22 August 2007.

Whether from tiredness, or the sadness of not being able to see our son, we felt terrible last night, couldn't sleep or chase the blues. It rained in the gray morning. By the time I met my partners at *Bon Saint Pourçain*, the streets were slick with standing pools.

Mabillon. Thursday 23 August 2007.

Lunch with Dominique Weinstein, busy again with work that keeps him in touch with American and European colleagues. At 49, he makes plans for retirement; the French system is amazing! He gave me some magazines with recent interviews of our friend Velasco. We also spoke of a large unknown object recently reported over the Channel. The British, who don't want any more cases in their public files, have washed their hands of it, stating with perfect bad faith that it flew over the French zone.

The Sillard project, with its committee of experts, remains a puzzle.

Weinstein and Louange have repeatedly suggested bringing me into the group, but some of their members, notably the mysterious "Parmentier," are against my participation. That is fine with me. Janine and I are about to travel to Germany to listen to the music of Beethoven she loves so dearly.

Bonn, Germany. Friday 24 August 2007.

Hotel Domicil, on Thomas Mann Strasse. We started from Paris at dawn and began the trip with a visit to Cologne (Koln) and a review of her history, from Roman roots to the French and the Dutch influence, and her uneasy ties to Prussia. The museum is admirable. We drove to nearby Bonn in the afternoon for the first concert in the annual Beethoven Festival series: Sir Andrew Davis and the London Philharmonic in the violin concerto (Leonidas Kavakos, soloist) along with two pieces by Elgar.

The news reports that three incendiary devices have been found at the HEC School of business near Paris where a top-level business meeting will take place in a week. Sarkozy will speak just before our own workshop on space development. Jose-Maria Barroso, head of the European commission, will be there as well. The bombs highlight the tensions that simmer in France under this quiet summer.

Germany, by contrast, rides high. The budget is in the black for the first time since re-unification, and one hears bitter criticism of the French economic plans, still based on deficit financing.

Bonn. Saturday 25 August 2007.

We went through the city center of Bonn today, and the stately university building overlooking the Rhine. The Roman-style *collégiale*, with its 12th century cloister, was worth a long visit, then Janine and I watched the relaxed crowd of locals and tourists dressed in every color and taste. There are amateur orchestras at every street corner.

The visit to Beethoven's house, or rather the small apartment where he was born in December 1770, would have been something of a disappointment (the pictures and documents it contains have been reproduced many times) if it were not for a private concert given by a local virtuoso on a curious piano with five pedals, including one that gives a soft, romantic color to the notes, as in the *Moonlight Sonata*, and another one that triggers percussive sounds.

In the evening we attended a long open-air concert including works by Beethoven but also Elgar, Haendel, and Gustav Holst, played by the Bonn Beethoven orchestra. Like most open-air concerts, this one was predictable but lively and good-natured.

On television, terrible pictures of the catastrophic fires in Greece have filled the screen for the last several days.

Bonn. Sunday 26 August 2007.

Two castles, typical of German 18th century architecture were on the program today: Benrath near Dusseldorf and the residence of the Great Elector in Bruhl. The former is a pretty hunting lodge and summer residence by the side of a lake. It is all pink and white, expensively decorated but soulless, as Janine observed.

The second one is even worse, a marble monstrosity worthy of Vegas with plaster angels and the flowing ostentation some German potentates copied from Versailles.

Tonight's concert included the *Pastorale* by the orchestra of Bremen under Paavo Jarvi, but the highlight was an astonishing performance by Olli Mustonen in a transcription for piano of Beethoven's violin concerto, that same piece we'd heard on Friday.

Mabillon. Monday 27 August 2007.

Built and rebuilt over many centuries, Cologne's cathedral features sophisticated stained glass and one unique item, the gold coffer containing relics of the Magi, the three kings who attended the Nativity of Christ.

I remain skeptical about their authenticity, but a panel of this shrine is opened once a year so that crowds can stare in amazement. We returned to Paris tired but enchanted with this long-overdue escapade that delighted Janine.

Mabillon. Thursday 30 August 2007.

My friends had arranged for me to meet Madame Laurence Parisot, the president of The Mouvement des Entreprises de France (MEDEF) (28) during their summer university in Jouy-en-Josas, on the campus of the HEC, one of the most prestigious and selective business schools in France. She is a smart, powerful young woman who has succeeded in taming the monsters of the French *patronat*, a cluster of tycoons with antiquated culture and conservative attitudes. If innovation is so little appreciated in France, it isn't for lack of creative people, but because new techniques threaten the established order. One of the arguments for our venture fund is that we can alert our investors to disruptive breakthroughs and help them adapt to them, but the message is a difficult one. Big companies have the power to delay technical change just as they can block social progress.

Nicolas Sarkozy, who spoke before some 3,000 leaders of French industry this afternoon, addressed the same issues. Seen in the flesh, his intensity comes through immediately, infusing the audience with palpable excitement; they had all voted for him. Not a great orator, he delivered his speech with the hurried style of a capricious boy on the verge of a temper tantrum.

Our workshop on space exploration followed, chaired by Jacques Arnould. Also attending were Giuliano Berretta, chairman of Eutelsat; François Auque of Astrium; Jean-Pierre Luminet of the Paris Observatory; and Pascale Sourisse of Thales-Alenia. We argued for two hours about the history, benefits, and dangers of the space business. Arnould gave me a ride back to Paris. We found we shared many impressions about the circus atmosphere surrounding ufology. He is skeptical of *Cometa* and Payan, but he's impressed by Dominique. He was not aware of the O'Hare sighting.

Pierre Lagrange told us that GEIPAN was on thin ice because CNES and the science community still don't take it seriously.

Mabillon. Sunday 2 September 2007.

Janine and I are alone again, happy together. On Thursday we had dinner at *Les Charpentiers*. Time had stopped in the soft night.

Château de Moullins. Friday 7 September 2007.

We just arrived in the quiet landscape of Sarthe, among what Philippe Favre lovingly calls his "pile of old stones." It is the end of a long week, spent between the laboratories of EADS in Suresnes and the offices of the Bank for European Investment in Luxembourg, rushing through Paris traffic with Alain Dupas and Philippe Richard, eating sandwiches on the train, and waiting for a TGV returning to Paris, which ended up pitifully stalling in the dark and deserted countryside near Metz.

Château de Moullins. Saturday 8 September 2007.

We had a sumptuous dinner last night, attended by Yves Messarovitch with his wife, Christine. Two musicians played medieval melodies for us on the minstrels' gallery, a finely-sculpted balcony overhanging the large room with its long table.

I presented Yves and Philippe with copies of my manuscript on French culture. Janine and I slept so well in the big four-poster bed that we were surprised to wake up at 10 o'clock this morning, in time to visit the restoration site in the main hall of what used to be the cloister, Philippe's formidable challenge.

Mabillon. Sunday 9 September 2007.

One last cup of coffee with Dominique, pleased that we reconnected him with Lagrange. We spoke of contacts in Tahiti, where recent observations of strange objects are still unexplained. Our conversation went back to Nazi mythology and its emergence out of groups that may still be active and could feed the ongoing manipulation of the belief in ETs.

Both of us continue to be struck by the link between such promotion and far-right politics.

A French novelist writes that we only discover the happiness of love when the affair breaks up or life separates the lovers, and they finally recognize what they miss.

Sterling, Virginia. Tuesday 11 September 2007.

Quality Inn, the cheapest place around. I meet Peter and Graham here for a presentation to BAE Systems while Janine flies on home. The Washington area, unsurprisingly, is warm and muggy, and gray, but the tiredness of the trip is already dissipating in the pressure of the presentations, and the thought of the flight home.

Hummingbird. Thursday 20 September 2007.

Hardly a week after returning from France, Janine had to leave again tomorrow for Charleston, where her brother Alain has suffered a severe liver crisis that sent him to the hospital.

My great pleasure: a cup of coffee and a pastry with my daughter at a Peninsula café. It's a fine autumn day; the weather is getting colder, re-awakening my spirits as it does every year at this time.

Athanor. Sunday 23 September 2007.

On her way back, Janine called me during a stopover in Chicago, asking me to make a doctor's appointment for her. For the last two weeks she's suffered from daily headaches and occasional blurred vision. She seemed all right when I picked her up at the airport, but she has felt worse since then; ordinary pain killers don't help. Perhaps the stress of her brother's illness, a week of intense care for him, have exhausted her.

She was well enough today for us to take a few hours' trip to the North coast, free of fog for once, the scenery luminous under the peaceful clouds that follow the rain.

A new tenderness has descended upon us, made of hopes and sadness, and the thousand little cares that come so naturally when we are together.

Over the weekend I worked hard on *Wonders* and checked a few items on the phone with Chris in Madrid. The manuscript will go out to the printers tonight to produce a mock-up, a first test version of the whole book.

Hummingbird. Thursday 27 September 2007.

Last night we went to the Opera with our Stanford friends to see *Tannhauser* with Peter Seiffert in the lead role, Petra Maria Schnitzer as Elisabeth, and Petra Lang as Venus, a flawed stage production in spite of the magnificent music.

Janine waited till this morning to tell me our doctor had called about her latest brain MRI, where he found an unmistakable lesion.

We walked over to his office in the brisk wind of a sunny morning. He's a balding, efficient, courteous professional who knows both of us well. He showed us the images, with a foreign spot about 2 centimeters in diameter in her right occipital region.

Next steps: An operation for her and a private talk for me with John Adler, the Stanford neurosurgeon who invented the Cyberknife at Accuray Systems, a company whose information I trust. I was an early investor and a member of the Board of Directors for four years.

In the afternoon I drove briefly to my office, to be away and hide tears. I stopped in San Mateo, suddenly eager to see the quiet lake. I did reach Dr. Adler in Shanghai; he promised to help. I gather documentation to educate myself. What else is there to do? And how can I stop the memories of our delights, all the big and small moments of our love arising in my mind to feed my terror?

Part Twenty

LABYRINTHS

16

Hummingbird. Saturday 29 September 2007.

The young surgeon came to the point quickly. "You just entered a new path," he told us, "one that begins with a serious operation, followed by the uncertainty of care once we know the nature of the lesion." He wants to operate soon, without a preliminary biopsy. The fact that the tumor is located in an accessible area is encouraging. So is the fact that Janine has lost no neurological function, except for occasional blurred vision.

I know the futility of noting all this, but it gives me the feeling that I can better control the anguish that seizes me when I look at her, so clear and vibrant. I also know, but only from books, the disturbing vagueness of reactions to disease, the sense of denial. It helps that Dr. John Adler has agreed to review the case. It helps that this morning a glorious sunrise has embraced the city all around us. We'll drive around the Bay to our special places and back to see Catherine, marvelous light in this storm.

Hummingbird. Sunday 30 September 2007.

I thought of asking Kit for counsel and caught him in his car with Kristin. I read out the MRI report to him, and he was immediately alert to our situation. He cut through the technical jargon and his comments gave us some hope that the lesion may be manageable. We felt much gratitude, and a new urgency for the operation.

Hummingbird. Wednesday 3 October 2007.

One day at a time. Janine slept well and is ready for this afternoon's surgery. The anguish of the past week resolves itself into a thousand contradictory thoughts: We have done all we could, and the medical services are superb. All our friends have called with support, and we keep re-affirming our luminous times together, as if any of it really mattered, faced with a lesion in the brain and a surgeon ready to saw into her skull. What does matter is her quiet courage, and a call that came from our son, marking the hope of a new day.

Later the same day.

We went to the hospital before noon. It was 6 pm when one of the surgical team members came to get us in the waiting room and brought us to Intensive Care. Groggy, caught in a web of tubes filled with fluids and oxygen, she was only able to speak softly, but her consciousness was intact as well as language and all motion. The scans have not shown any other suspicious site, so the main question now is the nature of the lesion.

Hummingbird. Thursday 4 October 2007.

Janine looked much better this morning, spoke normally and had all her bright faculties, but we still didn't know the diagnostic. I drove to Palo Alto to drop off a document at my office and to see Dr. Adler on the neurosurgery floor at Stanford. He picked up the phone and called the surgeon who had done the operation. They only exchanged a few words, after which John grabbed my arm, squeezed hard, and came straight to the point to say the things doctors never say: "It's glioblastoma, Jacques, a horrible disease. It's like crabgrass. It always comes back. People have tried many procedures over the last twenty years; nothing works." He looked me in the eye, squeezed harder: "You must get your affairs in order."

He explained the chemotherapy and the radiation treatments to come. He reached for a handful of tissues when he saw my reaction, standing there in the hallway full of electronics and technicians running around, charts in hand.

He also said the new vaccine experiments "might have value," offered introductions.

The thoughts of putting my wife, so vital and full of life, through all that were so poignant that all I wanted to do was to get home, all shades drawn, alone in the dark at last, and cry out your name.

When I came out of the hospital, the Blue Angels were screaming in the pale San Francisco sky, rehearsing for an air show this weekend. How irrelevant that seemed, the thundering power...

Hummingbird. Friday 5 October 2007.

Janine is regaining strength, so my spirits have picked up. What she needs now is music, and flowers, and happy thoughts, not my gloomy anguish. She has recovered so well that she is ready to come home. I left the hospital and took care of errands: the post office, the drugstore, the bank. I do everything on foot. I have to force my legs to move and my mind to focus because I get disoriented, I forget things, and lose my way like the distracted scientist I am. People tell me: "Have a nice weekend!" The bank teller recognizes my name and cheerfully asks, "How is your lovely wife?" I tell her, "She'll be back soon."

Hummingbird. Saturday 6 October 2007.

Today I brought Janine home, in this high castle where she says, "We could hold a siege." We may have to. The sky is a translucent blue; the sun bathes a succulent landscape at our feet.

In my scientific posturing, I assure her that dimensions like space and time don't really exist, they're just a convenience. I tell her that everything in the universe is eternal, like love. Didn't Einstein himself write to a bereaved friend that "the demarcation between past, present and future has only the significance of a persistent illusion?" This doesn't make sense to her, or to me, beyond the fact that everything must be linked together in the cosmos, and that we've always been together on the inner planes.

We spoke of practical things, of plans for the Athanor. We will empty the house of what is left of the books and sell the property; my UFO files will go into storage. I rarely work with them, anyway. If I had an office, an assistant, and a reasonable budget, I could pick up the research where I left it, if only to document many cases where I have drilled deeper than any of the research groups, even the Air Force, the DIA, or CNES. But I am more interested in the venture work: it makes a real difference in the world. She urges me to pursue it.

Hummingbird. Sunday 7 October 2007.

All my life, I now realize better than ever, I have been bathed in the light from her, her caring love, her beauty.

This morning a glorious sunrise enters the bedroom. This is her joy and one of our many little rituals: I get up and open the drapes for her so she can watch San Francisco waking up in the warmth of the new day.

Later the same day.

We had visitors today: Catherine and Rebecca, Tia Elena. Janine was bright and cheerful; I heard them laugh. When they left, we had our coffee, then drove down to Crissy Field and walked along the Bay Shore until the sun set over the hills near the Golden Gate.

"This is a new kind of peace," she said. We went home. We spoke of the journey of life, how we only discover its true nature now, the end in sight. I grasp at straws.

The human mind is incapable of coping with a universe that has no time and no space, and perhaps we do have souls that transcend such notions and merge eternally in the big ocean of consciousness. She laughs when I say that. As a little girl, she pictured her soul as a bar of *saindoux* (lard), very soft and very white.

Working on this Journal, I now wonder what it's for, what it could mean to any passerby.

Hummingbird. Monday 8 October 2007.

The fog is lifting over the City, so we're about to drive north to the Athanor to plan the sale of the house. Janine is up and active this morning, after her first restful night. I must not fall apart, I must go on setting goals and writing, to the extent these memoirs can preserve and transmit something of what we learned in a long search together.

Athanor. The same day (Columbus Day).

The trip has never been so beautiful, the air fresh and moist, puffs of ethereal fog hovering over the rocky shore. From the ridge, we discover a hundred miles of coastline and beaches, and the ocean's horizon beyond Tomales Point. We went through the house, selecting objects, things to give away, books to preserve. I packed up the first box of Blue Files, all the research records; they will go into storage tomorrow. We had our picnic at the shore among the rocks. We spoke of all the good friends we have been privileged to know, of our children. The wooded hillside was surrounded with so much grandeur and light that it seemed the whole planet was embracing us in her beauty, so splendid it hurt: a crystal blade through the heart.

Hummingbird. Wednesday 10 October 2007.

The apartment fills up with flowers from friends. My daughter worries about me. I know I must build a network of good counsel, as giving up to grief would help no one, but awareness of such truths is of little use. I take over most errands: the laundry, the banks, dinner from the Japanese restaurant down the street. Yesterday was a good day, a normal day, *like before*. But we learned that her brother Alain, in Charleston, was very ill again.

Hummingbird. Thursday 11 October 2007.

I am feeling chills, with weakness in my legs, shortness of breath, then the shaking and the tears. Our doctor tells me to watch out for signs of depression, loss of appetite, suicide thoughts, but he knows I fiercely plan to survive for us, for her. So I went to see Arthur Hastings at the Institute for Transpersonal Psychology. He offered comfort, a place to cry, conversation, and the psychomanteum (1) when I feel the need to transcend pain and meditate in a sacred space. He said I should expect days when I'll be unable to even get up from my chair.

There is pain, but oddly it isn't always the pain of despair and loss. It is the pain that comes with the height of love, the pure awareness of vertiginous culmination.

Arthur puts a hand on my shoulder and speaks of what comes beyond death. No separation, he says, only a change of the sense of presence. And like Janine herself, he assures me things are easier for those who leave, *because they know a time has come.*

Tonight, we took another quick trip to the Athanor at dusk as rain threatened. I loaded the Highlander with the remaining boxes of research that will go into storage, and more books we will save: the rarer ones in Spanish, Italian, and Russian, including the works of Kazantsev and Zigel. The unpublished Blue Files of all our UFO investigations themselves consist of 352 folders that fill 16 big boxes.

The sun was setting over the Pacific in thin blades of pink behind layers of darkness. The sky had heavy volumes of beautiful grays and whites that drew rounded spaceships, formidable lenses with things like portholes, equipped with beams and attractors in the depth of cloud masses.

We joked they were coming to lift us away.

Hummingbird. Friday 12 October 2007.

The rains have begun, in great swathes of blackness, drowning the freeways where one glimpses overturned cars in gullies, being picked up by cranes, among screaming ambulances.

We went to see the neurosurgeon this morning in the gray hospital and heard the awful news we expected.

It was a big relief to empty the Athanor. The body of new research I have developed here is based on heavy classification, detailed cataloguing, and historical compilation. The collections I've assembled are unique, both because of the variety of sources to which we've access and because I have sorted, organized, and pruned the various branches. The result is endowed with patterns that are as astounding today as they were when we first encountered them, but very few people care. The believers expect Aliens to land someday, missing the point. And government "experts" are no better.

I drove to Silicon Valley, my truck coasting along like a submarine. I dealt with my venture work, then deposited into storage fifty years of correspondence with researchers the world over, heavy boxes that no longer mean much to me.*

What is needed is support for the five-to-ten years of solid investigation it would take to scrub the worldwide data and match the phenomenon's complexity, beating it at its own games. Nobody will fund this, of course. They're all simply looking for propulsion and silly interplanetary scenarios, ignoring the real secrets, the treasures.

As I drove around the towns of the Valley, from Palo Alto and Menlo Park to Woodside and Belmont, visiting laboratories, speaking to colleagues, I saw that everything I knew has been first discovered with you, shared with you, and seen through your eyes in our common dreams.

Carl Jung, in *Alchemical Studies*: "The greatest and most important problems of our lives are fundamentally insoluble. They must be so, for they express the necessary polarity inherent in every self-regulating system. They can never be solved, but only outgrown."

Hummingbird. Sunday 14 October 2007.

Anguish lurks under the surface, but we manage to sleep through it, waking up several times during the night. Janine keeps our energies up and bright, with a cheerfulness that comes, she says, from simplifying our lives, disposing of things.

I continue to learn about the disease and to investigate resources. John Adler helped with an introduction to an experimental cancer program at Stanford, and we have new names of specialists at UCSF. The standard therapies have bleak results; the only hope for extended survival rests with advanced trials of novel drugs.

Yesterday gave us gorgeous Indian summer weather and another opportunity to take a long walk along the wetlands. After the rainstorm of Friday, the atmosphere was fresh and so clean the landscape stood out in all its beauty. She seems to have fully understood and accepted the process with an almost mystical sense of what happens *Beyond*. I have not, and cannot.

---

* Those records have now been preserved at Rice University, thanks to the dedication and vision of Dr. Jeff Kripal in the Department of Religion.

Hummingbird. Tuesday 16 October 2007.

In drizzle and greyness, we drove to UCSF to meet the neuro-oncology team, sharply aware that I'd driven Allen Hynek to that same huge hospital, over twenty years ago, for his cancer operation.

Medicine has made much progress since then, so Dr. Susan Chang gave us hopes that we could benefit from clinical trials for a new drug that everyone hopes will inhibit the ability of tumors to feed themselves by recruiting blood vessels.

Hummingbird. Wednesday 17 October 2007.

Mood changes shake me in slow oscillation from despair to a reluctant kind of acceptance, and an odd sense of the undercurrent of destiny that carries everything. I have piled up the Blue Files into a dark, cavernous storage place and felt the bitter loss of a certain future. We finished paying another mortgage today, reducing debts. I am signing a new agreement to put the Trilogy back into print, and I launch a new hardcover edition of this Journal. Someone watching our busy life would have no inkling that a monster has taken residence among us.

I twist in such anguish that Bob Johansen, when I saw him in downtown Palo Alto today, guessed something was wrong as soon as he saw my eyes. She is so lively, her figure svelte, and her face bright that it all seems like a bad dream. She urges me to resume my research, travel to meetings. It would be easy to believe that she's cured now, and that we will grow old together after all.

Las Vegas. Saturday 20 October 2007. Alexis Park Resort.

The International Remote Viewing Association has gathered some 150 studious folks in this quiet hotel (no gambling) where I've agreed to give the keynote speech at Ingo's urging.

Paul Smith, the organizer, took me to a Mexican lunch with Bob Durant, a well-informed East Coast ufologist I'd often heard mentioned. Like many researchers of our generation (he's a former airline pilot), he felt tired and discouraged by ufology, but he was happy with our meeting. He said he did believe in Roswell but thought it was useless to fight the government secrecy at the risk of becoming a target for counter-intelligence types who could mislead you or destroy your reputation with fake accusations in the process of pushing you away from the truth.

I asked him about Fred Beckman, with whom he is in irregular contact. He said Fred was still barely alive. He had suffered two strokes and was now in a retirement home.

Bob Bigelow kindly changed earlier plans in order to come and attend my lecture. We spoke of his space station prototypes that are now circling the Earth. He told me there were new events at the ranch, which he wants to discuss in private tomorrow.

Las Vegas. Sunday 21 October 2007.

We just had a big windstorm. It shook the palm trees around the hotel, hitting the walls like a battering ram for much of the night. After breakfast I attended Paul Smith's interesting presentation on dowsing and met a researcher named Eric Lash who has studied the "Rise of the Black Sun" in South America, where remnants of the SS keep their networks alive.

Bob Bigelow came back for our private conversation. He confided to me that he'd received a letter from the DIA expressing interest in UFO research. They want to learn more about events in Utah. One of their teams came to the ranch and saw something unexplained. The man who runs the project is a GS15 reporting to managers who are eager to move with a new program.

Says Bob: "They keep saying they don't know anything about UFOs, but every time I mention a case they already have all the details in mind...They also say their job is to look ahead 20 or 30 years..."

Hummingbird. Monday 22 October 2007.

There is sunshine, a warm wind, flowers all over the City. We had lunch in the garden at the *Magic Flute*, a delicate meal in the quiet shade. It almost felt like a vacation, an excursion *à deux*. But we'd spent the morning in the laboratories of UCSF and met the doctors who will take over the treatment.

We had to sign a bundle of papers. There is hope because all the neurology tests are normal; her mood is alert, which makes it tempting to simply deny the dangers. Tonight, we went out on foot, an ordinary couple shopping for groceries through San Francisco, so colorful, so unpretentious. What I love is our quiet time in the evening, when she asks me to read from the life of Beethoven, or to relate a funny item found in the newspapers.

Hummingbird. Wednesday 24 October 2007.

Jack Glazer, former general counsel of NASA-Ames, had me over his house on top of Nob Hill, near Grace Cathedral. He had much to tell me about what I should expect in coming months. His beautiful wife (he worships her memory still) was 52 when she was diagnosed with the same illness. Zelda only survived one year, became comatose, and died in his arms in that house after a terrible fight for her health and sanity that left this remarkable man with an exhausted mind and a broken heart.

He'd sold his law firm's building and devoted all his time to her medications and care. When he dies, the house will go to the UCSF neurology department, as lodging for visiting experts.

He gave me very stern advice, stressing that nobody can be the sole caregiver in such an ordeal, and that no time should be wasted before making the key decisions to dispose of property and simplify our lives, a fact John Adler had already impressed upon me. This illness moves fast; it kills in less than 11 months.

Walking over to his house, I passed the labyrinth outside Grace Cathedral, and also the inside one, a replica of the one at Chartres. I promised myself to use it as a tool for spiritual support. Then we escaped for a picnic at the Athanor. We had the beach to ourselves, the surf and the wind.

Hummingbird. Friday 26 October 2007.

I went back to see Henry "Jack" Glazer yesterday. He was amazed at the broken story of Red Planet Capital, said it was scandalous. He plans to raise the issue with the NASA general counsel next week in

Washington. He won't get anywhere; NASA is not the problem.

He'll try to learn the truth about the political deals, the blatant influence peddling that must have motivated the White House decision to kill all the venture plans (2).

Hummingbird. Sunday 28 October 2007.

In the world outside, now a secondary backdrop in our life, several processes move forward. Contacts for our new Fund are active, both in the US (Orbital Sciences, BAE Systems, Northrop, Loral…) and in Europe (EADS, Boeing France, AGF Private Equity, BEI). In two weeks, I'll be in Paris, to turn this interest into concrete decisions.

My work of the last decades is getting recognized, although ironically I have withdrawn from conferences and the media. Even my contribution to remote viewing is now known.

A scholar named Jeffrey Kripal, Chair of Religious Studies at Rice University, invites me to an Esalen seminar in June: "I am a historian of religions or comparativist by training. I have written four books now with the University of Chicago Press, all on different features of mystical literature from both the West and Asia, and from the ancient period to contemporary American culture. I am especially known for isolating and analyzing gender and sexual orientation patterns in mystical literature." (3)

He goes on: "I think you would find my positions there remarkably close to your own, despite the fact that I had not read your books then. My fourth book was a cultural history of Esalen, the human potential movement, and the New Age (*Esalen*, 2007). The latter involved, among many other subjects, mini-studies of psychical research, remote viewing, and UFOs in fact and fiction."

His insight into these modern developments led him to ask why academic thinkers were blind to the phenomenon: "The more I looked, the more I also realized that the deepest mystical doctrines of the human potential movement are carefully and systematically ignored in official American culture…These same doctrines, however, are widely embraced and even celebrated in fiction, in popular culture, and, especially, in superhero comics. Why is this? What is the relationship between the imagination and metaphysical truth? And

Fig. 17. Hard traces: preserving the UFO imprint from Soissons

Fig. 18. The labyrinth outside Grace Cathedral, San Francisco 2007.

also between religious truth and occult fiction?"

From there, he says, it was only a short step to my work: "One of the early conclusions ... is that the tropes of the Alien and the UFO are both originally and central to this entire mythical history.

"After all, Superman, the first real superhero, is quite literally an Alien who crash-lands in Kansas. This brought me to your books, which I have found particularly astonishing ... You are a scientist who does not write, at all, like a scientist. The scientists I know tend to be hermeneutically naïve, that is, they tend to be 'literalists' in their understanding of language and metaphor... But you are very different. Early on, with *Passport to Magonia* and *The Invisible College*, you saw that UFO phenomena must be contextualized comparatively in the broader history of folklore and religion, as well as the general field of psychical phenomena..."

I called him in Houston to tell him about *Wonders,* hoping he would give me an appraisal of my work with Chris Aubeck.

The powerful events we've all studied were hidden in plain sight all the time, but scholars are unable to see what stands before them in contemporary culture, he observed.

We have plans today, just a walk and lunch. Our grandson has sent us two colorful letters from Paris, filled with fun drawings and touching thoughts; this has restored Janine's mood and mine.

Hummingbird. Tuesday 30 October 2007.

General Pete Worden met with us this morning. NASA will try to revive Red Planet Capital and will work with us under a new Space Act Agreement for technology information.

Later, a long discussion with financier Mark McKee at the Fairmont about startup companies and my professional role in the investment community.

The mail brought the latest issue of *Flying Saucer Review*, badly edited, filled with loose arguments. Sadly, I will stop reading it. *Inforespace* has already died. The few serious newsletters have given up, swamped under Internet garbage, fake data.

We follow Glazer's advice to "lead as normal a life as possible."

Hummingbird. Wednesday 31 October 2007.

It's Halloween. From Rice University, Jeff Kripal sends me a picture of himself dressed as Spiderman, accompanied by a lovely woman. In San Francisco, people are variously costumed but the spirit of old evenings of fancy and passion has evaporated under threats of gang violence and the weight of marketing follies.

Hummingbird. Wednesday 7 November 2007.

This is week no.7; the treatment is going well. We get up at 6 am every day for the trip to Parnassus Hill. The radiation session itself only takes five minutes. The technician, a good-humored Chinese woman, hears us approaching when Janine's high heels click on the hard floor of the hallway. She's always ready with a smile and a compliment.

Annick arrived from Normandy this afternoon; she will make sure her sister is safe until I get back from France.

Mabillon. Saturday 10 November 2007.

The flight was sad because you should have been with me. Your voice reassured me, strong and lively when I called after landing.

I slept. I need lots of quiet, warm slumber, safely tucked in mounds of blankets, with books at my elbow, serious ones like Jeff Kripal's *Roads of Excess, Palaces of Wisdom*.

My vacillating awareness is layered with strange dreams. When death casts her shadow and threatens those we love, concerns with daily life become almost unbearable.

Everything I am and everything I know has been shaped with you, by you. Your touch, your taste, your wisdom is in the contours and colors of our life, in the light circle of the lamp, in the fine wood underfoot in this bedroom, in the landscape beyond this window.

Mabillon. Wednesday 14 November 2007.

The trains stopped running last night. The Metro and buses went to their depots. Once again, Paris is crippled by strikes; cabs are rare. The only relief comes from the bright sun that encourages those who ride or walk to work in the cold.

Reaching the European Space Agency this morning meant a brisk but not unpleasant 40-minute hike. Later I was lucky to find a cab to reach the Champs-Elysées and secure our funding for another, difficult year. Other meetings are going well, including a session yesterday at Boeing.

Mabillon. Thursday 15 November 2007.

Four more business meetings today. The strikes have thrown a messy troop of cyclists and pedestrians into the disorderly streets and heightened the ambiguous nature of the labor issues. Both sides in this conflict are right: Pensions need to be rationalized but no solution is fair because the French economy is too heavily burdened by bureaucracy and debt. The bureaucrats themselves will go on strike on Tuesday, demanding more bureaucracy, more debt...

Janine called and spoke gaily of plans for a concert when I get back to San Francisco. Moving away for a week was good for me; it gave me some reassurance. The key, Fred Adler told me as I confided to him, is to fight very hard to survive as long as possible in the expectation that research may come up with fresh answers.

Fred himself survived Hepatitis C at a time when most patients died; today, that disease is routinely treated. AIDS itself, once a death warrant, has been brought under control, even if not cured.

Mabillon. Friday 16 November 2007.

This day made the whole trip worthwhile, in spite of the strikes (two hours to catch a rare Metro just to reach Boulogne, then the fight with taxis and traffic jams).

At EADS Headquarters in Suresnes, our team met with two executives who report to Louis Gallois, the CEO. I led the presentation to the point where we discussed a letter of intent for an investment in both of our funds.

I left EADS to join Olivier on Île Saint-Louis, happy to embrace him at last. Maxim joined us. I gave him two boxes of *Fantastics* figures, soon embroiled in mock war on the café's tabletop, and then I took the taxi to the airport for the long flight home.

I am disoriented again, forgetful, tired from the French trip, often nauseous. I drive badly, while Janine has regained her dynamic spirit, helped by her sister's presence. Jeff Kripal will visit us from Houston next month to discuss research.

Hummingbird. Thursday 29 November 2007.

We saw Puccini's *La Rondine* at the opera last week after a visit at UCSF that made it clear that Janine's condition was stable: no visible disease. She does so well and has so much energy and zest that it would be easy to fall into the trap of forgetting the disease. The temptation is strong to simply pick up our life where we left it in September, to put all that behind us. The early-morning trips to Parnassus Hill at sunrise to the radiation sessions have become a special ritual for us.

Hummingbird. Saturday 8 December 2007.

Visit by Jeff Kripal yesterday. We discussed hermeneutics. By an amusing coincidence, he was in town for a speaking engagement on the Stanford campus, close to my own presentation at Tressider before some 50 French dignitaries on a tour of California.

Jeff writes: "Thank you, profusely, for opening your home and heart to me yesterday… What I saw was beauty, and a life that is whole in its insistence on fusing the scientific and the spiritual within a kind of modern esotericism. Along with the kindness and grace of your hospitality, I believe that what will stick with me most is the 'ritual space' of your study and shelves, the way the books are organized around a vision, the vision of Magonia."

He goes on: "Jung used to write about select individual's 'personal mythologies,' that is, the way certain individuals manage to create an entire worldview around and through their creative work. Jung did this in his Bollingen Tower. You have clearly done the same in your San Francisco Tower.

"I was also especially struck—'stunned' might not be too strong of a word—by how you work *sub rosa*, 'under the rose,' as you put it to me. Those windows! I hope we can continue to have discussions *sub rosa*, and that whatever I write about you will... transmit, as you might say, its deeper message under the rose. That anyway is how I always strive to write, on many levels, at the same time. In the language of *The Serpent's Gift*, I hiss forbidden secrets."

Hummingbird. Monday 10 December 2007.

This is the last week of radiation. We took a long walk yesterday in the subdued light of autumn, all the way around the foot of Russian Hill to North Beach, where we had lunch. The trees were red, purple, orange, and the City was at peace, "rejoicing in its splendor." We've had a quiet period of sacred peace.

I have replied to Jeff Kripal: "You realize, I am sure, how much your visit meant to me, at this point when I must question what I have done and how best to integrate the lessons from the various paths I have explored—paths where I have often stumbled and occasionally been rewarded with unexpected discoveries."

Hummingbird. Friday 14 December 2007.

The weather was balmy yesterday in San Diego as I joined Peter Banks for a visit to General Atomics, where we had lunch with co-founder Lynden Blue.

Dr. Jim Lemke, as he drove me back to Lindbergh Field, gave me an appraisal of energy futures. "The world consumes 13 terawatts a year," he said, "one third satisfied by products derived from oil, which has peaked and will decline. The US, with 4.5% of world population, consumes 25% of that energy. The total figure grows by 2% per year, so it will reach 23 terawatts or an added 10,000 gigawatts in 30 years. Well, one generating plant represents one gigawatt, and 30 years is 10,000 days, so to fill the gap you'd need to build one nuclear plant a day for the next 30 years, which obviously isn't going to happen.

"There's no new source of energy on the horizon, so the only outcome is massive restructuring, a catastrophe of civilization. The West has had the luxury of building its infrastructure at a time of cheap energy; we pity India and China for their late development, but they reply, '*Au contraire!* You have acquired all those bad habits we won't follow, and we have untapped reserves.'"

He added: "The real losers will be the third world, with extensive famines: Farmers will not be able to afford to work their fields. The move to biofuels is a myth, peddled by the farm lobby…"

Hummingbird. Monday 17 December 2007.

Annick will join us again tomorrow from Normandy, and Alain from Charleston. We walk every day, looking for Christmas gifts among the little shops of Polk Street. Then we only think of those we love.

Hummingbird. Monday 24 December 2007.

We were shocked when Alain emerged from the hallway in a wheelchair, unshaven, disoriented. He'd neglected his diabetes medication and barely recognized us. The next morning, he hardly had any pulse. The paramedics took him to Saint Francis emergency, where he spent the day, the four of us at his bedside.

The weather is sunny, with splendid views that please Max, who wants to see trees and nature. This afternoon, alone with him, I stopped at Grace Cathedral, and we walked the labyrinth together.

Hummingbird. Wednesday 26 December 2007.

Today, the weather still crisp and clear, I took Maxim to Golden Gate Park. We rented a boat to row around Stow Lake, followed by dozens of birds who eyed his hot dog. Alain is out of danger for now, but barely conscious.

In the middle of our cheerful banter, a fist of ice often grabs my heart when I least expect it, and squeezes it.

Hummingbird. Thursday 27 December 2007.

Janine seems to be losing energy. "What will become of us?" she asked. I could only answer by holding her even tighter, and I felt the overwhelming force of time passing over us, a thundering machine dragging lives away. The outside world doesn't bring us much reason to hope for the future. Benazir Bhutto was assassinated in Pakistan today by a man who blew himself up, tearing apart twenty people, shredding flesh and bones, scattering blood. In the name of what?

Hummingbird. Friday 28 December 2007.

Jeff Kripal sends me scholarly questions that force me to look up obscure references. Thus, perusing *Le Comte de Gabalis*, I was amused to encounter this passage, supposedly revealing the Kabbalistic secret of the birth of Melchisedek. The author claims that he was among the children of the Sylphs, along with Plato and Apollonius of Tyana:

"The Count asked: Do you know who was the father of Melchisedek? Actually, no, I said, because Saint Paul didn't know it. You should say that he wouldn't tell (said the Count) and that he was not allowed to reveal Kabbalistic Mysteries: He knew very well that the father of Melchisedek was a Sylph, and that this King of Salem was conceived inside the Arch by Sem's wife."

Jeff's questions have re-awakened the flame of my old erudition and my delight at the old books that surround me in this study where I work and sleep while our children and Annick use the beds in other rooms. I read the book on labyrinths by Lauren Artress, *Walking a Sacred Path*. She's a pioneer of the renaissance of Western spirituality and was instrumental in getting Grace Cathedral to build a replica of the eleven-circuit Chartres labyrinth.

Hummingbird. Wednesday 2 January 2008.

Bob Bigelow called yesterday with good wishes for 2008. He said his own wife, Diane, was about to undergo an MRI to explore suspicious traces on brain scans, so we shared our fears and hopes.

Bob went on to describe recent phenomena at the ranch, which seem to follow him wherever he goes. They are similar to Sturrock's "Alfies," round spots on photographs. The ranch manager is a woman who testifies to the phenomena, supported by the security officers.

The orbs are not seen with the naked eye but only appear on

photographs, which reinforces my hypothesis that they may be an artifact of the optics. Yet Bob insists that they've done other tests, notably by placing devices in a certain order in sealed rooms, only to find them altered by the poltergeist that seems to haunt the place.

Hummingbird. Thursday 3 January 2008.

A message from Bob Johansen tells us that Roy Amara died quietly on Saturday, at 82. Roy's steady leadership at the Institute for the Future was a striking contrast to the standard styles of management we read about in business books. He was a prince of tact and understanding, yet able to manage crises effectively, without an angry word or a threatening move. He built consensus through gentle suggestion and patience, and gave the credit and limelight to others, a real lesson to today's interrupt-driven, media-hungry CEOs.

One of the little-known facts of Roy's career was his role at SRI where he managed Engelbart's attempts to get his early projects funded. Always in the background, Roy was single-handedly responsible for getting Doug's proposals into a shape where they could be considered by the Air Force Office of Scientific Research, AFOSR, which launched his project. The rest is history.

Hummingbird. Tuesday 8 January 2008.

Today's MRI shows excellent healing of the area where the tumor was removed. Most importantly, it shows no new activity anywhere.

Jacques Patenet, responding to my good wishes for 2008, has invited me to join the College of Experts for CNES-GEIPAN that will pick up the UFO research work in Paris and Toulouse.

Hummingbird. Saturday 12 January 2008.

The fierce rainstorms have moved east, leaving the Bay Area scintillating in pristine clarity. Janine felt fine, so we took advantage of the sunshine to drive to Palo Alto do some shopping. It was a nostalgic trip, experienced as a return to the time when the entire world seemed available and vibrant. We found Palo Alto stirring with the faint awareness of spring. In the paradoxical California winter, some trees still had their yellow and orange leaves while others grew tender green shoots in warm air and clear light.

Hummingbird. Saturday 19 January 2008.

In the current financial desert, our long-awaited settlement with NASA has closed, and we can look more steadily at the future.

Lunch at Greens at Fort Mason with Mike Murphy, who wants to work with Jeff and me. In the evening, I attended a show of the paintings of Mike and George Kuchar, in an apartment near Guerrero. Their art is in the truculent style of Clovis Trouille, with gay themes, a mix of muscular heroes, and green monsters. Mike presented me with a copy of his movie, *Sins of the Fleshapoids*.

Mabillon. Saturday 26 January 2008.

Olivier met me for an animated lunch today on Île Saint-Louis. Our shared challenges and sorrows have restored what should never have been broken, the love and joy at being together.

Under Sarkozy, no adjustment has been made for the global economic turmoil unleashed by the US "subprime" crisis and the bad policies of the Bush White House, so the ship of France sails into the storm with the wrong sails, all proud pennants aflutter.

Mabillon. Wednesday 30 January 2008.

Our biotech meeting at Genopole reviewed two startup companies. I rode the train through the dreary southern suburbs of Paris, where nothing has been done to provide a human touch, a sign of hope.

Even the biotech campus, a showcase of French science, looks like a wasteland with no direction or plan. You cross busy highways with no walkways, you step into puddles along unpaved sidewalks.

Mabillon. Thursday 31 January 2008.

French "spacionaut" Jean-Jacques Favier briefs me on a new service for geoportals built on Google and Microsoft. Meanwhile, there is growing panic in Paris around Société Générale and the subprime crisis. The geniuses of trading and their financial bosses discover with amazement that, even after all their machinations, 2+2 still equals 4, a fact everyone had forgotten in the flames of speculation.

Mabillon. Friday 1 February 2008.

My life looks full and interesting to my friends, but my life is your life, in the environment you created. Even the little escapades, the peccadilloes, only made sense because there was a framework of humor and sanity, and those deeper levels. Thanks to you, I never created any fancy institute or joined any cabal. Thanks to you, I learned to be a traveler on the Earth with no allegiance to power.

At the Arab World Institute yesterday (a party given by EuroMed) people asked about you; you've touched everyone. They want to know you're still in their world, with your soft quiet smile. They can't imagine anything else, and my mind spins on, as I try to reassure them. Later I met twice with the leading researcher of the remarkable case near Soissons. Then a nostalgic dinner upstairs Chez Lipp with Elisabeth Antebi, watching the rain.

Hummingbird. Sunday 3 February 2008.

This is the 49th anniversary of our life as lovers. It finds us in rainy San Francisco, in a book-filled study rich with memories of trips, friends, and celebrations, bathed in echoes of Magonia, the music of the Spheres and a brave mystic quest. Outside, the soft sounds of Sunday, the hum of tires on wet pavement along the Van Ness corridor, and the fractured rumblings of the modern city.

Scanning the recent medical literature, there's some encouragement in papers describing developments in brain tumor treatment, researchers argue, citing the new drugs under investigation.

Hummingbird. Thursday 7 February 2008.

An ambulance came at noon to pick up Alain and Annick to take them to the airport where we said goodbye.

We tried to keep an upbeat mood, but we were sorry to see this man we had known so strong and joyful being wheeled out on a stretcher. He'll be staying in Normandy, where his sister will care for him, but the best we can hope is that he'll enjoy some pain-free days.

In the high-tech world, I note a curious new organization, Oxantium (4). Hal tells me he's now certain there is "hardware" in secret places. Of course, I said, we've always known that.

Hummingbird. Friday 8 February 2008.

Today was hard. Free from the distraction of caring for another sick person, I broke down again. I cry in secret, in my car or on the street, because Janine doesn't want any displays of sadness.

"There'll be time for that later," she says.

This emptiness, this loneliness, the prospect of waking up to a world without her, all that makes no sense, just as complete blackness makes no sense, as nothingness makes no sense.

Hummingbird. Monday 18 February 2008.

Kit's response to *Forbidden Science: Volume Two*: "I really did read it all, and every word. It was tough to put down. It is a wonderful book, and I have essentially zero edits or comments to make about anything that I was a party to, or remember. In fact, you refreshed my memory, and joyfully so. Your comments, especially toward the end about my recalcitrance and ambivalence, my obfuscation and confusion, and my reluctance to state definitely what I believed…were spot-on.

"You were prescient and accurate about what I was telling you, then. It was, as you so kindly implied, based on honesty and lack of access… not dissembling or an attempt to deceive."

Hummingbird. Saturday 23 February 2008.

We put things in order. We take every opportunity for short walks in the City. Janine reviews our files, throws away obsolete documents.

A big storm is sweeping towards San Francisco. Before it engulfed us in rain and wind, we escaped to Palo Alto for a concert at Stanford with Tia Elena, who is 78 today. Still employed full-time as the indispensable secretary at Stanford's statistics department, she keeps young by gardening and playing energetically with her grandsons.

The concert was organized by a friend, pianist Chryssie Nanou. Her Stanford students played pieces by Elliott Carter (*Dialogues, Three Poems of Robert Frost*) and Olivier Messiaen (*Trois Mélodies, Oiseaux Exotiques*), both born 100 years ago.

Hummingbird. Monday 25 February 2008.

I love those Sundays at home, working side by side on mundane things like editing books, corresponding with friends, watching a movie in the evening (*O Brother, Where Art Thou?*). Our uncertain future grinds on me, silently. I see it in my degraded alertness (my memory for names and faces, never good, keeps deteriorating) and in physical aches, tiredness, bad sleep. I feel cowardly. Small victory: a new Space Act Agreement, awarded to us by NASA for the exchange of high technology information.

Hummingbird. Monday 3 March 2008.

We had a good weekend of quiet talks. On Saturday the two of us strolled across town to Caffe Trieste for a snack of expresso and pastries and walked back in the mild sunshine. Janine was relaxed and happy, in a soft rose pullover and a black skirt, a shawl, a black vest.

This morning we drove up to the Athanor where our daughter was hard at work interviewing contractors, making plans to get the property on the market. The weather was balmy, the view divine across many miles of ocean and rocky shore on one side, the picturesque hills of Marin County to the east, and the road bordered by eucalyptus and gnarled old pines.

Hummingbird. Tuesday 4 March 2008.

The latest scan is very good. The images don't show any recurrence either in the area where the tumor was removed or in other zones, and the experimental spectroscopy gives no sign of new cancer. The physicians now consider trials of special vaccines, and I continue to educate myself in this complex area to be of good counsel. Much progress has been made at UCSF since the days, 20 years ago, when they operated on Allen Hynek.

A look at the news for the Primary results shows John McCain as the Republican candidate. Hillary Clinton won Texas and Ohio, beating Barack Obama in the Democrats' uphill battle.

Hummingbird. Saturday 8 March 2008.

Joel Hynek left a message for me. He's been working in Hollywood with Doug Trumbull (who was head of special effects for *CE3K*, and worked on *Bladerunner*) who plans to build a tracking system for UFOs and wants to discuss it. It consists of a telescope mounted on a Hummer, able to acquire and track unusual objects in the sky. He's visited the CIA, where he was assured UFOs were indeed real, and was encouraged in his project. Now he wants to talk to me.

Monterey. Monday 10 March 2008. Monterey Plaza Hotel.

A corner room over the ocean, with Cannery Row on one side. We woke up with the cries of seagulls and the sound of waves. I serve on a panel here, reviewing business plans. I will present Alter-G, our medical equipment company, based on a NASA invention. We take this retreat from the world as a chance to slowly recharge, simply talking about all the times we had lunch at the Crow's Nest on the harbor, as we did yesterday.

Tuesday 18 March 2008. Aboard a Virgin America flight to D.C.

This is only a short trip to visit Scott Pace at NASA Headquarters for an aerospace investment meeting. We've bought plane tickets for France at the end of the month, after some trepidation. I have convinced Janine we shouldn't miss this opportunity to be in Paris together. Six months have elapsed since the diagnosis. I feel enormous gratitude to the neuro-oncology team who've given us this time to value every hour we can still spend together. Even with this blessed interlude, things are hard. At work I deal with other uncertainties and steep learning curves that keep my mind occupied. The economy is in grave turmoil after six years of Bush's leadership. A global recession threatens; we strive hard to preserve innovative ventures.

Reston, Virginia. Thursday 20 March 2008.

On the History channel this evening, I stumbled on a UFO documentary entitled *Reverse Engineering*, purporting to show experts at work to prove that modern aircraft had been derived from Roswell... The cast included some ufologists, fascinated by drone-like devices in the California sky; a publisher; a French aviation hack promoting some spurious stories. Even John Schuessler, now retired in Littleton, Colorado, seemed to lend credibility to anonymous Internet rumors about a supposed secret project called CARET that re-invents the very tired MJ-12 myth.

After Bob Bigelow and Peter Sturrock discussing elusive spots on their digital photos, Hal and Eric chasing down government conspiracies, and now MUFON asserting that fiber optic technology must have come from Roswell, I see this as another reason to quietly return to my solid cases with real witnesses and proven data in the lab, away from the media.

Later the same day.

At this conference on aerospace, presenters speak glowingly of *Pax Americana* and of the transfer of key services, including military duties, to armed contractors and new mercenaries. It sounds almost as bizarre as the UFO "documentary" junk.

Peter Banks and I just had lunch with Scott Arnold of the Institute for Defense Analyses (IDA) who wants to help the government procure high tech that will "keep the nation secure." This assumes good people with good conscience in government while Bush, Cheney, and Rumsfeld have given us a bureaucracy that condones torture, tramples the Geneva Convention, and encourages contractors' abuses throughout the Middle East (5).

So this afternoon, as I made my way with thousands of other

travelers through the maze of security lines at Dulles that seem designed to test the ineptitude of laboratory rats, I suddenly understood: *Our enemies have won*. They have reduced this once-proud, free American people to a pliable crowd, docile to media hype and minor potentates. We have repudiated what made us unique, the values of the Constitution, the sanctity of independent minds, the freedom to confront authority in face-to-face debates, and the wisdom to keep the high moral ground.

An anecdote puts it in focus. Early for check-in, I tried in vain to confirm my ticket at a reluctant machine. Frustrated, I pushed all the buttons at once on the side of the screen and was surprised to see the actual code of the program that delivers passes. I could have entered a phantom passenger, even a criminal. Not only has our empire lost its soul, it has lost itself in its pretension, chaos of its own making.

Hummingbird. Wednesday 26 March 2008.

Tomorrow we fly to France together, cancer be damned. Your love was always my refuge.

I may not have this luxury much longer. May you remain always "my consolation from sorrow, the light in the black night, and at solitary times, my tumult." (Tibulus)

Mabillon. Monday 31 March 2008.

Janine enjoys being busy here. She recalls her childhood, the two years she spent with her godmother in Yvetot when her parents came back from Morocco after the war, in a country the conflict had devastated.

She recalled how her uncle once made wooden clogs for her and Annick. They were proud to wear them when they went to school through the fields.

TGV-East near Stuttgart. Wednesday 2 April 2008.

Yves Messarovitch, whom I met at the annual AFIC meeting at the Bourse, said I was well-regarded the small but influential venture circles of Paris. I saw many colleagues there. On the way to Germany, it was thrilling to roll smoothly into the country without seeing a border, or a slowdown of the train. Sunny weather between Ulm and Munich, a beautiful canal, forests on both sides of us.

Ottobrunne. Thursday 3 April 2008.

Philippe Richard and I met at EADS headquarters with all the CTOs of all major subsidiaries: Jean Boti, corporate CTO; Robert Lainé of Astrium; Patrick Gavin of Airbus; Yves Favenec of Eurocopter; and managers from MBDA, CASA, and EADS Defense and Security. We also met with the Airbus Finance group that manages the 13 billion euros cash reserve and the foreign exchange risk of the company.

There was unanimous interest in a venture operation, looking ahead. But the corporate offices are mired in politics, so our message may not reach the top office.

Later the same day. Aboard the German train back to Stuttgart.

I pass Ulm on the way back to France, the train at slow speed on the unimproved tracks. I plan to spend two days in Toulouse reviewing the files of CNES. As a student, Philippe Richard did an original analysis of the probability of life in the universe. He sent it to *La Recherche*, but of course such an august magazine couldn't print an article by a 22-year-old Army grunt, no matter how bright!

Philippe also told me the French networks monitoring thunderstorms had detected very powerful electromagnetic sources in the atmosphere on several occasions, but they were never identified, and not even reported to CNES.

Now Janine calls me on the train with positive news. Her latest test, done yesterday in Paris, shows her red blood cell count going up.

Toulouse. Sunday 6 April 2008.
Hotel Crowne Plaza, near Place du Capitole.

I just learned of the death yesterday of Dr. Hubert Larcher, president of Institut Métapsychique International, one of the few capable leaders of parapsychology research in France. Tomorrow I'll meet computer analyst Michael Vaillant at Place Jeanne d'Arc, and we will drive to CNES together.

The last two days have been full of happy moments with Max. Yesterday, he insisted on visiting the gardens of the Paris City Hall, where he'd deposited a moribund rat, evidently dying of poisoning. He dragged us through the tulips to visit the rat, who unfortunately had succumbed. One never knows what will happen when Max is around, and this unpredictability makes life delightful.

Toulouse. Monday 7 April 2008.

Visit to the GEIPAN, whose offices are in the Lagrange building. Where's the UFO library? Did someone take home all the books? The new staff is composed of a woman who does data entry, and Patenet's secretary. Michaël Vaillant works half-time. The annual budget had been set around 250,000 euros, but it will be cut by 30,000 euros.

Several Gendarmerie reports are misplaced, notably the ones for Trans-en-Provence and L'Amaranthe, two of the most solid, unexplained cases in the files. One of the folders is empty, with only a page that reads: "*Interesting case, has been transferred.*"

Toulouse. Tuesday 8 April 2008.

I found the files today, stored in two small offices in the basement of another building, near a video conference room. They hold the remains of a famous artillery shell that nearly hit a farmer near Royan, and some samples from another site with no identification. We looked in vain for the soil samples from Trans-en-Provence. The folders are in disarray because the Gendarmes' reports were extracted to be scanned, but never re-filed. One cabinet contains magazines, unsorted, including two ancient issues of my InfoMedia's *Planet News*!

Mabillon. Wednesday 9 April 2008.

Olympic celebrations. Ludicrous display of police power in Paris, with cops running alongside officers dressed as ordinary runners, in a futile effort to keep the flame safe from insults and riots.

The primary investigator from Soissons took me to see the plaster cast of the landing gear of the object, stored in a bank vault, so I was able to take measurements and photographs (figure 16).

The French economy is shaken by renewed inflation (3.5%) and the high euro (at $1.57), lethargic growth, and high debt. The cost of living keeps going up, says Yves Messarovitch, so many people feel trapped, crushed by anonymous masters, with shrinking ability to pay for the necessities of life. The men behind the throne are no longer the conservative (but competent and urbane) bosses of the Dassault, Michelin, or Jérôme Monod generation, but a new breed of brutish operators, the kind of sharks I once observed around Sarkozy.

On the Air France flight home. Sunday 13 April 2008.

Janine returned last night from a one-day trip to Normandy with bad news about Alain, now barely conscious. She did see him, possibly for the last time, at Caen hospital. The doctors told her they would not try any last minute, heroic treatments.

Hummingbird. Thursday 17 April 2008.

Mike Kuchar called as soon as we arrived. He'd seen a dark UFO over San Francisco about 7 pm on Saturday. The UFOTOG project by Doug Trumbull is taking shape. "Weirdly," he says, "my spooky type has tipped me off to some 'blimps' with super-muffled scramjets, and alerted me to their somewhat UFO appearance and performance, so I wouldn't get confused. He is helpful. As I said in the proposal, I'll vet military secret projects, I'm not interested in them anyway."

He adds, in answer to my questions: "I'm staying away from any kind of active radar or laser rangefinders at this time, because I don't want to emit any signals from our observing location."

Hummingbird. Sunday 20 April 2008.

Analyzing the official records from Soissons that I brought back from Toulouse, I discover that the various reports contain striking contradictions. In particular, the Gendarmes state that their surveillance of the site over the following two weekends disclosed nothing unusual... A blatant lie, since they did see an object that landed very close to them and left very obvious, deep traces, as in a French equivalent of the Socorro case. Not to mention they were paralyzed...

I spent last evening with Mike and George Kuchar, an entertaining experience. Mike prepared beef soup for us and told me the details of his extraordinary sighting of a large black object over San Francisco. The twins are always gentle and full of care for each other.

Hummingbird. Friday 25 April 2008.

Janine took the car and drove down the Peninsula yesterday to resume work with her colleagues, who had clamored for her to join them again, a big victory! She's regained her confidence; today her MRI was perfect, with no visible sign of tumor activity.

I saw Mike Kuchar again last night, then I went to the police station on Valencia to ask if they got any reports. They had not, but, as the young Chicano desk sergeant told me with a sad smile, they're more concerned with the area's intense criminal activity than with any Aliens... He was trained in biology and forestry, so he spoke to me about cryptozoology, one of his pet subjects.

Hummingbird. Sunday 27 April 2008.

I went back to the Mission today to post notices about Mike's sighting, calling for witnesses. At the Cave of Ali Baba, a middle-eastern restaurant on Valencia with a perfect view of the object's supposed trajectory, I had a lunch of shish-kebab and Diet Coke. It was a waste of time. None of their customers had reported anything.

Yesterday we had excellent news from France, where EADS has signed a Letter of Intent to invest in our proposed Fund—five million euros in the European structure and five million dollars in the American one, subject to us completing an investment syndicate.

This evening Doug Trumbull came over with his wife, Julia. Janine had surpassed herself with a great dinner, fine wines, and a gracious atmosphere that helped us bridge over some diverging views. Doug and Julia have become enamored of abduction research and ended up learning about physics from Sarfatti, who put them in touch with his own "CIA insider" contact in Florida.

The CIA guy has half-convinced them that the US had a pact with the Aliens, that the UFO presence will be revealed in 2012, and that the government plans "to slowly release information to prepare public opinion," an old disinformation plot we've been hearing forever.

I threw cold water over the idea: "Tomorrow we shave you for free!" used to be the joke in Europe about such promises. They laughed: Julia had already developed healthy skepticism about the issue.

Doug Trumbull's "CIA source" has given names of ten towns where "he'll see UFOs," so he'll take his equipment there.

Good luck, I said.

Hummingbird. Wednesday 30 April 2008.

The phone call came at four o'clock in the morning. We had expected it, of course. Alain was no longer conscious and the doctors had suspended treatment. Now it's the end of a brave, simple man who made everyone happy around him.

Alain had the life he wanted, dedicated to his friends and to the warm atmosphere he created. He opened *Le Midi* in Charleston 20 years ago and was known for the courteous and cheerful care he brought to his business dealings, for the warm, long-term friendships he formed with his customers, and for his magnificent cooking, repeatedly honored.

Born in 1942 in Morocco, where his father was stationed just before World War II, Alain was raised in Normandy after the war. He only had a primary school education and trained as a baker. Joining us in Chicago in 1965, he became a pastry chef (a demanding field for which he had an inspired flair) and learned the difficult skill of restaurant management.

When he moved again in 1970 to be with us in California, he opened several restaurants in Silicon Valley, notably the Little Store in Woodside where his trademark onion soup and delicious Napoléon pastries are fondly remembered to this day. His faithful customers included singer Joan Baez and early tycoons of the high-tech field. Alain was an artist, a man with a great heart.

Hummingbird. Sunday 4 May 2008.

Yesterday, to change our mood, we took advantage of the fine spring weather to enjoy out traditional snack and row around Stow Lake, the boat hidden in the reeds, yellow irises and the branches of pine trees among families of ducks, seagulls, and an array of turtles sunning themselves on floating logs. A couple of magnificent blue herons have a nest at the top of a tree on an islet where they raise their chicks, to the joy of nature lovers on nearby paths, equipped with telescopes.

Hummingbird. Tuesday 6 May 2008.

Alain's funeral took place in Yvetot today. Olivier represented us. Here the melancholy hangs over our thoughts, only distracted by the trip we plan to Charleston, his last home. We worry about the future of our own children: Who will be with them when they get old? We feel distraught and empty.

Montréal. Tuesday 13 May 2008. Hotel Sheraton "Le Centre."

I have found a small restaurant on Rue Sainte Catherine with French cuisine and a pianist who sings old Parisian tunes. My room looks out to the Mont Royal. The weather is wonderful, people in a good mood.

One of my financial appointments was rescheduled, so I took a long walk, east and down to the Old Town and the harbor. I had to go through a tourist section that looked like a cheap bazaar and smelled of grease, but I saw some charming enclaves in a mix of stately old buildings and stunning modern architecture. Trees are in bloom and the cherry blossoms enhance the glass and concrete towers I had found so forbidding on previous wintry visits.

May 13th is a historic date. Forty years ago, riots were about to erupt in Paris and Janine was about to give birth to our daughter. When I called her this morning, the two of them were about to catch the flight to Charleston.

As I walked along the Saint Laurent, my cellphone rang and the Soissons investigator told me that the gendarmerie superior officer in the case, a major, was willing to meet me. He was inviting us to lunch at his home next month to discuss the case. I dwell on the issues it raises: Why did they fail to report seeing the object up close in the official document I found in the CNES archives? Why did they lie to their superiors, stating that they went back for a stake-out *but saw nothing*? Finally, the key question: How could a massive object, over ten tons, emerge out of a simple wandering light?

Montreal. Wednesday 14 May 2008.

One or two more meetings with Québec financial institutions, and I will fly on to Charleston. My mind feels slow and bruised. The death of Alain weighs on me, even if we had little hope of healing him. My sorrow, the pain felt by my confused and tired brain, comes with the helplessness of time.

Yesterday I found restaurants nestled in courtyards or open to lively Rue Sainte Catherine. This city has an amazing number of stores selling clothes: every second boutique is full of dresses, shoes, jeans, or coats. At night the city feels safe, but I fail to discover its heart, perhaps because of the weakness in mine.

Charleston, South Carolina. Friday 16 May 2008.

Alain's house is almost empty now. Annick has already done much of the cleaning. Catherine, Olivier, and Eric have removed the furniture and cleared the garage, while Janine went through business papers. I am disoriented here, unused to the stupefying humidity, with only an occasional cooling breeze wafting from the marshes.

Alain had many friends here, they rush to talk of the happy times: companions of his adventures, colleagues and waitresses, neighbors and associates, and a few partners in various ventures who exploited his generosity. Now they hang around, hoping for souvenirs. I drive Janine into town to take care of the formal papers. A few items that vividly evoke her brother's memory will go to Normandy. Catherine will use his truck. In Alain's empty house we formed a circle of love, and said a somber *Adieu* to him.

17

Hummingbird. Thursday 22 May 2008.

Leaving Charleston, we flew back to the West Coast on Sunday night. Alain's picture now stands at a prominent place where we can see him, wave, and talk to him as we pass by, as if he were still among us.

Today, lunch at the Duck Club with two entrepreneurs who'd asked to see me to discuss UFO reverse engineering. Both advanced physicists, they've formed a startup company in stealth mode with a businessman friend as president. Their intent is to develop three products: (1) a Hydrogen-Lithium fusion device (HLFD) whose geometry can generate 100% fusion efficiency based on certain rules, (2) an electrogravity generator, and (3) a gravity propulsion engine.

The founder and his son have done many experiments with the first two devices. The fusion reaction using a proton beam from a Pelletron ion accelerator was an initial success, while the electrogravity generator failed. They may have used the wrong semiconductors (gallium phosphide and zinc selenide) with too high a resistivity, so they will try again. The devices are based on a new theory so revolutionary they've been thrown out by most of the physicists they consulted, an encouraging message indeed to any venture capitalist, given the big gaps in current physics.

I am struck by the parallels with what Poher is doing in France with his theory of Universons, and what Puthoff does in Texas with zero-point energy. Poher claims he can demonstrate actual motion of test objects in his lab.

Later the same day.

The ISS passed overhead last night, a nice throwback to our nights tracking satellites at Meudon. As computed, we enjoyed watching it as it appeared above Twin Peaks and flew its wide arc towards Berkeley. The station is very bright, all its modules and solar panels in place.

I was amused to read a recent *New Scientist* that reports on an interesting series of experiments on the effects of peer pressure. They show individuals casting aside what they actually enjoy from their own experience to adopt an inferior course of action when "everybody else is doing it."

The experiments sound fun. They involved rats who had a choice between attractive food and food they didn't like. When they were placed with a group of rats who were trained to feed on the bad food, they quickly conformed to their peers' choice instead of acting in the interest of their own taste. It now turns out humans behave in the same stupid way.

That particular issue (6) also had an article about a non-lethal weapon called a flash gun, designed to stop people in their tracks with a flashing light. One such device, the "Incapacitator" made by Optical Intelligent Systems in Torrance, is a big flashlight packed with multicolor diodes. The beam is bright enough to dazzle, but the colored lights are designed to pulse on and off in a particular sequence at a rate that causes disorientation, dizziness, and vertigo in two thirds of the people exposed.

The army also works on a strobing light mounted on a drone to control a mob from a few hundred meters. The light source, made by Peak Beam Systems in Pennsylvania, is a modified 15 million candela xenon lamp 100 times brighter than a car headlight. Tests showed people immobilized, falling down at 500 yards.

My files contain testimonies about such lights. Maurice Masse at Valensole told me about watching the object from below and seeing a dizzying array of multicolored flashing lights, an item I've never published. At Haravilliers, the bottom of the object had so many flashing colors it resembled a Christmas tree.

Studies of these effects in laboratories go back to the 1950s when helicopter pilots began complaining about strobing effects of the sun through rotor blades. Some experts are skeptical that strobing lights can have an impact on the brain, unless the person is subject to epileptic seizures.

I can only observe that once again, the UFO phenomenon seems to be a small step ahead of human technology, for better or worse.

Hummingbird. Saturday 24 May 2008.

Jeff Kripal spent the day here, going through my library, as he says, "to put another layer of insight" into an essay. That was my opportunity to invite our neighbor, Dr. Kevin Starr, for afternoon coffee.

Like Jeff, Kevin is a distinguished historian with special interest in spirituality. He promptly arrived with his own copy of Jeff's *Esalen* book for him to sign, a nice touch. This led to a sparkling exchange of academic references between the two scholars.

Athanor. Sunday 25 May 2008.

The weather was cool but sunny today, so we drove over to the Athanor for one last look. We've received an offer on the house, at a very fair price in the current depressed market. Down the hill from us, a developer is getting ready to build a dozen new homes. He doesn't have a building permit, but he's already cleared the trees and the bushes we (and the deer) loved so much.

We're leaving this town the same way we left New Jersey, and also our Spring Hill ranch, as the fine environment becomes insulted by too many disrespectful idiots. We ate a snack, sitting in the grass on top of the cliffs, with white wine for one last loving toast to the beauty of Bodega Bay.

NASA had some good news this evening as the Phoenix probe landed near the ice cap of Mars, an experiment I'd hoped I would live long enough to witness since my days working for De Vaucouleurs in Texas in 1962. Soon we should know whether or not there is water under the surface, and how much, and if life once existed there.

Hummingbird. Thursday 29 May 2008.

The latest Indiana Jones movie (*Indiana Jones and the Kingdom of the Crystal Skull*) ends with a series of scenes lifted from my novel, *FastWalker*: A crazed but inspired character leads the researchers to a cavern where a spacecraft has been hidden. It turns out to be an interdimensional machine, which lifts through the roof of the cave, needlessly blowing up the landscape.

Again, the concept of going through another dimension was lost on the scriptwriters who couldn't resist yet another sloppy explosion of their paper-mâché rock pile.

Universal had bought the rights to my novel years ago, so they didn't need my permission to betray it with Hollywood tricks.

Hummingbird. Friday 30 May 2008.

After spending a couple of hours at the pilot nanotechnology plant of Nanogram, I had lunch at the Duck Club with Peter Sturrock. He had trouble walking and told me he needed a knee operation. His scientific mind alert as ever, he's writing two papers for the journal *Science* and continues to study puzzling photographic "orbs."

The Esalen Institute. Monday 2 June 2008.

Esalen is not on any maps. It is nestled south of Big Sur in a fold of the coastal landscape, a cluster of wooden buildings linked by paths through flower beds and wide vegetable gardens. In this refined environment, Jeff Kripal has assembled a group of scholars of the paranormal and superpower comics. The program, which includes two presentations he asked me to give on remote viewing and UFO research, will allow me to become familiar with the work of Brenda Denzler, Wendy Doniger, and especially Dr. David Hufford, whose work on *The Terror That Comes in the Night* was in part influenced by *Passport to Magonia*.

This short interlude before my trip to France also enables me to appreciate Michael Murphy and especially Bertrand Méheust, with whom I share a room in the Big House. Other participants are Dean Radin, Russell Targ, and Roy Thomas (of *Dr. Strange* fame), cartoon artists like Arlen Schumer, Ramona Fradon, Christopher Knowles, and writers Victoria Nelson, Jorge Ferrer and Donna Freitas (*Sex and the Soul*).

Gordon Wheeler is the current president of Esalen, where Michael Murphy has redefined his role as research leader.

The Esalen Institute. Tuesday 3 June 2008.

Professor David Hufford, a researcher in psychiatry and folklore who teaches at Penn State, was the most interesting person I met here. He's concerned with what he calls "politically disadvantaged observations" and asks to what extent they are grounded in experience. He was involved in the failed Bigelow-Roper survey of abductions, arguing at the time that the link between Alien encounters and sleep paralysis was a deeply flawed assumption by Jacobs and Hopkins, based on misinterpretation of the science. (The abductionists didn't listen, and neither did their two high-society sponsors.)

The official rationalizations of extraordinary experiences rely on stigma, *lexical erasure* (such as calling them "nightmares"), *assimilation* (reducing them to anthropology or cultural bias), and *limited accommodation* (also known as "normal hallucinations").

The notion of "what is real" is not always objective, he added. For example, pain is undoubtedly real but not shareable or measurable.

Hufford then cited Stephen Jay Gould who said, "Facts do not go away while scientists debate theories to explain them."

Dean Radin argued that psychic anticipation of emotional events could be measured at about three second advance. He asked, "Is that the size of *now*?" But he went on to promote something called "intentional chocolate," sold over the Internet, and an unproven machine by Bill Tiller that reminded me of the claims of radionics. This illustrated for me the ambiguities of parapsychology.

"In her current circumstances," Janine didn't want to come with me to Esalen and meet researchers of the unknown beyond. She has been simplifying our records and those of Alain, with the quiet competence she puts into everything.

Air France flight to Paris. Wednesday 4 June 2008.

High above Hudson Bay, finally detached from the curtain of distractions we've created for these last few months, I dread the time when our blessed interlude may come to an end. I imagine her next to me. She was right not to come to Esalen; all our lofty talk of soul and survival was largely irrelevant.

Mabillon. Friday 6 June 2008.

When I opened the shutters, Paris was gray and cold, but the weather may yet lift and return to the mild sun we had yesterday. The high price of gasoline causes dislocations throughout France, hitting the fishing and trucking industry especially hard. People feel vulnerable, although many do enjoy early pensions, retirement as early as 55, and a much better social system than in the US. But the improvement in buying power promised by Sarkozy has failed to materialize.

Mabillon. Monday 9 June 2008.

We spent the day in a charming town in Picardie, near Amiens. The TGV stops at an isolated station in the middle of the fields, a short trip north of Charles de Gaulle Airport. The main witness of the Soissons landings, who came over to meet us, is a dynamic retired man in his late sixties. We passed an ancient castle to reach his house. His wife had prepared a French country lunch complete with *apéritif,* hors d'oeuvres, fish and meat, which we enjoyed while reviewing the case.

The Major didn't know what had happened to his report, so he was pleasantly surprised when I showed him the copy I'd discovered in the official CNES files in Toulouse.

We spent much time going over the details of what he saw at the site, which, as it turns out, is called *Le Trou du Diable*...The Devil's Hole. He was 30 meters away from the object when it seemed to emerge and drop down from the hovering light. So why is the official report silent on the main features of the case? Why does it simply note some superficial trace analyses, *without mentioning that two Gendarmes were present at the site, watching everything?* Their radio was out of commission and their minds so stunned they vaguely spoke of getting out of their car, but did nothing of the kind, contrary to the plans they had made.

Why doesn't CNES know about this? The answer is simple: The Major's superiors told him not to mention it because they would surely be brought before a shrink; their careers would be in jeopardy. The media would be crawling everywhere. It's another situation showing why the best cases never come before official panels.

Mabillon. Friday 13 June 2008.

I feel silly, alone in our apartment. Paris is heavily polluted; I have trouble sleeping. A big weight was lifted last night, however: Janine called to say there was no trace of the tumor on the latest images, and no need to resume chemotherapy. I prompted her to join me. She will be here on Sunday!

Paris has cooled down, dressed in her gray uniform. I have a dull headache after long sessions with our strategic committee. They agreed to extend our work for two more years, a good deal for them, consolidating our economic future.

Studiously working over the web, Chris Aubeck and I continue to trade updates for *Wonders*.

Mabillon. Saturday 14 June 2008.

Poor Nicolas Sarkozy: The French soccer team was flattened by Holland (four goals to one) and Ireland has just voted NO to the Lisbon treaty. Alas, there's no "Plan B" for Europe, lament the pundits in Brussels. Actually, the Lisbon treaty itself was Plan B, and it failed although hatched by Angela Merkel and Sarkozy. Now the elites, chastised by the Irish vote, try to figure out some maneuver to ram their overly-confusing scheme down the throat of their peoples, who might rally around a real plan for Europe, if it made sense.

Real estate in this area has shot up by another 14% since last year, to a range of 11,000 to 17,000 euros per square meter, or about 1,700 to 2,700 dollars per square foot. Fortunately, as president Sarkozy likes to repeat, "Inflation is under control."

Paris, Rue Copernic. Monday 16 June 2008.

Janine has joined me. We just had lunch at Le Suffren with Dominique Weinstein and Pierre Lagrange. They told us that Bertrand Méheust, our brilliant friend who teaches in Bourges, won an academic research position but it was suddenly "withdrawn." Of course, he sued and won reinstatement, but the new job he just earned "had been eliminated." The bureaucracy now denies him points of retirement pay for obscure reasons. What a waste!

Over lunch, I learned that Velasco did leave Toulouse with many books and some of the archives that he saved from bureaucratic destruction. As one generation uneasily replaces another, there are many such stories of data lost, dispersed, or stored away by uncommunicative researchers.

American scholarship isn't much better. When Pierre inquired about the Ruppelt files, now at the Center for UFO Studies (CUFOS), he was abruptly rebuffed by Michael Swords who answered with one of his faintly insulting letters. Nothing is left of SOBEPS in Brussels, except a bundle of reports Lagrange bought for a song.

Mabillon. Wednesday 18 June 2008.

Today the college of experts of GEIPAN met in Paris at CNES headquarters. Patenet, Louange, Rospars, Lagrange, and half a dozen other men listened to Erling Strand and another Norwegian researcher talk about the Hessdalen lights, with a pitch for an extensive new study. When I pointed out their presentation didn't take into account earlier work supposedly proving the lights were gaseous emanations linked to scandium (a rare mineral found in that valley), they brushed this aside, saying they "had new pictures." I came away puzzled.

Investigating Hessdalen is much safer than chasing most UFO cases, since the lights are concentrated in one location. Besides, they have an interesting geophysical connotation that makes them respectable. But is that going to convince anybody? No explanation is available.

Mabillon. Thursday 19 June 2008.

Jacques Zyss, president of the SNPE (a leading manufacturer of powders and explosives) invited us to dinner tonight with Alain Dupas, his wife, and another couple. They live in a beautiful apartment with high ceilings in the select seventh *arrondissement*, behind the National Assembly. The apartment was filled with fine paintings bought by Zyss' father, a Polish Jew of great taste who collected Dufy. Janine enjoyed the evening of conversation and superb food.

We walked all the way home, hand in hand. To my great joy, she is full of life, bright ideas, and as much energy as ever. There is sweetness in our life, along with a grave awareness of the uncertainty of fate. Ready to fly home, I savor this special time.

Hummingbird. Saturday 21 June 2008.

Summer has begun suddenly, hitting the Bay Area with a heat wave, over 100 degrees even in the City. My daughter greeted me joyfully at the airport, eager to guide me through the sale of the house on the coast. A part of my soul will always linger on that shoreline, so pure in the haze that rises from the beach and the rocks studded with purple and orange starfish, a place for simple picnics, sitting in a hollow in the rocks at low tide.

Hummingbird. Saturday 5 July 2008.

Our grandson has brought a new quality into our lives, the freshness of his eleven years, his new eyes on the world, and the energy he channels easily into a sharp interest for every living thing.

Yesterday, when we rowed around the lake in Golden Gate Park, we had to stop for every turtle and every baby duck. Life around him is fun, colorful, unpredictable, and busy.

Hummingbird. Sunday 13 July 2008.

We were coming back from the beach with Maxim, loaded with algae and the eleven crabs he caught, tired from the hot sun, when Robert Bigelow called to announce a breakthrough.

At our last meeting in Vegas, he had hinted he'd been approached by DIA to explore new research into UFOs, but I thought it mainly involved a few ongoing tests at the Utah ranch.

I was wrong because the new project is far more ambitious: "There's actual funding now, Jacques. The dollars have been delivered, the Agency has them. It's a five-year program of investigations, with annual appropriations. The first year is 10 million and it will ramp up according to results."*

Bob went on: "I'm writing the response to the RFP now; it'll be specific in terms of technical procedures, so we're in a good position to win. I'm looking at seven different approaches to the problem, including remote viewing."

He went on: "The staffing involves full-time people, 21 scientists and consultants, with a big emphasis on overseas research. There's money available for contracts. I've already lined up an administrator, John Gallagher who's a dean at UNLV. I'm looking for a deputy administrator and fifteen other good research people with a passion and the ability to manage projects. I want to cast a very broad net, embrace the science community…"

"Who's aware of the project at the moment?" I asked. "Can I mention it if I talk to Hal and Kit?"

"Yes, those two are aware of it, and so is John Schuessler, although he doesn't have the details yet. We're still a couple of months away from launching it."

He repeated that international contacts would be a very important part of the work. I made him aware of my plans.

Later the same day.

I've just closed the loop with Hal and raised some points of concern: Ten million dollars a year for UFO research at a time when Congress is clamping down on expenses? How long do they think such a project can be kept going without interference? Hal promised to tell me more about the political side, but even with top-level support, he said, that problem does remain.

Experience with the same kind of unstable funding at SRI is still present in both our minds. It will take a year to recruit the right team, and another year to train it.† By the end of the Condon project, three

---

* This new DIA-funded Bigelow project would turn out to be the Advanced Aerospace Weapon System Applications Program (AAWSAP), which was publicly revealed by *The New York Times* in December 2017 as "The Pentagon's Mysterious UFO Program" but wrongly attributed to the Advanced Aerospace Threat Identification Program (AATIP).

† I was wrong: the team was recruited in less than five months.

or four people on his staff had begun to grasp the complexity of the phenomenon (especially Dave Saunders), but too many mistakes had already been made along the way. We're not likely to have very much to show by the end of the first year.

Hal agreed and added another concern with the Agency: He wonders exactly how much access they have, citing anecdotes. After my own bad experience with NASA, I'm not about to invest a lot of trust into a new federal project, funded or not, but I will help Bob by joining his Board, as Hal encourages me to do. As for international contacts, I'll wait until I know more, and where that would fit.

Washington, Monday 14 July 2008.
The Comfort Inn, in Sterling.

Peter Banks and I are here to brief the top staff of EADS North America about venture prospects.

Returning my call this afternoon, Kit threw a completely different light on the project that Bob Bigelow and Hal had described to me. "Like you, when I first heard about it, I thought it just involved the ranch," he began.

"Only later, when I met with the man in Washington who is behind this, and when Hal and I met with another sponsor six weeks ago, I understood it was much more open-ended than what Bob said. *It's a very big project.*

"Bob has been picked for it because of his skill in executing cheaply on a large scale, but the whole thing is very down to earth, while Bob thinks of cosmic developments. The complete description includes a large secure building, and yes, international aspects are very important."

He added: "Bob is a proven performer for projects of that size, but he hasn't followed salary structures these days. He was assuming he could hire about 75 people, including PhDs, move them to Vegas with their families, get rid of those that wouldn't work out the first year, and pay the rest standard salaries for a year at a time, expecting them to work 80 hours a week...That's not the way things are done in technology today."

Later the same day.

Another name from the distant past: a woman I'll call "Babette," sent me a message, reminding me of our conversations decades ago, when she was in charge of organizing lectures at her college, and later as an intern at the White House. Now she's a well-established business woman after a stint as a Senatorial staffer and advanced studies in Middle Eastern affairs.

She said that one recent night in Michigan she'd observed a silent, *rectangular* object three stories high, flying slowly over the deserted road. She turned around trying to follow it and drove parallel to it until it seemed to shrink, giving the impression of moving away fast *while continuing to fly at its regular slow pace*. It vanished in this seemingly absurd geometric movement, melting into the night. It had a single main light and multiple smaller ones.

Mabillon, Sunday 20 July 2008.

Paris is sunny, clear of clouds and smoke, with a gentle breeze. Many people are away on their annual southern migration. Our building is oddly silent. Awake at 5 am, I taste the night, my anxious thoughts, and a landscape of burning mysteries to explore: ancient reports in *Wonders in the Sky* (Chris Aubeck and I are reaching the end of our screening of cases); modern reports like Haravilliers, Soissons, and others; then the long and fruitless search for definitive answers. And now, Bigelow's amazing new project.

Janine has lost faith in this research. She insists that my magistrate father was right when he spoke of the frailty of human testimony. Even when I replay for her my interview with the Major, who was in uniform and within feet of the huge Soissons object when it landed, she shakes her head: "All this has lasted too long, it remains too vague. You have no real evidence."

It's hard to argue with her view, which comes from someone with as much experience as I do. Many of our favorite cases have disintegrated under long-term scrutiny. The Dr. X story turned into a vaguely occult tale, photographic cases do not stand up, and the Costa Rica case, although undoubtedly real, may show a simple ball of volcanic gas if Dr. Banks is right. As for the experiments at Bigelow's Utah ranch, they have yielded puzzling enigmas and some reliable experiences but no more scientific clues than our own attempts at Spring Hill.

What is it, then, that made the three deep imprints at the Devils' Hole? What is it that flew over Haravilliers at dawn, startling six men on their way to hunt? Janine herself witnessed two unidentified lights at Spring Hill. As a child in Morocco, she had seen the face of what she thought was an impossible little boy outside a second-story window... Few people know the parameters of this giant puzzle better than the two of us: We've met every significant researcher and most of the influential witnesses in the last half century. They became part of our lives. We've heard all the theories and initiated a few of our own. Yet our quiet dialogue in the soft night boils down to this confession: that the physical reality of a transcendent unknown, which I see so clearly, cannot yet be formulated into a scientific statement that makes sense. I remain an optimist. I wonder, amidst all the confusion, if we are not closer than ever to an illuminating answer, hidden in plain sight, as Jeff Kripal says. I am delighted that Janine remains as intellectually brilliant and focused as she is physically active and fit.

We even spent Friday afternoon playing crazy games of "volley soccer" with Maxim at a nearby public tennis court. She ran with the ball, tossed it easily to us, and laughed at our clumsiness.

Mabillon. Friday 25 July 2008.

Philippe Richard and I spent the day in London on a visit to Rolls-Royce that furthered my understanding of the aerospace industry and its use of innovation. RR's offices are within a block of Buckingham Palace with its crowd of tourists and its rich park.

The Eurostar train now stops at St. Pancras, a modern, convenient station that puts the elderly, dusty, and confusing French train stations to shame, with their booming announcements over loudspeakers that echo incoherently like the bellow of inarticulate dinosaurs in bottomless caverns.

Mabillon. Sunday 27 July 2008.

Janine landed at Charles de Gaulle at noon, bringing back Maxim. We're happy together again. Dinner on Île Saint-Louis was relaxed.

Over the weekend, Chris Aubeck and I have negotiated our last substitutions of cases for *Wonders*. I am eager to get on with my analysis; this is a body of data I've long dreamed of assembling. Now it's there, inside my computer, ready to yield its secrets.

My friend and respected Spanish correspondent Vicente-Juan Ballester-Olmos has become skeptical of ufology. Echoing Janine's words to me, he writes:

"We are simply witnessing a continuing trend of misinterpretations of natural phenomena (especially relevant in the past) and conventional artificial objects, phenomena and processes (especially relevant today), interpreted according to current knowledge, fears and science myths of the epoch. This is hitting me nowadays in line with the sinking of major, classic cases."

I disagree, of course. What is slowly collapsing is a biased interpretation of the data that was faulty from the start. We aren't dealing with a simplistic Alien invasion; this isn't a sequel to a space movie from the 50s. It is more subtle in ways we've failed to grasp.

Mabillon. Monday 28 July 2008.

After coffee with Janine on Place Saint-Sulpice, I went to visit Olivier Orban at Plon with Yves Messarovitch.

"There isn't any intellectual life left in France," said Orban, one of the powerful publishers in Paris.

"The books that make money are filled with fluff and speculation about Sarkozy's women, reality shows, and scandal in high places. The thoughtful debates you find in American magazines are all absent from the French press. There isn't even any good show on TV, airing original ideas."

We leave everything behind tomorrow and start on the kind of trip I have dreamed of: a care-free wandering through the hills, valleys, and hidden villages of France, visiting friends.

Le Mans. Tuesday 29 July 2008.

Wonderful Didier Alliou! I found his workshop again, shook hands with the glass workers I remembered from my stay with the team, and I admired the four panels of the *Ascension*, the oldest example of stained glass still extant in Europe (at Le Mans cathedral). Didier and his team are studying and restoring this gorgeous work, which art historians have finally dated to 1098.

We had dinner with him in the medieval town (at *Le Plongeoir*) and spoke of tumors and doctors, alternative medicine and the need for a patient to remain captain of his own ship. His lung tumor was reduced by chemotherapy, but he knows that he must sell his unique enterprise. Like many Frenchmen we meet, he railed against Sarkozy and the insane complexity of French bureaucracy.

Saint-Rémy du Val. Wednesday 30 July 2008.

On the way from Le Mans, we stopped for lunch in Alençon, where in typical absurd French fashion all the shops were closed from noon to 3 pm. Then we drove to the marvelous domain of Philippe and Kathryn Favre. We found the medieval colony had expanded since our last visit. The donkey Marcus is the father of an adorable week-old kid, all smooth and gray. Work on the majestic Halle has improved, with the re-opening of one of the great gothic windows. I joined the team that carried the heavy square beams into the courtyard, to be cleaned of nails and rough spots.

Philippe remarked that French society had a unique series of barriers that even Sarkozy was unwilling to dislodge, with cozy relationships between the top managers of big companies and the political elite, so nothing will change for a while.

Poitiers. Thursday 31 July 2008.

The trip down to Poitiers only took three hours. We stopped for lunch in Tours, in the old town, an area of nice houses marred by advertising panels and a jumble of shops with no care for elegance. The weather is hot and heavy under a white sky of milky mugginess. Poitiers is clogged up with noisy cars in a tangle of one-way streets.

Joël and Helen Mesnard are in declining health. Joël said their six-room house in a Poitiers suburb was overrun with so many books and files that they had difficulty retrieving items. The demands of producing their fine magazine, *Lumières dans la Nuit* (*LDLN*), made it impossible to go away for even a short vacation.

Montflanquin. Friday 1 August 2008.

While looking at the map when we passed Limoges and Brive and took the road towards Cahors, Janine noticed that we would drive near this little town perched on top of a hill, where a teacher, a colleague of hers from school days, had a country home. They immediately invited us, so we had dinner with them at Moulin de Boulède. While sipping various local wines, they spoke of their life in retirement, their recent cruises to Egypt and Iceland.

Janine was delighted by this unplanned reunion with two of her closest friends.

Toulouse. Saturday 2 August 2008.

Claude Poher's beautiful house sits on top of a hill in an exclusive enclave between Ramonville and the urban sprawl of Toulouse. Neatly designed by Claude with environmental features such as cooling through the soil, its airy living room with an elegant metal fireplace and white tile floor is enlivened by modern sculptures.

Claude and Danièle, a slender blonde doctor in a flowing red and white dress, greeted us warmly, and the conversation came naturally to the latest experiments they've conducted in their laboratory, where Claude says he can demonstrate his Universon theory to visitors who deign to consider it.

A short refresher course in alternative physics teaches that modern theories of gravitation date back to 1669, when the French Academy held a debate proposed by Descartes, Roberval, Buot, and Huygens on a hypothetical "external pressure" as the cause of gravitation. This was superseded by Newton's theory of universal attraction, published in 1687.

In 1758 Swiss physicist LeSage proposed a quantized gravitation model where a flux of *corpuscules ultramondains* interacted by elastic collisions with matter. This was studied by Maxwell, Lord Kelvin, Lalande, Bernouilli, Lagrange, and others, but it was rejected around 1890 as it contradicted the inertia principle ("No force is required to maintain motion with constant velocity in a straight line, and absolute motion does not cause any observable physical effects.").

Finally, early in the 20th century Albert Einstein proposed his theory of General Relativity (GR), which hasn't been seriously challenged, although serious contradictions between relativity and quantum mechanics remain unsolved. In recent years, several developments of gravitation theory have been proposed, some of which are linked to interesting laboratory experiments. Three of them are summarized here.

1. Dr. Claude Poher's Universon theory

Claude holds a PhD in astrophysics from a French University. He is a former senior engineer with CNES. His experiments consist of electric discharges into superconductive ceramics with two layers having different superconductive critical temperatures, creating a propulsive kinetic momentum that is proportional to the energy of the electric discharge. This effect (which I have witnessed) is accompanied by acceleration of distant matter, induction of current in conductors, and induction of electric fields in distant dielectrics.

Poher, who finances his own work, explains these results by a hypothetical flux of quanta he calls "universons." He claims this flux is neither absorbed nor dispersed by matter. He believes the ceramics emit this quantized (not charged) propelling flux, which it extracts from a cosmologic flux of energy responsible for gravitation.

The model is compatible with the inertia principle, with Newton's law of inertia and gravitation, and with GR. It also predicts the acceleration of the Pioneer spacecraft, the Tully-Fisher and Faber-Jackson laws about the movement of stars in spiral and elliptical galaxies, and it eliminates the need for dark matter in astronomy. Most physicists who have read the theory are skeptical, but the experiments are compelling. Poher is preparing a paper describing his work, but there's been no peer-reviewed publication so far (7).

Both Peter Sturrock and Hal Puthoff have raised questions about Poher's theory. "Why come up with a new name for the hypothetical gravity particles," Hal asked, "rather than calling them *gravitons*, a name already in the mainstream literature? If universons do nothing more than being absorbed and re-emitted by matter, why a new theory?"

2. Dr. Harold Puthoff's zero-point energy theory

After serving in the Navy (1960-63) and at the NSA, Dr. Puthoff received a PhD from Stanford, where he became a lecturer in the electrical engineering department. In 1969, at age 33, he got a patent on a tunable Raman (infrared) laser he had invented. He co-authored *Fundamentals of Quantum Electronics* that became a standard textbook in physics. For over 30 years, Dr. Puthoff and his associates have developed hypotheses about gravity as a zero-point fluctuation (ZPF) force, based on a Sakharov model in which gravity is not a separate fundamental force but an induced effect of ZPF, in much the same way as the van der Waals (intermolecular) and Casimir forces. The work is sponsored by wealthy patrons.

It is one of the more bizarre predictions of quantum theory that each cubic centimeter of space contains an enormous amount of untapped electromagnetic energy known as zero-point energy, the point from which all other energies are measured. In his model, Hal shows that gravitational interaction begins with the fact that a particle situated in a sea of electromagnetic ZPF develops a "jitter" motion. It is the kinetic energy of this jitter ("zitterbewegung" in the physics literature) that constitutes what we know as the "mass" of the particle, through the relation, $E=mc^2$.

When two or more particles are in proximity, Puthoff argues, they are each influenced not only by the fluctuating background field, but by the field generated by all other particles. The inter-particle coupling due to those fields results in the attractive gravitational force. Under this theory, gravitation can thus be understood as an electromagnetic fluctuation force of the Casimir or van der Waals type, although of much longer range. The fact that gravity cannot be shielded is a consequence of the fact that high-frequency quantum noise in general cannot be shielded (8). Hal works on a model of UFO propulsion based on the polarization of the vacuum.

3. In stealth mode: the unified gravity model

A group of my friends, including a brilliant a PhD in theoretical physics from the University of California, have co-founded several successful software startups they sold profitably enough to return to physics with a vengeance: They are funding the work themselves.

Of the various theories I have examined, their model seems the most promising because (as mentioned in my 22 May entry) it yields a hydrogen-lithium fusion device, whose feasibility has already been demonstrated in preliminary experiments, but also an electricity generator and *a gravity propulsion engine* in which the kinetic energy from the alpha particles can be transferred into what they call "units of the fabric of space (FS)." This theory is also the most ambitious, since it represents a drastic departure from GR. It posits that the universe is composed of FS units with a rest mass of 2 proton masses able to store and transfer kinetic energy. They are responsible for the 3-degree Kelvin cosmic microwave background radiation.

This new gravity theory describes the gravitational interaction of photons and predicts the same results as GR for the three classical experimental tests of GR, (bending of light, gravitational redshift, precession of the perihelion of Mercury) *although for different reasons*. In addition, the equations predict the observed change in the period of binary pulsars without invoking gravitational radiation. It states that the gravity wavelength of an object is linearly proportional to its rest mass, and the coefficient of proportionality is the Avogadro number divided by a new physical constant, *atomic mass linear density*.

It further states that gravity occurs instantaneously as a result of a set of eight logarithmic singularities and a first-order singularity. Most physics experts, informally contacted, dismiss such a theory because it contradicts (or blatantly ignores) general relativity. Only one senior physicist has now agreed to serve as advisor, as well as a Washington-based expert.

Carcassonne. Sunday 3 August 2008.

We have decided to spend a second day in Carcassonne after visiting private researcher Franck Marie in Esperaza, in the craggy mountains of Cathar country at the foot of the Pyrénées. Five years ago, Franck, who lived near Paris, suffered a matrimonial collapse that left him penniless, without a car, and sadly separated from his two children. He took his files and books and moved to a small apartment in the beige and white stucco apartment building where we met him.

His research centers on a massive catalogue of anomalies, combined with lists of historical and esoteric events. He compiles it thanks to a network of correspondents, many in embassies and administrative positions. (I suspect they are high members of French free-masonry who share in his historical interests.) Like my friend Larry Hatch, he does everything alone with an old computer, looking for correlations between UFOs and human events.

He pulled out for us an index of his files until 1879 to match against my chronology of *Wonders*.

Franck's other work near Rennes-le-Château concerns historical research. Arguing with some reason that most current authors are wrong, he's gone back to genealogical documents like the wills of local families, the Blanchefort and the Negre, looking for clues about caves where the Cathar treasure might be buried "in the invisible castle under the mountain."

He has now located four places mentioned in such documents, where local peasants had been forbidden from gathering firewood.

Franck has also come into possession of the original slates (specially treated leaves) with Sanskrit inscriptions that workers reportedly found when restoring the foundations of Montségur castle. They are Zoroastrian or Manichaean magical texts sent by eastern bishops who spread Catharism in the West. His adventures when trying to translate these texts, which may have originated in Sri Lanka, are quite remarkable.

We had lunch with Franck at a local kitschy café and then we drove to Rennes-le-Château to admire the site again. We came back to Carcassonne through a landscape of mystery where it seems every hill supports the ruins of a castle with its own tale of treasures.

Franck has noted that the 1954 UFO wave began within only 10 days of the most powerful nuclear explosions by the US and USSR. Was that why Bergier had recommended to me that we look for correlations with atmospheric radioactivity?

Arles. Tuesday 5 August 2008.

We spent last night at Nîmes, after a detour through Alès to see Jacques Maniez, with whom I've occasionally corresponded (he was a frequent investigator and visitor at Valensole) but never met.

When I called his house, his wife cautioned me that he was in the early stages of Alzheimer and might not recall our correspondence. Yet our visit must have stimulated his mind because he greeted us happily when we joined him on Rue d'Uzès. We saw his home office, a touching reminder of what happens to amateurs when their passion overruns their living space. His wife, Simone, is a cheerful brunette with piercing blue eyes and a great deal of courage.

We went to lunch on a square in Alès in torrid weather and shared stories. He told us about a student, Christophe Fernandez, who took pictures of large orbs or balls of light in Uzès in 1974. Maniez himself had seen such a ball, pulsating as if alive, on the road in front of his motorcycle when he was 20 (in 1948). It took off at high speed and was soon lost in the sky.

I asked about the student's negatives. They were stolen, he said, or rather taken away by someone at CNES, and never returned. Another case he investigated was that of Assas in 1965, where the main witness (Gérard Barrascud) suffered physiological sequelae while his dog died within a day, its flesh falling away from its bones. Maniez gave me his notes.

Aix-en-Provence. Thursday 7 August 2008.

My French partner Philippe Richard and his German-born wife have offered us the hospitality of their home in Saint-Marc near Aix, next to a vast pine forest that extends all the way to Mont Sainte Victoire. There we rest, catch our breath, swim in the pool, and take long walks. Janine observes that the cities we've driven through seem dusty and decrepit, even under the summer sun. Great monuments like the Arènes at Nîmes and Arles are left to crumble. Many towns have become complicated by one-way streets and intractable circuits through ugly industrial suburbs.

Mabillon. Saturday 9 August 2008.

Here we are, in Paris again, with a rich harvest of new data and fresh ideas. I sat down at the computer and, 600 messages later, realized that a sea change was taking place in public attitudes towards UFOs. Yesterday two US political scientists, Profs. Alexander Wendt and Raymond Duvall, published a lengthy political science paper in the journal *Political Theory* (dated Aug. 1st), analyzing why governments refuse to take UFOs seriously.

Mabillon, Monday 11 August 2008.

More leaks. The *Herald Tribune* has an article by Billy Cox interviewing Vice-Admiral Thomas R. Wilson, who acknowledged he met with Edgar Mitchell and Steven Greer in April 1997. Yet Wilson denies that he ever tried to obtain documents about any secret UFO reverse-engineering program, while Mitchell and Greer swear the Admiral assured them he'd been rebuffed in his attempt to gain access, being told he did not have the need-to-know. They recall he was bitter because those who denied him access were not even DoD people, but corporate legal executives who'd agreed to meet with him only for one reason: to determine *how he had found them*.

I had lunch at Simonne Servais' apartment today. Since our last meeting she has contributed to several books as the last survivor of the Adenauer-DeGaulle meeting in June 1958. She feels diminished by her lengthy recovery, but at 86 she keeps a very clear mind.

Simonne concentrates on key questions. She is unwilling to meet anyone from Dominique's organization (DST) because of its murky political role in the Markovich affair under Pompidou (9). She thinks *Volume Two* of my journal should be published "because it is so completely honest." She remains upset with Payan and thoroughly despises Sarkozy, his ego and *esbrouffe* (bling-bling).

Hummingbird. Sunday 17 August 2008.

Hal has filled in the details of the Mitchell-Wilson story for me. It began when Commander Willard Miller (ex-Naval Intelligence, retired) set up a meeting with Wilson for Dr. Greer, who brought Ed Mitchell along. At that meeting, Mitchell told Wilson he'd grown up in Roswell and had personal testimony from local folks whose word he didn't doubt regarding a UFO crash and retrieval. Wilson promised to check. When Greer's book came out, claiming Wilson had been rebuffed, researcher Richard Dolan called him on the phone for an interview. Wilson stated "it's all poppycock" and hung up.

Well, I suggested to Hal there were two lessons to draw from this. One, all those so-called "super-secret" revelations that come through Joe Firmage, John Petersen, and others end up all over the Internet, so *they can't be very secret in the first place*. Two, nobody should make any claims that cannot be absolutely backed up with evidence. Edgar Mitchell himself is getting desperate, perhaps because he wants "the truth" before he gets too old, but where is the truth? He has no evidence except for the fact that he met with Wilson, and Wilson has no evidence, except that he was rebuffed.

Hal doesn't agree. "Wilson was indeed told what it was all about," he argues. But that's only another level in the cover, I said, eager to learn more.

Austin. Saturday 23 August 2008.

Hal had sent me a simple legal agreement with EarthTech International (ETI), which I signed, and a more complex three-page document with Bigelow, which I amended. Over dinner at Fonda San Miguel, our usual restaurant, he explained the structure of the project to me. Surprisingly, it started with an unclassified Request For Proposals (RFP) from DIA (Bolling AFB) entitled "Advanced Aerospace Weapons Systems Applications Program" dated 18 August, solicitation number HHM 40208R0211, with response expected by September 5. It is a "set-aside for small business" (eliminating Boeing or Lockheed) and demands prior performance in space, which restricts the field to three or four firms, including

Bigelow Aerospace.

"This white program has a black side," I learned. "The winning contractor must have a TS-rated facility and personnel. The leader will manage six projects that will contract with labs and universities for breakthrough products and processes, inspired by information already derived from UFO observations. We've been promised access to hardware and physiology data extracted from the current contractors, who are getting nowhere. In fact, their projects got so tangled up in their own compartments that 'the Senators' decided to turn to Bob's new company, BAASS (Bigelow Aerospace Advanced Space Systems) to do the job."

The government's project monitor is Dr. James T. Lacatski. The objective is to understand the physics and engineering of potential breakthrough technologies as they apply to "the foreign threat" from now through the year 2050. Primary focus is on applications that create discontinuities in currently-evolving technology trends.

Dr. Lacatski is an experienced nuclear physics major from the University of Tennessee, Knoxville. He's mentioned as a Visitor at Oak Ridge in 1982 and later as belonging to the System Planning Corporation in Arlington. He is cited in several articles about magnetic fusion reactors.

Austin. Sunday 24 August 2008.

Before meeting with Hal this morning, I went over yesterday's dinner conversation. "One corollary to the funding of the project is that there will be no premature disclosure to the public," he'd told me. "It would precipitate uncontrollable events that the Senators who support it don't want. On the other hand, an international approach for data gathering is expected. Bob has already spoken to Colonel de Brouwer and by coincidence (?) a classic triangle has been seen, tilted full face vertically, above his Montana ranch."

This puzzles me because data gathering is one thing, but talking about the project to people in other countries without proper guidelines seems the best way to expose its nature prematurely, given the propensity of ufologists to brag about the smallest bit of data, good or bad, with no checking. The Senators in question include Harry

Reid, majority leader in the Senate, and 84-year-old Ted Stevens of Alaska, currently indicted for corruption, who faces a difficult race in three months. There must be others I don't know.*

I told Hal about the inside story of the demise of Red Planet Capital and why it made me skeptical about any reliable funding dangled by DIA for a 5-year project, with funds only released one year at a time.

It bothers me that my friends often take their inspiration from sources like Jacobs or Hopkins, quoting incidents that were badly disfigured by bad hypnosis—or never happened.

Austin airport, later the same day.

I love those big Texas skies at sunset, with their black storm towers rising against huge pink and orange clouds. Hal and I spent the morning at the EarthTech office discussing the response to the project solicitation, where we toned down the "Alien" references. In that respect, Hal showed me a recent briefing paper that described the UFO problem wholly in terms of abductions. The author seemed convinced that telepathic robots built by Aliens were in the process of creating a hybrid race on Earth. I have misgivings about potential leaks. From what I've heard, I'm skeptical that the secrecy of the project can be maintained for more than a few months.‡

When Dr. Jim Lacatski went to the Utah ranch, he saw an apparition there, shaped like a "pale yellow pretzel." The ranch continues to be plagued with hauntings and poltergeists, so much so that one tough security man couldn't take it and resigned. A woman, who had just brought groceries from town, reportedly put the contents in the fridge and came back to the kitchen a few minutes later to find everything scattered around.

"So, what kind of extraterrestrial spacecraft does that?" I asked Hal jokingly. He acknowledged this took us beyond the equations of ordinary physics…and even extreme information theory.

---

* Mr. Stevens' corruption conviction was subsequently overturned.
‡ Actually, secrecy was properly maintained for nine years, until *The New York Times* broke the story in December 2017. But see my entry about Starstream on 11 March 2009.

A NASA manager named Al Holt has been approached to lead the BAASS project, but what if the project gets cut after one year, as was the case with our Red Planet Capital? Then the name of Ron Pandolfi came into the conversation. He's reportedly become an arch-enemy of any UFO-related research within the government, going as far as attacking people and their hard-won clearances.

My main point with Hal was that we'd never questioned our assumptions at NIDS, where everyone started out confidently looking for extraterrestrial craft, but we got every possible phenomenon, *except* evidence of craft, although Colm saw a fast-moving "unknown" in 1996. Now we have not one but two sets of unquestioned assumptions: that the craft do exist, and that the government keeps hidden hardware and bodies in contractors' labs.

One respected member of our team believes that there exists a group of Heads of State who have reliable knowledge of Aliens, based on his own Intelligence. If the project goes forward, he may try to activate these contacts. This led us to talk about Relativity. "One side of Einstein's equation describes the structure of time-space, the other side describes what you need to do to affect it," Hal said. "The challenge is that we're not able to master that second side to a large enough energy level to do anything."

It seems Bob never wanted to fully instrument the ranch; that might scare away the phenomena. EarthTech produced detectors to put in abductees' homes, but the abductees themselves were reluctant to use them, perhaps wisely, so no data was ever analyzed.

Las Vegas. Monday 25 August 2008. The Luxor.

At Bigelow headquarters on South Eastern, I was able to meet with Bob, who took me to lunch at the Country Club. On the way, I enquired about the condition of his wife, Diane, who still suffers some vision issues. I hand-delivered to Bob two documents from Hal (including the revised response to the solicitation) as well as signed NDAs from all of us, including Al Holt (40).

We spent much time discussing the paranormal events at the ranch, not only the woman's experience with the groceries, but another instance when she cleaned the top of the refrigerator and found a teleported coin there, which seemed to trigger another series of *apports*. Jim Lacatski reported a strange object that resembled the painting on the cover of a rock record *Tubular Bells* by Mike Oldfield. Jim was the only one to see it, as he had a clear view into the ranch manager's kitchen. One of the guards also reported a figure at the bedroom doorstep of the double-wide trailer.

Equally interesting, two keys that Diane had put into the glove compartment of her car were found impossibly linked together, which reminded me of extra dimensions again. Then, a typical "Belgian triangle" craft flew slowly next to Bob's Montana ranch, pointing down, with a bump on top like a cockpit and small orange lights emerging from it, shortly after he spoke to Colonel De Brouwer about those same Belgian triangle reports, possibly due to a 30-year-old US monitoring device, still confidential, like the devices the CIA unveiled for Doug Trumbull.

I mentioned to Bob that in serious spiritual traditions, *paranormal events are considered mere distractions on the road to enlightenment*...I gave him a copy of the new edition of *Messengers of Deception* and he told me about his plans for his aerospace company. He's decided to become involved in launchers and even capsules to be placed on top of the Ares V rocket (with Lockheed?) for the trip up to his space station, so things will get very exciting with the construction of a new, taller facility for assembly in Vegas.

Bob wants me involved with international affairs and the compilation of global databases, and liaison with foreign groups and governments, but I will proceed cautiously. Bob's main concern is to show a "product" at the end of Year-One. He will recruit about 30 people and move them to Vegas with their families.

"What happens if the funding stops?" I asked. "There are people in the 'community' who absolutely do not want to see such a project succeed. Not to mention those who presumably own 'hardware,' and have no plans to share it." By now, we know who they are.

Hummingbird. Wednesday 27 August 2008.

The weather is unusually hot in San Francisco, although nothing like the 108 degrees of Las Vegas.

Now Janine, who feels fine, is off at a birthday party with our Palo Alto friends. The Democratic National Convention goes on in Denver, with the historic event of the nomination of Barack Obama. Perhaps this beautiful country will finally get back on track, but it will take years to undo the recent damage inflicted upon the world.

I feel physically exhausted and mentally drained: too many plans, too many trips across time zones, too many moving parts, too many uncertainties, and those puzzling messages from Kit in Beijing talking about hidden hardware while promoting the dubious SERPO* project, supposedly a top-secret human exchange program with the Aliens, as if this crude hoax were a serious endeavor.

Actually, Kit may have his own reasons to maintain a keen interest in that expanding, silly SERPO charade. He is certain (1) that the tall tale comes from "current Executive Branch individuals," one of whom told him he was pushing the hoax *officially*, (2) that some meetings attended by himself and Hal over the last three years were secretly monitored, (3) that even a website *for which he has responsibility* was used to disseminate the poison of SERPO memes, and (4) that medical data on spinal cord injury and repair, a classified project about which he was briefed, are included in the material, *in violation of secrecy rules*. All that is like Chinese to me, unnecessarily obscure.

My friends at the stealthy physics startup have invited me to lunch at Boardwalk to pursue our discussions. I find myself wondering about the convergence of all these projects. Poher and Hal claiming they can duplicate UFO physics within General Relativity, this man and his brother scoffing at Einstein, and all of them trying to convince me that no extra dimensions are needed to explain UFOs.

In the midst of all this, I also find myself puzzled by the Nevada project. With its high risk of exposure and the fact that the major leaders (Bob and Hal, and now Al Holt) seem wedded to an answer I find to be dangerously incomplete, what are the chances that any real

---

* Rick Doty, a consultant to a ten-year project to monitor the Utah ranch, has been mentioned among possible conduits for the "SERPO" story. Earlier, he's also reported in the literature in connection with the fake data given Paul Bennewitz in Albuquerque about supposed signals from Aliens. Other researchers like Linda Howe have stated he provided documents about MJ-12 and hypnotic regressions.

secrets will be turned over? I've read Al Holt's papers on field-dependent propulsion (10), which didn't help much. I will go along, however, because I can in fact help a lot, and rapidly, with the databases, and I respect Bob's instincts as an exceptional leader.

Hummingbird. Sunday 7 September 2008.

Last night we walked down Van Ness Avenue to see Woody Allen's *Vicky Cristina Barcelona*, finally an intelligent movie about the complexities of carnal love. Today, we're off to Santa Rosa where I will work with Dr. Peter Banks, refining our investor presentations.

I have proposed a three-level plan to Bob for the creation of a very large data warehouse with an AI component; I call it *Capella*, like my earlier, private version of such a program.

Mabillon. Sunday 14 September 2008.

A jazz band plays on Rue Saint-André des Arts where Jim Morrison died. A tiny child, fascinated by the instruments, wanders next to the bass player and stares. His mother smiles, tourists take pictures. Maxim's eleventh birthday, celebrated in sunshine and chaotic horseplay, was a brilliant affair on Île Saint-Louis, with ten laughing kids, streamers, cakes, magic tricks, and much fanfare with the tearing of wrapping paper and the discovery of new gifts. I had a brief moment to speak with my son of his new job and his plans.

Paris was bright and joyfully busy today. The cafés are as full as ever. Discos and clubs overflow on sidewalks well past 3 am. I got caught in the mood of pleasure, mixed with anxiety for the current crisis; even Lehman Brothers is in jeopardy.

Mabillon. Monday 15 September 2008.

Bob Bigelow caught me just before I left. He'd already read the thinkpiece about the international database effort I proposed and liked it. He plans to hire a firm that can speed up our clearances.

When I called Admiral Pinon to ask about any results from a letter he wrote to the French President, he told me in a very kind and warm tone that he would be happy to discuss it with me when he returns to Paris. He expected that Sarkozy's entourage summarized his letter in a note, but he had no hope of direct contact. The minister of research has acknowledged his letter, however.

It's been a full year since Janine felt the headaches that led to her operation. Thankfully, she is free of visible disease, her blood test has practically returned to normal.

Mabillon. Tuesday 16 September 2008.

The global financial system has suddenly plunged deeper into chaos. Fear is palpable from Wall Street to Sand Hill Road. The usual patches and reassuring speeches won't work this time. Too many mistakes have been allowed by mindless politicians, greedy bankers, and the statisticians hired to erect flimsy scaffoldings of derivative devices that never deserved the technical term of art of "securities."

The unbelievable did happen: Lehman declared bankruptcy today, and will not be rescued. Merrill Lynch is a mere ghost, about to collapse into Bank of America. Major insurance companies are in trouble, while markets lose their footing all across the world.

The new Bigelow project, as I feared, may already be in some jeopardy. In the course of an interview with George Knapp, a long-time ufologist with a wide network made it clear that, at that level, access to secret data is the only thing worth searching for, and gossiping about. Can the real work go on quietly?

Reacting to all this from Beijing, Kit has expressed a surprisingly blunt opinion: "I view it as absolutely impossible that we will not be linked with a great nefarious and terrible set of web emendations. I am sure the blogs will pillory us... by name. Count on it." (11)

Another researcher alerts us to problems within the community: "Ron Pandolfi is certain to launch an investigation to seek the source of funds when he learns about the project," he warns us. "He'll claim that you guys have been finally successful at getting his Sister Organization to accept a fraud...So I have been arguing with the sponsor... He says, 'I know, I know...' and Bob says, 'We can manage this.'" I hope he's right, because the project is clean.

To which Kit comments: "Do I think the risk is worth the reward?

Yes. Do I think we will be professionally and personally attacked and besmirched? Yes. Do I think our security clearances can be jeopardized? Absolutely. Already have been. Will the bad things last? Probably not. But pain, in the meantime."

Mabillon. Thursday 18 September 2008.

The markets continue their spectacular plunge, as century-old economic behemoths either collapse or get taken over in heroic examples of government intervention.

The French are losing trust in their own system as they finally realize they will not be immune to the contagion, but they don't understand the underlying mechanism: nobody talks about the huge impact of hedge funds.

Mabillon. Sunday 21 September 2008.

Price increases in Paris are shocking, even compared to July. It is as if shop owners returning from vacation had suddenly decided to raise all prices by a hefty 15%. The sun is shining, and the pundits don't care if lower-income families and ordinary workers are squeezed by the system. They say "the markets are always right." Yet people begin to grasp the extent to which government and the banks had been spreading fairy dust all along.

This chaotic life of the traveler, with short overwhelming periods of afternoon slumber followed by wide-awake phases of introspection before dawn, threatens to upset whatever clarity of mind I can achieve. Over lunch *Chez Francis* I spent three hours with Pierre-Marc Johnson, former Premier of Québec. I face a tough time with my French investors, I told him: current results are poor, in line with market conditions. It's hard for startups to emerge. But the nights of Paris are soft with only a hint of autumn chill, sweet dreams after all.

Mabillon. Wednesday 24 September 2008.

Lunch today near the Sorbonne with Marie-Charlotte Delmas, wearing a purple top, a black skirt, and a coquettish hat. She is an expert on fairy faith, the Devil's Hunt, and Elfland. She told me her files included cases of fairies being abducted...by humans. (The fairies can be detected in crowds because they wear red clogs!)

She even knows of a case when chariots and horses were mysteriously stopped in motion, as modern cars are, and of medieval flying objects. Her friend and mentor, Claude Seignolle, has deeded his library to her. I treated myself to pancakes at a simple *crèperie* near the Beaubourg museum. Aflame in the light of projectors, it looked more than ever like a spaceship mistakenly landed in Paris.

Dominique has lent me *Le Nazisme Revisité* by Stéphane François, which argues convincingly that "nazi neopaganism must be sought among small neo-nazi groups that appeared after the Second World War," and that Bergier and Pauwels exaggerated the occult background behind Hitler in *The Morning of the Magicians*.

London. Friday 26 September 2008.

Across the street from the offices of Fleming Family & Partners, there's a funny restaurant called the Texas Embassy where I had some good coffee and a piece of pecan pie.

The financial crisis deepens again. After Bear Stearns and Lehman, Washington Mutual has collapsed, the largest bank failure in history, again the victim of absurd loan practices. This is no time to try raising money. Sarkozy keeps gesticulating while Bush and Paulsen go on posturing on television. They all look like a group of powerless shamans dancing in circles and invoking unseen powers, trying to convince themselves they can stave off disaster on a global scale. I wonder what I will find back in California, as McCain and Obama debate the sordid issues of war and the squeezing of money.

All during this trip I have enjoyed good weather. Today it culminates in one of those perfect, sunny afternoons when it seems you could drink the air itself as a warm, exciting nectar.

Aboard the Air France plane. Sunday 28 September 2008.

The cab driver who took me to the airport was a former butcher who recalled the area of Les Halles in the 1960s and their thrilling ambiance. Like me, he misses it, although the wholesale markets obviously needed to be moved, "but why couldn't they keep the retail shops, instead of eviscerating the city? Les Halles were not just its belly, but its soul!"

He lives in the Marais now, but even that area is getting gentrified, losing its character. He remembers the lively days and nights of erotic Rue Saint-Denis, where the Corsican mafia maintained tight order, and the cafés, bars, and all-night restaurants where he'd get a glimpse of Brassens, Jean Gabin, or Jacques Brel. One night, Brigitte Bardot drove up in a convertible with a friend and her dogs, so he sent over some bones from the shop.

"Come here, little butcher, I'll give you a kiss!" Brigitte shouted out to him.

He's a reader of Céline. He quoted entire passages by heart to me, about his hatred of war.

The papers are full of worsening news. Will Fortis fall in Europe, after the failure of Washington Mutual in the US? A few years ago, the stock of WaMu was beaten down by investors because the good managers resisted the pressure to invest in subprime mortgages, so even they are now forced to join the stupid herd, in spite of that good decision in the past.

Back in D.C., Congress is supposed to be at work day and night to avoid a collapse on Wall Street when the markets re-open tomorrow morning. Never have the pronouncements of experts and finance ministers sounded so vacuous.

In Paris, Sarkozy goes on with his speeches, condemning the greedy behavior in which his own closest supporters have indulged, and the feeding frenzy of the sharks. As for Bush and his finance gurus, on TV at all hours, they simply look exhausted and scared.

18

Hummingbird. Monday 29 September 2008.

Back in Silicon Valley, the only topic is the gloom of failed expectations. American finance is in crisis. The numbers flash, pitilessly on the tiny display of every mobile telephone: "Dow down 777 points," then: "Nasdaq crashing through the floor!" The television screens show White House briefers in disarray. Bush stammers about his vague "strategy to move forward." Obama and McCain are equally befuddled by the magnitude of the debacle. The enormous rescue package proposed by the Treasury (700 billion for the banking system) was just voted down by Congress.

On Wall Street, traders quote their old adage, "don't try to catch a falling knife!" Nobody is buying stocks. Or houses, for that matter.

Hummingbird. Tuesday 30 September 2008.

The DIA project was officially awarded to Bigelow last week. Bob doesn't see the need for a get-together to review what we learned from NIDS or to plan the new work. Instead, we now charge ahead with what he thinks the sponsor wants, namely technical stuff, "lift and propulsion" and the like. For the moment, I will try to forget the fact that UFOs have no lift and propulsion in any sense understood by our physics. I don't want to confuse anybody. I do hope to find out from George Hathaway what the prospects are for a more consistent plan when I meet him in Toronto on Monday.

Hummingbird. Thursday 2 October 2008.

Bob Bigelow called me twice today, first to tell me the project had been officially kicked off, and later to ask for help with the reports.

"The sponsor hasn't delivered anything of substance yet," he said with some bitterness. "We expected him to open certain doors, with other government parties…provide internal records…all that remains to be seen.* There's no doubt about the project, however. The goal is to ramp this up. There are more dollars coming, but we need to refine the strategy. I've been told, 'damn the torpedoes, full speed ahead!' Several times. I'm surprised by their eagerness to proceed. They've gone from *need to know* to *need to share*. But we're not yet on solid ground. This is the first month of the first year. It'll be hard to stop us; we've had lots of conversations about future years."

Having said that, all isn't clear about the hurdles we'll have to pass: "We'll need a *WOW! Factor*, something that would raise eyebrows in important places. And we need it three months before the fiscal year is up, which means May or June of '09. They'll want to know, what did we discover? Jim [the sponsor, Dr. James Lacatski] has told me he would fund us in two-year increments. It was supposed to be five years, but the lawyers came back with only two. We have to begin the hard research right away."

In terms of global data design and management, I noted that this urgency meant full-speed ahead with an initial structure that wouldn't demand years of training, as such projects do, yet would accommodate the higher levels I've designed.

We went back to the twelve areas of interest the sponsor has identified, two of which involve human experiences, and anything having to do with physiology, the financial system, religious beliefs, the wild factors. Is something wrong somewhere, which we haven't taken into account? What is of concern for world leaders? But Bob soberly conceded there was another aspect, not for discussion now, but that I should "park somewhere": What is it we are confirming? Witnesses, radar, photos, gun cameras? "All that can be dealt with," he remarked. But do we know what it means? Our reports may confirm that UFOs are solid objects.

"If so, how do we manage the confirmation? The subject has been

---

* The true reason for the government's failure to supply needed data didn't become obvious until many years later. The conversion from paper to digital records at DIA and CIA was badly managed: people had been given short deadlines to decide what was to be kept or destroyed. As reported in March 2022 by one executive, "Large bins were wheeled down each corridor and people randomly discarded what they felt they didn't need. No meetings, very little planning, close to wholesale chaos."

sub rosa for 60 years. People have taken secrets to their grave in fear of social disruption. Will this change? Does the phenomenon have an agenda? Where do foreign leaders stand? How would the public masses of the world react?"

I thought again of the danger of creating a market for every kind of charlatan and fanatic if we went too fast in that direction. Bob must have been thinking of the same thing, because he went on: "The human species is on a disturbing track. Look at Iran building nuclear bombs, look at terrorism...We need a larger agenda for this planet."

If the US government has determined the reality of the phenomenon, the news could increase the paranoia of terrorism, rather than decrease it. And it would not be legal for our project to influence the public, or precipitate disclosure.

Having parked this topic "off the main ramp," as Bob put it, we moved to the practical steps. "I have to produce numerous reports," he said, "including monthly progress statements. There are two or three options you might consider taking on. Try to identify specific assignments. I'll need milestones, schedules, action plans. I know you're very busy with your venture portfolio, but you can work from California. I've got another senior analyst working from home, full-time, 40 hours a week, not in Vegas [John Schuessler, a good choice]. The data warehouse approach is the most important, exactly along the lines you've already proposed."

Bob also said he was hoping to expand the community of sponsors. When I mentioned the need for training new scientist recruits, he understood the issue but didn't immediately jump on the idea. Yet I think that will be crucial, or we'll soon have 30 people working hard on a problem they don't understand in its totality. The people interviewed now aren't even told who the ultimate sponsor is. They have to start digging into a very confusing, vast literature of cases.

Hummingbird. Sunday 5 October 2008.

After some amendments, much arm-twisting, and a lot of pork-barrel additions, Congress has voted Bush's financial rescue package, which didn't impress Wall Street or prevent a further drop in the markets, so the whole world remains on the brink. The dollar is climbing against other currencies that are even more at risk.

While packing my suitcase for a visit to our investors in Canada, I keep thinking about Bigelow's offer. The Magonia library is finally reorganized. I'll soon be able to bring back some of the documents that linger in storage, along with exiled UFO books. The row of new filing cabinets is ready, too, designed to hold my most significant case studies and whatever new facts may come from BAASS.

Toronto. Monday 6 October 2008.
Novotel Centre, the Esplanade.

George Hathaway is in his fifties. He looks like my brother, a cordial fellow with a mustache and a black leather jacket, a keen sense of humor and a quick mind. A father with two daughters in their 30s, he is an engineer, not a physicist, he insists; he just "gets the equations from Puthoff and works with them." He kindly picked me up at the airport and took me to dinner at Canoe's, a trendy place high in a skyscraper from which we could see the lights of Toronto. He has been working for his current sponsors since 1979. In 1988 they "rescued Hal from the bureaucracy" by co-funding his fledgling research institute in Austin, but I told George I thought we couldn't assume the physical answers had to fit general relativity. Some interesting startups in my backyard and elsewhere were testing radically different formulations of mass and inertia. Hal is quite aware of this.

The main topic of the evening was the BAASS project and we were immediately on the same level, sharing plans but also concerns. Why wasn't there an organizing meeting that could have drawn the lessons from the shortcomings of NIDS? Why the contradictions between the plan to contact other nations to share data and the expectation of privileged information from Washington? Why the speculation about potential disclosure when a legal decision exists, precluding us from such disclosure?

George, who isn't a US citizen, isn't fully briefed but he knows that Bob Bigelow wanted a European sponsor to get involved, hence their trip with Hal and Kit, although that eminent contact isn't officially supposed to know the sponsor (as if he couldn't find out with two phone calls). That channel can open doors around the world, so

George encouraged me to go and discuss the subject in Europe. He also stated that my contribution with databases was a key factor in the project, as well as the "human interaction" topic, and asked what it would take for me to get fully involved?

I had to say that, in the present state of my fund and my partners, I couldn't commit to spending much time in Las Vegas. The truth is that I still don't understand enough about the project, and I must devote my essential attention to the care of my wife.

I was surprised to hear George talk about his interest in Rick Doty's material. Why take it at face value, when it is linked to a possible disinformation plot? Do we think we're so smart we'll see through the network of lies, professionally designed at such level? These reports mention selected people supposedly allowed to visit one Alien who survived the Roswell crash: The guard would instruct them before going in that they would hear things so horrible that they would never share them with anyone.

"More horrible than human history?" I had to ask. *"More horrible than Verdun? Or Vietnam? Come on! How silly can this get?"*

This reminded me of the endless—and to me, very childish—charades at Norton Air Force Base with General Scott and General Miller, and the teasing and dangling of so-called "evidence" that always evaporated, except when Linda Howe saw some MJ-12 documents obtained by Richard Doty, which researchers have argued *were official fakes.* And this is the world into which we're asked to enter in order to do scientific research?

George asked how I felt about disclosure. He observed that my build-up of contacts with aerospace CEOs could become handy if and when the project needed to reach out to industry. So I asked him why he thought the subject had suddenly gone to a *need to share* basis, after so many years of denial?

He thought someone must have died, someone high in the US Intelligence community, who had been keeping a lid on the secret military files.

Did somebody decide to play God? What if the phenomenon itself suddenly morphs into a new phase?

Back at the Esplanade, I catch up with the tough news: financial bloodbath around the world, the CAC40 down 9% in one day, the Dow Jones falling below 10,000 (then 9,000…), and Europe plainly unable to take joint action. The euro is still dropping.

Toronto. Tuesday 7 October 2008.

Markets worldwide continue to plunge even as central banks talk about measures to reverse the disastrous destruction of values reflected in bank failures, company restructurings, and the disintegration of the European financial system.

Today in Toronto, Peter Banks and I visited Brookfield, a huge real estate and financial empire. They advised us to contact a large fund called Mubadala and a public service pension plan that covers all Canadians, including the military. We also met with an ex-Microsoft senior executive, potentially interested in joining us.

Montréal. Wednesday 8 October 2008. Hotel de la Montagne.

Canadians will only discover economic reality after their election next week. The crisis is not yet visible in the streets: the sun is still warm, people are active, and Montréal is as pleasant as it was on my last visit, but the good restaurant on Rue Sainte Catherine where I wanted to take Peter Banks for dinner has gone out of business, an early victim of the spiraling economy.

Secretary Paulsen is on television, looking distraught. The Treasury will invest in banks to save them from a liquidity crisis; it will shore up Fannie and Freddie and buy mortgage-backed securities, all in efforts to stabilize plunging house values.

Air Canada flight. Thursday 9 October 2008.

Another pleasant, cordial, but fruitless trip. Investment groups in Québec, like BDC and FTQ (12), are so tied to political decisions, always vague and fleeting, that they are seldom able to put real innovation funding into place. Many Canadian entrepreneurs end up either taking ordinary jobs in Montréal, or leaving the country.

The global crisis cannot even clarify inconsistent policies.

Yesterday, the central banks of major countries took the unprecedented step of cutting interest rates in an effort to halt the slip of the markets. In the current stormy climate, that did little to reassure investors, who ignored the move and dumped stocks everywhere.

Many company valuations have been cut in half and continue to fall while the strident calls of experts sound increasingly irrelevant. The latest issue of *The Economist*, only a few days old, feels so obsolete that it reads as if it had been written on another planet.

My own thoughts return to BAASS. Given the agency's eagerness to launch it without reassessing the phenomenon as a whole, I don't feel the time is right to invoke new resources (second-level databases, or hard physical evidence cases). My first instinct is to remain disciplined and stand back until I gain some clarity.

Becoming an informal ambassador for a project with no acknowledged backer, no new facts, and the sole strategy of "going out on a limb" would take us nowhere.

I am suspicious of the physical models so hastily embraced, the same models we've heard of for years, based on questionable data from flawed abduction research, crash tales reshuffled by dramatization artists, or tabloid stories, TV garbage.

All that should be on the table.

Hummingbird. Sunday 12 October 2008.

Bob called me back at 8 am today. He was at his Montana ranch and wanted to continue yesterday's discussion. I told him I was bringing my files out of storage and would soon be ready to work on the project. Most of the conversation was about foreign contacts. "I've been given permission to admit to selected officials of other countries that we are sponsored by the federal government," he said. "You and I can work together. We just need to define the parameters, find what's comfortable for you."

I pointed out that any foreign official I approach with such a message would need to know more: "As soon as I leave their office, they'll be calling their closest contact at the US Embassy across town, asking for legitimate confirmation. The guy will fall off his chair and call Washington, and there goes all the confidentiality."

Bob was unimpressed. "Not necessarily," he replied, "because we'll ask everybody in the room to sign an NDA, and any violation would preclude going to the next level. Depending upon the relationship, a meeting could be arranged with our sponsor, at a non-government facility, once we have evolved to a certain level of concern. It's a step-by-step process. In terms of our own work, I see three levels: (1) study the advanced behavior of anomalous phenomena, (2) interact with these phenomena, and (3) reach global confirmation. That's where other countries could come in. Get them to admit the reality of the data, short of big press conferences of course. We need to increase the number of people who are interested. It's like global warming: See how long it took for the world to recognize it!"

When he puts it in those terms, the program does make sense. He continued: "We'll be in a position to give grants to major schools, Ivy League universities, to do studies in psychology and sociology to investigate why people report these things: $75,000 or $100,000 or more, in competition with each other, five universities on the same topic. I don't have a lot of time to work on this, given the financial crisis, and I have to pay attention to my own business, but the building is almost ready with the security upgrade, and furniture is moving in. I've got five people working part-time, and the guards, and I'm giving myself six to nine months to bring 32 people on board."

He went on: "You know, Jacques, we started on October 1st, we have four areas of research: psychosociology, physics, politics, and biology, and I need a 'WOW! Factor' within eight months, that's all there is to it. We need to affect the funding in a positive way, get the sponsor's attention. The WOW! could be progress on the political level with countries joining us, with some discreet meetings and a global agenda. Does the data show the phenomenon to be prolific? Is there activity of which we were not aware in the States? Also, I think there is actual Alien tissue somewhere; something has been done secretly [Kit hints that he was briefed about such a program]. The best scenario would be to walk their scientists somewhere, show them something tangible, some hardware or an Alien body. Just having a good meeting isn't sufficient; they'll need something to touch, a profound quantity of data."

When I hung up, there were still many questions in my mind. What does the sponsor expect? Can we rely on the guys in D.C.? How secure will the funding be under the next administration? Any professional-grade database effort is a 5-year project, not counting the AI phase I want to implement. If the project gets compromised within eight months, what will happen to the two-dozen people Bob is recruiting to work on my design? How much trust can we put in Kit's statements that there is Alien DNA somewhere? How seriously would authorities in friendly countries look at a project that rests on such a flimsy record?

Hummingbird. Monday 13 October 2008.

Columbus Day. Janine and I had a pleasant dinner on Friday night with scientist Burton Lee, Alain Dupas, and Aurélie Boudier (at Absinthe). Alain and Aurélie are in California on a search for deals on behalf of Astrium. They've already spoken to virtual reality experts in San Diego and Silicon Valley. Aurélie, whose appearance as a slim girl with glasses betrays her record as a smart project manager and private pilot, remembered our visit to her parents' home when she was a little girl. Her father recently organized a new committee called "Sigma Two" for the study of UFOs within a French aeronautical association. I have to wonder if they haven't picked up some rumor about the DIA project, or plans by the US Navy, because their statements (in line with the failed *Cometa* and Admiral Pinon's recent letter to Sarkozy) use very similar arguments.

Yesterday was a splendid time. We went rowing on Stow Lake, ate lunch at the island where a dozen turtles were sunning themselves among the branches of a big fallen tree, and came back to watch the television news of the G7 finance ministers stumbling over their inconsistent policies. In California, a democratic victory is a foregone conclusion.

Hummingbird. Wednesday 22 October 2008.

Another gorgeous day, celebrated over lunch with Catherine and her friends Christelle and Rebecca at the Cliff House. On the way, Diane told me about the Curse of Sutro Baths, a giant blaze, never elucidated, that happened in the Sixties before we came to California.

I've consulted Hal and Kit, asking how they thought I could best help the new project, and I have written to their European co-sponsors, suggesting a meeting in November. If I work with Bob as a special advisor, I will need someone to open doors in Europe. Yet the project remains full of contradictions. Kit states again that since 2000 he has seen new evidence in the form of DNA in the course of briefings and his private forensic work, but is it available?

Now Hal keeps stressing we should deal with "real physics data," in strong agreement with my pleas to upgrade our standards, but we have seen nothing of the kind yet. Bob tells me he will fund university studies about the psychology of witnesses, which will take years and certainly has nothing to do with physics.

The latest paper I have seen from Hal took inspiration from French "theorist" Eric Julien, who uses an assumed name, recycles tabloid data about abductions, and is on uncertain terms with authorities: Are we grasping at straws?

Hal states: "The goal is to stay out of controversy, not to do anything to influence public opinion, and to just focus on technical issues." This contradicts Bob's phone conversation with me when he listed politics and psycho-sociology as two of the four major areas of research, leading to a critical mass of countries. Who is right?

More concretely, Hal proposes a list of issues where the project could use my contribution:

"(1) Your Capella Project write-up to setup a useful, comprehensive database process is critical. In the Recommended Plan of Action white papers we are preparing, I've made that a critical startup issue; (2) of course, at some point, whatever dialogue you open in Europe is very important, but I imagine that will be further down the line; and (3) whatever files of your investigations you place into the database (that you design) about technical observables will be useful for tech types to attempt to cross-correlate with physics, anomalous or not (as in your novel *FastWalker*)."

He adds that briefing computer professionals about handling the labeling matrix is a prime requirement. I agree.

Hummingbird. Monday 27 October 2008.

Our European co-sponsors have answered me promptly, suggesting that we visit next one month. My first task, however, is to reposition our NASA venture fund in anticipation of presentations to corporate investors. Many startups still come to my attention, and I write up their technology (but only when they express interest) in the form of notes to NASA.

My enthusiasm is eroded by the somber atmosphere, however. The world cannot go on much longer this way, with economic values dropping between 3% and 10% every day in stock markets from Tokyo to Hong Kong and New York. My French business colleagues are disheartened.

Hummingbird. Wednesday 29 October 2008.

Kit called tonight from Washington after dinner with Bob and a meeting with Jim Lacatski. I had asked him how I could be of greatest use to BAASS, so he began with obvious areas: system software (a new collaboration program will be used to support private interaction) and the very large data warehouse I've discussed with Bob.

I had also expressed my concerns about the "catch and release" aspects of government funding, which could leave the staff suddenly shipwrecked if the agency stopped the money flow. Kit assured me the total projected budget might reach $240 million, with only the first $20 million firmly in the bank. Furthermore, staff members who do not obtain clearances may be re-employed in an unclassified facility, as Bob already does for his aerospace company.

Kit also reassured me there was no contradiction in Bob's "Wow Factor" expectations. The work already done (in ten white papers) assures continuation of funding: "Any objections within the government will be controlled, under a mandate from eight Congressmen who want to see the project move forward."

As for my concerns about contacting officials in other countries, Kit agrees that I should only do it if I carry official US credentials, under a model of cooperation between the project as an NGO, the US, and other nations. If someone balks at cooperation, or tries to run interference, "that's none of your business," Kit said, "That would be dealt with from Washington, backstopped, and fully open." Having covered all this with gusto, Kit did concede that he shared my concern about major contradictions: "I don't know all the answers I thought I did, about several fundamental areas."

Hummingbird. Thursday 30 October 2008.

Under the first rains of the season, I've had lunch in San Francisco with Colm Kelleher (at Le Charm). I hadn't seen him since his return to the Bay Area four years ago. He told me he was quitting Prosetta to join BAASS on November 10th. Initially, his family will remain in the East Bay, where his kids are in school, and he will commute every Monday to Vegas.

Colm has some of the same questions as I do about BAASS, wondering if the project was not precipitated by confidential breakthroughs in some other country. We both wondered about the advisability of involving the French or anyone else, until the politics were clarified. And Colm still believes that some of the mutilations, notably those on the Utah ranch, are paranormal in nature.

In the evening I got a call from Douglass Price-Williams, now retired and "a recluse," he says, because his wife is ill, a situation with which I can identify. His self-published book, *Life Dreams*, recounts our joint research (13). We hadn't spoken in eight years.

I have always thought that one of NIDS' missed opportunities was the failure to fully involve Douglass in a deep study of the ranch's anthropological and shamanic environment. There was miscommunication here. Another scholar of clinical psychology and anthropology, David Hufford, reflecting on our meeting at Esalen, remarks: "I believe the kind of comparative work you performed in *Magonia* is crucial to understanding any and all questions that lie (along with their answers) outside the modern paradigm. That is also the approach that I took in *The Terror That Comes in the Night*, in part thanks to the inspiration of your work. Yet, as crucial as the comparative method is, it is dismissed and reviled by both modern and postmodern scholars as 'essentialist.' So even those who pose as radical critics of contemporary culture adopt a stance that makes it impossible to take seriously, let alone learn from, the observations of other cultures and times: interesting implicit defenses!"

Now the rains have come in earnest. The sky is gray and heavy. Janine often feels tired and, like me, concerned about the future. How will our children fare in such a world of shrinking horizons? Will a historic victory by the Democrats next week, under the leadership of the brilliant Barack Obama, really open a new phase? America certainly needs it, and so does the world, after the presidency of George W. Bush and its cohort of unfocused ideologues.

Hummingbird. Sunday 2 November 2008.

Hal thinks it is a very good idea for me to visit our European contacts.

"They know what we do," he tells me, "Bob, Kit, and I went there to brief them, although we didn't tell them which agency was involved. If I'm ever polygraphed on this, I want to be able to say I didn't leak the name of the agency. But you don't need to hold back anything else. There have been private meetings with some Heads of State about this, although some are reluctant to get the subject mixed up with ongoing financial activities."

We talked about the Bigelow legal contracts. We agreed they included excessive intellectual property ownership requirements that neither Hal nor I could live under. They are designed not only to give Bigelow's company control of any future discoveries, but even ownership of everything we would bring into the project from our own past research.

As far as the secrecy goes about the sponsor, this also puzzles me as the request for proposals was on the government website, available to any good search engine. It even flaunted the agency's logo, with Dr. Lacatski's name. There's nothing really secret at that level; any smart journalist could figure it out. And did.

Janine and I saw Luisah Teish last night in her role as the leader of a *Festival of the Bones* that included sensational Congolese dances, four altars to the Ancestors, and very touching songs and stories. A recurring theme was to protect Obama from the extremists: some skinheads have already been arrested, intent on killing him.

Hummingbird. Wednesday 5 November 2008.

Last night we saw the San Francisco Opera's version of *Boris Godounov*, a far better production than the one we saw at Le Châtelet three years ago. The conductor was Vassily Sinaisky, and Samuel Ramey sang the title role, with Vitalij Kowaljow as Pimen, the monk-chronicler, with whom I privately identify.

Hummingbird. Saturday 8 November 2008.

We woke up early as the fog horn resounded in the misty dawn. Janine passed another test at UCSF yesterday, and the images were clean, so the next step for us is to plan our next European trip. We're amused by the French news, showing a wave of enthusiasm for Barack Obama among the same racist folks who've been complaining so bitterly about dark-skinned immigrants. Socialist luminaries like Fabius even claim Obama for their own camp, as if the new American president had learned the art of politics at the knee of French pundits who wouldn't last five minutes in the mean streets of Chicago's Southside.

What we expect to find in Europe is hardly conducive to starting a new venture fund. In one year, shares of Renault have dropped 80% (a loss of 26 billion euros!) and major firms like Veolia, Alcatel, Peugeot, Pinault-Printemps-Redoute, and Arcelor-Mittal have lost two thirds of their value. Saint-Gobain, Michelin, Air France, Axa, and Société Générale, as well as EDF, have lost half, an incredible debacle that isn't going to be rectified soon in the current climate. Yet those are the shares typically owned by "prudent men," pension funds, and many brave French families who counted on stock market growth for retirement.

On Thursday I had lunch with the gravity team in stealth mode. Their initial paper is published in a suitably obscure journal, and they now work on deriving quantum mechanics from their basic equations. They've looked at Poher's site with interest and think that their theory explains his tests better than his "Universons." The latest experiments they conducted gave confusing results, so they still don't know if they can generate a flow of alpha particles (two protons and two neutrons, as in the nucleus of helium) as their theory would predict.

Hummingbird. Tuesday 11 November 2008.

The prospect of working with BAASS has me both excited and troubled: too many intractable, unanswered questions. Not in Vegas, however, but back in Washington. In spite of Hal's fascination and Kit's enthusiasm, I remain reserved about the sponsor's assurances of support and the murky scientific agenda.

Damn the torpedoes. Charging ahead, I've submitted my design for Phase One of Capella, expecting to move it firmly into full-scale AI if funding can be secured beyond the two fundamental phases.

Now we must pack our suitcases for Europe again, wondering what we'll find amidst the human misery and financial turmoil there.

Mabillon. Sunday 16 November 2008.

Slow Sunday in gray Paris. We happily play with Max. Together, we read Heyerdahl's great adventure book *Kon-Tiki*. From Beijing, at the same time, Kit tells me he's unable to access my website to read my physics papers. Evidently, the Chinese must be unhappy at my published complaints about their censorship of the web in *Heart of the Internet*, so they censor my work.

The financial crisis has hit France with factory closings and deep losses in share prices, but you wouldn't know it when walking through Paris. I remember other bad times when restaurants and theaters were empty; to my surprise I see no such signs now. Perhaps the anticipation of Christmas, or some lingering trust in the government, keeps the crowd moving. Sarkozy's public support has gone up by several points.

We are happy here. In the last few months, we've experienced a new level of closeness, of tenderness, as the imminence of tragedy lifted. Janine has emerged from that terrible illness, and her brother's loss, like a prisoner escaping from the shadows, tasting freedom again, and pleasure.

Now Colm Kelleher calls from Las Vegas. Bob urges him to hurry in hiring people, including a database administrator to work on Capella. This is typical of a Bigelow operation. He won't wait for any recommendations for job descriptions, a full data structure, and reporting links, but I do like the sense of urgency.

Then Bob himself called, eager to arrange for my clearance, asking if I would be ready to renounce French citizenship if it sped up the process. I said NO, and in fact my passport will be important if I'm ever to serve in open liaison with European officials, as the project expects. But I am puzzled, and somewhat angry, at a project that encourages me to use my European contacts in research, but wants to punish me for having friends there!

Mabillon. Wednesday 19 November 2008.

Yves Messarovitch says the real crisis is going to hit here in three months, when large numbers of people start being laid off. So far, the government has done a good job of faking normalcy, keeping things relatively steady, but banks are plunging again, unable to estimate and mitigate risks.

London. Thursday 20 November 2008.

Endless travel, and my worries, take a physical and moral toll. In the harsh light of English hotels, mirrors send me back an unkind image of a chiseled, tired man: I look like my father when I thought of him as truly old. Yet there are many rewards for the work I do. Reviewing the ancient chronicles, I am astonished at their mysteries, but I wonder even more at life itself.

When I find myself reading these old records aboard a train speeding inside a tunnel under the English Channel, or when my webphone brings live pictures from NASA experiments in space, the joy in my mind pulls me into a happier realm, more secure.

Suresnes, near Paris. Friday 21 November 2008.

At a bistro on the main square, before a company meeting. Yesterday's trip to London left me tired. The beautiful train stank of stale tobacco. All investments are frozen in a landscape where the towers of the economy crumble like sugar cubes someone had just dipped into some hot liquid. The CAC40 dropped below 3000 points yesterday; the

Dow is at 7500 and the NASDAQ index has plunged to 1300.

We had visitors at Mabillon: our cousins from Luxembourg, with their son. Maxim came with his parents, and Annick as well for a warm, easy evening of conversation.

Zurich. Sunday 23 November 2008.

As soon as the train snaked out of Paris we saw the fields white with frost. There was snow on the ground as we got close to Strasbourg, but the rest of the trip, down through Colmar and Mulhouse, was sunny.

Zurich is cold but the pastry shop around the corner offers a place of good food and good cheer where proper Swiss gentlemen and ladies talk, work, or read the paper. We arrived early, intent on walking around the city, but the bitter wind soon sent us back to our room.

Aboard the TGV from Zurich. Monday 24 November 2008.

Our meeting with our potential co-sponsors was relaxed. They were urbane and simple. We sat by the fireplace in a vast office, while they apologized for the lingering smell of a wood fire.

My appeal for help in reaching cabinet-level people who might have access to the real files in Europe had little result, however; they found closed doors everywhere, so my initial reality-check of Bigelow's plan led to a negative conclusion. They made it clear that few people in political office would take the initiative of opening the real data until there was a clear, open signal from the United States, which has a history of carelessly exposing its friends.

Before leaving, we spoke of our venture fund's involvement in physics, the likelihood of breakthroughs in spacetime theory within ten years, and current experiments beyond those of which Europe is aware.

Mabillon. Friday 28 November 2008.

Cold air has swooped down over Paris, driving pedestrians to the cozy recesses of the Métro or into warm cafés. The homeless often die of exposure in these streets before they can be rescued. Unemployment is up sharply while the government dabbles in reforms, soon victim to messy political maneuvers or to the inertia of the bureaucracy. The deepening recession (France still in lonely denial) reduces Sarkozy's ideology to wishful thinking.

The new régime is ruthless. One friend, the CEO of SNPE, was a victim of it when Safran took over his company. He was summarily dismissed after years of good work at the helm of a business that he'd returned to profitability and growth, as Sarkozy places his minions in all key posts.

The new political culture is brutish and quietly corrupt.

Mabillon. Sunday 30 November 2008.

The sky has been gray all day. We spent last night with our son and grandson, Chrissie and Connie and Annick, celebrating Thanksgiving and Olivier's 45th birthday.

There were pies and balloons, wine and toys. The apartment could barely contain the happy confusion. Today is quieter; we watch the Shuttle Endeavor preparing to land while a Russian Progress supply ship docks to the ISS.

In the streets, Christmas displays are already up, studded with blue lights this year, in honor of the European Union.

Air France flight 084. Wednesday 3 December 2008.

Flying over Scotland, on the way back to the West Coast. I admire the snowy highlands, a steaming cup of coffee in my hand, reading *Le Canard Enchaîné*, wondering about the rapid changes in the world. I am always content in coach, as long as I have a window.

Hummingbird. Saturday 6 December 2008.

"Who needs museums?" asks Janine, pointing at the night-blue sky brushed with astonishing streaks of pink and purple. In contrast with the gray, cold gloom we left behind in Paris, San Francisco spreads its glamour before us in exquisite detail.

At a Venture Capital Association lunch yesterday, I heard Obama advisor Paul Begala speak of changes ahead. The audience was polite but on edge, aware that the economy is not likely to recover as fast as it did in previous recessions. The system is broken, and the usual models for recovery won't apply until some basic issues are fixed.

The federal investigator assigned to my clearance came to interview me at home. Very professional, he holds a PhD in psychology from Minnesota. It was a more relaxed exchange than I had expected. Also today I released *Volume Two* of this journal for general availability through online distributors like Amazon.

In a recent entry, Kit has reported: "Within the past few days I have had continuing discussions and analysis of medical data from a person (not a patient) who is totally sane from considered judgments; well educated, a superb writer, brilliant, holds a day job; is mature, appropriate sense of humor; supported by claims by parents, boss, and fiancé.*

"She has incredible stories of experiences—physical events claimed, that are not lucid dreaming. She was multiply abducted and impregnated: two partial-term vaginal births, with medical evidence of same. Clear evidence that first pregnancy was both non-parthenogenetic and not post-natural: IVF procedure with evidence to support; fascinating physical injuries and symptoms, dozens over years. Documented by physicians. She is not part of the soap opera, nor are any of the family members and friends. She was found by me, this is not a set-up... I am now more confused."

As we went rowing again today and ate our snacks at Turtle Island in the cold sun, I told Janine about Kit's observations. "What's the point?" she asked testily. "There's nothing specific. All you have are stories again, suppositions, words on a screen."

Yet such reports, coming up again, and again, point to a large unknown area we're failing to document, I said, to our great shame.

---

* When he reviewed this passage in May 2022, Dr. Green told me that he was surprised to have no clear recollection of these details. He would have been about to leave Beijing at the time, with his wife Kristin, after her stay on behalf of joint General Motors projects.

Las Vegas. Friday 12 December 2008.

The plane vibrated and undulated in the rainstorm like a noodle in a bowl of hot soup when I took off from Newark last night. I had spent the day in Manhattan with Peter Banks and the executives of L3 Communications. I left with a sense of anticipation of seeing Colm, now firmly established as the deputy administrator for BAASS.

Nevada leads the country in the percentage of foreclosures, and Las Vegas has seen a huge drop in business, tourism, and real estate values. There are idle cranes above the City Center, a massive condo and office development overlooking the Strip. The project is stalled even after a fresh injection of Middle Eastern cash.

Pending completion of the secure BAASS facility, Colm has the office next to Bob's at Park House on Eastern Avenue, so I met him there this morning, happy to resume our collaboration.

We sat in his office as he opened a white binder with my *Capella* report, which he had profusely, carefully underlined. We went over his questions and mine, trying to clarify what I perceived as the project's contradictions.

Bob then asked me what it would take to get me to lead the database effort on a full-time basis. I responded truthfully there were more qualified people than me to continue the job in Phase One, the initial data capture and conversion. He didn't take that for an answer, insisting my name and experience would guarantee the visibility of the work. The request came up again during lunch, so I suggested that I could spend a quarter of my time supervising the project, helping develop the data warehouse, but I wouldn't move to Vegas, concerned first with Janine's care and my ongoing commitments to my partners.

The conversation came back to the phenomena at the ranch. Bob maintains his interest in photographic "orbs," which I still suspect may be artifacts of the digital camera software; few people understand it at the code level. I'm willing to be proven wrong, naturally.

We discussed hybrid Aliens and Kit's conversion to the abduction scenario after years of calling it all "fugues and hallucinations."[*]

---

[*] Kit's conversion may have been "apparent" to me, but he insists he never embraced the common Alien abduction scenario.

It's very unlikely that intercourse with any Aliens, even if their DNA was close to ours, could be a viable method for producing a new race. I told Kit and Colm they would be better off reading the recent papers on hybridization by Dr. Miroslav Radman of Necker Hospital in Paris.

Intercourse with human victims will never repopulate any planet, no matter how often the Aliens are supposed to do it. So many aspects of the current belief system seem absurd to me, except as sociological indicators, or memes.

Spending the rest of the afternoon with Colm, we reflected on the old days of NIDS. He has now hired three leaders, including Doug Kurth, a sharp ex F-18 pilot from the *Nimitz*, who will start on Monday and get to work on my *Capella* project, but he expects more difficulty finding the three managers he seeks, who must have an advanced degree and 10 years of experience. Such people are unlikely to move to Nevada under current conditions.

Hummingbird. Saturday 13 December 2008.

Dick Haines sends me a sad message about the death of Jim McCampbell, which happened on the 7th of this month. Jim was a creative, knowledgeable man who dared to pursue his own intuitions. He was first to study the physiological effects of UFOs. His book remains a useful reference.

The year is about to end in an atmosphere of scandal and corruption beyond anything recently seen in the US. Coming on top of the disasters caused by the greed and arrogance of financiers, which have devastated retirement accounts and devalued most investments by 30% to 50% across the world, the arrest of the governor of Illinois for soliciting bribes and the $50 billion failure of the Bernie Madoff fund demonstrate the irresponsibility of a system out of control.

The Madoff case, a shameless pyramid scheme that hits banks, pension plans, and even Stephen Spielberg's charity foundation (along with BNP and other banks) is so gross that it forces admiration when one realizes that the pigeons were qualified, "sophisticated investors" recruited on the golf courses of the most prestigious country clubs: What could possibly go wrong?

Hummingbird. Wednesday 17 December 2008.

The Mission Skilled Nursing & Subacute Center in Santa Clara, where Larry Hatch spends his days and nights on a metal bed, is an intensive care facility for the poor, in a flat building with rows of rooms on either side of a central corridor.

When I visited him today with his brother Earl, I found the hallway busy with wheelchair patients taking their daily exercise. It would have been depressing were it not for the sunshine over the area and the big, colorful towers of the Winchester Mystery House nearby, one of my favorite landmarks.

Larry was as lucid and abrupt as I had known him a few years ago. He has suffered a stroke that left his left arm paralyzed and his legs so weak he cannot walk more than a few feet. He has fallen into depression, so he has been lying there, flat on his back, since 2006, refusing physical therapy or rehab, and has not done any new work on his excellent catalogue of UFO sightings. To cut costs down, his brother stopped his website.

I tried to cheer him up, bringing him a recent copy of *LDLN*, a French ufology magazine he loved.

He asked me about sightings in France and amazed me by recalling the details of a trip he took near Poitiers.

Hummingbird. Saturday 20 December 2008.

When I suggested to Kit that the woman he has studied (along with her mother and grandmother, who also speak of abduction experiences) might be the victim of non-Alien events, he confessed he was as confused as me. He now wants to talk about cult practices. Indeed, I can think of three cases in my files where we became familiar with people who had been subjected to intense esoteric recruiting and were left disoriented and scarred. On that subject, Kit recalled that he'd been the investigator who guided the detectives to Ira Einhorn's trunk where Holly's body was lying.

Back here, I need to move to a new office, more frugal than our big open place in Palo Alto. Our proposed Fund has no chance to find investors in the current crisis; a major California retirement fund has just announced a loss of 81 billion dollars!

Yesterday I invited Peter Sturrock to lunch and gave him the final version of *Volume Two*. He seemed a bit frail and mentioned he needed a second knee operation, perhaps the result of too much tennis, but he makes progress with his studies of solar neutrinos. His research shows that the core of the Sun is not perfectly spherical, changes shape with time, and spins more slowly than its atmosphere. Like Bigelow, Peter Sturrock remains fascinated with the orbs that show up on his digital photographs, and I can only respect his judgment.

Hummingbird. Wednesday 24 December 2008.

A very strange coincidence occurred this afternoon as Bob Bigelow and Colm Kelleher called me about the second project we've agreed I would do. They caught me at the wheel of the Highlander, as I had just parked it in Berkeley.

I was with Janine who had gone into a used bookstore to sell her brother's old vinyl records. Helping her carry the heavy boxes, one record on top of a pile caught my eye. It was Mike Oldfield's *Tubular Bells*, with the now-famous "pretzel" symbol on the cover, resembling the object that had appeared to Dr. Lacatski on his first visit to the Utah ranch.

"We're not selling this one," I told Janine, and I carried it back to the truck for safekeeping.

That's the exact moment when Bob and Colm called me on my cellphone. Hal comments on this, an obvious *intersign*: "Yes, sometimes it all looks like it is all scripted!" Now Roger Brenner tells me that *Tubular Bells* was used as the music for *The Exorcist*.

Later the same day.

It rains in San Francisco, the soft gray gentle rain I enjoy, putting a quiet blanket over sounds and sights of the city. We only have a small tree this Christmas; its tiny lights blink in the kitchen window high above the street. Few gifts: a few boxes of fruits and some chocolates brought back from Switzerland. We still have each other. That is the great miracle we need to savor.

Doug Trumbull has just sent me a DVD of his Academy of Motion Picture presentation with Tom Hanks about the special effects in *2001: Space Odyssey*. In his cover letter, he suggests that I join him in his explorations through the west in early spring aboard his Touareg 4X4 equipped with telescopes and high-tech recorders.

Next, I called Hal in Texas and we spoke at length about BAASS. I briefed him about my report on *Capella*, which he hadn't seen, and he told me about his 9-point plan for the project, which Bob had not shared with me either. This kind of compartmentalization is not helpful because Hal needs to know all about my database structure, and I need to know his comments and critiques as a prime user. He told me his first job had consisted in putting together a program plan, timeline, and list of collaborators. That had taken 45 days with Eric and George Hathaway, but he had to price it by the hour, the method favored by Bob, who only wanted to pay at the end.

Bob now recommended that the Agency should open some doors.

The section about human effects includes a mention of my research in Colares with a recommendation to go back and get the original reports. Easier said than done, I pointed out. One reason Brazil keeps those reports secret is that they don't want them to leak out to "Norteamericanos," which they rightly view as arrogant and insensitive. The fact that Kit still argues their medical "events" are bogus may not help the credibility of our efforts. The doctors were real, he insists, but the subsources were fake.

Another section talks about configurations of craft seen, and other parts address computing and physics. The next project to be done by EarthTech will assemble about 30 detail papers written by experts who may not know the full extent of the sponsor's interests. One of these papers, concerned with spatio-temporal manipulation, will be written by Hal and Eric themselves, and will use the relativistic model. "The equations we use yield every magical thing the objects do, and the resulting signatures," he insists. I may have questions about that because they've preselected their cases. The method excludes more features than it explains.

When I spoke of "the sponsor," Hal corrected me. "There are two levels of sponsors," he said, "and that agency represents the lower level. The top level is composed of politicians who hold the dollars, the agenda, and are driven by their own concerns about the big picture. They've selected this particular agency to manage the funds and the project, and to expedite dollars and clearances, but if the work was halted at that level, the program would continue. The agency channel is expendable. This is amusing because the managers don't want to hear the 'U' word, while the Senators know exactly what we do."

I told Hal where I stood with my second project and my reluctance to drive forward blindly to try and open relationships in France. Bob tells me he needs access to the CNES files "in the next few weeks," unaware (like most American ufologists) that the French data has always been freely available on the web. I have answered Colm, stressing the need to build long-term trust before charging into foreign lands, France or Brazil, with dollars and big tape recorders. I certainly don't want to damage international contacts by grabbing other people's data, even if given full access to it, without giving them information in return, or at least an indication of what we plan.

Furthermore, I don't want to get into a position where I'm asked to compile a report but cannot have access to what I've written a few months later for lack of the right clearance. Gérard De Vaucouleurs taught me this a long time ago in Austin. After he delivered his report about Mars exploration, he wasn't allowed to see it again, even to fix the misspellings! And I won't pursue the relationship with BAASS if my clearance hinges on giving up my dual citizenship with France.

One project member said he was in a similar situation and was forced to withhold his data and deeper plans. "I've been building a relationship with an aerospace company that's trying to get me in through the backdoor," he told us. "I'm pretty sure they have some hardware, but if I talk about it, someone from D.C. will try to force his way in through the front door and everybody will scatter. Those corporate guys hate the government, which they see as nothing but a source of dirty politics and business trouble. They want to keep the bureaucrats away. Same thing with some of the hardware-related Bluebook files; the guy in charge never put them into the security system, so nobody even knows they exist. He told his security officer to only allow access to names on a list he gave him. We'll have to design the rules as we go."

"By the way," I added, "when we can talk freely, I should tell you about my visit to Europe."

"Yes, we should discuss that," Hal replied. "I was there just after you. They want to push for a high-level meeting, preferably at the White House. They want you to be there to discuss long-term interaction with the phenomenon, manifesting for centuries..."

"They must have read my manuscript," I said, "or perhaps my mind..." I added with a wink in Hal's direction, encouraged to see how close his thinking was to mine.

Hummingbird. Thursday 1 January 2009.

We were alone last night, happy to share a quiet evening and the birth of the New Year. We savor those moments. Janine prepared a cream of shrimp soup, *boudin* with baked apples, and English trifle with Amaretto and Champagne. We hardly saw the City's fireworks, low on the Bay and half-eaten by the fog, but we were quite content to put the year behind us. It has been a hard period with Alain's woes and the worries of the economic collapse on top of Janine's fight against the illness. Even if our own finances remain stable, the small startups in my current Fund, which has two more years to run, and new offices* face survival issues and demand a lot of work.

Today, the city was fogged in again, so we stayed home and enjoyed our little talks with a mix of excitement and apprehension. She has gathered some dead branches to make an enticing perch on our wide deck for the birds that fly up from the streets, little ordinary birds eating the food she hangs from the balcony. She delights in seeing them, so alive and fragile, so simple.

Hummingbird. Friday 2 January 2009.

Troubled sleep, my lungs inflamed by asthma, anxiety, and the uncertainty that haunts Bob Bigelow's visionary research program.

---

* Our space was taken over by our neighbor, Peter Thiel's Palantir Technologies, which was expanding operations.

I've begun serious work on two catalogues and prepared a plan of action with Colm, but the long-term view is still in question for me.

It rains hard today; Nob Hill is drenched in gray patches. At UCSF where Janine has just taken new tests, the doctor gives us the bad news: a new lesion, small but badly placed, so they cannot operate. This means new and difficult treatment with a drug that restricts the blood vessels and depresses the whole body. She takes it all with her extraordinary courage, but I am a poor match for her.

Hummingbird. Sunday 4 January 2009.

My brother called me yesterday morning. He and his wife are doing "as well as can be expected." Gabriel is 84, quietly retired and beyond worry about the spreading economic crisis.

Janine suggested a long walk along Mission Street, with its loud music, bright colors, and good smells of Mexican cooking. We expand our excursions around the City, places to visit or simple haunts of interesting folks, like the Valhalla bookstore, well-hidden off Mission Street. Every second is to be savored now, with an acute awareness that sums up our life together.

Hummingbird. Monday 5 January 2009.

I must continue to go to work, interact with others, and push on projects. When I called him to give him my New Year wishes, Fred Adler commented on the current crisis, saying he'd never experienced anything like it. He wakes up at night not knowing what to do, can't get back to sleep. In a reflective mode, Fred recalled being six years old in Brooklyn when his father was unable to pay the mortgage and they lost their home, the brick house he loved.

He walked down the street, staring back at the house like a stunned automaton, and hit a light pole. His mother cleaned up his bleeding head. The Great Depression spread in America.

Today, an equally stunning debacle is in progress in the entire world. Most savers who owned stocks or retirement plans have lost 30 to 40% of their savings, another kind of bloodbath.

We've heard again from Bill McGarity, the security officer at Area

51 we met over dinner in Austin a couple of years ago. He says the "missing" Blue Book files about Alien hardware are stored there. Now he wonders if he should share this with higher-ups for fear they will send a bunch of goons and come up with nothing.

Hummingbird. Sunday 11 January 2009.

For the last three days the sun was so fine and the air so clean and fragrant it felt like the blissful awakening of spring. We walked all over: yesterday to Haight Ashbury, amused by the young people with big hair, in jeans and tie-dyes who got there forty years too late, mixing with the Goth fellows in black capes, and silly druggies singing to their dogs.

Janine lost a glove along the way, a gift from Catherine. I was sure I could find it again if I went back by myself, and sure enough, it was there on the sidewalk, a small but precious victory, at a time when small victories count an awful lot.

Later the same day.

My futurist friends now identify three ages of modern civilization.

The first one was the *Age of the Producer*. Power centered on manufacturing. The focus was the Worker. The symbolic object was the time clock. During World War II, solution to problems was rationing. Key examples of success are GE and Dow Chemical.

The second phase, they say, was the *Age of the Consumer*. Power was in marketing, not manufacturing, because factories could make far more stuff than was needed. The focus shifted to the Consumer and the symbolic object became the credit card. Solution to problems was to keep buying, wasting instead of rationing, inciting the public's desires through television. Key examples of success are Procter & Gamble and CBS.

The third phase is the *Age of the Pro-sumer*, the creator economy. Cooperative creation holds the power. The focus is the innovator. The symbolic object is the mouse. Key examples: Wikipedia and Google.

I hope they're right, but I don't see much evidence of it yet. Instead, power moves from nations to geographically-centered city states like

Singapore or the Bay Area. This was demonstrated when California Governor Arnold Schwarzenegger and Tony Blair gave a joint press conference in L.A., announcing environmental measures bluntly opposed to those of President Bush, and when the attorney general of California sued the Federal government and five major car companies for failing to implement pollution regulations.

Hummingbird. Thursday 15 January 2009.

Is Dr. Green ready to drink the Cool-Aid? He now acknowledges there are unexplained events at the Utah ranch, including physiological effects on humans. He even suggests that we should study them together under a new project for BAASS. He also takes abduction stories more seriously.

After repeated assurances that nothing would happen in our research on Brazil without our team being involved (part of my current work is to compile all my unpublished notes on Colares), the opposite message has come down: All information about the files will be used to directly contact Brazilian authorities. I responded that I hoped they realized any untimely approach would wipe out our chances of getting real information released, a looming fiasco.

Yesterday morning I drove Janine to Mount Zion Hospital for her first injection of Avastin, our last hope, an experimental drug that restricts the ability of tumors to grow their own blood supply. It was hard to take this new step, and I spent the rest of the day emotionally and physically exhausted. Fortunately, our grandson has been sending her color drawings that brightened the day for her.

Later the same day.

Colm has explained to me, with his dry Irish humor, the odd request about Brazil: "It's not the sponsor acting like a bull in a China shop; it's Bob pushing them to act like bulls in a China shop...He worries that we're four months into a 12-month contract, and we don't have results to show yet, so the sponsor had better do what they promised and get us the materials we need."

Well, yeah, I pointed out, but in dealing with a very complex foreign culture like Brazil, a country the size of the US where Bob has never set foot, and where the US is not trusted (for a mix of both good and bad reasons), such a move will have the opposite effect.

With luck, a military attaché who speaks some Portuguese (is there such a person?) can open new contacts on the subject with his counterparts in Brasilia, but I seriously doubt it.

Hummingbird. Friday 16 January 2009.

For the last few days, I have felt exhausted and generally at the end of my mental rope, even though Janine shows no sign of neurological problems or loss of energy. On the contrary, today she drove off to Nevada with our daughter and reports gaily on the progress of their business. I need to rest for a few days, concentrate on the advanced coding of the databases, and try to sleep.

Reading Allen Greenfield's well-researched book on the late 18th century's Hermetic Brotherhood of Light, which contains reprints of several works by Pascal Beverly Randolph, I find references to the "Intelligences of Space" at several places in the "sacred and confidential" private letter entitled *The Ansairetic Mystery*. Thus, teaching no.25 promises "to have mental dalliance with the powers of Space," while teaching no.80 concerns "coming *en rapport* with the purely Intellectual Powers of Space."

Elsewhere, the book offers to unveil the science. "The fee is $250 in gold..." Randolph could have saved the DIA a lot of money.

Hummingbird. Sunday 18 January 2009

I have completed the first task I'd agreed to do for BAASS, putting in place the initial *Capella* version of the old NIDS catalogue, the reader to be uploaded on the private net.

Lunch *Chez Moi* near Fillmore and Union, where we like to walk around the shops and cafés. The sun was warm. We ate crêpes by the open door. People were playing with their kids, or sat at outside tables reading the newspaper, anticipating Barack Obama's inauguration on Tuesday. The guns are silent in the Middle East, at least for now, but the economic crisis rages on.

19

Las Vegas. Friday 23 January 2009.

It feels like a new America now, with a young President, a restructured administration, and the anticipation that Barack Obama's charisma can rally energies across the world to overcome the financial debacle that throws good people out of work and out of their houses. Las Vegas remains a ghost town, only tolerable today because a spring-like sun puts happy touches on the ochre walls.

The secure BAASS facility isn't ready, so we met at Park House on South Eastern. Colm introduced me to Doug Kurth, his first recruit, a tall, dynamic former Marines pilot from the USS *Nimitz* who brings his experience and enthusiasm to the building of our databases. I installed our first *Capella* file on his computer and trained him in its use. It represents the first 668 cases from the NIDS investigations, expanded into the six layers of the Vallee-Davis model (14).

Over lunch with Colm (Doug wasn't asked to join us), he said he'd resign if his clearance didn't come through. I feel the same way: How can I build an information system for people who are not allowed to talk to me?

Colm has been asked to hire two people a week for the next 20 weeks, so his time is taken with interviews and reference checks.

"I don't understand the frenzied urgency of this program," he confessed as we ate our chicken salads. "The sponsor has already established some contacts to retrieve the Colares files from Brazil, and he's going to Area 51 to get the data we've identified in their vault: data from the days of Project Grudge and a mysterious 'artifact' file that was kept away from Blue Book."

In the evening, Hal arrived, so we went to his hotel to compare notes about technology. Hal gave me a list of the twelve fundamental "research area" papers that EarthTech has generated, and I gave him the executive summary of the *Capella* development. We also went over the definitive story of MJ-12: The whole charade started with Admiral Edward Burkhalter, then Chief of Naval Intelligence (15).

His counter-intel staff doctored up authentic documents that referred to a project, indeed active (but classified) back in the fifties, *to mislead the Soviets* about technology developments, as Eric had already found out through his own contacts.

The doctored documents were leaked (reportedly through Rick Doty and his colleagues?) and dropped into the mailbox of an innocent ufologist who turned it into a major story, still a major source of bewilderment among the believers who treat it like gospel.

Three representatives of MUFON arrive tonight to meet with us and discuss a potential alliance for data acquisition and field research: A new beginning for well-funded research?

Las Vegas. Saturday 24 January 2009.

The three MUFON representatives (James Carrion, Jan Harzan, and Chuck Modlin) are ready to help us with their data. John Schuessler was there as well, with his usual well-informed, patient restraint. We met at 8 am at Park House, where Bob Bigelow brought his attorney, Steve Stefani.

Bob led the meeting, listing his requests. He proposed to pay $50,000 a month to MUFON in return for access to all their files and current sighting information, as well as first right of refusal on any recovered materials, and right of co-investigation.

Mr. Bigelow's tough management style, his greatest asset, is less effective when it comes to running a science project, so I don't hold much hope for long-term collaboration. Fortunately, the MUFON team took it all calmly, did not attempt to negotiate on the spot, and gave us a nice demonstration of their corporate-style case assignment system (16).

Later, Doug Kurth gave me a detailed description of an encounter off the coast of Mexico on 8 December 2004. As commanding officer of an F-18 squadron, the VMFA-232 Red Devils, he had taken off from the deck of the *Nimitz* on a maintenance test flight. They were vectored to check on a disturbance in the water that corresponded to an unidentified blip picked up on radar by several ships. He did see the disturbance and heard the conversation between other pilots who saw the object, a white rounded cylinder shaped like a "tic-tac" candy, which outmaneuvered them and flew up at enormous speed. It was picked up on infrared and tracked.

The event was reported in Navy routine. Nobody was told to keep it secret, and it was the subject for much joking aboard the carrier.

Hummingbird. Wednesday 28 January 2009.

Last night we celebrated Janine's birthday on a floating restaurant, the Sherman, anchored south of San Francisco airport, *en famille* with Tia Elena and our daughter. I gave her the first printed copy of *Wonders in the Sky*.

Hummingbird. Sunday 1 February 2009.

The project has hit a snag. All of us are frustrated in attempts to find any of the promised documentation in Washington: A search on the "U-word" turned up a hundred hits, but only one was a sighting report. Hal now recognizes that "there's no science office there anymore," although it was once the source of much of the SRI funding. Anyway, my data warehouse project is both large and self-sufficient, well structured, and needs all my attention.

In the middle of a phone conversation with Hal, as he was reminiscing about his contacts in Burkhalter's office, his cellphone suddenly went dead, a situation he attributes to "the Friendlies." This has happened to us before whenever we touched on sensitive subjects. We don't know whether to feel warmly protected or insulted by the relentlessly indiscretions, but it doesn't make for a very creative environment.

Timber Cove. Tuesday 3 February 2009.

For several weeks Northern California has enjoyed insolent weather, balmy temperatures, and blue skies over blooming flowers and budding trees, so perfect that experts, always in contrarian moods, predict drought in the spring and firestorms in summer. This morning we drove away to escape computers, cellphones, and bureaucracies to celebrate our 50 years together in the secret paradise of the Pacific

North Coast. As we left home, a joyful surprise: a courier brought roses from Olivier.

We picked up fresh croissants at our favorite pastry shop on Fillmore and drove through Mill Valley, the warm smell filling the car. We took the long way north through Muir Woods, Olema, Stinson Beach, to lunch by the side of the road in Tomales, then on to the mouth of the Russian River at Jenner and the tumbling rocks and towering pyramids that jut out of the sea like the ruins of fabled Lemuria, drowned in patches of sunlight.

The evening comes, we rest after watching the sunset. The only sound is that of the quiet waves licking the shore. Fifty years ago, you bravely welcomed me into your life. Our intimacy, this tenderness, the silence of our easy understanding, all that has deepened, and nothing else matters as we look beyond the night, beyond life itself.

Hummingbird. Wednesday 4 February 2009.

We woke up early in Timber Cove. The weather was changing, still beautiful and mild, but with that haze over the shore and that pink hesitancy in the sky that presages coming of rain. Janine suggested a drive on to Ukiah for old time's sake: Why not try to see Spring Hill and our observatory one more time? So we rejoined the highway traffic at Healdsburg and retraced the road so often travelled, up north to Redwood Valley.

Not much has changed along the way. Little towns like Cloverdale and Hopland are redolent of neglect and blight. In an effort to capture the passing tourist, the wineries are the only touches of relative luxury in that tapestry of fine hillsides where man has stitched his ambitions in torn shreds of fading fabric. In Ukiah, decrepit service stations, greasy garages, boarded up shops, and deserted halls where earlier generations held proud meetings or lively political rallies testify to a darker economic page, so it wasn't surprising to find that the locals had turned the land around our observatory into a junkyard. So we will have no regrets; I wouldn't want the place today if they gave it to us.

At the bottom of the driveway, we met Mary Cleveland's old companion on his way to town. He remembered us and said she was up at the house, so we drove on, noticing the new barriers erected against her neighbors. We found her handicapped by poor eyesight but as crusty as ever.

We remarked on the clutter on our old property: a broken-down bus and debris covered with tarp, the grand old willow tree cut up into pieces, the obvious disrepair, and all the mud. She sighed and told us the ranch had been sold twice since we left. The first man wanted to cut down the redwoods; she fought him in Court for five years. Finally, a local winery family bought it and finished trashing it. Her father, a real estate man, once told her, "After you sell a property, you should never go back to look at it!"

Hummingbird. Friday 6 February 2009.

Doug Trumbull and Julia invited us to lunch today to discuss their project. We met at Silks in the Mandarin Oriental Hotel. Doug explained his current notion of secretly equipping ten sites with sophisticated all-sky cameras. Seeking funding in Hollywood, he found a group of "TV reality" producers who could fund the enterprise, but he remains leery of instant entertainment.

The producers told him, after much initial enthusiasm, that ufology appeared so complex that the mind got lost, leading to that mix of fascination and ridicule that surrounds the subject.

Doug is in touch with a supposed CIA man he met through Sarfatti, who assures him that John Mack was assassinated. He knows that's ridiculous; Mack never knew anything worthy of murder and all the circumstances of the accident are known. The next step is a test of Doug's equipment, mounted on an all-terrain truck, in Colorado or New Mexico; or a series of all-sky cameras hidden in mundane objects. I agreed to take part in the experiment if it materialized..

The US economy, meanwhile, continues in free fall, a drama illustrated by the incompetence of bickering politicians and the tragedy of families thrown out of their homes in increasing numbers.

Hummingbird. Tuesday 10 February 2009.

This morning I introduced my friends in the physics startup to an investment firm downtown, but chances of funding are slim. They have given me an assessment of the material samples I've recovered from close encounter sites: "Your calculation of the optical power from the craft is in line with the requirements to lift a vessel. To counteract earth's gravity, our patent says that an 11-ton vessel like the one in France only needs 148 kW of power output. As for the ejection of material, this could be a safety measure. In order to support the propulsion, they could focus about half of the fusion byproducts in a linear direction. The energy of the byproducts in the other hemisphere can be harnessed by electrogravity: in our model, a strong magnetic field is needed to focus the 8.6 MeV helium system for propulsion.

"If fusion is occurring when the focusing magnetic field is lost (even for a second), then the fusion byproducts revert to spherically symmetric radial trajectories. This results in the fusion energy heating up the focusing magnet.

"If this happens to an 11-ton craft hovering over the ground, the heat energy would destroy the magnet and possibly melt other systems. The safest thing to do would be to dump the heated material."

They went on: "For the material analysis, one of your cases found aluminum and zinc. We can only speculate this might be part of a focusing device for the protection byproducts. In another case, the one you documented above the lake, there was iron, strontium, chromium, tin, nickel, and cadmium. Many elements you found are ferrite material, used in magnets."

Las Vegas. Friday 13 February 2009.

The new offices of BAASS occupy the building where NIDS used to be on South Polaris, now refurbished according to the sponsor's guidelines for tighter security. Located near the intersection of Tropicana and Dean Martin Boulevard, it looks like an ordinary office facility on top of which a large, humorous flying saucer, complete with dome and portholes, seems to have crashed.

At 8 am, Franck, the uniformed guard, gave us a form to sign and handed me a badge. Doug, the IT manager, checked my portable drive that only held one file, the pilot sightings database. He locked up my cellphone, after which he gave me a tour of the facility where Colm and his secretary were already at work. Three rooms downstairs are secured for classified material, although none has yet been received from the sponsor.

Much of the day was spent updating the *Capella* system. Doug has taken control of the structure, adding new items and collecting updates to the NIDS files. He asked me about priorities. I would put the emphasis on electromagnetic effect cases and medical injuries or physiological impact, I said, in order to get the scientists and especially Kit started as soon as possible. But the atmosphere is not conducive to the best teamwork; for security, all the Utah ranch data is kept segregated. One guard has refused to return to the ranch, scared at the level of unexplained activity there.

Doug asked me to brief two new investigators about the challenges of witness interviews. I made it clear I was never trained professionally like them (one comes from a career in federal law enforcement, the other from AFOSI), but I stressed the perils of sterile questionnaires and the importance of establishing trust. Witnesses first need to be reassured before being bombarded with questions, and a good visit from a specialist can have a therapeutic effect well beyond the acquisition of data. I was relieved to hear that everyone was open-minded but with healthy skepticism towards extreme abduction claims.

Unsurprisingly, we had no news of the sponsor's efforts to gain access to the Colares files through the US embassy in Brasilia. Nor did they seem to know about the dramatic events at Itatira, which José continues to document daily, including medical injuries to terrified witnesses. Brazilian intelligence teams at the scene have not taken the Pentagon into their confidence. The local policemen who keep us informed are scared of the *chupas* and even more of their own government. They're risking their jobs, so I have no intention of talking until more guidelines are in place. The negative effects of secrecy (particularly needless secrecy, as is the case here) are already being felt. Communication within our group, which used to be lively and productive, has fallen very low, so that I find myself forced to withhold data about various events and projects. It is a common flaw of overly-protective structures to strangle its own channels, enforce erroneous interpretations of data, and ultimately become blind to important facts. The misplaced temptation of cleared personnel to feel smarter and uniquely-informed also becomes irresistible. Next come the easy slide into arrogance, isolation, and fundamental errors.

Hummingbird. Monday 16 February 2009.

A big storm has come over San Francisco, bringing heavy rains that pound our building, blur the view of the Bay, and shake the windows. Janine works with a sense of urgency, wrapping up her brother's estate and cleaning up records. We know the worst is yet to come, but we don't know when, or what form it will take.

The release of *Volume Two* on the Amazon open market has brought warm messages: Pierre Lagrange in France, Bill Chalker in Australia, researchers in Germany and Italy, and even Jerry Clark, who had been a frequent critic of my work.

Hummingbird. Wednesday 18 February 2009.

Another low point today, a sense of aimless drifting. Last night I expressed my concerns about BAASS in a message to Hal and Kit. The latter immediately called me from Beijing.

"The medical claims are unique," he said. "The details began to emerge ten years ago, of claimed genetic IVF/ICSI procedures and neuro-degenerative disease and neuro-regenerative stem-cell CNS injury repair... notably movement disorder treatments and spinal cord injury repair processes. The recent stories have anticipated some discoveries that had not yet been put into practice, and knowledge not known until very recently. These reports do not contradict (except very superficially) possible medical or genetic experiments. Indeed, it is unlikely persons other than fertility specialists or geneticists, or neurologists and rehabilitation physician-psychiatrists, would even recognize certain sophisticated elements of the stories."

He adds that this fact supports *weakly* the most credible, small percentage of abduction stories, but he also speculates about "a real epidemic...possibly pandemic...of *increased incidence of UFO-abduction and UFO-technology-rich paranoid schizophrenia and schizoaffective disorders in persons under 40, and growing prevalence of post-40 paraphrenia* in Western nations.

"An explanation for this phenomenon is the creation of an Alternative Reality being fed by contemporary sociological, and anthropological elements, which is not healthy."

These are strong observations from an expert in scientific intelligence, but I don't understand his appraisal when he adds that the purpose must be "non-traditional generation-after-next requirements for far-forward analysis" He adds: "Like minds are needed, they exist in a virtual world where the coin is knowledge of secrets."

Hummingbird. Saturday 21 February 2009.

Yesterday was tough, driving Janine to blood tests and MRI. Solutions are lacking and basic research is weak, behind the biochemical verbiage. The disease has travelled, crabgrass-like, to another zone, in spite of biweekly Avastin injections.

Every day brings me two or three Internet reports on brain research, new trials, new medication, but no bright hope, even after I spoke to the leader of Novocure in Israel and communicated again with Dr. Adler, who only said the Cyberknife "might help."

Hummingbird. Sunday 22 February 2009.

BAASS makes progress now. Colm was in Washington this week, and Hal has obtained his clearance in record time: "Six to eight weeks, and I'm fully cleared, beyond SRI days. What gives?! And introductions that I would never have imagined a month ago. As the song says, something is going on here..."

Keeping up with social graces and a sense of normalcy we can still afford, we had dinner at the French consulate with Ambassador Pierre Vimont, General Consul Pierre-François Mourier, and his wife. The guests were Sequoia venture capitalist Pierre Lamont and his wife, Partech's Vincent Worms and Eric Benhamou. This afternoon, on a welcome break, we went over to St. Mark where our extraordinary friend Mahan Esfahani played Bach's seven Toccatas for harpsichord at a concert of the Early Music Society, beyond the Earth plane...

Las Vegas. Alexis Park. Thursday 26 February 2009.

The economic crisis has humbled this city. I find Vegas nicer when it is subdued. Its magical power remains intact even as the stock market tumbles (the Dow barely above 7,000 today, still dropping) and as new questions get raised about Obama's plan to inject trillions of dollars into the economy, with deleterious side effects. The most direct result will be to fatten the bureaucracy.

Stanton Friedman, who recently came to Vegas, spoke to Bigelow of his research at the National Archives, where he did find many UFO file drawers off-limits, as he did at the Reagan and Clinton Presidential Libraries. It is understandable that strategic material would still be classified; this means nothing in terms of a possible cover-up of UFO data, I said. No smoking gun so far, according to Colm, who is irritated at the situation because he still doesn't have his clearance.

No news from Brazil either. We're told that two US attachés met with the minister of defense who promised to review the documents and decide what could be released. In the meantime, in Itatira, I follow reports about a woman who was injured by *chupas* in an area of uranium mines, space facilities, and military installations.

Still on the unclassified topics, Bob seeks to educate the world about the phenomenon. To that end, he plans to fund public studies abroad. He interprets the recent release of UFO files by several nations as a move towards imminent disclosure: Denmark and Canada have followed the example of France, Spain, and Great Britain. But I told him we could just as easily interpret these releases as a way for the politicians to wash their hands of an annoying PR problem.

Las Vegas. Friday 27 February 2009.

First full, exciting day at the BAASS office. Doug picked me up early in his gray Mercury Mariner hybrid. Spring has come to Vegas, with mild weather and a delightful breeze. Trees and flowers are blooming. Whatever one thinks of Vegas with its constant teasing and fake marble façades, there is also true wonder and lightness in the morning air as the sun rises above the mountains and brings the desert to life.

The first thing that hits you as you enter the building, after you sign in with Frank and get your security badge, is the silly music: songs from twenty years ago, with their undistinguishable lyrics, ever-present in the background.

Capella, the project's first product, was the morning topic. Should they integrate the new files that have their own structure? How should they build searches? What will the sponsor want to see? Doug has added the unclassified UFOCAT files to the mix, linked to the MUFON daily updates. The team would prefer keeping them as they are, rather than integrating them with the data warehouse. If they do that (and I'm almost certain I will lose this battle, so superficially seductive is the programming), they will be unable to merge these diverse datasets for any sophisticated statistics, and they won't take advantage of the model of the phenomenon Eric Davis and I have built. In one year, they will have hundreds of thousands of entries in incompatible formats, and it will be another sinking cathedral.

So I made my recommendations, turned over my final report and my handwritten notes from our 1988 trip to Colares, and kept my peace. Much of my time now is devoted to Janine's care, I told Bob, and I can't take any additional assignment within BAASS.

On the way to Park House, I asked about Dick Haines and NARCAP. Dick has changed his mind on his initial agreement to turn over full copies of his files to BAASS. After much discussion about his possible role, he decided to sever the ties. There are other subjects of friction: Colm puts a low priority on certain hot topics like abductions, and Bob, while a great business manager, puts enormous pressure on everyone.

It was fun, however, to drive to Arby's for cheap fast-food in Bob's red full-scale Mercedes to pick up hamburgers and fries (just a salad for me, please).

Hummingbird. Thursday 5 March 2009.

The stock market remains in free fall. Europe and Japan are scared of their dropping economies. There seems to be no workable solution. Washington is in the grips of empty ideological battles; many high offices have not yet been staffed. More Americans lose their jobs and their houses every day. Misery and anguish are spreading far and wide.

Hummingbird. Friday 6 March 2009.

Lunch with Peter Sturrock who now believes he can prove that the surface of the sun spins faster than the core. The core is not even spinning on the same axis, he says, and there's a correlation between surface phenomena (luminance) and the flow of neutrinos, which is unexplained; effects should take much longer to reach the surface.

Solar physicists have their own club and don't care about Peter's neutrinos, while most neutrino physicists are not interested in the sun...However Peter has submitted one more proposal to NSF after he had thought his academic career was behind him. He talks about traveling again, giving lectures. I encouraged him: In this age of global warming, people don't realize that most categories of energy (including fossil fuels) are simply solar energy in another form.

Bob Bigelow was in the news today when his funding of MUFON was prematurely splashed across the Internet. No fewer than 50 scientists at BAASS, says the article, will be analyzing what MUFON researchers will uncover in the field! Bob is upset at the leak, but it had to happen. The pretense of sophistication in secrecy cannot be maintained when an amateur organization is hired to deploy two hundred volunteers to dredge up sensational stories across the land. You can't have it both ways.

Hummingbird. Monday 9 March 2009.

When I expressed my dismay about the ill-timed MUFON press release, I heard that Jim Carrion and his companions were just as upset. They suspect that one of their state directors issued the proclamation, now picked up around the world.

Once again, the team has come back from Washington disappointed with the status of the data at the sponsor's office. "I don't think the Agencies have anything of real value anymore," Hal told me. "They can't even get his hands on the DIA's own report they wrote about the Tehran sighting."

It turns out that in the early 1990s the Defense department had a big move to "efficiency," so they rushed to go from paper to computer files: "People were told to keep only one set of paper documents from a single file drawer in their office; everything else would be scanned and digitized. But there were never enough personnel or funds, so the files were shredded!"

The urgency of the project now rests on claims of specific threats: The realization that nuclear sites have been compromised by UFOs in both the US and Russia, *including the initiation of launch sequences*, and the hostile episodes in Brazil reported by Bob Pratt and by me, with definite injuries. Yet I pointed out that under the compartmentalization now imposed, Hal and Kit didn't have access to my latest report about Colares, while I am pushing for the development of *Capella* beyond the first three databases I edited myself. I was told that "The data could get lost."*

If that's the reason for the tight management, I can only agree, but this is no way to achieve long-term, global results.

Hummingbird. Wednesday 11 March 2009.

The rains are over. Every morning, Janine delights in watching the sunrise over San Francisco. I have convinced her to brave the MRI images and fly to France with me.

Now the web brings a surprisingly detailed article from *Starstream*, a site produced by Gary S. Bekkum, in collaboration with Jack Sarfatti. He claims to have inquired about interest in the use of paranormal phenomena by the DIA: "In the past few weeks, we have received additional confirmation that anomalous mental and 'paraphysical' phenomena continue to elicit interest. A highly placed source has confirmed that the strange events investigated by Las Vegas businessman Bob Bigelow's National Institute of Discovery Science have been the subject of discussion at DIA sponsored meetings on the threats of emerging technologies."

The leaked statement goes on: "This particular 'fish-story' lends at least some credence to the rumors of continued government interest in

---

* The data can get lost, or at least misplaced. In 2021 the highly-classified records from Capella were reportedly offered for public access over the web by a private company. The circumstances under which it was given the data were never clear to me, but the privacy of witnesses may have been placed in jeopardy at the time.

accessing paranormal paraphysical phenomena in the guise of advanced technology. In other words, 'they' want to reverse-engineer technology not of this world. Of course, it is likely that some of the information is provided as cover for a larger set of activities. Our source for this particular tidbit is a former officer with CIA/OSI Life Sciences Division. He is presently a member on a DIA sponsored committee tasked with monitoring developments in future technologies that might pose a surprise threat to the national security."

Who is in a position to be the mysterious leaker? *Starstream* goes on, referencing Colm's book: "There has been a lot of discussion of the bizarre *paranormal* activity at Bigelow's Utah-based 'Skinwalker Ranch.' Strange creatures, strange objects, floating black triangles, animal mutilations, disintegrated dogs, telepathic messages—a smorgasbord of every strange and imaginable terror has been served to those unfortunates that spent any time at the ranch... A Starstream contact who teaches at the University of Utah, Salt Lake City, and is not prone to flights of fantasy, actually observed a floating black triangle above the mountains...

"Our high-level source confirmed that NIDS data has been discussed by members of an elite DIA committee, at least informally. Life sciences are probably more concerned these days with the avian virus. But never underestimate the appetite for weird and wild science, even at an official level. A list of names of committee members involved in this particular wild 'tiger tail' apparently was intercepted by the NSA. Or so we are told."

The reference to a "tiger tail" is not innocent, since the elite group is known as the DIA Tiger team, which includes Dr. Green. But the informer knows a lot of details: "On a private level, the NIDS investigation of the 'Skinwalker' phenomena was flawed as a result of budget constraints. One of the lead investigators, a physicist who has recently worked under government contract, lamented the lack of available detection equipment. Some of the '*creatures*' on the ranch could only be seen using ITT night vision binoculars. The lack of a color thermal imager meant there was no means of determining if the *shadowy* beings emitted heat. This particular '*entity*' was completely invisible to the unaided eye."

Why would DIA show so much interest in past and present events at the ranch? "The ability to enter an environment without detection and interact with the local surroundings would be of immense interest to the DIA. *Paranormal* stealth was a driving force behind the original StarGate *psychic* spy programs. Worse yet, the ability of an unseen entity to enter top-secret American government installations should send up red flags throughout the military community. Covert psychic spying was heralded as a useful supplement to conventional intelligence gathering, but the real diamond in the rough was *remote perturbation*—the desire to use psychokinesis to affect command and control systems."

The report continues: "Consider the implications. Physics tells us that all information requires physical representation, but information is no longer considered an abstract quality. Information is the driving physical mechanism that controls the national defense from the operation of electronics on the battlefield, to the bio-physical mental functioning of the Commander in Chief."

This is very good analysis. *Starstream* goes on, correctly, to assess the impact of such phenomena on modern science, although I believe they accept the nature of phenomena at the ranch a little too quickly, contradicting their own observation that detection equipment and good standards are lacking.

The article states: "'Science' is a moving target. And there is never a shortage of researchers looking to upset the status quo. The problem nowadays for the would-be "alternative scientist" is that the mainstream is getting back into the game as well. Not only are some of the mainstream leaders discovering exciting possibilities in previously forbidden ground, but there is data coming in that looks to support a whole new view of man, mind, and the (multi/mega) universe."

Mabillon. Saturday 14 March 2009.

We found Paris quiet and mild, the streets surprisingly uncluttered by honking cars. The absence of traffic jams is the only visible sign of the economic slowdown, perhaps because financial changes here take more time to manifest than in America. It doesn't take much digging to find evidence of social unrest, however. Sarkozy's reforms are shipwrecked on a rocky island of layoffs and factory closings. The media pretend everything is fine, shunning economic news, highlighting fashion shows and their glittering dresses.

We brought gifts and comfort for a difficult passage: the challenge of a deteriorating job climate strikes especially hard in finance.

Olivier now teaches part-time at Paris University, which helps a bit in the transition.

Later the same day.

In response to a message from Colm, Kit has clarified the rumors reported by *Starstream*: "This was first written in 2006. Bekkum's sources are Pandolfi, Paul Murad, Mark Pesses and, in part, me. There was a TIGER discussion, around a coffeepot during a break with the chair, ex-Deputy Director for Science and Technology of the CIA, Dr. Ruth David. Paul Murad was there, and Jim Dearlove [DWO chief scientist], and the sponsor of the TIGER and myself. Bekkum later mis-identified the discussion as part of the official agenda."

He goes on: "Paul (Murad) had just read Colm's *Hunt for the Skinwalker*. There had been conversation about Bigelow, led by Pandolfi, who had an office next to Paul, and also Mark Pesses."

Kit stresses: "The *Tiger* never discussed Bigelow, but there was an unrelated incident in 2008 when I was asked to talk to senior Academy officials with Dr. Ruth David to see if the Tiger would do a BAASS study: The request was that I first check with Ruth, then John Gannon, then the Academy vice-president, and then, if approved in principle, I was to go to Bob and convince him to carve out some dollars from BAASS to Tiger. Ruth and John and I agreed. So did the actual DIA DWO sponsor and boss of Murad.

"Very soon after, I spoke to Bob who said reluctantly yes, but it was clear he didn't want to do it. Jim and Bob, several months later briefed [name withheld] on BAASS. He refused to have anything to do with it, or the proposed Tiger study. Independently, the Academy Board said they wouldn't accept any money from a private corporation for such a study, and Ruth withdrew support as well."

Mabillon. Tuesday 17 March 2009.

Over lunch at Le Suffren, Dominique Weinstein has just introduced me to Professor Yves Sillard, head of GEIPAN. We discussed Hessdalen and my venture work in technology. I was amused to discover that Sillard didn't know he could get GPS data on his new iPhone until I activated the application to show him the near-real-time satellite view of the area where we were having lunch.

Kit is in Beijing, which doesn't facilitate conversation, but we both felt an intense need to compare notes about BAASS. He told me that a recent summary of my progress with *Capella,* which he received from Vegas, mixed in with some concerns, "fits new spins" in his own situation.

Mabillon. Saturday 21 March 2009.

Janine has returned from a quick trip to Normandy with Annick. I met her at Saint Lazare station, frail and tired from an emotional visit to her brother's grave, yet as sharp as ever, ready to boost everyone's spirit with sane advice.

Everything seems normal now. Maxim stays with us tonight. Friends are coming over for lunch: Yannis Deliyannis and Marie-Charlotte Delmas, two fine experts on medieval folklore. This should be a simple day for pleasure, good cheer and conversation, but I secretly mourn the precious balance we've lost. Then, on the bus on the way home, Janine whispered to me she wanted her ashes to rest in Normandy.

Hummingbird. Sunday 5 April 2009.

On Friday we drove up to Marin County with Mike Kuchar and his friend, performance artist Mark Arthur, to attend the screening of *It Came from Kuchar* at George Lucas' Skywalker Ranch.

The fine weather, which comes with morning sunbursts over the Bay leading to mild evenings in the parks and over the shoreline of the Pacific, helps in keeping our spirits up.

When we moved our venture capital offices on Friday, Janine was there in Palo Alto, directing the work, getting every room ready. In the evening we read the second draft of *Volume Three* of my journal together. This is a special moment: she comments brightly on my notes and corrects my recollections.

We relive those years, the decade of the 1980s when the experience of Spring Hill and our children's coming of age dominated our lives.

Now Doug Kurth has sent me the User's Guide he has compiled for *Capella*, a fine piece of work covering the six databases now assembled. This is excellent work, and I am proud to have started it and built the structure, but most of the cases they've collected (perhaps as much as 80%) have nothing to do with a new phenomenon, except in a peripheral, sociological or cultural sense. The second phase, if I remain involved, will be a massive statistical re-calibration and quality control effort, but I doubt if anyone realizes the need for this, so inebriated are they with the hundreds of thousands of entries we have inside those computers, potentially a source of big errors, mere shadows in cyberspace if we don't compile the difficult screens.

Hummingbird. Sunday 12 April 2009.

Low point again today. Through the venture network, I keep investigating experiments about vaccines, gene therapy, and Novocure's tests with electro-magnetic fields, but they are uncertain and the outcome isn't the breakthrough we're hoping for.

I do know just enough, from my experiences financing Accuray and watching other companies, to understand the grim reality behind the clinical reports.

Fortunately Catherine came over with Easter delicacies and later drove us to Dolores Park, where San Francisco offered one of its unique and colorful displays, a celebration of the 25th anniversary of the Sisters of Perpetual Indulgence, a gay group that has been a consistent support for the sick and the best example of charitable work, at a time when other organizations, particularly the Catholic church, behaved so despicably towards AIDS victims, expected to rot in their garrets, and burn in Hell. The sun beamed over a thousand people. The walk home helped a bit in restoring my spirits.

Hummingbird. Thursday 16 April 2009.

Last night, the French Consulate gave a dinner in honor of Nathalie Kosciuzko-Morizet, French minister for the digital economy, formerly in charge of environmental issues under Jean-Louis Borloo. Tonight, a cocktail with another ambitious minister, clever Valérie Pécresse, currently in charge of higher education and research.

Hummingbird. Sunday 19 April 2009.

California spring. Down the Peninsula the trees are in full bloom; flowers cascade down the slopes; well-kept houses rest behind trimmed bushes and clean lawns, as if everything was fine with the world. We had dinner with our daughter and spent the night at her home. In the morning I watched the ballet of the squirrels, reminding me of similar scenes when we lived in Belmont, decades ago. I read an old book on the redwood deck: I am becoming a fan of Alexis de Tocqueville! For a Norman aristocrat, he had a fine grasp not only of his own country but of American democracy.

I've had no contact with BAASS, Kit, or Hal since my latest visit to Vegas, other than occasional email dealing with ongoing research. I continue to prepare a trip to Marley Woods, assembling charts and data. I will join Ted Phillips and Doug Trumbull there as I resume my independent field research. Next month there is a potential trip to Washington to see NASA, and a meeting at Esalen organized by Jeff Kripal. Then it will be June: time for another trip to Paris.

Hummingbird. Saturday 25 April 2009.

The Foundation for Mind-Being Research (FMBR), founded 27 years ago by Bill Gough and some of his buddies from Stanford and SRI, held an interesting meeting in Los Altos last night. We attended it with Catherine. The FMBR is presided by Yevgeny Gorodetsky, a graduate from the Institute of Biosensory Psychology in Russia. They showed *The Living Matrix*, a movie by Greg Becker that discusses the role of information in medicine, particularly "spontaneous remissions," which naturally interest me sharply. Experts like Dean Radin, Marilyn

Schlitz, and Edgar Mitchell testified, along with HearthMath researchers and Dr. Bruce Lipton.

Although the argument had weaknesses and many terms like "fields" and "energy" remained poorly defined, the movie was well-documented and clear.

We drove back to Catherine's house and spent another restful night there before coming home. I've made an appointment with Dr. Cobbs at California-Pacific. I track down experts, and I explore connections at Duke and UCLA.

Hummingbird. Sunday 26 April 2009.

This morning I reconnected with Colm, who had tried to reach me during the week (cellphones are forbidden at BAASS, which does not make for easy connections). He sounded a bit dejected: "The sponsor has not delivered anything so far," he said again. It was classic Washington. Even the Brazil connection has only given superficial stuff, as I'd expected; some attachés from the US Embassy were sent out to contact a one-star general who may (or may not) control the files. He flew into a rage when they approached him because he was once rebuffed on an unrelated Brazilian request to the US. He told them he just wouldn't deal with them.

John Schuessler has now learned of the newer sightings there and mentioned them to BAASS, but I doubt if the Brazilians will talk about what goes on. The connection with MUFON is yielding some good data but it is meager. Contrary to earlier claims of "400 to 600 cases per month," there were less than six items of interest in April. When the new dispatchers verify details with witnesses, most cases evaporate. "The amount of quality data is low," I'm told. "We need to upgrade the methodology."

Privately, I see BAASS following the same trajectory as Dr. Hynek's CUFOS under Alan Hendry in the 70s, when they started checking cases carefully and found that much of the "evidence" disappeared under serious scrutiny.

BAASS is running a vacuum cleaner over the field of international ufology and falls into the trap about which the wise Major Murphy warned me, ending up with 95% of the information...but missing the five percent that really matter.

Kit was in Vegas on Thursday, giving the group a background lecture on the remote viewing program, SRI, Uri Geller, and the early developments. Colm wants me to teach a parallel track. BAASS now employs 38 people, including nine investigators and three analysts, most of them dedicated to the *Capella* development project and its derivatives. In the evening I called Dr. Richard Niemtzow, still with the Air Force in Washington. When he heard about Janine's condition he was immediately helpful, so he boosted my hopes.

Springfield, Missouri. Tuesday 28 April 2009.

Springfield is greenish-gray and extremely flat. As sensible Midwesterners, or as a private joke, the citizens have placed their cemetery at the end of the airport runway. Everything else is owned by a Mr. Hammons, who has built a tall black tower downtown and pasted his name on the stadium. The local business paper deplores government control of the banks and worries about Obama "plunging the country into socialism"!

Marley Woods. Wednesday 29 April 2009.

Adam Johnson and Tom Ferrario picked me up at the hotel in their black Jeep and we reached Site One about 1 pm after a stop for lunch in West Plains, where I was surprised to get a call from Bigelow's secretary. She said my "clearance was ready, it only remained for me to sign a "security side-letter." Shortly thereafter, Jim Lacatski called cheerfully from Washington to confirm next week's arrangements.

Ted Phillips, now white-haired but as full of energy as ever, joined us in the afternoon. He showed me the various buildings, including a neat one-story construction with an observation tower, intended for use by the team. The owner is a local banker whose family has owned the farm for generations. He's become fascinated by the phenomena there. We also met "Gopher," the caretaker who lives in a trailer on the property. In the evening we had dinner with Douglas Trumbull. We surveyed the land, calibrating cameras at Site 1 until 4 am. The weather was overcast, with occasional fine rain, but good visibility.

Marley Woods. Thursday 30 April 2009.

I spent a short, uneasy night on the sofa in the upstairs room of the observation building. It is a peculiar environment, which the enthusiastic owners have filled with every possible corny artifact of American ufology, from inflatable Aliens to plastic spaceships, all of which detracts from the atmosphere of serious study Ted and his assistants would have liked to see. We went to lunch in Thomasville with Douglas, still tired from his trip. Later, we drove out to Sites 2 and 3 to get a general idea of the environment.

Most of the incidents Ted and his team described to me were peculiar lights. Typically, they rise over the rolling landscape of grassy fields and dogwood clusters. There are creeks and ponds, but no hill above 1,000 feet.

This is dairy country; the night is busy with the sounds of chickens, cows, and turkeys running loose, and the peacock up on the roof who cries out like a woman in pain.

Washington. Wednesday 6 May 2009. Holiday Inn Rosslyn.

We saw Dr. Charles Cobbs recently. He gave us hopes that trials of Valcyte might work against the cytomegalovirus, possibly instrumental in the development of brain tumors. Janine doesn't suffer from any diminished function twenty months after her operation, contrary to predictions; this may enable us to take advantage of the newest research, and it allowed me to take this trip to D.C. At the New Executive building that houses the Executive Office of the President and OSTP, I spent an hour describing venture capital and its impact on technology to a seasoned bureaucrat from the Obama transition team charged with the revival of job creation. She had no concept of venture capital and didn't understand how innovation turns into an enterprise, so I wasted my time and hers, not an unusual experience in D.C.

Eric Davis called me, suggesting I give an interview on UFO reverse engineering to Bill Scott at *Aviation Week*, who has been a source of information on some projects. I declined. At this point, I'm not eager to get my name into the media. BAASS has grown, with new employees in temporary offices at Park House. Most of the new hires are investigators, plus two French and one Portuguese translator for *Capella*, and three researchers on the Northern Tier and the best NIDS cases. My initial data warehouse now holds nine databases.

Later the same day.

Strange how the prospect of separation, the horrible idea of no longer being able to speak with you, to hold you, to hear your voice, has made our intimacy closer and more tender, with an acceptance of something infinite over us, even as we fight the disease with every resource we can muster. Medicine's progress, which was unable to help poor Allen Hynek, has given us this marvelous interlude. Janine's silky hair has returned to its full length. Today, her alertness, her quickness of mind, are preserved treasures. I watch her, and I have stopped caring very much about anything else.

I continue with some projects (*Wonders* with Chris Aubeck, work with my partners) because I must keep my own strength to help her.

Washington. Friday 8 May 2009.

Holiday Inn at Key Bridge. I finally met Jim Lacatski this morning. He took me to a lady in his office who sternly explained why my clearance had been stalled because of my frequent trips abroad. This creates a potential risk "when a person is bound by affection, or may otherwise be obligated to individuals who are not US citizens."

This may be a logical precaution, but it left me puzzled about an Intelligence agency suspicious of someone with some international savvy, familiar with faraway cities and cultures, especially after earlier requests by the same Agency to use that background to build open bridges with research abroad. The same contradiction also helped me understand the fiascos in Brazil.

There are concerns about Russia, China, Europe: What about crashed material all over the years? In the afternoon, returning to my extension of Red Planet Capital, I went over to the NASA administrator's office to brief George Whitesides, open and helpful.

Hummingbird. Friday 15 May 2009.

We went to a Haendel concert last night (Bernard Labadie conducting, with Richard Paré at the organ) and happily came back on foot after listening to the organ concerto in G minor and the splendid *Dettingen Te Deum*.

Now we await the results of new blood tests. I learned from Fred Adler that it's often unrealistic to expect a "cure" of such a disease, but if one survives long enough on one therapy to be a candidate for the next trial, and the next clinical experiment, one may in fact beat the illness for a long time. That was the case for AIDS, and for Hep. C, so why not for glioma?

Hummingbird. Saturday 16 May 2009.

Bob and Colm will have a meeting with the sponsor to discuss monitoring equipment, among other topics. Bob is reviewing his engineers' design of an overly-complex observing station and hopes the government will provide experience in advanced monitoring. Hal shares my frustration about the lack of data from Skinwalker Ranch, where he'd proposed installing instruments from George Hathaway, like those already used at Chaco Canyon.

I remarked that after seven years of monitoring, we had nothing definite to show our scientific colleagues, so Bob has a point.

The Esalen Institute. Sunday 17 May 2009.

Astounding Esalen, amazing Big Sur. Stunned, people stop their cars by the side of the precipitous road to stare in wonder beyond the abyss. Suspended above the cold Pacific, the cliffs are subtly brushed by the swirls of the spray and the fog that rises from the heaving ocean. That combination of vertiginous drops, the abrupt infinity of the water, the translucent filters of the haze playing with the sunlight make the landscape at once dangerous and seductive, profoundly disturbing to the soul, yet a unique inspiration.

Jeff Kripal, once again, has assembled a group of gifted artists, scientists, and academics to plumb the secrets of what is left of our reality. It includes some of those I met last June like Dean Radin from the Institute of Noetic Sciences, writer Victoria Nelson, Doug Moench who writes the Batman comics, Chris Knowles, author of *Our Gods Wear Spandex*, and of course Michael Murphy, Esalen's founder.

There were new people too, like editor Mitch Horowitz of Tarcher-Penguin, who took an instant interest in my mock-up of *Wonders*; along with Erik Davis, author of *TechGnosis;* and cinematographer Scott Jones, who has been filming our presentations for a movie about Kripal's work; Larry Sutin, author of a Crowley biography (*Do What Thou Wilt*) and a Philip K. Dick biography (*Divine Invasions*); Paul Selig, a medium from New York; and Christopher Partridge, a professor of religious studies at Lancaster University.

Discussing why people like science-fiction, Victoria Nelson observes many folks need "a world big enough to breathe in." But others may feel they are a character in someone else's novel: "We are being written."

Another remark I heard: "Millionaires don't believe in astrology, but billionaires do," could apply to ufology. Much interesting discussion of Philip K. Dick and Bishop Pike's last, fatal trip to the Judean desert. I hadn't realized he'd invited Michael Murphy to join him.

The Esalen Institute. Monday 18 May 2009.

Doug Moensch had recommended that I look up the "Mithras" Liturgy in the *Paris Codex* for an initiatory journey that parallels the abduction experience. Indeed, I find that the document, interpreted by scholars as "a journey of the soul," is remarkably specific, almost technological:

> The Great God *Helios Mithras* "ordered that it be revealed to me by his archangel, so that I may ascend into heaven alone as an inquirer, and behold the universe… It is impossible for me, born mortal, to rise with the golden brightnesses of the immortal brilliance… Draw in breath from the rays, drawing up three times as much as you can, and you will see yourself being lifted up and ascending to the height, so that you seem to be in mid-air."

The text goes on:

> The visible gods will appear through the disk of god... and in similar fashion the so-called "pipe," the origin of the ministering wind. For you will see it hanging from the sun's disk like a pipe... And when the disk is open, you will see the fireless circle, and the fiery doors shut tight. Then, open your eyes and you will see the doors open, and the world of the gods that is within the doors.

The invocation itself is a gorgeous text:

"Hail, O Guardians of the pivot, O sacred and brave youths, who turn at one command the revolving axis of the vault of heaven, who send out thunder and lightning and jolts of earthquakes and thunderbolts..."

Hummingbird. Saturday 30 May 2009.

In discussions with Ed May, and separately with my stealth-mode buddies (at Boardwalk in Los Altos, eating a Chili Dog and fries with a Coke, which felt very good after two days of overly healthy Tofu at Esalen), I have clarified my notes about the current state of physics, well summarized in a recent *New Scientist* article by Marcus Chown (15 April 2009): "General relativity breaks down when gravity is very strong—when describing the big bang, for example, or the heart of a black hole. And the standard model of particle physics (a quantum description of the matter around us and all forces other than gravity) has to be stretched to breaking point to account for the masses of the universe's fundamental particles. *The two theories are incompatible, having entirely different notions of time.*" (my emphasis)

Bob Bigelow, when I called him this morning, was warm and relaxed. We had a congenial conversation about the project, NASA, and the future of the American space program, which he saw as entering a challenging period since the Shuttle will stop flying in two years. There is no replacement for it other than the Ares-Orion combination, a pork-barrel project NASA's own experts detest and want to cancel.

In the last several years, the Agency has started, funded, and then stopped nine different projects! Bob is pushing for private space projects using the Atlas V rocket and an improved design of the Orion capsule. He's also developing his own model for a lunar base.

BAASS has sent a team of seven members to Brazil. I haven't heard the results.

We've agreed I would travel to Vegas soon after my return from Europe in three weeks.

Mabillon. Friday 5 June 2009.

Almost midnight. At the China Basin facility of UCSF, Janine must be out of the big magnet. My daughter is with her. Waves of sleep wash over me, then I wake up again and think of them.

What courage in your voice, my love; what knowledge you must have of infinity, to face this. "Don't rush back," you said. "Don't get people alarmed about me."

Mabillon. Friday 12 June 2009.

A *bistrot* on Boulevard de Sébastopol, for a glass of juice before my meeting at CNES. Yesterday our team (including Graham) had lunch after our partnership strategic session.

This is my last effort. I've cancelled all my meetings next week, including plans to visit the Bourget Air Show. I will be with Janine tomorrow evening. UCSF hopes to try a new therapy.

My son is in London for two days, so I picked up Maxim for dinner (at Mandarin in Saint-Germain-des-Prés) and he spent the night at Mabillon. Almost twelve now, conversations with him are animated, fun, and insightful, so we enjoy each other's company, a rare source of pleasure for me in these troubled days.

Hummingbird. Thursday 18 June 2009.

On Tuesday, back in San Francisco, we drove out for a picnic at Diana's Grove, a delightful little park on the cliff overlooking the gray Pacific. The weather was cold, breezy, and foggy, but we enjoyed the suspension of time, simply sitting on a bench for a welcome break. Today we walked all the way to the top of Strawberry Hill, an area filled with flowers and ancient trees. We climbed up above the waterfall in the glow of sunshine brushed by the approaching Pacific fog, alive with its fresh caress.

Hummingbird. Tuesday 30 June 2009.

BAASS has some 55 employees now, with enough investigators to cover domestic and international field work. Plans include remote viewing sessions. Colm tells me the staff is fully absorbed with the preparation of the ten-month report to the sponsor.

Hummingbird. Sunday 5 July 2009.

Maxim and Olivier are here, brightening our life. Our son needs to reconnect to his roots and get over a recent divorce. I took Maxim to Turtle Island. We ate our hot dogs in the boat, like old fishermen.

I've read again that remarkable Soviet novel by the Strugatsky brothers, *Definitely Maybe*, where a character observes: "The conclusion is that there are no aliens and no ancient wise men, but something else, some force—and our work is getting in its way."

Where did the Russians find the information? How did their conclusion converge with ours, from completely separate data sets?

George Kuchar just called to say John Keel died in New York on Friday, of heart failure. The poor man had been very ill for a long time. I sent my sympathy to his friends, all those I knew.

Later the same day.

A typical private report from a reader, one of many: "I was a teacher in a private college prep school in Arlington, Texas, 12 years ago. At lunch one day in the faculty lounge I was lightly touching on UFOs, something I do with great care to save myself from being labeled as an 'odd duck.'

"The light remark passed blithely over the faculty, causing only a momentary pause in their pursuit of the latest Harlequin romance.

"The bell rang and all left, save the music teacher and myself. She was a fabulous, gifted teacher, not one to entertain any fringe thoughts of any sort. She lingered with a pale expression. She told me she'd never told anyone what had happened to her family when she was a child; that her mother wouldn't allow her or her siblings to discuss it in her presence, it so terrified her.

"The family was on a vacation trip in the summer, through New Mexico. They were driving at night when a 'star' caught her mother's attention.

"She commented on how bright it was: almost instantly it zoomed over their car, illuminating the area. Everyone was terrified, screaming.

"The UFO violently shook the car and then zoomed away as quickly. I will never forget the total fear in her eyes and ashen face as she told me this."

Hummingbird. Sunday 12 July 2009.

Last night the Silent Film Festival was screening *Aelita, Queen of Mars*. I expected to join a few dozen folks like me, crazy enough to spend two hours watching a 1934 silent Soviet film in black and white, but I was delighted to find the line taking up three sides of the block. The theater was full by the time legendary organist Dennis James sat at the Mighty Wurlitzer (with Theremin), accompanied by Mark Goldstein on Buchla Lightning.

Hummingbird. Thursday 16 July 2009.

The due diligence work on the new immunology treatment keeps me busy. Tonight, we'll have dinner in Atherton with the Herzenbergs, the inventors of the Stanford cell sorting machine.

Three military investigators from the government team, one each from the Army, Navy, and Air Force, have come to the Utah ranch and found themselves frozen, unable to reach the old homestead; 125 feet away, their legs couldn't move, while they felt intense terror. Yet a security guard who followed them was able to walk all over. The second night they were scanning the mesa with generation-3 night-vision devices when they saw a distinct object two thirds the size of a car, only visible in infrared. All four saw it with a different shape (oval, lozenge, rectangle, and "disk").

Hummingbird. Saturday 25 July 2009.

Every night, I wake up between 3 and 4 am, distraught in spite of the hope for new treatments.* Fortunately, Maxim is with us, fun and lively. He helps us through all this. I took him back to the Academy of Sciences in Golden Gate Park to see the planetarium and the bugs' exhibit we'd missed on an earlier visit.

Yesterday we spent the afternoon at a Texas barbecue given by a colleague in the hills of Portola Valley. Some 80 people gathered in his large garage amidst race cars, including a 1959 Cadillac, a Cobra convertible, and even an Ariel Evans that Max and I admired together.

Hummingbird. Sunday 9 August 2009.

We went back to see Dillon Beach today, the Bay and the ocean as stupendous as ever in the sublime light of the coast. Our Athanor stands on the edge of the bluff, stately as always, but we don't regret selling the property, our new life more frugal. We hiked down to the beach and rested in the warm sand.

Janine was pleased to get away from the City but tonight she was very tired. Some options remain, at the National Cancer Institute.

Hummingbird. Tuesday 11 August 2009.

The setting sun puts its orange flames all over the buildings on Nob Hill while the fog starts rolling in behind us, San Francisco deploying its glory. I get ready for another trip to Las Vegas, and next week a visit to Hal in Austin.

In anticipation of my day-long lecture at BAASS, Colm writes: "Virtually nobody knows the identity of the sponsor, for now. A sizeable portion of your audience will be retired police and military

---

* The nanoliposome formuklation of CPT-11 had no positive effect in the patients recruited at UCSF.

intelligence officers, many of whom have little background in the complexity of the UFO phenomenon." He adds: "We'll have some analysts, translators, a couple of biologists and a couple of physicists in the audience. As a group they're skeptical, which is good."

Las Vegas. Wednesday 12 August 2009. Alexis Park.

I arrived aboard a full plane, so I told my cab driver, "Some people still have money, your business must be picking up," to which he laughed and replied, philosophically, "Yeah, it's all the folks who've lost their jobs—they come here, they've no other place to go!"

Dinner with Bob Bigelow and Colm at McCormick & Schmick's. Bob spoke about the Utah ranch, then Colm briefed me on current reports: MUFON teams are improving their investigations and BAASS now backs them up with its own resources. One significant case, originally reported to Sturrock, involves a blue light that interfered with a car. The driver suffered severe consequences.

When the conversation turned to other countries, I asked: "So, what did you find out in Brazil?"

"We split the group into two teams" Colm replied. "We went to Fortaleza and also Brasilia, but everyone had to go on a tourist visa. We attended a UFO conference where we met local researchers who agreed to share their data. We had portable scanners, so we brought back lots of material we now need to translate. We also met with General Uchoa, the son of the notorious ufologist. He promised to put us in touch with the government."

"What about the cases southwest of Fortaleza, in the uranium zone?"

He replied: "There was little we could document."

The large photos, which Bob had prepared in a special folder, are indeed stunning, but I still wonder if they could have been triggered by point-size random reflections enhanced by the digital process.

More directly, the guards have started seeing unusual animals, such as a large beaver, indifferent to people as it walks straight across the land and disappears. The same crypto-animals have been reported in Marley Woods, so I wonder if UFO intrusions into our world do not draw in weird flotsam. In Marley Woods one of the sightings was of a dozen hooded beings with wolfish snouts as in some ancient fairy tale like *Little Red Riding Hood*. This isn't the sort of thing you can take to the Academies, although it is classic Magonia. So is the feeling of terror experienced by the hardened military types at the ranch, including a commando-trained woman; or the experience (very discouraging to a scientist) of four observers describing four completely different things when they scrutinize an object with night-vision binoculars.

Janine reminds me again that as a child in Morocco, she used to see a little Arab wearing a round bonnet at her second-floor bedroom window. She adds: "We were so scared, we would have made up almost anything."

Las Vegas. Thursday 13 August 2009.

A full day of lecturing, with only a short lunch break with Colm and Bob. About 30 people filed into the boardroom at Bigelow headquarters, intimidated by the huge marble table and the big retro-projectors. I already knew several of them, including Doug who managed the computer projections. Others introduced themselves: a Frenchman and also the chief of investigations.

I said I was glad such a professional group was finally assembled to study a problem that had long been the province of amateurs or lone scientists working in their spare time, as I did.

We spent the morning going over case investigations and the history of the field. I stressed that I would only speak about situations I had encountered myself.

There were questions about Brazil, physical samples, and about history, but not as many as I'd expected, perhaps because the group (now over 50 people) has not yet coalesced into a team where members are comfortable challenging common ideas. One statement I made to get their attention, "By now you must have realized that 90% of the data is irrelevant," was apparently a direct hit.

Over lunch, Bob and I spoke about NASA's lack of vision and the problems in Washington, where Obama struggles to get his healthcare reforms approved by Congress. When he was approached to help the BAASS project, John Podesta unexpectedly "ran the other way," clearly eager to avoid getting the administration mixed up in ufology.

I don't blame him, but I had been given the opposite impression of the man's intentions.

Bob reflected sadly on the changes in America, the new culture of "everything for nothing" and ineffective laws that fail to protect anyone but promote costly legal entanglements. He laughed: "Vegas takes the money from all those outsiders who dream of making easy millions, not just the gamblers but the promoters, the corporate giants," Bob said. "They come here, invest lavishly, and leave a few years later with their pockets empty."

In the afternoon, I made two more presentations to provide a sense of the challenges of methodology. We ended with remote viewing, which left them a bit stunned since they hadn't been told that psychic techniques might be used.

I was happy to see I still had the stamina to spend an entire day in intense, occasionally confrontational work.

We ended up in Colm's office where Doug brought me up to date on *Capella* before driving me back to Alexis Park. We now have nine databases, including a Colares and a Canadian silo, and a team of four assistants who fill out the data screens.

The deep, real secret will be in the structure, I told them, rarely in the data; and we won't get to it until the end of Phase Two, in a couple of years. This time can't be compressed, even by hiring more people.

Good AI is like making babies: No matter how many women you marry, making a baby still takes nine months.

Las Vegas. Friday 14 August 2009.

I stayed in Vegas an extra day so I could have dinner with George Knapp. We met at the Italian restaurant of the Hard Rock Casino. I was impressed at George's professionalism. He told me he'd declined to join BAASS and to get a clearance, which keeps him out of some relevant loops, but he felt ties with the government would be incompatible with his work as a journalist. We spoke of the strategy without getting into details. He knew that the sponsors didn't have a row of filing cabinets with data which BAASS could access: Wasn't that going to be the whole point?

The most surprising news from George came with his statement that he was still getting email from and about Gordon Novel, who claimed he could build his flying saucer with blueprints from recovered hardware, linked with Hal's research. They were still trying to raise money for the project, he added. Could this be what Hal referred to when he told me he was meeting with Kit next week to discuss "a project he was running for an overseas sponsor"? If so, it is puzzling. As for mutilations of cattle, they still go on and seem carefully staged to appear human-made, as we found out under the NIDS effort when such obvious props as batteries or syringes were left at the site, next to the impossible carcasses. We've made no progress in that investigation.

Hummingbird. Saturday 15 August 2009.

The Vegas trip has left me a bit discouraged. Evidently, the sponsor has his own agenda and his own bundle of innuendoes, and so do some researchers with side deals. I'm worried about the team sliding into uncritical beliefs about phenomena at the ranch. Some members are now convinced that spirits interact with their digital cameras modulated by human emotions, resulting in the orbs on the photographs. I'm not ready to follow them, and neither is Colm.

Equally naïve is the belief (shared by many) that the recent release by several countries like Canada, Denmark, and the U.K. of their so-called "secret" UFO files indicates a change in policy. Let's apply reverse thinking, I tell them: These files were never truly secret in the first place. This may simply indicate a desire on the part of these governments to wash their hands of the political mess.

Hummingbird. Tuesday 17 August 2009.

Back in old Palo Alto, lunch with Russell Targ today at Joanie's. Latest stories about survival: speaking through a medium, a dead grand master has played 60 moves against Korchnoi.

Russell thinks highly of Ed May, who is redoing the silver experiments.

Now Richard Niemtzow has agreed to see us on Saturday.

Bethesda, Maryland. Friday 21 August 2009.

The Hyatt Regency, and the moist summer furnaces of Washington. This morning a well-organized shuttle service drove Janine and me to the huge clinical center at NIH, the largest research hospital in the country. We returned to the hotel in early afternoon after a thorough assessment of her condition.

The storm that travelled in the wake of the offshore hurricane blew in, cooling the atmosphere in time for us to have a cup of coffee on the plaza to review the data we had been so eager to obtain from our doctors.

As the top-level federal health agency, NIH manages its own clinical trials in addition to those it delegates to leading hospitals. Dr. Howard Fine gave us a clear view of the research avenues open to us if the current treatment fails to reverse the growth of the tumors. There is no magical drug, but we feel relieved to have more complete knowledge of the state of research.

We met with Richard Niemtzow, who recounted his sighting of a bizarre flying craft. "I knew it wasn't a flock of birds, or a helicopter," he told us as we sat in a booth at the Daily Grill.

Janine has recovered her bright outlook and her fighting spirit. For me, the visit is the culmination of a long search on the right set of questions, even if the answers elude us—as they do the best scientists.

Washington–Dulles airport. Saturday 22 August 2009.

Colonel Niemtzow came again to meet us at the Hyatt where we had lunch, after which he very kindly drove us to Dulles airport in his new Cadillac, the color of hazelnut cream. He told us he didn't follow the literature and he seemed only vaguely aware of NIDS. He did report seeing something he considered to be a UFO, as he was jogging in College Park about 6 pm on 26 July, a Sunday.

"I saw it for about five minutes," he said, "and then, all of a sudden, it was gone. Next, a dark disk came towards me, moving in the same direction where the first object had disappeared. It turned into a black ball and vanished as well."

Hummingbird. Wednesday 26 August 2009.

Senator Ted Kennedy, who was treated at Duke University for glioblastoma, died yesterday at age 77. He had battled the disease since being diagnosed in May 2008, 15 months, a bit longer than the statistics for patients overall. If any evidence was needed, this shows that no amount of scientific knowledge or access to the very best doctors can yet provide a cure from this terrible condition.

We approach the two-year mark. Janine retains her fine mind and her sharp judgment, although she gets increasingly tired under the treatment. I read books to her and try to help as I can, but the illness is ever-present. After many years without any citation, I've had two tickets for moving violations in the same week, and I'm increasingly distracted and forgetful. I have to concentrate on every task, schedule every move, and drive with special care.

Hummingbird. Sunday 6 September 2009.

A week ago, I asked Ted Phillips about his plans. "As far as I'm concerned you've been an adviser and member of the team since April. As such, you'll be working with us in any way you wish," he replied.

This doesn't resolve my quandary with respect to Marley Woods because BAASS engineers are eager to plant "special" devices at that location, and nothing indicates that I (or Ted's team, for that matter) would know what they do and what they detect. So this is yet another instance where a classified setup gets in the way of real research.

Ted adds some news about the site: "In the past week there have been two mutilated calves at Site 3, two calves disappeared from the same spot overnight on Site 1 with no traces of violence, an oval landing site at Site 3, which was swirled and depressed, central area undisturbed.

"I found a roughly circular area at the north end of the oval which was radioactive and indicated EM residue."

Things got even stranger with Douglas Trumbull's own equipment, securely installed at Site 3 inside the deer stand with the floor eight feet above ground, set on a heavy tripod and tightened to the point where it could not be moved with both hands, as I can testify.

Ted writes: "We drove back to Site 1 and powered up a computer to check the camera's viewing position. As recorded on image one, the camera was activated by motion 20 minutes after we had left it. The second image also showed the camera was rotated several degrees from the original position.

"We returned to the deer stand....The camera tripod was in the same position and I could not rotate the camera in either direction with both of my hands, so how did 'they' move it?"

Hummingbird. Thursday 10 September 2009.

On Tuesday we received a letter mistakenly addressed to "Jasmine" and the same evening we watched *Secondhand Lions*, a movie where one of the characters is named Jasmine. On Wednesday, we spoke to Olivier, who had just hired an au-pair girl to take care of Maxim in Paris, her name was... *Jasmine*.

Austin, Texas. Saturday 12 September 2009.

Staying at the home of Hal and Adrienne, in a beautiful wooded area near Chaparral stadium. Hal and Eric had come to pick me up at the airport this afternoon, and we spent the rest of the day discussing ongoing research, especially the study of Brazilian cases, with the hope of obtaining the internal reports of Project Prato.

Austin, Texas. Sunday 13 September 2009.

Eric briefed me today about the work of a leading Lockheed aircraft designer named Nathan C. Price, who took several early patents on advanced propulsion (16). As part of Kelly Johnson's legendary aircraft design group, he would have been in a position to know about any Roswell materials. The thought now is that the most secret stuff at Lockheed would be in Sunnyvale, not at the Skunk Works. There is increasingly credible evidence that the Roswell crash did happen. My own study of memory metals at Battelle starting in the late forties (and giving rise to Nitinol) under Howard Cross of Pentacle Memorandum fame reinforces this impression. Kit is back in the US; Kristin's work in China on the environment, pollution control, and materials having come to an end. He studies cases of reported interference with orbs.

A recent remote viewing session has convinced the government to keep the activity going. There was a secret Chinese atomic test where the satellites saw no mushroom cloud, suggesting the bomb was a dud. Other reports, however, told of happy celebrations among the technicians. Remote viewers, given the coordinates and the date, described a situation where the parachute failed to open and the bomb buried itself, but it did explode. This was later confirmed by simulations at Lawrence Livermore.

Some of the phenomena described at Marley Woods, such as the strange animal, have also happened at the Utah ranch where a large beaver-like beast was seen roaming around; it had spikes on its back, unlike any living animal. And one agent has been plagued by poltergeists, back in Virginia, following her stay at the ranch.

Bob is negotiating with NASA to hook up his Sundancer to the ISS. The Bigelow unit generates less secondary radiation than the Station and provides better shelter. Bigelow has other projects with Lockheed, buying six of their Atlas rockets.

Hummingbird. Sunday 20 September 2009.

Dinner with Madame Idrac on Wednesday, at the French Consulate. She is the Minister of Foreign Trade in Fillon's government. The discussions are interesting and I enjoy the brilliant conversation, but nothing will come of it, political expediency being what it is.

I stayed home all day today, wrote a quote for Ed May's book and spoke to Ted Phillips, puzzled by his latest talk with BAASS. He wonders why conditions keep changing: "It's as if they hadn't heard what Bob said about my keeping control at Marley. Now they want to send ten to twelve of their people to the property: a non-starter."

Hummingbird. Tuesday 22 September 2009. Autumn Equinox.

I have received a remarkable letter from a senior Intelligence analyst in Reston. He has become "a student of hidden power structures in the world," adding: "I have learned that, at least for the period of time from the 1920s through WWII, there was an immensely powerful network of industrial interests, with its center of gravity in Germany. This network was not only instrumental in bringing Hitler to power, but it was simultaneously capable of wielding considerable influence over the governments of the US, Great Britain, France, the Netherlands, and elsewhere." He sends me a disk with the text of a book entitled *All Honorable Men* by James Stewart Martin, who exposed people who helped the Nazi. The letter adds: "It becomes conceivable that a behind-the-scenes power structure could manipulate governments on matters of great importance."

Whether or not this is the case with ufology as a vector is speculation, but he writes that he first became interested when he heard privately from a trusted pilot of a military reconnaissance aircraft who had observed a large UFO in the early 1980s: "He and his crewmates had captured 20 minutes of photographic, video and radio frequency data on the UFO, which flew in close formation in broad daylight. A few hours after they landed, they were debriefed by an anonymous, plain-clothes team who confiscated all their evidence."

Prior to hearing this story, he insists, he had been an arch skeptic. But what followed took the enigma to an even higher level: "*The debriefing team ignored all rules of classified material accountability* when confiscating the mission materials. The mission had been an operational signal intelligence mission, and all photos and other data were classified Top Secret/Sensitive Compartmented Information (TS/SCI) subject to two-person integrity regulations. *Yet the debriefing team signed for nothing*. They simply put the tapes and film in a pouch and just walked off. *There's nothing on paper regarding these materials*, nothing to file a FOIA request."

My correspondent is a defense analyst for the Federal government who spent half his career working with special access programs. He's shocked by this situation: "In all my experience, the higher the classification, the stricter the adherence to the rules of material handling and the more dire the consequences of violating security regulations. So I was extremely baffled by this case. A behind-the-scenes power structure exists, which is able to manipulate the CIA,

NSA, Air Force OSI, or whoever grabbed the data, then perhaps this power structure is able to break all the rules and get away with it."

Hummingbird. Thursday 24 September 2009.

I turn 70 today, but given the circumstances this calls for no celebration. We will spend the evening with one friend and our daughter for a quiet dinner. My brother Gabriel called along with his wife, which made me happy. He was going well.

Water has been discovered on the moon. "Why didn't they find it before?" I asked Peter Banks. "They dismissed water in the moon rocks as terrestrial contamination," he said. "Actually, the amount is small, a monolayer on the surface, no usable volume."

Hummingbird. Friday 25 September 2009.

Ted Phillips called me as I drove to Palo Alto this morning. He said Colm has just conveyed to him that the team was too busy with to deal with Marley Woods, which didn't surprise me.

As a result, Ted wanted to re-engage privately with Douglas and me. I told him we were having dinner with Douglas tomorrow, and lunch with a friend of mine known as the "best antenna expert" in Silicon Valley, who could help monitor the electro-magnetic spectrum at the property in a professional manner.

Janine's blood tests show improvement, so it looks like I will be able to go to Europe on schedule; she can rely on Annick and Catherine during my short absence.

20

Mabillon. Thursday 1 October 2009.

What if the UFO phenomenon is not describable by purely technical analysis? I asked my friends at BAASS.

Hal Puthoff concedes that current physics fails to account for much of the data. At the Utah ranch, paranormal events are increasingly intense and flamboyant. A woman whose husband is an investigator with the tribal police saw a 7-foot being at short range (60 feet) at 10 o'clock in the morning on 11 September. It leaped from the top of an 11-foot barn and cleared a fence. The same woman saw "a four-legged black creature running through her garden. It was very dark brown, looked like it had skin, not hair, was definitely humanoid and covered about 40 yards to the treeline in four graceful zig zag leaps in broad daylight."

Intrigued, Colm has interviewed the head of the Department of Fish and Wildlife who'd seen "a very pale grayish smaller being" two years ago, and a bizarre creature terrified his horses. The same individual has had several spectacular sightings outside the ranch.

Mabillon. Friday 2 October 2009.

The weather in Paris has been mild since I arrived, the morning grayness lifting every afternoon. Internet mail brought important news today, first with a contract by Tarcher-Penguin for *Wonders in the Sky*, then a terribly sad notice from Philippe Favre announcing the death of our good friend, glass-master Didier Alliou. He had gone on vacation to Italy, rebuilding his strength.

On August 25 he went for his chemo in Paris: "Beatrice brought him back late afternoon, and he suffered an attack of tachycardia. His doctor managed to get him back to normal, but a later attack proved too much."

We had thought, as he did, that he'd beaten lung cancer.

Mabillon. Sunday 4 October 2009.

In the current depressed climate, there are few venture meetings (Lyon, Toulouse). I do enjoy finding Paris again, from the arches of Notre-Dame to the wandering alleys of the Marais where I go shopping for a piece of fabric, or a gadget to amuse my grandson.

I had to get away for a few days, for my own sanity. Yet I am powerless to manage this anguish, the immense fear of failing you.

When we discussed my trip you said, vulnerable and sad, "You are my only support."

Mabillon. Monday 5 October 2009.

Dominique Weinstein, to whom I gave a copy of *All Honorable Men*, was not surprised by the book. He has focused his research on the foo-fighters of WW2. He's convinced that the objects were man-made, originated in Germany, and were simply designed to interfere with bombing raids. While most of them were plain fireballs that flew up from the ground, his research shows some were also dropped from above. A few Allied planes were downed by the devices, which scrambled radar.

How advanced was Germany in atomic physics? What else was being explored? Beyond Operation Paperclip, what German scientists were protected in 1945? And to what extent was Berman able (or allowed) to transfer financial and economic power to Argentina, Chile, Brazil, and other places where advance bases had been established? Their managers may not have had great power, but they still could wield influence through major firms.

Not much happens in France. Sillard prepares a report that revisits the theses of *Cometa*, inspired by Payan and restricted to nuts-n-bolt data. He points the finger at the secrecy of America while everyone knows that at least three hoards of unreleased UFO data exist in France: the Gendarmerie's own files (not always sent to CNES), and those of the Air Force and the Defense Ministry. The files of cases like Quarouble or Valensole, where extensive analysis was conducted by multiple agencies, do not appear anywhere.

After the death of Didier Alliou, another blow. Attorney Craig Johnson, an old friend and celebrated venture expert in Silicon Valley, died of a massive stroke on Saturday.

Mabillon. Wednesday 7 October 2009.

A prominent Parisian lady, with whom I had breakfast at Deux Magots this morning, recounts for me an anecdote about the Chinese ambassador to Paris, who was her frequent dinner guest at the time when France was about to sell six frigates to Taiwan. Ignoring official channels, he contacted her to obtain an urgent meeting with Prime Minister Michel Rocard.

My friend had the home number of Rocard's secretary and arranged for an emergency meeting, where the ambassador explained that such a sale might force Beijing to intervene militarily. Rocard took steps to cancel the transaction that very afternoon, but he was unaware that Mitterrand and a prominent minister were getting money under the table in the form of illegal commissions for the deal. Mitterrand made sure it went through and fired Rocard, summarily replaced with Edith Cresson.

Mabillon. Sunday 11 October 2009.

Our neighbor Professor Bokias tells me (over lunch at Procope) about his latest trip to Greece. He found the country even more corrupt than before, as highlighted by the disastrous fires inspired by crooked promoters to get rid of "protected" forests around Athens and build up new suburbs once the land was cleared. Even the Orthodox Church is filling its coffers by peculiar means: One elderly pope, 95 years old, was arrested for embezzling a million euros. His excuse was that he felt the need to save money…for his old days.

Hummingbird. Friday 16 October 2009.

Meeting with NASA today, Peter, Graham, and I heard conflicting statements today about future budgets, decisions about innovation and staffing, even the fate of the Ames Research Center. Typical bureaucratic fumbling. Even the potential cancelation of human missions is on the table.

My own research leads me into three novel tracks: (1) More detailed insight into ancient sightings: in Paris I spent two very interesting hours with scholar Yannis Deliyannis reviewing the latest mock-up of *Wonders in the Sky*. (2) The realization, at Marley Woods and the Utah ranch, of a cryptozoology component that can't be ignored any more, reminiscent of the novels of John Fowles. (3) A suggestion of increasing interest in the subject by industrial firms. The problem needs to be tackled in new ways. Is there a cartel, as my D.C. friends believe? Or a Brotherhood?

Hummingbird. Saturday 24 October 2009.

A consultant to the BAASS project has invited me to confirm some of his recent research findings

"All I see is a big vacuum cleaner running over everything," I said. "That's how the data warehouse I designed is being driven, but it wasn't meant to be limited in that way. I don't mind if the team exploits my investigations of 30 years ago, like my records about Brazil, but at some point we'll just end up with junk. Lots of things have happened in those 30 years."

I must have hit a nerve, because the man looked at me squarely and replied: "That's exactly my own experience. I've been modestly active, no more than 20 hours of consulting in the last three months. I gave a 9-hour seminar in Vegas, as you and others have done, and I was asked to look at one case, but they didn't want to spend money on follow-up. They asked me about your cases: I told them you had the files. Did they ever contact you?"

"No. All I saw was one brief email, no follow-up," I had to admit. "Did they ever show you *Capella*, where I'd designed specific fields for the human factors?"

He shook his head: "I only had one brief demo. No chance to test it myself." This made me angry:

"*Capella* was designed to run as a live service to users—like you in your area and Hal in physics—not as a dead, closed file or a simple repository!"

He just nodded, and went on: "The most puzzling thing was that after all this time and the clearances, they have yet to see a single classified piece of paper from the sponsors."

That's bizarre, but I have no insight to offer, so I jumped to another subject: "Do you know about the orbs in Utah? I was shown a file of color prints with lots of orbs, possibly responding to brain impulses from the security personnel."

"I've seen the same thing," the consultant said with a sigh.

"There may be some physical orbs, but frankly, until I get more details and do some tests, I believe the images may be artifacts of the digital camera software, so I'm staying clear," I confessed.

"I've given up on the orbs myself," the man said again, "but Bob is convinced some hidden force is operating. So it's interesting to monitor everything, as they do."

"Is there enough time?" I asked. "I hear funding may not get renewed after the two-year point. If the project dies, it'll be another missed opportunity."

"Yes, but it won't be a surprise," was the answer. "I had dinner with Jack Gibbons last night. You probably remember..."

"Presidential science advisor to Clinton, in the days of the Rockefeller Initiative," I recalled.

"Well, he told me the inside story. He really didn't know anything about UFOs, but he had these 'important persons' coming to his office, insisting he should do research on a bunch of dead Aliens at Roswell!"

He laughed, recalling the scene: "He had to get rid of them somehow... Now he wonders..."

Back to work: I have legal papers from medical equipment giant Becton-Dickinson on my desk in Palo Alto, proposing to acquire Handylab.

Hummingbird. Sunday 25 October 2009.

"Your wife is a miracle," exclaims a consulting physician who's agreed to give us new advice on the frontiers of brain tumor research.

Janine has now survived for more than two years and shows little if any neurological impact, other than occasional confusion with numbers. But how long can we fight the intractable disease?

The miracle was obvious today as we walked three miles, hoping to have lunch at the Yacht Club. But they turned up their noses when they saw us and refused to serve us, since we're not members!

I felt stupid (I should have known), but Janine just laughed, and we found a nice restaurant on trendy Chestnut Street. The sun was out; we enjoyed our walk through the City.

Hummingbird. Wednesday 4 November 2009.

Such a bright day. The landscape is insolently sunny and clear from the Pacific to the Berkeley hills and beyond, a beautiful backdrop for my sorrow: This time the images are bad. Our doctors at UCSF tell us flatly, as doctors do, that they've have run out of options.

Tears eventually coalesce into words, fearful phrases that form awkward sentences I do not care to write.

Bethesda, Maryland. Friday 6 November 2009.

In the huge structures of NIH, attendants accompany patients on wheelchairs; others stumble in with relatives. Like us they hug, hold hands, and try to smile.

Old men come alone, holding their medical forms in shaky hands, looking for the right office.

The sick children are the most distressing; somehow, they don't seem to belong in a monstrous place called the National Cancer Institute. They break our hearts, clutching their toys.

Janine strolled in on my arm, elegant in a pink sweater and her brunette wig.

The medical team spoke to us carefully of the few remaining treatments we might try. They made it clear we've reached the place where knowledge ends.

The wooded Washington suburbs display the full palette of their fall colors in the cold sun. Congress in in session, arguing about the future of healthcare in America, what to do about the scandalous impunity of

Fig. 19. Boulevard Saint Michel, 1959-2009: 50 years have passed!

Fig. 20. Marley Woods, Missouri: with Doug Trumbull (left), Ted Phillips and Tom Ferrario, April 2009.

insurance companies, and how to avoid pushing patients into even deeper financial disasters in the next few years.

Most of today's news is about an Army psychiatrist who went berserk and killed 13 soldiers at Fort Hood, near Austin. A devout Muslim, he wanted to halt to military deployment in Iraq.

Now a group of pundits, psychologists, and academic legal experts are trying to "analyze his motivations," as if the insanity of all wars and the contradictions of religious dogma weren't plain enough.

Bethesda. Saturday 7 November 2009.

Washington can offer a delightful face when the sun shines on its overgrown monuments, designed to impress upon the world the scope and wealth of the American Republic. The parks are well-maintained, yet areas that were decrepit 30 years ago, when I often came here on behalf of the early Internet, still crumble in squalor.

Yesterday Janine and I had dinner at the fancy "America" restaurant inside Union Station, and then we took a stroll at night around the Capitol. Today we met Phil Meade for lunch at Sequoia on the harbor, after which we walked around in the White House area.

The House of Representatives has just passed the limited Healthcare program ("Obamacare") proposed by the Democrats; the political arguments move to the Senate amidst a storm cloud of lobbyists.

Hummingbird. Tuesday 10 November 2009.

Through a phone call from South America, we've just learned of the death of Dr. Hans Rasmussen in Mar del Plata. Our old Viking friend, the companion of many an excursion since Chicago days, suffered a heart attack and died in the arms of his Argentinian girlfriend. Our private labyrinth keeps getting narrower.

Most days are still normal, however, thanks to our daughter who comes over to help with dinner and daily walks. San Francisco greets each morning with its insolent beauty, the caress of the sun on a landscape so perfect every tiny detail of the Victorians stands out, responding to the warmth of the air with its own offer of a kiss.

Close to the center of the labyrinth we huddle, unable to hide or disguise our fears any more, sheltering in a love that becomes essential as everything around it seems to fracture away.

Hummingbird. Saturday 21 November 2009.

Wonders in the Sky is finished, thanks to last-minute improvements of the text and refinements of references by Yannis and Chris. If we had foreseen the amount of research and editing labor such a book demanded, I don't know we would have embarked on this journey, but we're proud of the result.

Janine is increasingly sleepy and occasionally confused with numbers, but her memory is intact; her awareness of things and people, her humor and her logical mind remain. Thankfully, she has no pain other than passing headaches.

I don't go to the office anymore, except for quick trips to sign papers or meet someone. She's never alone and our closeness is sweeter than ever. Oddly, this time of anguish and tears is also uniquely precious, tender, caring. Several times a day I read aloud to her, either from this journal of our past days or from books and letters people send me. She treasures those moments and I cherish her comments.

Jack Glazer, the legal expert, had instructed me, "Keep life as normal as possible, as long as possible." Today we plan for lunch by the bay at Sinbad's and tomorrow our friends in Palo Alto have invited us to a baby shower. Next week we go back to Washington for the third time, as part of a new experimental treatment at NIH. Annick arrives early in December, and Olivier with my grandson in time for Christmas. There will be time for joy, and time for tears.

Hummingbird. Sunday 29 November 2009.

I haven't spent much time on the BAASS project in the last few weeks, but my interest was revived today. Colm Kelleher, home for Thanksgiving, met me for coffee on Union Street. He said the ranch remains a focus of activity: all six sponsor personnel have had experiences there. They're fascinated by the issue of detection and stealthy penetration such observations represent. Yet in spite of our clearances, neither the Air Force nor others will talk to us until an SAP is setup.

From France, Bertrand Méheust tells me that Rémy Chauvin has died, the last great man from the generation that dared to question and explore: Aimé Michel, Costa de Beauregard, and Pierre Guérin. With Chauvin, they were the four mentors who guided and inspired me.

Chantilly. Sunday 6 December 2009.

This hotel is a forlorn outpost catering to frugal airline crews on the edge of Dulles airport. There are few amenities. I crossed the frozen parking lot to Applebee's for a soggy sandwich and came back to my room, preparing the research papers I will need on hand when I meet Peter Banks tomorrow. Washington is dark and cold.

I led Janine to NIH again last week. A bit confused by the huge center, she took the medical tests and the first cycle of their latest clinical trial. If we could only stabilize the tumor until the spring, there might be a chance to join yet another program which promises to penetrate the brain-blood barrier, the main obstacle to current treatments.

The doctors at UCSF, who just told us to go home in comfort until the end, don't know that we're made of stronger stuff and that she can rely on the certainty that I will be her champion forever—fighting with her for every breath, extending my contacts through the clever venture networks that parallel and occasionally extend inquisitive fingers beyond their own research.

I am increasingly aware that Ingo Swann is right, there's a psychic "signal line" that we can grasp, provided we don't let ourselves be distracted by the ambient noise, the so-called "opportunities" of the intellectual marketplace, all the empty visions. We can tune in to the information it contains and follow its thread. What I've noted as *intersigns* are little beeps along that signal line, pointing the way.

When I called you in San Francisco, I marveled at the fact that in the last few months I have learned so much more about your mind and the trust you place in me. I should have known these things a long time ago, but I am grateful that I still have this opportunity to learn new ways to love you.

Hummingbird. Sunday 27 December 2009.

The phenomena keep growing at Marley Woods. Ted Phillips tells me of new cattle events, unspeakable terror and missing animals. This is now centered at Site 3, where mutilations happened before in connection with unexplained objects in the woods. Amber lights manifest again. One owner found himself surrounded by small *visible* orbs (those physical "orbs" again, not just photographs this time) after which he cannot recall anything. I left messages for Doug Trumbull, who continues to build increasingly sophisticated cameras. All that seems very tentative to me, but the phenomena themselves continue.

Hummingbird. Monday 28 December 2009.

Suddenly, Janine is getting weaker. The day after Christmas she pulled me close to her, squeezed my hand very hard. We spoke of sacred things: "What a journey we had, *ma chérie!*" I said after reassuring her she would be at home until the end, with me.
 "Do you have any regrets?" I added.
 "Oh no," she replied emphatically, "I adore you." She felt my tears, stroked my face: "I'm causing so much grief…"
 "What you're creating is love, not grief," I lied about the sorrow..
 She sighed: "Love…that's what I take with me, then."
 Her eyes were on me, more profound than ever, a desperate perspective onto the unreachable infinity she already seemed to inhabit. The best part of me felt drawn into it.
 "What do you think I should do?" I asked, hopelessly lost.
 "Anything, anything you like," she whispered urgently. "Go on with your research."
 She found the strength to tell me: "You did all you could; you went beyond the limits."
 "Love has no limit, my darling."
 "But life does," she said; "Life does."

Reflections

It was only in early January 2010 that we entered the final phase. The day came when I had to face reality, abandon the idea of leading Janine through more airports and more tests, cancel our fourth trip to NIH, and call the Hospice organization to follow the doctors' advice to keep her as comfortable as possible at home, until the end. I did call with a profound sense of personal failure.

The person they sent noticed the books on our shelves: She was a daughter of Barney Oliver, the legendary Hewlett-Packard vice-president of engineering who had helped start SETI. Her warmth and competence helped us over the difficult transition from intense treatment to acceptance of the end.

During this period Janine did remain comfortable, to her own surprise. She insisted on hearing me read to her, so I spent many precious hours by her side, relishing the rich memoirs of Abbé Mugnier (1), or last year's entries from my journal.

Those readings took us beyond time, to a special place that summed up our life. I was astonished to experience such peace, even as my eyes filled with tears. I even read to her my most private entries—desperate words I had not intended for her to hear, but it was best for her to know my feelings at the end. There would be no other opportunity.

One afternoon (January 8th) as I read to her, she suddenly asked me to pause, saying she felt "the end of the process" approaching. She begged me not to cry. She said something oddly poetic, looking at my chiseled face: "It's too hard to see all these wooden boards covered with tears."

Then we were just lying together, listening to music. I could only savor the closeness of her and the touch of her fragile hand. Again, these moments were both marvelous and deeply tragic. We were aware of Annick's and Catherine's quiet loving presence.

Of the rest of the world, there was nothing left. Grieving, unable to stay home, I went and spent an hour at Grace Cathedral in the majesty of the labyrinth before returning in the cold, indifferent evening. The

Haitian earthquake loomed over the news, with the awesome presence of death.

The following night, she was even weaker, vacillating in and out of consciousness. At 4 am on Sunday 17 January, she took her last deep breaths and expired in my arms, with the three of us embracing her. Looking at her, so peaceful in our pale green bedroom, under the well-framed gaze of Fragonard's plump angels, I could not imagine that her presence, the source of all grace and tenderness and beauty in my life, had been extinguished.

Before she was taken away, I played for her the old record that had brought us together in Paris so many years ago, Mahalia Jackson's beautiful rendition of *In the Upper Room*. She left our home at dawn. I took the elevator with the mortuary employees, staying with her as long as I could, and I watched the limo drive her away.

In the dreadful time before dawn, the City was morose, wrapped in a cold drizzle, shaken by sudden bursts of wind matching the helpless sorrow that froze my heart.

That Monday, Annick and I went on sorting papers, emptying drawers, saving small treasures, softly crying. Strong storms swept the Bay Area and lasted all week. In the gray background, only a small flame remained in my shattered life. It was the light of hope she would have wanted me to keep, but I did not have the strength to think about the future.

After that, one sad day just followed another. Our neighbor Sheila offered hospitality. People started calling, saying they'd never known a couple more in love than we were, and offering a memorial. I told them she had wanted no ritual, no flowers, and no fuss; she felt we were merely travelers who must leave no trace.

The storms went on raging over San Francisco, with stunning effects of light and color, darkness at noon, thunder and lightning, flooding and the usual threats of catastrophic landslides.

That Wednesday Annick flew home. Then I was alone, compiling dozens of letters and messages—sorrowful or warm, heart-breaking. I was left with the sense that I had failed her, that I should have been able to do just that little bit of extra research that would have saved my wife: an unrealistic emotion, given the overwhelming disease, yet the guilt lingered. There must be a reason our home was so empty, the wind howling so lugubriously, the sky so gloomy, and as the sole survivor it must be my fault. At other times, it felt like she was simply away on vacation, or recovering somewhere, and would join me again soon. Then I could tell her about all the people who had called. She would be pleased when she heard it, and I would see her smile again.

A nurse from the hospice organization called to check up on me. She commented she'd always remember how I kept reading aloud to Janine almost until the end, how beautiful she'd found it. "That hasn't changed," I told her truthfully. "I still read to her every night."

It was still raining the following Monday when I collected the black box with her ashes. Back home, in darkness only punctuated by a small candle and the dreamy lights of San Francisco, I played Beethoven's divine violin concerto, which we'd heard in Germany.

Over the web the messages kept coming, the wisest from Drs. Lee and Len Herzenberg, speaking of joy: "We are saddened to hear of her passing; still, we are glad to realize that her long ordeal has now moved to the point where she can rest, and where hopefully you can be more at peace now that you know she will not suffer any more. Being of an age where we can well see ourselves in your places, we understand the sadness with which Janine left you to live life without her, and the sadness with which you now face that life. We hope that you can also see the joy in continuing to live for the two of you, now, and to enjoy quietly all the things that you enjoyed together."

What hurt most were the absurd ideas that continued to sneak up on me and catch me unaware. I would open up an especially moving message of condolences and the first rush of my thought would be, "I must show her this wonderful tribute …" only to fall into the void, tripped by my failure to face the loss of her presence and the awful fact that for the first time in my life I held something of beauty that I would be unable to share with her.

That horrible month of January finally came to an end. I had survived the worst of it with the help of good friends: caring advice from colleagues, recommendations by doctors, a warm meeting with Douglas Trumbull and Julia, and an invitation to a guitar concert from Roger Brenner, a brief, happy interlude. Yet I was left with an immense sense of distress and vulnerability that accompanied me when I drove to Sacramento to pick up the California forms that would allow me to carry the ashes out of state and back to Normandy. To make things worse, the date was February 3rd; it would have been our 51st anniversary.

There was a break in the weather that day. Sacramento had a spring-like feeling and the road was easy, but the passenger seat was empty. The storm returned with unusual fury the next day. The letters that kept coming reopened my wounds with their caring words. I thought I was going crazy when I accomplished the formalities to gather certificates, authenticate signatures, and obtain the state's *apostille,* and the Consulate's clearances for French Customs.

The trip to Paris felt like an absurd dream; the ashes traveled in a black box sealed with a red, white, and blue ribbon and the wax seal of the French consulate. I thought Janine, wherever she was, would be surprised, or amused, to leave America under national colors.

Paris was quiet, in the icy grip of winter. Messages of condolences kept coming...some of them long emotional letters. She had touched people at many levels, even those who had never met her were shocked and saddened. Martial arts master Douglas Crosby, who had only spoken to her on the phone but knew her from my journals, wept after he heard the news.

Thérèse de Saint-Phalle assured me that the soul was immortal, that we would be together again. Yet with all my past exposure to psychical research, I did not feel her presence anywhere near me.

It seemed she was simply gone, and that was that.

I started missing her in new ways. Oddly, I especially missed the demanding routine of her illness, our early-morning drives to the labs, the long waits for medical visits, all the hardship shared so tenderly in anguish so tangible. I missed caring for her, as I did when she became weak and had to rely on my clumsy help. I still cry today for that sense of shared sorrow that swept down over us when I stopped going to work altogether and spent all my time with her, both of us knowing what would happen, accepting it, ignoring the world and embracing our love so exclusively, because we knew nothing else was left.

The trip to Normandy took the form of a sacred duty, the

accomplishment of the commitment I had made, that she would be going back to a place that held such high value for her, yet it broke beyond my emotional limits: I felt close to insanity as I waited at Saint-Lazare station. I held the package very hard against me all the way, afraid I would somehow lose it in the bustling crowds, or it might be taken from me by some unforeseen accident, or by strangers bent on stealing her. I spoke to her softly, describing to her the snowy landscape the train was traversing under a cold sky that became very clear and blue after Mantes-la-Jolie.

Caen was sunny but muddy with dirty melting snow. Annick was devastated. She had a cold and a fever. We felt helpless and sadder than we could ever express.

On February 14, I took the train to Chartres, hoping that the cathedral would heal the turmoil in my soul and help me build on the magnificent memories we had accumulated there: the stained glass of the axial window we had helped restore (but why did my artistic mentor, masterful Didier Alliou have to die so soon?). I saw the labyrinth, learned its history, and felt hope among kindred spirits who had revived it as a pure mystical path.

On Tuesday, February 23, I went to Yvetot with Annick and my son to join a small group of family and close friends. We buried her ashes as she had wanted, in the tomb where her brother Alain and her father already rested. Thankfully, the sun came out for a couple of hours, pushing aside the ugly black clouds of rain that had turned the Norman landscape to mud in previous days. I had not planned to make any speech, but Annick gave me the courage to thank the good people who had come. I reminded them that Janine's family had yielded her to me over a half-century before and was taking her back, and that her wishes were now safely fulfilled, to return to her beloved Normandy, a few feet from the church where she prayed as a little girl.

I spoke of the perils of cheating death, as we'd tried to do so hard for three years, a desperate push against elusive medical frontiers. My son and I took the train in Valognes and returned to Paris that evening. The rains came back, hard. I was drained, devastated, and confused, with a deepening awareness of her cruel absence that passed all understanding.

Notes and References

Introduction

1. Grace Paley, who died in 2007, was an American short story author, poet, teacher, and political activist.
2. Tom Dolby (born in London in January 1975) is an American filmmaker, producer, and novelist.
3. Thanks to Professor Jeff Kripal, in the Department of Religion in the School of the Humanities at Rice University, who founded the Archives of the Impossible, I was able to preserve trusted sources of veridical data through donation of many research files, including those I used in the present work.

Part Seventeen: Athanor Transition

1. The three Euro-America Funds, raised from European, Japanese, and Canadian financial institutions, insurance companies, banks, and retirement funds, invested in over 60 high-technology and medical startups in the US and Europe between 1987 and the first decade of the present century. We specialized in early-stage venture capital, creating a number of modern enterprises.
2. Mercury Interactive, a US-Israeli company, revolutionized software quality control and other domains. It went public on Nasdaq and was purchased by Hewlett-Packard for 4.5 billion dollars, one of half a dozen "unicorns" we helped create.
3. The files of APRO (Aerial Phenomena Research Organization) were donated to two individual researchers in 1988 following the death of founders Coral and Jim Lorenzen.
4. Dr. Douglas Engelbart (1925-2013) was an information science pioneer. Working at the Stanford Research Institute in Menlo Park, California, he assembled a team that pioneered in computer-human interaction, notably through the Augmentation Research Center (SRI-ARC). Several inventions that are common now, such as the computer mouse, came from his work, but his major contributions were in advanced software architectures for human communication.

5. Robert Bigelow, based in Las Vegas, Nevada, is an American space entrepreneur who has used his real estate wealth to finance advanced research in spacecraft design and habitability. He founded the National Institute for Discovery Science (NIDS) in 1995. It ceased activity in 2004.
6. Colonel John B. Alexander, born in 1937, commanded Special Forces teams in Vietnam and Thailand, among other important assignments. As a retired infantry officer, he is best known for his work in the development of "non-lethal weapons" at Los Alamos National Laboratory.
7. Dr. Peter Sturrock, born in England in 1924, served as professor of applied physics at Stanford University. He is the author of five books on solar physics, astrophysics, and plasma theory, as well as over 200 publications in related fields, including the study of UFOs. He pioneered research on isotopic analysis of unidentified materials related to the phenomenon. He also served as the founder of the Society for Scientific Exploration in 1982. I worked with him on astrophysics at Stanford in 1970 and 1971 and our collaboration continued after that date.
8. The "Utah Ranch," now known as "Skinwalker Ranch," was bought by Robert Bigelow in 1995. Located near Ballard, Utah, the 512-acre property has been the site of numerous anomalous phenomena, including bizarre animals. It served as an observation and research outpost for NIDS until it was sold to a new owner, Mr. Brandon Fugal, in 2016.
9. Dr. Peter M. Banks, who began his academic career at Stanford and later served at the Office of Naval Research in Washington, D.C., held positions as professor of physics at University of California, San Diego, and Stanford before moving to the University of Michigan as chairman of the Engineering Department in 1989. A member of the JASON group, he is an active advisor on many space projects. He joined me and legal expert Graham Burnette in founding the Red Planet Capital fund for NASA in 2007.
10. The Haravilliers case of January 10, 1998, involves a remarkable series of observations of a flying disk by five retired men in different locations, plus a farm worker. They were getting ready for a hunting party at 7 am in a wooded area where they used an isolated lodge. The object induced an unexplained loss of memory in the men and disappeared as it flew low over the forest.
11. In various American tall tales and uncontrolled rumors, the Moon has been said to be used by Aliens as a staging area to monitor the Earth and occasionally to abduct its inhabitants.

12. Jean-Jacques Velasco, born in 1946, is an engineer at the CNES (French Space Agency) who served with courage and dedication as the head of its UFO project (1983 to June 2004).
13. Luisah Teish, an African-American woman of Yoruba ancestry, was born in New Orleans. Her book *Jambalaya* (published by Harper in 1988) is considered a classic in modern ritual literature. She is a passionate teacher, writer, and leader of traditional communities in California and beyond.
14. "Roger Brenner" was the pseudonym I used for our friend Ron Brinkley, who was part of many research trips in California and New Mexico. He was killed by a careless driver on his way to his work in Albuquerque in August 2018.
15. The MEDEA program was led by "a taciturn group of about 60 scientists in academia and industry who advise the nation's intelligence agencies on the use of secret data to study the Earth." The name stood for Measurement of Earth Data for Environmental Analysis. Established under Al Gore in 1993, the controversial program was shut down in the George W. Bush administration, restarted in 2010, and concluded in 2015. (William J. Broad, "US Will Deploy its Spy Satellites on Nature Mission," *New York Times*, 27 Nov. 1995. Also, *Nature*, 22 Sept. 2011, "Shared Intelligence.")
16. "Carlos Allende" or "Carl Allen" was the name or pseudonym of a man who claimed that a destroyer active in WW2, the USS *Eldridge*, had become invisible during physical experiments. The claim has been thoroughly exposed, but it has remained one of the cherished hoaxes of American ufology.
17. Frederick R. Adler, born in New York on April 4, 1926, and deceased on January 24, 2022, was an important contributor to the structure and practice of venture capital in the US. Data General, Intersil, Daisy Systems, and Life Technologies were some of his major successes. I worked with him as a member of the General Partner of the three Euro-America Funds.
18. The late Gilbert Payan, "the man in the shadows" according to Dr. J-P Petit, was a graduate of Ecole Polytechnique and an adviser to various high-technology groups in France, notably through the research branch of the French Defense ministry.
19. Dr. Christopher ("Kit") Green, MD, a graduate of Northwestern University, served for many years at the CIA Life Sciences division (1969-85) before joining the General Motors corporation as CTO for Asia-Pacific region. Joining the Wayne School of Medicine as Assistant

Dean, he continues to serve on committees of the US and the Chinese Academy of Sciences. He researches brain imaging and unexplained injuries of personnel exposed to unidentified phenomena.

20. Jack Parsons, born Marvel Whiteside Parsons in L.A. (2 October 1914) was an American rocket engineer and a principal founder of the Jet Propulsion Laboratory in Pasadena. A follower of Aleister Crowley's "Thelema" magical system, he died under mysterious circumstances in an explosion at his home on 17 June 1952.
21. George Kuchar (1942-2011) was an American underground film director and video artist. He taught cinema at the San Francisco Art Institute during the time when Janine and I knew him, and we became close friends. He is survived by his equally gifted twin brother, Mike.
22. The Genopole is a French institution for research into biology and medicine, based south of Paris in the town of Evry. Its campus gathers advanced laboratories, biological enterprises, and startup companies.
23. In June 2009, Dr. Hal Puthoff did a series of experiments at Wisconsin University to test the hypothesis that the structure of the hydrogen atom was related to zero-point energy. The experiments were inconclusive, according to Hal.
24. SEPRA (Service d'Etudes sur les Phénomènes Rares Aérospatiaux) replaced the GEPAN in November 1988. Jean-Jacques Velasco continued as director, based in Toulouse. SEPRA was in turn replaced by GEIPAN (Groupe d'Etudes et d'Information sur les Phénomènes Aérospatiaux non Identifiés) in 2005. GEIPAN is still active as of 2022.
25. Dr. Marcello Truzzi (1935-2003) was one of the founders of the skeptical "Committee for the Scientific Investigation of Claims of the Paranormal" (CSICOP). He also founded a journal called *The Zetetic Scholar*. In later years he accused CSICOP of "pseudo-skepticism" and exposed its antiscientific positions taken *a priori*.
26. The "Chapin Case" in Northern California involved an older couple who owned a property in the Klamath valley where they were looking for gold ore. They saw an object land on their claim on three occasions and eventually reported it. I visited their property several times and instrumented it with an automated camera.
27. FUFOR (Fund for UFO Research) was founded in 1979 in Maryland. It ceased activity in about 2011. During its active years, it counted Don Berliner and Bruce Maccabee as active members. It awarded grants totaling $700,000 to various organizations, researching topics from MJ-12 to the history of Project Blue Book.
28. Mr. Dominique Weinstein served as a distinguished member of the

French DST (Défense de la Sûreté du Territoire), similar to the FBI, until his retirement in 2017. He is the author of the first comprehensive catalogue of officially recorded pilot observations of UFOs.
29. Ubatuba (Brazil) is the site of an unexplained observation and recovery of material from a UFO that exploded over the beach in 1957. A Brazilian researcher, Dr. Olavo Fontes, obtained several samples that he transmitted to the APRO organization in Arizona for further analysis. In turn, some of the material was turned over to Professor Sturrock at Stanford University, and then to me.
30. Willamette Pass, Oregon, was the site of a claimed UFO photograph in November 1966 that was eventually exposed as a hoax by Irwin Wieder. (*Journal of Scientific Exploration* Vol.7, No.2, 1993)
31. Mr. Paul Bennewitz (1927-2003) was an engineer and businessman who built electronic measurement devices for the US Air Force in Albuquerque, New Mexico, through his company, Thunder Scientific. In about 1979 he became convinced that he was recording signals and observing objects of extraterrestrial origin, without realizing that what he detected was US classified technology. He became the target of a sophisticated disinformation project involving Bill Moore, Agent Rick Doty, and even Dr. Hynek, to convince him that he was in fact observing and photographing UFOs. The stress reportedly drove him to near-insanity, as I can testify, and he died a broken man in 2003.
32. CyberIQ was a startup high technology company in the Euro-America portfolio.
33. *Basic Patterns in UFO Observations* (co-authored with Claude Poher) AIAA paper 75-42, delivered at the 13th Aerospace Sciences Meeting, Pasadena, CA. January 20-22, 1975.
34. Book review of *UFOs and Abductions* by Dr. David Jacobs (2000). *Journal of Scientific Exploration*, 2001.
35. Aimé Michel (1919-1992) was an erudite French writer, radio engineer, and philosopher of spiritual and cultural research. He was a friend of Jean Cocteau and Pierre Schaeffer, and a close collaborator of Jacques Bergier and Louis Pauwels, the founders of *Planète*. His book, *Mystérieux Objets Célestes*, published in 1958, revolutionized research in ufology. It encouraged me to apply computer techniques to conduct research into the phenomenon.
36. French engineer René Hardy, a scientist with numerous credentials in civilian and military aeronautics, had a long-term interest in UFOs. He died mysteriously on June 12, 1975 at 7:45 am while at home in the "Claret" area of Toulon. He had stated to colleagues that he was close to

explaining the extra-dimensionality of UFOs with a scientific theory.
37. The *Cometa* report was reportedly based on the earlier document mentioned here.
38. Gulf Breeze was the site of a series of UFO hoaxes in November 1987 that created much excitement among American ufologists. The photos of the "UFO" resulted in the publication a popular book prefaced by Dr. Bruce Maccabee.
39. The NARCAP organization, dedicated to the investigation of UFO reports by pilots, was created by Dr. Richard Haines in 1999. See narcap.org.
40. Carlo Bartalini, opera singer and artist, was our neighbor and close friend until his death in San Francisco in January 2001.
41. "Hilltop Curve" is the name I gave to the distribution of UFO reports from the public as a function of their degree of what Hynek used to call "strangeness."
42. Dr. Gregory Chaitin is an IBM expert in mathematical logic. He is the author of three books in which he argues that mathematics should be viewed as an experimental rather than an exact science.
43. Paul Hill was a well-respected scientist who had a UFO sighting in 1950. He later acted as an informal clearinghouse for reports at NASA. His important book, *Unconventional Flying Objects*, was published after his death. It argued that UFOs follow the laws of physics and that their observed behavior can be explained by current science.
44. Vice-Admiral Thomas R. Wilson was born March 4, 1946. He became the director of the Defense Intelligence Agency in 1999 and held this post until 2022.
45. *The Four Elements of Financial Alchemy* was a guide on financial investment I published in 2001 through Ten Speed Press. Subtitle: A new formula for personal prosperity.
46. Mr. Gilbert Payan. See entry (**18**).
47. "AFFA," which was supposed to be an interplanetary entity communicating through a medium, was taken seriously enough by some officers in the US Navy (including Admiral Herbert Bain Knowles) for them to conduct a series of séances in which the entity announced the arrival of a UFO, instructing those in attendance to "go to the window." In a stunning development, they all saw an unknown object in the sky, while radars inexplicably went down in that section of Washington. Mr. Art Lundahl confirmed the event to me in person.
48. James Westwood was retired from a classified unit that designed fake documents on behalf of the US in order to disinform foreign intelligence

agents. He was also an expert in the analysis of Soviet documents obtained by US Intelligence.
49. Dr. Federico Faggin is an American physicist and engineer of Italian origin who co-invented the microprocessor as the leader of the Intel 4004 chip design team. He was born in Vicenza on December 1, 1941, and emigrated to the US in 1968.
50. This "secret project" refers to the statements attributed to Admiral Wilson, later discussed in the famous memo by Dr. Eric Davis. See entry (44).

Part Eighteen: September Eleven

1. The book in question was *The Heart of the Internet: An Insider's View of the Origin and Promise of the On-Line Revolution.* (Hampton Roads, 2003)
2. Our friend Oberon (Tim Otter Zell) was writing a study of the Gaia concept of the oneness of the Earth. We discussed the fact that it derived from an earlier concept called "Le Géon," first introduced in France in the early 20th century.
3. My weekly column in *Le Figaro* ran from June 1997 to October 1998 and again (by popular demand?) from September 2002 to December 2003.
4. Dr. Colm Kelleher's article had to do with DNA and enlightenment. Testing the transcription levels of transposons in the blood cells of individuals pursuing meditation might lead to better understanding of near-death experiences, or close encounters with UFOs.
5. Dr. Gregory Chaitin has published three books on the nature of mathematics, namely: *The Limits of Mathematics* (1997), *The Unknowable* (1999), and *Exploring Randomness* (2001). All three were published by Springer-Verlag in London.
6. Howard Cross, a metallurgist, was head of a group at Battelle that wrote *Project Blue Book Special Report No. 14*. At the time of the Robertson Panel, he sent a classified letter (which I later referred to as the "Pentacle Memorandum"), insisting that more research was necessary before such a panel could be useful. His recommendation was ignored by the Air Force (under pressure from the CIA, the real organizer of the panel).
7. Dr. Brenda Denzler, the author of *Lure of the Edge* (University of California Press), received her doctorate from Duke University and works an as editor.
8. *Kleinsteins* (or "Acme Klein bottles") was the name given by gifted

physicist and computer scientist Dr. Cliff Stoll to his series of beautiful glass vessels that were folded in space (as the 3D equivalent of a Moebius strip). They can hold a liquid, although their volume, naturally, is zero.

9. Heinrich Cornelius Agrippa (1486-1535) is the most influential writer of Renaissance esoterica, and of Western occultism. His book is entitled *De Occulta Philosophia*.

10. *The Bureau and the Mole: The Unmasking of Robert Philip Hanssen, The Most Dangerous Double Agent in FBI History*, by David A. Vise. (Grove Atlantic, 2002).

11. Project Jenifer (or "Project Azorian") had to do with the "impossible" recovery of a modern Soviet submarine that had sunk to the bottom of the Pacific in 1974.

12. The book *Mort d'un Général* by John Ralston Saul (Seuil 1977) discusses the probability that General Ailleret was assassinated by a group of French rivals through a technical sabotage operation on the aircraft that brought him back to France from Réunion Island in 1988. The book is a thinly-veiled novel, where some names have been changed.

13. I gave the name "Pentacle Memo" to a secret document (a classified letter) asking the government to postpone the review of UFO files by the Robertson Panel. See entry (**6**).

14. The names of Thérèse, Caroline, Henriette, Louise, and Marie belong to the bells in the sublime *carillon* of the church of Saint Sulpice, our neighbor in Paris.

15. The Vivendi debacle happened in July 2002 when the conglomerate assembled by Jean-Marie Messier was unable to refinance its monumental amount of debt.

16. Mobilian, Inc. was one of the startup companies in which Euro-America III invested. It was technically successful but did not grow fast enough in the ebullient market for advanced telephony. Its technology and patents, however, were viable enough to be acquired by Intel.

17. Victor Sheymov, whom I met when I visited his startup company (Invicta), died aged 73 on December 6, 2019. Sheymov was the inventor of the "variable cyber coordinates" method of information security.

18. Victor Sheymov is prominently featured in the book *The Bureau and the Mole* by David A. Vise.

19. Jacques Bergier (possibly born as Yakov Mikhailovitch Berger on 8 August 1912 in Odessa), was a chemist and prolific writer who served as a member of an early team of French scientific spies during World

War Two. After the war, he was an editor of *Planète* and a prominent publisher of science fiction and other works. He died in Paris on 23 November 1978.
20. *The Strange case of Vintrix Polbarton* by Ian Marshall was published in 1929 by Thomas Nelson. Curiously, the French version published on 21 October 1931, *Le Docteur Frégalle*, bears a fictitious author's name of "Oswald Dallas," as I was able to verify.
21. Norton Air Force Base, where video and movie archives of the military were kept for research and for the frequent use by Hollywood studios, served for many years as the depository of films showing actual UFOs, according to statements made to Dr. Hynek by the site managers.
22. The ThyoPro Pharmaceuticals Corporation filed on 13 September 2002 in the State of New York. It was dissolved on 27 October 2010.
23. Robert Kingery Buell (1908-1971) was also the author of the books *Wild White Wings*, *My Land of Dreams*, and *California Stepping Stones*.
24. Abraham Maslow and Anthony Sutich were the founders of Transpersonal Psychology.
25. *Firestorm* is the title of an excellent biography of Dr. James E. MacDonald (1920-1971) by Mrs. Ann Druffel, published in 2006 by Granite Publishing.
26. "UMMO" is the name of a fictitious cosmic organization of planets. The UMMO hoax seems to have been created by an Intelligence group in Spain, rather than by an amateur organization, but this has not been positively established.
27. The SOBEPS organization (formed in 1971 in Belgium) was an active, well-managed amateur UFO research group that ceased activity in December 2007.
28. LBOs, or "leveraged buyouts," are a common form of financial "exit" for new companies when acquired by a larger company.
29. Dr. Eric Davis & Admiral Wilson controversy: See the entry for 2 October 2003.
30. The Perception Technology Corporation "designs, manufactures and markets voice processing products." Curiously, there are 15 companies listed by this name in various states. The earliest one was listed in Massachusetts in December 1968.
31. Hopkinsville, Kentucky, was the site of a famous 1955 incident in which a family experienced a fantastic attack on their farm, coming from small creatures that were able to "float" as they moved and were impervious to bullets.
32. The Robertson Panel was convened in January 1953, assembling leading

physicists to review the best data extant in the Air Force files.
33. Vico cigarette: There are other cases in the files, in which witnesses were given food or a smoke. But the parallel is even more striking in a "Magonia" context, since the pattern is a standard one in the fairy tradition. Ancient books recommend refusing (politely) offers of food or drink from fairies when one is abducted by them.

Part Nineteen: Pacific Heights

1. *"Cometa"* is the name of a French document authored by retired military officers, ostensibly written for President Chirac, regarding the extent of the UFO phenomenon. It blamed the US for withholding its data. It turned out that the authors had received no such Presidential request, and the name of the main author (Gilbert Payan) was hidden from readers. Oddly advertised as a "secret study," it was printed and distributed by a popular magazine tabloid. See reference (**37**) above.
2. Mr. James Westwood. See entry (**48**) above in Part 17.
3. The "Lead Mask mystery" has to do with the death of two Brazilian technicians on 17 August 1966.They climbed the "Morro do Vintem" peak near Rio in anticipation of a meeting with supposed extraterrestrials but were found dead at the site, wearing crude masks made of lead.
4. Nanogram Devices, Inc. was a Silicon Valley nanotechnology company in which I invested through the Euro-America venture funds. The company was later acquired by a Japanese conglomerate.
5. The files of Tina Choate and Brian Myers included the massive body of documents (estimated number: 15,000) they had received from the APRO organization developed by Carol and Jim Lorenzen following the death of the founders, much to the chagrin of competing ufologists.
6. *The Golden Builders,* by Tobias Churton, published in 2004, discusses the works of Alchemists, Rosicrucians, and the first Freemasons in "a breathtaking span of detailed research."
7. Vandenberg (Southern California) is the West Coast equivalent of Cape Canaveral.
8. The drug plane is supposed to have been detected through its infrared signature only. My research uncovered first-hand information conflicting with this statement. Pilots who were debriefed shortly after the flight later reported privately that several unknown objects were involved and were seen visually. This fact was never published.
9. Testimonies (including mine) given at the Al Gore Congressional Hearings, along with the strong recommendations of the Panel, had been

published in the Library of Congress document: *Congressional Testimony on Information Technology for Emergency Management.* Washington: U.S. Govt. Printing Office 1984. Congressional Research Service (CRS) report for the Subcommittee on Investigations and Oversight, Committee on Science and Technology, U.S. House of Representatives, Ninety-eight Congress, second session, Serial HH. Softbound, dated October 9, 1984. (Note: Introduction by Al Gore. With a letter from McManis on behalf of the CIA, and lists of participants.) My testimony covered my work related to crisis management and nuclear safety, since we were linking emergency response teams in six countries.
10. The Chinese River, known as "Huangpu Jiang" or Yellow Bank River, is a tributary of the Yangtse River ("Chang Jiang").
11. Dr. Kevin Starr's book, *Coast of Dreams* (Vintage) was hailed by critics as a "vivid, precise and astute" probing of the possible collapse of the California dream in the years 1990-2003. The title may have been an *homage* to Robert Kingery Buell's earlier book *My Land of Dreams*.
12. Dr. Patrick Bailey was a senior executive with Lockheed at the time of writing this book.
13. "Secrets of the Milky Way," *New Scientist,* 14 May 2005.
14. Velasco, Jean-Jacques, *OVNI: 60 ans de Désinformation.* Co-authored with François Parmentier. Preface by Vladimir Volkoff. (Le Rocher, 22 April 2004).
15. My first meeting with Director Stephen Spielberg, as recounted by Marcia Seligson in *New West* (May 1977), clarified the facts around the French character in *Close Encounters of the Third Kind.*
16. The PEAR Lab (Princeton Engineering Anomalies Research) "flourished for nearly three decades under the aegis of Princeton" and closed, "having completed its study of the interaction of human consciousness with sensitive physical systems." See pearlab.icrl.org.
17. Bertrand Méheust published this correspondence with Aimé Michel in 2008 under the title *Apocalypse Molle* (Aldane). It covers the years 1978 to 1990.
18. The Clearstream Affair was a French political scandal in the runup to the 2007 presidential election won by Nicolas Sarkozy. The name refers to a Luxembourg bank alleged to have aided French politicians and companies in evading taxes. It also helped them launder money arising from bribes surrounding the 1991 sale of six frigates to Taiwan. (*Wikipedia*).
19. Webster Hubbell, assistant attorney general under President Clinton,

mentions the topic in his book *Friends in High Places* (William Morrow, 1997).
20. *Heraclitean Fire: Sketches From a Life before Nature*, by Erwin Chargaff: Rockefeller University Press. June 1978.
21. The China-Berlin route of Lufthansa provides a remarkable illustration of the early development of international air travel. The books by Swedish writer Sven Hedin (particularly *To the Forbidden Land* and his *Trans-Himalaya: Discoveries and Adventures in Tibet*) are essential to understanding the context of the Roerich observation of a supposed early UFO.
22. The group assembled by Colonel John Alexander was restricted to military and intelligence personnel with Top-Secret clearances and above, which constrained the information they reviewed. Predictably, they concluded there was no hidden project—and in particular, no hidden hardware—available to the United States after more than 50 years of UFO investigation. Any such secret would probably have been classified at a higher level.

Restriction of high-level discussion to a narrow group of qualified but specialized individuals has been a hallmark of American approaches to the problem, and an important factor in their ultimate, failures since the 1950 era.
23. Oberon Zell-Ravenheart was born on 30 November 1942 in Saint Louis. He is a prolific and careful neo-Pagan writer, speaker, and founder of the Church of All Worlds.
24. The Fermi paradox simply has to do with the fact that no sign of Alien life has been detected, while such civilizations should be abundant in the galactic neighborhood, given modern telescopes and radio techniques.
25. Madame de la Tour du Pin was born in 1770 in a family of old aristocracy, and barely escaped the "Terreur" of the 1789 French Revolution, eventually fleeing to America with her family. Her *Memoirs* are remarkable for the accuracy of her reports and the depth of her understanding of historical events.
26. Mrs. Ruann Ernst Pengov, one of the early *Grandes Dames* of Silicon Valley, served as one of the Trustees in NASA's Red Planet Capital fund. She was a department head at HP for much of her brilliant career.
27. Jérome Garrido is a contemporary artist born and living in Paris. He "re-purposes" fragments of old writings that are pasted into compositions where yellow and especially red colors dominate.
28. The MEDEF is the organization representing the *patrons* (leaders) of French industry.

Part Twenty: Labyrinths

1. The Psychomanteum is a small, enclosed area where a subject can sit in front of a mirror angled so it does not reflect any object (and is therefore available for unique visions). It is used for meditation and the evocation of spirits or other entities. It was first used by Raymond Moody, originator of the term Near-Death Experience.
2. NASA venture plans were designed over four years, in response to the need for innovative devices and procedures in future missions of increasing sophistication. They also responded to the need to finance inventions that could benefit society, such as the "Alter-G" device my partners and I financed under the Red Planet Capital fund in 2005.
3. Dr. Jeffrey J. Kripal chaired the Department of Religion in the School of the Humanities at Rice University when I first met him. His books include *Kali's Child, Esalen, Authors of the Impossible, The Serpent's Gift*. At this writing, he is Associate Dean in the School of the Humanities.
4. Oxantium Ventures is based in Washington, D.C., with activities in Austin, Texas, and other places. Mr. Lester Hyman is listed as the firm's principal.
5. Abuses were reported throughout the word as a result of the US government condoning torture as a tool against terrorism during the years covered by this book. This obviously went contrary to the US military's traditions of high standards and the Rule of Law. It ended up feeding terrorism itself.
6. "Flashgun," mentioned in *New Scientist* (19 June 2008) and *Science* (DOI: 10:1126/science.1157846), among other places, is an optical development designed to disable human opponents. It emits an extremely rapid, well-focused wave of differently colored light pulses.
7. Dr. Claude Poher, the founder of GEPAN within the French Space Agency in 1977, was born in 1936. His doctorate is in astrophysics. Following his retirement from CNES in 1996, he continues his personal research into the physics of gravitation.
8. Shielding (of high-frequency quantum noise) may be relevant to experiments in antigravity.
9. The Markovic Affair during the Pompidou era was a major disruption in French political life in 1968, following the discovery of his body on October 1st. Stephan Markovic was an employee of actor Alain Delon and the frequent organizer of "special soirées" during which compromising photographs had been taken. One of them claimed

(falsely) to show Mr. Pompidou's wife.
10. Alan Holt, who retired from NASA after 50 years of service (Apollo lunar missions, Skylab, and the ISS), holds an MS in astrophysics from the University of Houston (1979).
11. Dr. Green worked in China during this period on a joint project. He also served as a member of the Chinese Academy of Sciences.
12. BDC is the Business Development Bank of Canada, while FTQ stands for Fonds des Travailleurs du Québec, a retirement fund for union workers based in Montréal.
13. *Life Dreams*, by Professor Douglas Price-Williams of UCLA, is subtitled: "Field Notes on Psi, Synchronicity and Shamanism." (Pioneer Imprints, 2008).
14. The Vallée-Davis model was first presented at the international forum on "Science, Religion and Consciousness" in Porto, Portugal, October 2003. The actual title was: "Incommensurability, Orthodoxy and the Physics of High Strangeness: a 6-layer model for Anomalous Phenomena."
15. Vice-Admiral Edward Burkhalter (born in Roanoke in 1928) served on nuclear submarines and was later named deputy director of Naval Intelligence. A close friend of William J. Casey, he died in 2020 of a heart attack. He was 91.
16. MUFON representatives included: 1. International Director James Carrion, from Colorado, who had served in the military and ran a small computer support company; 2. Jan Harzan, former IBM manager from Costa Mesa, who reportedly followed Dr. Greer's research philosophy; and 3. Chuck Modlin, a retired engineer from Lawrence Livermore with experience in radar and missiles "and good Midwestern common sense.")

Reflections

1. Abbé Mugnier (1859-1944) kept a diary of sacerdotal life over 60 years, during which he confessed duchesses and notable literary figures in Paris. A frequent guest in the best salons of Paris, he was always dressed in the rough clothes and square shoes of a country curate. A man of remarkable style, insight, and kindness, he stated that Hell did exist, "but there isn't anybody in it."

INDEX OF NAMES

A

AAAS (Amer. Assoc. for Adv. of Science), 180
AAWSAP (Adv. Aerosp. Weapon Syst. App. prog), 412, 426
Abelio, Raymond (Georges Soulès), 302
Abramson, general -, 201
Abu Dhabi, 441
Accuray Systems, Inc., 366, 483
Ackroyd, Dan, 119
Adamski, George, 42, 48, 153
Addington, David, 341
Adler, Frederick, 22, 24, 54, 103, 126, 268, 307, 382, 462, 489
Adler, Dr. John, 366, 367, 373
Aelita, Queen of Mars, 494
Aerospace Corporation, 232
AFFA, 83
Afghanistan, 106, 111, 120
AFIO, 204, 227
AFOSI, 272, 472
AFOSR, 388
Agobard (Saint -), 86, 87
Agrippa, Cornelius, 124
AIAA, 53, 313, 325
AIDS, 382, 384, 489
Ailleret, General Charles -, 140, 150
Airbus Corp., 356, 396
Akhenaton, 110, 111
Al Qaida, 224
Albuquerque, 319Alcatraz, 66
Aldridge, Pete, 187-189, 197
Aldrin, Buzz, 349
Aleph Zero, 67
Alexander, Col. John, 19, 23, 34, 67, 148-151 (Fig.5), 201, 229, 230, 260, 299, 308
Alexander, Victoria, 34, 88

Algrin, 44, 239
Alintel, 232, 235
Alix, Stéphane, 304
All Honorable Men, 504
Allah, 85, 181
Allende, Carlos, 24
Allin, Mark W., 358
Allioux, Didier, 317, 323, 346, 417, 506, 508, 522
Almaden, CA, 308
Alter-G, Inc., 337
Altschuler, Dr., 118
Alzheimer's disease, 182, 186, 423
Amara, Dr. Roy, 387
Ames, see NASA-Ames
Annick (Saley), see Thoby, Jeanne
Antébi, Elizabeth, 91
Antony, France, 31
Apple Computers, 9, 62
APRO, 12, 168, 231
Area51, 54, 78, 300, 462, 466
Arenal, 139, 142
Arisem Corp., 11
Ariane rocket, 349
Army Science Board, 204
Arnold, Kenneth, 345, 357
Arnold, Scott, 394
Arnould, Jacques, 363
ARPA, 63, 168, 243 – see DARPA
Arquila, John, 238
Art Magic, 124, 137
Artress, Lauren, 387
Asahi, 84
Ashcroft, John David, 175
Astrium Corp., 349; 355, 444
Attali, Jacques, 31
Aubeck, Chris, 132, 138, 206, 209, 210 (Fig.7), 224, 256, 267, 297, 303, 306, 322, 338, 381, 416
Auque, François, 349, 363
Aviation Week, 487

Index

Axelrod, 21, 218
Ayn Rand, 244
Azhazha, Vladimir, 84

B

BAASS, 426, 428, 439, 442, 446, 447, 450, 455, 459, 460, 464, 466, 471, 473-4, 476-7, 481-2, 484-6, 492-3, 495-6, 497-8, 501, 503, 506, 509, 514
Baghdad, 178, 181-183, 194, 233
Bailey, Patrick, 171, 180, 264
Balland publishers, 184, 211
Ballester-Olmos, V-J, 416
Balzar, 91
Banks, Dr. Peter, 20, 23, 46, 74, 78, 102, 136, 152, 154, 238, 273, 306, 309, 320, 321, 340, 342, 345, 384, 394, 413, 441, 455, 505, 515
Baran, Paul, 119, 121, 346
Barbarin, Cardinal -, 260
Barrascud, Gérard, 424
Bartalini, Carlo, 65, 66
Basiago, Andrew D., 242
Battelle Memorial Institute, 116, 121, 147, 199, 213, 502
Bayrou, François, 97, 350-351
Beaverton, OR, 68
Bechtel Corporation, 198-199
Beckman, Fred, 70, 192, 242, 375
Becton-Dickinson, 510
Beijing, China, 84, 255, 430
Bekkum, Gary, 54, 270, 478, 481
Belfond, Jean-Daniel, 272, 278, 284
Belgium, 20, 41, 117, 132
Bell, Art, 72, 273
Belmont, CA, 26, 138, 215, 279, 375, 484
Benedetti, Arnaud, 271, 276-277, 313
Benedict-XVI (Pope -), 328
Benford, Gregory, 40
Bensoussan, Dr. Alain, 170, 236
Bennett, Colin, 153, 358
Bennion, Christa, 128, 129, 297
Bennewitz, Paul, 51, 430
Bentwaters, UK, 91
Beren, Peter, 357
Bergier, Jacques, 189, 423, 434
Berkeley, CA, 67, 403, 458, 511
Big Brother, 20
Bigelow, Robert, 14, 19, 33, 48, 54, 57, 63, 66, 80, 83 114, 116, 117, 135, 146, 193, 204, 217, 226, 228, 229, 230, 234, 295-297, 308, 319, 375, 387, 412, 426, 448, 450, 452, 458, 461, 467, 475, 477-9, 481, 486, 491, 496-7, 503
Bin Laden, Osama, 116, 149
Bingham, Jeff, 340
Bishop, Greg, 285, 287
Bishop Pike, 490
Blackburn, Dr. Ron, 201, 204, 205, 274
Blades, Joe, 103
Blair, Tony, 464
Blasband, Richard, 242
Blue Book, 20, 53, 213, 264, 463, 466
Blue Border, 23
Blue, Linden, 384
BNP-Paribas Bank, 456
Bodega Bay, 36, 49, 56
Body Snatchers in the Desert, 285
Boëdec, Jean-François, 354
Boeing Corp., 81, 329, 342, 349, 352, 378, 382, 426
Boitte, Franck, 195
Bokias, Prof., 11, 58, 71, 91, 127, 163, 172, 184, 278, 337, 354, 508
Borges, Jorge-Luis, 14, 358

Boris Godouvov, 301, 449
Boston Globe, 202
Boudier, Alain, 155, 162, 356
Boudier, Aurélie, 444
Bourdais, Gildas, 74
Bourgeois, Denis, 184
Bourget Air show, 356, 492
Bowart, Walter, 274
Bozhich, 180
Brain Trust, 274
Brasserie Lipp, Paris, 156, 162, 262, 310
Brazil, 21, 138, 218, 225, 247-248, 267-268, 290, 294, 459, 460, 464-6, 472, 475, 478, 485, 488, 492, 496, 497, 502, 507, 509
Breck, Ren, 12, 68, 191
Breen, Walter, 243, 244
Briggs, Michael, 98, 244, 287, 290
Brinkley, Ron (alias Brenner, Roger), 22, 23, 30, 56, 57, 151 (Fig.6), 217, 520
Brookfield Fund, 443
Brown, T. Townsend, 149, 299
Brownstein, Neil, 168
Brummel, Antoine, 289
Brune (Father -), 59
Brunei, 24, 85, 122
Bryant, Colonel Joseph -, 272
Buell, Robert K., 192
Burkhalter (Colonel -), 228, 466, 468
Burnette, Graham, 12, 30, 41, 47, 51, 58, 62, 71, 79, 92, 199, 309, 311-312, 358, 365
Bush, Pres. George W., 57, 62, 64, 85, 175, 200, 227, 256, 259, 333, 436
Bush, Vannevar, 121, 224

C

CAC40, 441, 451
Cache City, UT, 75
Cache Logan, 118
Caisse des Dépôts, 38, 62, 240
Callahan, John, 169
Calsters, 30, 245
Calvert, Bill, 267, 295
Camp Detrick, MD, 182
Canada, 138, 184, 186, 208, 439, 475, 499
Capella data warehouse system, 431, 455, 450, 455-6, 459, 459, 465, 466, 472, 476, 478, 482, 483, 486, 488, 509
Carcosa, 87
Cardano, Girolame, 8
Cardozo, Joao, 179, 180
Carlisle Group, 149, 291
Carlucci, Franck, 149
Carpenter, John, 34
Carter (sheriff Darius -), 75, 76
Carter, John, 29
Carteret (NJ), 118
Cash-Landrum incident, 91, 300
Casimir force, 232, 420
Cassilda (song of -), 87
Cayce, Edgar, 298, 306
Cerf, Dr. Vint, 164, 168
Chaitin, Gregory, 67, 117
Chalker, Bill, 473
Chaos Telecom, Inc., 154
Chapman, Philip, 126
Chargaff, Dr. Erwin, 322-323
Chartrand, Robert, 245-246, 250, 287
Chartres (cathedral), 275, 305, 324, 326, 334 (Fig.13), 522
Chatelain, Maurice, 105
Chauvin, Prof. Rémy, 59, 515
Cheney, Dick, 175, 341, 394
Cheng, Edgar, 291-292

Childress, David Hatcher, 56
Chile, 47, 53, 244, 508
China, 182, 230, 238, 253-255
Chinavest, 253, 254, 291
Chirac, Jacques (Pres.), 140, 221, 222
Choate, Tina, 161, 168, 231
CIA, 66, 70, 95, 131, 164, 185, 195, 213, 238, 400, 470, 479, 481, 506
CINCLANT, 45
CIPA, 28, 69, 73, 74, 135
Cisco, Inc.60, 78, 157
Clark, Jerome ("Jerry"), 473
Clearstream scandal, 314
Clérebaut, Michel, 353
Clinton, Pres. Bill, 63, 200
Clinton, Hilary, 394
Close Encounters of the Third Kind, 393
CNES, 89, 124, 127, 133, 152, 156, 160, 170, 215, 223, 236, 262, 276, 277, 301, 313, 344, 347, 354, 363, 388, 396, 408, 460, 492, 507
CNN, 84, 85, 106
CNRI, 186
CNRS, 277
Coast Guard (US), 161
Cochet, Yves (Minister), 128
Col de Vence (France), 162
Colares, 459, 464, 466, 472, 478, 498, 501
Colby, William Egan, 196, 231
Coleman, Loren, 192, 228
Columbia (shuttle accident), 174
COM-21, Inc., 302
Cometa report, 61, 74, 81, 94, 223, 239, 245, 338, 363, 444, 507
Confrontations, 42
Congress (US), 47, 180, 191, 203, 436, 439

Congressional Hearings, 19
Contras, in Latin America, 36
Cook, Nick, 258
Cooper, Gordon, 49, 53, 258
Cooper, William Milton, 118
Corbally, Father Chris -, 209
Cornell University, 244
Cornet, Bruce, 234
Corréard, Roger, 58
Corso (Col. Philip J.), 30, 131, 205, 225, 226, 333
Costa Rica, 109 (Fig. 4), 139, 140, 152, 415
Covelo, CA, 50
Cradle of the Sun, 232, 250, 334 (Fig. 14)
Crane, Hue, 13
Crawford, Admiral-, 204
Creighton, Gordon, 72, 104, 192
Crosby, Douglas, 102, 103, 121, 126, 261, 521
Cross, Howard (Battelle), 121, 147, 213, 502
Crowley, Dr. Robert, 135
CSIS, 246
CUFOS, 12, 410
Curien, Hubert (Minister -), 127
CyberIQ, Inc., 52
Cyberknife, 366, 474

D

Dakin, Henry, 22, 96, 153
Dale, John, 67, 237
Dallas, TX, 23
Daly, Judith, 204
Dames, Major Ed -, 273
Daniels, Neil, 20
DARPA, 188, 353 (see also ARPA)
David, Dr. Ruth -, 481
Davis, Dr. Eric, 23, 27, 34, 35, 45, 53, 66, 67, 76, 77, 83, 130, 131, 133, 135, 136, 202, 203,

224, 252, 273, 296, 313, 332,
  459, 467, 476, 487, 502
Davis, Kathy, 159, 217
Davis, Congressman Tom-, 175,
  186
Davos, Switzerland, 175
de Brosses, Marie-Thérèse, 59
de Brouwer, Colonel Walter -
  (Belgium), 260, 427, 429
de Duve, Prof. Christian, 208
de Grossouvre, François, 262, 263,
  314, 337
de Maigret, Pamela, 218, 247
de Marenches, Alexandre, 262, 263
De Occulta Philosophia, 124
de Saint-Phalle, Thérèse, 72, 190,
  211, 262, 272, 278 289, 337,
  346, 521
de Scitivaux, Thierry, 359
de Tocqueville, Alexis, 484
de Villepin, Dominique, 288, 309
Defense Special Weapons Agency
  (DSWA), 188
Definitely Maybe (Strugatsky), 493
Deforge, Gérard, 31, 32, 37, 43, 49,
  59, 93 (Fig.2), 105, 214, 241,
  261, 277, 303
Delangle, 25, 241
Deliyannis, Yannis, 485, 509, 514
Delmas, Marie-Charlotte, 433, 482
Deluol, Jean-François, 302
Demopoulos, Dr. Harry, 191
Denderah (Egypt), 108, 109 (Fig.3),
  110
Deng Zhao Ping, 253
Denzler, Brenda, 122, 406
Derrida, Jacques, 260
Des Mousseaux, 138
Desrochers, Réal, 30
DeVaucouleurs, Gérard &
  Antoinette, 318, 462

DIA, 45, 198, 202-204, 227, 228,
  336, 375, 376, 4142 426, 436,
  479, 480, 481
Diamond, Henry, 169
Dick, Philip K., 170, 490
Dietz, Jean & Richard, 147
Digital Universe, Inc., 331
Discovery Channel, 14
Discovery (Shuttle -), 318
Dolan, Richard, 425
Dolby, Tom, 8
Doty, Richard, 228, 274, 285, 332,
  359, 440, 441
Dow Jones index, 69, 82, 216, 359,
  436, 441
Druffel, Ann, 194
Duck Club, 21, 47, 54, 160, 197,
  346, 403, 406
Dupas, Alain, 155, 333, 342, 355
Durant, Frederick C., 250, 272
Durant, Robert, 375
Dyson, Freeman, 208

E

EADS Corp., 364, 383, 399, 413
Eagelton, James, 228
EarthTech Int'l, 203, 426, 427, 429,
  459, 466
Easenergy (EDF), 274, 284
Eckert, Paul, 342, 349
Eco, Umberto, 26
Edberg, John, 283, 318
Edwards AFB, 49, 52, 149, 161
EDF, 239, 274, 284, 449
EG&G Corporation, 202, 227, 299
Einhorn, Ira, 42, 43, 48, 96, 166,
  458
Einstein, Dr. Albert, 369, 419, 428
El Grenada, 20
Elohim, 173
Emenegger, Robert, 190, 228
Energia (Russia), 150

Engelbart, Dr. Doug, 13, 63, 93 (Fig.1), 268
Eragny, France, 105, 261
Ernst, Ruann-Pengov, 321, 355
ESA (European Space Agency), 382
Esalen, CA, 378, 405-406, 447, 484, 489-491
Escary, Jean-Louis, 25
Esfahani, Mahan, 236, 474
Estero, CA, 36
Euler, 27
Euro-America, 12, 105, 302
Evrard, Luc, 57
Evry, France, 31
Exon (General) 130, 131
Eyes Wide Shut, 26
Ezekiel, 346

F

FAA, 229
Fabius, (Prime Minister Laurent -), 39, 278, 449
Fadiman, Jim, 305
Faggin, Federico, 88, 92, 121, 138, 242
"Falcon," 226, 228, 330
Farmer, Michael, 186, 197
FastWalker, 27, 62, 188, 189, 235, 244, 340, 406
Fatima, 207, 209, 210 (Fig.8), 211
Favier, Jean-Jacques, 349, 389
Favre, Philippe, 317, 323, 328, 364, 417, 506
FBI, 68, 70, 164, 169, 217
Feinler, Elizabeth ("Jake"), 63, 93 (Fig.1)
Fernandez, Joaquim, 207
Ferrario, Tom, 486, 512 (Fig.20)
Festival of the Bones, 448
Finland, 40
Fiorina, Carla, 99
Firestorm (James McDonald), 194

Firmage, Joe, 22, 28, 30, 31, 56, 62, 63, 69, 74, 76, 77, 135, 152, 189, 197, 198, 201, 204, 265, 297, 331, 425
Fisher (- information), 28
Flickinger, Dr. Donald, 134, 231
Flying Saucer Review, 72, 380
Foucault's Pendulum, 26
Fouéré, Françoise, 59
Four Elements, 12, 56, 70, 72, 79
Ford, John, 23
Fort Mason, San Francisco, 138, 388
Fowles, John, 512
Friend, Colonel Robert -, 83, 161
Freud, Dr. Sigmund, 64
Friedman, Stanton, 44, 285, 298, 475
FTQ (Fonds des Travails. du Québec), 120, 442
FUFOR group, 42
Fuller, William ("Bill"), 178

G

Gaia, 80, 103
Gajdusek, Dr. Carleton, 182
Galileo, 253
Gansler, Dr. Jacques, 197, 200, 204
Garcia Family, 67
Garland, general-, 213
Gauguin, Philippe Alexandre, 222, 232
Gauss-Bonnet, 27
Genentech, 9
General Atomic, 20, 384
General Motors Corp., 185, 195, 231
Genodyssée, Inc., 25
Genopole (Evry), 11, 31, 60, 81, 91, 176, 309, 345, 349, 389
Georgetown University, 199
George Washington University, 169

GEPAN, 124, 125, 127, 276, 314, 363, 482 (also "GEIPAN")
Ghoia, Phil, 358
Gibbons, Dr. Jack, 95, 510
Giraud, Colonel René-, 214
Giscard d'Estaing, Valéry (Pres.), 276
Glazer, Jack, 379, 381, 392, 514
Glomar Explorer, 134, 231
Goddard, see NASA
Gold, Stephen, 208
Good, Timothy, 340
Google, 9, 295, 335, 389, 463
Gore, Al (Vice-President), 245, 287
Goss, Porter, 246
Gough, Bill, 279, 484
Gould, Dr. Stephen Jay, 208, 407
Graal (Auberge du Saint-), 32
Grace Cathedral (San Francisco), 377, 379 (Fig.18)
Graff, Dale, 77, 228
Greason, Jeff, 252
Great Falls, MT, 68
Greece, 40, 43, 107, 163, 278, 362, 508
Green, Dr. Christopher ("Kit"), 29, 57, 76, 124-126, 131, 133, 149, 159, 164, 185, 194-196, 204, 215, 216, 230, 236, 243, 268, 275, 290, 294, 297, 340, 367, 391, 433, 446-8, 450, 454-458, 472-3, 478, 481-2, 484, 486, 499, 503
Green, Kristin, 147, 195-196, 230, 283, 367, 454n, 503
Greenwood, Barry, 168
Greer, Dr. Steven, 45, 47, 83, 84, 96, 97, 197, 202, 204
Greger, Ed, 191
Griffin, Mike (NASA), 320, 322
Gulf Breeze, 61
Guérin, Dr. Pierre, 56, 58, 60, 61, 91

Guez, Laurent, 162, 262
Gunn, Moira, 226, 219

H

Haggadah, 3
Haines, Dr. Richard, 22, 23, 54, 63, 73, 80, 88, 122, 139, 140, 152, 160, 171, 179, 180, 187, 274, 279, 352, 456, 476
Haisch, Dr. Bernie, 28, 46, 69, 76, 135, 169, 171, 179, 189, 197, 201, 204, 236, 279, 297, 331, 352, 357
Haight-Ashbury, 463
Hall, Richard, 185
Hamilton Field, 82
Hampton Roads (publ.), 135, 142, 158
Hamre, John, 200, 246, 250
Handylab, Inc., 114, 136, 193, 196, 256, 275, 283
Haravilliers, 21, 25, 29, 31, 34, 37, 43, 49, 59, 88, 93 (Fig.2), 241, 404
Harary, Dr. Keith, 124, 297
Hardy, Christine, 60, 165
Hardy, Dr. René, 59, 104, 133
Harrison, Dr. Albert, 151 (Fig.5), 229
Hastings, Dr. Arthur, 193, 274, 372
Hatch, Larry, 54, 158, 422, 457
Hathaway, George, 436, 439, 459, 489
Hawaii, 56, 137
Heart of the Internet (The), 56, 119, 135, 158, 170, 174, 184, 189, 193, 450
Hegarty, Diane, 78, 153
Helms, Richard (CIA), 231
Henry, Dr. Richard ("Dick"), 169
Hermeneutics, 385
Hermetic Brotherhood of Light, 467

Herzenberg, Dr. Leonard & Leonore, 495, 520
Hessdalen, Norway, 410, 482
Hilbert, David, 67
Hildegard (Sainte -), 344
Hill, Betty & Barney, 256, 258, 275
Hill, Paul, 76
Hilltop curve, 67
Hitchcock, Alfred, 49
Hoffmann, Dr. Jeffery, 337
Hollanda Lima, Colonel, 267, 295
Hollande, Pres. François, 278
Hollingsworth, Kathleen, 19, 34
Holloman AFB, 35, 150, 226, 227, 231
Holt, Al, 76, 428, 429
Holy City, CA, 76
Honolulu, 279 (Fig.10)
Hong Kong, 253
Hopkins, 48, 57, 119, 159
Hopkinsville, KY, 212
Horowitz, Mitch, 493
Houellebeck, Michel, 144, 145
Howe, Linda, 228, 432, 443
Huawei, 292
Hubbell, Webster, 319, 320
Hufford, Dr. David, 406-8, 447
Hughes, General Patrick -, 204
Hunt for the Skinwalker, 479, 481
Hussein, Saddam, 215
Hutin, Serge, 107
Hynek, Dr. J. Allen, 38, 48, 51, 83, 98, 191, 194, 213, 228, 264, 305, 314, 333

I

IBM Corporation, 68, 117
Idrac, Anne-Marie, 97, 503
Igbal, Dr. Muzzafar -, 208
IHEDN, France, 38, 223
Imhoff, François, 302

IMI (Inst. Métapsychique Int'l, 304, 396
In the Upper Room (Mahalia Jackson), 519
In-Q-Tel (CIA), 257, 321-322
Indole, 115
InfoMedia Corp., 40, 63, 294
Inforespace, 195, 353, 380
INRIA, France, 170
Institute for Advanced Studies, 203
Institute for the Future, 168, 212, 238, 273, 285, 387
Institute of Noetic Sciences (IONS), 18, 79, 185, 286
Institute of Transpersonal Psychology, 193, 274, 371
INTEL Corp., 47, 68, 105, 206
Internet (The), 26, 54, 62, 72, 168
Interop Show, 35
Invicta, Inc., 168, 169
Irby, Charles, 63
Isis (Goddess), 107
Isobe, Tsuyoki, 62, 85
Israel, 25, 96, 111, 137, 176, 320, 474
ISSO, 22, 23, 69

J

Jacobs, David, 48, 241
JAFCO, 84
Jahn, Prof. Robert -, 289
Japan, 61, 84, 99
Jennifer, Project, 134, 231
Johansen, Dr. Robert, 63, 259, 285
Johnson, Adam, 486
Johnson, Craig, 508
Johnson, Greg, 511
Johnson, Kelley, 502
Johnson, Pierre-Marc, 434
Jonkers, Ray K., 228
Jospin, Lionel, 48, 82
JPL (Jet Propulsion Lab.), 331, 336

Judd, Dean, 229, 230
Jung, Dr. Cark Gustav, 373, 384

K
Kabul, 106, 120
Kahle, Brewster, 306
Kahn, Dr. Robert, 168, 186
Kaku, Dr. Michio, 169
Kaminski, Paul, 204
Karatidi, Olga, 28
Kazantsev, Alexander, 104, 372
Kean, Leslie, 73, 167, 169, 180, 187, 190, 202
Kecksburg, PA, 197
Keel, John, 57, 140, 496
Kelleher, Dr. Colm, 27, 34, 53, 66, 67, 77, 83, 91, 114, 115, 117, 121, 134, 135, 146-148, 181, 182, 191, 193, 194, 197, 215, 216, 218, 229, 231 (Fig.9), 256, 273,447, 450, 458, 514
Kennedy, Senator Ted -, 504
Kerry (Senator John), 54, 256, 257
Keyhoe, Donald, 48, 247
KGB, 169
King in Yellow (The), 87
Kisling, Jean, 156, 157
"Kit", see Green, Dr. Christopher
Klein, Gérard, 170, 288
Kleinrock, Dr. Leonard, 168
KMT, 291
Knapp, George, 435, 502
Knoll, Julien, 332
Koestler, Arthur, 152
Korolev, Sergei Pavlovich, 89
Kostelnick, Brig. General, 204
Kripal, Prof. Jeff, 376, 379, 382, 384-5, 387, 405-6, 415, 484, 489, 490
Kubrick, Stanley, 26
Kuchar, George, 30, 57, 388
Kuchar, Mike, 389, 398-9, 482

Kurth, Doug, 456, 466-7, 483

L
Labbé, Thierry, 60
Lacatski, Dr. James T., 426, 428, 429, 437, 448, 458, 486, 488
Lago de Cote, 109 (Fig. 4), 140, 143, 152, 156
Lagrange, Dr. Pierre, 43, 170, 214, 363, 364, 410, 473
Lampson, Nick, 187
Landsman, Larry, 190, 191, 197
Lapaz, Dr. Lincoln, 212
Larcher, Dr. Hubert, 396
Lawrence Livermore Lab, 77, 503
Lazar, Bob, 204, 300
Le Canard Enchaîné, 58, 199
Le Carré, John, 290
Le Chien qui Fume, 156
Le Comte de Gabalis, 386
Le Docteur Frégalle, 190
Le Figaro, 49, 106, 155, 157, 162, 221, 262, 278
Les Charpentiers, 11
Lecomte, Marina L., 222, 233
Lee, Dr. Burton -, 444
Leftheriotis, Dr. Georges, 215, 287
Lehman Brothers, 432, 435
Lehtman, Harvey, 63, 305
Le Pen, 140, 239
Le Ruel, 25
Le Suffren, 271
Le Train Bleu, 79
Lead Mask mystery, 225
Legba, 123
Leir, Dr. Roger, 83
Lemke, Dr. Jim, 154, 384
Lemke, Larry, 76, 77, 122, 160, 171, 180, 189, 352, 357
Les Halles (Paris), 313, 435
Letty (Général), 81, 214, 223
Levitt, Creon, 22, 69, 74, 274

546   Index

Lewis, Spencer, 107
Libération, 43
Libby, Scooter, 341
Life Dreams, 447
Lignon (Prof.-), 59
Lilith, 226
Lille, France, 59, **374**
Lindeman, Michael, 76
Lindner, Dr. Robert Mitchell, 225
LINUX, 68
Lobos (Gal. Mario Avila-), 53
Lockheed, 69, 149, 201, 204, 232, 329, 339, 502
Lockyer, Lisa, 315, 329
Logan-Cashe airport, 75
Lomas, Robert, 272
London (UK), 58, 253, 255, 258, 269, 272, 282-3, 288, 374 416, 434, 451, 492
Los Alamos, 33, 67, 117, 136, 185, 195, 196, 202, 229, 299, 308
Louange, François, 127, 152, 156, 177, 181, 215, 262, 287-288, 314, 335
Louie, Gilman, 321-322, 355
Lovins, Dr. Amory, 121
LSD, 14, 88
Lundahl, (Sir Arthur), 247
Lungren, Eve, 159
Luxor (Egypt), 106, 107
Lyon (France), 43, 60, 79, 92, 237, 260-1, 310

M

Maccabee, Dr. Bruce, 95, 169
Mack, Prof. John -, 57, 148, 153, 225, 252, 253, 255, 258
Mad Cow Disease, 181, 186
Madoff, Bernie, 459
Magonia, 207, 345, 352, 380, 384, 390, 406, 439, 447, 497
Maillard, Charlotte, 97

Maillard, Nicolas, 43
Major Murphy, 488
Manhattan, 26, 54, 102, 157, 200, 240, 349, 457
Manhattan Project, 244
Maniez, Jacques, 283, 288, 423
ManyOne Systems, 189
Mao Tse Tung, 253
Marais, Marin, 12, 297
Marcel, Jesse, 131
Marie, Franck, 241, 424
Markoff, John, 105, 280, 285
Markovitch (affaire -), 424,
Marley Woods, 484, 486-7, 496, 501, 504, 505, 509, 512 (Fig.20), 516
Mars (planet), 152, 205, 218, 333, 336
Marshall Plan, 190
Marshall, CA, 50
Martin, James Stewart, 504
Masonry (Free-), 265
Masse, Maurice, 180, 404
Mattoon, 175, 187
Maxfield, Myles, 134
May, Dr. Edwin, 286, 295, 491, 499
McCain, Senator John -, 394, 437, 438
McCampbell, Jim, 160, 180, 192
McDonald, Dr. James, 194
McDonnell aircraft, 125, 188, 195, 205
McGarity, Bill, 80, 299, 300, 462
McIlwan, Carl, 345
McLindon, Connie, 168, 186
McMoneagle, Joe, 258, 259
McVeigh, Timothy, 118
Meade, Frank, 149
Meade, Phil, 517
Mecca, 85
MEDEA Project, 23

Meessen, Prof. August, 206, 208, 211, 353
Meet the Press, 84
Méheust, Dr. Bertrand, 59, 312, 406, 409, 515
Meier, Billy, 265, 297
Melchizedek, 275, 324, 386
Mellon, Christopher, 164
Menant, Marc, 80
Mendel Rivers, (Representative Lucius -), 246
Menehune (Hawaii), 137, 281
Menlo Park, CA, 21, 63, 305, 373
Menzel, Prof. Donald, 205, 268, 298
Mercury Interactive, Inc., 12
Mergui, Gabriel, 25, 31, 60, 81, 91, 262, 349
Mesnard, Joël, 418
Mérieux, Alain, 92
Messarovitch, Yves, 106, 155, 157, 278, 314, 323, 364, 395, 417, 451
Messengers of Deception, 319, 431
Messier, Jean-Marie, 157, 165, 183, 191
Mexico, 84, 163, 467
Michaelmas, 155
Michel, Aimé, 85, 91, 98, 218, 312
Michigan, 20
Millard, Stephen, 53, 119
Miller, Comm. Willard, 44, 45, 47, 121, 202, 204, 425
Miller (General Glenn E. -), 161
Millstadt, MO., 12
Milner, Terry, 270, 271
Mind-Brain Research, 279
Minot AFB, 67, 168
Mission Bay, San Diego, 78
Mitchell, Captain Edgar, 28, 45, 97, 187, 197, 198, 204, 229, 250, 424, 425
Mithra, 493

Mitterrand, Pres. François, 263, 269, 508
MJ-12, 298, 394, 430
Mobilian, Inc., 158, 206
Mobius, 286
Mojave Desert, 252, 356
Monroe, Robert, 193
Montagnier, Dr. Paul, 191
Montana, 53, 232, 234, 427, 429, 443
Montara, CA, 20
Monteverdi restaurant, 190
Montpellier, France, 195
Montréal, Canada, 119-120, 165, 199, 245, 283, 296, 306, 401, 441-2
Mount Shasta, 50, 57
Moody, Robert J., 23
Moore, Bill, 51, 228
Morgane, 245
Morning Glory, 29, 136, 350
Morning of the Magicians, 436
Moss Beach, 20
Mubarak (Presdt.), 110, 111
MUFON (- Journal), 15, 53, 191, 274, 394, 467, 476, 477, 485, 496
Mugnier, Abbé -, 518
Murad, Paul, 481
Murphy, Mike, 388, 406, 485, 490
Mysterious Skin, 188

N

Nanogram Devices, Inc., 226, 406
NARCAP, 63, 112, 160, 171, 179, 352, 476
NASA, 22, 33, 53, 80, 97, 122, 160, 185 (Goddard), 286, 306, 309, 315, 318, 341, 343, 348, 352, 355, 357, 378, 379, 381, 389, 392, 393, 405, 413, 428, 446,

548   Index

451, 484, 488, 491, 497, 503, 508
NASDAQ, 82, 105, 216, 436, 452
National Science Foundation (NSF), 168, 477
NATO, 30, 199
Nautilus Biotech, Inc., 91
Nature (Journal), 21
Naxos, 43
Neal, Dr. Richard, 125
NeoPhotonics, Inc., 188, 290, 292, 325 (Fig.11)
Network Revolution, 280
Neuron Data, Inc., 163
New Scientist, 275, 404
New West, 284
New York City, 19, 54, 101, 183
New York Times, 105, 412n, 428
NICAP, 185, 272
NIDS, 14, 19, 20, 22, 23, 27, 34, 46, 48, 53, 61, 66, 83, 104, 114-116, 146, 149, 151 (Fig.5), 191, 194, 256, 428
Niemtzow, Dr. Richard, 52, 64, 123-126, 131, 133, 196, 264, 314, 486, 499, 500
NIH (Nat'l Inst. of Health), 182, 500, 511, 514, 515, 518
Nimitz (carrier), 456, 467
Ninth Gate (The), 26
Nippon Investment & Finance, 62, 84
Nixon, Pres. Richard, 204
NNSA, 204
Nomura (Japan), 19
Northrop-Grumman, Inc., 232, 298
Norton AFB, 190, 231, 440
Norway, 124
Novel, Gordon, 499
Noxon, MT, 54, 66, 216
NRO, 232, 358
Nunley, Wesley, 23

O

Obama, President Barack, 9, 390, 392, 430, 436, 449, 454, 465, 466, 475, 486, 487, 497, 513
O Globo, 225
O'Hare airport (Chicago), 352
Oakland, CA, 22, 123
Oberg, James, 319
Oberon Zell, 29, 56, 57, 102, 103, 136
Oliver, Dr. Barney, 522
OneCosmos, Inc., 69
ONERA, 333, 342
Onet, Dr. George, 66, 118, 148
ONI (Off. Naval Intelligence), 270
Operation Mind Control, 274
Operation Paperclip, 511
Oregon, 68, 96, 124, 154
Orwell, George, 20
Oshun, 123
Osiris, 107-108
Ossendowski, 37
Oswald Dallas, 190
OUSDAT, 204
Out There, 119
Oxantium, 392
Oxindole, 115

P

Pace, Scott, 331, 336
Palantir Technologies, Inc., 461
Paley, Grace, 8
Palo Alto, CA, 69
Pandolfi, Dr. Ronald, 66, 70, 96, 140, 230, 232, 308, 332, 340, 428, 432, 481
Papon, Maurice, 342
Parisot, Mme Laurence, 363
Parmentier, François, 238
Parsons, Jack, 29
Passavant Family, 138, 350

Passport to Magonia, see "Magonia"
Paté-Cornell, Dr. Elizabeth, 97, 351
Patenet, Jacques, 314, 347, 388
Payan, Gilbert, 24, 38, 41-45, 55, 74, 81, 94, 124, 125, 131, 162, 170, 223, 238, 425
Pécresse, Valérie (French Minister), 484
Pearl Harbor, 101
Pearl River, China, 292
Pegasus project, 242
Pellat, (Prof. -), 127
Pellucidar, 62
Penetration (Swann), 21, 217
Penngrove, 29
Pentacle Memorandum, 62, 85, 116, 121, 199, 213
Pentagon, 44, 45, 47, 101, 131
Perception Technology Corp., 205
Petersen, John, 45, 67, 88, 89, 96, 301, 332, 425
Petit, Dr. Jean-Pierre, 73
Petrakis, Perry, 195
Phillips, Ted, 484, 486, 501, 503, 505, 512 (Fig.20), 516
Pierret, Christian, 39
Piltz, Dr. Marty, 33, 151 (Fig. 5), 229
Pinkerton, Dr. Brian, 186
Pinon, admiral Gilles -, 214, 301, 432, 445
Pissarro, 94
Plaza Hotel, 126, 165, 183, 190
Plon publishers (Paris), 419
Pocantico report, 21, 44, 85, 127, 134, 160
Podesta, John, 167, 169
Poher, Dr. Claude, 53, 124, 179, 180, 197, 211, 313, 360, 403, 418, 431
Point Loma, 78, 88

Point Reyes, 26, 32, 39, 46, 50, 97
Polanski, Roman, 26
Polko, 228
Pontoise, 15-18, 26, 32, 59, 85, 90, 94, 155, 190, 222
Popular Mechanics, 85, 217
Portugal, 179, 206
Poughkeepsie, NY, 54
Pouletty, Dr. Philippe, 80, 262
Pouliquen (Gal), 44
Pratt, Bob, 298
Prévert, Jacques, 81
Price, Nathan, 502
Price, Pat, 270, 271
Price-Williams, 447
Priory de Sion, 235
Progeria, 300
Project Beta, 285
Project CARET (manufactured fake), 394
Project Prato, 267
Project UFOTOG, 398
Prosetta, Inc., 186, 193, 197, 273
Puech, Jean-François, 60
Puthoff, Dr. Harold (Hal), 23, 28, 31, 34-36, 76, 77, 83, 89, 116, 135, 149, 151 (Fig. 5), 257, 270, 332, 359, 390, 403, 413, 420, 425, 439, 445,506
Puthoff, Brendan, 332
Pyewackit, 116

Q

Quarouble, France, 507
Québec, Canada, 442

R

Radford, Admiral -, 299
Radin, Dr. Dean, 185, 192, 295, 407, 484, 490
Randolph, Pascal Beverly -, 465

550   Index

Random House, 103
Ranky, Eric, 59
Rasmussen, Dr. Hans, 22, 513
Rauley, Eric, 80, 91, 163, 241
Ravenheart Family, 22, 29, 56, 86, 136
Ray Charles, 238
Rayl, Sally, 252
Raytheon Corp., 201, 232
Reagan, Pres. Ronald, 250
Red Planet Capital, 306, 309, 315, 317, 318, 321, 330, 380, 428
Redfern, Nick, 285, 287
Reid, Senator Harry -, 320, 427
Rémi, Roger, 300
Remote viewing, 23, 40, 77, 189, 192-3, 204, 208, 225, 227, 243, 258-260, 270, 273-4, 298, 306, 340, 375, 378, 406, 412, 486, 493, 498, 503
Rendlesham Forest, UK, 197
Revel, Jean-François, 71
Revelations, 91
Ribera, Antonio, 104
Ricard, Matthieu, 208
Rich County, UT, 75
Richard, Philippe -, 333, 342, 396, 416
Rice University, 375, 382
Rickover, Admiral -, 148, 298
RightPoint Corp., 206
Roberts, Dr. Larry, 168
Robertson report, 89, 213, 250, 272
Rocard, Prof. Yves, 81, 82, 131
Rocard, Prime Minister Michel -, 511
Rockefeller, Laurance, 42, 57, 95
Rockwell, Ted, 33, 83, 148
Rodeghier, Dr. Mark, 12
Roe, Ted, 122, 160, 169, 180
Rogers, Kenny, 224, 273
Rohrabacher, Dana, 19, 34

Rommel (ex-FBI), 68
Rosenberg, Jerry, 77
Rosicrucians, 111, 233
Rosin, Carol, 96
Rospars, Dr. Jean-Pierre, 214, 412
Roswell, NM, 28, 33, 41, 61, 62, 72, 77, 83, 90, 92, 96, 130, 131, 134, 189, 198, 212, 231, 375, 425
Roswell, as a failed medical experiment, 298
Rothschild, Ed, 169, 175, 186
Rumsfeld, Donald, 175, 178, 199, 237, 394
Ruppelt, Col. Ed, 48, 121, 213, 412
Russell, Richard, 341
Russia, 17, 22-24, 90-91, 95, 113, 169, 203-4, 225, 247-8, 272, 296, 301, 312, 321, 323, 339, 343, 374, 453, 478, 484, 488, 493
Rutan, Burt, 252

S

Saffo, Paul, 116, 175, 205, 225
Safran Corp., 455
Sagan, Dr. Carl, 69, 268
Sahara, 37
SAIC (Science Applications, Inc), 286
Saint Agobard, 192, 193, 261, 359
Saint Anthony, 47
Saint Louis (island), 26
Saint Sulpice, 72, 221, 417
Sainte Chapelle, 346
Sakharov, Dr. Andrei Dmitrievitch, 420
Saley, Alain (Janine's brother), 52, 65, 205, 337, 365, 385, 390, 400
Saley, Annick – see Thoby
Salez, Morvan, 185, 214

Samaël, 226
Samizdat, 83, 90
Samothrace, 137
San Antonio, TX, 57
San Diego, CA, 52, 78, 88, 103,
  121-3, 133-4, 154, 158, 174,
  218, 329, 345, 385, 444
Sanders, Dr. Dave -, 415
Santa Claus, 14
Santa Rosa, CA, 147
Santilli, 131-2
SAPOC, 200, 202-204, 246
SARA, 46
Sarfatti, Jack, 22, 49, 51, 232, 235,
  243, 253, 400, 470, 478
Sarkozy, Pres. Nicolas, 238, 288,
  351, 360, 363, 409, 425, 435,
  435, 444, 450, 453, 481
Sarraute, Ms. Claude, 71
Saudi Arabia, 323, 328
Sawyer, Steve, 268
Schirra, Wally, 53
Schlitz, Marilyn, 79
Schuessler, John, 34, 53, 196, 205,
  229, 394, 438, 467, 485
Schwartz, Stephen, 286, 298
Schwarzenegger, Governor
  Arnold -, 464
Sci-Fi Channel, 191, 197, 216
Scott, General Norman -, 358
Schultz, George, 97, 148
Secret Onion, 201
Seignolle, Claude, 434
Senior Soda, 299
Seligson, Marcia, 284
SEPRA, 38, 42, 74, 94, 127, 181,
  211, 215, 223, 236
SERPO (Govt. Hoax ?), 430, 431
Serres, Prof. Michel -, 91
Servais, Simonne, 38, 41-45, 49, 81,
  92, 425
SETI, 357, 518

SFF, 318
Shannon, Oke, 202
Sheehan, Daniel, 96, 153
Sheehan, General Jack -, 199, 202,
  224, 236, 250
Shenzhen, China, 254, 290, 325
  (Fig.11)
Sheymov, Dr. Victor Ivanovitch -,
  169
Shocker (operation -), 90
Shuttle Endeavor, 348 (Fig.15)
Sicaud, Marceau, 59, 214
Sillard, Yves, 288, 313, 335, 347,
  360
Simmons, Jerry, 75
Singapore, 85, 291
Sirag, Dr. Saul-Paul, 22
Sisters of Perpetual Indulgence, 483
Skinwalker Ranch, 67, 85, 479, 481,
  489
Smith, Dan, 150, 330
Smith, Paul, (remote viewer), 375
Smith, Ruthie -, 294
Snelson, Robin, 319
SNPE, France, 349, 410, 453
SOBEPS (Belgium), 195, 353, 410
Society for Scient. Exploration
  (SSE): 260
Socorro, NM, 185, 401
Soissons, 159, 348 (Fig.16), 379
  (Fig.17), 394, 398, 402, 408,
  415
Solem, John Dale, 33, 117
Sommer, Goeffrey, 180
Sorbonne, 16, 91
Sous le Fouet du Simoun, 37
SpaceShip-One, 356
Space Shuttle, 116, 174, 318, 336,
  341, 348 (Fig.15), 453, 491
Space Station, 33, 147, 174, 296,
  318, 329, 331, 336, 340-341,
  375, 403, 503

Space-X, 296, 341
Sparks, Brad, 168, 212, 213
Spielberg, Steven, 115, 167, 261, 284, 456
Spottiswood, 69
SRI International, 23, 63, 91, 164, 204, 270, 286, 289, 340
Stahl, Dr, 132, 134
Stalin, Joseph, 89
Stanford, Dr. Ray, 185
Stanford University, 12, 13, 328
Stapleton, Grant, 235
Star Gate Archive, 258
Starr, Dr. Kevin- and Sheila, 257, 405
Starstream Research, 307-308, 479, 480, 481
Stevens, Senator Ted, 427
Stoll, Dr. Cliff, 123
Stow Lake, 268
Strand, Erling, 412
Stratagem (novel), 278, 284, 289, 293, 303
Strauss-Kahn, Dominique, 82, 278
Strieber, Whitley, 57, 83
Stringfield, Len, 125
Strugatsky Brothers, 493
Sturrock, Prof. Peter, 20-22, 46, 47, 54, 55, 130, 150, 159, 160, 169, 179, 180, 186, 187, 231, 242, 287, 346, 357, 406, 420, 458, 477, 496
Swann, Ingo, 30, 217, 306, 376, 515
Swift, Prof. David -, 251 (Fig.10), 279, 330
Swigart, Rob, 277, 302, 305, 306, 354
Switch, Robert, 306
Switzerland, 60, 458

T

Table d'Emeraude, 24
Tahiti, 364
Tales of the City, 40
Taliban, 113, 116, 180
Tahoe (lake), 29, 206
Tanaka, Dr. Toshiyuki, 182
Tarcher-Penguin, 493
Targ, Russell, 78, 135, 142, 153, 192, 259, 274, 286, 295, 406, 499
TechNation, 226, 249
Tehran, Iran, 340, 477
Teish, Luisah, 22, 102, 103, 123
The Economist, 442
The Jet-Propelled Couch, 225
The Lure of the Edge, 122
The Terror that comes in the Night, 408, 447
Theil, Peter, 461
Theory of Everything, 275
Thoby, Annick Jeanne, 63, 65, 67, 80, 205, 271, 302
Thomas, Roy, 407
Thomson-CSF, 314
Thurston, Herbert, 56
Thyopro Corp., 191
Tia Helena, 370
Tlon, Uqbar, Orbis Tertius, 231, 358
Todd, Olivier, 58
Tokyo, 62, 84-85, 98, 235, 446
Tomales Bay, 26, 40, 47, 98, 102, 153, 158, 268
Tomlin, Lily, 103
Tormé, Tracy, 247
Toulouse, France, 64, 276
Trans-en-Provence, 397
Tremonton film, 213
Troadec, Jean-Pierre, 195
Trudeau, (General -), 226, 333

Trumbull, Douglas, 393, 398, 400, 429, 459, 470, 484, 486, 501, 512 (Fig.20), 516, 520
Truzzi, Marcello, 40, 175
TRW, 28, 77, 232
Tubular Bells, 429, 458
Tucson, AZ, 23, 209
Tulien, Tom, 167
TWA-800, 161

U

Ubatuba, Brazil, 21, 298
Uchoa, General -, 297-298, 496
UFOCAT, 476
Ukiah, CA, 14
UMMO, 195
United Airlines, 20, 161
United Nations (UN), 174, 200
Universons (re. Poher), 179, 211, 360, 403, 419, 420
USSR, 156
US Air Force, 21, 52, 53, 67, 101, 116, 123, 200, 205, 134, 149-150, 156, 157, 161, 180, 186, 188, 202, 213, 227, 229, 237, 247-248, 257, 264, 267-268, 272, 277, 295, 330, 331, 333, 352, 369, 388, 440, 486, 494, 505, 507, 515
Utah, 49, 67, 85, 104, 114
Utts, Prof. Jessica, 229

V

Vagenende, 113
Vaillant, Michaël, 396-397
Valdez (Corporal in Chile), 244, 245
Valdez, Gabe, 114, 299
Valensole, France, 82, 180, 404, 507
VALIS (Philip Dick), 55
Vallée, Gabriel (father), 15
Vallée, Dr. Gabriel (brother), 15, 17, 50, 58, 61, 155, 163, 222, 335, 462, 505
Vallée, Madeleine (mother), 15-17, 21, 50
Vallée, Maxime, 37, 54, 63, 80, 91, 95, 97, 105, 122, 155, 214, 222, 286, 314, 338, 355, 386, 411, 415, 416, 431, 452, 482, 492, 493, 495, 502
Vallée, Olivier, 31, 54, 56, 63, 65, 71, 80, 97, 103, 113, 114, 138, 157, 214
Valognes, France, 522
Van Allen, Dr. James, 345
Vandenberg, CA, 230, 234
Varvoglis, Mario, 304
Vatican Observatory (Tucson, AZ), 209
Velasco, Jean-Jacques, 21, 42, 47, 55, 64, 127, 156, 160, 170, 177, 211, 223, 236, 245, 347, 360, 410
Venturini, Jean-Claude, 301
Vilchez, Carlos & Ricardo, 139
Vilenskaya, Larissa, 91
Vivendi Corp., 157, 158, 162, 164, 183, 191
Vorilhon, Claude (Raël), 172
Vorona, Dr. Jack, 228
Voronej (Russia), 90
Voyager Project, 46, 69
VUCA University, 259
Vulcan Ventures, 252

W

Wall Street, 432, 436
Walter, Jean-Jacques, 176
Walter-Reed (hospital), 132
Warcollier, René, 289
Ward (Maj. Gal Marshall H -), 200
Ward, Tom, 306

Ware, Donald, 300
Washington Post, 46
Watts, Alan, 51
Wayback Machine, 305
Wayne State University, 185
Weinstein, Dominique, 47, 54, 61, 63, 73, 74, 80, 81, 89-91, 106, 122, 127, 133, 156, 164, 168, 172, 177, 179, 211, 214, 215, 222, 238, 262, 271, 335, 358, 360, 409, 482, 507
Weisbuch, Dr. Claude -, 91
Weiss, Robert K., 119, 126
West, Dr. Jim -, 19
Westwood, Jim, 23, 33, 131, 204, 224, 237, 250, 272, 283
Whidby Island, WA, 63
Whinnery, General Jim -, 43, 34, 229, 230
Whitesides, George -, (NASA), 488
Williamette Pass, OR, 48, 49
Williams, Dr. Robert Parvin, 135
Willits, CA, 50
Willow, CA, 50
Wilson, Thomas, 12, 202, 224, 227, 236, 250, 424, 425
Winchester Mystery House, San Jose, 457
Winterhaven, 299
Wolf, Fred, 79
Wolverton (sheriff), 68
Wonders in the Sky, 256, 303, 381, 409, 414, 416, 422, 468, 488, 490, 506, 509, 514
Woo, Harry, 213
Wood, Dr. Robert, 88
Woodside, CA, 80
Woolsey, James (CIA), 96
Worden, Pete (NASA-Ames), 329, 357, 381
Wright, Frank Lloyd, 84
Wright-Patterson AFB, 77, 117

X, Y

X-Cor, Inc., 25
Yahoo!, 78
Yeti, 42
Yilnaz, Hüsseyin, 205
Yolla Bolly, 50
Yuba River, 83
Yvetot, 395, 401, 522

Z

Zebra Imaging, 339, 340
Zell, Timothy Otter, 29
Zen, 51
Zenia, CA, 50
Zodiac killer, 35
Zodiac Project, 77
Zyss, Jacques, 349, 41

INDEX OF SUBJECTS

A

abductions
 - files of J. Carpenter, 34
 - French approach, 42
 - general: 61, 64, 79, 138-9, 147-148, 159, 191, 204, 225, 230, 241, 267-268, 301, 357, 400, 407, 427, 442, 445, 457, 464, 473, 476, 490
 - Spielberg series, 167
 - as "daimonic," 297
absurdity factor, 95, 152, 159, 238, 357, 414, 456
advanced aerospace threats, 414
advanced propulsion, 96, 164
advanced technology, 188, 189, 201, 227, 238, 243, 252, 257, 404, 426, 443, 478,
AIDS, 383, 483, 489
aircraft accidents, 161
alchemy, 107, 233, 305
alien bodies, 70, 77, 131, 216, 319, 430
alien tissue samples, 132
alien hybrid, 241, 242, 427, 455
analysis, of UFO materials, 408, 471, 507
antimatter, 149
artificial life, 138
assassination, 256, 388, 472
asteroids, 100, 230
astronauts, 33, 53, 148, 193, 229, 329, 333, 335, 341, 349, 341
atom, 35, 115, 421, 508
atom bomb, 212, 503

B

balls of light, 212, 300, 423, 508
beams, 37, 59, 117, 141, 305, 374, 403, 404
behavior, 77, 223, 443
biology, 203, 208, 343, 399, 444
black ball, 500
black hole, 205, 491
black projects, 36, 73, 76, 77, 149, 196, 197, 200-202, 204, 213, 237, 242, 299, 426
black Sun, 377
black triangle, 46, 479
blue files, 48, 329, 373, 374, 376
blue gel, 115
brain, 159, 182 (kuru), 194, 195, 297, 330, 406, 487, 510, 511

C

carbon dioxide, 143, 152, 143, 152
cattle, 94, 181, 186, 224, 237, 290, 499, 516
cerebral incident, 29, 315, 316
channeling, 265
classification (of cases), 42, 135, 204, 250, 374, 504
clearances (secret), 66, 77, 230, 231, 250, 300, 428, 431, 433, 448, 451, 454, 460, 462, 468, 474, 475, 486, 488, 500, 510, 515
coincidences, 60, 91, 164, 190, 212, 311, 384, 428, 458
cold fusion, 203, 230, 265, 332
collaboration software, 446
communication, 33, 35, 67, 154, 206, 225, 252, 308, 319, 346
 - with the Dead, 59
 - with Aliens, 195
computers, 287, 292, 305, 483
consciousness, 28, 57, 96, 124, 146, 149, 164, 206, 208, 266, 289, 315, 372

contact, 21, 88,103, 132, 147, 154,163, 188,198
coordinate remote viewing, 506
corruption, 241, 255, 291, 314, 427, 453, 456, 508
counter-intelligence, 33, 83, 377
coverup, 45, 167, 168, 185, 187, 250
crashes, financial, 9, 31, 436
crashes, UFOs, 23, 28, 30, 33, 36, 72, 77, 131, 132, 134, 147, 156, 167, 187, 197, 231, 250, 267, 298, 307, 319, 333, 345, 381, 425, 440, 442, 472, 489, 503
creatures, 122, 242, 479
crime, 68, 124,182, 225, 234, 341
crop circles, 141
cults, 59, 79, 107, 167, 172, 265, 458

D

Database
- of pilot cases, 73,
- of NIDS, 122
- patterns, 130, 267
- Larry Hatch extensions, 158
- of CNES, 160
- "Corpus", 163
- analysis, 203, 217
- classified Capella, 431, 445, 450, 451, 455, 456, 459, 465-7, 472, 476, 478, 482, 484, 486, 488, 498, 509, 510
- of Brazilian cases, 498
- with built-in AI, 444
datamining, 303
day after, 333
deception, 89, 196
delusion, 79, 243, 330
demonology, 112, 122, 124

directed energy, 300
disaster, 45, 138, 230, 264, 290, 435, 456, 513
disclosure, 9, 76, 77, 83, 84, 96, 213, 300, 426, 439, 440-441, 475
disinformation, 47, 55, 83, 84, 89, 131, 204, 216, 226, 228, 232, 238, 285, 398, 440, 442
disk-shaped, 38, 52, 84, 89, 116, 131, 142-144, 152, 156, 217, 241, 299, 308, 339, 352, 491, 495, 500
dot-com, 54, 63
dowsing, 375
dreams, 454
drones, 154
drugs, 14, 55, 67, 88, 115, 235, 298, 305, 375-376, 382-383, 390, 462, 463-464, 496, 500

E

electricity, 137, 217, 419, 420, 421
electro-magnetism, 32, 73, 118, 296, 396, 421, 472
energy, 179, 257, 265, 320, 352, 384-385, 419
- "free" energy, 22, 187, 331, 420
- directed -, 300
- "zero-point" energy, 28, 35, 179, 205, 252, 331, 353, 403, 420, 421, 430
- in orbit, 33
- entities of -, 226
- dark -, 303
- Department of -, 217
environment, 417, 464, 484, 487, 503
esoterica, 27, 57, 60, 162, 233, 302, 384, 422, 457

extraterrestrial, 55, 61, 77, 96, 122, 127, 132, 139, 179, 209, 217, 305, 338, 358, 427-8

F

false UFO experiences:
- fake images, 62
- false disclosure claims, 77, 87, 228
- fake documents, 228
- religions, 176, see also "cults"

far-right politics, 44, 239, 364
fiberoptics, 92, 187, 264, 394
fields, 308, 420, 421, 431, 471, 483-485
finance, 261, 419, 435-6, 444
flashes (of light), 308, 406
flying triangle, 12, 25, 37, 46, 127, 155, 157, 299, 426, 429, 479
folklore, 381, 407, 482
fraud, 73, 77, 163, 432
free-energy systems, see "energy"
French, 259, 260, 266, 276, 277, 287, 301, 349
- economy, 240, 261-262, 333, 355, 360, 361, 363, 382, 398, 416-418, 433, 442, 452
- politics, 238, 269, 274, 295, 314, 342, 350, 351, 434, 486, 504
- spirit, 241, 337, 346, 418
- media, 257, 278, 296, 333, 376, 394, 448
- research, 262, 271, 289, 299, 387

Fundamentalism, 159, 175, 208
fusion reaction, 403, 421, 426, 471-472
- cold fusion, see "cold" above
futures research, 37, 285, 333, 384

G

Gendarmes, 42, 73, 343, 344, 397, 399, 408
Genetics, 77, 229
Geophysics, 180
Ghost, 60, 260, 308, 124
Globular, 346
Government, 330, 340, 341, 355, 358, 359, 375, 394, 400, 424, 425, 427, 430, 434-440, 442, 444-7, 449, 479-480, 489, 496, 499, 504
- French -, 335, 450, 452, 503
- Brazilian -, 472
Gravity, 74, 96, 116, 136, 146, 179, 228, 229, 335, 360, 403, 419-422, 449, 471, 491
Gravitons, 179, 420
Greys, 122
Gyroscopes, 73

H

hallucinations,, 407, 455
healing, 60, 208, 264
Hearings, 19, 20, 34, 46, 187, 191, 197, 245-246, 287, 333
helicopters, 55, 66, 67, 75-76, 82, 118, 405, 500
Helium, 449, 471
Hell, 122, 483
hippies, 14, 136
hoaxes, 49, 72, 134, 161, 196, 297, 357, 430 homeless, 452
hostage, 248
humanoids, 125, 506
hydrogen, 35
hydrogen-lithium, 403, 421
Hypnosis, 79, 427

I

Immigration, 295, 449
implants, 34, 42, 114, 230, 236
Indians (American -), 34, 50, 272, 373
inertia, 28, 360, 421, 422, 439
information, 22, 28, 31, 35, 40, 47, 55, 61, 68, 82, 83, 84, 89, 95, 117, 162, 179, 185, 198, 203, 204, 216, 226, 228, 232, 238, 246, 268, 285, 305, 340, 359, 381, 400, 427, 439, 440, 460, 464, 466, 467, 479-480, 484, 485, 487, 493, 504, 515
Infrared, 235, 420, 468, 495
Initiation, 136, 303
innovation, 16, 21, 39, 119, 120, 165, 199, 234, 239, 252, 262, 276, 363, 418, 441, 487, 508
intelligence, 267, 270-271, 285, 288, 295, 322, 340, 351, 375, 425, 428, 440, 465, 466, 472, 474, 480, 488, 496, 503, 504
interdimensional theory, 96
interference, 413, 447, 503
Internet, 9, 15, 25, 26, 37, 40, 43, 49, 52, 54, 62, 67, 69, 72, 91, 119, 131, 142, 163, 164, 168, 179, 199, 200, 206, 208, 260, 270, 286, 292, 302, 323, 331, 332, 345, 356, 380, 394, 407, 425, 474, 478, 506, 513
Internet Archive, 306
interplanetary, 319, 373
intersign, 226, 458, 515
invisible, 103, 171, 245, 326, 422, 479
ionization, 300
ischemia, 317, 330

J, K, L

Jews, 31, 107, 152, 233, 342, 349, 410
Jupiter, 64, 117, 152, 249
Kabbala, 386
King, of Salem, 386
King, in yellow, 87
Kings, Valley of the -, 111, 112
King Hassan II, 195
Korea, 291
lasers, 27, 28, 74, 117, 229, 238, 398, 420
lawsuits, 18, 168, 278
lens-shaped, 90, 372
lenses, 372
lies, 137, 440
life sciences, 21, 31, 479-480
lights, unidentified, 12, 25, 141, 162, 223, 245, 247, 261, 300, 346, 404, 410, 415, 487, 516

M

magnetism, 59, 137
magnetic, 23, 32, 53, 73, 118, 195, 230, 236, 296, 396, 421, 426, 471-2, 483, 505
manipulation, 181, 226, 263, 364
material samples, 36, 77, 78, 121, 130, 131, 134, 146, 147, 156, 183, 185, 196, 203, 226, 227, 229, 270, 471-472, 502
medical issues, 16, 123, 132, 134, 164, 215, 268, 285, 294, 298, 337, 454, 459, 472, 473, 475
medical investments, 51, 91, 292, 393
medium, 163, 490, 499
memory, 38, 314, 392, 514
memory metal, 502
meteorites (with bacteria), 333
microgravity, 136, 146, 228, 229

microwaves, 179, 180, 421
mutilations, 53, 61, 66, 67, 75, 77, 90, 94, 104, 115, 117, 118, 140, 146, 148, 181-182, 186, 195, 224, 237, 274, 290, 308, 447, 479, 499, 516
mysticism, 107, 108, 112, 209, 257, 303, 347, 374, 378, 390, 522
mythology, 226, 364 (Nazi)

N

neo-nazi, 434
neutrinos, 130, 458, 477
nightmare, 407
non-lethal, 229, 404
nuclear war, 90, 244, 273, 303, 345, 423, 440
nuclear plants, 90, 215, 217, 284, 385
nuclear energy, 230, 265, 426
nun, 153, 193
nurse, 15, 16, 319, 520

O

occult, 26, 124, 274, 378, 415, 434
optics, 187, 264, 387
orbs, 346, 348, 387, 406, 423, 455, 458, 499, 503, 510, 516
out-of-body, 192

P

pagans, 29, 80, 191, 233, 351, 434
paralysis, 180, 399
paralysis (sleep-), 297, 407
paranoia, 72, 152, 438
paranormal, 9, 14, 21, 24, 42, 56, 59, 84, 113, 118, 119, 124, 189, 214, 260, 261, 290, 305, 406, 428, 447, 480, 509
parapsychology, 41, 43, 48, 59, 69, 149, 185, 192, 232, 241, 259, 274, 286, 289, 298, 324, 330, 340, 396, 407
pattern, 28, 59, 111, 146, 162, 209, 352, 372
pattern, - of lights, 90
photographs, 38, 130, 152, 288, 335, 346, 387, 394, 398, 406, 414, 437, 440, 456, 458, 496, 499, 504, 516
 - in Costa Rica, 131, 140, 142, 143, 144, 152, 156, 159, 161
 - at Willamette Pass, 48, 49
 - of humanoids, 125, 196,
physical traces, 159, 185, 191, 216, 379 (Fig. 17), 398, 503
physiology, 208, 426, 440
pilot sightings, 20, 22, 23, 34, 41, 49, 53, 63, 66, 70, 73, 76, 80, 88-90, 104, 122, 130, 154, 156, 157, 171, 179, 211, 223, 235, 247, 252, 262, 268, 298, 308, 335, 352, 377, 407, 446, 458, 467, 471, 504
planetary, 124, 277, 332
plant, 36, 90, 113, 140
plasma, 252
police, 12, 34, 101, 108, 111, 270, 342, 397, 399, 497
 - tribal, 506
 - in mutilation, 68, 75, 117
 - in France, 239, 277, 296, 309, 339
 - in Brazil, 294, 472
poltergeist, 60, 297, 387, 427, 503
precognition, 185, 192, 295
propulsion, 22, 23, 42, 96, 116, 227, 252, 296, 375, 403, 421, 431, 436, 471, 502
protestant, 326
psychiatry, 42, 195, 260, 330, 409, 4763 513

psychic, 69, 78, 214, 230, 242, 243, 256, 260, 279, 286, 289, 298, 330, 346, 379, 381, 407, 480, 500, 515, 522
psychological warfare, 95, 224, 272, 301
psychomanteum, 371

Q

quantum electrodynamics, 27, 419, 420
- mechanics, 28, 243, 360, 419-420, 449, 491
- entanglement, 28, 121,
- gravity, 359

R

radar, 66, 72, 160, 307, 398, 437, 467, 507
radiation, 48, 90, 284, 344, 367, 380, 382, 383, 420, 421, 503
rationalism, 58, 79
reality manipulation, 180, 225
religion, 51, 106, 107, 136, 137, 171, 175, 205, 207, 208, 232, 258, 327, 372n, 377, 379
remote viewing, 16, 22, 40, 76, 188, 191, 192, 203, 204, 224, 242, 257-259, 269, 272, 297, 305, 339, 374, 377, 405, 412, 480, 486, 493, 498, 503
remote perturbation, 480
reptilians, 118
reverse engineering, 34, 88, 186, 202, 203, 223, 269, 395, 402, 424, 479, 487
radio frequency, 504
ritual, 135, 265, 333, 370, 382, 519
robots, 118, 153, 217, 221, 427
rumors, false, 44, 60, 69, 75-76, 82, 83, 89, 91, 109, 113, 124, 149, 151, 164, 191, 204, 248, 254, 289, 307, 393, 444, 478, 481

S

sample analysis, 11, 20, 21, 48, 65, 77, 83, 109 (Fig.4), 114, 115, 130, 132, 143, 163, 185, 298, 327, 397, 471, 497
satellites, 23, 84, 86, 90, 154, 157, 169, 196, 212, 280, 320, 404, 482, 503
saucer, 23, 30, 36, 72, 77, 89, 90, 105, 119, 131, 137, 150, 180, 185, 187, 203, 216, 217, 224, 241, 243, 297, 308, 339, 347, 357, 380, 472, 499, 500
schizophrenia, 473
sects, 47, 76, 172, 235
semiconductors, 13, 403
shaman, 447
shuttle, 116, 174, 318, 336, 341, 348 (Fig. 15), 453, 491
sidereal time, in databases, 69, 130, 260, 287
skeptics, 19, 24, 123, 124, 144, 147, 167, 225, 236, 319, 363, 400, 405, 416, 420, 472, 496, 504
software, 59, 136, 206, 255, 273, 308, 357, 421, 446, 456, 510
solar physics, 212, 458, 478
special effects, 393, 459
spheres, 73, 140, 300, 390
spirits, 124, 138, 237, 499
stained glass, 232, 249, 266, 272, 275, 276, 295, 303,-305, 310, 317, 324, 326-328, 333, 344, 362, 417, 522
statistics, 13, 34, 41, 69, 73, 98, 170, 229, 330, 393, 476, 483
stealth, 127, 308, 403, 421, 430, 449, 480, 491, 514
stigma, 188, 407

suicide, 55, 59, 137, 150, 196, 255, 283, 303, 371
- of Larissa Vilenskaya, 91
- of René Hardy, 59

T

Taiwan, 291, 314, 508
telepathy, 275, 308
terrorism, 103, 119, 174, 177, 178, 216, 440
theory,
- wormhole, 27
- quantum electrodynamics, 28
- depends on data selection, 41
- semantic fields, 60
- ET origin, 77
- Westwood's -, 94
- universons (Poher), 179, 419
- TOE, 275
- zero-point, 420
- unified gravity, 421-422
- information physics, 428
- spacetime folding, 452
threat, 412n, 426, 478, 479
titanium, 116, 121, 147, 185
trans-communication, 59
transistor, 13, 92
triangles, 12, 25, 37, 46, 127, 155, 157, 299, 426, 429, 479

U

UFO hardware, 30, 44, 77, 89, 131, 189, 196, 197, 198, 202, 204, 223, 224, 227, 285, 301, 333, 340, 359, 390, 426, 428-429, 443, 460-463, 499
- bases, 34, 54
- catalogues, 241, 260, 262, 352, 372, 422, 457, 462, 465
- crash, see "crashes"
- detectors, 431
- photographs, 38, 48, 49, 125, 130, 131, 140, 142, 143, 144, 152, 156, 159, 161, 196, 288, 335, 346, 387, 394, 398, 406, 414, 437, 455, 458, 496, 499, 504
- medical effects, 132, 134, 215, 268, 285, 294, 298, 454, 472-474
- fakes, 33, 61, 84, 90, 205, 227, 297, 357, 440
undercurrent, 89, 226, 374
unicorn, 56, 80, 87
US Constitution, 175, 341, 395

V

vacuum polarization, 421
venture capital, 21, 22, 31, 38, 39, 39, 54, 60, 69, 74, 79, 80, 84, 98, 128, 135, 138, 157, 158, 164, 165, 176, 183, 190, 200, 213, 216, 234, 239, 259, 268, 273, 306, 307, 308, 316, 317, 318, 322, 329, 330, 341, 351, 355, 363, 369, 373, 377, 393, 395, 397, 413, 439, 446, 449, 451, 454, 475, 480-481, 513
veterinary medicine, 68
videos, of UFOs, 56, 57, 67, 84, 85, 141, 277, 504
VR technology, 154, 195, 286, 358, 444, 474
visions (optics), 211, 299, 300, 479, 496, 497
visitors (as Aliens), 345, 347
voices, 59, 176, 308

W, X, Y, Z

warp (drive), 117
water (samples), 109 (Fig.4), 143
- on Mars, 152, 218, 405

- on the Moon, 505
weapon systems, 74, 188, 238, 318
   - in space, 84, 425
   - biological, 182, 258
   - non-lethal, 229, 404
   - nuclear, 248, 307,
web, 8, 11, 13, 20, 46, 54, 64, 65, 81, 123, 167, 256, 259, 267, 297, 304, 307, 307, 318, 321, 329, 356, 409, 432, 434, 448, 450, 451, 457, 460, 478, 520
whitewash, of cattle mutilation reports, 68
witches, 87, 117, 300
wormhole, 27, 113, 257
zero-point energy, 28, 35, 179, 205, 252, 331, 353, 404, 420

CPSIA information can be obtained
at www.ICGtesting.com
Printed in the USA
LVHW040336070323
740989LV00016BA/1182